www.wadsworth.com

wadsworth.com is the World Wide Web site for Wadsworth and is your direct source to dozens of online resources.

At *wadsworth.com* you can find out about supplements, demonstration software, and student resources. You can also send email to many of our authors and preview new publications and exciting new technologies.

wadsworth.com
Changing the way the world learns®

Criminology

The Core

Larry J. Siegel

University of Massachusetts–Lowell

THOMSON

™

WADSWORTH

Australia • Canada • Mexico • Singapore
Spain • United Kingdom • United States

THOMSON

WADSWORTH

Senior Executive Editor, Criminal Justice: Sabra Horne
Development Editor: Shelley Murphy
Assistant Editor: Jana Davis
Editorial Assistant: Elise Smith
Technology Project Manager: Susan DeVanna
Marketing Manager: Terra Schultz
Marketing Assistant: Annabelle Yang
Advertising Project Manager: Stacey Purviance
Project Manager, Editorial Production: Jennie Redwitz
Art Director: Vernon Boes/Carolyn Deacy
Print/Media Buyer: Barbara Britton

Permissions Editor: Joohee Lee
Production Service: The Cooper Company
Text Designer: Lisa Delgado
Photo Editor/Researcher: Linda L Rill
Copy Editor: Kay Mikel
Indexer: Do Mi Stauber
Illustrators: John and Judy Waller, Scientific Illustrators
Cover Designer: Yvo
Cover Image: Noah Woods
Compositor: R&S Book Composition
Text and Cover Printer: Quebecor World/Dubuque

Printed in the United States of America
1 2 3 4 5 6 7 08 07 06 05 04

For more information about our products, contact us at:
Thomson Learning Academic Resource Center
1-800-423-0563
For permission to use material from this text or product, submit a request online at **http://www.thomsonrights.com**. Any additional questions about permissions can be submitted by email to **thomsonrights@thomson.com**.

Library of Congress Control Number: 2003112735

Student Edition: ISBN 0-534-62937-7

Instructor's Edition: ISBN 0-534-62938-5

Thomson Wadsworth
10 Davis Drive
Belmont, CA 94002-3098
USA

Asia
Thomson Learning
5 Shenton Way #01-01
UIC Building
Singapore 068808

Australia/New Zealand
Thomson Learning
102 Dodds Street
Southbank, Victoria 3006
Australia

Canada
Nelson
1120 Birchmount Road
Toronto, Ontario M1K 5G4
Canada

Europe/Middle East/Africa
Thomson Learning
High Holborn House
50/51 Bedford Row
London WC1R 4LR
United Kingdom

Latin America
Thomson Learning
Seneca, 53
Colonia Polanco
11560 Mexico D.F.
Mexico

Spain/Portugal
Paraninfo
Calle Magallanes, 25
28015 Madrid, Spain

This book is dedicated to my children,
Julie, Andrew, Eric, and Rachel,
and to my wife, Therese J. Libby

BRIEF CONTENTS

CONTENTS

PART 4 ▪ THE CRIMINAL JUSTICE SYSTEM   347

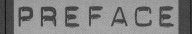

n October 17, 2003, Franklin C. Brown, the former chief counsel of Rite Aid Corp. drug store chain, was convicted of taking part in a conspiracy to falsely inflate the drugstore chain's earnings and mislead federal investigators. He was the first person to be convicted of criminal charges in the wake of the recent accounting scandals that have plagued the nation and caused the collapse of prestigious companies such as the Arthur Anderson accounting firm and Enron, the energy trading and producing empire. Brown, 75, was convicted of conspiracy, several obstruction charges, witness tampering, and five counts of lying to the Securities and Exchange Commission. He was found to have conspired to inflate income at the drugstore chain, backdated severance letters so he and other senior executives could collect big payouts, and misled internal and federal investigators.

The Brown indictment is one of the many high-profile criminal cases involving wealthy corporate executives whose illegal acts have shaken the public's confidence in the business community. Why would people who have so much resort to theft and deception to acquire even more? Though staggering, Brown's thievery seems relatively insignificant when compared to other executives who are alleged to have misappropriated hundreds of millions of dollars from their companies. And while the media seems incapable of ever losing interest in notorious killers, serial murderers, drug lords, and sex criminals, the Brown case and others like it show that crime can reach into the most prestigious corporate boardrooms. It is not surprising then that many Americans are concerned about crime and are worried about becoming the victims of crime: having our houses broken into, our cars stolen, and/or our pension funds misappropriated. We alter our behavior to limit the risk of victimization, and we question whether legal punishment alone can control criminal offenders. We watch movies about law firms, clients, fugitives, and stone-cold killers. We are shocked by graphic accounts of school shootings, police brutality, and sexual assaults in the news.

I have had a life-long interest in crime, law, and justice. Why do people behave the way they do? What causes one person to become violent and antisocial, while another channels his or her energy into work, school, and family? Why are some adolescents able to resist the "temptation of the streets" and become law-abiding citizens, while others join gangs and embark upon a criminal career? Conversely, what accounts for the behavior of the multimillionaire who cheats on his or her taxes or engages in fraudulent schemes? The lower-class adolescent has nothing yet is able to resist crime; the millionaire has everything and falls prey to its lure.

For the past 30 years I have been able to channel this interest into a career as a teacher of criminology. My goal in writing this text is to help students generate the same interest in criminology that has sustained me during my teaching career. What could be more important or fascinating than a field of study that deals with such wide-ranging topics as the motivation for mass murder, the effects of violent media on young people, drug abuse, and organized crime? Criminology is a dynamic field, changing constantly with the release of major research studies, Supreme Court rulings, and governmental policy. Its dynamism and diversity make it an important and engrossing area of study.

One reason that the study of criminology is so important is that debates continue over the nature and extent of crime and the causes and prevention of criminality. Some view criminals as society's victims who are forced to violate the law because of poverty and the lack of opportunity. Others view aggressive, antisocial behavior as a product of mental and physical abnormalities, present at birth or soon after, which are stable over the life course. Still another view is that crime is a function of the rational choice of greedy, selfish people who can only be deterred through the threat of harsh punishments.

Because interest in crime and justice is so great and so timely, I have written *Criminology: The Core* to help students develop an understanding of these ongoing issues. It is meant as a broad overview of the field, designed to whet the reader's appetite and encourage further and more in-depth exploration.

TOPIC AREAS

Criminology: The Core, Second Edition, is a concise yet thorough introduction to this fascinating field and is intended for students in introductory-level courses in criminology. It is divided into four main sections or topic areas.

Part 1 provides a framework for studying criminology. The first chapter defines the field and discusses its most basic concepts: the definition of crime, the component areas of criminology, the history of criminology, criminological research methods, the concept of criminal law, and the ethical issues that confront the field. Chapter 2 covers the nature, extent, and patterns of crime. Chapter 3 is devoted to the concept of victimization, including the nature of victims, theories of victimization, and programs designed to help crime victims.

Part 2 contains six chapters that cover criminological theory: Why do people behave the way they do? Why do they commit crimes? These views focus on choice (Chapter 4), biological and psychological traits (Chapter 5), social structure and culture (Chapter 6), social process and socialization (Chapter 7), social conflict (Chapter 8), and human development (Chapter 9).

Part 3 is devoted to the major forms of criminal behavior. The chapters in this section cover violent crime (Chapter 10), common theft offenses (Chapter 11), white-collar and organized crimes (Chapter 12), and public order crimes, including sex offenses and substance abuse (Chapter 13).

Part 4 contains a single chapter covering the criminal justice system (Chapter 14). This chapter provides an overview of the entire justice system, including the process of justice, the major organizations that make up the justice system and concepts and perspectives of justice.

GOALS AND OBJECTIVES

The text has been carefully structured to cover relevant material in a comprehensive, balanced, and objective fashion. Every attempt has been made to make the presentation of material interesting and contemporary. No single political or theoretical position dominates the text; instead, the many diverse views that are contained within criminology and characterize its interdisciplinary nature are presented. While the text includes analysis of the most important scholarly works and scientific research reports, it also includes a great deal of topical information on recent cases and events, such as the rape accusation lodged against basketball star Kobe Bryant and the conviction of Dr. Sam Waksal for insider trading in the Imclone case in 2003.

In sum, the primary goals in writing this text are

- to provide students with a thorough knowledge of the criminology in a brief format,

- to be as thorough and up to date as possible,

- to be objective and unbiased,
- to describe current theories, crime types, and methods of social control, and analyze their strengths and weaknesses.

NEW IN THE SECOND EDITION

■ **Chapter 1** now begins with the story of Kobe Bryant, the star athlete arrested in Eagle, Colorado, on July 4, 2003, on rape charges. The chapter has a review of research on mating behaviors and crime. Global trends in crime are reviewed in a new box on crime booms around the world. There is data on treatment for state prisoners and how it can be used to break the drug–crime cycle among parole violators. A number of new cases are analyzed, including the 2003 case *Smith v. Doe,* which concerned the Alaska Sex Offender Registration Act, and an important 2003 case, *Lawrence v. Texas,* in which the Supreme Court declared that laws banning sodomy were unconstitutional.

■ **Chapter 2** begins with a discussion of Eric Rudolph, who was arrested and charged with the deadly bombing of an Atlanta abortion clinic. It has a new discussion of the NIBRS data, which is the future of the Uniform Crime Report. There is an analysis of important research, including Steven Levitt's work on understanding why crime rates fell in the 1990s, as well as new research explaining neighborhood drug arrest rates, and the reporting of sexual victimization to the police. There is also the latest data from the Monitoring the Future study, the National Crime Victimization Survey, and the Uniform Crime Reports—these are the focus of a Concept Summary on data collection methods. A Policy and Practice in Criminology box on gun control has been updated.

■ **Chapter 3** starts with the story of Waterbury, Connecticut, Mayor Philip Giordano, a married father of three, who was convicted of engaging in sexual relations with minors as young as nine years old. The chapter contains material on the System Costs as part of the economic loss due to the victimization. A Current Issues in Crime box explores the problems faced by adolescent victims of violence. A review of the book *Aftermath: Violence and the Remaking of a Self,* by rape victim Susan Brison, tells of her experiences in the aftermath of sexual assault. There is also a box focusing on rape on campus. The concept of moral guardianship is explored, as well as the latest data on the Victim of Crime Act. Among the research studies now integrated within the chapter are ones covering the effect of victimization on hostility and risk factors for the sexual victimization of women.

■ **Chapter 4** reviews a number of important new research studies, including Steven Levitt and Sudhir Alladi Venkatesh's investigation of drug wars and Bruce Jacobs' research on robbers who target drug dealers. There is also analysis of data on the association between the level of police and crime rates and the effect of deterrent measures on crime prevention, the success of a breath-analyzed ignition interlock device to prevent drunk driving, the effects of closed-circuit television on crime, and whether the police can prevent homicide. A Current Issues in Crime box answers the question: Can crime pay dividends? A new Concept Summary compares crime control methods.

■ **Chapter 5** has a new Current Issues in Crime box, "Are You What You Eat?," and also includes the latest findings from the Minnesota study of twins reared apart. It has updated research on such topics as the effects of prenatal exposure to mercury and data from the most extensive assessment ever of Americans' exposure to environmental chemicals. It covers the intergenerational transmission of antisocial behavior; the effects of a depressed mood on delinquency, cognitive ability, and delinquent behavior; and research on juvenile sex offenders.

■ **Chapter 6** has a new Race, Culture, Gender, and Criminology box called "Bridging the Racial Divide." It has new research on the effects of housing on mental health, the role of culture in a socially disorganized area, and the structural correlates of homicide rates. It expands coverage of community cohesion and shows how it influences risks of victimization. There is new information on the neighborhood context of policing, as well as the association of neighborhood structure and parenting processes. The latest NCVS and census data are presented. Neighborhood ecology and victimization are explored.

■ **Chapter 7** reviews a number of new research studies examining the effects of socialization on criminality. It covers the importance of family and school in shaping adolescent deviance as well as the influence of early work experiences on adolescent deviance and substance abuse. There is new material on the intergenerational transmission of antisocial behavior, the effects of pairing aggressive and nonaggressive children in social relations, and the influence of parental monitoring on adolescents' delinquent behavior. The sections on stigma, labeling, and delinquency have all been updated.

■ **Chapter 8** now includes a major section on the effects of globalization on crime and well-being. It contains research on a wide variety of conflict theory topics, including the effects of racial profiling and whether human empathy can transform the justice system. A gendered theory of crime is analyzed, as well as the issues linking crime to the justice system.

■ **Chapter 9** now contains material on how marriage helps reduce the likelihood of chronic offending. It has a detailed analysis of David Farrington's new integrated cognitive antisocial potential (ICAP) theory. Reports on new research cover such topics as childhood predictors of offense trajectories, stability and change in antisocial behavior, the relationship of childhood and adolescent factors to offending trajectories, the intergenerational transmission of antisocial behavior, and the relationship between race, life circumstances, and criminal activity. Nan Lin's new book on social capital is analyzed.

■ **Chapter 10** has expanded coverage on the causes of violence. There are also new sections on psychological and social learning views of rape causation. Rape law changes have been updated with a new section on consent. There has been an expansion of the sections on murder and homicide, including material on who is at risk to become a school shooter. There are new materials on causes of child abuse and parental abuse. There are new sections on acquaintance robbery and expanded material on hate crimes and terrorism, including responses to terrorism by the FBI and the Department of Homeland Security.

■ **Chapter 11** begins with a vignette on the Winona Ryder shoplifting case. The chapter contains new material on shoplifting control, including the use of electronic tagging of products. The chapter lists the cars and car parts crooks love best. There is more information on credit card theft and what is being done to control the problem. There is new material on burglary, including repeat burglary and infectious burglary. The section on arson has been expanded.

■ **Chapter 12** has been retitled **Enterprise Crime: White-Collar Crime, Cyber Crime, and Organized Crime** to reflect the growing importance of cyber crimes and cyber criminals. Cyber crimes involve people using the instruments of modern technology for criminal purpose. Among the topics now covered are Internet securities fraud and identity theft. There are sections on enforcement issues and a new box on controlling cyber crime, which covers recent efforts to control computer- and Internet-based criminal activities. Data from the most recent Computer Crime and Security Survey by the Computer Security Institute are analyzed. A new Race, Culture, Gender, and Criminology box covers Russian organized crime. A number of new cases involving white-collar crime, including the Imclone case that involved TV personality Martha Stewart and the Securities and Exchange Commission investigation of leading Wall Street brokerage firms, are covered.

■ **Chapter 13** now has material on changes in the distribution of pornography via the Internet. There is more on the international trade in prostitution, including a new box on the "Natasha Trade," the coercion of women from the former Soviet Union into prostitution. There is an analysis of Judith Levine's book *Harmful to Minors: The Perils of Protecting Children from Sex,* which caused a stir when it was published. A number of important legal cases are summarized, including *Dale v. Boy Scouts of America,* which upheld the Boy Scouts' right to ban gay men from becoming scout masters; *Lawrence v. Texas,* which made it impermissible for states to criminalize nonheterosexual sex; and *Ashcroft, Attorney General, et al. v. Free Speech Coalition,* which dealt with the government's right to control Internet pornography. There is a new section on cyber prostitution. The latest data on drug use and the association between substance abuse and crime are included.

■ **Chapter 14** now includes a number of new cases, including *Hope v. Pelzer,* regarding prisoners' rights. It has the latest material on important criminal justice issues, including the police, courts, and corrections. There are updated data on the number of people behind bars and trends in the correctional population. There is new information on justifiable homicides by police officers and how police interactions with citizens affect satisfaction with the police. There is an analysis of the 2003 case *Wiggins v. Smith,* which helped define attorney competence. A great deal of attention is paid to the concept of inmate re-entry and how it affects the community.

FEATURES OF THE SECOND EDITION

This text contains pedagogy intended to help students analyze material in greater depth and also to link it to other material in the book.

- **Current Issues in Crime** are boxed inserts that review important issues in criminology. For example, in Chapter 2, a box called "Explaining Crime Trends" discusses the social and political factors that cause crime rates to rise and fall.

- **Policy and Practice in Criminology** are boxes that show how criminological ideas and research can be put into action. A Policy and Practice in Criminology box in Chapter 2, "Should Guns Be Controlled?," examines the pros and cons of the gun control debate.

- **Race, Culture, Gender, and Criminology** boxes cover issues of racial, sexual, and cultural diversity. For example, in Chapter 6, a Race, Culture, Gender, and Criminology box, "Bridging the Racial Divide," discusses the work and thoughts of William Julius Wilson, one of the nation's leading sociologists.

- Each of these boxes are accompanied by **critical thinking questions and links to articles** in the InfoTrac College Edition Research online database.

- **Connections** are short inserts that help link the material to other areas covered in the book. For example, a Connections box in Chapter 11 shows how efforts to control theft offenses are linked to the choice theory of crime discussed in Chapter 4.

- **Find It on InfoTrac College Edition**

- **Chapter Outlines**

- **Chapter Learning Objectives** (NEW to this edition)

- **Checkpoints**

- A **running glossary** in the margins ensures that students understand words and concepts as they are introduced.

- **Chapter-opening vignettes linked to CNN video clips on the student CD-ROM** (NEW to this edition)

- **Thinking Like a Criminologist** sections at the end of each chapter present challenging questions or issues that students must use their criminological knowledge to answer or confront. Applying the information learned in the text will help students begin to "think like criminologists."

- **Doing Research on the Web** (NEW to this edition) sections accompany every Thinking Like a Criminologist box and guide students to Web pages that will help them answer the criminological questions posed by the "Thinking" box.

- Each chapter ends with a list of **Key Terms** and **Critical Thinking Questions,** which help develop students' critical thinking skills.

ANCILLARIES

A number of supplements, available to qualified adopters, are provided by Wadsworth to help instructors use *Criminology: The Core,* Second Edition in their courses and to aid students in preparing for exams. Please consult your local sales representative for details.

For the Instructor

Instructor's Manual   The manual includes lecture outlines, discussion topics, student activities, Internet connections, media resources, and testing suggestions that will help time-pressed teachers more effectively communicate with their students and also strengthen the coverage of course material. Each chapter has multiple-choice and true/false test items, as well as sample essay questions.

WebTutor™ Toolbox   is preloaded with content and available free via pincode when packaged with this text. WebTutor ToolBox for WebCT pairs all the content of this text's rich Book Companion Web Site with all the sophisticated course management functionality of a WebCT product. Instructors can assign materials (including online quizzes) and have the results flow *automatically* to their gradebooks. ToolBox is ready to use at log on—or, instructors can customize its preloaded content by uploading images and other resources, adding Web links, or creating their own practice materials. Students have access only to student resources on the Web site. Instructors can enter a pincode for access to password-protected Instructor Resources. Contact a Thomson Wadsworth representative for information on packaging WebTutor ToolBox with this text.

ExamView®   This computerized testing software helps instructors create and customize exams in minutes. Instructors can easily edit and import their own questions and graphics, change test layouts, and reorganize questions. This software also offers the ability to test and grade online. It is available for both Windows and Macintosh.

CNN® Today Videos   Exclusively from Thomson Wadsworth, the CNN Today Video series offers compelling videos that feature current news footage from the Cable News Network's comprehensive archives. Criminology Volumes I through V each provide a collection of 2- to 8-minute clips on hot topics in criminology such as children who murder, the insanity defense, hate crimes, cyber terrorism, and much more. Available to qualified adopters, these videotapes are great lecture launchers as well as classroom discussion pieces.

Wadsworth Criminal Justice Video Library   The Wadsworth Criminal Justice Video Library offers an exciting collection of videos to enrich lectures. Qualified adopters may select from a wide variety of professionally prepared videos covering various aspects of policing, corrections, and other areas of the criminal justice system. The selections include videos from *Films for the Humanities & Sciences, Court TV* videos that feature provocative one-hour court cases to illustrate seminal high-profile cases in depth, *A&E American Justice Series* videos, *National Institute of Justice: Crime File* videos, *ABC News* videos, and *MPI Home videos.*

Opposing Viewpoints Resource Center This online center allows instructors to expose their students to all sides of today's most compelling issues, including genetic engineering, environmental policy, prejudice, abortion, health care reform, media violence, and dozens of other topics. The Opposing Viewpoints Resource Center draws on Greenhaven Press's acclaimed social issues series, as well as core reference content from other Gale and Macmillan Reference USA sources. The result is a dynamic online library of current event topics—the facts as well as the arguments of each topic's proponents and detractors. Special sections focus on critical thinking (and walk students through how to critically evaluate point–counterpoint arguments) and researching and writing papers. To take a quick tour of the OVRC, visit http://www.gale.com/OpposingViewpoints/index.htm.

For the Student

Student CD-ROM **Packaged free with text and NEW to this edition.** Included on the CD are chapter-based CNN video clips with critical thinking questions relating to key points from the text. Student responses can be saved and emailed to instructors.

Study Guide An extensive student study guide has been developed for this edition. Because students learn in different ways, a variety of pedagogical aids are included in the guide to help them. Each chapter is outlined, major terms are defined, and summaries and sample tests are provided.

Companion Web Site The Student Companion Web Site provides chapter outlines and summaries, tutorial quizzing, a final exam, textbook glossary, flashcards, crossword puzzle, concentration game, InfoTrac College Edition exercises, Web links, a link to OVRC, and the multi-step Concept Builder that includes review, application, and exercise questions on chapter-based key concepts.

InfoTrac® College Edition Students receive four months of real-time access to InfoTrac College Edition's online database of continuously updated, full-length articles from hundreds of journals and periodicals. By doing a simple keyword search, users can quickly generate a list of related articles, then select relevant articles to explore and print out for reference or further study.

Crime Scenes: An Interactive Criminal Justice CD-ROM This highly visual and interactive program casts students as the decision makers in various roles as they explore all aspects of the criminal justice system. Exciting videos and supporting documents put students in the midst of a juvenile murder trial, a prostitution case that turns into manslaughter, and several other scenarios. This product received the gold medal in higher education and silver medal for video interface from *NewMedia Magazine's Invision Awards.*

Mind of a Killer CD-ROM Based on Eric Hickey's book *Serial Murderers and Their Victims,* this award-winning CD-ROM offers viewers a look at the psyches of the world's most notorious killers. Students can view confessions of and interviews with serial killers, and they can examine famous cases through original video documentaries and news footage. Included are 3-D profiling simulations, which are extensive mapping systems that seek to find out what motivates these killers.

Careers in Criminal Justice Interactive CD-ROM, Version 3.0 This engaging self-exploration CD-ROM provides an interactive discovery of the wide range of careers in criminal justice. The self-assessment helps steer students to suitable careers based on their personal profile. Students can gather information on various careers from the job descriptions, salaries, employment requirements, sample tests, and video profiles of criminal justice professionals presented on this valuable tool.

Seeking Employment in Criminal Justice and Related Fields, Fourth Edition Written by J. Scott Harr and Kären Hess, this practical book helps students develop a search strategy to find employment in criminal justice and related fields. Each chapter includes "insider's views," written by individuals in the field and addressing promotions and career planning.

Guide to Careers in Criminal Justice This concise 60-page booklet provides a brief introduction to the exciting and diverse field of criminal justice. Students can learn about opportunities in law enforcement, courts, and corrections and how they can go about getting these jobs.

Criminal Justice Internet Investigator III This handy brochure lists the most useful criminal justice links on the World Wide Web. It includes the most popular criminal justice and criminology sites featuring online newsletters, grants and funding information, statistics, and more.

Internet Guide for Criminal Justice Developed by Daniel Kurland and Christina Polsenberg, this easy reference text helps newcomers as well as experienced Web surfers use the Internet for criminal justice research.

Internet Activities for Criminal Justice This 60-page booklet shows how to best utilize the Internet for research via searches and activities.

Criminology: An Introduction Using MicroCase ExplorIt, Fourth Edition This book features real data to help students examine major criminological theories such as social disorganization, deviant associations, and others. It has 12 one-hour exercises and five independent projects in all, covering dozens of topic areas and offering an exciting view of criminological research.

ACKNOWLEDGMENTS

My colleagues at Wadsworth did their typically outstanding job of aiding me in the preparation of the text and putting up with my seasonal angst. Sabra Horne, my wonderful editor, is always there with encouragement, enthusiasm, and advice; Shelley Murphy, a terrific developmental editor, is always there with a kind word and a pat on the back. Linda Rill did her usual thorough, professional job in photo research (she is almost a member of the family). I have worked with Cecile Joyner, the book's production editor, many times and she is always great (and very patient). The sensational Jennie Redwitz somehow pulls everything together as production manager, and Terra Schultz serves as marketing manager extraordinaire.

Finally, I would like to thank the following reviewers for their valuable comments: Stephen J. Brodt, Ball State University; Yvonne Downs, Hilbert College; Catherine F. Lavery, Sacred Heart University; Danielle Liautaud-Watkins, William Patterson University; Larry A. Long, Pioneer Pacific College; Scott Wagner, Columbus State Community College; and Jay R. Williams, Duke University.

Larry Siegel
Bedford, New Hampshire

part 1

Concepts of Crime, Law, and Criminology

How is crime defined? How much crime is there, and what are the trends and patterns in the crime rate? How many people fall victim to crime, and who is likely to become a crime victim? How did our system of criminal law develop, and what are the basic elements of crimes? What is the science of criminology all about? These are some of the core issues that will be addressed in the first three chapters of this text.

Chapter 1 introduces students to the field of criminology: its nature, area of study, methodologies, historical development, and the evolution of criminal law. The other two chapters of Part 1 review the various sources of crime data to derive a picture of crime in the United States. Chapter 2 focuses on the nature and extent of crime, and Chapter 3 is devoted to victims and victimization. Important, stable patterns in the rates of crime and victimization indicate that these are not random events. The way crime and victimization are organized and patterned profoundly influences how criminologists view the causes of crime.

Crime and Criminology

Chapter Objectives

1. Understand what is meant by the field of criminology.
2. Know the historical context of criminology.
3. Recognize the differences between the various schools of criminological thought.
4. Be familiar with the various elements of the criminological enterprise.
5. Be able to discuss how criminologists define crime.
6. Recognize the concepts of criminal law.
7. Know the difference between evil act and evil intent.
8. Describe the various defenses to crime.
9. Show how the criminal law is undergoing change.
10. Be able to discuss ethical issues in criminology.

HEN BASKETBALL IDOL KOBE BRYANT WAS ARRESTED IN EAGLE, COLORADO, ON JULY 4, 2003, AND CHARGED WITH felony sexual assault on July 18, a strong ripple went through all levels of American society. Bryant was alleged to have assaulted a 19-year-old girl who worked at a luxury hotel in Colorado where Bryant was staying after knee surgery in late June. The case dominated the media for months.

CNN. View the CNN video clip of this story and answer related critical thinking questions on your Criminology: The Core 2e CD.

ESPN told viewers that a bellman saw the woman leaving Bryant's room with marks on her face and neck. *People* magazine reported that Kobe Bryant bought his wife a $4 million, 8-carat pink diamond ring. Other reports said that Bryant's accuser overdosed on pills two months before the alleged incident. A married man with an infant daughter, Bryant himself used the media to announce that he had committed adultery with the woman but insisted the sex was consensual. The Bryant case certainly raises questions about the media's role in high-profile criminal trials. How is it possible to select a fair and impartial jury and carry out an objective trial if the case has already been tried in the press? Is it fair to expose the victim's name and medical history? How do details from her past contribute to deciding the truth of a criminal matter?

ace shouldn't be a factor in the Bryant case, but a criminal charge against a famous black athlete facing an accusation from a white woman causes many Americans to view the case through the lens of race. Is Kobe Bryant another O. J. Simpson? Are African American men routinely and falsely accused by the justice system?

And if he did indeed attack the young girl, what factors could have motivated a wealthy and famous athlete to commit a violent act? Could he possess an impulsive personality that limited his ability to exercise self-control over his actions?

The questions about crime and its control raised by the Bryant case and other similar high-profile crimes have spurred the development of **criminology,** an academic discipline that uses scientific methods to study the nature, extent, cause, and control of criminal behavior. Unlike political figures and media commentators, whose opinions about crime may be colored by personal experiences, biases, and election concerns, criminologists remain objective as they study crime and its consequences.[1]

Criminology is an **interdisciplinary** science. Criminologists hold degrees in a variety of diverse fields, most commonly sociology,

Connections

For the criminological view on the relationship between media and violence, see Chapter 5. For more on acquaintance rape, go to Chapter 10.

criminology
The scientific study of the nature, extent, cause, and control of criminal behavior.

interdisciplinary
Involving two or more academic fields.

but also criminal justice, political science, psychology, economics, and the natural sciences. For most of the twentieth century, criminology's primary orientation was sociological, but today it can be viewed as an integrated approach to the study of criminal behavior.

A Brief History of Criminology

The scientific study of crime and criminality is a relatively recent development. During the Middle Ages (1200–1600), people who violated social norms or religious practices were believed to be witches or possessed by demons.[2] It was common practice to use cruel torture to extract confessions. Those convicted of violent or theft crimes suffered extremely harsh penalties, including whipping, branding, maiming, and execution.

Classical Criminology

By the mid-eighteenth century, social philosophers began to argue for a more rational approach to punishment. They sought to eliminate cruel public executions, which were designed to frighten people into obedience. Reformers stressed that the relationship between crime and punishment should be balanced and fair. This more moderate view of criminal sanctions can be traced to the writings of an Italian scholar, Cesare Beccaria (1738–1794), who was one of the first scholars to develop a systematic understanding of why people committed crime.

Beccaria believed in the concept of **utilitarianism:** In their behavior choices, people want to achieve pleasure and avoid pain. Crimes occur when the potential pleasure and reward from illegal acts outweigh the likely pains of punishment. To deter crime, punishment must be sufficient—no more, no less—to counterbalance criminal gain. Beccaria's famous theorem was that in order for punishment to be effective it must be public, prompt, necessary, the least possible in the given circumstances, proportionate, and dictated by law.[3]

The writings of Beccaria and his followers form the core of what today is referred to as **classical criminology.** As originally conceived in the eighteenth century, classical criminology theory had several basic elements:

1. In every society, people have free will to choose criminal or lawful solutions to meet their needs or settle their problems.
2. Criminal solutions may be more attractive than lawful ones because they usually require less work for a greater payoff.
3. A person's choice of criminal solutions may be controlled by his or her fear of punishment.
4. The more severe, certain, and swift the punishment, the better able it is to control criminal behavior.

This classical perspective influenced judicial philosophy, and sentences were geared to be proportionate to the seriousness of the crime. Executions were still widely used but gradually came to be employed for only the most serious crimes. The catch phrase was "let the punishment fit the crime."

Positivist Criminology

During the nineteenth century, a new vision of the world challenged the validity of classical theory and presented an innovative way of looking at the causes of crime. The scientific method was beginning to take hold in Europe and North America. Scientists were using careful observation and analysis of natural phenomena to explain how the world worked. New discoveries were being made in biology, astronomy, and chemistry. If the scientific method could be applied to the study of nature, then why not use it to study human behavior?

utilitarianism
The view that people's behavior is motivated by the pursuit of pleasure and the avoidance of pain.

classical criminology
The theoretical perspective suggesting that (1) people have free will to choose criminal or conventional behaviors; (2) people choose to commit crime for reasons of greed or personal need; and (3) crime can be controlled only by the fear of criminal sanctions.

■ Early positivists believed the shape of the skull was a key determinant of behavior. These drawings from the nineteenth century illustrate "typical" criminally shaped heads.

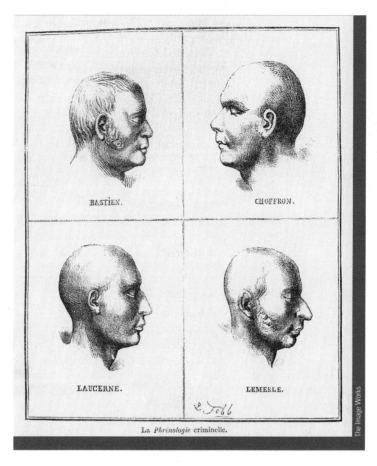

La *Phrénologie* criminelle.

FIND IT ON INFOTRAC
College Edition

Positivism can be used as an orientation in shaping the content of the law. To read about this perspective, look up:

Claire Finkelstein, "Positivism and the Notion of an Offense," *California Law Review*, March 2000 v88 i2 p335

Connections

We have grown up with movies showing criminals as "homicidal maniacs." Some may laugh, but *Freddie vs. Jason* was a big hit in 2003. For more on psychosis as a cause of crime, go to Chapter 5.

positivism
The branch of social science that uses the scientific method of the natural sciences and suggests that human behavior is a product of social, biological, psychological, or economic forces.

Auguste Comte (1798–1857), considered the founder of sociology, argued that societies pass through stages that can be grouped on the basis of how people try to understand the world in which they live. People in primitive societies believe that inanimate objects have life (for example, the sun is a god); in later social stages, people embrace a rational, scientific view of the world. Comte called this the positive stage, and those who followed his writings became known as positivists.

Positivism has two main elements:

1. Positivists see human behavior as a function of external forces that are often beyond individual control. Some are social, such as wealth and class; others are political and historical, such as war and famine. Personal factors, such as an individual's brain structure and biological makeup or mental ability, also influence human behavior.

2. Positivists rely on the scientific method. They would agree that an abstract concept such as "intelligence" exists because it can be measured by an IQ test. They would challenge a concept such as the "soul" because it cannot be verified by the scientific method.

Early Positivism   The earliest "scientific" studies examining human behavior now seem quaint and primitive. Physiognomists, such as J. K. Lavater (1741–1801), studied the facial features of criminals and found that the shape of the ears, nose, and eyes and the distances between them were associated with antisocial behavior. Phrenologists, such as Franz Joseph Gall (1758–1828) and Johann K. Spurzheim (1776–1832), studied the shape of the skull and bumps on the head and concluded that these physical attributes were linked to criminal behavior.

By the early nineteenth century, abnormality in the human mind was being linked to criminal behavior patterns. Phillipe Pinel, one of the founders of French psychiatry, coined the phrase *manie sans delire* to denote what eventually was referred to as a psychopathic personality.

In 1812 an American, Benjamin Rush, described patients with an "innate preternatural moral depravity."[4] English physician Henry Maudsley (1835–1918) believed that insanity and criminal behavior were strongly linked.[5] These early research efforts shifted attention to brain functioning and personality as the keys to criminal behavior.

Biological Determinism   In Italy Cesare Lombroso (1835–1909), known as the "father of criminology," began to study the cadavers of executed criminals in an effort to determine scientifically how criminals differed from noncriminals. Lombroso was soon convinced that serious and violent offenders had inherited criminal traits. These "born criminals" suffered from "atavistic anomalies"; physically, they were throwbacks to more primitive times when people were savages and were believed to have the enormous jaws and strong canine teeth common to carnivores and savages who devour raw flesh. Lombroso's version of criminal anthropology was brought to the United States via articles and textbooks that adopted his ideas.[6] By the beginning of the twentieth century, American authors were discussing "the science of penology" and "the science of criminology."[7]

Although Lombroso's version of strict biological determinism is no longer taken seriously, some criminologists have recently linked crime and biological traits. Because they believe that social and environmental conditions also influence human behavior, the term **biosocial theory** has been coined to reflect the assumed link between physical and social traits and their influence on behavior.

Sociological Criminology

At the same time that biological views were dominating criminology, another group of positivists was developing the field of sociology to study scientifically the major social changes that were taking place in nineteenth-century society. The foundations of **sociological criminology** can be traced to the work of pioneering sociologists L. A. J. (Adolphe) Quetelet (1796–1874) and (David) Émile Durkheim (1858–1917).[8]

Quetelet was a Belgian mathematician who (along with a Frenchman, Andre-Michel Guerry) used social statistics that were just being developed in Europe to investigate the influence of social factors on the propensity to commit crime. In addition to finding a strong influence of age and sex on crime, Quetelet uncovered evidence that season, climate, population composition, and poverty were also related to criminality.[9] He was one of the first criminologists to link crime rates to alcohol consumption.[10]

According to Durkheim's vision of social positivism, crime is normal because it is virtually impossible to imagine a society in which criminal behavior is totally absent.[11] Durkheim believed that crime is inevitable because people are so different from one another and use such a variety of methods and forms of behavior to meet their needs. Even if "real" crimes were eliminated, human weaknesses and petty vices would be elevated to the status of crimes. Durkheim suggested that crime can be useful and occasionally even healthful for society because it paves the way for social change. To illustrate this concept, Durkheim offered the example of the Greek philosopher Socrates, who was considered a criminal and put to death for corrupting the morals of youth simply because he expressed ideas that were different from what people believed at that time.

In his famous book *The Division of Labor in Society,* Durkheim described the consequences of the shift from a small, rural society, which he labeled "mechanical," to the more modern "organic" society with a large urban population, division of labor, and personal isolation.[12] From the resulting structural changes flowed **anomie,** or norm and role confusion. An anomic society

biosocial theory
Approach to criminology that focuses on the interaction between biological and social factors as they relate to crime.

sociological criminology
Approach to criminology, based on the work of Quetelet and Durkheim, that focuses on the relationship between social factors and crime.

anomie
A lack of norms or clear social standards. Because of rapidly shifting moral values, the individual has few guides to what is socially acceptable.

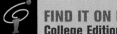

FIND IT ON INFOTRAC
College Edition

To learn more about how socialization affects human development, use "socialization" as a key
word on InfoTrac College Edition.
To learn how TV affects socialization, you may want to look at this
article:

Susan D. Witt, "The Influence of Television
on Children's Gender Role Socialization,"
Childhood Education, Midsummer 2000 v76
i5 p322

Connections

Did your mother ever warn you
about staying away from "bad
neighborhoods" in the city? If she
did, how valid were her concerns?
To find out, go to Chapter 6 for a
discussion of the structural conditions that cause crime.

is in chaos, experiencing moral uncertainty and an accompanying loss of traditional values. People who suffer anomie may become confused and rebellious. Might the dawning of the "Internet age" create anomie in our own
culture?

The Chicago School   The primacy of sociological positivism was secured
by research begun in the early twentieth century by Robert Ezra Park (1864–
1944), Ernest W. Burgess (1886–1966), Louis Wirth (1897–1952), and their
colleagues in the sociology department at the University of Chicago. The
scholars who taught at this program created what is still referred to as the
Chicago School in honor of their unique style of doing research.

These urban sociologists examined how neighborhood conditions, such as
poverty levels, influenced crime rates. They found that social forces operating
in urban areas created a crime-promoting environment; some neighborhoods
were "natural areas" for crime.[13] In urban neighborhoods with high levels of
poverty, the fabric of critical social institutions, such as the school and the
family, became undone. Their traditional ability to control behavior was undermined, and the outcome was a high crime rate.

Chicago School sociologists argued that crime was not a function of personal traits or characteristics but rather a reaction to an environment that
was inadequate for proper human relations and development. Thus, they
challenged the widely held belief that criminals were biologically or psychologically impaired or morally inferior. Instead, crime was a social phenomenon and could be eradicated by improving social and economic conditions.

Socialization Views   During the 1930s and 1940s, another group of sociologists began conducting research that linked criminal behavior to the quality
of an individual's relationship to important social processes, such as education, family life, and peer relations. They found that children who grew up in
homes wracked by conflict, attended inadequate schools, or associated with
deviant peers became exposed to pro-crime forces. One position, championed
by the preeminent American criminologist Edwin Sutherland, was that people
learn criminal attitudes from older, more experienced law violators. Another
view, developed by Chicago School sociologist Walter Reckless, was that crime
occurs when children develop an inadequate self-image, which renders them
incapable of controlling their own misbehavior. Both of these views linked
criminality to the failure of **socialization**—the interactions people have with
the various individuals, organizations, institutions, and processes of society
that help them mature and develop.

Conflict Criminology

While most criminologists embraced either the ecological view or the socialization view of crime, the writings of another social thinker, Karl Marx
(1818–1883), had sown the seeds for a new approach in criminology.[14]

In his *Communist Manifesto* and other writings, Marx described the oppressive labor conditions prevalent during the rise of industrial capitalism.
Marx was convinced that the character of every civilization is determined by
its mode of production—the way its people develop and produce material
goods. The most important relationship in industrial culture is between the
owners of the means of production, the capitalist bourgeoisie, and the people
who do the actual labor, the proletariat. The economic system controls all
facets of human life; consequently, people's lives revolve around the means of
production. The exploitation of the working class, he believed, would eventually lead to class conflict and the end of the capitalist system.

Although these writings laid the foundation for a Marxist criminology, it
was not until the social and political upheaval of the 1960s, fueled by the Vietnam War, the development of an antiestablishment counterculture movement,
the civil rights movement, and the women's movement, that **conflict theory**

Chicago School
Group of urban sociologists who studied
the relationship between environmental
conditions and crime.

socialization
Process of human development and enculturation. Socialization is influenced by
key social processes and institutions.

conflict theory
The view that human behavior is shaped
by interpersonal conflict and that those
who maintain social power will use it to
further their own ends.

© AP/Wide World Photos

■ Firefighters and rescue workers struggle to put out fires in the aftermath of the 9/11 attack. According to conflict theory, violence is a function of the political, economic, and social conflict that divides people. The 9/11 attack is an extreme instance of the violent effects of political rage.

took hold. Young sociologists interested in applying Marxist principles to the study of crime began to analyze the social conditions in the United States that promoted class conflict and crime. What emerged from this intellectual ferment was a Marxist-based radical criminology that indicted the economic system as producing the conditions that support a high crime rate. The Marxist tradition has played a significant role in criminology ever since.

Contemporary Criminology

These various schools of criminology, developed over 200 years, have been constantly evolving. Classical theory has evolved into modern **rational choice theory,** which argues that criminals are rational decision makers. They use available information to choose criminal or conventional behaviors, and their choice is structured by the fear of punishment. Lombrosian theory has evolved into contemporary biosocial and psychological views. Criminologists no longer believe that a single trait or inherited characteristic can explain crime, but some are convinced that biological and psychological traits interact with environmental factors to influence all human behavior, including criminality. Biological and psychological theorists study the association between criminal behavior and such factors as diet, hormonal makeup, personality, and intelligence.

The original Chicago School vision has been updated in **social structure theory,** which maintains that the social environment directly controls criminal behavior. According to this view, people at the bottom of the social hierarchy, who cannot achieve success through conventional means, experience anomie, strain, failure, and frustration; they are the most likely to turn to criminal solutions to their problems. The social process view is also still prominent. Some theorists believe that children learn to commit crime by interacting with and modeling their behavior after others they admire; others find that criminal offenders are people whose life experiences have shattered their social bonds to society.

The writings of Marx and his followers continue to be influential. Many criminologists still view social and political conflict as the root cause of crime. The inherently unfair economic structure of the United States and other advanced capitalist countries is the engine that drives the high crime rate. Some contemporary criminologists are now combining elements from each of these views into complex developmental theories of criminal careers that integrate a number of these theoretical concepts. Each of the major perspectives is summarized in Figure 1.1.

What Criminologists Do

rational choice theory
The view that crime is a function of a decision-making process in which the potential offender weighs the potential costs and benefits of an illegal act.

social structure theory
The view that disadvantaged economic class position is a primary cause of crime.

Regardless of their background or training, criminologists are primarily interested in studying crime and criminal behavior. Their professional training, occupational role, and income are derived from a scientific approach to the study and analysis of crime and criminal behavior.[15]

Several subareas exist within the broader arena of criminology. Taken together, these subareas make up the field of criminology. Criminologists may specialize in a subarea in the same way that psychologists might specialize in a subfield of psychology, such as child development, perception, personality, psychopathology, or sexuality. Some of the more important criminological specialties are described in the following sections and summarized in Figure 1.2.

Figure 1.1
Criminology Perspectives
The major perspectives of criminology focus on *individual* (biological, psychological, and choice theories), *social* (structural and process theories), *political and economic* (conflict theory), and *multiple developmental* factors.

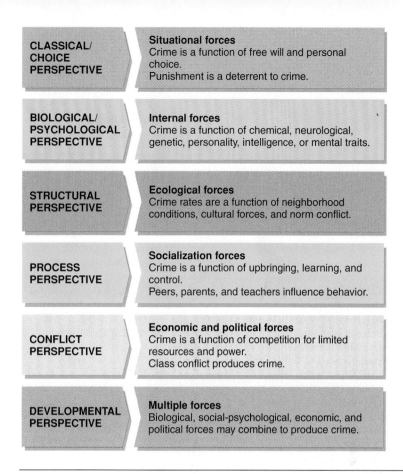

CLASSICAL/ CHOICE PERSPECTIVE
Situational forces
Crime is a function of free will and personal choice.
Punishment is a deterrent to crime.

BIOLOGICAL/ PSYCHOLOGICAL PERSPECTIVE
Internal forces
Crime is a function of chemical, neurological, genetic, personality, intelligence, or mental traits.

STRUCTURAL PERSPECTIVE
Ecological forces
Crime rates are a function of neighborhood conditions, cultural forces, and norm conflict.

PROCESS PERSPECTIVE
Socialization forces
Crime is a function of upbringing, learning, and control.
Peers, parents, and teachers influence behavior.

CONFLICT PERSPECTIVE
Economic and political forces
Crime is a function of competition for limited resources and power.
Class conflict produces crime.

DEVELOPMENTAL PERSPECTIVE
Multiple forces
Biological, social-psychological, economic, and political forces may combine to produce crime.

Figure 1.2
The Field of Criminology
These subareas constitute the field/ discipline of criminology.

Subarea | Primary Focus

CRIMINAL STATISTICS
Gathering valid crime data
Devising new research methods
Measuring crime patterns and trends

SOCIOLOGY OF LAW
Determining the origin of law
Measuring the social, historical, political, and economic factors that change laws and society

THEORY CONSTRUCTION
Predicting individual behavior
Understanding the cause of crime rates and trends

CRIMINAL BEHAVIOR SYSTEMS
Determining the nature and cause of specific crime patterns
Studying violence, theft, organized, white-collar, and public order crimes

PENOLOGY
Studying the correction and control of criminal behavior

VICTIMOLOGY
Studying the nature and cause of victimization
Aiding crime victims

RACE, CULTURE, GENDER, AND CRIMINOLOGY

International Crime Trends

International crime rate comparisons involving two or more countries are often difficult to make because the legal definitions of crime vary from country to country. There are also differences in the way crime is measured. For example, in the United States crime may be measured by counting criminal acts reported to the police or by using victim surveys, whereas in many European countries the number of cases solved by the police is used for measures of crime. Despite these problems, valid comparisons about crime across different countries can still be made using a number of reliable data sources. For example, the United Nations Survey of Crime Trends and Operations of Criminal Justice Systems (UNCJS) is the best-known source of information on cross-national data. The International Crime Victims Survey (ICVS) is conducted in 60 countries and managed by the Ministry of Justice of the Netherlands, the Home Office of the United Kingdom, and the United Nations Interregional

Crime and Justice Research Institute. There is also the United Nations International Study on the Regulation of Firearms, and INTERPOL, an international police agency, collects data from police agencies in 179 countries. The *European Sourcebook of Crime and Criminal Justice Statistics* provides data from police agencies in 36 European nations. What do these various sources tell us about international crime rates?

While crime rates are trending downwards in the United States, they seem to be increasing abroad:

- In 1980 the United States clearly led the Western world in overall crime, but a decade later statistics show a marked decline in U.S. property crime. Overall crime rates for the United States dropped below those of England and Wales, Denmark, and Finland.

- No matter what part of the world is surveyed, over a five-year period two out of three inhabitants of big

cities are victimized by crime at least once. Risks of being victimized are highest in Latin America and (sub-Saharan) Africa.

- Homicide rates are still higher in the United States than all nations except those in political and social turmoil. Colombia, for instance, had 63 homicides per 100,000 people, and South Africa 51, compared to less than 6 in the United States.

- Until 1990, U.S. rape rates were higher than those of any Western nation, but by 2000, Canada took the lead. The lowest reported rape rates were in Asia and the Middle East. Less than one in three female victims of violence report their victimization to the police. Violence against women, like most serious crime, is related to economic hardship and is inversely related to the social status of women. Where women are more emancipated, the rates of violence against women are lower.

Criminal Statistics/Crime Measurement

The subarea of criminal statistics/crime measurement involves calculating the amount and trends of criminal activity: How much crime occurs annually? Who commits it? When and where does it occur? Which crimes are the most serious?

Criminologists interested in computing criminal statistics try to create **valid** and **reliable** measurements of criminal behavior. For example, to analyze the activities of police and court agencies, they formulate techniques for collecting and analyzing institutional records and activities. To measure criminal activity not reported to the police, they develop survey instruments that estimate the percentage of people who actually commit crimes but who escape detection by the justice system. They also develop measures that identify the victims of crime, especially those who have not reported their victimization to the police.

The study of criminal statistics is a crucial aspect of the criminological enterprise. Without valid and reliable data sources, efforts to conduct research on crime and create criminological theories would be futile. One of the more challenging aspects of developing criminal statistics is devising methods to compare international crime rates. This is the topic of the Race, Culture, Gender, and Criminology feature.

valid
Actually measuring what one intends to measure; relevant.

reliable
Producing consistent results from one measurement to another.

- As of 2000, countries with more reported robberies than the United States included England and Wales, Portugal, and Spain. Countries with fewer reported robberies included Germany, Italy, and France, as well as Middle Eastern and Asian nations.

- As of 2000, the United States had lower burglary rates than Australia, Denmark, Finland, England and Wales, and Canada. It had higher reported burglary rates than Spain, Korea, and Saudi Arabia. Globally, two in three victims of burglaries report their victimization to the police.

- Australia, England and Wales, Denmark, Norway, Canada, France, and Italy now have higher rates of vehicle theft than the United States.

- Contrary to the common assumption that Europeans are virtually unarmed, the 15 countries of the European Union have an estimated 84 million firearms. Of that 67 million (80 percent) are in civilian hands. With a total population of 375 million people, this amounts to 17.4

guns for every 100 people. (In the United States there are about 100 guns for every 100 people.)

- Only one in five serious cases of violence is ever brought to the attention of the police. Reporting is particularly low in the countries of Asia and Latin America.

Why are crime rates increasing around the world while leveling off in the United States? In some developing nations, crime rates may be spiraling upward because they are undergoing a rapid change in their social and economic makeup. In Eastern Europe, for example, the fall of communism has brought about a transformation of the family, religion, education, and the economy. These changes increase social pressures and can result in crime rate increases. Other societies, such as China, are undergoing rapid industrialization as traditional patterns of behavior are disrupted by urbanization and the shift from agricultural to industrial and service economies. In some areas, such as Asia and the Middle East, political turmoil has resulted in a surge in crime rates.

Critical Thinking

The United States is notorious for employing much tougher penal measures than Europe. Do you believe our tougher measures explain why crime is declining here while increasing abroad?

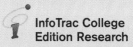

InfoTrac College Edition Research

What is being done in Europe to combat the latest crime boom? To find out, use "international crime" as a key term on InfoTrac College Edition.

SOURCES: Gene Stephens, "Global trends in crime: crime varies greatly around the world, statistics show, but new tactics have proved effective in the United States. To keep crime in check in the twenty-first century, we'll all need to get smarter, not just tougher," *The Futurist* 37 (2003): 40–47; Graeme Newman, *Global Report on Crime and Justice* (New York: Oxford University Press, 1999); Gary Lafree and Kriss Drass, "Counting crime booms among nations: evidence for homicide victimization rates, 1956–1998," *Criminology* 40 (2002): 769–801; *The Small Arms Survey* (2003), http://www.smallarmssurvey.org/ [accessed July 10, 2003].

Sociology of Law

The sociology of law is a subarea of criminology concerned with the role social forces play in shaping criminal law and the role of criminal law in shaping society. Criminologists study the history of legal thought in an effort to understand how criminal acts, such as theft, rape, and murder, evolved into their present form.

Often criminologists are asked to join the debate when a new law is proposed to outlaw or control a particular behavior. For example, across the United States a debate has been raging over the legality of artworks, films, photographs, and even music that some people find offensive and lewd and others consider harmless. Criminologists help determine the role that the law will play in curbing public access to controversial media. They may be called upon to help answer relevant questions: Do children exposed to pornography experience psychological harm? Will they later go on to commit violent crime? The answers to these questions may one day shape the direction of legislation controlling the sexual content of the Internet.

Criminologists also help lawmakers alter the content of the criminal law in response to changing times and conditions. For example, computer fraud, theft from automatic teller machines, Internet scams, and illegal tapping of television cable lines are behaviors that did not exist when criminal law was

FIND IT ON INFOTRAC
College Edition

To learn more about the sociology
of law, use "sociological jurispru-
dence" as a subject guide. You
may also want to look at the following paper:

George P. Fletcher, "The Nature and
Function of Criminal Theory," *California Law
Review*, May 2000 v88 i3 p687

originally conceived. The law must be constantly revised to reflect cultural, societal, and technological adaptations of common acts. For example, in a 2003 case *Smith v. Doe,* the U.S. Supreme Court ruled that the Alaska Sex Offender Registration Act, which required an incarcerated sex offender or child kidnaper to register with the Department of Corrections within 30 days before his or her release, was legal and may be required even for inmates convicted before the Act's passage and that this was not a violation of the Constitution's ban on **ex post facto laws.**[16] The Court reasoned that the Registration Act was nonpunitive and designed to protect the public from sex offenders rather than to punish those who had committed the act. The Court's ruling reflects the public's concern about sexual predators and the desire to create and maintain sex offender registries. Could the Court have just as easily ruled that making people register as sex offenders was a violation of their basic civil rights? After all, we do not make robbers and burglars register even though they present a danger to society! Was the Court's legal interpretation influenced by public opinion?

Developing Theories of Crime Causation

Criminologists also explore the cause of crime. Some who have a psychological orientation view crime as a function of personality, development, social learning, or cognition. Others investigate the biological correlates of antisocial behavior and study the biochemical, genetic, and neurological linkages to crime. Sociologists look at the social forces producing criminal behavior, including neighborhood conditions, poverty, socialization, and group interaction.

Sometimes criminologists investigate crime causation by conducting research on common behavioral practices in order to understand how they may influence crime. For example, in a recent study Ronald Simons and his colleagues looked at a sample of 236 young adults and their romantic partners to find out the influence of mating behaviors on crime.[17] They discovered that people who engaged in delinquent behaviors when they were adolescents were more likely to choose antisocial romantic partners as young adults. Involvement with an antisocial romantic partner then reinforced his or her criminal activities. The effect of antisocial romantic partners differed between the sexes: Females were much more likely to be influenced by criminal boyfriends; males were more likely to be influenced by criminal peers rather than their mates. The Simons research helps criminologists address the question of continuity of crime: Why do some adolescent delinquents become adult criminals whereas others desist from crime? For females, the choice of a romantic partner may be a key element; for males, it is rejection of deviant friends.

Understanding the true cause of crime remains a difficult problem. Criminologists are still unsure why, given similar conditions, some people choose criminal solutions to their problems while others conform to accepted social rules of behavior.

Connections

Criminologists have sought to reconcile the differences among
these visions of crime by combining or integrating them into unified
but complex theories of criminality.
At their core, these integrated theories suggest that, as people develop over the life course, a variety
of factors—some social, others
personal—shape their behavior
patterns. What these factors are
and the influence they have on
human behavior is discussed in
Chapter 9.

ex post facto law
A law applied retroactively to punish acts
that were not crimes before its passage,
or that raises the grade of an offense,
or that renders an act punishable in a
more severe manner than it was when
committed.

white-collar crime
Illegal acts that capitalize on a person's
status in the marketplace. White-collar
crimes may include theft, embezzlement,
fraud, market manipulation, restraint of
trade, and false advertising.

Understanding and Describing Criminal Behavior

Another subarea of criminology involves research on specific criminal types and patterns: violent crime, theft crime, public order crime, organized crime, and so on. Numerous attempts have been made to describe and understand particular crime types. Marvin Wolfgang's famous 1958 study, *Patterns in Criminal Homicide,* is considered a landmark analysis of the nature of homicide and the relationship between victim and offender.[18] Edwin Sutherland's analysis of business-related offenses helped coin a new phrase, **white-collar crime,** to describe economic crime activities of the affluent.

Penology

The study of **penology** involves the correction and control of known criminal offenders. Some criminologists are advocates of **rehabilitation;** they direct their efforts at identifying effective treatment strategies for individuals convicted of law violations. Others argue that crime can be prevented only through a strict policy of social control; they advocate such measures as **capital punishment** and **mandatory sentences.** Criminologists also help evaluate correctional initiatives to determine if they are effective and how they impact people's lives.

Victimology

Criminologists recognize the critical role of the victim in the criminal process and that the victim's behavior is often a key determinant of crime.[19] **Victimology** includes the following areas of interest:

- Using victim surveys to measure the nature and extent of criminal behavior and to calculate the actual costs of crime to victims
- Calculating probabilities of victimization risk
- Studying victim culpability in the precipitation of crime
- Designing services for crime victims, such as counseling and compensation programs

Victimology has taken on greater importance as more criminologists focus attention on the victim's role in the criminal event.

Deviant or Criminal? How Criminologists Define Crime

Criminologists devote themselves to measuring, understanding, and controlling crime and deviance. How are these behaviors defined, and how do we distinguish between them?

Criminologists view deviant behavior as any action that departs from the social norms of society.[20] **Deviance** thus includes a broad spectrum of behaviors, ranging from the most socially harmful, such as rape and murder, to the relatively inoffensive, such as joining a religious cult or cross-dressing. A deviant act becomes a **crime** when it is deemed socially harmful or dangerous; it then will be specifically defined, prohibited, and punished under the criminal law.

Crime and deviance are often confused because not all crimes are deviant and not all deviant acts are illegal or criminal. For example, recreational drug use such as smoking marijuana may be a crime, but is it deviant? A significant percentage of the population has used recreational drugs (including some well-known politicians). To argue that all crimes are behaviors that depart from the norms of society is probably erroneous. Similarly, many deviant acts are not criminal, even though they may be shocking or depraved. For example, a passerby who observes a person drowning is not required to jump in and render aid. Although the general public would probably condemn the person's behavior as callous, immoral, and deviant, no legal action could be taken because citizens are not required by law to effect rescues. In sum, many criminal acts, but not all, fall within the concept of deviance. Similarly, some deviant acts, but not all, are considered crimes.

Criminologists are often concerned with the concept of deviance and its relationship to criminality. The shifting definition of deviant behavior is closely associated with our concepts of crime: Where should society draw the line between behavior that is merely considered deviant and unusual and behavior that is considered dangerous and criminal? For example, when does sexually oriented material stop being merely erotic and suggestive (deviant) and become obscene and pornographic (criminal)? Can a clear line be drawn

penology
Subarea of criminology that focuses on the correction and control of criminal offenders.

rehabilitation
Treatment of criminal offenders aimed at preventing future criminal behavior.

capital punishment
The execution of criminal offenders; the death penalty.

mandatory sentences
A statutory requirement that a certain penalty shall be carried out in all cases of conviction for a specified offense or series of offenses.

victimology
The study of the victim's role in criminal events.

deviance
Behavior that departs from the social norm but is not necessarily criminal.

crime
An act, deemed socially harmful or dangerous, that is specifically defined, prohibited, and punished under the criminal law.

separating sexually oriented materials into two groups, one that is legally acceptable and a second that is considered depraved or obscene? And if such a line can be drawn, who gets to draw it? If an illegal act, such as viewing Internet pornography, becomes a norm, should society reevaluate its criminal status and let it become merely an unusual or deviant act?

Professional criminologists usually align themselves with one of several schools of thought or perspectives. Each of these perspectives maintains its own view of what constitutes criminal behavior and what causes people to engage in criminality. A criminologist's choice of orientation or perspective depends, in part, on his or her definition of crime. The three most common concepts of crime used by criminologists are the consensus view, the conflict view, and the interactionist view.

The Consensus View of Crime

According to the **consensus view,** crimes are behaviors that all elements of society consider to be repugnant. The rich and powerful as well as the poor and indigent are believed to agree on which behaviors are so repugnant that they should be outlawed and criminalized. Therefore, the **criminal law**—the written code that defines crimes and their punishments—reflects the values, beliefs, and opinions of society's mainstream. The term *consensus* implies general agreement among a majority of citizens on what behaviors should be prohibited by criminal law and hence be viewed as crimes.[21]

This approach to crime implies that it is a function of the beliefs, morality, and rules inherent in Western civilization. Ideally, the laws apply equally to all members of society, and their effects are not restricted to any single element of society.

The Conflict View of Crime

Although most practicing criminologists accept the consensus model of crime, others take a more political orientation toward its content. The **conflict view** depicts society as a collection of diverse groups—such as owners, workers, professionals, and students—who are in constant and continuing conflict. Groups able to assert their political power use the law and the criminal justice system to advance their economic and social position. Criminal laws, therefore, are viewed as acts created to protect the haves from the have-nots. Conflict criminologists often contrast the harsh penalties exacted on the poor for their "street crimes" (burglary, robbery, and larceny) with the minor penalties the wealthy receive for their white-collar crimes (securities violations and other illegal business practices). Whereas the poor go to prison for minor law violations, the wealthy are given lenient sentences for even the most serious breaches of law.

The Interactionist View of Crime

According to the **interactionist view,** the definition of crime reflects the preferences and opinions of people who hold social power in a particular legal jurisdiction. These people use their influence to impose their definition of right and wrong on the rest of the population. They maintain their power by stigmatizing or labeling people who fall outside their definition of right and wrong. Criminals therefore are individuals that society labels as outcasts or deviants because they have violated social rules. In a classic statement, sociologist Howard Becker argued, "The deviant is one to whom that label has successfully been applied; deviant behavior is behavior people so label."[22] Crimes are outlawed behaviors because society defines them that way, not because they are inherently evil or immoral acts.

consensus view
The belief that the majority of citizens in a society share common values and agree on what behaviors should be defined as criminal.

criminal law
The written code that defines crimes and their punishments.

conflict view
The belief that criminal behavior is defined by those in a position of power to protect and advance their own self-interest.

interactionist view
The belief that those with social power are able to impose their values on society as a whole, and these values then define criminal behavior.

Figure 1.3
The Definition of Crime
The definition of crime affects how criminologists view the cause and control of illegal behavior and shapes their research orientation.

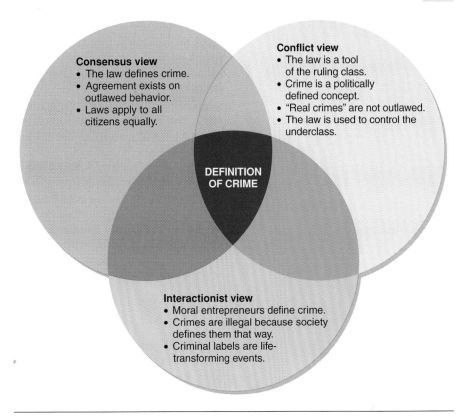

Consensus view
- The law defines crime.
- Agreement exists on outlawed behavior.
- Laws apply to all citizens equally.

Conflict view
- The law is a tool of the ruling class.
- Crime is a politically defined concept.
- "Real crimes" are not outlawed.
- The law is used to control the underclass.

DEFINITION OF CRIME

Interactionist view
- Moral entrepreneurs define crime.
- Crimes are illegal because society defines them that way.
- Criminal labels are life-transforming events.

Interactionists see criminal law as conforming to the beliefs of "moral crusaders" or moral entrepreneurs, who use their influence to shape the legal process as they see fit.[23] Laws against pornography, prostitution, and drugs are believed to be motivated more by moral crusades than by capitalist sensibilities. Consequently, interactionists are concerned with shifting moral and legal standards.

A Definition of Crime

Because of their diverse perspectives, criminologists have taken a variety of approaches in explaining crime's causes and suggesting methods for its control (see Figure 1.3). Considering these differences, we can take elements from each school of thought to formulate an integrated definition of crime such as the following:

> Crime is a violation of societal rules of behavior as interpreted and expressed by the criminal law, which reflects public opinion, traditional values, and the viewpoint of people currently holding social and political power. Individuals who violate these rules are subject to sanctions by state authority, social stigma, and loss of status.

This definition combines the consensus view that the criminal law defines crimes, the conflict perspective's emphasis on political power and control, and the interactionist concept of stigma. Thus, crime as defined here is a political, social, and economic function of modern life.

No matter which definition of crime we embrace, criminal behavior is tied to the criminal law. It is therefore important for all criminologists to have some understanding of the development of criminal law, its objectives, its elements, and how it evolves.

Crime and the Criminal Law

The concept of criminal law has been recognized for more than 3,000 years. Hammurabi (1792–1750 B.C.), the sixth king of Babylon, created the most famous set of written laws of the ancient world, known today as the **Code of Hammurabi.** Preserved on basalt rock columns, the code established a system of crime and punishment based on physical retaliation ("an eye for an eye"). The severity of punishment depended on class standing: If convicted of an unprovoked assault, a slave would be killed, whereas a freeman might lose a limb.

More familiar is the **Mosaic Code** of the Israelites (1200 B.C.). According to tradition, God entered into a covenant or contract with the tribes of Israel in which they agreed to obey his law (the 613 laws of the Old Testament, including the Ten Commandments), as presented to them by Moses, in return for God's special care and protection. The Mosaic Code is not only the foundation of Judeo-Christian moral teachings but also a basis for the U.S. legal system. Prohibitions against murder, theft, perjury, and adultery preceded, by several thousand years, the same laws found in the modern United States.

Common Law

After the Norman conquest of England in 1066, royal judges began to travel throughout the land, holding court in each county several times a year. When court was in session, the royal administrator, or judge, would summon a number of citizens who would, on their oath, tell of the crimes and serious breaches of the peace that had occurred since the judge's last visit. The royal judge would then decide what to do in each case, using local custom and rules of conduct as his guide. Courts were bound to follow the law established in previous cases unless a higher authority, such as the king or the pope, overruled the law.

The present English system of law came into existence during the reign of Henry II (1154–1189), when royal judges began to publish their decisions in local cases. Judges began to use these written decisions as a basis for their decision making, and eventually a fixed body of legal rules and principles was established. If a new rule was successfully applied in a number of different cases, it would become a **precedent.** These precedents would then be commonly applied in all similar cases—hence the term **common law.** Crimes such as murder, burglary, arson, and rape are common-law crimes whose elements were initially defined by judges. They are referred to as *mala in se,* or inherently evil and depraved. When the situation required, the English Parliament enacted legislation to supplement the judge-made common law. Crimes defined by Parliament, which reflected existing social conditions, were referred to as *mala prohibitum,* or **statutory crimes.**

Before the American Revolution, the colonies, then under British rule, were subject to the common law. After the colonies acquired their independence, state

■ Common law was created by English judges during the Middle Ages. It unified local legal practices into a national system of laws and punishments. Common law serves as the basis for the American legal system.

Code of Hammurabi
The first written criminal code, developed in Babylonia about 2000 B.C.

Mosaic Code
The laws of the ancient Israelites, found in the Old Testament of the Judeo-Christian Bible.

precedent
A rule derived from previous judicial decisions and applied to future cases; the basis of common law.

common law
Early English law, developed by judges, which became the standardized law of the land in England and eventually formed the basis of the criminal law in the United States.

statutory crimes
Crimes defined by legislative bodies in response to changing social conditions, public opinion, and custom.

A. C. Cooper, Ltd., by permission of The Inner Temple, London

legislatures standardized common-law crimes such as murder, burglary, arson, and rape by putting them into statutory form in criminal codes. As in England, whenever common law proved inadequate to deal with changing social and moral issues, the states and Congress supplemented it with legislative statutes, creating new elements in the various state and federal legal codes.

Contemporary Criminal Law

Criminal laws are now divided into felonies and misdemeanors. The distinction is based on seriousness: A **felony** is a serious offense; a **misdemeanor** is a minor or petty crime. Crimes such as murder, rape, and burglary are felonies; they are punished with long prison sentences or even death. Crimes such as unarmed assault and battery, petty larceny, and disturbing the peace are misdemeanors; they are punished with a fine or a period of incarceration in a county jail.

Regardless of their classification, acts prohibited by the criminal law constitute behaviors considered unacceptable and impermissible by those in power. People who engage in these acts are eligible for severe sanctions. By outlawing these behaviors, the government expects to achieve a number of social goals (see Figure 1.4).

■ **Enforcing social control.** Those who hold political power rely on criminal law to formally prohibit behaviors believed to threaten societal well-being or to challenge their authority. For example, U.S. criminal law incorporates centuries-old prohibitions against the following behaviors harmful to others: taking another person's possessions, physically harming another person, damaging another person's property, and cheating another person out of his or her possessions. Similarly, the law prevents actions that challenge the legitimacy

Figure 1.4
Purposes of the Criminal Law

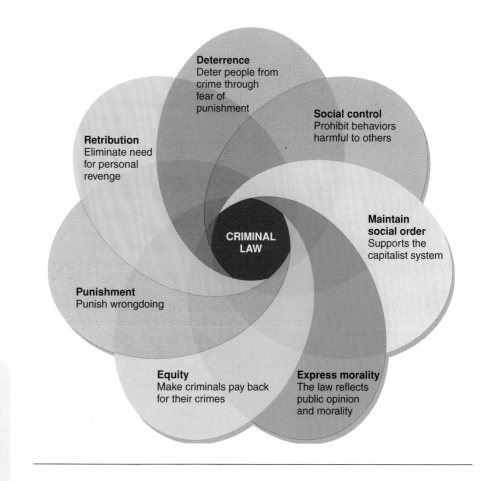

Deterrence
Deter people from crime through fear of punishment

Social control
Prohibit behaviors harmful to others

Retribution
Eliminate need for personal revenge

CRIMINAL LAW

Maintain social order
Supports the capitalist system

Punishment
Punish wrongdoing

Equity
Make criminals pay back for their crimes

Express morality
The law reflects public opinion and morality

felony
A serious offense that carries a penalty of imprisonment, usually for one year or more, and may entail loss of political rights.

misdemeanor
A minor crime usually punished by a short jail term and/or a fine.

of the government, such as planning its overthrow, collaborating with its enemies, and so on.

■ **Discouraging revenge.** By punishing people who infringe on the rights, property, and freedom of others, the law shifts the burden of revenge from the individual to the state. As Oliver Wendell Holmes stated, this prevents "the greater evil of private retribution."[24] Although state retaliation may offend the sensibilities of many citizens, it is greatly preferable to a system in which people would have to seek justice for themselves.

■ **Expressing public opinion and morality.** Criminal law reflects constantly changing public opinions and moral values. *Mala in se* crimes, such as murder and forcible rape, are almost universally prohibited; however, the prohibition of legislatively created *mala prohibitum* crimes, such as traffic offenses and gambling violations, changes according to social conditions and attitudes. Criminal law is used to codify these changes.

■ **Deterring criminal behavior.** Criminal law has a social control function. It can control, restrain, and direct human behavior through its sanctioning power. The threat of punishment associated with violating the law is designed to prevent crimes before they occur. During the Middle Ages, public executions drove this point home. Today criminal law's impact is felt through news accounts of long prison sentences and an occasional execution.

■ **Punishing wrongdoing.** The deterrent power of criminal law is tied to the authority it gives the state to sanction or punish offenders. Those who violate criminal law are subject to physical coercion and punishment.

■ **Creating equity.** Criminals benefit from their misdeeds. People who violate business laws make huge profits from their illegal transactions; the drug dealer accumulates wealth because of his trafficking in illegal substances. Through fines, forfeiture, and other economic sanctions, the criminal law redistributes illegal gains back to society thereby negating the criminal's unfair advantage.

■ **Maintaining social order.** All legal systems are designed to support and maintain the boundaries of the social system they serve. In medieval England, the law protected the feudal system by defining an orderly system of property transfer and ownership. Laws in some socialist nations protect the primacy of the state by strictly curtailing profiteering and individual enterprise. Our own capitalist system is also supported and sustained by criminal law. In a sense, the content of criminal law is more a reflection of the needs of those who control the existing economic and political system than a representation of some idealized moral code.

The Evolution of Criminal Law

The criminal law is constantly evolving in an effort to reflect social and economic conditions. Sometimes legal changes are prompted by highly publicized cases that generate fear and concern. For example, a number of highly publicized cases of celebrity stalking, including Robert John Bardo's fatal shooting of actress Rebecca Schaeffer on July 18, 1989, prompted more than 25 U.S. states to enact stalking statutes. Such laws prohibit "the willful, malicious, and repeated following and harassing of another person."[25] Similarly, after 7-year-old Megan Kanka of Hamilton Township, New Jersey, was killed in 1994 by a repeat sexual offender who had moved into her neighborhood, the federal government passed legislation requiring that the general public be notified of local pedophiles (sexual offenders who target children).[26] California's sexual predator law, which took effect on January 1, 1996, allows people convicted of sexually violent crimes against two or more victims to be committed to a mental institution after their prison terms have been served. This law has already been upheld by **appellate court** judges in the state.[27]

The criminal law may also change because of shifts in culture and social conventions and reflect a newfound tolerance for behavior condemned only a

appellate court
Court that reviews trial court procedures to determine whether they have complied with accepted rules and constitutional doctrines.

Connections

As the information highway sprawls toward new expanses, the nation's computer network advances, and biotechnology produces new substances, criminal law will be forced to address threats to the public safety that today are unknown. These new forms of Internet-related techocrimes are discussed in more detail in Chapter 12.

few years before. For example, in an important 2003 case, *Lawrence v. Texas*, the Supreme Court declared that laws banning sodomy were unconstitutional because they violated the due process rights of citizens because of their sexual orientation.[28]

The future direction of U.S. criminal law remains unclear. Certain actions, such as crimes by corporations and political corruption, will be labeled as criminal and given more attention. Other offenses, such as recreational drug use, may be reduced in importance or removed entirely from the criminal law system. In addition, changing technology and its ever-increasing global and local roles in our lives will require modifications in criminal law. For example, such technologies as automatic teller machines and cellular phones have already spawned a new generation of criminal acts such as identity theft and software piracy. ✔ **Checkpoints**

Criminological Research Methods

Criminologists use a wide variety of research techniques to measure the nature and extent of criminal behavior. To understand and evaluate theories and patterns of criminal behavior, it is important to understand how these data are collected. This understanding also shows how professional criminologists approach various problems and questions in their field.

✔ Checkpoints

✔ The American legal system is a direct descendant of the British common law.

✔ The criminal law has a number of different goals, including social control, punishment, retribution, deterrence, equity, and the representation of morality.

✔ Each crime has both a physical and a mental element.

✔ Persons accused of crimes can defend themselves either by denying the criminal act or by presenting an excuse or justification for their actions.

✔ The criminal law is constantly changing in an effort to reflect social values and contemporary issues and problems.

To quiz yourself on this material, go to questions 1.1–1.14 on the Criminology: The Core 2e Web site.

sampling
Selecting a limited number of people for study as representative of a larger group.

population
All people who share a particular characteristic, such as all high school students or all police officers.

cross-sectional research
Interviewing or questioning a diverse sample of subjects, representing a cross-section of a community, at the same point in time.

longitudinal research
Tracking the development of the same group of subjects over time.

Survey Research

Survey research can measure the attitudes, beliefs, values, personality traits, and behavior of participants. A great deal of crime measurement is based on analysis of survey data, which are gathered using techniques such as self-report surveys and interviews. Both types of surveys involve **sampling,** the process of selecting for study a limited number of subjects to represent a larger group, called a **population.** For example, a criminologist might interview a sample of 3,000 prison inmates drawn from the population of more than 1 million inmates in the United States; in this case, the sample represents the entire population of U.S. inmates. The characteristics of people or events in a randomly selected sample should be quite similar to those of the population at large.

One common type of survey simultaneously interviews or questions a diverse sample of subjects, representing a cross-section of a community, about research topics under consideration. This method is referred to as **cross-sectional research.** For example, all youths in the tenth grade in a public high school can be surveyed about their substance abuse. If most youths in this community attend public school, the survey will contain a sample that represents a cross-section of the community: rich and poor, males and females, users and nonusers, and so on.

Self-report surveys may ask participants to describe in detail their recent and lifetime criminal activities. Victimization surveys seek information from people who have been victims of crime. Attitude surveys measure the attitudes, beliefs, and values of different groups, such as prostitutes, students, drug addicts, police officers, judges, or juvenile delinquents.

Statistical analysis of data gathered from randomly drawn samples enables researchers to generalize their findings from small groups to large populations. Although cross-sectional research measures subjects at a single point in time, survey questions can elicit information on subjects' prior behavior as well as their future goals and aspirations.[29]

Cohort Research

Longitudinal research involves observing a group of people who share some common characteristic over a period of time. Such a group is known as a **cohort.** For example, researchers might select all girls born in Albany, New York, in 1984 and then follow their behavior patterns for 20 years. The research data might include their school experiences, arrests, hospitalizations, and information about their family life (such as divorces or parental relations). The subjects might be given repeated intelligence and physical exams, and their diets might be monitored. Data can be collected directly from the subjects, or without their knowledge from schools, police, and other sources. If the research is carefully conducted, it may be possible to determine which life experiences, such as growing up in a troubled home or failing at school, typically preceded the onset of crime and delinquency.

Record Data Analysis

Aggregate record data can tell us about the effects of social trends and patterns on the crime rate. Criminologists use large government agency and research foundation databases, such as those from the U.S. Census Bureau, Labor Department, and state correctional departments. The most important of these sources is the **Uniform Crime Report (UCR),** compiled by the Federal Bureau of Investigation (FBI).[30] The UCR collects records of the number of crimes reported by citizens to local police departments and the number of arrests made by police agencies in a given year.

Record data can be used to focus on the social forces that affect crime. For example, to study the relationship between crime and poverty, criminologists can use Census Bureau data to obtain information about income, the number of people on welfare, and single-parent families in a given urban area. They can then cross-reference this information with police records from the same locality.

Connections

The FBI's Uniform Crime Report remains the most important source of official crime statistics and is discussed more completely in Chapter 2.

Experimental Research

Sometimes criminologists want to study the direct effect of one factor on another. For example, they may wish to test whether watching a violent TV show will cause viewers to act aggressively. Answering this type of question requires **experimental research**—manipulating or intervening in the lives of subjects to observe the outcome or effect of a specific intervention. True experiments usually have three elements: (1) random selection of subjects, (2) a control or comparison group, and (3) an experimental condition.

To study the effects of violent TV, a criminologist might have one group of randomly chosen subjects watch an extremely violent and gory film (such as *Scream* or *Psycho*) while another randomly selected group views something more mellow (like *Finding Nemo* or *The Parent Trap*). The behavior of both groups would be monitored, and if the subjects who had watched the violent film were significantly more aggressive than those who had watched the nonviolent film, an association between media content and behavior would be supported. The fact that both groups were randomly selected would prevent some preexisting condition from invalidating the results of the experiment.

When it is impossible to select subjects randomly or manipulate conditions, a different type of experiment is used. For example, a criminologist may want to measure the change in driving fatalities and drunk driving arrests brought about by a new state law that mandates jail sentences for persons convicted of driving while intoxicated (DWI). Because police cannot randomly arrest drunk drivers, criminologists need to find an alternative strategy, such as comparing the state's DWI arrest and fatality trends with those of nearby states that have more lenient DWI statutes. Although not a true experiment, this approach would give some indication of the effective-

cohort
A group of subjects that is studied over time.

Uniform Crime Report (UCR)
Large database, compiled by the Federal Bureau of Investigation (FBI), of crimes reported and arrests made each year throughout the United States.

experimental research
Manipulating or intervening in the lives of subjects to observe the outcome or effect of a specific intervention. True experiments usually include (1) random selection of subjects, (2) a control or comparison group, and (3) an experimental condition.

■ One form of criminological research involves observing and interviewing people as they go about their daily activities. For example, some criminologists become involved with the homeless in order to understand the problems they face on the streets and the survival skills they use in order to endure in their very difficult daily environment.

© Joe Raedle/Getty Images

ness of mandatory sentences because the states are comparable except for their drunk driving legislation.

Observational and Interview Research

Sometimes criminologists focus their research on relatively few subjects, interviewing them in depth or observing them as they go about their activities. This research often results in the kind of in-depth data absent in large surveys; for example, Claire Sterk focused on the lives of middle-class female drug abusers.[31] The 34 interviews she conducted provide insight into a group whose behavior might not be captured in a large survey. Sterk found that these women were introduced to cocaine at first "just for fun." One 34-year-old lawyer told her, "I do drugs because I like the feeling. I would never let drugs take over my life."[32] Unfortunately, many of these subjects succumbed to the power of drugs and suffered both emotional and financial stress.

Another common criminological method is to observe criminals firsthand in order to gain insight into their motives and activities. This may involve going into the field and participating in group activities, as was done in sociologist William Whyte's famous study of a Boston gang, *Street Corner Society*.[33] Other observers conduct field studies but remain in the background, observing but not being part of the ongoing activity.[34]

Still another type of observation involves bringing subjects into a structured laboratory setting and observing how they react to a predetermined condition or stimulus. This approach is common in experimental studies testing the effect of observational learning on aggressive behavior. For example, subjects may be asked to view violent films, and their subsequent behavior is monitored.

Criminology, then, relies on many of the basic research methods common to other fields, including sociology, psychology, and political science. Multiple methods are needed to achieve the goals of criminological inquiry.

✔ Checkpoints

✔ Criminologists use a wide variety of research methods.

✔ Surveys employ samples of subjects who are asked about their behavior and attitudes.

✔ Cohort research follows a group of people who share some characteristic.

✔ Record studies use large databases collected by institutions such as police and correctional agencies, schools, and hospitals.

✔ Experimental research involves introducing a stimulus to determine the effect of the intervention.

✔ Observational studies focus on the daily lives and activities of particular individuals or groups.

🖱 To quiz yourself on this material, go to question 1.15 on the Criminology: The Core 2e Web site.

✔ Checkpoints

Ethical Issues in Criminology

A critical issue facing criminology students involves recognizing the field's political and social consequences. All too often criminologists forget the social responsibility they bear as experts in the area of crime and justice. When government agencies request their views of issues, their pronouncements and opinions may become the basis for sweeping social policy.

The lives of millions of people can be influenced by criminological research data. Debates over gun control, capital punishment, and mandatory sentences are ongoing and contentious. Some criminologists have argued successfully for social service, treatment, and rehabilitation programs to reduce the crime rate; others consider these a waste of time, suggesting instead that a massive prison construction program coupled with tough criminal sentences can bring the crime rate down. By accepting their roles as experts on law-violating behavior, criminologists place themselves in a position of power. The potential consequences of their actions are enormous. Therefore, they must be both aware of the ethics of their profession and prepared to defend their work in the light of public scrutiny. Major ethical issues include what to study, whom to study, and how to conduct those studies.

- **What to study.** Criminologists must be concerned about the topics they study. It is important that their research not be directed by the sources of funding on which research projects rely. The objectivity of research may be questioned if studies are funded by organizations that have a vested interest in the outcome of the research. For example, a study on the effectiveness of the defensive use of handguns to stop crime may be tainted if the funding for the project comes from a gun manufacturer whose sales may be affected by the research findings. It has been shown over the past decades that criminological research has been influenced by government funding linked to the topics the government wants research on and those it wishes to avoid. Recently funding by political agencies has increased the likelihood that criminologists will address drug issues while spending less time on topics such as incapacitation and white-collar crime.[35] Should the nature and extent of scientific research be shaped by the hand of government, or should it remain independent of outside interference?

- **Whom to study.** Another ethical issue in criminology concerns selection of research subjects. Too often criminologists focus their attention on the poor and minorities while ignoring middle-class white-collar crime, organized crime, and government crime. For example, a few social scientists have suggested that criminals have lower intelligence quotients than the average citizen and that because the average IQ score is lower among some minority groups, their crime rates are high.[36] This was the conclusion reached in *The Bell Curve,* a popular but highly controversial book written by Richard Herrnstein and Charles Murray.[37] Although such research is often methodologically unsound, it brings to light the tendency of criminologists to focus on one element of the community while ignoring others.

- **How to study.** A third area of concern involves the methods used in conducting research. One issue is whether subjects are fully informed about the purpose of research. For example, when European American and African American youngsters are asked to participate in a survey of their behavior or to take an IQ test, are they told in advance that the data they provide may later be used to demonstrate racial differences in their self-reported crime rates? Criminologists must also be careful to keep records and information confidential in order to maintain the privacy of research participants. But ethical questions still linger: Should a criminologist who is told in confidence by a research subject about a future crime report her knowledge to the police? How far should a criminologist go to protect her sources of information; should stated intentions to commit offenses be disclosed?[38]

In studies that involve experimentation and treatment, care must be taken to protect those subjects who have been chosen for experimental and control groups. For example, is it ethical to provide a special program for one group while depriving others of the same opportunity just so they can later be compared? Conversely, criminologists must be careful to protect subjects from experiments that may actually cause harm. An examination of the highly publicized "Scared Straight" program, which brings youngsters into contact with hard-core felons in a prison setting, found that participants may have been harmed by their experience. Rather than being frightened into conformity, subjects actually increased their criminal behavior.[39] Finally, criminologists must take extreme care to ensure that research subjects are selected in a random and unbiased manner.[40]

Summary

- Criminology is the scientific approach to the study of criminal behavior and society's reaction to law violations and violators. It is essentially an interdisciplinary field; many of its practitioners were originally trained as sociologists, psychologists, economists, political scientists, historians, and natural scientists.

- Criminology has a rich history, with roots in the utilitarian philosophy of Beccaria, the biological positivism of Lombroso, the social theory of Durkheim, and the political philosophy of Marx.

- The criminological enterprise includes subareas such as criminal statistics, the sociology of law, theory construction, criminal behavior systems, penology, and victimology.

- When they define crime, criminologists typically hold one of three perspectives: the consensus view, the conflict view, or the interactionist view.

- The consensus view holds that criminal behavior is defined by laws that reflect the values and morals of a majority of citizens.

- The conflict view states that criminal behavior is defined in such a way that economically powerful groups can retain their control over society.

- The interactionist view portrays criminal behavior as a relativistic, constantly changing concept that reflects society's current moral values. According to the interactionist view, behavior is labeled as criminal by those in power; criminals are people society chooses to label as outsiders or deviants.

- The criminal law is a set of rules that specify the behaviors society has outlawed.

- The criminal law serves several important purposes: It represents public opinion and moral values, it enforces social controls, it deters criminal behavior and wrongdoing, it punishes transgressors, it creates equity, and it banishes private retribution.

- The criminal law used in U.S. jurisdictions traces its origin to the English common law. In the U.S. legal system, lawmakers have codified common-law crimes into state and federal penal codes.

- The criminal law is undergoing constant reform. Some acts are being decriminalized—their penalties are being reduced—while penalties for others are becoming more severe.

- Criminologists use various research methods to gather information that will shed light on criminal behavior. These methods include surveys, longitudinal studies, record studies, experiments, and observations.

- Ethical issues arise when information-gathering methods appear biased or exclusionary. These issues may cause serious consequences because research findings can significantly impact individuals and groups.

Thinking Like a Criminologist

You have been experimenting with various techniques in order to identify a surefire method for predicting violent behavior in delinquents. Your procedure involves brain scans, DNA testing, and blood analysis. Used with samples of incarcerated adolescents, your procedure has been able to distinguish with 80 percent accuracy between youths with a history of violence and those who are exclusively property offenders. Your research indicates that if all youths were tested with your techniques, potentially violence-prone career criminals could be easily identified for special treatment. For example, children in the local school system could be tested, and those identified as violence-prone could be carefully monitored by teachers. Those at risk for future violence could be put into special programs as a precaution.

Some of your colleagues argue that this type of testing is unconstitutional because it violates the subjects' Fifth Amendment right against self-incrimination. There is also the problem of error: Some children may be falsely labeled as violence-prone.

How would you answer your critics? Is it fair or ethical to label people as potentially criminal and violent even though they have not yet exhibited any antisocial behavior? Do the risks of such a procedure outweigh its benefits?

Go to the Criminology: The Core 2e Web site to review the content of this chapter.

Doing Research on the Web

For an up-to-date list of URLs, go to

http://www.cj.wadsworth.com/siegel_crimcore2e

Go to these sites for information on the biological testing of criminals:

http://www.wiu.edu/library/govpubs/guides/dnacrmnl.htm

http://www.forensic-evidence.com/site/Biol_Evid/BioEvid_dna_jones.html

You can read Nicole Rafter's take on biological theories of crime at:

http://www.albany.edu/museum/wwwmuseum/criminal/curator/nicole.html

To read about the effects of stigma at it pertains to mental health, go to:

http://www.cmha-tb.on.ca/stigma.htm#what

Pro/Con discussions and Viewpoint Essays on some of the topics in this chapter may be found at the Opposing Viewpoints Resource Center:

http://www.gale.com/OpposingViewpoints

Key Terms

criminology 3
interdisciplinary 3
utilitarianism 4
classical criminology 4
positivism 5
biosocial theory 6
sociological criminology 6
anomie 6
Chicago School 7
socialization 7
conflict theory 7
rational choice theory 8
social structure theory 8
valid 10
reliable 10

ex post facto law 12
white-collar crime 12
penology 13
rehabilitation 13
capital punishment 13
mandatory sentences 13
victimology 13
deviance 13
crime 13
consensus view 14
criminal law 14
conflict view 14
interactionist view 14
Code of Hammurabi 16
Mosaic Code 16

precedent 16
common law 16
statutory crimes 16
felony 17
misdemeanor 17
appellate court 18
sampling 19
population 19
cross-sectional research 19
longitudinal research 19
cohort 20
Uniform Crime Report (UCR) 20
experimental research 20

Critical Thinking Questions

1. What are the specific aims and purposes of the criminal law? To what extent does the criminal law control behavior? Do you believe that the law is too restrictive? Not restrictive enough?

2. If you ran the world, which acts, now legal, would you make criminal? Which criminal acts would you legalize? What would be the likely consequences of your actions?

3. Beccaria argued that the threat of punishment controls crime. Are there other forms of social control? Aside from the threat of legal punishment, what else controls your own behavior?

4. What research method would you employ if you wanted to study drug and alcohol abuse at your own school?

5. Would it be ethical for a criminologist to observe a teenage gang by hanging with them, drinking, and watching as they steal cars? Should the criminologist report that behavior to the police?

The Nature and Extent of Crime

Chapter Objectives

1. Become familiar with the various forms of crime data.
2. Understand the problems associated with collecting valid crime data.
3. Be able to discuss the recent trends in the crime rate.
4. Be able to identify the factors that influence crime rates.
5. Understand the patterns in the crime rate.
6. Recognize age, gender, and racial patterns in crime.
7. Be able to discuss the association between social class and crime.
8. Describe the various positions on gun control.
9. Be familiar with Wolfgang's pioneering research on chronic offending.
10. Understand the influence the discovery of the chronic offender has had on criminology.

N MAY 31, 2003, ERIC RUDOLPH WAS ARRESTED BEHIND A GROCERY STORE IN RURAL WESTERN NORTH CAROLINA after five years on the run. He was accused of detonating a bomb that exploded outside a Birmingham abortion clinic on January 29, 1998, killing a police officer and critically injuring a clinic nurse. He was also charged with setting off a bomb that killed one person and injured 150 others in a park in downtown Atlanta during the 1996 Olympics. Additional evidence indicates that Rudolph was involved in the 1997 bombings of a gay nightclub and a building that housed an abortion clinic.

CNN. View the CNN video clip of this story and answer related critical thinking questions on your Criminology: The Core 2e CD.

Rudolph's crime spree is believed to have been motivated by his extreme political beliefs. He was reputedly a member of a white supremacist group called the Army of God. His relatives told authorities that Rudolph was an ardent anti-Semite who claimed that the Holocaust never happened and that the Jews now control the media and the government. Ironically, soon after he was arrested, the court appointed attorney Richard S. Jaffe, a practicing Jew, to lead Rudolph's defense team.[1]

The Rudolph case made national headlines in 2003, an illustration of the undercurrent of violence that is still all too common on the American landscape. Although the Rudolph case is a shocking reminder of the damage a single person can inflict on the public, the overall crime rate seems to be in decline. The United States has the reputation of being an extremely violent nation, but violence rates here are dropping while increasing abroad. How can this phenomenon be explained? What causes the rise and fall in crime rates and trends?

o answer these and similar questions, criminologists have devised elaborate methods of crime data collection and analysis. Without accurate data on the nature and extent of crime, it would not be possible to formulate theories that explain the onset of crime or to devise social policies that facilitate its control or elimination.

In this chapter, we review how data are collected on criminal offenders and offenses and what this information tells us about crime patterns and trends. We also examine the concept of criminal careers and discover what available crime data can tell us about the onset, continuation, and termination of criminality. We begin with a discussion of the most important sources of crime data.

The Uniform Crime Report

The Federal Bureau of Investigation's **Uniform Crime Report (UCR)** is the best-known and most widely cited source of aggregate criminal statistics.[2] The FBI receives and compiles records from more than 17,000 police departments serving a majority of the U.S. population. Exhibit 2.1 defines the eight most serious offenses, or **index crimes,** included in the UCR. The FBI tallies and annually publishes the number of reported offenses by city, county, standard metropolitan statistical area, and geographical division of the United States. In addition to these statistics, the UCR shows the number and characteristics (age, race, and gender) of individuals who have been arrested for these and all other crimes, except traffic violations.

The UCR uses three methods to express crime data. First, the number of crimes reported to the police and arrests made are expressed as raw figures (for example, 16,204 murders occurred in 2002). Second, crime rates per 100,000 people are computed. That is, when the UCR indicates that the murder rate was 5.6 in 2002, it means that about 6 people in every 100,000 were murdered between January 1 and December 31 of 2002. This is the equation used:

$$\frac{\text{Number of reported crimes}}{\text{Total U.S. population}} \times 100,000 = \text{Rate per 100,000}$$

EXHIBIT 2.1 Uniform Crime Report: Index Crimes

CRIME	DESCRIPTION
Criminal homicide	a. Murder and nonnegligent manslaughter: the willful (nonnegligent) killing of one human being by another. Deaths caused by negligence, attempts to kill, assaults to kill, suicides, accidental deaths, and justifiable homicides are excluded. Justifiable homicides are limited to (1) the killing of a felon by a law enforcement officer in the line of duty and (2) the killing of a felon, during the commission of a felony, by a private citizen. b. Manslaughter by negligence: the killing of another person through gross negligence. Traffic fatalities are excluded.
Forcible rape	The carnal knowledge of a female forcibly and against her will. Included are rapes by force and attempts or assaults to rape. Statutory offenses (no force used—victim under age of consent) are excluded.
Robbery	The taking or attempting to take anything of value from the care, custody, or control of a person or persons by force or threat of force or violence and/or by putting the victim in fear.
Aggravated assault	An unlawful attack by one person upon another for the purpose of inflicting severe or aggravated bodily injury. This type of assault usually is accompanied by the use of a weapon or by means likely to produce death or great bodily harm. Simple assaults are excluded.
Burglary/breaking and entering	The unlawful entry of a structure to commit a felony or a theft. Attempted forcible entry is included.
Larceny/theft (except motor vehicle theft)	The unlawful taking, carrying, leading, or riding away of property from the possession or constructive possession of another. Examples are thefts of bicycles or automobile accessories, shoplifting, pocket picking, or the stealing of any property or article that is not taken by force and violence or by fraud. Attempted larcenies are included. Embezzlement, con games, forgery, worthless checks, and so on are excluded.
Motor vehicle theft	The theft or attempted theft of a motor vehicle. A motor vehicle is self-propelled and runs on the surface and not on rails. Specifically excluded from this category are motorboats, construction equipment, airplanes, and farming equipment.
Arson	Any willful or malicious burning or attempt to burn, with or without intent to defraud, a dwelling house, public building, motor vehicle or aircraft, personal property of another, or the like.

SOURCE: FBI, Uniform Crime Report, 2002.

Third, the FBI computes changes in the number and rate of crimes over time. For example, murder rates declined 4.5 percent between 1998 and 2002.

Validity of the UCR

The accuracy of the UCR is somewhat suspect. Surveys indicate that fewer than half of all crime victims report incidents to police. Those who don't report may believe that the victimization was "a private matter," that "nothing could be done," or that the victimization was "not important enough."[3] Some victims do not trust the police or have confidence in their ability to solve crimes. Others do not have property insurance and therefore believe it is useless to report theft. In other cases, victims fear reprisals from an offender's friends or family or in the case of family violence from their spouse, boyfriend, or girlfriend.[4] Or they may believe that they are themselves somehow responsible for the crime: for example, the date rape victim who was drinking or had taken drugs prior to the attack.[5]

There is also evidence that local law enforcement agencies make errors in their reporting practices. Some departments may define crimes loosely— for example, reporting an assault on a woman as an attempted rape— whereas others pay strict attention to FBI guidelines.[6] Ironically, what appears to be a rising crime rate may simply be an artifact of improved police record-keeping ability.[7]

Methodological issues also contribute to questions regarding the UCR's validity. The complex scoring procedure used by the FBI means that many serious crimes are not counted. For example, during an armed bank robbery, the offender strikes a teller with the butt of a handgun. The robber runs from the bank and steals an automobile at the curb. Although the offender has technically committed robbery, aggravated assault, and motor vehicle theft, because robbery is the most serious offense, it is the only one recorded in the UCR.[8] Clearly, a more reliable source for crime statistics is needed. The most common issues affecting the validity of the UCR are summarized in Exhibit 2.2.

EXHIBIT 2.2 Factors Affecting the Validity of the Uniform Crime Reports

1. No federal crimes are reported.
2. Reports are voluntary and vary in accuracy and completeness.
3. Not all police departments submit reports.
4. The FBI uses estimates in its total crime projections.
5. If an offender commits multiple crimes, only the most serious is recorded. Thus, if a narcotics addict rapes, robs, and murders a victim, only the murder is recorded. Consequently, many lesser crimes go unreported.
6. Each act is listed as a single offense for some crimes but not for others. If a man robbed six people in a bar, the offense would be listed as one robbery; but if he assaulted or murdered them, it would be listed as six assaults or six murders.
7. Incomplete acts are lumped together with completed ones.
8. Important differences exist between the FBI's definition of certain crimes and those used in a number of states.
9. Victimless crimes often go undetected.
10. Many cases of child abuse and family violence are unreported.

SOURCE: Leonard Savitz, "Official Statistics," in *Contemporary Criminology*, ed. Leonard Savitz and Norman Johnston (New York: John Wiley, 1982), pp. 3–15; updated 2000.

Uniform Crime Report (UCR)
Large database, compiled by the Federal Bureau of Investigation (FBI), of crimes reported and arrests made each year throughout the United States.

index crimes
The eight most serious offenses included in the UCR: murder, rape, assault, robbery, burglary, arson, larceny, and motor vehicle theft.

The National Incident-Based Reporting System

To improve the validity of the UCR, in 1982 a five-year redesign effort was undertaken to provide more comprehensive and detailed crime statistics. The effort resulted in the National Incident-Based Reporting System (NIBRS), which collects data on each reported crime incident. Instead of submitting statements of the kinds of crime that individual citizens reported to the police and summary statements of resulting arrests, the new program requires local police agencies to provide at least a brief account of each incident and arrest, including the incident, victim, and offender information. Under NIBRS, law enforcement authorities will provide information to the FBI on each criminal incident involving 46 specific offenses, including the 8 Part I crimes that occur in their jurisdiction; arrest information on the 46 offenses plus 11 lesser offenses is also provided in NIBRS. These expanded crime categories include numerous additional crimes, such as blackmail, embezzlement, drug offenses, and bribery, and would allow a national database on the nature of crime, victims, and criminals to be developed. Other information to be collected includes statistics gathered by federal law enforcement agencies, as well as data on hate or bias crimes.

So far 22 states have implemented their NIBRS program and 12 others are in the process of finalizing their data collections. When this new UCR program is fully implemented and adopted across the nation, it should bring about greater uniformity in cross-jurisdictional reporting and improve the accuracy of official crime data.

Victim Surveys

The second source of crime data is surveys that ask crime victims about their encounters with criminals. Because many victims do not report their experiences to the police, and therefore are not included in the UCR, victim surveys are considered a method of getting at the unknown figures of crime. The **National Crime Victimization Survey (NCVS)** is the current method of assessing victimization in the United States.

Each year data are obtained from a large nationally representative sample; in 2002, 42,340 households and 76,050 people age 12 or older were interviewed.[9] People are asked to report their victimization experiences with such crimes as rape, sexual assault, robbery, assault, theft, household burglary, and motor vehicle theft. Because of the care with which the samples are drawn and the high completion rate, NCVS data are considered a relatively unbiased, valid estimate of all victimizations for the target crimes included in the survey.

NCVS Findings

The NCVS finds that many crimes go unreported to police. For example, the UCR shows that about 95,000 rapes or attempted rapes occurred in 2002, but the NCVS estimates that about 247,000 actually occurred. The reason for such discrepancies is that fewer than half of violent crimes, fewer than one-third of personal theft crimes (such as pocket picking), and fewer than half of household thefts are reported to police. Victims seem to report to the police only crimes that involve considerable loss or injury. If we are to believe NCVS findings, the official UCR statistics do not provide an accurate picture of the crime problem because many crimes go unreported to the police.

Validity of the NCVS

Like the UCR, the NCVS may also suffer from some methodological problems. As a result, its findings must be interpreted with caution. Among the potential problems are the following:

Connections

Victim surveys provide information not only about criminal incidents that have occurred but also about the individuals who are most at risk of falling victim to crime, and where and when they are most likely to become victimized. Recent NCVS data are used in Chapter 3 to draw a portrait of the nature and extent of victimization in the United States.

National Crime Victimization Survey (NCVS)
The ongoing victimization study conducted jointly by the Justice Department and the U.S. Census Bureau that surveys victims about their experiences with law violation.

PLEASE INDICATE HOW OFTEN IN THE PAST 12 MONTHS YOU DID EACH ACT. (CHECK THE BEST ANSWER.)

	Never did act	One time	2–5 times	6–9 times	10+ times
Stole something worth less than $50					
Stole something worth more than $50					
Used cocaine					
Been in a fistfight					
Carried a weapon such as a gun or knife					
Fought someone using a weapon					

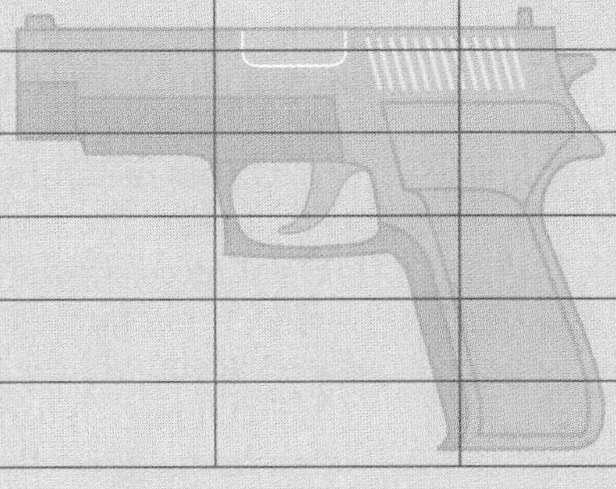

Figure 2.1
Self-Report Survey Questions

- Overreporting due to victims' misinterpretation of events. For example, a lost wallet may be reported as stolen, or an open door may be viewed as a burglary attempt.

- Underreporting due to the embarrassment of reporting crime to interviewers, fear of getting in trouble, or simply forgetting an incident.

- Inability to record the personal criminal activity of those interviewed, such as drug use or gambling; murder is also not included, for obvious reasons.

- Sampling errors, which produce a group of respondents who do not represent the nation as a whole.

- Inadequate question format that invalidates responses. Some groups, such as adolescents, may be particularly susceptible to error because of question format.[10]

Self-Report Surveys

The third source of crime data, **self-report surveys,** asks people to reveal information about their own law violations. Most often, self-report surveys are administered to groups of subjects through a mass distribution of questionnaires. The basic assumption of self-report studies is that the assurance of anonymity and confidentiality will encourage people to describe their illegal activities accurately. Self-reports are viewed as a mechanism to get at the "dark figures of crime," the figures missed by official statistics. Figure 2.1 illustrates some typical self-report items.

Most self-report studies have focused on juvenile delinquency and youth crime.[11] But self-reports are not restricted to youth crime; they are also used to examine the offense histories of prison inmates, drug users, and other segments of the population. Also, because most self-report instruments contain items measuring subjects' attitudes, values, personal characteristics, and behaviors, the data obtained from them can be used for various purposes, including testing theories, measuring attitudes toward crime, and computing the association between crime and important social variables, such as family relations, educational attainment, and income.[12]

In general, self-reports, like victimization surveys, indicate that the number of people who break the law is far greater than the number projected by official statistics. Almost everyone questioned is found to have violated some law at some time.[13] Furthermore, self-reports dispute the notion that criminals and delinquents specialize in one type of crime or another; offenders seem to engage in a "mixed bag" of crime and deviance.[14]

self-report surveys
A research approach that requires subjects to reveal their own participation in delinquent or criminal acts.

Accuracy of Self-Reports

Various techniques have been used to verify self-report data.[15] For example, the "known group" method compares youths who are known to be offenders with those who are not to see whether the former report more delinquency. Research shows that when kids are asked if they have ever been arrested or sent to court their responses accurately reflect their true, life experiences.[16]

Critics of self-report studies frequently suggest that it is unreasonable to expect people to candidly admit illegal acts. This is especially true of those with official records, who may be engaging in the most criminality. At the same time, some people may exaggerate their criminal acts, forget some of them, or be confused about what is being asked. Some surveys contain an overabundance of trivial offenses, such as shoplifting small items or using false identification, often lumped together with serious crimes to form a total crime index. Consequently, comparisons between groups can be highly misleading.

The "missing cases" phenomenon is also a concern. Even if 90 percent of a school population voluntarily participate in a self-report study, researchers can never be sure whether the few who refuse to participate or are absent that day comprise a significant portion of the school's population of persistent high-rate offenders. Research indicates that offenders with the most extensive prior criminality are also the most likely to "be poor historians of their own crime commission rates."[17] Institutionalized youths, who are not generally represented in the self-report surveys, are not only more delinquent than the general youth population but are also considerably more misbehaving than the most delinquent youths identified in the typical self-report survey.[18] Consequently, self-reports may measure only nonserious, occasional delinquents while ignoring hard-core chronic offenders who may be institutionalized and unavailable for self-reports.

Finally, there is evidence that reporting accuracy differs between racial, ethnic, and gender groups. For example, one recent study found that girls were more willing than boys to disclose drug use but that Hispanic girls underreport their drug usage. Such differences might provide a skewed and inaccurate portrait of criminal or delinquent activity, such as that Hispanic girls use fewer drugs than other females.[19]

Evaluating Crime Data

Each source of crime data has strengths and weaknesses. The FBI survey contains data on the number and characteristics of people arrested, information that the other data sources lack. Some recent research indicates that for serious crimes, such as drug trafficking, arrest data can provide a meaningful measure of the level of criminal activity in a particular neighborhood environment that other data sources cannot provide. It is also the source of information on particular crimes such as murder, which no other data source can provide.[20] The UCR remains the standard unit of analysis upon which most criminological research is based. However, this survey omits the many crimes victims choose not to report to police, and it is subject to the reporting caprices of individual police departments.

The NCVS includes unreported crime and important information on the personal characteristics of victims. However, the data consist of estimates made from relatively limited samples of the total U.S. population, so that even narrow fluctuations in the rates of some crimes can have a major impact on findings. It also relies on personal recollections that may be inaccurate. The NCVS does not include data on important crime patterns, including murder and drug abuse.

Self-report surveys can provide information on the personal characteristics of offenders, such as their attitudes, values, beliefs, and psychological profiles that is unavailable from any other source. Yet, at their core, self-reports rely on the honesty of criminal offenders and drug abusers, a population not generally known for accuracy and integrity.

Although their tallies of crimes are certainly not in synch, the crime patterns and trends they record are often quite similar.[21] For example, all three sources generally agree about the personal characteristics of serious criminals (such as age and gender) and where and when crime occurs (such as urban areas, nighttime, and summer months). In addition, the problems inherent in each source are consistent over time. Therefore, even if the data sources are incapable of providing a precise and valid count of crime at any given time, they are reliable indicators of changes and fluctuations in yearly crime rates.

What do these data sources tell us about crime trends and patterns?

Crime Trends

Crime is not new to this century.[22] Studies indicate that a gradual increase in the crime rate, especially in violent crime, occurred from 1830 to 1860. Following the Civil War, this rate increased significantly for about 15 years. Then, from 1880 up to the time of the First World War, with the possible exception of the years immediately preceding and following the war, the number of reported crimes decreased. After a period of readjustment, the crime rate steadily declined until the Depression (about 1930), when another crime wave was recorded. Crime rates increased gradually from the 1930s until the 1960s, and then the growth rate increased rapidly. The homicide rate, which had actually declined from the 1930s to the 1960s, also began a sharp increase that continued through the 1970s and 1980s.

In 1991, police recorded about 14.6 million crimes. Both the number and rate of crimes have been declining ever since. For example, between 1995 and 1999, the crime rate declined by 16 percent. In 2002 about 11.8 million crimes were reported to the police, an almost identical number as the year before. Despite this recent stabilization, the number of reported crimes has declined by about 3 million from the 1991 peak (see Figure 2.2).

Even teenage criminality, a source of national concern, has been in decline during this period, decreasing by about one-third over the past 20 years. The teen murder rate, which had remained stubbornly high, has also declined during the past few years.[23] The factors that help explain the upward and downward movements in crime rates are discussed in the Current Issues in Crime feature.

Trends in Violent Crime

The violent crimes reported by the FBI include murder, rape, assault, and robbery. In 2002, about 1.4 million violent crimes were reported to police, a rate of around 500 per 100,000 Americans. According to the UCR, violence in the United States has decreased significantly during the past decade, reversing a long trend of skyrocketing increases. The total number of violent crimes declined about 11 percent between 1997 and 2002, and the violence rate dropped more than 17 percent; violent crimes declined more than 25 percent during the past decade.

Figure 2.2
Crime Rate Trends
After years of steady increase, crime rates declined between 1993 and 2002.

SOURCE: FBI, Uniform Crime Report, 2002.

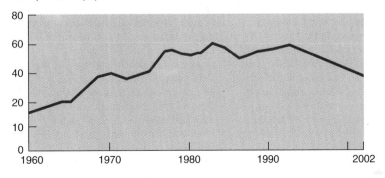

Rate per 1,000 population

CURRENT ISSUES IN CRIME

Explaining Crime Trends

Crime experts have identified a variety of social, economic, personal, and demographic factors that influence crime rate trends. Although crime experts are still uncertain about how these factors impact crime rate trends, change in their direction seems to be associated with changes in crime rates.

Age

Because teenagers have extremely high crime rates, crime experts view change in the population age distribution as having the greatest influence on crime trends: as a general rule, the crime rate follows the proportion of young males in the population. With the "graying" of society in the 1980s and a decline in the birth rate, it is not surprising that the overall crime rate declined between 1991 and 2002. The number of juveniles should be increasing over the next decade, and some crime experts fear that this will signal a return to escalating crime rates. However, the number of senior citizens is also expanding, and their presence in the population may have a moderating effect on crime rates (seniors do not commit much crime), offsetting the effect of teens.

Economy

There is debate over the effect the economy has on crime rates. It seems logical that during an economic downturn people, especially those who are unemployed, will become more motivated to commit theft crimes. However, some crime experts believe a poor economy actually helps lower crime rates because unemployed parents are at home to supervise children and guard their possessions. Because there is less to spend, a poor economy reduces the number of valuables worth stealing. Also, it seems unlikely that law-abiding, middle-aged workers will suddenly turn to a life of crime if they are laid off during an economic downturn.

Not surprisingly, most research efforts fail to find a definitive relationship between unemployment and crime. For example, recent research (2002) on the relationship between unemployment and crime conducted by Gary Kleck and Ted Chiricos reinforced the weak association between the two factors. Kleck and Chiricos discovered no relationship between unemployment rates and the rate of most crimes including those that desperate unemployed people might choose such as the robbery of gas stations, banks, and drugstores. Nor did unemployment influence the rate of nonviolent property crimes including shoplifting, residential burglary, theft of motor vehicle parts, and theft of automobiles, trucks, and motorcycles.

It is possible that over the long haul a strong economy helps lower crime rates, whereas long periods of sustained economic weakness and unemployment may eventually lead to increased rates. Crime rates fell when the economy surged for almost a decade during the 1990s; a long-term economic recession may produce increases in the crime rate.

Social Malaise

As the level of social problems increases—such as single-parent families, dropout rates, racial conflict, and teen pregnancies—so too do crime rates. For example, crime rates are correlated with the number of unwed mothers in the population. It is possible that children of unwed mothers need more social services than children in two-parent families. As the number of kids born to single mothers increases, the child welfare system will be taxed and services depleted. The number of teenage births began to decrease in the late 1980s, and 15 years later crime rates followed.

Racial conflict may also increase crime rates. Areas undergoing racial change, especially those experiencing an in-migration of minorities into predominantly white neighborhoods, seem prone to significant increases in their crime rate. Whites in these areas may be using violence to protect what they view as their home turf. Racially motivated crimes actually diminish as neighborhoods become more integrated and power struggles are resolved.

Abortion

In a controversial work, John Donohue III and Steven Levitt found empirical evidence that the recent drop in the crime rate can be attributed to the availability of legalized abortion. In 1973, *Roe v. Wade* legalized abortion nationwide. Within a few years of *Roe v. Wade,* more than 1 million abortions were being performed annually, or roughly one abortion for every three live births. Donohue and Levitt suggest that the crime rate drop, which began approximately 18 years later, in 1991, can be tied to the fact that at that point the first groups of potential offenders affected by the abortion decision began reaching the peak age of criminal activity. They find that states that legalized abortion before the rest of the nation were the first to experience decreasing crime rates and that states with high abortion rates have seen a greater fall in crime since 1985.

The abortion-related reduction in crime rates is predominantly attributable to a decrease in crime among the young. It is possible that the link between crime rates and abortion is the result of two mechanisms: (1) selective abortion on the part of women most at risk to have children who would engage in criminal activity, and (2) improved child-rearing or environmental circumstances caused by better maternal, familial, or fetal circumstances because women are having fewer children. If abortion were illegal, they suggest that crime rates might be 10 to 20 percent higher than they currently are with abortion. If these estimates are correct, legalized abortion can explain about half of the recent fall in crime. All else being equal, they predict that crime rates will continue to fall slowly for an additional 15 to 20 years as the full effects of legalized abortion are gradually felt.

Guns

The availability of firearms may influence the crime rate, especially the proliferation of weapons in the hands of teens. There is evidence that more guns than ever before are finding their way into the hands of young people. Surveys of high school students indicate that between 6 and 10 percent carry guns at least some of the time. Guns also cause escalation in the seriousness of crime. As the number of gun-toting students increases, so too will the seriousness of violent crime as, for example, a schoolyard fight turns into murder.

Gangs

Another factor that affects crime rates is the explosive growth in teenage gangs. Surveys indicate that there are more than 850,000 gang members in the United States. Boys who are members of gangs are far more likely to possess guns than non–gang members; criminal activity increases when kids join gangs. According to Alfred Blumstein, gangs involved in the urban drug trade recruit juveniles because they work cheaply, are immune from heavy criminal penalties, and are "daring and willing to take risks." Arming themselves for protection, these drug-dealing children present a menace to their community, which persuades non–gang-affiliated neighborhood adolescents to arm themselves for protection. The result is an arms race that produces an increasing spiral of violence.

The recent decline in the crime rate may be tied to changing gang values. Some streetwise kids have told researchers that they now avoid gangs because of the "younger brother syndrome"—they have watched their older siblings or parents caught in gang or drug-related activities and want to avoid the same fate.

Drug Use

Some experts tie increases in the violent crime rate between 1980 and 1990 to the "crack epidemic," which swept the nation's largest cities, and drug-trafficking gangs that fought over drug turf. These well-armed gangs did not hesitate to use violence to control territory, intimidate rivals, and increase market share. As the crack epidemic has subsided, so too has the violence in New York City and other metropolitan areas where crack use was rampant.

Media

Some experts argue that the availability and use of violent media can influence the direction of crime rates. As the availability of media with violent themes skyrocketed with the introduction of home video players, DVDs, cable TV, computer and video games, and so on, so too did teen violence rates. According to a recent analysis of all available scientific data conducted by Brad Bushman and Craig Anderson, watching violence on TV is correlated to aggressive behaviors, especially for people with a preexisting tendency toward crime and violence. This conclusion is bolstered by research showing that the more kids watch TV the more often they get into violent encounters. For example, Jeffrey Johnson and his associates at Columbia University found that 14-year-old boys who watched less than one hour of TV per day later got into an average of 9 fights resulting in injury. In contrast, adolescent males watching one to three hours of TV per day got into an average of 28 fights; those watching more than three hours of TV got into an average of 42 fights. Of those watching one to three hours per day, 22.5 percent later engaged in violence, such as assaults or robbery, in their adulthood; 28.8 percent of kids who regularly watched more than three hours of TV in a 24-hour period engaged in violent acts as adults.

Medical Technology

Some crime experts believe that the presence and quality of health care can have a significant impact on murder rates. According to research conducted by Anthony Harris and his associates, murder rates would be up to five times higher than they are today without the medical breakthroughs developed over the past 40 years. They estimate that the United States would suffer between 50,000 and 115,000 homicides per year, as opposed to the current number of around 16,000, without these advances in medical care. Looking back more than 40 years, they found that the aggravated assault rate has increased at a far higher pace than the murder rate, a fact they attribute to the decrease in mortality of violence victims in hospital emergency rooms. The big breakthrough occurred in the 1970s when technology developed to treat injured soldiers in Vietnam was applied to trauma care in the nation's hospitals. Since then, murder rates can be linked to the level and availability of emergency medical services.

Justice Policy

Some law enforcement experts have suggested that a reduction in crime rates may be attributed to adding large numbers of police officers and using them in aggressive police practices that target "quality of life" crimes such as panhandling, graffiti, petty drug dealing, and loitering. By showing that even the smallest infractions will be dealt with seriously, aggressive police departments may be able to discourage potential criminals from committing more serious crimes. For example, Michael White and his associates have recently shown that cities employing aggressive, focused police work may be able to lower homicide rates in the area.

It is also possible that tough laws targeting drug dealing and repeat offenders with lengthy prison terms can affect crime rates. The fear of punishment may inhibit some would-be criminals, and placing a significant number of potentially high-rate offenders behind bars may help lower crime rates. As the nation's prison population has expanded, the crime rate has fallen.

Crime Opportunities

Crime rates may drop (a) when market conditions change or (b) when an alternative criminal opportunity develops. For example, the decline in the burglary rate over the past decade may be explained in part by the abundance and subsequent decline in price of commonly stolen merchandise such as VCRs, TVs, and cameras. Improving home and commercial security devices may also turn off would-be burglars, convincing them to turn to other forms of theft such as theft from motor vehicles. These are nonindex crimes and do not contribute to the national crime rate.

Critical Thinking

While crime rates have been declining in the United States, they have been increasing in Europe. Is it possible that

(continued)

CURRENT ISSUES IN CRIME

Explaining Crime Trends (continued)

factors that correlate with crime rate changes in the United States have little utility in predicting changes in other cultures? What other factors may increase or reduce crime rates?

InfoTrac College Edition Research

Gang activity may have a big impact on crime rates. To read about the effect, see: John M. Hagedorn, Jose Torres, and Greg Giglio, "Cocaine, Kicks, and Strain: Patterns of Substance Use in Milwaukee Gangs," *Contemporary Drug Problems,* Spring 1998 v25 n1 p113–145
Mary E. Pattillo, "Sweet Mothers and Gangbangers: Managing Crime in a Black Middle-Class Neighborhood," *Social Forces,* March 1998 v76 n3 p747(28)

SOURCES: Steven Levitt, "Understanding why crime fell in the 1990s: four factors that explain the decline and six that do not," *Journal of Economic Perspectives* (in press, 2004); Michael White, James Fyfe, Suzanne Campbell, and John Goldkamp, "The police role in preventing homicide: considering the impact of problem-oriented policing on the prevalence of murder," *Journal of Research in Crime and Delinquency* 40 (2003): 194–226; Jeffrey Johnson, Patricia Cohen, Elizabeth Smailes, Stephanie Kasen, and Judith Brook, "Television viewing and aggressive behavior during adolescence and adulthood," *Science* 295 (2002): 2468–2471; Brad Bushman and Craig Anderson, "Media violence and the American public," *American Psychologist* 56 (2001): 477–489; Gary Kleck and Ted Chiricos, "Unemployment and property crime: a target-specific assessment of opportunity and motivation as mediating factors," *Criminology* 40 (2002): 649–680; Anthony Harris, Stephen Thomas, Gene Fisher, and David Hirsch, "Murder and medicine: The lethality of criminal assault 1960–1999," *Homicide Studies* 6 (2002): 128–167; Steven Messner, Lawrence Raffalovich, and Richard McMillan, "Economic deprivation and changes in homicide arrest rates for white and black youths, 1967–1998: a national time-series analysis," *Criminology* 39 (2001): 591–614; John Laub, "Review of the crime drop in America," *American Journal of Sociology* 106 (2001): 1820–1822; John J. Donohue III and Steven D. Levitt, "Legalized Abortion and Crime" (University of Chicago, June 24, 1999, unpublished paper); Donald Green, Dara Strolovitch, and Janelle Wong, "Defended neighborhoods, integration, and racially motivated crime," *American Journal of Sociology* 104 (1998): 372–403; Robert O'Brien, Jean Stockard, and Lynne Isaacson, "The enduring effects of cohort characteristics on age-specific homicide rates, 1960–1995," *American Journal of Sociology* 104 (1999): 1061–1095; Darrell Steffensmeier and Miles Harer, "Making sense of recent U.S. crime trends, 1980 to 1996/1998: age composition effects and other explanations," *Journal of Research in Crime and Delinquency* 36 (1999): 235–274; Desmond Ellis and Lori Wright, "Estrangement, interventions, and male violence toward female partners," *Violence and Victims* 12 (1997): 51–68; Joseph Sheley and James Wright, *In the Line of Fire: Youth, Guns, and Violence in Urban America* (New York: Aldine de Gruyter, 1995).

■ Though national crime surveys tell us that crime rates have declined, the public is bombarded by media accounts of brutal violence. Here William Striler, a disgruntled client, was caught on a TV camera as he shot his attorney Jerry Curry outside a Los Angeles courthouse. Curry survived and Striler was arrested for assault with a deadly weapon.

Particularly encouraging has been the decrease in the number and rate of murders. The murder statistics are generally regarded as the most accurate aspect of the UCR. Figure 2.3 illustrates homicide rate trends since 1900. Note that the rate peaked around 1930, then held relatively steady at about 4 or 5 per 100,000 population from 1950 through the mid-1960s, at which point the rate started rising to a peak of 10.2 per 100,000 population in 1980. From 1980 to 1991, the homicide rate fluctuated between 8 and 10 per 100,000 population; in 1991 the number of murders topped 24,000 for the first time in the nation's history. Between 1991 and 2000, homicide rates per capita fell from 9.8 to 5.5 per 100,000, a drop of 44 percent. Since that time, homicide rates have been steady. The decline in the violence rate has been both unexpected and welcome. Some major cities, such as New York, report a decline of more than 50 percent in their murder rates.

Trends in Property Crime

The property crimes reported in the UCR include larceny, motor vehicle theft, and arson. In 2002, about 10.4 million property crimes were reported, a rate of about 3,624 per 100,000 population. Property crime rates have declined in recent years, though the drop has not been as dramatic as that experienced by the violent crime rate. Between 1992 and 2002, the total number of prop-

Figure 2.3
Homicide Rate Trends,
1900–2002

SOURCE: Bureau of Justice Statistics, *Violent Crime in the United States* (Washington, D.C.: Author, 1992; updated 2002).

Rate per 100,00 population

erty crimes declined about 17 percent, and the property crime rate declined about 26 percent.

Trends in Self-Reports and Victimization

Table 2.1 contains data from a self-report study called *Monitoring the Future* (MTF), which researchers at the University of Michigan Institute for Social Research (ISR) conduct annually. This national survey of more than 2,500 high school seniors, one of the most important sources of self-report data, shows a widespread yet stable pattern of youth crime since 1978.[24] Young people self-report a great deal of crime: about 30 percent of high school seniors now report stealing in the last 12 months; 20 percent said they were involved in a gang fight, and more than 10 percent injured someone so badly that the victim had to see a doctor; almost 25 percent engaged in breaking and entering. The fact that so many—at least 33 percent—of all U.S. high school students engaged in theft and that about 20 percent committed a serious violent act during the past year shows that criminal activity is widespread and is not restricted to a few "bad apples." However, the MTF survey does not report any major upswing in teen crime, and if anything, there has been a slight decline in self-reported behavior in recent years.

Self-report results appear to be more stable than the UCR. When the results of recent self-report surveys are compared with various studies conducted over a 20-year period, a uniform pattern emerges. The use of drugs and alcohol increased markedly in the 1970s, leveled off in the 1980s, and then began to increase in the mid-1990s until 1997, when drug use began to decline. Theft, violence, and damage-related crimes seem more stable. Although a self-reported crime wave has not occurred, neither has there been any visible reduction in self-reported criminality.

According to the National Crime Victimization Survey (NCVS), in 2002 U.S. residents age 12 or older experienced about 23 million violent and property victimizations. This represents a significant downward trend in reported victimization that began in 1994 and that has resulted in the lowest number of criminal victimizations since 1973, when an estimated 44 million victimizations were recorded. Between 1993 and 2002 the violent crime rate has decreased 54 percent, from 50 to 23 victimizations per 1,000 persons age 12 or older, and the property crime rate declined 50 percent (from 319 to 159 crimes per 1,000 households). For example, in 2002 the rate for rape was 0.4 per 1,000 persons age 12 or older, 60 percent of the 1993 rate; the rate for robbery was down 63 percent.

TABLE 2.1 Self-Reported Delinquent Activity During the Past 12 Months among High School Seniors, 2002

TYPE OF CRIME	TOTAL COMMITTING WHO COMMITTED CRIME ONCE OR MORE (%)	COMMITTED ONLY ONCE (%)	COMMITTED MORE THAN ONCE (%)
Set fire on purpose	3	1	2
Damaged school property	11	5	6
Damaged work property	7	3	4
Auto theft	5	2	3
Auto part theft	5	2	3
Break and enter	23	10	13
Theft less than $50	29	12	17
Theft greater than $50	10	5	5
Shoplift	28	11	17
Gang fight	17	9	8
Hurt someone badly	12	6	6
Used force to steal	3	1	2
Hit teacher or supervisor	3	1	2
Gotten into serious fight	12	6	6

SOURCE: *Monitoring the Future, 2002* (Ann Arbor, Mich.: Institute for Social Research, 2003).

✔ Checkpoints

✔ The FBI's Uniform Crime Report is an annual tally of crime reported to local police departments. It is the nation's official crime database.

✔ The National Crime Victimization Survey (NCVS) samples more than 50,000 people annually to estimate the total number of criminal incidents, including those not reported to police.

✔ Self-report surveys ask respondents about their own criminal activity. They are useful in measuring crimes rarely reported to police, such as drug usage.

✔ Crime rates peaked in the early 1990s and have been in sharp decline ever since. The murder rate has undergone a particularly steep decline.

✔ A number of factors are believed to influence the crime rate, including the economy, drug use, gun availability, and crime control policies including adding police and putting more criminals in prison.

✔ It is difficult to gauge future trends. Some experts forecast an increase in crime, whereas others foresee a long-term decline in the crime rate.

To quiz yourself on this material, go to questions 2.1–2.11 on the Criminology: The Core 2e Web site.

Figure 2.4 shows the recent trends in violent crime, and Figure 2.5 tracks property victimizations. Although the official crime statistics indicate that the crime rate drop may be stabilizing, the victim data indicate that the crime drop continues unabated.

What the Future Holds

It is always risky to speculate about the future of crime trends because current conditions can change rapidly. But some criminologists have tried to predict future patterns. Criminologist James A. Fox predicts a significant increase in teen violence if current trends persist. The United States has approximately 50 million school-age children, many of them under age 10. Although many come from stable homes, others lack stable families and adequate supervision. These children will soon enter their prime crime years. As a result, Fox predicts a wave of youth violence.[25]

Although Fox's predictions are persuasive, not all criminologists believe we are in for an age-driven crime wave. Steven Levitt, for example, does not believe that the population's age makeup contributes as much to the crime rate as Fox and others suggest.[26] Levitt argues that even if teens do commit more crime in the future, their contribution may be offset by the aging of the population, which will produce a large number of senior citizens and elderly in the population, a group with a relatively low crime rate.[27] Levitt believes that keeping large numbers of people in prison and adding more police may add to the drop in crime rates. In the future, two factors—the rising numbers of police officers and the availability of legalized abortion—are likely to help keep the crime rate down (the waning of the crack epidemic and the peaking of the prison population will reduce the effect of these two important contributors to the crime rate decline). Levitt also sees a threat ahead: the maturation of "crack babies" who spent their early childhood years in families and neighborhoods ravaged by crack. Coupled with a difficult home environment, these children may turn out to be more prone to criminal activity. Overall, however, Levitt believes that continued crime declines over the next decade are a real possibility.

Although such prognostication may be reassuring, there is no way of telling what future changes may influence crime rates. For example, technological developments such as the rapid expansion of e-commerce have cre-

Figure 2.4

Violent Crime Rates

Violent victimization rates have declined since 1994, reaching the lowest level ever recorded in 2002.

SOURCE: Callie Marie Rennison and Michael Rand, *Criminal Victimization 2002* (Washington, D.C.: Bureau of Justice Statistics, 2003).

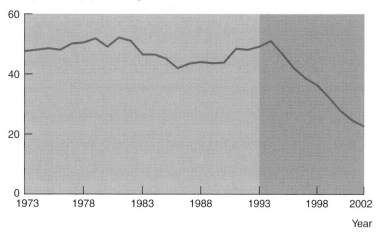

Rate per 1,000 population age 12 and over

Figure 2.5

Property Crime Victimization Rates

Property crime victimizations continue to decline.

SOURCE: Callie Marie Rennison and Michael Rand, *Criminal Victimization 2002* (Washington, D.C.: Bureau of Justice Statistics, 2003).

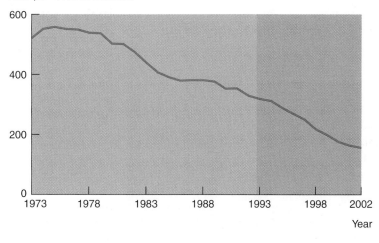

Rate per 1,000 households

ated new classes of crime, and the threat of war, terrorism, and economic recession may have some influence. So, while crime rates have trended downward, it is too early to predict that this trend will continue into the foreseeable future. ✔ Checkpoints

Crime Patterns

To gain insight into the nature of crime, criminologists look for stable crime rate patterns. If crime rates are consistently higher at certain times, in certain areas, and among certain groups, this knowledge might help explain the onset or cause of crime. For example, if criminal statistics show that crime rates are consistently higher in poor neighborhoods in large urban areas, then crime may be a function of poverty and neighborhood decline. If, in contrast, crime rates were spread evenly across the social structure, this would provide little evidence that crime has an economic basis; instead, crime might be linked to socialization, personality, intelligence, or some other trait unrelated to class position or income. In this section we examine traits and patterns that may influence the crime rate.

The Ecology of Crime

Most reported crimes occur during the warm summer months of July and August. During the summer, teenagers, who usually have the highest crime levels, are out of school and have greater opportunity to commit crime. People also spend more time outdoors, making them easier targets. Two exceptions to this trend are murders and robberies, which occur frequently in December and January (although rates are also high during the summer). Robbery rates increase in the winter partly because the Christmas shopping season means more money in the cash registers of potential targets.[28]

Crime rates also may be higher on the first day of the month than at any other time. Government welfare and Social Security checks arrive at this time, and with them come increases in such activities as breaking into mailboxes and accosting recipients on the streets. Also, people may have more disposable income at this time, and the availability of extra money may relate to behaviors associated with crime, such as partying, drinking, and gambling.[29]

Weather effects, such as temperature swings, may also affect violent crime rates. Crime rates increase with rising temperatures up to a point (about 85 degrees), but then begin to decline, perhaps because it becomes too hot for physical exertion.[30] However, the rates of some crimes, such as domestic assault, continue to increase as temperatures rise.[31]

Large urban areas have by far the highest violence rates; rural areas have the lowest per capita crime rates.

■ One reason that violence rates remain so high in the United States is the proliferation of hand guns and firearms. Here a shooting victim sits in a chair while being attended to by paramedics in Los Angeles County on April 20, 2003. The shooting was considered "gang related."

Use of Firearms

Firearms play a dominant role in criminal activity. According to the NCVS, firearms are typically involved in about 20 percent of robberies, 10 percent of assaults, and 6 percent of rapes. In 2002, the UCR reported that almost 70 percent of all murders involved firearms; most of these weapons were handguns.

According to international criminologists Franklin Zimring and Gordon Hawkins, the proliferation of handguns and the high rate of lethal violence they cause is the single most significant factor separating the crime problem in the United States from the rest of the developed world.[32] Differences between the United States and Europe in nonlethal crimes are only modest at best.[33] Because this issue is so important, the Policy and Practice in Criminology feature on pages 42–43 discusses gun control issues.

Social Class and Crime

Traditionally crime has been thought of as a lower-class phenomenon. After all, people at the lowest rungs of the social structure have the greatest incentive to commit crimes. Those unable to obtain desired goods and services through conventional means may resort to theft and other illegal activities—such as selling narcotics—to obtain them. These activities are referred to as **instrumental crimes.** Those living in poverty are also believed to engage in disproportionate numbers of **expressive crimes,** such as rape and assault, as a means of expressing their rage, frustration, and anger against society. Alcohol and drug abuse, common in impoverished areas, helps fuel violent episodes.[34]

Official statistics indicate that victimization rates for both males and females in inner-city, high-poverty areas are generally higher than those in suburban or wealthier areas.[35] Studies using aggregate police statistics (arrest records) have consistently shown that crime rates in lower-class areas exceed those in wealthier neighborhoods. Another "official" indicator of a class–crime relationship comes from surveys of prison inmates, which consistently show that prisoners were members of the lower class and unemployed or underemployed in the years before their incarceration.

An alternative explanation for these findings is that the relationship between official crime and social class is a function of law enforcement practices, not actual criminal behavior patterns. Police may devote more resources to poor areas, and consequently apprehension rates may be higher there. Simi-

instrumental crimes
Offenses designed to improve the financial or social position of the criminal.

expressive crimes
Offenses committed not for profit or gain but to vent rage, anger, or frustration.

■ Although some criminologists believe that criminals tend to be members of the lower class, members of the upper class commit crime as well. Here Defense Attorney David Rudolf (left) is shown at novelist Michael Peterson's trial for the murder of his wife Kathleen. Despite his claims of innocence, Peterson was convicted of the crime.

© 2003 AP/Wide World Photos

larly, police may be more likely to formally arrest and prosecute lower-class citizens than those in the middle and upper classes, which may account for the lower class's overrepresentation in official statistics and the prison population.

Class and Self-Reports   Self-report data have been used extensively to test the class–crime relationship. If people in all social classes self-report similar crime patterns, but only those in the lower class are formally arrested, that would explain higher crime rates in lower-class neighborhoods. However, if lower-class people report greater criminal activity than their middle- and upper-class peers, it would indicate that official statistics accurately represent the crime problem.

Surprisingly, self-report studies generally do not find a direct relationship between social class and youth crime.[36] Socioeconomic class is related to official processing by police, courts, and correctional agencies, but not to the actual commission of crimes. While lower- and middle-class youths self-report equal amounts of crime, the lower-class youths have a greater chance of getting arrested, convicted, incarcerated, and becoming official delinquents.[37] More than 20 years ago, Charles Tittle, Wayne Villemez, and Douglas Smith concluded that little if any support exists for the contention that crime is primarily a lower-class phenomenon. They argued that official statistics probably reflect class bias in processing lower-class offenders.[38]

Weighing the Evidence for a Class–Crime Relationship   Tittle's research has sparked significant debate. Many self-report instruments include trivial offenses such as using a false ID or drinking alcohol. Their inclusion may obscure the true class–crime relationship because affluent youths frequently engage in trivial offenses such as petty larceny, using drugs, and simple assault. Those who support a class–crime relationship suggest that if only serious felony offenses are considered, a significant association can be observed.[39] Studies showing middle- and lower-class youths to be equally delinquent rely on measures weighted toward minor crimes (for example, using a false ID or skipping school); when serious crimes, such as burglary and assault, are compared, lower-class youths are significantly more delinquent.[40] There is also debate over the most appropriate measure of class. Should it be income? Occupation? Educational attainment? Findings may be skewed if the measurement of class used is inappropriate or invalid. Finally, research shows that class affects crime rates for nonwhites more than it does for whites.[41]

The weight of recent evidence seems to suggest that serious, official crime is more prevalent among the lower classes, whereas less serious, self-reported crime is spread more evenly throughout the social structure.[42] Income inequality, poverty, and resource deprivation are all associated with the most serious violent crimes, including homicide and assault.[43] Communities that lack economic and social opportunities also produce high levels of frustration; their residents believe that they are relatively more deprived than residents of more affluent

Connections

If class and crime are unrelated, then the causes of crime must be found in factors experienced by members of all social classes—psychological impairment, family conflict, peer pressure, school failure, and so on. Theories that view crime as a function of individual traits are discussed in Chapter 5, and theories that view crime as a function of social problems experienced by members of all social classes are reviewed in Chapter 7.

POLICY AND PRACTICE IN CRIMINOLOGY

Should Guns Be Controlled?

The 2002 sniper killings in the Washington D.C. area focused a spotlight on a long-running policy debate in the United States: Should guns be controlled? According to the 2003 Small Arms Survey, the United States has by far the largest number of publicly owned firearms in the world and is approaching the point where there is one gun for every American. About 280 million! An estimated 50 million of these guns are illegal. Handguns are linked to many violent crimes, including 20 percent of all injury deaths (second to autos) and 60 percent of all homicides and suicides. They are also responsible for the deaths of about two-thirds of all police officers killed in the line of duty. Cross-national research conducted by Anthony Hoskin found that nations with high levels of privately owned firearms, including the United States, also have the highest levels of homicide. To some critics the deadly sniper attacks that paralyzed the Virginia-Maryland area in October 2002 were a sad result of the widespread availability of deadly rifles and handguns.

Research by Matthew Miller and his associates shows that in areas where household firearm ownership rates are high, a disproportionately large number of people die from homicide. The association between guns and crime has spurred many Americans to advocate controlling the sale of handguns and banning the cheap mass-produced handguns known as "Saturday night specials."

In contrast, gun advocates view control as a threat to personal liberty and call for severe punishment of criminals rather than control of handguns. They argue that the Second Amendment of the U.S. Constitution protects the right to bear arms. A 2001 survey by Robert Jiobu and Timothy Curry found that the typical gun owner has a deep mistrust of the federal government; to them, a gun is an "icon for democracy and personal empowerment" (p. 87).

Gun Control Efforts

Efforts to control handguns have come from many different sources. The states and many local jurisdictions have laws banning or restricting sales or possession of guns; some regulate dealers who sell guns. The Federal Gun Control Act of 1968, which is still in effect, requires that all dealers be licensed, fill out forms detailing each trade, and avoid selling to people prohibited from owning guns such as minors, ex-felons, and drug users. Dealers must record the source and properties of all guns they sell and carefully account for their purchase. Gun buyers must provide identification and sign waivers attesting to their ability to possess guns. Unfortunately, the resources available to enforce this law are meager.

On November 30, 1993, the Brady Handgun Violence Prevention Act was enacted, amending the Gun Control Act of 1968. The bill was named after former Press Secretary James Brady, who was severely wounded in the attempted assassination of President Ronald Reagan by John Hinckley in 1981. The Brady Law imposes a waiting period of five days before a licensed importer, manufacturer, or dealer may sell, deliver, or transfer a handgun to an unlicensed individual. The waiting period applies only in states without an acceptable alternate system of conducting background checks on handgun purchasers. Beginning November 30, 1998, the Brady law changed, providing an instant check on whether a prospective buyer is prohibited from purchasing a weapon. Federal law bans gun purchases by people convicted of or under indictment for felony charges, fugitives, the mentally ill, those with dishonorable military discharges, those who have renounced U.S. citizenship, illegal aliens, illegal drug users, and those convicted of domestic violence misdemeanors or who are under domestic violence restraining orders (individual state laws may create other restrictions). The Brady Law now requires background approval not just for handgun buyers but also for those who buy long guns and shotguns.

Although gun control advocates see this legislation as a good first step, some question whether such measures will ultimately curb gun violence. For example, when Jens Ludwig and Philip Cook compared two sets of states, 32 that installed the Brady Law in 1994 and 18 states plus the District of Columbia that already had similar types of laws prior to 1994, they found no evidence that implementing the Brady Law contributed to a reduction in homicide.

Another approach is to severely punish people caught with unregistered handguns. The most famous attempt to regulate handguns using this method is the Massachusetts Bartley-Fox Law, which provides a mandatory one-year prison term for possessing a handgun (outside the home) without a permit. A detailed analysis of violent crime in Boston after the law's passage found that the use of handguns in robberies and murders did decline substantially (in robberies by 35 percent and in murders by 55 percent in a two-year period). However, these optimistic results must be tempered by two facts: rates for similar crimes dropped significantly in comparable cities that did not have gun control laws, and the use of other weapons, such as knives, increased in Boston.

Some jurisdictions have tried to reduce gun violence by adding extra punishment, such as a mandatory prison sentence for any crime involving a handgun. California's "10-20-life" law requires an additional 10 years in prison for carrying a gun while committing a violent felony, 20 years if the gun is fired, and if someone is injured the penalty increases to from 25 years to life in prison.

Can Guns Be Outlawed?

Even if outlawed or severely restricted, the government's ability to control guns is problematic. Even if legitimate gun stores were strictly regulated, private citizens could still sell, barter, or trade handguns. Unregulated gun fairs and auctions are common throughout the United States; many gun deals are made at gun shows with few questions asked. People obtain firearms illegally through a multitude of unauthorized sources including unlicensed dealers, corrupt licensed dealers, and "straw" purchasers.

If handguns were banned or outlawed, they would become more valuable; illegal importation of guns might increase as it has for another controlled substance, narcotics. Increasing penalties for gun-related crimes has also met with limited success because judges may be reluctant to alter their sentencing policies to accommodate legislators. Regulating dealers is difficult, and tighter controls on them would only encourage private sales and bartering. Relatively few guns are stolen in burglaries, but many are sold to licensed gun dealers who circumvent the law by ignoring state registration requirements or making unrecorded or mis-recorded sales to individuals and un-licensed dealers. Even a few corrupt dealers can supply tens of thousands of illegal handguns.

Is There a Benefit to Having Guns?

Not all experts are convinced that strict gun control is a good thing. Gary Kleck, a leading advocate of gun ownership, argues that guns may actually inhibit violence. Along with Marc Gertz, Kleck conducted a national survey that indicates that Americans use guns for defensive purposes up to 2.5 million times a year. This figure seems huge, but it must be viewed in the context of gun ownership: about 47.6 million households own a gun, more than 90 million, or 49 percent of the adult U.S. population, live in a household with guns, and about 59 million adults personally own guns. Considering these numbers it is not implausible that 3 percent of the people (or 2.5 million people) with access to a gun could have used one defensively in a given year.

Guns have other uses. In many assaults, Kleck reasons, the aggressor does not wish to kill but only scare the victim. Possessing a gun gives aggressors so much killing power that they may actually be inhibited from attacking. For example, research by Kleck and Karen McElrath found that during a robbery guns can control the situation without the need for illegal force. Guns may also enable victims to escape serious injury. Victims may be inhibited from fighting back without losing face; it is socially acceptable to back down from a challenge if the opponent is armed with a gun. Guns then can de-escalate a potentially

violent situation. Kleck, along with Michael Hogan, finds that people who own guns are only slightly more likely to commit homicide than nonowners. The benefits of gun ownership, he concludes, outweigh the costs.

Kleck's findings have been supported by research conducted by John Lott and David Mustard. Using cross-sectional data for the United States, they found that jurisdictions that allow citizens to carry concealed weapons also have lower violent crime rates. If all states allowed citizens to carry concealed weapons, their analysis indicates that 1,500 murders, 4,000 rapes, 11,000 robberies, and 60,000 aggravated assaults would be avoided yearly. The annual social benefit from each additional concealed handgun permit is as high as $5,000, saving society more than $6 billion per year.

Does Defensive Gun Use Really Work?

While Kleck and his associates support the use of guns for defensive purposes, other research efforts show that defensive gun use may be more limited than believed. It works sometimes and only for some people. Moreover, research shows that having a gun in a violent situation is more likely to produce a negative outcome than any other kind of weapon (for example, knives or clubs). Even people with a history of violence and mental disease are less likely to kill when they use a knife or other weapon than when they employ a gun. "Do guns kill people or do people kill people?" Research indicates that even the most dangerous people are less likely to resort to lethal violence if the gun is taken out of their hands.

Critical Thinking

1. Should the sale and possession of handguns be banned?

2. Which of the gun control methods discussed do you feel would be most effective in deterring crime?

InfoTrac College Edition Research

One method of reducing gun violence may be to make guns safer. Read more about this plan in:

Krista D. Robinson, Stephen P. Teret, Susan DeFrancesco, and Stephen W. Hargarten, "Making Guns Safer," *Issues in Science and Technology,* Summer 1998 v14 n4 p37(4)

SOURCES: *The Small Arms Survey,* 2003 http://www.smallarmssurvey.org/ (accessed July 10, 2003); Matthew Miller, Deborah Azrael, and David Hemenway, "Rates of household firearm ownership and homicide across US regions and states, 1988–1997," *American Journal of Public Health* 92 (2002): 1988–1993; Stephen Schnebly, "An examination of the impact of victim, offender, and situational attributes on the deterrent effect of gun use: A research note," *Justice Quarterly* 19 (2002): 377–399; William Wells and Julie Horney, "Weapon effects and individual intent to do harm: influences on the escalation of violence," *Criminology* 40 (2002): 265–296; John Lott Jr., "More guns, less crime: understanding crime and gun-control laws," *Studies in Law and Economics,* 2nd ed. (Chicago, Ill.: University of Chicago Press, 2001); John Lott Jr. and David Mustard, "Crime, deterrence, and right-to-carry concealed handguns," *Journal of Legal Studies* 26 (1997): 1–68; Anthony A. Braga and David M. Kennedy, "The illicit acquisition of firearms by youth and juveniles," *Journal of Criminal Justice* 29 (2001): 379–388; Anthony Hoskin, "Armed Americans: the impact of firearm availability on national homicide rates," *Justice Quarterly* 18 (2001): 569–592; J. Robert Jiobu and Timothy Curry, "Lack of confidence in the federal government and the ownership of firearms," *Social Science Quarterly* 82 (2001): 77–87; Jens Ludwig and Philip Cook, "Homicide and suicide rates associated with the implementation of the Brady Violence Prevention Act," *Journal of the American Medical Association* 284 (2000): 585–591; Julius Wachtel, "Sources of crime guns in Los Angeles, California," *Policing* 21 (1998): 220–239; Gary Kleck and Michael Hogan, "National case-control study of homicide offending and gun ownership," *Social Problems* 46 (1999): 275–293; Garen Wintemute, Mora Wright, Carrie Parham, Christina Drake, and James Beaumont, "Denial of handgun purchase: a description of the affected population and a controlled study of their handgun preferences," *Journal of Criminal Justice* 27 (1999): 21–31; Shawn Schwaner, L. Allen Furr, Cynthia Negrey, and Rachelle Seger, "Who wants a gun license?" *Journal of Criminal Justice* 27 (1999): 1–10; Gary Kleck and Marc Gertz, "Armed resistance to crime: the prevalence and nature of self-defense with a gun," *Journal of Criminal Law and Criminology* 86 (1995): 150–187; Colin Loftin, David McDowall, Brian Wiersma, and Talbert Cottey, "Effects of restrictive licensing of handguns on homicide and suicide in the District of Columbia," *New England Journal of Medicine* 325 (1991): 1615–1620.

areas and may turn to criminal behavior to relieve their frustration.[44] Family life is disrupted and law-violating youth groups thrive in a climate that undermines adult supervision.[45] Conversely, when the poor are provided with economic opportunities via welfare and public assistance, crime rates drop.[46]

Age and Crime

There is general agreement that age is inversely related to criminality.[47] Regardless of economic status, marital status, race, sex, or other factors, younger people commit crime more often than their older peers. Research indicates that this relationship has been stable across time periods ranging from 1935 to the present.[48]

Official statistics tell us that young people are arrested at a disproportionate rate to their numbers in the population; victim surveys generate similar findings for crimes in which assailant age can be determined. Whereas youths ages 13 to 17 collectively make up about 6 percent of the total U.S. population, they account for about 25 percent of index crime arrests and 17 percent of arrests for all crimes. As a general rule, the peak age for property crime is believed to be 16, and for violence, 18 (see Figure 2.6). In contrast, adults 45 and over, who make up more than 30 percent of the population, account for less than 10 percent of index crime arrests.

The elderly are particularly resistant to the temptations of crime; they make up more than 12 percent of the population and less than 1 percent of arrests. Elderly males 65 and over are arrested predominantly for alcohol-related matters (public drunkenness and drunk driving) and elderly females for larceny (shoplifting). The elderly crime rate has remained stable for the past 20 years.[49] The fact that people commit less crime as they mature is referred to as **aging out** or **desistance.**

Why does aging out occur? One view is that there is a direct relationship between aging and crime. Psychologists note that young people, especially the indigent and antisocial, tend to discount the future.[50] They are impatient, and, because their future is uncertain, they are unwilling or unable to delay gratification. As they mature, troubled youths are able to develop a long-term life view and resist the need for immediate gratification.[51] Kids may view crime as fun, a risky but exciting social activity. As they grow older, life patterns such as job and marriage become inconsistent with criminality; people literally grow out of crime.[52]

Although most people age out of crime, some do pursue a criminal career. Yet even career criminals eventually slow down as they age. Crime is too dangerous, physically taxing, and unrewarding (and punishments too harsh and long-lasting) to become a long-term way of life for most people.[53] By middle age, even the most chronic offenders terminate criminal behavior.

Figure 2.6

The Relationship between Age and Serious Violent Crime

Violent crime rates peak in the late teens and then decline rapidly.

SOURCE: FBI, Uniform Crime Report, 2002, pp. 244–245.

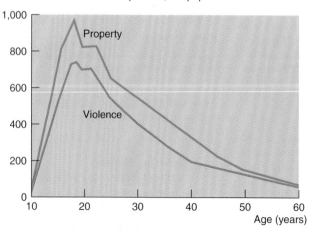

Violent Crime Index arrests per 100,000 population

aging out (desistance)
The fact that people commit less crime as they mature.

Gender and Crime

■ While males are still significantly more likely to commit crimes than females, the female crime rate has been on the rise. Here Fallon Tallent looks at her family during her arraignment on charges of first degree murder after she struck and killed two police officers during a high-speed chase on Interstate 40 in Tennessee on July 9, 2003.

Connections

Gender differences in the crime rate may be a function of androgen levels; these hormones cause areas of the brain to become less sensitive to environmental stimuli, making males more likely to seek high levels of stimulation and to tolerate more pain in the process. Chapter 5 discusses the biosocial causes of crime and reviews this issue in greater detail.

masculinity hypothesis
The view that women who commit crimes have biological and psychological traits similar to those of men.

All three data-gathering criminal statistics tools support the theory that male crime rates are much higher than those of females. Victims report that their assailant was male in more than 80 percent of all violent personal crimes. The Uniform Crime Report arrest statistics indicate that the overall male–female arrest ratio is about 3.5 male offenders to 1 female offender; for serious violent crimes, the ratio is closer to 5 males to 1 female; murder arrests are 8 males to 1 female. Recent self-report data collected by the Institute for Social Research at the University of Michigan also show that males commit more serious crimes, such as robbery, assault, and burglary, than females. However, although the patterns in self-reports parallel official data, the ratios seem smaller. In other words, males self-report more criminal behavior than females, but not to the degree suggested by official data.

Trait Differences   Why are there gender differences in the crime rate? Early criminologists pointed to emotional, physical, and psychological differences between males and females to explain the differences in crime rates. They maintained that because females were weaker and more passive, they were less likely to commit crimes. Cesare Lombroso argued that a small group of female criminals lacked "typical" female traits of "piety, maternity, undeveloped intelligence, and weakness."[54] Lombroso's theory became known as the **masculinity hypothesis;** in essence, a few "masculine" females were responsible for the handful of crimes that women commit.[55]

Although these early writings are no longer taken seriously, some criminologists still consider trait differences a key determinant of crime rate differences. For example, some criminologists link antisocial behavior to hormonal influences by arguing that male sex hormones (androgens) account for more aggressive male behavior; thus, gender-related hormonal differences can explain the gender gap in the crime rate.[56]

Socialization Differences   By the mid-twentieth century, criminologists commonly portrayed gender differences in the crime rate as a function of socialization. Female criminals were described as troubled individuals, alienated at home, who pursued crime as a means of compensating for their disrupted personal lives.[57] The streets became a "second home" to girls whose physical and emotional adjustment was hampered by a strained home life marked by such conditions as absent fathers or overly competitive mothers. The relatively few females who committed violent crimes actually had a home and family relationship that was more troubled than those experienced by males.[58] For example, in a 2002 study of delinquent girls sent to adult prisons, Emily Gaarder and Joanne Belknap found that many of these young women had troubled lives that set them on a criminal career path.[59] One girl told them how her father had attacked her yet her mother shortly let him return home:

> I told her I'd leave if he came back, but she let him anyway. I was thinking, you know, she should be worrying about me. I left and went to my cousin's house. Nobody even called me. Mom didn't talk to me for two weeks, and Dad said to me "Don't call." It was like they didn't care. I started smoking weed a lot then, drinking, skipping school, and shoplifting...I had no [delinquency] record before this happened.

Feminist Views   In the 1970s, liberal feminists focused their attention on the gender differences in social and economic roles and its relationship to female crime rates.[60] They suggested that the traditionally lower crime rate for women could be explained by their "second-class" economic and social position. Gender disparities in income, education, economic opportunities, and political

Connections

Critical criminologists view gender inequality as stemming from the unequal power of men and women in a capitalist society and the exploitation of females by fathers and husbands. This perspective, along with radical feminism, is considered more fully in Chapter 8.

power made women vulnerable to predatory men. When women did turn to violent crime, it was because of their hopelessness and rage, which developed because they were so vulnerable to abusive partners.[61]

Feminists predicted that as women's social roles changed and their lifestyles became more like those of men, their crime rates would converge.[62] Their prognostications may be borne out by recent trends in the crime rate. Although arrest rates are still considerably higher for males than for females, female arrest rates seem to be increasing at a faster pace. For example, between 1992 and 2002, male arrests actually decreased about 4 percent, whereas female arrests increased almost 18 percent. During this period, female violent crime arrests rose about 24 percent, while male violent crime arrests declined 16 percent. The arrests of teenage girls increased during this period (26 percent), whereas those of male teenagers declined (about –12 percent), suggesting that young females are increasing their offense rates at a pace equal or even greater than their older sisters.

Race and Crime

Official crime data indicate that minority group members are involved in a disproportionate share of criminal activity. According to UCR reports, African Americans make up about 12 percent of the general population, yet they account for about 37 percent of violent crime arrests and 31 percent of property crime arrests.

Self-Reports and Race   Another approach to examining this issue is to compare the racial differences in self-report data with those found in official delinquency records. Charges of racial discrimination in the arrest process would be supported if racial differences in self-report data were insignificant.

Nationwide studies of youth have found few racial differences in crime rates, although black youths were much more likely to be arrested and taken into custody.[63] These self-report studies seem to indicate that the criminal behavior rates of black and white teenagers are generally similar and that differences in arrest statistics may indicate a differential selection policy by police.[64]

Causes of Racial Disparity in the Crime Rate   Racial differences in the crime rate remain an extremely sensitive issue. Although official arrest records indicate that African Americans are arrested at a higher rate than members of other racial groups, some question whether this is a function of crime rate differences or discrimination in the way the law is enforced.[65] There are a number of views on this issue, and the two most prominent are discussed here:

Connections

According to some criminologists, racism has created isolated subcultures that espouse violence as a way of coping with conflict situations. Exasperation and frustration among minority group members who feel powerless to fit within middle-class society are manifested in aggression. This view is discussed further in Chapter 10 in the review of the subculture of violence theory.

1. *Racial threat.* According to the **racial threat view,** as the size of the black population increases, the perceived threat to the white population increases, resulting in a greater amount of social control imposed against blacks. African Americans are arrested more often because they are viewed as an economic and social threat to the white population.

Is this position valid? The research shows that suspects who are poor, minority, and male are more likely to be formally arrested than suspects who are white, affluent, and female.[66] Some police officers have used "racial profiling" to stop African Americans and search their cars without probable cause or reasonable suspicion. Some cynics have gone so far as to suggest that police officers have created a new form of traffic offense called DWB—driving while black.[67] The effects of racial threat are most noticeable when there are increases in black-on-white crime; in contrast, no such effect is typically observed for black-on-black crime. This finding indicates that it is not black crime rates per se that motivate the decision to arrest but the threat posed by interracial crimes.[68]

Empirical evidence shows that, at least in some jurisdictions, young African American males are treated more harshly by the criminal and juvenile justice systems than are members of any other group.[69] Under some circumstances (for example, if they have a prior record), African American youths are more likely to be punished severely than are white youths.[70] It is possible that some judges view poor blacks as "social dynamite," considering them more

racial threat view
As the size of the black population increases, the perceived threat to the white population increases, resulting in a greater amount of social control imposed against blacks.

dangerous and likely to recidivate than white offenders.[71] Yet black victims of crime receive less public concern and media attention than white victims.[72]

2. *Racial inequality.* The UCR may reflect discriminatory police practices in that African Americans are arrested for a disproportionate amount of violent crime, such as robbery and murder. But it is improbable that police discretion alone accounts for these proportions. It is doubtful that police routinely ignore white killers, robbers, and rapists while arresting violent black offenders. Many criminologists today concede that recorded differences in the black and white violent crime arrest rates cannot be explained away solely by racism or differential treatment within the criminal justice system.[73] To do so would be to ignore the social problems that exist in the nation's inner cities.

According to the racial inequality view, African Americans have suffered through a long history of racism in the United States that has left long-lasting emotional scars.[74] Differences in the black–white crime rate are a function of the impact of economic deprivation and the legacy of racism and discrimination.[75] Racism is still an element of daily life in the African American community, undermining faith in social and political institutions and weakening confidence in the justice system.[76]

African Americans living in lower-class slums may be disproportionately violent because they are exposed to more violence in their daily lives than other racial and economic groups. This exposure is a significant risk factor for violent behavior.[77] In a significant research effort, sociologist Julie Philips finds that if whites were subjected to the same economic and social disabilities as minorities, interracial homicide rate differences would be dramatically reduced.[78]

In sum, the weight of the evidence shows that although there is little difference in self-reported overall crime rates by race, African Americans are more likely to be arrested for serious violent crimes. The causes of minority crime have been linked to poverty, racism, hopelessness, lack of opportunity, and urban problems experienced by all too many African Americans. ✔ Checkpoints

The Chronic Offender

Crime data show that most offenders commit a single criminal act and, upon arrest, discontinue their antisocial activity. Others commit a few, less serious crimes. Finally, a small group of persistent offenders accounts for a majority of all criminal offenses. These persistent offenders are referred to as career criminals or **chronic offenders.**

The concept of the chronic or career offender is most closely associated with the research efforts of Marvin Wolfgang, Robert Figlio, and Thorsten Sellin.[79] In their landmark 1972 study, *Delinquency in a Birth Cohort,* they used official records to follow the criminal careers of a cohort of 9,945 boys born in Philadelphia in 1945, from the time of their birth until they reached 18 years of age in 1963. Official police records were used to identify delinquents. About one-third of the boys (3,475) had some police contact. The remaining two-thirds (6,470) had none. The best-known discovery of Wolfgang and his associates was the phenomenon of the chronic offender. They identified a group of 627 boys who had been arrested five times or more. This group was responsible for a total of 5,305 offenses, or 51.9 percent of all the offenses committed by the cohort. Even more striking was their involvement in serious criminal acts. Though comprising only about 6 percent of the entire sample, they committed 71 percent of the homicides, 73 percent of the rapes, 82 percent of the robberies, and 69 percent of the aggravated assaults.

Wolfgang and his associates found that arrests and court experience did little to deter the chronic offender. In fact, punishment was inversely related to chronic offending: The more stringent the sanction chronic offenders received, the more likely they were to engage in repeated criminal behavior. Wolfgang's pioneering effort to identify the chronic career offender has since been replicated by a number of other researchers in a variety of locations in the United States and abroad.[80]

chronic offenders
A small group of persistent offenders who account for a majority of all criminal offenses.

The findings of the cohort studies and the discovery of the chronic offender have revitalized criminological theory. If relatively few offenders become chronic, persistent criminals, then perhaps they possess some individual trait that is responsible for their behavior. Most people exposed to troublesome social conditions, such as poverty, do not become chronic offenders, so it is unlikely that social conditions alone can cause chronic offending.

Traditional theories of criminal behavior failed to distinguish between chronic and occasional offenders. They concentrated more on explaining why people begin to commit crime and paid scant attention to why people stop offending. The discovery of the chronic offender 25 years ago forced criminologists to consider such issues as persistence and desistance in their explanations of crime; more recent theories account not only for the onset of criminality but also for its termination.

Summary

- The three primary sources of crime statistics are the Uniform Crime Reports, based on police data accumulated by the FBI; self-reports from criminal behavior surveys; and victim surveys.

- Each data source has its strengths and weaknesses, and, although quite different from one another, they actually agree on the nature of criminal behavior.

- The crime data indicate that rates have declined significantly in the past few years and are now far less than they were a decade ago. Suspected causes for the crime rate drop include an increasing prison population, more cops of the street, the end of the crack epidemic, the availability of abortion, and the age structure of society.

- The data sources show stable patterns in the crime rate.

- Ecological patterns show that crime varies by season and by urban versus rural environment.

- There is also evidence of gender patterns in the crime rate: Men commit more crime than women.

- Age influences crime. Young people commit more crime than the elderly. Crime data show that people commit less crime as they age, but the significance and cause of this pattern are still not completely understood.

- Similarly, racial and class patterns appear in the crime rate. However, it is still unclear whether these are true differences or a function of discriminatory law enforcement.

- One of the most important findings in the crime statistics is the existence of the chronic offender, a repeat criminal responsible for a significant amount of all law violations. Chronic offenders begin their careers early in life and, rather than aging out of crime, persist into adulthood.

Thinking Like a Criminologist

The planning director for the State Department of Juvenile Justice has asked for your advice on how to reduce the threat of chronic offenders. Some of the more conservative members of her staff seem to believe that these young offenders need a strict dose of rough justice if they are to be turned away from a life of crime. They believe that juvenile delinquents who are punished harshly are less likely to recidivate than youths who receive lesser punishments, such as community corrections or proba-

tion. In addition, they believe that hard-core, violent offenders deserve to be punished; excessive concern for offenders and not their acts ignores the rights of victims and society in general.

The planning director is unsure whether such an approach can reduce the threat of chronic offending. Can tough punishment produce deviant identities that lock young offenders into a criminal way of life? She is concerned that a strategy stressing punishment will have relatively little impact on chronic offenders and, if any-thing, may cause escalation in serious criminal behaviors.

She has asked you for your professional advice. On one hand, the system must be sensitive to the adverse effects of stigma and labeling. On the other hand, the need for control and deterrence must not be ignored. Is it possible to reconcile these two opposing views?

Go to the Criminology: The Core 2e Web site to review the content of this chapter.

Doing Research on the Web

For an up-to-date list of URLs, go to

http://www.cj.wadsworth.com/siegel_crimcore2e

To help formulate your answer, review some of these web-based resources:

"Recommendations to Strengthen Criminal Justice as It Relates to Juveniles," by former Attorney General William P. Barr,

http://www.juvenilejustice.com/wbarr.html

"Turning Chronic Juvenile Offenders Into Productive Citizens: Comprehensive Model Emerging," by Eric B. Schnurer and Charles R. Lyons

http://www.cnponline.org/Issue%20Briefs/Statelines/statelin0101.htm

For an International view, see:

"Juvenile Offending: Predicting Persistence and Determining the Cost-Effectiveness of Intervention,"

http://www.lawlink.nsw.gov.au/bocsar1.nsf/pages/r33textsection1

Pro/Con discussions and Viewpoint Essays on some of the topics in this chapter may be found at the Opposing Viewpoints Resource Center:

http://www.gale.com/OpposingViewpoints

Key Terms

Uniform Crime Report (UCR) 29
index crimes 29
National Crime Victimization Survey (NCVS) 30

self-report surveys 31
instrumental crimes 40
expressive crimes 40
aging out (desistance) 44

masculinity hypothesis 45
racial threat view 46
chronic offenders 47

Critical Thinking Questions

1. Would you answer honestly if a national crime survey asked you about your criminal behavior, including drinking and drug use? If not, why not?

2. How would you explain gender differences in the crime rate? That is, why do you think males are more violent than females?

3. Assuming that males are more violent than females, does that mean that crime has a biological rather than a social basis (because males and females share a similar environment)?

4. The UCR tells us that crime rates are higher in large cities than in small villages. What does that tell us about the effect of TV, films, and music on teenage behavior?

CHAPTER 3

Victims and Victimization

Chapter Objectives

1. Understand the concept of victimization.

2. Describe the nature of victimization.

3. Be able to discuss the problems of crime victims.

4. Be familiar with the costs of victimization.

5. Be able to discuss the relationship between victimization and antisocial behavior.

6. Recognize the age, gender, and racial patterns in victimization data.

7. Be able to discuss the association between lifestyle and victimization.

8. Understand the term *victim precipitation*.

9. List the routine activities associated with victimization risk.

10. Be able to discuss the various victim assistance programs.

I N 2001 THE STATE OF CON-

NECTICUT WAS ROCKED

WHEN WATERBURY MAYOR

PHILIP GIORDANO, A MARRIED

father of three, was arrested for engag-

ing in sexual relations with minors as

young as 9 years old. Giordano was a

highly respected officeholder who had

been the Republican candidate for U.S.

Senator in the 2000 campaign (he lost to

incumbent Joseph Lieberman). During an

FBI investigation into city corruption, a

View the CNN video clip of this story and answer
related critical thinking questions on your
Criminology: The Core 2e CD.

17-year-old girl came forward and charged that Giordano had paid her to have sex with him in
his private law office and to watch him have sex with her aunt, Guitana Jones. The teenager told
state officials that from the time she was 12 Jones often arranged for sexual encounters between
her and men for pay, a practice that Jones called "going to wash windows." The FBI investigation
also found that Jones was providing her two daughters, ages 8 and 10, to Giordano for sexual
encounters.[1]

n March 25, 2003, a federal jury convicted Giordano of violating the
civil rights of the two young girls. He was also found guilty of conspiracy and using an interstate device—a cell phone—to arrange the
meetings with the girls. Giordano, 40, faces up to life in prison.[2] The
Giordano case is shocking because it involves a high public official.
And though it is unusual for its sordidness, it is not unique. A recent
multinational survey concluded that each year in the United States
325,000 children are subjected to some form of sexual exploitation,
which includes sexual abuse, prostitution, use in pornography, and
molestation by adults.[3]

The Giordano case also illustrates the importance of understanding the victim's role in the crime process. Why do people become targets of predatory criminals? Is victimization a matter of chance, or do
people become victims because of their lifestyle and environment?
Can a victim somehow deflect or avoid criminal behavior? And most
importantly in the Giordano case, what can be done to protect victims, and, failing that, what can be done to help them in the aftermath of crime?

The Victim's Role

For many years, crime victims were not considered an important topic for criminological study. Victims were viewed as the passive recipients of a criminal's anger, greed, or frustration; they were considered to be people "in the wrong place at the wrong time." In the late 1960s, a number of pioneering studies found that, contrary to popular belief, the victim's own behavior is important in the crime process. Victims were found to influence criminal behavior by playing an active role in a criminal incident, as when an assault victim initially provokes an eventual attacker. Victims can also play an indirect role in a criminal incident, as when a woman adopts a lifestyle that continually brings her into high-crime areas.

The discovery that victims play an important role in the crime process has prompted the scientific study of victims, or **victimology**. Criminologists who focus their attention on crime victims refer to themselves as **victimologists**.

In this chapter, we examine victims and their relationship to the criminal process. First, using available victim data, we analyze the nature and extent of victimization. We then discuss the relationship between victims and criminal offenders. In this context, we look at various theories of victimization that attempt to explain the victim's role in the crime problem. Finally, we examine how society has responded to the needs of victims and consider what special problems they still face.

Problems of Crime Victims

The National Crime Victimization Survey (NCVS) indicates that the annual number of victimizations in the United States is about 23 million incidents. Being the target or victim of a rape, robbery, or assault is a terrible burden that can have considerable long-term consequences. The costs of victimization can include such things as damaged property, pain and suffering to victims, and the involvement of the police and other agencies of the justice system. The pain and suffering that is inflicted on an individual from an assault or robbery can result in medical care, lost wages from not being able to go to work, as well as reduced quality of life from debilitating injuries and/or fear of being victimized again, which can result in not being able to go to work, long-term medical care, and counseling.

Economic Loss

When the costs of goods taken during property crimes is added to productivity losses caused by injury, pain, and emotional trauma, the cost of victimization is estimated to be in the hundreds of billions of dollars.

System Costs   Part of the economic loss due to victimization is the cost to American taxpayers of maintaining the justice system. For example, violent crime by juveniles alone costs the United States $158 billion each year.[4] This estimate includes some of the costs incurred by federal, state, and local governments to assist victims of juvenile violence, such as medical treatment for injuries and services for victims, which amounts to about $30 billion. The remaining $128 billion is due to losses suffered by victims, such as lost wages, pain, suffering, and reduced quality of life. Not included in these figures are the costs incurred trying to reduce juvenile violence, which include early prevention programs, services for juveniles, and the juvenile justice system.

Juvenile violence is only one part of the crime picture. If the cost of the justice system, legal costs, treatment costs, and so on are included, the total loss due to crime amounts to $450 billion annually, or about $1,800 per U.S. citizen.[5]

victimology
The study of the victim's role in criminal events.

victimologists
Criminologists who focus on the victims of crime.

Individual Costs In addition to these societal costs, victims may suffer long-term losses in earnings and occupational attainment. Victim costs resulting from an assault are as high as $9,400, and costs are even higher for rape and arson; the average murder costs around $3 million.[6] Research by Ross Macmillan shows that Americans who suffer a violent victimization during adolescence earn about $82,000 less than nonvictims; Canadian victims earn $237,000 less. Macmillan reasons that victims bear psychological and physical ills that inhibit first their academic achievement and later their economic and professional success.[7]

Abuse by the System

The suffering endured by crime victims does not end when their attacker leaves the scene of the crime. They may suffer more victimization by the justice system.

While the crime is still fresh in their minds, victims may find that the police interrogation following the crime is handled callously, with innuendos or insinuations that they were somehow at fault. Victims have difficulty learning what is going on in the case; property is often kept for a long time as evidence and may never be returned. Some rape victims report that the treatment they receive from legal, medical, and mental health services is so destructive that they can't help feeling "re-raped."[8] Victims may also suffer economic hardship because of wages lost while they testify in court and find that authorities are indifferent to their fear of retaliation if they cooperate in the offenders' prosecution.[9]

Long-Term Stress

Victims may suffer stress and anxiety long after the incident is over and the justice process has been forgotten. Experiencing abuse is particularly traumatic for adolescents who quite often suffer hostility and **posttraumatic stress disorders (PTSD)**.[10] For example, girls who were psychologically, sexually, or physically abused as children are more likely to have lower self-esteem and be more suicidal as adults than those who were not abused.[11] They are also placed at greater risk to be re-abused as adults than those who escaped childhood victimization.[12] Children who are victimized in the home are more likely to run away to escape their environment, which puts them at risk for juvenile arrest and involvement with the justice system.[13] Many who undergo traumatic sexual experiences later suffer psychological deficits such as eating disorders and mental illness and social problems such as homelessness and repeat victimization.[14] For example, a recent study of homeless women found that they were much more likely than other women to report childhood physical abuse, childhood sexual abuse, adult physical assault, previous sexual assault in adulthood, and a history of mental health problems.[15]

Stress does not end in childhood. Spousal abuse victims suffer an extremely high prevalence of depression, posttraumatic stress disorder (an emotional disturbance following exposure to stresses outside the range of normal human experience), anxiety disorder, and obsessive-compulsive disorder (an extreme preoccupation with certain thoughts and compulsive performance of certain behaviors).[16] One reason may be that abusive spouses are as likely to abuse their victims psychologically with threats and intimidation as they are to use physical force; psychological abuse can lead to depression and other long-term disabilities.[17]

Some victims are physically disabled as a result of serious wounds sustained during episodes of random violence, including a growing number that suffer paralyzing spinal cord injuries. And if victims have no insurance, the long-term effects of the crime may have devastating financial as well as emotional and physical consequences.[18]

posttraumatic stress disorder
Psychological reaction to a highly stressful event; symptoms may include depression, anxiety, flashbacks, and recurring nightmares.

■ People who have suffered crime victimization remain fearful long after their wounds have healed. Even if they have escaped attack themselves, hearing about another's victimization may make them timid and cautious. Here a woman looks out of her window in fear at police officers during the hunt for the D.C. snipers on October 22, 2002, in Aspen Hill, Maryland.

© Stefan Zaklin/Getty Images

Fear

People who have suffered crime victimization remain fearful long after their wounds have healed. Even if they have escaped attack themselves, hearing about another's victimization may make people timid and cautious. For example, a recent effort to reduce gang crime and drug dealing in some of Chicago's most troubled housing projects failed to meet its objectives because residents feared retaliation from gang boys and possible loss of relationships; joining an effort to organize against crime placed them at extreme risk.[19]

Victims of violent crime are the most deeply affected, fearing a repeat of their attack. There may be a spillover effect in which victims become fearful of other forms of crime they have not yet experienced; people who have been assaulted develop fears that their house will be burglarized.[20] In a moving book, *Aftermath: Violence and the Remaking of a Self,* rape victim Susan Brison recounts the difficult time she had recovering from her ordeal. The trauma of rape disrupted her memory, cut off events that happened before the rape from those that occurred afterward, and eliminated her ability to conceive of a happy or productive future. Although sympathizers encouraged her to forget the past, she found that confronting it can have healing power.[21]

Antisocial Behavior

There is growing evidence that crime victims are more likely to commit crimes themselves. Being abused or neglected as a child increases the odds of being arrested, both as a juvenile and as an adult.[22] People, especially young males, who were physically or sexually abused are much more likely to smoke, drink, and take drugs than are nonabused youth. Incarcerated offenders report significant amounts of posttraumatic stress disorder as a result of prior victimization, which may in part explain their violent and criminal behaviors.[23]

The abuse–crime phenomenon is referred to as the **cycle of violence**.[24] Research shows that both boys and girls are more likely to engage in violent behavior if they were (1) the target of physical abuse and were (2) exposed to violent behavior among adults they know or live with, or exposed to weapons.[25] ✔ Checkpoints

✔ Checkpoints

✔ Victimology is the branch of criminology that examines the nature and extent of crime victimization.

✔ The total economic loss from crime victimization amounts to hundreds of billions of dollars annually.

✔ Victims may suffer long-term trauma, including posttraumatic stress disorder.

✔ Many victims become fearful and go through a fundamental life change.

✔ People who are victims may be more likely to engage in antisocial acts themselves.

To quiz yourself on this material, go to questions 3.1–3.5 on the Criminology: The Core 2e Web site.

cycle of violence
Victims of crime, especially childhood abuse, are more likely to commit crimes themselves.

The Nature of Victimization

Connections

As we saw in Chapter 2, the NCVS is currently the leading source of information on the nature and extent of victimization. It uses a sophisticated sampling methodology to collect data; statistical techniques then estimate victimization rates, trends, and patterns for the entire U.S. population.

How many crime victims are there in the United States, and what are the trends and patterns in victimization? According to the NCVS, an estimated 23 million criminal events occurred during 2002.[26]

As you may recall from Chapter 2, like the Uniform Crime Report, the NCVS finds that crime rates have been declining (Figure 3.1). All told, between 1993 and 2002 the violent crime rate decreased 54 percent, from 50 to 23 victimizations per 1,000 persons age 12 or older, and the property crime rate declined 50 percent (from 319 to 159 crimes per 1,000 households).

Patterns in the victimization survey findings are stable and repetitive, suggesting that victimization is not random but is a function of personal and ecological factors. The stability of these patterns allows judgments to be made about the nature of victimization; policies can then be created in an effort to reduce the victimization rate. Who are victims? Where does victimization take place? What is the relationship between victims and criminals? The following sections discuss some of the most important victimization patterns and trends.

The Social Ecology of Victimization

The NCVS shows that violent crimes are slightly more likely to take place in an open, public area, such as a street, a park, or a field, in a school building, or at a commercial establishment such as a tavern, during the daytime or early evening hours than in a private home during the morning or late evening hours. The more serious violent crimes, such as rape and aggravated assault, typically take place after 6 P.M. Approximately two-thirds of rapes and sexual assaults occur at night—6 P.M. to 6 A.M. Less serious forms of violence, such as unarmed robberies and personal larcenies like purse snatching, are more likely to occur during the daytime.

Neighborhood characteristics affect the chances of victimization. Those living in the central city have significantly higher rates of theft and violence than suburbanites; people living in rural areas have a victimization rate almost half that of city dwellers. The risk of murder for both men and women is

Figure 3.1

Victimization Rates, 1973–2002

The National Crime Victimization Survey reveals long-term declines in victimization rates, resulting in the lowest per capita rates in nearly 30 years.

SOURCE: Callie Marie Rennison and Michael Rand, *Criminal Victimization 2002* (Washington, D.C.: Bureau of Justice Statistics, 2003).

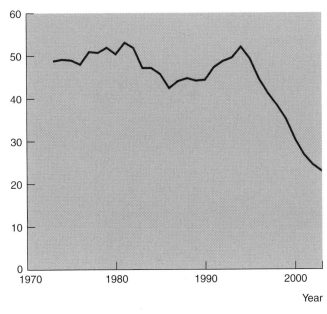

Rate per 1,000 population

(a) Violent victimization rates in population age 12 or over

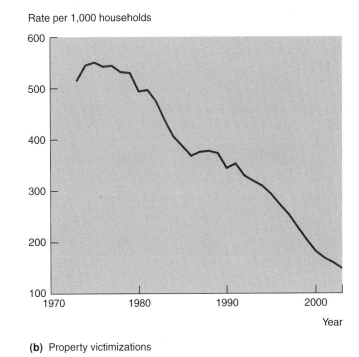

Rate per 1,000 households

(b) Property victimizations

significantly higher in disorganized inner-city areas where gangs flourish and drug trafficking is commonplace.

The Victim's Household

The NCVS tells us that within the United States, larger, African American, Western, and urban homes are the most vulnerable to crime. In contrast, rural, European American homes in the Northeast are the least likely to contain crime victims or be the target of theft offenses, such as burglary or larceny. People who own their homes are less vulnerable than renters.

Recent population movement and changes may account for recent decreases in crime victimization. U.S. residents have become extremely mobile, moving from urban areas to suburban and rural areas. In addition, family size has been reduced; more people than ever before are living in single-person homes (about 25 percent of households). It is possible that the decline in household victimization rates during the past 15 years can be explained by the fact that smaller households in less populated areas have a lower victimization risk.

Victim Characteristics

Social and demographic characteristics also distinguish victims and nonvictims. The most important of these factors are gender, age, social status, and race.

Gender As Figure 3.2 shows, gender affects victimization risk. Except for the crimes of rape and sexual assault, males are more likely than females to be the victims of violent crime. Men are almost twice as likely as women to experience robbery. Women, however, are six times more likely than men to be victims of rape or sexual assault. For all crimes, males are more likely to be victimized than females. However, the gender differences in the victimization rate appear to be narrowing.

Females were most often victimized by someone they knew, whereas males were more likely to be victimized by a stranger. Of those offenders victimizing females, about two-thirds were described as someone the victim knew or was related to. In contrast, only about half of male victims were attacked by a friend, relative, or acquaintance.

Figure 3.2
Violent Crime Rates by Gender of Victim

For most crimes, men are much more likely to become victims than are women.

SOURCE: Bureau of Justice Statistics, 2003.

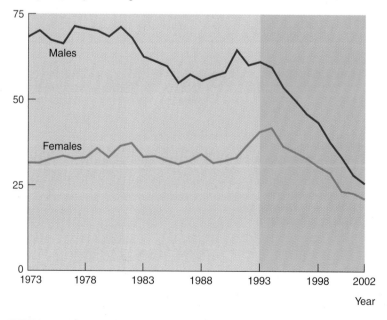

Figure 3.3
Violent Crime Rates by Age of Victim
Young people are much more likely to become victims than are the elderly.

SOURCE: Bureau of Justice Statistics, 2003.

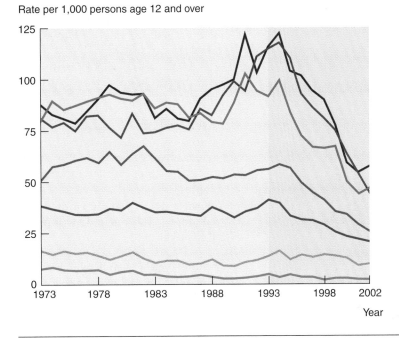

Rate per 1,000 persons age 12 and over

Age Victim data reveal that young people face a much greater victimization risk than do older persons. As Figure 3.3 shows, victim risk diminishes rapidly after age 25. The elderly, who are thought of as the helpless targets of predatory criminals, are actually much safer than their grandchildren. People over 65, who make up about 15 percent of the population, account for only 1 percent of violent victimizations; teens 12 to 19, who also make up 15 percent of the population, typically account for more than 30 percent of victimizations. For example, teens 16 to 19 suffer 58 violent crimes per 1,000 whereas people over 65 experience only 3.

Although the elderly are less likely to become crime victims than the young, they are most often the victims of a narrow band of criminal activities from which the young are more immune. Frauds and scams, purse snatching, pocket picking, stealing checks from the mail, and committing crimes in long-term care settings claim more older than younger victims. The elderly are especially susceptible to fraud schemes because they have insurance, pension plans, proceeds from the sale of homes, and money from Social Security and savings that make them attractive financial targets. Because many elderly live by themselves and are lonely, they remain more susceptible to telephone and mail fraud. Unfortunately, once victimized the elderly have more limited opportunities to either recover their lost money or earn enough to replace what they have lost.[27]

Social Status The poorest Americans are also the most likely victims of violent and property crime. This association occurs across all gender, age, and racial groups. Although the poor are more likely to suffer violent crimes, the wealthy are more likely targets of personal theft crimes such as pocket picking and purse snatching. Perhaps the affluent, who sport more expensive attire and drive better cars, attract the attention of thieves.

Marital Status Marital status also influences victimization risk. Never-married males and females are victimized more often than married people.

Connections
The association between age and victimization is undoubtedly tied to lifestyle: Adolescents often stay out late at night, go to public places, and hang out with other young people who have a high risk of criminal involvement. Teens also face a high victimization risk because they spend a great deal of time in the most dangerous building in the community: the local school!

Figure 3.4

Violent Crime Rates by Race of Victim

African Americans are more likely than European Americans to be victims of violent crime.

SOURCE: Bureau of Justice Statistics, 2003.

Rate per 1,000 persons age 12 and over

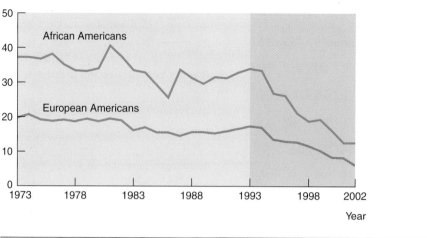

Widows and widowers have the lowest victimization risk. This association between marital status and victimization is probably influenced by age, gender, and lifestyle:

1. Many young people, who have the highest victim risk, are actually too young to have been married.

2. Young single people also go out in public more often and sometimes interact with high-risk peers, increasing their exposure to victimization.

3. Widows and widowers suffer much lower victimization rates because they are older, interact with older people, and are more likely to stay home at night and to avoid public places.

Race and Ethnicity   As Figure 3.4 shows, African Americans are more likely than European Americans to be victims of violent crime: Per every 1,000 persons in that racial group, 28 blacks, 23 whites, and 15 persons of others races sustained a violent crime.

Why do these discrepancies exist? Because of income inequality, racial and minority group members are often forced to live in deteriorated urban areas beset by alcohol and drug abuse, poverty, racial discrimination, and violence. Consequently, their lifestyle places them in the most "at-risk" population group.

Repeat Victimization   Does prior victimization enhance or reduce the chances of future victimization? Individuals who have been crime victims have a significantly higher chance of future victimization than people who have remained nonvictims.[28] Households that have experienced victimization in the past are the ones most likely to experience it again in the future.[29]

What factors predict chronic victimization? Most repeat victimizations occur soon after a previous crime has occurred, suggesting that repeat victims share some personal characteristic that makes them a magnet for predators.[30] For example, children who are shy, physically weak, or socially isolated may be prone to being bullied in the schoolyard.[31] David Finkelhor and Nancy Asigian have found that three specific types of characteristics increase the potential for victimization:

1. *Target vulnerability.* The victims' physical weakness or psychological distress renders them incapable of resisting or deterring crime and makes them easy targets.

2. *Target gratifiability.* Some victims have some quality, possession, skill, or attribute that an offender wants to obtain, use, have access to, or manipulate.

Having attractive possessions such as a leather coat may make one vulnerable to predatory crime.

3. *Target antagonism.* Some characteristics increase risk because they arouse anger, jealousy, or destructive impulses in potential offenders. Being gay or effeminate, for example, may bring on undeserved attacks in the street; being argumentative and alcoholic may provoke barroom assaults.[32]

Repeat victimization may occur when the victim does not take defensive action. For example, if an abusive husband finds out that his battered wife will not call police, he repeatedly victimizes her; or if a hate crime is committed and the police do not respond to reported offenses, the perpetrators learn they have little to fear from the law.[33]

The Victims and Their Criminals

The victim data also tell us something about the relationship between victims and criminals. Males were more likely to be violently victimized by a stranger, and females were more likely to be victimized by a friend, an acquaintance, or an intimate.

Victims report that most crimes were committed by a single offender over age 20. Crime tends to be intraracial: African American offenders victimize blacks, and European Americans victimize whites. However, because the country's population is predominantly white, it stands to reason that criminals of all races will be more likely to target white victims. Victims report that substance abuse was involved in about one-third of violent crime incidents.[34]

Although many violent crimes are committed by strangers, a surprising number of violent crimes are committed by relatives or acquaintances of the victims. In fact, more than half of all nonfatal personal crimes are committed by people who are described as being known to the victim. Women are especially vulnerable to people they know. More than six in ten rape or sexual assault victims stated the offender was an intimate, a relative, a friend, or an acquaintance. Women were more likely than men to be robbed by a friend or acquaintance: Seventy-four percent of males and 43 percent of females stated the individuals who robbed them were strangers. ✔ **Checkpoints**

✔ Checkpoints

✔ Males are more often the victims of crime than females; women are more likely than men to be attacked by a relative.

✔ The indigent are much more likely than the affluent to be the victims of violent crime; the wealthy are more likely to be the targets of personal theft.

✔ Younger, single people are more often targets than older, married people.

✔ Rates of violent victimization are much higher for African Americans than for European Americans. Crime victimization tends to be intraracial.

✔ Some people and places are targets of repeat victimization.

🌐 To quiz yourself on this material, go to questions 3.6–3.9 on the Criminology: The Core 2e Web site.

Theories of Victimization

For many years criminological theory focused on the actions of the criminal offender; the role of the victim was virtually ignored. More than 50 years ago scholars began to realize that the victim was not simply a passive target in crime but someone whose behavior can influence his or her own fate, who "shapes and molds the criminal."[35] These early works helped focus attention on the role of the victim in the crime problem and led to further research efforts that have sharpened the image of the crime victim. Today a number of different theories attempt to explain the causes of victimization.

Victim Precipitation Theory

victim precipitation theory
The view that victims may initiate, either actively or passively, the confrontation that leads to their victimization.

active precipitation
Aggressive or provocative behavior of victims that results in their victimization.

According to **victim precipitation theory,** some people may actually initiate the confrontation that eventually leads to their injury or death. Victim precipitation can be either active or passive.

Active precipitation occurs when victims act provocatively, use threats or fighting words, or even attack first.[36] In 1971, Menachem Amir suggested that female rape victims often contribute to their attack by dressing provocatively or pursuing a relationship with the rapist.[37] Although Amir's findings are controversial, courts have continued to return not guilty verdicts in rape cases if a victim's actions can in any way be construed as consenting to sexual intimacy.[38]

In contrast, **passive precipitation** occurs when the victim exhibits some personal characteristic that unknowingly either threatens or encourages the attacker. The crime can occur because of personal conflict, such as when two people compete over a job, promotion, love interest, or some other scarce and coveted commodity. For example, a woman may become the target of intimate violence when she improves her job status and her success results in a backlash from a jealous spouse or partner.[39] In other situations, although the victim may never have met the attacker or even known of his or her existence, the attacker feels menaced and acts accordingly.[40]

Lifestyle Theories

Some criminologists believe that people may become crime victims because their lifestyle increases their exposure to criminal offenders. Victimization risk is increased by such behaviors as associating with young men, going out in public places late at night, and living in an urban area. Conversely, one's chances of victimization can be reduced by staying home at night, moving to a rural area, staying out of public places, earning more money, and getting married. The basis of such **lifestyle theories** is that crime is not a random occurrence; rather, it is a function of the victim's lifestyle.

■ People who live high-risk lifestyles—such as walking alone at night in high crime areas—face a greater chance of victimization than those who avoid risky behaviors. Here relatives of Sakia Gunn, killed by two men at a bus stop in Newark, New Jersey, comfort one another at a memorial rally. The fifteen-year-old, who was returning home from a late night in New York City, rebuffed the sexual advances of two men who then stabbed her to death.

High-Risk Lifestyles   People who have high-risk lifestyles—drinking, taking drugs, getting involved in crime—have a much greater chance of victimization.[41] For example, young runaways are at high risk for victimization; the more time they are exposed to street life, the greater their risk of becoming crime victims.[42]

Teenage males have an extremely high victimization risk because their lifestyle places them at risk both at school and once they leave the school grounds.[43] They spend a great deal of time hanging out with their friends and pursuing recreational fun.[44] Their friends may give them a false ID so they can go drinking in the neighborhood bar. They may hang out in taverns at night, which places them at risk because many fights and assaults occur in places that serve liquor. Those who have a history of engaging in serious delinquency, getting involved in gangs, carrying guns, and selling drugs have an increased chance of being shot and killed.[45]

Lifestyle risks continue into young adulthood. College students who spend several nights each week partying and who take recreational drugs are much more likely to be victims of violent crime than those who avoid such risky academic lifestyles (see the Current Issues in Crime feature for more on this issue).[46] Lifestyle risks continue into young adulthood. As adults, those who commit crimes increase their chances of becoming the victims of homicide.[47]

Criminal Lifestyle   One element of lifestyle that may place some people at risk for victimization is an ongoing involvement in a criminal career. Both convicted and self-reported criminals are much more likely to suffer victimization than are noncriminals.[48]

For example, analysis of data from the Rochester and Pittsburgh Youth Studies, two ongoing surveys tracking thousands of at-risk youth, found that kids who get involved in gangs and carry a weapon are up to four times more likely to become victims of serious crime than non–gang members. About 40 percent of males involved in gang/group fights had themselves been seriously injured; among females, 27 percent of those involved in gang/group fights had been seriously injured. Carrying a weapon was another surefire way to

passive precipitation
Personal or social characteristics of victims that make them "attractive" targets for criminals; such victims may unknowingly either threaten or encourage their attackers.

lifestyle theories
The view that people become crime victims because of lifestyles that increase their exposure to criminal offenders.

CURRENT ISSUES IN CRIME

Rape on Campus: Lifestyle and Risk

Due to their lifestyle and demographic makeup, college campuses contain large concentrations of young women who may be at greater risk for rape and other forms of sexual assault than women in the general population. How common is campus rape? Who are its victims? And what actions do they take after they are assaulted?

To answer these important questions, Bonnie Fisher and her colleagues conducted a telephone survey of a randomly selected, national sample of 4,446 women who were attending a 2- or 4-year college or university during the fall of 1996.

Based on their findings, they estimated that a college with 10,000 female students could experience more than 350 rapes a year. At first glance, the fact that "only" about 1 in 36 college women (2.8 percent) experience a completed rape or attempted rape in an academic year does not signify that campus rape has reached epidemic proportions. However, the results must be interpreted with caution. When compared with the FBI estimate of about 6 women per 10,000 in the population are rape victims each year and the NCVS estimate of about 20 women per 10,000, the college rape statistics are startling. Also, the college "year" is only about seven months long. In addition, many women experience other forms of sexual coercion on campus, including unwanted or uninvited sexual contacts; more than one-third of the sample reported incidents like these.

College rape is a serious social problem, but it remains below the radar screen because few incidents of sexual victimization are reported to law enforcement officials; fewer than 5 percent of completed and attempted rapes are reported. In about two-thirds of the rape incidents, the victim did tell another person. However, most often this person was a friend, not a family member or a college official.

When and Where Does Sexual Victimization Occur, and Who Are the Perpetrators?

Fisher and her colleagues found that most (90 percent) of the victims knew the person who sexually victimized them. Most often this was a boyfriend, ex-boyfriend, classmate, friend, acquaintance, or coworker; college professors were not identified as committing any rapes or sexual coercions.

The vast majority of sexual victimizations occurred in the evening (after 6 P.M.), typically (60 percent) in the students' living quarters. Other common crime scenes were other living quarters on campus and fraternity houses (about 10 percent). Off-campus sexual victimizations, especially rapes, also occurred in residences. Incidents where women were threatened or touched also took place in settings such as bars, dance clubs or nightclubs, and work settings. Though a majority of incidents took place off campus, most involved a victim who was engaged in an activity connected to her life as a student at the college she attended, for example, attending a student party.

Fighting Back

For nearly all forms of sexual victimization, the majority of female students reported attempting to take protective actions during the incident. Fisher found that those women who fought back were less likely to experience successful attacks, a finding that suggests the intended victim's willingness or ability to take protective action might be one reason attempts to rape or coerce sex failed.

The most common protective action was using physical force against the assailant. Nearly 70 percent of victims of attempted rape used this response—again, a possible reason many of these acts were not completed. Other common physical responses included removing the offender's hand, running away, and trying to avoid the offender. Verbal responses also were common, including pleading with the offender to stop, screaming, and trying to negotiate with the offender.

Who Gets Victimized?

Is lifestyle connected to victimization? Fisher and her colleagues found that four main factors consistently increased the risk of sexual victimization: (1) fre-

quently drinking enough to get drunk, (2) being unmarried, (3) having been a victim of a sexual assault before the start of the current school year, and (4) living on campus (for on-campus victimization only).

Fisher also found that many women do not believe their sexual victimizations were a crime, some because they blame themselves for their sexual assault. Others did not clearly understand the legal definition of rape, or they did not want to define someone they knew who victimized them as a rapist.

The Fisher research reinforces the lifestyle theory of victimization. Young college women are at greater risk than other women because of their lifestyle: they are more likely to associate with dangerous peers; that is, young men who are more likely to drink and live alone.

Critical Thinking

1. Considering Fisher's findings, would you advise a female high school senior to attend an all girls school in order to be safe? Or would you propose another course of action?

2. There have been a number of recent sexual assault cases at the nation's service academies (West Point, Air Force Academy, Naval Academy). Do you believe women who attend these schools are at greater risk than those who attend traditional colleges and universities?

InfoTrac College Edition Research

To learn more about sexual victimization by acquaintances on college campuses and elsewhere, use "date rape" and "acquaintance rape" as subject guides on InfoTrac College Edition.

SOURCE: Bonnie Fisher, Francis Cullen, and Michael Turner, *The Sexual Victimization of College Women* (Washington, D.C.: National Institute of Justice, 2001).

become a crime victim. Males who carried weapons were approximately three times more likely to be victimized than those who did not carry weapons—33 percent of the weapons carriers became victims as opposed to only 10 percent who did not carry weapons.[49] These data indicate that criminals and victims may not be two separate and distinct groups. Rather, the risk of victimization is directly linked to the high-risk lifestyle of young, weapon toting gang boys.

Deviant Place Theory

According to **deviant place theory,** victims do not encourage crime but are victim prone because they reside in socially disorganized high-crime areas where they have the greatest risk of coming into contact with criminal offenders, irrespective of their own behavior or lifestyle.[50] Neighborhood crime levels may be more important for determining the chances of victimization than individual characteristics or lifestyle. Consequently, there may be little reason for residents in lower-class areas to alter their lifestyle or take safety precautions because personal behavior choices do not influence the likelihood of victimization.[51]

Deviant places are poor, densely populated, highly transient neighborhoods in which commercial and residential properties exist side by side.[52] The commercial establishments provide criminals with easy targets for theft crimes, such as shoplifting and larceny. Successful people stay out of these stigmatized areas. They are home to "demoralized kinds of people" who are easy targets for crime: the homeless, the addicted, the retarded, and the elderly poor.[53]

People who live in more affluent areas and take safety precautions significantly lower their chances of becoming crime victims; the effect of safety precautions is less pronounced in poor areas. Residents of poor areas have a much greater risk of becoming victims because they live in areas with many motivated offenders; to protect themselves, they have to try harder to be safe than do the more affluent.[54]

Routine Activities Theory

FIND IT ON INFOTRAC
College Edition

To read articles on this subject, use "routine activities theory" as a subject guide on InfoTrac College Edition.

deviant place theory
The view that victimization is primarily a function of where people live.

routine activities theory
The view that victimization results from the interaction of three everyday factors: the availability of suitable targets, the absence of capable guardians, and the presence of motivated offenders.

suitable targets
Objects of crime (persons or property) that are attractive and readily available.

capable guardians
Effective deterrents to crime, such as police or watchful neighbors.

motivated offenders
People willing and able to commit crimes.

Routine activities theory was first articulated in a series of papers by Lawrence Cohen and Marcus Felson.[55] Cohen and Felson assume that both the motivation to commit crime and the supply of offenders are constant.[56] Every society will always have some people who are willing to break the law for revenge, greed, or some other motive. Therefore, the volume and distribution of predatory crime (violent crimes against a person and crimes in which an offender attempts to steal an object directly) are closely related to the interaction of three variables that reflect the routine activities of the typical American lifestyle:

1. The availability of **suitable targets,** such as homes containing easily salable goods.
2. The absence of **capable guardians,** such as police, homeowners, neighbors, friends, and relatives.
3. The presence of **motivated offenders,** such as a large number of teenagers.

The presence of these components increases the likelihood that a predatory crime will take place. Targets are more likely to be victimized if they are poorly guarded and exposed to a large group of motivated offenders such as teenage boys.[57] The interacting components of routine activities theory are illustrated in Figure 3.5.

Cohen and Felson argue that crime rates increased between 1960 and 1980 because the number of adult caretakers at home during the day

Figure 3.5
Routine Activities Theory
Crime and victimization involve the interaction of three factors.

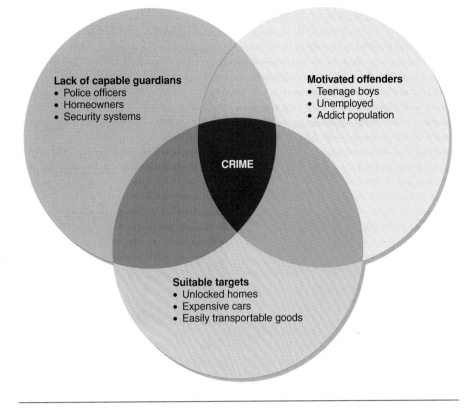

Lack of capable guardians
- Police officers
- Homeowners
- Security systems

Motivated offenders
- Teenage boys
- Unemployed
- Addict population

CRIME

Suitable targets
- Unlocked homes
- Expensive cars
- Easily transportable goods

(guardians) decreased as a result of increased female participation in the workforce. While mothers are at work and children in day care, homes are left unguarded. Similarly, with the growth of suburbia and the decline of the traditional neighborhood, the number of such familiar guardians as family, neighbors, and friends diminished. At the same time, the volume of easily transportable wealth increased, creating a greater number of available targets.[58] A recent study by Steven Messner and his associates found that between the years of 1967 and 1998 as adult unemployment rates *increased,* juvenile homicide arrest rates *decreased.* It is possible that juvenile arrests decreased because unemployed adults were at home to supervise their children and make sure they did not get in trouble or join gangs; these data support the effect of adult supervision on juvenile crime predicted by routine activities theory.[59]

Routine Activities and Lifestyle Routine activities theory and the lifestyle approach have a number of similarities. They both assume that a person's living arrangements can affect victim risk and that people who live in unguarded areas are at the mercy of motivated offenders. These two theories both rely on four basic concepts: (1) proximity to criminals, (2) time of exposure to criminals, (3) target attractiveness, and (4) guardianship.[60]

Based on the same basic concepts, these theories share five predictions: People increase their victimization risk if they (1) live in high-crime areas, (2) go out late at night, (3) carry valuables such as an expensive watch, (4) engage in risky behavior such as drinking alcohol, and (5) are without friends or family to watch or help them.[61] For example, young women who drink to excess in bars and fraternity houses may elevate their risk of date rape because (1) they are easy targets and (2) their attackers can rationalize raping them because they are intoxicated ("She's loose and immoral, so I didn't think she'd care."). Intoxication is sometimes seen as making the victim culpable for the crime.[62] Conversely, people can reduce their chances of

✔ Checkpoints

✔ Victim precipitation theory suggests that crime victims may trigger attacks by acting provocatively.

✔ Some experts link victimization to high-risk lifestyles.

✔ Some people live in places that are magnets for criminals.

✔ The routine activities approach suggests that the risk of victimization may be an interaction among suitable targets, effective guardians, and motivated criminals. Victims present attractive targets with insufficient protection to motivated criminals.

To quiz yourself on this material, go to questions 3.10–3.13 on the Criminology: The Core 2e Web site.

■ According to routine activities theory motivated offenders will commit crimes if presented with suitable, unguarded targets. Here Robert Tulloch, a Vermont youth, is shown in custody of New Hampshire law enforcement agents after his arrest in 2001 for the murder of two Dartmouth professors after a routine break-in of their homes.

repeat victimization if they change their lifestyle and adopt crime-suppressing routines such as getting married, having children, or moving to a small town.[63]

The Current Issues in Crime feature on Crime and Everyday Life shows how these relationships can be influenced by cultural and structural change.

✔ Checkpoints on p. 63

Caring for the Victim

National victim surveys indicate that almost every American age 12 and over will one day become the victim of a common-law crime, such as larceny or burglary, and in the aftermath suffer financial problems, mental stress, and physical hardship.[64] Surveys show that upward of 75 percent of the general public have been victimized by crime at least once in their lives. As many as 25 percent of the victims develop posttraumatic stress syndrome, with symptoms that last for more than a decade after the crime occurred.[65]

Helping the victim to cope is the responsibility of all of society. Law enforcement agencies, courts, and correctional and human service systems have come to realize that due process and human rights exist not only for the criminal defendant but also for the victim of criminal behavior.

Because of public concern over violent personal crime, President Ronald Reagan created a Task Force on Victims of Crime in 1982.[66] This group suggested that a balance be achieved between recognizing the victim's rights and providing the defendant with due process. Recommendations included providing witnesses and victims with protection from intimidation, requiring restitution in criminal cases, developing guidelines for fair treatment of crime victims and witnesses, and expanding programs of victim compensation.[67]

As a result, Congress passed the Omnibus Victim and Witness Protection Act, requiring the use of victim impact statements at sentencing in federal criminal cases, greater protection for witnesses, more stringent bail laws, and the use of restitution in criminal cases. In 1984, the Comprehensive Crime Control Act and the Victims of Crime Act authorized federal funding for state victim compensation and assistance projects.[68] With these acts, the federal government recognized the plight of the victim and made victim assistance an even greater concern of the public and the justice system.

FIND IT ON INFOTRAC
College Edition

Did you know that a great deal of victimization occurs in school buildings? Though school violence may be declining, about one-third of all students are injured in a physical altercation each year. To learn more about this phenomenon, read:

"Violence Decreasing in U.S. High Schools," *The Brown University Child and Adolescent Behavior Letter,* December 1999 v15 i12 p3

CURRENT ISSUES IN CRIME

Crime and Everyday Life

A core premise of routine activities theory is that, all things being equal, the greater the *opportunity* to commit crime, the higher the crime and victimization rates. Marcus Felson elaborates on this thesis in his classic book, *Crime and Everyday Life*. Using a routine activities perspective, Felson shows why he believes American crime rates are so high and why U.S. citizens suffer such high rates of victimization.

According to Felson, there are always impulsive, motivated offenders willing to take the chance, if conditions are right, of committing crime for profit. Therefore, crime rates are a function of changing social conditions. Crime increased in the United States as the country changed from a nation of small villages and towns to one of large urban environments. In a village, not only could a thief easily be recognized, but the items that were stolen could be identified long after the crime occurred. Cities provided a critical population mass, enabling predatory criminals to hide and evade apprehension. After the crime, criminals could blend into the crowd, disperse their loot, and make a quick escape using the public transportation system.

The modern-day equivalent of the urban center is the shopping mall. Here, strangers converge in large numbers and youths "hang out." The interior is filled with people, so drug deals can be concealed in the pedestrian flow. Stores have attractively displayed goods, encouraging shoplifting and employee pilferage. Substantial numbers of cars are parked in areas that make larceny and car theft virtually undetectable. Cars that carry away stolen merchandise have an undistinguished appearance: Who notices people placing items in a car in a shopping mall lot? Also, shoppers can be attacked in parking lots as they walk in isolation to and from their cars.

As American suburbs grew in importance, labor and family life began to scatter away from the household, decreasing guardianship. Microwave ovens, automatic dishwashers, and fast-food meals have freed adolescents from common household chores. Rather than help prepare the family dinner and wash dishes afterward, adolescents are free to meet with their peers and avoid parental control. As car ownership increases, teens have greater access to transportation outside parental control. Greater mobility and access to transportation makes it impossible for neighbors to know if a teen belongs in an area or is an intruder planning to commit a crime. As schools become larger and more complex, they provide ideal sites for crime. The many hallways and corridors prevent teachers from knowing who belongs where; spacious school grounds reduce teacher supervision.

Felson finds that these changes in the structure and function of society have been responsible for changes in the crime rates. He concludes that, rather than trying to change people, crime prevention strategies must reduce the opportunity to commit crime.

Critical Thinking

1. What recent technological changes have influenced crime rates? The Internet? Video and computer games? Paging systems? Fax machines? Automatic teller systems?

2. Would increased family contact decrease adolescent crime rates, or would it increase the opportunity for child abuse?

InfoTrac College Edition Research

To see how the routine activities approach is used to explain violent victimizations, read:

Thoroddur Bjarnason, Thordis J. Sigurdardottir, and Thorolfur Thorlindsson, "Human Agency, Capable Guardians, and Structural Constraints: A Lifestyle Approach to the Study of Violent Victimization," *Journal of Youth and Adolescence,* February 1999 v28 i1 p105(1)

SOURCE: Marcus Felson, *Crime and Everyday Life: Insights and Implications for Society,* 3rd ed. (Thousand Oaks, Calif.: Sage, 2002).

Victim Service Programs

victim–witness assistance programs
Government programs that help crime victims and witnesses; may include compensation, court services, and/or crisis intervention.

compensation
Financial aid awarded to crime victims to repay them for their loss and injuries; may cover medical bills, loss of wages, loss of future earnings, and/or counseling.

An estimated 2,000 **victim–witness assistance programs** have been developed throughout the United States. These programs are organized on a variety of government levels and serve a variety of clients. We will look briefly at some prominent forms of victim assistance operating in the United States.[69]

Victim Compensation   One of the primary goals of victim advocates has been to lobby for legislation creating crime victim **compensation** programs.[70] As a result of such legislation, the victim ordinarily receives compensation from the state to pay for damages associated with the crime. Rarely are two compensation schemes alike, however, and many state programs suffer from a lack of both adequate funding and proper organization within the criminal justice system. Compensation may be provided for medical bills, loss of wages,

FIND IT ON INFOTRAC
College Edition

Use "victims rights" as a key term on InfoTrac College Edition to conduct research on this topic.

loss of future earnings, and counseling. In the case of death, the victim's survivors may receive burial expenses and aid for loss of support.[71] Awards typically range from $100 to $15,000. Occasionally, programs will provide emergency assistance to indigent victims until compensation is available. Emergency assistance may come in the form of food vouchers or replacement of prescription medicines.

In 1984, the federal government created the Victim of Crime Act (VOCA), which grants money to state compensation boards derived from fines and penalties imposed on federal offenders. The money is distributed each year to the states to fund both their crime victim compensation programs and their victim assistance programs, such as rape crisis centers and domestic violence shelters. Victims of violent crime and their families received benefits totaling $460 million in federal fiscal year 2002—$90 million more than the year before and $140 million more than just two years ago. In 2003, VOCA will distribute about $600 million; it is estimated that $625 million will be spent in fiscal year 2004.[72]

Court Services   A common victim program helps victims deal with the criminal justice system. One approach is to prepare victims and witnesses by explaining court procedures: how to be a witness, how bail works, and what to do if the defendant makes a threat. Lack of such knowledge can cause confusion and fear, making some victims reluctant to testify in court procedures. Many victim programs also provide transportation to and from court and counselors who remain in the courtroom during hearings to explain procedures and provide support. Court escorts are particularly important for elderly and disabled victims, victims of child abuse and assault, and victims who have been intimidated by friends or relatives of the defendant.

Victim Impact Statements   Most jurisdictions allow victims to make an impact statement before the sentencing judge. This gives the victim an opportunity to tell of his or her experiences and describe the ordeal; in the case of a murder trial, the surviving family can recount the effect the crime has had on their lives and well-being.[73] The effect of victim/witness statements on sentencing has been the topic of some debate. Some research finds that victim statements result in a higher rate of incarceration, but others find that victim/witness statements are insignificant.[74] Those who favor the use of impact statements argue that because the victim is harmed by the crime the victim has a right to influence the outcome of the case. After all, the public prosecutor is allowed to make sentencing recommendations because the public has been harmed by the crime. Logically the harm suffered by the victim legitimizes his or her right to make sentencing recommendations.[75]

Public Education   More than half of all victim programs include public education to help familiarize the general public with their services and with other agencies that help crime victims. In some instances, these are primary prevention programs, which teach methods of dealing with conflict without resorting to violence. For example, school-based programs present information on spousal and dating abuse, followed by discussions of how to reduce violent incidents.[76]

Crisis Intervention   Most victim programs refer victims to specific services to help them recover from their ordeal. Clients are commonly referred to the local network of public and private social service agencies that can provide emergency and long-term assistance with transportation, medical care, shelter, food, and clothing. In addition, more than half of all victim programs provide **crisis intervention** for victims who feel isolated, vulnerable, and in need of immediate services. Some programs counsel at their offices; others visit victims in their homes, at the crime scene, or in the hospital.

Victim–Offender Reconciliation Programs   **Victim–offender reconciliation programs (VORP)** use mediators to facilitate face-to-face encounters

FIND IT ON INFOTRAC
College Edition

The National Center for Victims of Crime (NCVC) in Arlington, Virginia, conducts research on the effectiveness of state constitutional amendments and other laws designed to protect victims. To learn more about its work, read:

Julie Brienza, "Crime Victim Laws Sometimes Ignored," *Trial*, May 1999 v35 i5 p103

crisis intervention
Emergency counseling for crime victims.

victim–offender reconciliation programs
Mediated face-to-face encounters between victims and their attackers, designed to produce restitution agreements and, if possible, reconciliation.

FIND IT ON INFOTRAC
College Edition

To read about how reconciliation
is used in other cultures, go to:

Jonathan Rudin, "Aboriginal Alternative
Dispute Resolution in Canada—A Case Study,"
International Journal of Public Administration,
Nov 2002 v25 i11 p1403-1426

Connections

Reconciliation programs are based on the concept of restorative justice, which rejects punitive correctional measures and instead suggests that crimes of violence and theft should be viewed as interpersonal conflicts that need to be settled in the community through noncoercive means. See Chapter 8 for more on this approach.

✔ Checkpoints

To quiz yourself on this material, go to questions 3.14–3.15 on the Criminology: The Core 2e Web site.

between victims and their attackers. The aim is to engage in direct negotiations that lead to restitution agreements and, possibly, reconciliation between the two parties involved.[77] More than 120 reconciliation programs currently in operation handle an estimated 16,000 cases per year. Designed at first to handle routine misdemeanors such as petty theft and vandalism, programs now commonly hammer out restitution agreements in more serious incidents such as residential burglary and even attempted murder.

Victims' Rights

Because of the influence of victims' rights advocates, every state now has a set of legal rights for crime victims in its code of laws, often called a Victims' Bill of Rights.[78] These generally include the right:

- To be notified of proceedings and the status of the defendant.
- To be present at criminal justice proceedings.
- To make a statement at sentencing, and to receive restitution from a convicted offender.
- To be consulted before a case is dismissed or a plea agreement entered.
- To a speedy trial.
- To keep the victim's contact information confidential.

Assuring victims' rights may involve an eclectic mix of advocacy groups—some independent, others government-sponsored, and some self-help. Advocates can be especially helpful when victims need to interact with the agencies of justice. For example, advocates can lobby police departments to keep investigations open as well as request the return of recovered stolen property. They can demand that prosecutors and judges provide protection from harassment and reprisals by, for example, making "no contact" a condition of bail. They can help victims make statements during sentencing hearings as well as probation and parole revocation procedures. Victim advocates can also interact with news media, making sure that reporting is accurate and that victim privacy is not violated. Victim advocates can be part of an independent agency similar to a legal aid society. If successful, top-notch advocates may eventually open private offices, similar to attorneys, private investigators, or jury consultants.[79]

Summary

- Criminologists now consider victims and victimization a major focus of study.

- About 23 million U.S. citizens are victims of crime each year.

- Like the crime rate, the victimization rate has been in sharp decline.

- The social and economic costs of crime are in the billions of dollars annually.

- Victims suffer long-term consequences such as experiencing fear and posttraumatic stress disorder.

- Research shows that victims are more likely than non-victims to engage in antisocial behavior.

- Like crime, victimization has stable patterns and trends.

- Violent crime victims tend to be young, poor, single males living in large cities, although victims come in all ages, sizes, races, and genders.

- Females are more likely than males to be victimized by somebody they know.

- Adolescents maintain a high risk of being physically and sexually victimized. Their victimization has been linked to a multitude of subsequent social problems.

- Many victimizations occur in the home, and many victims are the target of relatives and loved ones.

CONCEPT SUMMARY **3.1 Victimization Theories**

THEORY	MAJOR PREMISE	STRENGTHS	RESEARCH FOCUS
Victim precipitation	Victims trigger criminal acts by their provocative behavior. Active precipitation involves fighting words or gestures. Passive precipitation occurs when victims unknowingly threaten their attacker.	Explains multiple victimizations. If people precipitate crime, it follows that they will become repeat victims if their behavior persists over time.	Victim's role, crime provocation, victim–offender relationship
Lifestyle	Victimization risk is increased when people have a high-risk lifestyle. Placing oneself at risk by going out to dangerous places results in increased victimization.	Explains victimization patterns in the social structure. Males, young people, and the poor have high victimization rates because they have a higher-risk lifestyle than females, the elderly, and the affluent.	Personal activities, peer relations, place of crime, type of crime
Deviant places	People who live in deviant places are at high risk for crime. Victim behavior has little influence over the criminal act.	Places the focus of crime on deviant places. Shows why people with conventional lifestyles become crime victims.	Ecology of victimization, victimization and economic status, victim rates and community decline
Routine activities	Crime rates can be explained by the availability of suitable targets, the absence of capable guardians, and the presence of motivated offenders.	Can explain crime rates and trends. Shows how victim behavior can influence criminal opportunity. Suggests that victimization risk can be reduced by increasing guardianship and/or reducing target vulnerability.	Opportunity to commit crime, effect of police and guardians, population shifts and crime rates

- There are a number of theories of victimization (see Concept Summary 3.1).

- One view, called victim precipitation, is that victims provoke criminals.

- Lifestyle theories suggest that victims put themselves in danger by engaging in high-risk activities, such as going out late at night, living in a high-crime area, and associating with high-risk peers.

- Deviant place theory argues that victimization risk is related to neighborhood crime rates.

- The routine activities theory maintains that a pool of motivated offenders exists and that these offenders will take advantage of unguarded, suitable targets.

- Numerous programs help victims by providing court services, economic compensation, public education, and crisis intervention.

- Most states have created a Victims' Bill of Rights.

Thinking Like a Criminologist

The director of the state's department of human services has asked you to evaluate a self-report survey of adolescents ages 10 to 18. She has provided you with the following information on physical abuse.

Adolescents experiencing abuse or violence are at high risk of immediate and lasting negative effects on health and well-being. Of the high school students surveyed, an alarming one in five (21 percent) said they had been physically abused. Of the older students, ages 15 to 18, 29 percent said they had been physically abused. Younger students also reported significant rates of abuse: 17 percent responded "yes" when asked whether they had been physically abused. Although girls were far less likely to report abuse than boys, 12 percent said they had been physically abused. Most abuse occurs at home; it occurs more than once; and the abuser is usually a family member. More than half of those physically abused had tried alcohol and drugs, and 60 percent had admitted to a violent act. Nonabused children were significantly less likely to abuse substances, and only 30 percent indicated they had committed a violent act.

How would you interpret these data? What factors might influence their validity? What is your interpretation of the association between abuse and delinquency?

Go to the Criminology: The Core 2e Web site to review the content of this chapter.

Doing Research on the Web

For an up-to-date list of URLs, go to

http://www.cj.wadsworth.com/siegel_crimcore2e

To help address this issue, explore the following sites:

Blending Perspectives and Building Common Ground, A Report to Congress on Substance Abuse and Child Protection

http://aspe.hhs.gov/hsp/subabuse99/subabuse.htm

National Center on Substance Abuse and Child Welfare (NCSACW), a service of the Substance Abuse and Mental Health Services Administration's (SAMHSA) Center for Substance Abuse Treatment

http://www.ncsacw.samhsa.gov/

Adam M. Tomison, Child Maltreatment and Substance Abuse

http://www.aifs.org.au/nch/discussion2.html

Pro/Con discussions and Viewpoint Essays on some of the topics in this chapter may be found at the Opposing Viewpoints Resource Center:

http://www.gale.com/OpposingViewpoints

Key Terms

victimology 52
victimologists 52
posttraumatic stress disorder 53
cycle of violence 54
victim precipitation theory 59
active precipitation 59

passive precipitation 60
lifestyle theories 60
deviant place theory 62
routine activities theory 62
suitable targets 62
capable guardians 62

motivated offenders 62
victim–witness assistance programs 65
compensation 65
crisis intervention 66
victim–offender reconciliation
    programs 66

Critical Thinking Questions

1. Considering what you have learned in this chapter about crime victimization, what measures can you take to better protect yourself from crime?

2. Do you agree with the assessment that a school is one of the most dangerous locations in the community? Did you find your high school to be a dangerous environment?

3. Do people bear some of the responsibility for their victimization if they maintain a lifestyle that contributes to

the chances of becoming a crime victim? That is, should we "blame the victim"?

4. Have you ever experienced someone "precipitating" crime? If so, did you do anything to help the situation?

5. What would you advise freshman girls to do to lower the risk of being sexually assaulted?

part

2

Theories of Crime Causation

An important goal of the criminological enterprise is to generate valid and accurate theories of crime causation. Social scientists have defined theory as sets of statements that explain why and how several concepts are related.

In this section, theories of crime causation are grouped into six chapters. Chapters 4 and 5 focus on theories that hold that crime is either a free-will choice made by an individual or a function of personal psychological or biological abnormality, or both. Chapters 6 through 8 investigate theories based in sociology and political economy. Chapter 9 is devoted to theories that combine or integrate these various concepts into a cohesive, complex view of human development.

CHAPTER 4

Choice Theory: Because They Want To

Chapter Objectives

1. Understand the concept of rational choice.
2. Know the work of Beccaria.
3. Be able to discuss the concepts of offense- and offender-specific crime.
4. Be able to discuss why violent and drug crimes are rational.
5. Summarize the various techniques of situational crime prevention.
6. Be able to discuss the association between punishment and crime.
7. Be familiar with the concepts of certainty, severity, and speed of punishment.
8. Understand what is meant by specific deterrence.
9. Be able to discuss the issues involving the use of incapacitation.
10. Understand the concept of "just desert."

N CALIFORNIA, UNDER THE "THREE STRIKES LAW," A JUDGE MAY IMPOSE A SENTENCE OF 25 YEARS TO LIFE for any felony conviction if the criminal was previously convicted of two serious or violent felonies.[1] This draconian punishment was approved in 1994 amid public furor over the kidnapping and murder of 12-year-old Polly Klaas by Richard Allen Davis, a repeat offender out on parole at the time of the murder. In 1995 a career criminal

CNN. View the CNN video clip of this story and answer related critical thinking questions on your Criminology: The Core 2e CD.

named Leandro Andrade was convicted of stuffing videotapes down his pants at two southern California Kmart stores. Andrade had previous burglary convictions, making him eligible for extra punishment under California's three-strikes law. His sentence meant that Andrade would be eligible for parole in 2046 when he will be 87. He argued that the sentence violated the constitutional ban on "cruel and unusual" punishment but the Supreme Court disagreed and upheld the sentence.

Three strikes and other tough legal measures seem to rely on the belief that criminals choose to commit crime and they can be convinced not to if when caught they will be punished severely. Implementing such tough measures assumes that the decision to commit crime involves rational and detailed planning and decision making, designed to maximize personal gain and avoid capture and punishment.

his suggests that the decision to commit crime can involve rational and detailed planning and decision making, which is designed to maximize personal gain and avoid capture and punishment. Some criminologists go as far as suggesting that any criminal violation—committing a robbery, selling drugs, attacking a rival, or filing a false tax return—is based on rational decision making. Such a decision may be based on a variety of personal reasons, including greed, revenge, need, anger, lust, jealousy, thrill-seeking, or vanity. But if it is made after weighing the potential benefits and consequences, then the illegal act is a **rational choice.** This view of crime is referred to here as **choice theory.**

In this chapter, we review the philosophical underpinnings of choice theory—the view that criminals rationally choose crime. We then turn to theories of crime prevention and control that flow from the concept of choice: situational crime control, general deterrence theory, specific deterrence theory, and incapacitation. Finally, we take a brief look at how choice theory has influenced criminal justice policy.

rational choice
The view that crime is a function of a decision-making process in which the potential offender weighs the potential costs and benefits of an illegal act.

choice theory
The school of thought holding that people choose to engage in delinquent and criminal behavior after weighing the consequences and benefits of their actions.

The Development of Rational Choice Theory

Connections

As you may recall from Chapter 1, Beccaria believed that criminals weighed the benefits and consequences of crime before choosing to violate the law. They would be unlikely to choose crime if punishment was swift, certain, and severe.

Rational choice theory has its roots in the classical school of criminology developed by the Italian social thinker Cesare Beccaria, whose utilitarian approach powerfully influenced the criminal justice system and was widely accepted throughout Europe and the United States.[2] It seemed more rational to let the "punishment fit the crime" than to punish criminals in a cruel and capricious manner. Beccaria's vision was influential in the move away from torture and physical punishment in the nineteenth century and toward prison sentences geared to fit the severity of the crime. These practices were the cornerstone of what is known today as **classical criminology,** a view that remained popular for a century.

By the end of the nineteenth century, the popularity of the classical approach began to decline, and by the middle of the twentieth century, the perspective was neglected by mainstream criminologists. During this period, positivist criminologists focused on internal and external factors—poverty, IQ, education—rather than personal choice and decision making.

Beginning in the late 1960s, a number of criminologists began to revisit classical ideas, producing books and monographs expounding the theme that criminals are rational actors who plan their crimes, could be controlled by the fear of punishment, and deserve to be penalized for their misdeeds. In the 1960s, Nobel Prize–winning economist Gary Becker applied his views on rational behavior and human capital (that is, human competence and the consequences of investments in human competence) to criminal activity. He argued that with the exception of a few mentally ill people, criminals behave in a predictable or rational way when deciding to commit crime. They engage in a cost-benefit analysis of crime, weighing what they expect to gain against the risks they must undergo and the costs they may incur, such as going to prison.[3] Instead of regarding criminal activity as irrational behavior, Becker viewed criminality as rational behavior that might be controlled by increasing the costs and reducing the potential for gain.

In *Thinking About Crime,* political scientist James Q. Wilson observed that people who are likely to commit crime are unafraid of breaking the law because they value the excitement and thrills of crime, have a low stake in conformity, and are willing to take greater chances than the average person. If they could be convinced that their actions would bring severe punishment, only the totally irrational would be willing to engage in crime.[4]

From these roots has evolved a more contemporary version of classical theory, based on intelligent thought processes and criminal decision making; today this is referred to as the rational choice approach to crime causation.[5]

The Concepts of Rational Choice

classical criminology
The theoretical perspective suggesting that (1) people have free will to choose criminal or conventional behaviors; (2) people choose to commit crime for reasons of greed or personal need; and (3) crime can be controlled only by the fear of criminal sanctions.

According to the rational choice approach, law-violating behavior is the product of careful thought and planning. Offenders choose crime after considering both personal needs—money, revenge, thrills, entertainment—and situational factors, such as how well a target is protected and the efficiency of the local police force. The reasoning criminal evaluates the risk of apprehension, the seriousness of expected punishment, the potential value of the criminal enterprise, and his or her immediate need for criminal gain.

The decision to commit a specific type of crime, then, is a matter of personal choice made after weighing and evaluating available information. Conversely, the decision to forgo crime may be based on the criminal's perception that the potential rewards of the criminal act are not worth the risk of apprehension. For example, burglars may choose not to commit crime if they believe a neighborhood is well patrolled by police.[6] In fact, when police concentrate patrols in a particular area of the city, crime rates tend to increase in adjacent areas because calculating criminals view them as being safer.[7]

Offense- and Offender-Specific Crime

Rational choice theorists view crime as both offense- and offender-specific.[8] Crime is said to be **offense-specific** because offenders react selectively to the characteristics of particular crimes. Deciding to commit a particular burglary, for example, might involve evaluating the target's likely cash yield, the availability of resources such as a getaway car, and the probability of capture by police.[9]

Crime is **offender-specific** because criminals are not simply driven people who, for one reason or another, engage in random antisocial acts. Before deciding to commit crime, they analyze whether they have what it takes to be successful; they carefully evaluate their skills, motives, needs, and fears. A criminal act might be ruled out, for example, if potential offenders perceive that they can reach a desired personal goal through legitimate means, such as a part-time job or borrowing money from a relative.

Note the distinction made here between crime and criminality.[10] Crime is an event; criminality is a personal trait. Criminals do not commit crime all the time; conversely, even the most honest citizens may, on occasion, violate the law. On one hand, some high-risk people lacking opportunity may never commit crime; on the other hand, given enough provocation or opportunity, a low-risk, law-abiding person may commit crime.

Structuring Criminality

A number of personal factors condition people to choose criminality; one important factor is the promise of significant financial rewards that could not be attained in legitimate jobs. In contrast, offenders are likely to desist from crime if they believe (1) that their future criminal earnings will be relatively low and (2) that attractive and legal opportunities to generate income are available.[11]

One reason for the decision to commit crime is that criminals may consistently overestimate the value of potential criminal rewards. Some may know people who have made "big scores" and are quite successful at crime.[12] When Steven Levitt and Sudhir Alladi Venkatesh studied the financial rewards of being in a drug gang, they found that despite enormous risks to their health, life, and freedom, average gang members earned slightly more than what they could in the legitimate labor market (about $6 to $11 per hour).[13] Why did they stay in the gang? They believed that there was a strong potential for future riches if they stayed in the drug business and earned a "management" position (gang leaders earned a lot more). In this case, the rational choice is structured by the person's perception of the potential for future criminal gain versus the reality of conventional alternatives and opportunities.[14]

Learning and experience may be important elements in structuring criminality.[15] Career criminals may learn the limitations of their powers; they know when to take a chance and when to be cautious. Experienced criminals may turn from a life of crime when they develop a belief that the risk of crime is greater than its potential profit.[16]

Personality and lifestyle also affect criminal choices. Criminals appear to be more impulsive and have less self-control than other people; they seem unaffected by fear of criminal punishment.[17] They are typically under stress or facing some serious personal problem or condition that forces them to choose risky behavior.[18]

Connections

Rational choice theory dovetails with routine activities theory, which you learned about in Chapter 3. Although not identical, these approaches both claim that crime rates are a product of criminal opportunity. They suggest that increasing the number of guardians, decreasing the suitability of targets, or reducing the offender population should lower crime rates. Conversely, increased opportunity and reduced guardianship will increase crime rates.

offense-specific
The idea that offenders react selectively to the characteristics of particular crimes.

offender-specific
The idea that offenders evaluate their skills, motives, needs, and fears before deciding to commit crime.

Structuring Crime

According to the rational choice approach, the decision to commit crime, regardless of its substance, is structured by (1) where it occurs, (2) the characteristics of the target, and (3) available means.

FIND IT ON INFOTRAC
College Edition

Evidence suggests that the design of a property has a considerable impact on building security. The configuration of doors, hallways, exits, and other parts of a building can lower the incidence of crime rates. To find out more, use "crime prevention" and "architectural designs" as key words on InfoTrac College Edition.

✔ Checkpoints

✔ Choice theory can be traced to Beccaria's view that crime is rational and can be prevented by punishment that is swift, severe, and certain.

✔ Crime is said to be offense-specific because criminals evaluate the characteristics of targets to determine their suitability.

✔ Crime is offender-specific because criminals evaluate their skills, motivations, and needs before committing a specific crime.

✔ Criminal choice involves such actions as choosing the place of crime, selecting targets, and learning criminal techniques.

To quiz yourself on this material, go to questions 4.1–4.6 on the Criminology: The Core 2e Web site.

Choosing the Place of Crime   Criminals carefully choose where they will commit their crime. Criminologist Bruce Jacobs's interviews with 40 active crack cocaine street dealers in a Midwestern city showed that dealers carefully evaluate the desirability of their sales area before setting up shop.[19] Dealers consider the middle of a long block the best choice because they can see everything in both directions; police raids can be spotted before they occur.[20] Another tactic is to entice new buyers into spaces between apartment buildings or into back lots. Although the dealers may lose the tactical edge of being on a public street, they gain a measure of protection because their colleagues can watch over the operation and come to the rescue if the buyer tries to "pull something."[21]

Choosing Targets   Evidence of rational choice may also be found in the way criminals locate their targets. Victimization data indicate that while the affluent are rarely the victims of violent crimes, high-income households are the most likely targets of burglary.[22] Interviews with burglars find that they check to make sure that no one is home before they enter a residence. Some call ahead; others ring the doorbell, preparing to claim they had the wrong address if someone answers. Some find out which families have star high school athletes because those that do are sure to be at the weekend football game, leaving their houses unguarded.[23] Others seek unlocked doors and avoid the ones with deadbolts; houses with dogs are usually considered off-limits.[24] Burglars also report being sensitive to the activities of their victims. They note that homemakers often develop predictable behavior patterns, which helps them plan their crimes.[25] Burglars seem to prefer "working" between 9 A.M. and 11 A.M. and in midafternoon, when parents are either working or dropping off or picking up children at school. Burglars appear to monitor car and pedestrian traffic and avoid selecting targets on heavily traveled streets.[26] It does not seem surprising that well-organized communities that restrict traffic and limit neighborhood entrance and exit routes have experienced significant declines in property crime.[27]

Learning Criminal Techniques   Criminals report learning techniques of crime to help them avoid detection (see Exhibit 4.1). Research conducted by Leanne Fiftal Alarid and her partners found that women drawn into dealing drugs learn the trade in a businesslike manner. One young dealer told Alarid how she learned the techniques of the trade from an older male partner:

> He taught me how to "recon" [reconstitute] cocaine, cutting and repacking a brick from 91 proof to 50 proof, just like a business. He treats me like an equal partner, and many of the friends are business associates. I am a catalyst....I even get guys turned on to drugs.[28]

Note the business terminology used. This coke dealer could be talking about taking a computer training course at a major corporation! If criminal acts are treated as business decisions, in which profit and loss potential must be carefully calculated, then crime must indeed be a rational event.

In sum, rational choice involves both shaping criminality and structuring crime. Personality, age, status, risk, and opportunity seem to influence the decision to become a criminal; place, target, and techniques help to structure crime.[29]   ✔ Checkpoints

Is Crime Rational?

It is relatively easy to show that some crimes are the product of rational, objective thought, especially when they involve an ongoing criminal conspiracy centered on economic gain. For example, when prominent bankers in the savings and loan industry were indicted for criminal fraud, their elaborate financial schemes not only showed signs of rationality but exhibited brilliant, though flawed, financial expertise.[30] Similarly, the drug dealings of organized

EXHIBIT 4.1 Female Crack Dealers' Arrest Avoidance Techniques

Projected Self-Image

Female crack dealers learn the art of conveying a sense of normalcy and ordinariness in their demeanor and physical appearance to avoid attention. Female crack dealers avoid typical male behavior. They refuse to dress provocatively or wear flashy jewelry but instead dress down, wearing blue jeans and sweat pants to look like a "resident." Some affect the attire of crack users, figuring the police will not think them worth the trouble of an arrest.

Stashing

Female crack dealers learn how to hide drugs on their person, in the street, or at home. One dealer told how she hid drugs in the empty shaft of a curtain rod; another wore hollow earmuffs to hide crack. Knowing that a female officer has to do body cavity searches gives the dealers time to get rid of their drugs before they get to the station house. Dealers are aware of legal definitions of possession. One said she stashed her drugs 250 feet from her home because that was beyond the distance (150 feet) police considered a person legally to be in "constructive possession" of drugs.

Selling Hours

The women are aware of the danger of dealing at the wrong time of day. For example, it would be impossible to tell police you were out shopping at 3 A.M. If liquor stores are open, a plausible story could be concocted: I was out buying beer for a party. Dealers who sell from their homes cultivate positive relations with neighbors who might otherwise be tempted to tip off police. Some had barbecues and even sent over plates of ribs and pork to those who did not show up for dinner.

Routine Activities/Staged Performances

Dealers camouflage their activities within the bustle of their daily lives. They sell crack while hanging out in a park or shooting hoops in a playground. They meet their customers in a lounge and try to act normal, having a good time, anything not to draw attention to themselves and their business. They use props to disguise drug deals.

SOURCE: Bruce Jacobs and Jody Miller, "Crack Dealing, Gender, and Arrest Avoidance," *Social Problems* 45 (1998): 550–566.

crime bosses demonstrate a reasoned analysis of market conditions, interests, and risks. But what about crimes that are immediate rather than ongoing? Do they show signs of rationality?

Are Street Crimes Rational?

There is evidence that even seemingly "unplanned" street crimes may also be the product of careful risk assessment, including environmental, social, and structural factors. Target selection seems highly rational. Ronald Clarke and Patricia Harris found that auto thieves are very selective in their choice of targets. Vehicle selection seems to be based on attractiveness and suitability for a particular purpose; for example, German cars are selected for stripping because they usually have high-quality audio equipment that has good value on the second-hand market.[31]

There are also signs of rationality in the choices made by armed robbers. They generally choose targets close to their homes or in areas to which they routinely travel. Familiarity with the area gives them ready knowledge of escape routes; this is referred to as their "awareness space."[32] Robbers may be wary of people who are watching the community for signs of trouble; research by Paul Bellair shows that robbery levels are relatively low in neighborhoods where residents keep a watchful eye on their neighbors' property.[33] Many robbers avoid freestanding buildings because they can more easily be surrounded by police; others select targets that are known to do a primarily cash business, such as bars, supermarkets, and restaurants.[34] Robbers also tend to shy away from victims who are perceived to be armed and potentially dangerous.[35] However, some target people who themselves engage in deviant or antisocial behaviors, such as drug dealers.[36] Though these fellow criminals may be dangerous, robbers recognize that people with "dirty hands" are unlikely to call police and get entangled with the law.

Is Drug Use Rational?

Did actor Robert Downey Jr. make an objective, rational choice to abuse drugs and potentially sabotage his career? Did comedian Chris Farley make a rational choice when he abused alcohol and other drugs to the point that it killed him? Is it possible that drug users and dealers, a group not usually associated with clear thinking, make rational choices? Research does in fact show that at its onset drug use is controlled by rational decision making. Users report that they begin taking drugs when they believe the benefits of substance abuse outweigh its costs: They believe drugs will provide a fun, exciting, thrilling experience. They choose what they consider safe sites to buy and sell drugs.[37] Their entry into substance abuse is facilitated by their perception that valued friends and family members endorse and encourage drug use and abuse substances themselves.[38]

Drug dealers approach their profession in a businesslike fashion. According to criminologist George Rengert's study of drug markets, drug dealers face many of the same problems as legitimate retailers. If they are too successful in one location, rivals will be attracted to the area, and stiff competition may drive down prices and cut profits. The dealer can fight back by discounting the cost of drugs or increasing quality, as long as it doesn't reduce profit margins.[39] Steven Levitt and Sudhir Alladi Venkatesh found that dealers may start drug wars on their rivals' turf, not so much to put them out of business as to drive customers away from such a dangerous area and onto safer ground that they control; in retaliation, rivals may cut prices to lure customers back. In other words, drug dealers face many of the same problems as legitimate businesspeople; they differ in that they use violence to help settle disputes.[40]

Can Violence Be Rational?

Is it possible that violent acts, through which the offender gains little material benefit, are the product of reasoned decision making? Evidence confirms that even violent criminals select suitable targets by picking people who are vulnerable and lack adequate defenses.[41] For example, when Richard Wright and Scott Decker interviewed active street robbers in St. Louis, Missouri, their subjects expressed a considerable amount of rational thought before choosing a robbery, which may involve violence, over a burglary, which involves stealth and cunning.[42] One told them why he chose to be a robber:

> I feel more safer doing a robbery because doing a burglary, I got a fear of breaking into somebody's house not knowing who might be up in there.... On robbery I can select my victims, I can select my place of business. I can watch and see who all work in there, or I can rob a person and pull them around in the alley or push them up in a doorway and rob them.[43]

Violent offenders avoid victims who may be armed and dangerous.[44]

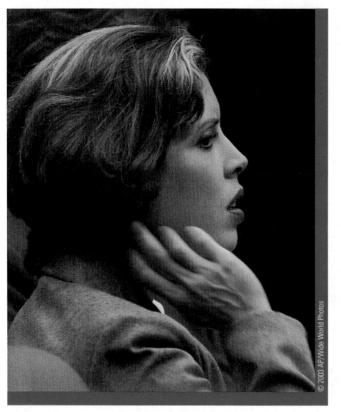

© 2003 AP/Wide World Photos

■ Is drug use rational? How can we explain substance abuse by the wealthy and powerful? Noelle Bush, daughter of Florida governor Jeb Bush, was sentenced to 10 days in jail for contempt of court after she was caught with a rock of crack cocaine in her shoe while in court-ordered rehabilitation at the Center for Drug-Free Living.

Connections

As you may recall from this chapter, criminals may also find that despite its risks crime can provide economic rewards that are far higher than they could hope to achieve in conventional employment. Many overestimate the profits from crime, though most seem to realize that the chances of a big payoff are remote.

FIND IT ON INFOTRAC
College Edition

Use "shoplifting" as a key word to
find out how retail establishments
are using situational crime prevention techniques to prevent retail
theft and limit "sneaky thrills."

In his book, *Robbing Drug Dealers: Violence Beyond the Law,* Bruce Jacobs shows that some robbers specialize in targeting drug dealers because
they believe that even though their work is risky it has rewards. In some
ways, drug dealers represent the perfect victim. They are plentiful, visible,
accessible, and carry plenty of cash. Their merchandise is valuable, easily
transportable, and can be used by the robber or sold to another. Drug dealers
are not particularly popular, so they cannot rely on bystanders to come to
their aid. Nor can they call the police and ask them to recover their stolen
goods! Of course drug dealers may be able to "take care of business" themselves, but, surprisingly, Jacobs finds that many do not choose to carry a pistol. Police have become too aggressive, and dealers are now more afraid of
getting arrested than of getting robbed. In Jacobs work we can see how a
seemingly senseless act, stealing from a well-armed dangerous criminal, can
have a rational basis.[45]

Why Do People Commit Crime?

Assuming that crime is rational, why—knowing its often unpleasant consequences—do people choose to commit crime? Rational choice theorists believe
that crime is a natural choice people make after weighing such issues as their
personal needs, mental state, legitimate alternatives such as a job, the risks
of getting caught, and the threat of punishment. All these factors are considered before the decision is made to commit crime. Consequently, even the
most desperate criminal might hesitate to attack a well-defended target,
whereas a group of teens might choose to rip off an unoccupied home on the
spur of the moment.[46]

For many people, crime is a more attractive alternative than law-abiding
behavior. It brings rewards, excitement, prestige, or other desirable outcomes
without lengthy work or effort. Whether it is violent or profit-oriented, crime
has an allure that some people cannot resist. Crime may produce a natural
"high" and other positive sensations that are instrumental in maintaining
and reinforcing criminal behavior.[47] Some law violators describe the "adren-
aline rush" that comes from successfully executing illegal activities in
dangerous situations. This has been termed **edgework:** the "exhilarating,
momentary integration of danger, risk, and skill" that motivates people to try
a variety of dangerous criminal and noncriminal behaviors.[48]

Sociologist Jack Katz argues that there are, in fact, immediate benefits
to criminality. These situational inducements, which he labels the **seductions of crime,** directly precede the commission of crime and draw offenders
into law violations. For example, someone challenges their authority or
moral position, and they vanquish their opponent with a beating; or they
want to do something exciting, so they break into and vandalize a school
building.[49]

According to Katz, choosing crime can help satisfy personal needs. For
some people, shoplifting and vandalism are attractive because getting away
with crime is a thrilling demonstration of personal competence (Katz calls
this "sneaky thrills"). Even murder can have an emotional payoff: Killers behave like the avenging gods of mythology, choosing to have life-or-death control over their victims.[50] The fact that crime can provide benefits to the
criminal is the subject of the Current Issues in Crime feature.

If committing crime is a rational choice, it follows that crime can be controlled or eradicated by convincing potential offenders that crime is a poor
choice—that it will not bring them rewards but bring pain, hardship, and
deprivation. Evidence shows that jurisdictions with relatively low incarceration rates also experience the highest crime rates.[51] As we have seen, according to rational choice theory, street-smart offenders know which areas offer
the least threat and plan their crimes accordingly. A number of potential
strategies flow from this premise. The following sections discuss each of these
crime reduction or control strategies based on the rationality of criminal
behavior. ✔ Checkpoints

✔ **Checkpoints**

✔ Theft crimes appear rational
because thieves and burglars typically
choose targets that present little risk,
and they plan their attacks carefully.

✔ Robbers report that they select
vulnerable targets who are unlikely to
fight back. Some like to attack drug
dealers who have lots of cash and
cannot call the police when it is taken.

✔ Drug users and dealers use
elaborate ploys to avoid detection.
They employ businesslike practices in
their commercial enterprises.

✔ Even serial killers use cunning and
thought to avoid detection.

✔ Crime is seductive. People may
rationally choose crime because it
provides them with psychological and
social benefits. It helps them solve
problems.

To quiz yourself on this material,
go to questions 4.7–4.8 on the
Criminology: The Core 2e Web site.

edgework
The excitement or exhilaration of successfully executing illegal activities in dangerous situations.

seductions of crime
The situational inducements or immediate
benefits that draw offenders into law
violations.

CURRENT ISSUES IN CRIME

Can Crime Pay Dividends?

The criminal lifestyle fits well with people who organize their life around risk taking and partying. Criminal events provide money for drugs and are ideal for displaying courage and fearlessness to one's running mates. Rather than create overwhelming social problems, a criminal way of life may be extremely beneficial to some people, helping them overcome the problems and stress they face in their daily lives.

According to sociologist Timothy Brezina, crime helps some achieve a sense of control or mastery over their environment. Adolescents in particular may find themselves feeling "out of control" because society limits their opportunities and resources. Antisocial behavior gives adolescents the opportunity to exert control over their own lives and destinies by helping them avoid situations they find uncomfortable or repellant (for example, cutting school or running away from an abusive home) or to obtain resources for desired activities and commodities (for example, stealing or selling drugs to buy stylish outfits).

Crime may help adolescents boost their self-esteem by attacking, symbolically or otherwise, perceived enemies (for example, by vandalizing the property of an adult who has given them grief). Drinking and drug taking may help some people ward off depression and compensate for a lack of positive experiences; they learn how to self-medicate. Some teens, angry at their mistreatment, may turn to violence to satisfy a desire for revenge or retaliation.

Brezina found a great deal of evidence that suggests that people engage in antisocial acts to solve problems. The literature on drug and alcohol abuse is replete with examples of research showing how people turn to substance abuse to increase their sense of personal power, to become more assertive, and to reduce tension and anxiety. Some people embrace deviant lifestyles, such as joining a gang, to offend conventional society and at the same time compensate for their feelings of powerlessness or ordinariness. Engaging in risky behavior helps people to feel alive and competent. There is also evidence that antisocial acts can provide positive solutions to problems. Violent kids, for example, may have learned that being aggressive with others is a good way to control the situation and to get what they want; counterattacks may be one means of controlling people who are treating them poorly.

Why do people age out of crime? As a short-run, problem-solving solution, crime may be appealing to adolescents, but it becomes less attractive as people mature and begin to appreciate the dangers of using crime to solve problems. Going to a drunken frat party may sound appealing to sophomores who want to improve their social life, but the risks involved to safety and reputation make them off limits to older grads. As people mature, their thinking extends farther into the future, and risky behavior is a threat to long-range plans.

Critical Thinking

According to Brezina, as people mature, their thinking extends farther into the future, and risky behavior is a threat to long-range plans. Does this vision adequately explain the aging out process? If so, why do some people continue to commit crime in their adulthood?

InfoTrac College Edition Research

How do people learn to solve problems? To find out, go to InfoTrac College Edition and use "problem solving" as a subject guide.

SOURCES: Timothy Brezina, "Delinquent problem-solving: an interpretive framework for criminological theory and research," *Journal of Research in Crime and Delinquency* 37 (2000): 3–30; Andy Hochstetler, "Opportunities and decisions: interactional dynamics in robbery and burglary groups," *Criminology* 39 (2001): 737–763.

Preventing Crime

Rational choice theory suggests that because criminal activity is offense-specific, crime prevention, or at least crime reduction, can be achieved through policies that convince potential criminals to desist from criminal activities, delay their actions, or avoid a particular target. Criminal acts will be avoided if (1) potential targets are carefully guarded, (2) the means to commit crime are controlled, and (3) potential offenders are carefully monitored. Desperate people may contemplate crime, but only the truly irrational will attack a well-defended, inaccessible target and risk strict punishment.

One way of preventing crime, then, is to reduce the opportunities people have to commit particular crimes. This approach is known as **situational crime prevention.** It was first popularized in the United States in the early 1970s by Oscar Newman, who coined the term **defensible space.** The idea is that crime can be prevented or displaced through the use of residential designs that reduce criminal opportunity, such as well-lit housing projects that maximize surveillance.[52]

situational crime prevention
A method of crime prevention that seeks to eliminate or reduce particular crimes in narrow settings.

defensible space
The principle that crime can be prevented or displaced by modifying the physical environment to reduce the opportunity individuals have to commit crime.

Crime Prevention Strategies

Situational crime prevention involves developing tactics to reduce or eliminate a specific crime problem (such as shoplifting in an urban mall or street-level drug dealing). According to criminologists Ronald Clarke and Ross Homel, crime prevention tactics used today generally fall into one of four categories:

- Increase the effort needed to commit crime.
- Increase the risks of committing crime.
- Reduce the rewards for committing crime.
- Induce guilt or shame for committing crime.

These basic techniques and some specific methods that can be used to achieve them are summarized in Exhibit 4.2.

Some of the tactics to increase effort include target-hardening techniques such as putting unbreakable glass on storefronts, locking gates, and fencing yards. Even simple prevention measures can work. Removing signs from store windows, installing brighter lights, and instituting a pay-first policy have helped reduce thefts from gas stations and convenience stores.[53]

Technological advances can also make it more difficult for would-be offenders to commit crimes; for example, having an owner's photo on credit cards should reduce the use of stolen cards. New security products such as steering locks on cars have reduced the incidence of theft.[54] Similarly, installing a locking device on cars that prevents drunken drivers from starting the vehicle (Breath Analyzed Ignition Interlock Device) significantly reduces drunk-driving rates among people with a history of driving while intoxicated.[55] Closed circuit TV cameras have been shown to reduce the amounts of car theft from parking lots while reducing the need for higher cost security personnel.[56]

Target reduction strategies are designed to reduce the value of crime to the potential criminal. These include making car radios removable so they can be kept in the home at night, marking property so that it is more difficult to sell when stolen, and having gender-neutral phone listings to discourage obscene phone calls. Tracking systems, such as those made by the Lojack Corporation, help police locate and return stolen vehicles.

Inducing guilt or shame might include such techniques as setting strict rules to embarrass offenders. For example, publishing "John lists" in the newspaper punishes those arrested for soliciting prostitutes. Facilitating compliance by providing trash bins might shame chronic litterers into using them. Ronald Clarke found that caller ID in New Jersey resulted in significant reductions in the number of obscene phone calls, presumably because of the shame presented by the threat of exposure.[57]

© 2003 AP/Wide World Photos

■ Surveillance techniques are one of the numerous situational crime prevention strategies now in use. Here pedestrians at Chicago's Navy Pier walk under a portable surveillance unit. The units, which are equipped with night vision, 360-degree tilt and zoom capabilities, and blue flashing lights, are encased in a bulletproof box and will be mounted to light and telephone poles in high-crime areas of the city.

Displacement, Extinction, Discouragement, and Diffusion

Situational crime prevention efforts, however, may produce unforeseen and unwanted consequences. Preventing crime in one location does not address or deter criminal motivation. People who desire the benefits of crime may choose alternative targets, so that crime is not prevented but deflected or displaced.[58] For example, beefed-up police patrols in one area may shift crimes to a more vulnerable neighborhood.[59] Although crime **displacement** certainly does not solve the general problem of crime, it has been shown to reduce the frequency of crime or produce less serious offense patterns.[60]

displacement
An effect of crime prevention efforts in which efforts to control crime in one area shift illegal activities to another.

EXHIBIT   **4.2 Sixteen Techniques of Situational Prevention**

INCREASING PERCEIVED EFFORT	INCREASING PERCEIVED RISKS	REDUCING ANTICIPATED REWARDS	INDUCING GUILT OR SHAME
1. *Target hardening* Slug rejector devices Steering locks Bandit screens	5. *Entry/exit screening* Automatic ticket gates Baggage screening Merchandise tags	9. *Target removal* Removable car radio Women's refuges Phone card	13. *Rule setting* Harassment codes Customs declaration Hotel registrations
2. *Access control* Parking lot barriers Fenced yards Entry phones	6. *Formal surveillance* Burglar alarms Speed cameras Security guards	10. *Identifying property* Property marking Vehicle licensing Cattle branding	14. *Strengthening moral condemnation* "Shoplifting is stealing" Roadside speedometers "Bloody idiots drink and drive"
3. *Deflecting offenders* Bus stop placement Tavern location Street closures	7. *Surveillance by employees* Pay phone location Park attendants Closed-circuit TV systems	11. *Reducing temptation* Gender-neutral phone lists Off-street parking	15. *Controlling disinhibitors* Drinking age laws Ignition interlock Server intervention
4. *Controlling facilitators* Credit card photo Caller ID Gun controls	8. *Natural surveillance* Defensible space Street lighting Cab driver ID	12. *Denying benefits* Ink merchandise tags PIN for car radios Graffiti cleaning	16. *Facilitating compliance* Improved library checkout Public lavatories Trash bins

SOURCE: Ronald Clarke and Ross Homel, "A Revised Classification of Situational Crime Prevention Techniques," in *Crime Prevention at a Crossroads,* ed. Steven Lab (Cincinnati: Anderson, 1997), p. 4.

extinction
The phenomenon in which a crime prevention effort has an immediate impact that then dissipates as criminals adjust to new conditions.

diffusion of benefits
An effect that occurs when efforts to prevent one crime unintentionally prevent another, or when crime control efforts in one locale reduce crime in other nontarget areas.

discouragement
An effect that occurs when limiting access to one target reduces other types of crime as well.

There is also the problem of **extinction:** Crime reduction programs may produce a short-term positive effect, but benefits dissipate as criminals adjust to new conditions. They learn to dismantle alarms or avoid patrols. They may also try new offenses they had previously avoided. For example, if every residence in a neighborhood has a foolproof burglar alarm system, motivated offenders may turn to armed robbery, a riskier and more violent crime.

Although displacement and extinction may create problems, there may also be advantages.[61] **Diffusion of benefits** occurs (1) when efforts to prevent one crime unintentionally prevent another or (2) when crime control efforts in one locale reduce crime in other nontarget areas. For example, diffusion would occur if closed circuit cameras reduced car theft in a parking lot that employed them and in the lot across the street that had not installed the cameras. What causes diffusion? First, crime prevention efforts may produce a generalized fear of apprehension. For example, video cameras set up in a mall to reduce shoplifting can also reduce property damage because would-be vandals fear they will be caught on camera. Or intensive police patrol efforts targeting neighborhood drug dealers may convince prostitutes that it is too dangerous to ply their trade in that area.[62]

Situational crime prevention efforts may also produce **discouragement:** Limiting access to one target convinces would-be lawbreakers that crime no longer pays in general. For example, evaluations of the Lojack auto protection system, which uses a hidden radio transmitter to track stolen cars, have found that the device helps lower car theft rates. Not only does Lojack deter auto thieves, it also seems to disrupt the operation of "chop shops," where stolen vehicles are taken apart for the resale of parts. Stolen car buyers cannot be sure if a stolen vehicle they purchase contains Lojack, which the police can trace to their base of operations.[63] Thus, a device designed to protect cars from theft also has the benefit of disrupting the sale of stolen car parts.

General Deterrence

According to the rational choice view, motivated people will violate the law if left free and unrestricted. The concept of **general deterrence** is that, conversely, the decision to commit crime can be controlled by the threat of criminal punishment. If people fear being apprehended and punished, they will not risk breaking the law. An inverse relationship should exist between crime rates and the severity, certainty, and speed of legal sanctions. If, for example, the punishment for a crime is increased and the effectiveness and efficiency of the criminal justice system are improved, then the number of people engaging in that crime should decline.

The factors of severity, certainty, and speed of punishment may also be interactive. For example, if a crime—say, robbery—is punished severely, but few robbers are ever caught or punished, the severity of punishment for robbery will probably not deter people from robbing. On the other hand, if the certainty of apprehension and conviction is increased by modern technology, more efficient police work, or some other factor, then even minor punishment might deter the potential robber.

Do these factors actually affect the decision to commit crime and, consequently, general crime rates?

Certainty of Punishment

According to deterrence theory, if the certainty of arrest, conviction, and sanctioning increases, crime rates should decline. Rational offenders will soon realize that the increased likelihood of punishment outweighs any benefit they perceive from committing crimes. Crime persists because most criminals believe (1) that there is only a small chance they will get arrested for committing a particular crime, (2) that police officers are sometimes reluctant to make arrests even if they are aware of crime, and (3) that even if apprehended there is a good chance of receiving a lenient punishment.[64] If people believed that their criminal transgressions would result in apprehension and punishment, then only the truly irrational would commit crime.[65]

This issue is far from settled. However, a number of research efforts do show a direct relationship between crime rates and the certainty of punishment, and some noted scholars have concluded that the threat of criminal sanctions can reduce crime rates.[66] The certainty of punishment seems to have a greater impact than its severity. In other words, people will more likely be deterred from crime if they believe that they will get caught; what happens to them after apprehension seems to have a lesser impact.[67]

Level of Police Activity

If certainty of apprehension and punishment deters criminal behavior, then increasing the number of police officers on the street should cut the crime rate. Moreover, if these police officers are active, aggressive crime fighters, would-be criminals should be convinced that the risk of apprehension outweighs the benefits they can gain from crime.

The deterrent power of adding police has also been the topic of some debate.[68] Some early studies failed to show that increasing the number of police officers in a community can, by itself, lower crime rates, but more recent research efforts, using different methodologies, have found that police presence may actually reduce crime levels and that adding police may bring crime levels down.[69]

In addition to their mere presence on the street, it is possible that the added police will make more arrests, another factor that helps lower the crime rate. Traditionally about 20 percent of all crimes reported to the police are cleared by arrest. Research indicates that if police could make an arrest in at least 30 percent of all reported crimes, the crime rate would decline significantly.[70] If there were greater police resources, police departments would have the luxury of engaging in aggressive, focused crime fighting initiatives

general deterrence
A crime control policy that depends on the fear of criminal penalties, convincing the potential law violator that the pains associated with crime outweigh its benefits.

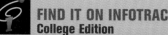
FIND IT ON INFOTRAC
College Edition

To read more about the concept of
"general deterrence" use it as a
key term on InfoTrac College
Edition.

with the result being more arrests and a greater deterrent effect.[71] For example, UCR data show that index crimes are the ones most often cleared by arrest. Due to the visibility of homicide in the media and the importance police agencies place on homicide clearances, homicide detectives work aggressively to clear all homicides regardless of where they occur or the personal characteristics of homicide victims.[72] It is possible that this aggressive approach to solving crime, spurred on by media attention to high-profile cases, has helped lower the homicide rate.

To lower crime rates, some police departments have instituted **crackdowns**—sudden changes in police activity designed to increase the communicated threat or actual certainty of punishment. For example, a police task force might target street-level narcotics dealers by using undercover agents and surveillance cameras in known drug-dealing locales. These efforts have not proven to be successful mechanisms for lowering crime rates.[73] In an analysis of 18 police crackdowns, Lawrence Sherman found that the crackdown initially deterred crime but that crime rates returned to earlier levels once the crackdown ended.[74] Although these results contradict the deterrence concept, research shows that more focused efforts may reduce crime levels. Crime rates are reduced when police officers use aggressive problem-solving and community improvement techniques, such as increasing lighting and cleaning vacant lots, to fight particular crimes in selected places.[75]

Although there is some conflicting data, the weight of the evidence suggests that if punishment became more certain, crime rates would drop. The effect would be enhanced if certainty reached a level sufficient to convince the most dedicated criminal that the risks of crime outweigh the rewards.

Severity of Punishment

According to deterrence theory, the introduction or threat of severe punishment should also bring the crime rate down. Some studies have found that people who believe that they will be punished severely for a crime will forgo committing criminal acts.[76] Nonetheless, there is little consensus that strict punishments alone can reduce criminal activities.[77] The certainty rather than severity of punishment seems to have a greater deterrent effect.

Capital Punishment

It stands to reason that if severity of punishment can deter crime, then fear of the death penalty, the ultimate legal deterrent, should significantly reduce murder rates. Because no one denies its emotional impact, failure of the death penalty to deter violent crime jeopardizes the validity of the entire deterrence concept.

Various studies have tested the assumption that capital punishment deters violent crime. The research can be divided into three types: immediate impact studies, comparative research, and time-series analysis.

Immediate Impact   If capital punishment is a deterrent, the reasoning goes, then its impact should be greatest after a well-publicized execution. Robert Dann tested this assumption in 1935 and found an average of 4.4 more homicides during the 60 days following an execution than during those preceding it, suggesting that the overall impact of executions might actually be to increase the incidence of homicide.

The fact that executions may actually increase the likelihood of murders' being committed is a consequence referred to as the **brutalization effect.** The basis of this theory is that potential criminals may begin to model their behavior after state authorities: If the government can kill its enemies, so can they.[78] The brutalization effect means that after an execution murders may increase, causing even more deaths of innocent victims.[79]

Although many criminologists question the utility of capital punishment, claiming that it causes more harm than it prevents, others believe that, in

crackdown
The concentration of police resources on a particular problem area to eradicate or displace criminal activity.

brutalization effect
The belief that capital punishment creates an atmosphere of brutality that enhances rather than deters the level of violence in society.

FIND IT ON INFOTRAC
College Edition

Some advocates of the death penalty believe that the punishment's deterrent effect would increase if people could watch executions on television. Could such a strategy actually work, or would it have unforeseen consequences? To learn more about this, read:

Don Corrigan, "Viewing Executions: Does the Public Have a Right to See?" *St. Louis Journalism Review*, March 1999 v29 i14 p1(2)

the short run, executing criminals can bring the murder rate down.[80] In sum, a number of criminologists find that executions actually increase murder rates, whereas others argue that their immediate impact is to lower murder rates.

Comparative Research   Another type of research compares the murder rates in jurisdictions that have abolished the death penalty with the rates in those that employ the death penalty.[81] Two pioneering studies, one by Thorsten Sellin (1959) and the other by Walter Reckless (1969), showed little difference in the murder rates of adjacent states, regardless of their use of the death penalty; capital punishment did not appear to influence the reported rate of homicide.[82] More recent research gives little reason to believe that executions deter homicide.[83] Studies have compared murder rates in jurisdictions having a death penalty statute with those that don't, and have also taken into account the number of people actually executed. These comparisons indicate that the death penalty—whether on the books or actually used—does not deter violent crime.[84]

The failure to show a deterrent effect of the death penalty is not limited to comparisons among U.S. states. Research conducted in 14 nations around the world found little evidence that countries with a death penalty have lower violence rates than those without. In fact, homicide rates decline after capital punishment is abolished, a direct contradiction to its supposed deterrent effect.[85]

Time-Series Analysis   Statistical analysis has allowed researchers to gauge whether the murder rate changes when death penalty statutes are created or eliminated. The most widely cited study is Isaac Ehrlich's 1975 work, in which he used national crime and execution data to reach the conclusion that each execution in the United States would save seven or eight people from being murdered.[86] Ehrlich's research has been widely cited by advocates of the death penalty as empirical proof of the deterrent effect of capital punishment. However, subsequent research that attempted to replicate Ehrlich's analysis showed that his approach was flawed and that capital punishment is no more effective as a deterrent than life imprisonment.[87] For example, a recent test of the deterrent effect of the death penalty during the years 1984–1997 in Texas found no association between the frequency of execution and murder rates.[88]

Why Capital Punishment Fails   In sum, studies that have attempted to show the deterrent effect of capital punishment on the murder rate indicate that executing convicted criminals has relatively little influence on behavior.[89] Although it is still uncertain why the threat of capital punishment has failed as a deterrent, the cause may lie in the nature of homicide itself. Murder is often an expressive "crime of passion" involving people who know each other and who may be under the influence of drugs or alcohol. Murder is also a by-product of the criminal activity of people who suffer from the burdens of poverty and income inequality.[90] These factors may either prevent or inhibit rational evaluation of the long-term consequences of an immediate violent act.

The deterrent power of the death penalty may be reduced because executions are conducted within the privacy of a correctional center, and the relatively benign lethal injection has replaced the more horrendous forms of death such as the electric chair and gas chamber. As legal historian Stuart Banner points out, when it was first used as a deterrent, executions were conducted in the public square, drew huge crowds, and were conducted in a brutal fashion. In some cases bodies were actually dissected after the execution, a practice viewed as a punishment beyond death, to enhance the deterrent effect of capital punishment.[91]

It is also possible that capital punishment fails as a deterrent because, as Steven Levitt points out, it just isn't used frequently enough for the threat of execution to deter a rational criminal. Even among those on death row, the annual execution rate is only 2 percent, or just twice the death rate from accidents and violence among all American men.[92]

The failure of the "ultimate deterrent" to deter the "ultimate crime" has been used by critics to question the validity of the general deterrence hypothesis that severe punishment will lower crime rates. In general, there is little direct evidence that severity of punishment alone can reduce or eliminate crime.

Swiftness of Punishment

A core element of general deterrence theory is that people who believe that they will be swiftly punished if they break the law will abstain from crime.[93] Again, the evidence on the association between perceived punishment risk and crime has been mixed. Some research efforts have found a relationship;[94] others have not.[95]

The threat of swift retaliation seems to work best when would-be criminals believe they will be subjected to very harsh punishments.[96] However, even this fear may be negated or overcome by the belief that a crime gives them a significant chance for large profit; greed overcomes fear![97]

Critique of General Deterrence

Some experts believe that the purpose of the law and justice system is to create a "threat system."[98] The threat of legal punishment should, on the face of it, deter lawbreakers through fear. Nonetheless, the relationship between crime rates and deterrent measures is far less than choice theorists might expect. Despite efforts to punish criminals and make them fear crime, there is little evidence that the fear of apprehension and punishment alone can reduce crime rates. How can this discrepancy be explained?

Rationality Deterrence theory assumes a rational offender who weighs the costs and benefits of a criminal act before deciding on a course of action. Criminals may be desperate people who choose crime because they believe there is no reasonable alternative. Some may suffer from personality disorders that impair their judgment and render them incapable of making truly rational decisions. Psychologists believe that chronic offenders suffer from an emotional state that renders them both incapable of fearing punishment and less likely to appreciate the consequences of crime.[99] For example, research on repeat sex offenders finds that they suffer from an elevated emotional state that negates the deterrent effect of the law.[100] There is also evidence that drinking alcohol may impede a person's ability to reasonably assess the costs and benefits of crime.[101] If the benefits of crime are exaggerated, the law's deterrent effect may be deflated.

Certainty, Severity, and Speed As Beccaria's famous equation tells us, the threat of punishment involves not only its severity but its certainty and speed. The American legal system is not very effective. Only 10 percent of all serious offenses result in apprehension. Half of these crimes go unreported, and police make arrests in only about 20 percent of reported crimes. Even when offenders are detected, police officers may choose to warn rather than arrest.[102] The odds of receiving a prison term are less than 20 per 1,000 crimes committed. As a result, some offenders believe that they will not be severely punished for their acts and consequently have little regard for the law's deterrent power. Even those accused of murder are often convicted of lesser offenses and spend relatively short amounts of time behind bars.[103] In making their "rational choice," offenders may be aware that the deterrent effect of the law is minimal.

Some Offenders Are More "Deterrable" Than Others Research by Greg Pogarsky indicates that deterrent measures may have greater impact on

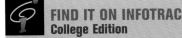

FIND IT ON INFOTRAC
College Edition

To read a study that did find a specific deterrence effect, go to:

James Lasley, "The Effect of Intensive Bail Supervision on Repeat Domestic Violence Offenders," *Policy Studies Journal*, May 2003 v31 i2 p187–208

some people while having a lesser effect on others: *Acute conformists* obey the law because of their own moral beliefs and values; the *deterrable* are those people influenced by the threat of legal sanctions; the *incorrigible* are immune to the threat of legal sanctions. Of the three groups identified by Pogorsky, only the deterrable will respond to the threat of legal sanctions.[104]

Are there people who cannot be deterred? Among some groups of high-risk offenders, such as teens living in economically depressed neighborhoods, the threat of formal sanctions is irrelevant. Young people in these areas have little to lose if arrested; their opportunities are few, and they have little attachment to social institutions such as school or family. Even if they truly fear the consequences of the law, they must commit crime to survive in a hostile environment. Similarly, some people may be suffering from personality disorders and mental infirmity, which make them immune to the deterrent power of the law.[105]

Summary   Studies measuring the perception of punishment agree with studies using aggregate criminal justice data that the certainty of punishment has a greater deterrent effect than its severity. Nonetheless, neither the perception nor the reality of punishment can deter most crimes.

Specific Deterrence

The theory of **specific deterrence** (also called special or particular deterrence) holds that criminal sanctions should be so powerful that known criminals will never repeat their criminal acts. According to this view, the drunk driver whose sentence is a substantial fine and a week in the county jail should be convinced that the price to be paid for drinking and driving is too great to consider future violations. Similarly, burglars who spend five years in a tough, maximum-security prison should find their enthusiasm for theft dampened.[106] In principle, punishment works if a connection can be established between the planned action and memories of its consequence; if these recollections are adequately intense, the action will be unlikely to occur again.[107]

Research on specific deterrence does not provide any clear-cut evidence that punishing criminals is an effective means of stopping them from committing future crimes. Research on chronic offenders indicates that arrest and punishment seem to have little effect on experienced criminals and may even increase the likelihood that first-time offenders will commit new crimes.[108] About two-thirds of all convicted felons are re-arrested within three years of their release from prison, and those who have been punished in the past are the most likely to commit a new offense.[109] **Incarceration** may sometimes slow down or delay **recidivism** in the short term, but the overall probability of re-arrest does not change following incarceration.[110] In fact, some research efforts have shown that, rather than reducing the frequency of crime, severe punishment may backfire and actually increase re-offending rates.[111] For example, even the criminals who receive probation are less likely to recidivate than those who are sent to prison for committing similar crimes; specific deterrence theory would predict that those punished severely (given prison time) should have lower recidivism rates than those treated leniently (given probation).[112] It is possible that punishment may bring defiance rather than deterrence, and the stigma of apprehension may help lock offenders into a criminal career. Criminals who are punished may also believe that the likelihood of getting caught twice for the same type of crime is remote: "Lightning never strikes twice in the same spot," they may reason. "No one is that unlucky."[113]

Although these results are not encouraging, some studies show that arrest and conviction may, under some circumstances, lower the frequency of re-offending, a finding that supports specific deterrence.[114] These contradictory findings suggest that further research is needed to clarify the impact of formal sanctions on individual decision making. The effects of specific deterrence in preventing domestic violence are discussed in the Race, Culture, Gender, and Criminology feature.

specific deterrence
The view that criminal sanctions should be so powerful that offenders will never repeat their criminal acts.

incarceration
Confinement in jail or prison.

recidivism
Repetition of criminal behavior.

RACE, CULTURE, GENDER, AND CRIMINOLOGY

Deterring Domestic Violence

Is it possible to use a specific deterrence strategy to control domestic violence? Would the memory of a formal police arrest reduce the incidence of spousal abuse? Despite the fact that domestic violence is a prevalent, serious crime, police departments have been accused of rarely arresting suspected perpetrators. Lack of forceful action may contribute to chronic episodes of violence, which obviously is of great concern to women's advocacy groups. Is it possible that prompt, formal action by police agencies might prevent the reoccurrence of this serious crime that threatens and even kills so many women?

In the famous Minneapolis domestic violence study, Lawrence Sherman and Richard Berk had police officers randomly assign treatments to the domestic assault cases they encountered on their beats. One approach was to give some sort of advice and mediation; another was to send the assailant from the home for a period of eight hours; and the third was to arrest the assailant. They found that when police took formal action (arrest), the chance of recidivism was substantially less than with less punitive measures, such as warning offenders or ordering offenders out of the house for a cooling-off period. A six-month follow-up found

that only 10 percent of those who were arrested repeated their violent behavior, whereas 19 percent of those advised and 24 percent of those sent away repeated their offenses. Sherman and Berk's interviews of 205 victims demonstrated that arrests were somewhat effective in controlling domestic assaults: 19 percent of the women whose attackers had been arrested reported their mates had assaulted them again; in contrast, 37 percent of those whose mates were advised and 33 percent of those whose mates were sent away reported further assaults. Sherman and Berk concluded that a formal arrest was the most effective means of controlling domestic violence, regardless of what happened to the offender in court.

The Minneapolis experiment deeply affected police operations around the nation. Atlanta, Chicago, Dallas, Denver, Detroit, New York, Miami, San Francisco, and Seattle, among other large cities, adopted policies encouraging arrests in domestic violence cases. A number of states adopted legislation mandating that police either take formal action in domestic abuse cases or explain in writing their failure to act.

Although the findings of the Minneapolis experiment received quick acceptance, government-funded research replicating the experimental design in

five other locales, including Omaha, Nebraska, and Charlotte, North Carolina, failed to duplicate the original results. In these locales, formal arrest was not a greater deterrent to domestic abuse than warning or advising the assailant. Christopher Maxwell and his associates recently pooled the findings from all the replication studies to provide an overall picture of the arrest/deterrence relationship. Although positive, the effect of arrest on re-offending was at best modest. What seemed more important predictors of repeat offending were the batterer's prior criminal record and his age.

Why Is the Deterrent Effect Minimal?

There are a number of reasons arrest does not deter domestic violence. Sherman and his associates found that in some instances the effect of arrest quickly decays and, in the long run, may escalate the frequency of repeat domestic violence.

Explaining why the initial deterrent effect of arrest decays over time is difficult. It is possible that offenders who are arrested initially fear punishment, but eventually replace fear with anger and violent intent toward their mates when their cases do not result in severe punishment. Many repeat abusers do not fear arrest, believing that formal

Incapacitation

incapacitation effect
The idea that keeping offenders in confinement will eliminate the risk of their committing further offenses.

It stands to reason that if more criminals are sent to prison, the crime rate should go down. Because most people age out of crime, the duration of a criminal career is limited. Placing offenders behind bars during their prime crime years should lessen their lifetime opportunity to commit crime. The shorter the span of opportunity, the fewer offenses they can commit during their lives; hence, crime is reduced. This theory, known as the **incapacitation effect,** seems logical, but does it work?

In the past 20 years we have witnessed significant growth in the number and percentage of the population held in prisons and jails. Today more than 2 million Americans are incarcerated. Advocates of incapacitation suggest that this effort has been responsible for the decade-long decline in crime rates. However, critics counter that what appears to be an incapacitation effect may actually reflect the effect of some other legal or social phenomenon. The economy has improved, police may be more effective, and the crack cocaine epidemic has waned. Crime rates may be dropping simply because potential police action will not cause them harm. They may be aware that police are reluctant to make arrests in domestic violence cases unless there is a significant chance of injury to the victim, for example, when a weapon is used.

It is also possible that the threat of future punishment may have little impact on repeat offenders who have already become involved in the justice system. For example, D. Alex Heckert and Edward Gondolf surveyed men in an abuse prevention program and found that the subjects were aware of potential punishment but that it was unlikely to be sufficiently harsh to deter their spousal abuse. Similarly, Robert Davis and his associates also found little association between the severity of punishment for past spousal abuse and re-arrest on subsequent charges. Men were just as likely to recidivate if their case was dismissed, if they were given probation, or even if they were sent to jail. It is possible that people who have already experienced arrest and punished on spouse abuse charges perceive the law as less severe than they had imagined, encouraging rather than deterring future violations.

These studies indicate that there is little reason to believe that domestic violence can be controlled through the administration of harsh punishments. Treating offenders within a rehabilitative setting using counseling and other techniques may be a more effective

method, especially if, as Jill Gordon and Laura Moriarty found, the abuser takes the program seriously and completes all treatment sessions.

Critical Thinking

1. Why do arrests seem to have little effect on future domestic violence? Could it be that getting arrested increases feelings of strain and hostility and does little to reduce the problems that led to domestic conflict in the first place? Explain how you think this works.

2. What policies would you suggest to reduce the reoccurrence of domestic violence?

InfoTrac College Edition Research

Would police be more efficient in combating domestic violence if they feared lawsuits from victims? To find out, read:

Lisa Gelhaus, "Civil Suits against Police Change Domestic Violence Response," *Trial*, (35) September 1999: 103

SOURCES: Jill Gordon and Laura Moriarty, "The effects of domestic violence batterer treatment on domestic violence recidivism: the Chesterfield County experience," *Criminal Justice and Behavior* 30 (2003): 118–1s35; Christopher Maxwell, Joel H. Garner, and Jeffrey A. Fagan, "The effects of arrest in intimate partner violence: new evidence," *Spouse Assault*

Replication Program (Washington, D.C.: National Institute of Justice, 2001); D. Alex Heckert and Edward Gondolf, "The effect of perceptions of sanctions on batterer program outcomes," *Journal of Research in Crime and Delinquency* 37 (2000) 369–391; Robert Kane, "Patterns of arrest in domestic violence encounters: identifying a police decision-making model," *Journal of Criminal Justice* 27 (1999): 65–79; Dana Jones and Joanne Belknap, "Police responses to battering in a progressive pro-arrest jurisdiction," *Justice Quarterly* 16 (1999): 249–273; Robert Davis, Barbara Smith, and Laura Nickles, "The deterrent effect of prosecuting domestic violence misdemeanors," *Crime and Delinquency* 44 (1998): 434–442; Amy Thistlethwaite, John Wooldredge, and David Gibbs, "Severity of dispositions and domestic violence recidivism," *Crime and Delinquency* 44 (1998): 388–398; J. David Hirschel, Ira Hutchison, and Charles Dean, "The failure of arrest to deter spouse abuse," *Journal of Research in Crime and Delinquency* 29 (1992): 7–33; Franklyn Dunford, David Huizinga, and Delbert Elliott, "The role of arrest in domestic assault: the Omaha experiment," *Criminology* 28 (1990): 183–206; Lawrence Sherman, Janell Schmidt, Dennis Rogan, Patrick Gartin, Ellen Cohn, Dean Collins, and Anthony Bacich, "From initial deterrence to long-term escalation: short-custody arrest for domestic violence," *Criminology* 29 (1991): 821–850; Lawrence Sherman and Richard Berk, "The specific deterrent effects of arrest for domestic assault," *American Sociological Review* 49 (1984): 261–272; Michael Steinman, "Lowering recidivism among men who batter women," *Journal of Police Science and Administration* 17 (1990):124–131; and Susan Miller and Leeann Iovanni, "Determinants of perceived risk of formal sanction for courtship violence," *Justice Quarterly* 11 (1994): 282–312.

criminals now recognize and fear the tough new sentencing laws that provide long mandatory prison sentences for drug and violent crimes. What appears to be an incapacitation effect may actually be an effect of general deterrence.[115]

Can Incapacitation Reduce Crime?

There has long been debate among criminologists over the effect of incarceration on the crime rate.[116] Some experts question the effect of incarceration.[117] Others find that it can reduce crime.[118]

Considering that criminals are unable to continue their illegal activities while housed in a prison or jail, incapacitation should be an excellent crime control strategy. For example, a study of 201 heroin abusers in New York City found that, if given a one-year jail sentence, they would not have been able to commit their yearly haul of crimes: 1,000 robberies, 4,000 burglaries, 10,000 shopliftings, and more than 3,000 other property crimes.[119]

There are also those who question whether incapacitation really controls crime rates. For one thing, there is little evidence that incapacitating criminals

■ Simply put, if dangerous criminals were incapacitated, they would never have the opportunity to prey upon others. One of the most dramatic examples of the utility of incapacitation is the case of Lawrence Singleton, who in 1978 raped a young California girl, Mary Vincent, and then chopped off her arms with an axe. He served eight years in prison for this vile crime. Upon his release, he moved to Florida, where in 1997 he killed a woman, Roxanne Hays. Vincent is shown here as she testified at the penalty phase of Singleton's trial; he was sentenced to death. Should a dangerous predator such as Singleton ever be released from incarceration? Is rehabilitation even a remote possibility?

three strikes and you're out
Policy whereby people convicted of three felony offenses receive a mandatory life sentence.

will deter them from future criminality and even more reason to believe that they may be more inclined to commit crimes upon release. Prison has few specific deterrent effects: The more prior incarceration experiences inmates have, the more likely they are to recidivate (and return to prison) within 12 months of their release.[120] The short-term crime reduction effect of incapacitating criminals is negated if the prison experience has the long-term effect of escalating the frequency of criminal behavior upon release. By its nature, the prison experience exposes young, first-time offenders to higher-risk, more experienced inmates who can influence their lifestyle and help shape their attitudes. Novice inmates also run an increased risk of becoming infected with AIDS and other health hazards, and that exposure reduces their life chances after release.[121]

Furthermore, the economics of crime suggest that if money can be made from criminal activity, there will always be someone to take the place of the incarcerated offender. New criminals will be recruited and trained, offsetting any benefit accrued by incarceration. Imprisoning established offenders opens new opportunities for competitors who were suppressed by the more experienced criminals. For example, incarcerating organized crime members may open drug markets to new gangs. The flow of narcotics into the country may actually increase after the more experienced organized crime leaders are imprisoned because newcomers are willing to take greater risks.

Another reason incarceration may not work is that most criminal offenses are committed by teens and very young adult offenders, and it is unlikely that they will be sent to prison for a single felony conviction. At the same time, many incarcerated criminals, aging behind bars, are already past the age when they are likely to commit crime. As a result, a strict incarceration policy may keep people in prison beyond the time they are a threat to society while a new cohort of high-risk adolescents is on the street. It is possible that the most serious criminals are already behind bars and that adding less dangerous offenders to the population will have little appreciable effect while adding tremendous costs to the correctional system.[122]

An incapacitation strategy is terribly expensive. The prison system costs billions of dollars each year. Even if incarceration could reduce the crime rate, the costs would be enormous. Are U.S. taxpayers willing to spend billions more on new prison construction and annual maintenance fees? A strict incarceration policy would result in a growing number of elderly inmates whose maintenance costs, estimated at $69,000 per year, are three times higher than those of younger inmates. In 2003 there will be more than 125,000 of these elderly inmates, and by 2005 about 16 percent of the prison population will be over age 50.[123]

Three Strikes and You're Out

Some experts maintain that incapacitation can work if it is focused on the most serious chronic offenders. For example, the **three strikes and you're out** policy, giving people convicted of three felony offenses a mandatory life sentence, has received widespread publicity. Many states already employ habitual offender laws that provide long (or life) sentences for repeat offenders. Criminologists retort that although such strategies are politically compelling, they will not work, for several reasons:

■ Most three-time losers are at the verge of aging out of crime anyway.
■ Current sentences for violent crimes are already quite severe.

■ Some critics believe that three strikes laws are "cruel and unusual" because they provide extremely long sentences for relatively minor crimes. Joanna Verduzco, ten, of Riverside, California, whose father, Pedro Verduzco, seen in photo, is in jail for twenty-nine years to life for possession of 0.6 grams of methamphetamine, pauses during a protest against California's three strikes law, March 9, 2002, at the federal building in the Westwood area of Los Angeles. The event was organized by Families to Amend California's Three Strikes (FACTS) and other groups.

© 2002 AP/Wide World Photos

✔ Checkpoints

✔ Situational crime prevention efforts are designed to reduce or redirect crime by making it more difficult to profit from illegal acts.

✔ General deterrence models are based on the fear of punishment that is severe, swift, and certain.

✔ Specific deterrence aims at reducing crime through the application of severe punishments. Once offenders experience these punishments, they will be unwilling to repeat their criminal activities.

✔ Incapacitation strategies are designed to reduce crime by taking known criminals out of circulation, preventing them from having the opportunity to commit further offenses.

To quiz yourself on this material, go to questions 4.9–4.15 on the Criminology: The Core 2e Web site.

■ An expanding prison population will drive up already high prison costs.

■ There would be racial disparity in sentencing.

■ The police would be in danger because two-time offenders would violently resist a third arrest, knowing they face a life sentence.[124]

■ The prison population probably already contains the highest-frequency criminals.

Those who support a selective incapacitation strategy argue that criminals who are already in prison (high-rate offenders) commit significantly more crimes each year than the average criminal who is on the outside (low-rate offenders). If a broad policy of incarceration were employed, requiring mandatory prison sentences for all those convicted of crimes, more low-rate criminals would be placed behind bars.[125] It would be both costly and nonproductive to incarcerate large groups of people who commit relatively few crimes. It makes more economic sense to focus incarceration efforts on known high-rate offenders by lengthening their sentences.

Before the use of incarceration as a crime control strategy is abandoned, we should recall that there is highly sophisticated research linking incarceration with reductions in the crime rate.[126] A strict incarceration policy may also have residual benefits. For example, Ilyana Kuziemko and Steven Levitt found that the number of prisoners incarcerated on drug-related offenses rose dramatically (1500 percent) between 1980 and 2000. This policy had an impact on drug markets. The cost of cocaine rose by 10 to 15 percent, which resulted in a drop of cocaine usage by as much as 20 percent.[127] Concept Summary 4.1 outlines the various methods of crime control and their effects. ✔ Checkpoints

CONCEPT SUMMARY **4.1 Crime Control Methods**

CRIME CONTROL METHOD	CORE CONCEPT	IS IT SUCCESSFUL?
Situational Crime Control	Reduce the payoff of crime	Some methods seem to reduce particular crimes
General Deterrence	Scare would-be criminals	Certainty of punishment more effective than severity
Specific Deterrence	Scare known criminals	Limited effectiveness underscored by high recidivism rates
Incapacitation	Reduce criminal opportunity	As prison rates have increased, the crime rate has declined

Policy Implications of Choice Theory

From the origins of classical theory to the development of modern rational choice views, the belief that criminals choose to commit crime has influenced the relationship among law, punishment, and crime. Although research on the core principles of choice theory and deterrence theories has produced mixed results, these models have had an important impact on crime prevention strategies.

When police patrol in well-marked cars, it is assumed that their presence will deter would-be criminals. When the harsh realities of prison life are portrayed in movies and TV shows, the lesson is not lost on potential criminals. Nowhere is the idea that the threat of punishment can control crime more evident than in the implementation of tough mandatory criminal sentences to control violent crime and drug trafficking.

Despite its questionable deterrent effect, some advocates argue that the death penalty can effectively restrict criminality; at least it ensures that convicted criminals never again get the opportunity to kill. Many observers are dismayed because people who are convicted of murder sometimes kill again when released on parole. One study of 52,000 incarcerated murderers found that 810 had been previously convicted of murder and had killed 821 people following their previous release from prison.[128] About 9 percent of all inmates on death row have had prior convictions for homicide. Death penalty advocates argue that if these criminals had been executed for their first offenses, hundreds of people would be alive today.[129]

The concept of criminal choice has also prompted the development of justice policies that treat all offenders equally, without regard for their background or personal characteristics. This is referred to as the concept of **just desert.** The just desert position has been most clearly spelled out by criminologist Andrew Von Hirsch in his book, *Doing Justice*.[130] Von Hirsch argues that while punishment is needed to preserve the social equity disturbed by crime, it should be commensurate with the seriousness of the crime.[131] Von Hirsch's views can be summarized as follows:

1. Those who violate others' rights deserve to be punished.
2. We should not deliberately add to human suffering; punishment makes those punished suffer.
3. Punishment may prevent more misery than it inflicts, which justifies the need for desert-based punishment.[132]

Desert theory is also concerned with the rights of the accused. It alleges that the rights of the person being punished should not be unduly sacrificed for the good of others (as with deterrence). The offender should not be treated as more (or less) blameworthy than is warranted by the character of his or her offense. For example, Von Hirsch asks the following question: If two crimes, A and B, are equally serious, but if severe penalties are shown to have a deterrent effect only with respect to A, would it be fair to punish the person

just desert
The principle that those who violate the rights of others deserve punishment commensurate with the seriousness of the crime, without regard to their personal characteristics or circumstances.

who has committed crime A more harshly simply to deter others from committing the crime? Conversely, it is unfair for a merciful judge to impose a light sentence on a teenage criminal, because in so doing he arbitrarily makes the younger offender less blameworthy than an older criminal who commits the same act. All offenders must be treated the same on the basis of what they did, not who they are.

In sum, the just desert model suggests that retribution justifies punishment because people deserve what they get for past deeds. Punishment based on deterrence or incapacitation is wrong because it involves an offender's future actions, which cannot be accurately predicted. Punishment should be the same for all people who commit the same crime. Criminal sentences based on individual needs or characteristics are inherently unfair because all people are equally blameworthy for their misdeeds. The influence of Von Hirsch's views can be seen in mandatory sentencing models that give the same punishment to all people who commit the same type of crime.

Summary

- Choice theories assume that criminals carefully choose whether to commit criminal acts. These theories are summarized in Concept Summary 4.2.

- People are influenced by their fear of the criminal penalties associated with being caught and convicted for law violations.

- The choice approach is rooted in the classical criminology of Cesare Beccaria, who argued that punishment should be certain, swift, and severe enough to deter crime.

- Today, choice theorists view crime as offense- and offender-specific.

- Offense-specific means that the characteristics of the crime control whether it occurs. For example, carefully protecting a home makes it less likely to be a target of crime.

- Offender-specific refers to the personal characteristics of potential criminals. People with specific skills and needs may be more likely to commit crime than others.

- Research shows that offenders consider their targets carefully before deciding on a course of action. Even violent criminals and drug addicts show signs of rationality.

- By implication, crime can be prevented or displaced by convincing potential criminals that the risks of violating the law exceed the benefits.

- Situational crime prevention is the application of security and protective devices that make it more difficult to commit crime or reduce criminal rewards.

- Deterrence theory holds that if criminals are indeed rational, an inverse relationship should exist between punishment and crime.

- The certainty of punishment seems to deter crime. If people do not believe they will be caught, even harsh punishment may not deter crime.

- Deterrence theory has been criticized on the grounds that it wrongfully assumes that criminals make a rational choice before committing crimes, that it ignores the intricacies of the criminal justice system, and that it does not take into account the social and psychological factors that may influence criminality.

- A big disappointment for deterrence theory is the fact that the death penalty does not seem to reduce murders.

- Specific deterrence theory holds that the crime rate can be reduced if known offenders are punished so severely that they never commit crimes again.

- There is little evidence that harsh punishment actually reduces the crime rate. Most prison inmates recidivate.

- Incapacitation theory maintains that if deterrence does not work, the best course of action is to incarcerate known offenders for long periods so that they lack criminal opportunity.

- Research efforts have not proved that increasing the number of people in prison—and increasing prison sentences—will reduce crime rates.

CONCEPT SUMMARY **4.2 Choice Theories**

THEORY	MAJOR PREMISE	STRENGTHS	RESEARCH FOCUS
Rational choice	Law-violating behavior occurs after offenders weigh information on their personal needs and the situational factors involved in the difficulty and risk of committing a crime.	Explains why high-risk youths do not constantly engage in delinquency. Relates theory to delinquency control policy. It is not limited by class or other social variables.	Offense patterns, where, when, and how crime takes place
Routine activities	Crime and delinquency are functions of the presence of motivated offenders, the availability of suitable targets, and the absence of capable guardians.	Can explain fluctuations in crime and delinquency rates. Shows how victim behavior influences criminal choice.	Guardianship, target availability, offender populations
General deterrence	People will commit crime and delinquency if they perceive that the benefits outweigh the risks. Crime is a function of the severity, certainty, and speed of punishment.	Shows the relationship between crime and punishment. Suggests a real solution to crime.	Perception of punishment, effect of legal sanctions, probability of punishment and crime rates
Specific deterrence	If punishment is severe enough, criminals will not repeat their illegal acts.	Provides a strategy to reduce crime.	Recidivism, repeat offending, punishment type and crime
Incapacitation	Keeping known criminals out of circulation will reduce crime rates.	Recognizes the role that opportunity plays in criminal behavior. Provides a solution to chronic offending.	Prison population and crime rates, sentence length and crime

Thinking Like a Criminologist

The attorney general has recently funded a national survey of state sentencing practices and received the following data.

Felony Convictions in State Courts

		PERCENT CONVICTED AND SENTENCED TO:		
YEAR	NUMBER CONVICTED	PRISON	JAIL	PROBATION
1992	893,600	44	26	30
1994	872,200	45	26	29
1996	998,000	38	31	31
1998	927,700	44	24	32
2000	924,700	40	28	3

Average Maximum Sentence Length (in months)

MOST SERIOUS CONVICTION OFFENSE	TOTAL	INCARCERATION		
		PRISON	JAIL	PROBATION
All offenses	36 mo	55 mo	6 mo	38 mo
Violent offenses	66 mo	91 mo	7 mo	44 mo
Property offenses	27 mo	42 mo	6 mo	38 mo
Drug offenses	30 mo	47 mo	6 mo	36 mo
Weapons offenses	25 mo	38 mo	7 mo	36 mo
Other offenses	22 mo	38 mo	6 mo	40 mo

The attorney general wants you to make some recommendations about criminal punishment. Is it possible, he asks, that the type of criminal sentences and the way they are served can have an impact on crime rates? What could be gained by either increasing punishment or requiring inmates to spend time behind bars before their release? Are we being too lenient or too punitive? As someone who has studied choice theory, how would you interpret these data, and what do they tell you about sentencing patterns? How might crime rates be affected if the way we punished offenders were radically changed?

Go to the Criminology: The Core 2e Web site to review the content of this chapter.

Doing Research on the Web

For an up-to-date list of URLs, go to

http://www.cj.wadsworth.com/siegel_crimcore2e

To read the actual report from which these data are taken, go to:

http://www.ojp.usdoj.gov/bjs/pub/pdf/fssc00.pdf

See also:

http://www.ojp.usdoj.gov/bjs/pub/pdf/fdluc98.pdf

Another good site for information on sentencing is the Sentencing Project, which is devoted to alternative sentencing programs and research and advocacy on criminal justice policy:

http://www.sentencingproject.org/about.cfm

Pro/Con discussions and Viewpoint Essays on some of the topics in this chapter may be found at the Opposing Viewpoints Resource Center:

http://www.gale.com/OpposingViewpoints

Key Terms

rational choice 73
choice theory 73
classical criminology 74
offense-specific 75
offender-specific 75
edgework 79
seductions of crime 79
situational crime prevention 80

defensible space 80
displacement 81
extinction 82
diffusion of benefits 82
discouragement 82
general deterrence 83
crackdown 84
brutalization effect 84

specific deterrence 87
incarceration 87
recidivism 87
incapacitation effect 88
three strikes and you're out 90
just desert 92

Critical Thinking Questions

1. Are criminals rational decision makers, or are most motivated by noncontrollable psychological and emotional drives or social forces such as poverty and despair?

2. Would you want to live in a society where crime rates are quite low because they are controlled by extremely harsh punishments, such as flogging for vandalism?

3. Which would you be more afraid of if you were caught by the police while shoplifting: receiving criminal punishment or having to face the contempt of your friends or relatives?

4. Is it possible to create a method of capital punishment that would actually deter murder—for example, by televising executions? What might be some of the negative consequences of such a policy?

CHAPTER 5

Trait Theory: It's in Their Blood

Chapter Objectives

1. Be familiar with the concept of sociobiology.
2. Know what is meant when biosocial theorists use the term *equipotentiality*.
3. Be able to discuss the relationship between diet and crime.
4. Be familiar with the association between hormones and crime.
5. Be able to discuss why violent offenders may suffer from neurological problems.
6. Know the factors that make up the ADHD syndrome.
7. Be able to discuss the role genetics plays in violent behavior.
8. Be familiar with the concepts of evolutionary theory.
9. Be able to discuss the psychodynamics of criminality.
10. Understand the association between media and crime.
11. Discuss the role of personality and intelligence in antisocial behaviors.

NDREW LUSTER, AN HEIR TO THE MAX FACTOR COSMETIC FORTUNE, LIVED A PRIVILEGED LIFE OF SUN AND FUN IN A beach house in an exclusive community near Santa Barbara. However, Andrew has a darker side, which came to light on July 17, 2000, when he was arrested after a young woman accused him of drugging her with the "date rape" drug GHB and then having sex with her while she was unconscious. When police served a war-

CNN. View the CNN video clip of this story and answer related critical thinking questions on your Criminology: The Core 2e CD.

rant on his home, they found tapes indicating Luster had a habit of drugging women and raping them while they were comatose. Halfway through the trial, Luster jumped bail, disappeared, and was declared a fugitive from justice. In his absence, the jury found him guilty on 86 of the 87 counts, and he was eventually sentenced to more than 100 years in prison. Five months later, he was captured in the resort town of Puerto Vallarta, Mexico, by bounty hunter Duane "Dog" Chapman. On July 3, 2003, an appellate court denied Luster's appeal of his guilty verdicts because he had jumped bail.

ow can we explain the bizarre behavior of Andrew Luster? Why would a wealthy, handsome man drug and rape unsuspecting women? Could his acts possibly be the result of calculation and planning, or are they the product of some mental aberration or personality disturbance?

The image of a disturbed, mentally ill offender seems plausible because a generation of Americans has grown up on films and TV shows that portray violent criminals as mentally deranged and physically abnormal. Beginning with Alfred Hitchcock's film *Psycho,* producers have made millions depicting the ghoulish acts of people who at first seem normal and even friendly but turn out to be demented and dangerous. Lurking out there are deranged roommates (*Single White Female*), abnormal girlfriends (*Fatal Attraction*) and boyfriends (*Fear*), and lunatic high school friends (*Scream*) who evolve into even crazier college classmates (*Scream II*) and then grow up to become nutty young adults (*Scream III*). No one is safe when the psychologists and psychiatrists who are hired to treat these disturbed people turn out to be demonic murderers themselves (*Silence of the Lambs, Hannibal, Red Dragon*). Is it any wonder that we respond to a particularly horrible crime by saying of the perpetrator, "That guy must be crazy" or "She is a monster"?

This chapter reviews the theories that suggest that criminality is a matter of abnormal human traits. These **trait theories** can be

trait theory
The view that criminality is a product of abnormal biological or psychological traits.

subdivided into two major categories: one stressing biological makeup and the other stressing psychological functioning. Although these views often overlap (for example, brain function may have a biological basis), each branch has its unique characteristics and will be discussed separately.

The Development of Trait Theory

The view that criminals have physical or mental traits that make them different and abnormal is not restricted to movie viewers but began with the Italian physician and criminologist Cesare Lombroso. The early research of Lombroso and his contemporaries is today regarded as historical curiosity, not scientific fact. The research methodology they used was slipshod, and many of the traits they assumed to be inherited are not really genetically determined but are caused by environment and diet. As criticism of their work mounted, biological explanations of crime fell out of favor and were abandoned in the early twentieth century.[1]

In the early 1970s, spurred by the publication of *Sociobiology* by Edmund O. Wilson, biological explanations of crime once again emerged.[2] **Sociobiology** differs from earlier theories of behavior in that it stresses that biological and genetic conditions affect how social behaviors are learned and perceived. It suggests that both animal and human behavior is determined in part by the need to ensure survival of offspring and replenishment of the gene pool. These perceptions, in turn, are linked to existing environmental structures.

Sociobiologists view biology, environment, and learning as mutually interdependent factors. These views revived interest in finding a biological or psychological basis for crime and delinquency. It prompted some criminologists to conclude that personal traits must separate the deviant members of society from the nondeviant. Possessing these traits may help explain why, when faced with the same life situation, one person commits crime whereas another obeys the law. Put another way, living in a disadvantaged neighborhood will not cause a well-adjusted person to commit crime; living in an affluent area will not stop a maladapted person from offending.[3] All people may be aware of and even fear the sanctioning power of the law, but some are unable to control their urges and passions.

Connections

As you may recall (Chapter 1), Lombroso's work on the born criminal was a direct offshoot of applying the scientific method to the study of crime. His identification of primitive, atavistic anomalies was based on what he believed to be sound empirical research using established scientific methods.

Contemporary Trait Theory

Contemporary trait theorists do not suggest that a single biological or psychological attribute adequately explains all criminality. Rather, each offender is considered physically and mentally unique; consequently, there must be different explanations for each person's behavior. Some may have inherited criminal tendencies; others may be suffering from neurological problems; still others may have blood chemistry disorders that heighten their antisocial activity. Criminologists who focus on the individual see many explanations for crime because, in fact, there are many differences among criminal offenders.

Contemporary trait theorists focus on basic human behavior and drives that are linked to antisocial behavior patterns. Because humans are not all born with equal potential to learn and achieve (**equipotentiality**), the combination of physical traits and the environment produces individual behavior patterns. There is a significant link between behavior patterns and physical or chemical changes in the brain, autonomic nervous system, and central nervous system.[4]

Trait theorists today recognize that having a particular physical characteristic does not, in itself, produce criminality. Crime-producing interactions involve both personal traits (such as defective intelligence, impulsive personality, and abnormal brain chemistry) and environmental factors (such as family life, educational attainment, socioeconomic status, and neighborhood conditions). People may develop physical or mental traits at birth or soon after that affect their social functioning over the life course and influence their behavior choices; they suffer some biological or psychological condition

sociobiology
The view that human behavior is motivated by inborn biological urges to survive and preserve the species.

equipotentiality
The view that all humans are born with equal potential to learn and achieve.

FIND IT ON INFOTRAC
College Edition

When males desire younger females, sociobiologists suggest
that they are engaging in a procre-
ation strategy that will maximize
the chance of producing healthy
offspring. Females prefer older
males because the survival of
their offspring will be enhanced by
someone with greater prestige
and wealth. To learn more, use
"sociobiology" as a subject guide.

or trait that renders them incapable of resisting social pressures and problems.[5] For example, low birth weight babies have been found to suffer poor
educational achievement later in life; academic deficiency, in turn, has been
linked to delinquency and drug abuse.[6] A condition present at birth or soon
after can thus affect behavior across the life span. Although some people may
have a predisposition toward aggression, that does not mean that they will
necessarily or automatically engage in violent behaviors; environmental stimuli can either suppress or trigger antisocial acts.[7]

Trait theories have gained prominence recently because of what is now
known about chronic recidivism and the development of criminal careers. If
only a few offenders become persistent repeaters, then what sets them apart
from the rest of the criminal population may be an abnormal biochemical
makeup, brain structure, genetic constitution, or some other human trait.[8]
Even if crime is a choice, the fact that some people make that choice repeatedly
could be linked to their physical and mental makeup. According to this view, biological makeup contributes significantly to human behavior. ✔ **Checkpoints**

Biological Trait Theories

Connections

Biosocial theory focuses on the violent crimes of the lower classes
while ignoring the white-collar
crimes of the upper and middle
classes. That is, although it may
seem logical to believe there is a
biological basis to aggression and
violence, it is more difficult to explain how insider trading and fraud
are biologically related. The
causes of white-collar crime are
discussed in Chapter 12.

One branch of contemporary trait theory focuses on the biological conditions
that control human behavior. Criminologists who work in this area typically
refer to themselves as biocriminologists, biosocial criminologists, or biologically oriented criminologists; the terms are used here interchangeably.

The following sections examine some important subareas within biological criminology (Figure 5.1). First we review the biochemical factors that are
believed to affect how proper behavior patterns are learned. Then we consider
the relationship between brain function and crime. Next we analyze current
ideas about the association between genetic factors and crime. Finally, we
evaluate evolutionary views of crime causation.

Biochemical Conditions and Crime

Some trait theorists believe that biochemical conditions, including both those
that are genetically predetermined and those that are acquired through diet
and environment, influence antisocial behavior. This view of crime received
national attention in 1979 when Dan White, who confessed to killing San

✔ Checkpoints

✔ Early criminologists such as Cesare
Lombroso suggested that some people
had crime-producing biological traits.

✔ Some contemporary criminologists
believe that human traits interact with
environmental factors to produce
criminal behaviors.

✔ No single trait is responsible for all
crime. Suspected crime-producing
traits include neurological problems,
blood chemistry disorders, and
personality disorders.

✔ People are not all born physically
and psychologically equal; if they were,
all people living in the same environment would act in a similar fashion.

To quiz yourself on this material,
go to questions 5.1–5.2 on the
Criminology: The Core 2e Web site.

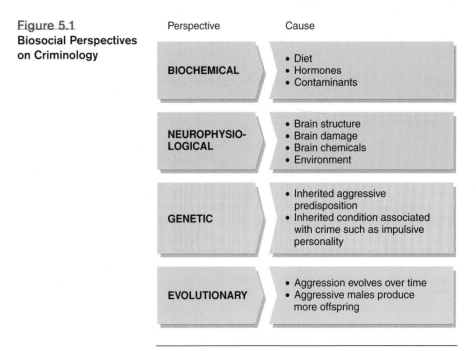

Figure 5.1
Biosocial Perspectives on Criminology

Connections

Should a person be excused from crime if he or she suffers from a disease that impairs judgment? If eating junk foods can excuse crime, what about drinking alcohol? Go to Chapter 1 for more on criminal defenses.

hypoglycemia
A condition that occurs when glucose (sugar) in the blood falls below levels necessary for normal and efficient brain functioning.

androgens
Male sex hormones.

Francisco Mayor George Moscone and City Councilman Harvey Milk, claimed that his behavior was precipitated by an addiction to sugar-laden junk foods.[9] White's successful "Twinkie defense" prompted a California jury to find him guilty of the lesser offense of diminished-capacity manslaughter rather than first-degree murder. (White committed suicide after serving his prison sentence.) Some of the biochemical factors that have been linked to criminality are set out in detail here.

Chemical and Mineral Influences   Biocriminologists maintain that minimal levels of minerals and chemicals are needed for normal brain functioning and growth, especially in the early years of life. Research conducted over the past decade shows that an over- or undersupply of certain chemicals and minerals, including sodium, mercury, potassium, calcium, amino acids, monoamines, and peptides, can lead to depression, mania, cognitive problems, memory loss, or abnormal sexual activity. In some cases, the relationship is indirect: chemical and mineral imbalance leads to cognitive and learning deficits and problems, and these factors in turn are associated with antisocial behaviors.[10]

What people eat and take into their bodies may influence their behavior. Some medicines may have detrimental side effects. For example, recent research has linked sildenafil, more commonly known as Viagra, with aggressive and violent behavior. Although the cause is still unknown, it is possible that sildenafil exerts various biochemical and physiologic effects in the brain that affect information processing.[11] Even common food additives such as calcium propionate, which is used to preserve bread, have been linked to problem behaviors.[12] Aggressive behavior has also been linked to a diet especially high in carbohydrates and sugar.[13] Experiments altering children's diets so that sweet drinks were replaced with fruit juices, table sugar was replaced with honey, and so on indicate that these changes can reduce aggression levels.[14] Although these results are impressive, some recent research efforts have failed to find a link between sugar consumption and aggressive behavior.[15] The issue of diet and crime is explored further in the Current Issues in Crime feature.

Hypoglycemia   **Hypoglycemia** occurs when blood glucose (sugar) falls below levels necessary for normal and efficient brain functioning. Symptoms of hypoglycemia include irritability, anxiety, depression, crying spells, headaches, and confusion. Research studies have linked hypoglycemia to outbursts of antisocial behavior and violence.[16] Several studies have related assaults and sexual offenses to hypoglycemic reactions.[17] Studies of jail and prison inmate populations have found a higher than normal level of hypoglycemia.[18] High levels of reactive hypoglycemia have been found in groups of habitually violent and impulsive offenders.[19]

Hormonal Influences   Biosocial theorists note that males are biologically and naturally more aggressive than females, whereas women are more nurturing toward the young.[20] This discrepancy has been linked to gender-based hormonal differences. Hormones cause areas of the brain to become less sensitive to environmental stimuli. Abnormally high hormone levels require people to seek excess stimulation and to be willing to tolerate pain in their quest for thrills. Hormones are linked to brain seizures that, under stressful conditions, can result in emotional volatility. They also affect the brain structure itself: They influence the left hemisphere of the neocortex, the part of the brain that controls sympathetic feelings toward others.[21] These effects promote violence and other serious crimes by causing people to seek greater levels of environmental stimulation and to tolerate more punishment, and by increasing impulsivity, emotional volatility, and antisocial emotions.[22]

Biosocial research has found that abnormal levels of male sex hormones (**androgens**) do in fact produce aggressive behavior.[23] Other androgen-related male traits include sensation seeking, impulsivity, dominance, and

CURRENT ISSUES IN CRIME

Are You What You Eat?

stephen Schoenthaler, a well-known biocriminologist, has conducted a number of studies that indicate a significant association between diet and aggressive behavior patterns. In some cases, the relationship is direct; in others, a poor diet may compromise individual functioning, which in turn produces aggressive behavior responses. For example, a poor diet may inhibit school performance, and children who fail at school are at risk for delinquent behavior and criminality.

In one study of 803 New York City public schools, Schoenthaler found that the academic performance of 1.1 million schoolchildren rose 16 percent after their diets were modified. The number of "learning disabled" children fell from 125,000 to 74,000 in one year. No other changes in school programs for the learning disabled were initiated that year. In a similar experiment conducted in a correctional institution, violent and nonviolent antisocial behavior fell an average of 48 percent among 8,047 offenders after dietary changes were implemented. In both these studies, the improvements in behavior and academic performance were attributed to diets containing more vitamins and minerals as compared with the old diets. The greater amounts of these essential nutrients in the new diets were believed to have corrected impaired brain function caused by poor nutrition.

More recently, Schoenthaler conducted three randomized controlled studies in which 66 elementary school children, 62 confined teenage delinquents, and 402 confined adult felons received dietary supplements—the equivalent of a diet providing more fruits, vegetables, and whole grains. To avoid experimental bias, neither subjects nor researchers knew who received the supplement and who received a placebo. In each study, the subjects receiving the dietary supplement demonstrated significantly less violent and nonviolent antisocial behavior when compared to the control subjects who received placebos. The carefully collected data verified that a very good diet, as defined by the World Health Organization, has significant behavioral benefits beyond its health effects.

Schoenthaler and his associates have also evaluated the relationship between nutrition and intelligence. These studies involved 1,753 children and young adults in California, Arizona, Oklahoma, Missouri, England, Wales, Scotland, and Belgium. In each study, poorly nourished subjects who were given dietary supplements showed a greater increase in IQ—an average of 16 points—than did those in the placebo group. (Overall, IQ rose more than 3 points.) The differences in IQ could be attributed to about 20 percent of the children who were presumably inadequately nourished prior to supplementation. The IQ research was expanded to include academic performance in two studies of more than 300 schoolchildren ages 6 to 14 in Arizona and California. In both studies, children who received daily supplements at school for three months achieved significantly higher gains in grade level compared to the matched control group taking placebos. The children taking a supplement improved academically at twice the rate of the children who took placebos.

Schoenthaler concludes that parents with a child who behaves badly, or does poorly in school, may benefit from having the child take a blood test to determine if concentrations of certain nutrients are below the reference norms; if so, a dietary supplement may correct the child's conduct and performance. There is evidence that 19 nutrients may be critical; low levels appear to adversely affect brain function, academic performance, intelligence, and conduct. When attempting to improve IQ or conduct, it is critical to assess all these nutrients and to correct deficiencies as needed. If blood nutrient concentrations are consistently in the normal range, physicians and parents should consider looking elsewhere for the cause of a child's difficulties.

Though more research is needed before the scientific community reaches a consensus on how low is "too low," Schoenthaler finds evidence that vitamins, minerals, chemicals, and other nutrients from a diet rich in fruits, vegetables, and whole grains can improve brain function, basic intelligence, and academic performance. These are all variables that have been linked to antisocial behavior.

Critical Thinking

1. If Schoenthaler is correct in his assumptions, should schools be required to provide a proper lunch for all children?

2. How would Schoenthaler explain the "aging out" process? Hint: Do people eat better as they mature? What about after they get married?

InfoTrac College Edition Research

To read more about the relationship between nutrition and behavior, use "nutrition and behavior" as key terms in InfoTrac College Edition.

SOURCES: Stephen Schoenthaler, "Intelligence, academic performance, and brain function," California State University, Stanislaus, 2000. See also S. Schoenthaler and I. Bier, "The effect of vitamin–mineral supplementation on juvenile delinquency among American schoolchildren: A randomized double-blind placebo-controlled trial," *Journal of Alternative and Complementary Medicine: Research on Paradigm, Practice, and Policy* 6 (2000): 7–18.

---

reduced verbal skills; all of these androgen-related traits are also related to antisocial behavior.[24] A growing body of evidence suggests that hormonal changes are also related to mood and behavior. Adolescents experience more intense mood swings, anxiety, and restlessness than their elders, explaining in part the high violence rates found among teenage males.[25]

FIND IT ON INFOTRAC
College Edition

Some biologists have claimed that the only difference between men and women is a hormonal system that renders men more aggressive. To research this phenomenon further, use "testosterone" and "violence" as key words.

Testosterone, the most abundant androgen, which controls secondary sex characteristics such as facial hair and voice timbre, has been linked to criminality.[26] Research conducted on both human and animal subjects has found that prenatal exposure to unnaturally high levels of testosterone permanently alters behavior. Girls who were unintentionally exposed to elevated amounts of testosterone during their fetal development display an unusually high, long-term tendency toward aggression. Conversely, boys who were prenatally exposed to steroids that decrease testosterone levels display decreased aggressiveness.[27] Gender differences in the crime rate, therefore, may be explained by the relative difference in testosterone and other androgens between the two sexes. Females may be biologically protected from deviant behavior in the same way they are immune from some diseases that strike males.[28] Hormone levels also help explain the aging-out process: levels of testosterone decline during the life cycle, and so too do violence rates.[29]

Premenstrual Syndrome The suspicion has long existed that the onset of the menstrual cycle triggers excessive amounts of the female sex hormones, which stimulate antisocial, aggressive behavior. This condition is commonly referred to as **premenstrual syndrome (PMS).**[30] The link between PMS and delinquency was first popularized more than 30 years ago by Katharina Dalton, whose studies of English women indicated that females are more likely to commit suicide and to be aggressive and otherwise antisocial just before or during menstruation.[31]

Although the Dalton research is often cited as evidence of the link between PMS and crime, methodological problems make it impossible to accept her findings at face value. There is still significant debate over any link between PMS and aggression. Some doubters argue that the relationship is spurious; it is equally likely that the psychological and physical stress of aggression brings on menstruation and not vice versa.[32] However, Diana Fishbein, a noted expert on biosocial theory, concludes that there is in fact an association between elevated levels of female aggression and menstruation. Research efforts, she argues, show that (1) a significant number of incarcerated females committed their crimes during the premenstrual phase and (2) at least a small percentage of women appear vulnerable to cyclical hormonal changes that make them more prone to anxiety and hostility.[33]

The debate is ongoing, but the overwhelming majority of females who suffer anxiety and hostility before and during menstruation do not engage in violent criminal behavior. Thus, any link between PMS and crime is tenuous at best.[34]

Environmental Contaminants Dangerous amounts of copper, cadmium, mercury, and inorganic gases, such as chlorine and nitrogen dioxide, are found in the ecosystem. In January 2003 the Center for Disease Control released a very extensive evaluation of chemical and mineral contamination and found that despite some significant improvements there are still many dangerous substances in the environment.[35] Of critical importance is lead contamination. New data on blood lead levels in children aged 1 to 5 years indicate that about 2.2 percent had elevated blood lead levels, down from 4.4 percent a decade ago.

The improvement is welcome, but exposure of children to lead in homes containing lead-based paint and lead-contaminated dust remains a serious public health concern because research indicates that these environmental contaminants can influence behavior. At high levels, these substances can cause severe illness or death; at more moderate levels, they have been linked to emotional and behavioral disorders.[36] A number of recent research studies have linked lead ingestion to problem behavior.[37] Criminologist Deborah Denno investigated the behavior of more than 900 African American youths and found that lead poisoning was one of the most significant predictors of male delinquency and persistent adult criminality.[38] Another recent study

testosterone
The principal male hormone.
premenstrual syndrome (PMS)
The idea that several days prior to and during menstruation, excessive amounts of female sex hormones stimulate antisocial, aggressive behavior.

found that delinquents were 3.7 times more likely to have high bone lead levels than children in the general population.[39]

Lead is not the only environmental contaminant linked to social and psychological problems. Exposure to the now banned PCB (polychlorinated biphenyls), a chemical once used in insulation materials, has been shown to influence brain functioning and intelligence levels.[40]

Neurophysiological Conditions and Crime

Some researchers focus their attention on **neurophysiology,** or the study of brain activity.[41] They believe that neurological and physical abnormalities acquired as early as the fetal or perinatal stage or through birth delivery trauma control behavior throughout the life span.[42] Studies conducted in the United States and elsewhere have shown a significant relationship between impairment in executive brain functions (such as abstract reasoning, problem solving, and motor skills) and aggressive behavior.[43] Research using memorization and visual awareness tests, short-term auditory memory tests, and verbal IQ tests indicate that this relationship can be detected quite early and that children who suffer measurable neurological deficits at birth or in adolescence are more likely to become criminals later in life.[44]

Studies using an electroencephalograph (EEG)—a device that records electrical impulses in the brain—have found far higher levels of abnormal EEG recordings in violent criminals than in nonviolent or one-time offenders.[45] Although about 5 percent of the general population show abnormal EEG readings, about 50 to 60 percent of adolescents with known behavior disorders display abnormal recordings.[46] Behaviors highly correlated with abnormal EEG readings include poor impulse control, inadequate social adaptation, hostility, temper tantrums, and destructiveness.[47]

Newer brain-scanning techniques using electronic imaging, such as positron emission tomography (PET), brain electrical activity mapping (BEAM), and the superconducting interference device (SQUID), have made it possible to assess which areas of the brain are directly linked to antisocial behavior.[48] Both violent criminals and substance abusers have been found to have impairment in the prefrontal lobes, thalamus, medial temporal lobe, and superior parietal and left angular gyrus areas of the brain.[49] Chronic violent criminals have far higher levels of brain dysfunction than the general population; murderers exhibit brain pathology at a rate 32 times greater than that in the general population.[50]

Minimal Brain Dysfunction   Related to abnormal cerebral structure, **minimal brain dysfunction (MBD)** has been defined as an abruptly appearing, maladaptive behavior that interrupts an individual's lifestyle and life flow. One type of minimal brain dysfunction is manifested in episodic periods of explosive rage. This form of the disorder is considered an important cause of behaviors such as spouse and child abuse, suicide, aggressiveness, and motiveless homicide. One perplexing feature of this syndrome is that people who are afflicted with it often maintain warm, pleasant personalities between episodes of violence. Studies measuring the presence of minimal brain dysfunction in offender populations have found that up to 60 percent exhibit brain dysfunction on psychological tests.[51] More sophisticated brain-scanning techniques, such as PET, have also shown that brain abnormality is linked to violent crime.[52]

Attention Deficit Hyperactivity Disorder   Many parents have noticed that their children do not pay attention to them—they run around and do things in their own way. Sometimes this inattention is a function of age; in other instances it is a symptom of **attention deficit hyperactivity disorder (ADHD),** in which a child shows a developmentally inappropriate lack of attention, impulsivity, and hyperactivity. The various symptoms of ADHD are

neurophysiology
The study of brain activity.

minimal brain dysfunction (MBD)
An abruptly appearing, maladaptive behavior such as episodic periods of explosive rage.

attention deficit hyperactivity disorder (ADHD)
A developmentally inappropriate lack of attention, along with impulsivity and hyperactivity.

■ This scan compares a normal brain (left) and an ADHD brain (right). Areas of orange and white demonstrate a higher rate of metabolism, while areas of blue and green represent an abnormally low metabolic rate. Why is ADHD so prevalent in the United States today? Some experts believe that our immigrant forebears, risk takers who impulsively left their homelands for life in a new world, may have brought with them a genetic predisposition for ADHD.

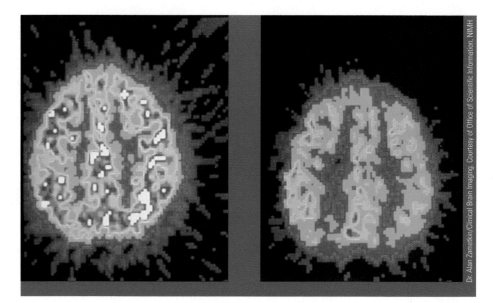

Dr. Alan Zametkin/Clinical Brain Imaging. Courtesy of Office of Scientific Information, NIMH

listed in Exhibit 5.1. About 3 percent of U.S. children, most often boys, are believed to suffer from this disorder, and it is the most common reason children are referred to mental health clinics. The condition has been associated with poor school performance, grade retention, placement in special needs classes, bullying, stubbornness, and lack of response to discipline.[53]

Although the origin of ADHD is still unknown, suspected causes include neurological damage, prenatal stress, and even reactions to food additives and chemical allergies. Recent research has suggested a genetic link.[54] There are also links to family turmoil: Mothers of ADHD children are more likely to be divorced or separated, and ADHD children are much more likely to move to new locales than non-ADHD children.[55] It may be possible that emotional turmoil either produces symptoms of ADHD or, if they already exist, causes them to intensify.

Research studies now link ADHD to the onset and maintenance of a delinquent career.[56] Both boys and girls who suffer from ADHD are impaired both academically and socially, factors that are related to long-term antisocial behaviors.[57] Children diagnosed as having ADHD are more likely to be suspended from school and to engage in criminal behavior as adults. This ADHD–crime association is important because symptoms of ADHD seem stable through adolescence into adulthood.[58]

Early diagnosis and treatment of children with ADHD may enhance their life chances. Today the most typical treatment is doses of stimulants, such as Ritalin, which ironically help control emotional and behavioral outbursts. The relationship between chronic delinquency and attention disorders may also be mediated by school performance. Children who are poor readers are the most prone to antisocial behavior; many poor readers also have attention problems.[59] Early school-based intervention programs may thus benefit children with ADHD.

Brain Chemistry **Neurotransmitters** are chemical compounds that influence or activate brain functions. Those studied in relation to aggression include dopamine, norepinephrine, serotonin, monoamine oxidase (MOMA), and gamma-aminobutryic acid (GABA). Evidence exists that abnormally low levels of these chemicals are associated with aggression.[60] For example, when Avshalom Caspi and his colleagues examined groups of people who had been abused during adolescence, they found that people endowed with an abundance of MOMA were significantly more likely to cope with the effects of an unhappy or abusive childhood and lead a normal adult life than those born with lower levels of the enzyme. Male victims of child abuse in the study were

neurotransmitters
Chemical compounds that influence or activate brain functions.

EXHIBIT 5.1 Symptoms of Attention Deficit Hyperactivity Disorder

Lack of Attention

Frequently fails to finish projects

Does not seem to pay attention

Does not sustain interest in play activities

Cannot sustain concentration on schoolwork or related tasks

Is easily distracted

Impulsivity

Frequently acts without thinking

Often "calls out" in class

Does not want to wait his or her turn in lines or games

Shifts from activity to activity

Cannot organize tasks or work

Requires constant supervision

Hyperactivity

Constantly runs around and climbs on things

Shows excessive motor activity while asleep

Cannot sit still; is constantly fidgeting

Does not remain in his or her seat in class

Is constantly on the go like a "motor"

SOURCE: Adapted from American Psychiatric Association, *Diagnostic and Statistical Manual of Mental Disorders,* 4th ed. (Washington, D.C.: American Psychiatric Press, 1994).

nine times as likely to engage in antisocial activity if they maintained low-levels of MOMA when compared to a group of equally abused children who had above normal levels.[61] Studies of habitually violent criminals show that low serotonin levels are associated with poor impulse control and hyperactivity, increased irritability, and sensation seeking.[62]

What is the link between brain chemistry and crime? Prenatal exposure of the brain to high levels of androgens can result in a brain structure that is less sensitive to environmental inputs. Affected individuals seek more intense and varied stimulation and are willing to tolerate more adverse consequences than individuals not so affected.[63] It has also been suggested that individuals with a low supply of the enzyme monoamine oxidase (MAO) engage in behaviors linked with violence and property crime, including defiance of punishment, impulsivity, hyperactivity, poor academic performance, sensation seeking and risk taking, and recreational drug use. Abnormal MAO levels may explain both individual and group differences in the crime rate. For example, females have higher MAO levels than males, which may explain gender differences in the crime rate.[64]

Because this linkage has been found, it is not uncommon for violence-prone people to be treated with antipsychotic drugs such as Haldol, Stelazine, Prolixin, and Risperdal. These drugs, which help control levels of neurotransmitters (such as serotonin or dopamine), are sometimes referred to as chemical restraints or chemical straitjackets.

Arousal Theory According to **arousal theory,** for a variety of genetic and environmental reasons, people's brains function differently in response to environmental stimuli. All of us seek to maintain a preferred or optimal level of arousal: too much stimulation leaves us anxious and stressed, whereas too little makes us feel bored and weary. However, people vary in the way their

arousal theory
The view that people seek to maintain a preferred level of arousal but vary in how they process sensory input. A need for high levels of environmental stimulation may lead to aggressive, violent behavior patterns.

brains process sensory input. Some nearly always feel comfortable with little stimulation, whereas others require a high degree of environmental input to feel comfortable. The latter group of "sensation seekers" looks for stimulating activities, which may include aggressive, violent behavior patterns.[65]

Although the factors that determine a person's level of arousal are not fully understood, suspected sources include brain chemistry (such as serotonin levels) and brain structure. Some brains have many more nerve cells with receptor sites for neurotransmitters than others. Another view is that people with low heart rates are more likely to commit crime because they seek stimulation to increase their arousal to normal levels.[66]

Genetics and Crime

Another biosocial theme is that the human traits associated with criminality have a genetic basis.[67] This line of reasoning was spotlighted in the 1970s when genetic testing of Richard Speck, the convicted killer of eight Chicago nurses, allegedly found that he had an abnormal XYY chromosomal structure (XY is normal in males). There was much public concern that all people with XYY chromosomes were potential killers and should be closely controlled. Civil libertarians expressed fear that all XYY males could be labeled dangerous and violent regardless of whether they had engaged in violent activities.[68] When it was disclosed that neither Speck nor most violent offenders actually had an extra Y chromosome, interest in the XYY theory dissipated.[69] However, the Speck case drew researchers' attention to looking for a genetic basis of crime.

Researchers have carefully explored the heritability of criminal tendencies by looking at a variety of factors. Some of the most important are described here.

Parental Deviance   If criminal tendencies are inherited, then the children of criminal parents should be more likely to become law violators than the offspring of conventional parents. A number of studies have found that parental criminality and deviance do, in fact, powerfully influence delinquent behavior.[70] Some of the most important data on parental deviance were gathered by Donald J. West and David P. Farrington as part of the long-term Cambridge Youth Survey. These cohort data indicate that a significant number of delinquent youths have criminal fathers.[71] Whereas 8.4 percent of the sons of noncriminal fathers eventually became chronic offenders, about 37 percent of youths with criminal fathers were multiple offenders.[72] In another important analysis, Farrington found that one type of parental deviance, schoolyard aggression or bullying, may be both inter- and intragenerational. Bullies have children who bully others, and these second-generation bullies grow up to father children who are also bullies, in a never-ending cycle.[73]

Farrington's findings are supported by some recent research data from the Rochester Youth Development Study (RYDS), a longitudinal analysis that has been monitoring the behavior of 1,000 area youths since 1988. RYDS researchers have also found an intergenerational continuity in antisocial behavior, though their data do not allow them to definitively determine whether it is a result of genetics or socialization.[74]

In sum, there is growing evidence that crime is intergenerational: criminal fathers produce criminal sons who then produce criminal grandchildren. Although there is no certainty about the relationship between parental and child deviance, it is possible that at least part of the association is genetic.[75] How can this relationship be more definitively tested?

Twin Behavior   If, in fact, inherited traits cause criminal behavior, we might expect that twins would be quite similar in their antisocial activities. However, because twins are usually brought up in the same household and exposed to the same social conditions, determining whether their behavior is

■ There is a link between parental deviance and a child's criminality, although it is still unsure whether it is a function of learning, environment, or genetics. Here, Judy Gould, 27, and William Gould, 38, both of Jackson, Michigan, are arraigned before District Judge Carlene Walz, in Jackson County District Court, on three counts of contributing to the delinquency of a minor, and one count of receiving stolen property valued at more than $100. Police say the couple kept three of their six children, ages 8, 10, and 12, padlocked in the basement of their home at night without access to a bathroom, and forced the children to steal thousands of dollars in collectible items by day. Between $30,000 and $50,000 of stolen items were recovered from the couple's Jackson home.

© 2003 AP/Wide World Photos

a result of biological, sociological, or psychological conditions is difficult. Trait theorists have tried to overcome this dilemma by comparing identical, **monozygotic (MZ) twins** with fraternal, **dizygotic (DZ) twins.**[76] MZ twins are genetically identical, whereas DZ twins have only half their genes in common. If heredity determines criminal behavior, we should expect that MZ twins would be much more similar in their antisocial activities than DZ twins.

Studies conducted on twin behavior detected a significant relationship between the criminal activities of MZ twins and a much lower association between those of DZ twins, and these genetic effects can be seen in children as young as 3 years old.[77] A review of relevant studies found that 60 percent of MZ twins shared criminal behavior patterns (if one twin was criminal, so was the other), whereas only 30 percent of DZ twins were similarly related.[78] These and other findings may be viewed as powerful evidence of a genetic basis for criminality.[79] Although the behavior of twin pairs may be influenced by their environment, some twins share behavior similarities that can only be explained by their genetic similarity.[80] One famous study of twin behavior still under way is the Minnesota Study of Twins Reared Apart. This research compares the behavior of MZ and DZ twin pairs that were raised together with others who were separated at birth and in some cases did not even know of each other's existence. The study shows some striking similarities in behavior and ability for twin pairs raised apart. An MZ twin reared away from a co-twin has about as good a chance of being similar to the co-twin in terms of personality, interests, and attitudes as one who has been reared with his or her co-twin. The conclusion: similarities between twins are due to genes, not

monozygotic (MZ) twins
Identical twins.

dizygotic (DZ) twins
Fraternal (nonidentical) twins.

> ══EXHIBIT══ **5.2 Findings from the Minnesota Study of Twins Reared Apart**
>
> ■ If you are a DZ twin and your co-twin is divorced, your risk of divorce is 30%. If you are an MZ twin and your co-twin is divorced, your risk of divorce is 45%, which is 25% above the rates for the Minnesota population. Because this was not true for DZ twins, we can conclude that genes do influence the likelihood of divorce.
>
> ■ MZ twins become *more* similar with respect to abilities such as vocabularies and arithmetic scores as they age. As DZ (fraternal) twins get older, they become less similar with respect to vocabularies and arithmetic scores.
>
> ■ A P300 is a tiny electrical response (a few millionths of a volt) that occurs in the brain when a person detects something unusual or interesting. For example, if a person were shown nine circles and one square, a P300 brain response would appear after seeing the square because it's different. Identical (MZ) twin children have very similar looking P300s. By comparison, children who are fraternal (DZ) twins, do not show as much similarity in their P300s. These results indicate that the way the brain processes information may be greatly influenced by genes.
>
> ■ An EEG is a measure of brain activity or brain waves that can be used to monitor a person's state of arousal. MZ twins tend to produce strikingly similar EEG spectra, whereas DZ twins show far less similarity.
>
> SOURCE: *Minnesota Study of Twins Reared Apart,* 2001 [Online]. Available: http://www.psych.umn.edu/psylabs/mtfs/special.htm

the environment. Because twins reared apart are so similar, the environment, if anything, makes them different (Exhibit 5.2).[81]

Not all research efforts have found that MZ twin pairs are more closely related in their criminal behavior than DZ or ordinary sibling pairs, and some have found an association that is at best modest.[82] Yet many experts conclude that individuals who share genes are alike in personality regardless of how they are reared; environment, they argue, induces little or no personality resemblance in twin pairs.[83]

Adoption Studies   It seems logical that if the behavior of adopted children is more closely aligned to that of their biological parents than to that of their adoptive parents, then the idea of a genetic basis for criminality would be supported. If, on the other hand, adoptees' behavior is more closely aligned to the behavior of their adoptive parents than of their biological parents, an environmental basis for crime would seem more valid.

Several studies indicate that some relationship exists between biological parents' behavior and the behavior of their children, even when they have had no contact.[84] In what is considered the most significant study in this area, Barry Hutchings and Sarnoff Mednick analyzed 1,145 male adoptees born in Copenhagen, Denmark, between 1927 and 1941. Of these, 185 had criminal records.[85] After following up on 143 of the criminal adoptees and matching them with a control group of 143 noncriminal adoptees, Hutchings and Mednick found that the biological father's criminality strongly predicted the child's criminal behavior. When both the biological and the adoptive fathers were criminal, the probability that the youth would engage in criminal behavior greatly increased. Of the boys whose adoptive and biological fathers were both criminals, 24.5 percent had been convicted of a criminal law violation. Only 13.5 percent of those whose biological and adoptive fathers were not criminals had similar conviction records.[86]

FIND IT ON INFOTRAC
College Edition

Twin studies show that some traits, such as bulimia, are environmental, whereas schizophrenia, autism, and bipolar (manic-depressive) disorder seem to be genetic. To learn more about this phenomenon, read:

Peter McGuffin and Martin Neilson, "Behaviour and Genes," *British Medical Journal*, 3 July 1999 v319 i7201 p37

Connections

The relationship between evolutionary factors and crime has just begun to be studied. Criminologists are now exploring how social organizations and institutions interact with biological traits to influence personal decision making, including criminal strategies. See the discussion of latent trait theories in Chapter 9 for more about the integration of biological and environmental factors.

cheater theory
A theory suggesting that a subpopulation of men has evolved with genes that incline them toward extremely low parental involvement. Sexually aggressive, they use deceit for sexual conquest of as many females as possible.

The findings of the twin and adoption studies tentatively support a genetic basis for criminality. However, those who dispute the genes–crime relationship point to inadequate research designs and weak methodologies in the supporting research. Newer, better-designed research studies, critics charge, provide less support than earlier, less methodologically sound studies.[87]

Evolutionary Views of Crime

Some criminologists believe that the human traits that produce violence and aggression have been advanced by the long process of human evolution.[88] According to this evolutionary view, the competition for scarce resources has influenced and shaped the human species.[89] Over the course of human existence, people whose personal characteristics allowed them to accumulate more than others were the most likely to breed and dominate the species. People have been shaped to engage in actions that promote their well-being and ensure the survival and reproduction of their genetic line. Males who are impulsive risk takers may be able to father more children because they are reckless in their social relationships and have sexual encounters with numerous partners. If, according to evolutionary theories, such behavior patterns are inherited, impulsive behavior becomes intergenerational, passed down from parents to children. It is therefore not surprising that human history has been marked by war, violence, and aggression.

The Evolution of Gender and Crime   Evolutionary concepts that have been linked to gender differences in violence rates are based loosely on mammalian mating patterns. To ensure survival of the gene pool (and the species), it is beneficial for a male of any species to mate with as many suitable females as possible, because each can bear his offspring. In contrast, because of the long period of gestation, females require a secure home and a single, stable, nurturing partner to ensure their survival. Because of these differences in mating patterns, the most aggressive males mate most often and have the greatest number of offspring. Therefore, over the history of the human species, aggressive males have had the greatest impact on the gene pool. The descendants of these aggressive males now account for the disproportionate amount of male aggression and violence.[90]

Crime rate differences between the genders, then, may be less a matter of socialization than of inherent differences in mating patterns that have developed over time.[91] Among young men, reckless, life-threatening risk proneness is especially likely to evolve in cultures that force them to find suitable mates to ensure their ability to reproduce. Unless they are aggressive with potential mates and potential rivals for those suitable mates, they will remain childless.[92] Reproductive aggressiveness and similar evolutionary processes may explain why women of child-bearing age are more attractive targets of rapists (and rapist-murderers) than women who are no longer able to bear children and therefore unlikely to serve as desirable mates.[93]

High rates of spouse abuse in modern society may be a function of aggressive men seeking to control and possess mates. Men who feel most threatened over the potential of losing mates to rivals are the most likely to engage in sexual violence. Research shows that women in common-law marriages, especially those who are much younger than their husbands, are at greater risk of abuse than older, married women. Abusive males may fear the potential loss of their younger mates, especially if they are not bound by a marriage contract, and may use force for purposes of control and possession.[94]

"Cheater" Theory   According to **cheater theory,** a subpopulation of men has evolved with genes that incline them toward extremely low parental involvement. They are sexually aggressive and use cunning to achieve sexual conquest of as many females as possible. Because females would not willingly choose them as mates, they use stealth to gain sexual access, including such tactics as mimicking the behavior of more stable males. They use devious, illegal means to acquire resources they need for sexual domination. These deceptive reproductive tactics spill over into other endeavors, where their irresponsible, opportunistic behavior supports their antisocial activities. Deceptive reproductive strategies, then, are linked to a deceitful lifestyle.[95]

Psychologist Byron Roth notes that cheater-type males may be especially attractive to younger, less intelligent women who begin having children at a very early age. State-sponsored welfare, claims Roth, removes the need for potential mates to have the resources required of stable providers and family caretakers.[96] With the state meeting their financial needs, these women are drawn to men who are physically attractive and flamboyant. Their fleeting courtship produces children with low IQ scores, aggressive personalities, and little chance of proper socialization in father-absent families. Because the criminal justice system treats them leniently, argues Roth, sexually irresponsible men are free to prey upon young girls. Over time, their offspring will make up an ever-expanding supply of cheaters who are both antisocial and sexually aggressive.

Evaluation of the Biological Branch of Trait Theory

Biosocial perspectives on crime have raised some challenging questions. Critics find some of these theories racist and dysfunctional. If there are biological explanations for street crimes such as assault, murder, or rape, the argument goes, and if, as official crime statistics suggest, the poor and minority-group members commit a disproportionate number of such acts, then by implication, biological theory says that members of these groups are biologically different, flawed, or inferior.

Biological explanations for the geographic, social, and temporal patterns in the crime rate are also problematic. Is it possible that more people are genetically predisposed to crime in the South and the West than in New England and the Midwest? Furthermore, biological theory seems to divide people into criminals and noncriminals on the basis of their genetic and physical makeup, ignoring self-reports that indicate that almost everyone has engaged in some type of illegal activity.

Biosocial theorists counter that their views should not be confused with Lombrosian, deterministic biology. Rather than suggesting that there are born criminals and noncriminals, they maintain that some people carry the potential to be violent or antisocial and that environmental conditions can sometimes trigger antisocial responses.[97] This would explain why some otherwise law-abiding citizens perform a single, seemingly unexplainable antisocial act and, conversely, why some people with long criminal careers often behave conventionally. It also explains geographic and temporal patterns in the crime rate; people who are predisposed to crime may simply have more opportunities to commit illegal acts in the summer in Los Angeles and Atlanta than in the winter in Bedford, New Hampshire, and Minot, North Dakota.

The most significant criticism of biosocial theory has been the lack of adequate empirical testing. Most research samples are relatively small and nonrepresentative. A great deal of biosocial research is conducted with samples of adjudicated offenders who have been placed in clinical treatment settings. Methodological problems make it impossible to determine whether findings apply only to offenders who have been convicted of crimes and placed in treatment or to all criminals.[98] More research is needed to clarify the relationships proposed by biosocial researchers and to silence critics. The major elements of biosocial theory are found in Concept Summary 5.1. **✔ Checkpoints**

✔ Checkpoints

✔ Brain chemistry and hormonal differences are related to aggression and violence.

✔ Most evidence suggests that there is no relationship between sugar intake and crime.

✔ The male hormone testosterone is linked to criminality.

✔ Neurological impairments have been linked to crime.

✔ Genetic theory holds that violence-producing traits are passed on from generation to generation.

✔ According to evolutionary theory, instinctual drives control behavior. The urge to procreate influences male violence.

✔ Biological explanations fail to account for the geographic, social, and temporal patterns in the crime rate; critics question the methodology used.

To quiz yourself on this material, go to questions 5.3–5.11 on the Criminology: The Core 2e Web site.

CONCEPT SUMMARY 5.1 Biosocial Theories

THEORY	MAJOR PREMISE	STRENGTHS	RESEARCH FOCUS
Biochemical	Crime, especially violence, is a function of diet, vitamin intake, hormonal imbalance, or food allergies.	Explains irrational violence. Shows how the environment interacts with personal traits to influence behavior.	Diet; hormones; enzymes; environmental contaminants; lead intake
Neurological	Criminals and delinquents often suffer brain impairment, as measured by the EEG. Attention deficit hyperactivity disorder and minimal brain dysfunction are related to antisocial behavior.	Explains irrational violence. Shows how the environment interacts with personal traits to influence behavior.	ADD, ADHD, learning disabilities; brain injuries; brain chemistry
Genetic	Criminal traits and predispositions are inherited. The criminality of parents can predict the delinquency of children.	Explains why only a small percentage of youth in high-crime area become chronic offenders.	Twin behavior; sibling behavior; parent–child similarities
Evolutionary	As the human race evolved, traits and characteristics have become ingrained. Some of these traits make people aggressive and predisposed to commit crime.	Explains high violence rates and aggregate gender differences in the crime rate.	Gender differences; understanding human aggression

Psychological Trait Theories

The second branch of trait theory focuses on the psychological aspects of crime, including the associations among intelligence, personality, learning, and criminal behavior (Figure 5.2). This view has a long history, and psychologists, psychiatrists, and other mental health professionals have long played an active role in formulating criminological theory.

Among nineteenth-century pioneers in this area were Charles Goring (1870–1919) and Gabriel Tarde (1843–1904). Goring studied 3,000 English convicts and found little difference in the physical characteristics of criminals and noncriminals. However, he uncovered a significant relationship between crime and a condition he referred to as "defective intelligence," which involved such traits as feeblemindedness, epilepsy, insanity, and defective social instinct.[99] Tarde was the forerunner of modern learning theorists, who hold that people learn from one another through imitation.[100]

In their quest to understand and treat all varieties of abnormal mental conditions, psychologists have encountered clients whose behavior falls within the categories that society has labeled as criminal, deviant, violent, and antisocial. A number of different psychological views have been associated with criminal behavior causation. The most important of these perspectives are discussed in the following sections.

Psychodynamic Perspective

Psychodynamic (or **psychoanalytic**) psychology was originated by Viennese psychiatrist Sigmund Freud (1856–1939) and has remained a prominent segment of psychological theory ever since.[101] Freud believed that we all carry with us residue of the most significant emotional attachments of our childhood, which then guides our future interpersonal relationships.

According to Freud's version of psychodynamic theory, the human personality has a three-part structure. The **id** is the primitive part of people's mental makeup, present at birth, that represents unconscious biological drives for food, sex, and other life-sustaining necessities. The id seeks instant

psychodynamic (psychoanalytic)
Theory originated by Freud that the human personality is controlled by unconscious mental processes developed early in childhood, involving the interaction of id, ego, and superego.

id
The primitive part of people's mental makeup, present at birth, that represents unconscious biological drives for food, sex, and other life-sustaining necessities. The id seeks instant gratification without concern for the rights of others.

Figure 5.2
Psychological Perspectives on Criminality

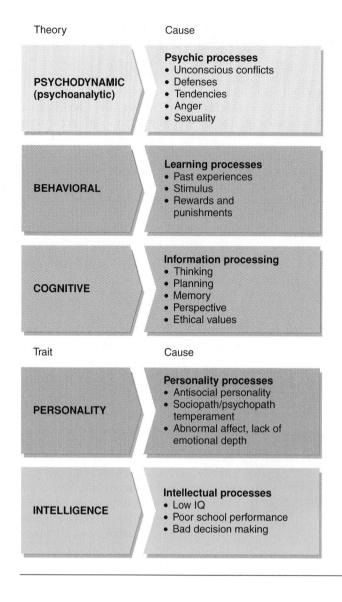

gratification without concern for the rights of others. The **ego** develops early in life, when a child begins to learn that his or her wishes cannot be instantly gratified. The ego is the part of the personality that compensates for the demands of the id by helping the individual guide his or her actions to remain within the boundaries of social convention. The **superego** develops as a result of incorporating within the personality the moral standards and values of parents, community, and significant others. It is the moral aspect of people's personalities; it judges their behavior.

Psychodynamics of Abnormal Behavior Psychodynamic theory originally used the term **neurotic** to refer to people who experienced feelings of mental anguish and feared that they were losing control of their personalities. People who had completely lost control and who were dominated by their primitive id were referred to as **psychotic**. Today these terms have, for the most part, been replaced by the term **disorder**, as in anxiety disorders, mood disorders, and conduct disorders. The most serious disorder is **schizophrenia**, marked by hearing nonexistent voices, seeing hallucinations, and exhibiting inappropriate responses.

Schizophrenics have illogical, incoherent thought processes and lack insight into their behavior. They may experience delusions and hallucinate. For example, they may see themselves as agents of the devil, avenging angels, or the recipients of messages from animals and plants. Serial killer David

Berkowitz, dubbed "Son of Sam" or the "44-calibre killer," claimed that his 1976–1977 killing spree began after he received messages from a neighbor's dog. Paranoid schizophrenics suffer complex behavioral delusions involving wrongdoing or persecution—they think everyone is out to get them.

Psychodynamics of Criminal Behavior   Psychodynamic theorists view criminals as id-dominated persons who suffer from one or more disorders that render them incapable of controlling impulsive, pleasure-seeking drives.[102] The psychodynamic model of the criminal offender depicts an aggressive, frustrated person dominated by events that occurred early in childhood. Perhaps as a result of unhappy experiences in childhood or families that could not provide proper love and care, criminals suffer from weak or damaged egos that make them unable to cope with conventional society. Weak egos are associated with immaturity, poor social skills, and excessive dependence on others. People with weak egos may be easily led into crime by antisocial peers and drug abuse. Some offenders have underdeveloped superegos and consequently lack internalized representations of those behaviors that are punished in conventional society. They commit crimes because they have difficulty understanding the consequences of their actions.[103]

Offenders, then, have various mood and behavior disorders. They may be histrionic, depressed, antisocial, or narcissistic.[104] They may exhibit conduct disorders (long histories of antisocial behavior) or mood disorders (disturbance in expressed emotions). Among the latter is **bipolar disorder,** in which moods alternate between periods of wild elation and deep depression.[105] Some offenders are driven by an unconscious desire to be punished for prior sins, either real or imaginary. They may violate the law to gain attention or punish their parents.

From this perspective, then, crime is a manifestation of feelings of oppression and people's inability to develop the proper psychological defenses and rationales to keep these feelings under control. Criminality allows troubled people to survive by producing positive psychic results: It helps them feel free and independent, and it gives them the possibility of excitement and the chance to use their skills and imagination. In addition, it allows them to blame others for their predicament (for example, the police), and it gives them a chance to rationalize their sense of failure ("If I hadn't gotten into trouble, I could have been a success").[106]

Crime and Mental Illness   Psychodynamic theory suggests a linkage between mental illness and crime. Although the association appears clear-cut, empirical evidence has been contradictory. Some research has shown that offenders who engage in serious, violent crimes suffer from some sort of mental disturbance, such as depression.[107] The diagnosed mentally ill appear in arrest and court statistics at a rate disproportionate to their presence in the population.[108] There is also research linking mental illness to violent crimes. Existing data suggest that certain symptoms of mental illness are connected to violence: for example, the feeling that others wish the person harm, or that the person's mind is dominated by forces beyond his or her control, or that thoughts are being put into the person's head by others.[109]

Studies of adolescent males accused of murder found that 75 percent could be classified as having some mental illness, including schizophrenia.[110] Abusive mothers have been found to have mood and personality disorders and a history of psychiatric diagnoses.[111] Nor is this relationship unique to the United States. Forensic criminologist Henrik Belfrage studied mental patients in Sweden and found that 40 percent of those discharged from institutional care had a criminal record as compared to less than 10 percent of the general public.[112] Australian men diagnosed with schizophrenia are four times more likely than the general population to be convicted for serious violence.[113] And a recent Danish study found a significant positive relationship between mental disorders such as schizophrenia and criminal violence.[114]

Connections

Chapter 1 discussed how some of the early founders of psychiatry tried to understand the criminal mind. Early theories suggested that mental illness and insanity were inherited and that deviants were inherently mentally damaged by their inferior genetic makeup.

bipolar disorder
An emotional disturbance in which moods alternate between periods of wild elation and deep depression.

■ Some psychologists believe that crime is caused by mental illness or other psychological disorders. Here Rebekah Amaya is escorted outside a Colorado courthouse on October 20, 2003, where she is being tried for killing her two children. She told authorities that she drowned them after getting a sign from a spider that crawled across her hand.

behavior theory
The view that all human behavior is learned through a process of social reinforcement (rewards and punishment).

social learning theory
The view that people learn to be aggressive by observing others acting aggressively to achieve some goal or being rewarded for violent acts.

behavior modeling
Process of learning behavior (notably aggression) by observing others. Aggressive models may be parents, criminals in the neighborhood, or characters on television or in movies.

Despite this evidence, questions remain as to whether the mentally ill population has a greater inclination toward criminal behavior than the mentally sound. The mentally ill may in fact be more likely to withdraw or harm themselves than to act aggressively toward others.[115] Even research that finds a mental illness–crime association indicates that the great majority of known criminals are not mentally ill and that most mentally ill people are not criminals.[116] It is possible that any link between mental illness and crime is caused by some intervening variable: the mentally ill find it difficult to gain employment and are forced to live in poor high-crime areas, which leaves them crime prone; the mentally ill have conflict ridden social relationships, which make them prone to both violence and victimization.[117] And it is also possible that the factors that cause mental illness also cause crime: stressful life events, living in a crime-ridden neighborhood, and suffering social problems such as physical abuse. Consequently, both mental illness and crime may have common antecedents.[118]

Behavioral Perspective: Social Learning Theory

Behavior theory maintains that human actions are developed through learning experiences. The major premise of behavior theory is that people alter their behavior according to the reactions it receives from others: Behavior is supported by rewards and extinguished by negative reactions or punishments. The behaviorist views crimes, especially violent acts, as learned responses to life situations, which do not necessarily represent abnormality or moral immaturity.

The branch of behavior theory most relevant to criminology is **social learning theory**.[119] Social learning theorists, most notably Albert Bandura, argue that people are not actually born with the ability to act violently; rather, they learn to be aggressive through their life experiences. These experiences include personally observing others acting aggressively to achieve some goal or watching people being rewarded for violent acts on television or in movies. People learn to act aggressively when, as children, they model their behavior after the violent acts of adults. Later in life, these violent behavior patterns persist in social relationships. For example, the boy who sees his father repeatedly strike his mother with impunity is likely to become a battering parent and husband.

Although social learning theorists agree that mental or physical traits may predispose a person toward violence, they believe a person's violent tendencies are activated by factors in the environment. The specific form of aggressive behavior, the frequency with which it is expressed, the situations in which it is displayed, and the specific targets selected for attack are largely determined by social learning. However, people are also self-aware and engage in purposeful learning. Their interpretations of behavior outcomes and situations influence the way they learn from experiences. One adolescent who spends a weekend in jail for drunk driving may find it the most awful experience of her life—one that teaches her never to drink and drive again. Another person, however, may find it an exciting experience about which he can brag to his friends.

Social learning theorists view violence as something learned through a process called **behavior modeling.** In modern society, aggressive acts are usually modeled after three principal sources:

1. **Family interactions.** Studies of family life show that aggressive children have parents who use similar tactics when dealing with others. For example, the children of wife batterers are more likely to use aggressive tactics themselves than children in the general population, especially if the victims (their mothers) suffer psychological distress from the abuse.[120]

■ According to behavioral theory, people learn to become violent when they learn to be aggressive through their life experiences. These experiences include personally observing others acting aggressively to achieve some goal or watching people being rewarded for violent acts on television or in movies. Here, O. J. Simpson explains in a Miami court how he got into a confrontation with a motorist, Jeffrey Pattinson, which began when Pattinson flashed his lights and blared his horn. How would a behaviorist explain the onset of incidents of "road rage"?

© 2001 AP/Wide World Photos

2. **Environmental experiences.** People who reside in areas where violence occurs daily are more likely to act violently than those who dwell in low-crime areas whose norms stress conventional behavior.

3. **Mass media.** Films and television shows commonly depict violence graphically. Moreover, violence is often portrayed as acceptable, especially for heroes who never have to face legal consequences for their actions.[121] Viewing violence is believed to influence behavior in a number of ways, which are summarized in Exhibit 5.3.

Social learning theorists have tried to determine what triggers violent acts. One position is that a direct, pain-producing, physical assault will usually trigger a violent response. Yet the relationship between painful attacks and aggressive responses has been found to be inconsistent. Whether people counterattack depends, in part, on their fighting skill and their perception of the strength of their attackers. Verbal taunts and insults have also been linked to aggressive responses. People who are predisposed to aggression by their learning experiences are likely to view insults from others as a challenge to their social status and to react violently.

Still another violence-triggering mechanism is a perceived reduction in one's life conditions. Prime examples of this phenomenon are riots and demonstrations in poverty-stricken inner-city areas. Studies have shown that discontent also produces aggression in the more successful members of lower-class groups, who have been led to believe they can succeed but then have been thwarted in their aspirations. Although it is still uncertain how this relationship is constructed, it is apparently complex. No matter how deprived some individuals are, they will not resort to violence. People's perceptions of their relative deprivation have different effects on their aggressive responses.

In summary, social learning theorists suggest that the following four factors may contribute to violent or aggressive behavior:

1. **An event that heightens arousal.** For example, a person may frustrate or provoke another through physical assault or verbal abuse.

2. **Aggressive skills.** Learned aggressive responses picked up from observing others, either personally or through the media.

EXHIBIT **5.3 How the Media Influence Violence**

- Media violence provides aggressive scripts that children store in memory. Repeated exposure to these scripts can increase their retention and change attitudes.

- Children learn from what they observe. In the same way they learn cognitive and social skills from their parents and friends, children learn to be violent by watching television.

- Television violence increases the arousal levels of viewers and makes them more prone to act aggressively. Studies measuring the galvanic skin response of subjects—a physical indication of arousal based on the amount of electricity conducted across the palm of the hand—show that viewing violent television increases arousal levels in young children.

- Watching television violence promotes negative attitudes such as suspiciousness and the expectation that the viewer will become involved in violence. Those who watch television frequently view aggression and violence as common, socially acceptable behavior.

- Television violence allows aggressive youths to justify their behavior. Rather than causing violence, television may help violent youths rationalize their behavior as socially acceptable.

- Television violence may disinhibit aggressive behavior, which is normally controlled by other learning processes. Disinhibition takes place when adults are viewed as being rewarded for violence and when violence is seen as socially acceptable. This contradicts previous learning experiences in which violent behavior was viewed as wrong.

SOURCES: UCLA Center for Communication Policy, *Television Violence Monitoring Project* (Los Angeles, 1995); Jonathan Freedman, "Television Violence and Aggression: A Rejoinder," *Psychological Bulletin* 100 (1986): 372–378; Wendy Wood, Frank Wong, and J. Gregory Chachere, "Effects of Media Violence on Viewers' Aggression in Unconstrained Social Interaction," *Psychological Bulletin* 109 (1991): 371–383.

3. **Expected outcomes.** The belief that aggression will somehow be rewarded. Rewards can come in the form of reducing tension or anger, gaining some financial reward, building self-esteem, or gaining the praise of others.

4. **Consistency of behavior with values.** The belief, gained from observing others, that aggression is justified and appropriate, given the circumstances of the current situation.

Cognitive Theory

One area of psychology that has received increasing recognition in recent years is **cognitive theory.** Psychologists with a cognitive perspective focus on mental processes—how people perceive and mentally represent the world around them and solve problems. The pioneers of this school were Wilhelm Wundt (1832–1920), Edward Titchener (1867–1927), and William James (1842–1920). Today the cognitive area includes several subdisciplines. The moral development branch is concerned with how people morally represent and reason about the world. Humanistic psychology stresses self-awareness and getting in touch with feelings. **Information-processing theory** focuses on how people process, store, encode, retrieve, and manipulate information to make decisions and solve problems.

When cognitive theorists who study information processing try to explain antisocial behavior, they do so in terms of mental perception and how people use information to understand their environment. When people make decisions, they engage in this sequence of cognitive thought processes: First, they encode information so that it can be interpreted; next, they search for a proper response and decide on the most appropriate action; and finally, they act on their decision.[122]

According to this cognitive approach, people who use information properly, who are better conditioned to make reasoned judgments, and who can make quick and reasoned decisions when facing emotion-laden events are best able to avoid antisocial behavior choices.[123] In contrast, crime-prone people may have cognitive deficits and use information incorrectly when they

cognitive theory
Psychological perspective that focuses on mental processes: how people perceive and mentally represent the world around them and solve problems.

information-processing theory
Theory that focuses on how people process, store, encode, retrieve, and manipulate information to make decisions and solve problems.

CONCEPT SUMMARY **5.2 Psychological Theories**

THEORY	MAJOR PREMISE	STRENGTHS	RESEARCH FOCUS
Psychodynamic	The development of the unconscious personality early in childhood influences behavior for the rest of a person's life. Criminals have weak egos and damaged personalities.	Explains the onset of crime and why crime and drug abuse cut across class lines.	Mental illness and crime personality
Behavioral	People commit crime when they model their behavior after others they see being rewarded for the same acts. Behavior is reinforced by rewards and extinguished by punishment.	Explains the role of significant others in the crime process. Shows how family life and media can influence crime and violence.	Media and violence; effects of child abuse
Cognitive	Individual reasoning processes influence behavior. Reasoning is influenced by the way people perceive their environment.	Shows why criminal behavior patterns change over time as people mature and develop their reasoning powers. May explain the aging-out process.	Perception; environmental influences

make decisions.[124] They view crime as an appropriate means to satisfy their immediate personal needs, which take precedence over more distant social needs such as obedience to the law.[125]

One reason for this is that they may be relying on mental scripts learned in childhood that tell them how to interpret events, what to expect, how they should react, and what the outcome of the interaction should be.[126] Hostile children may have learned improper scripts by observing how others react to events; their own parents' aggressive, inappropriate behavior would have considerable impact. Some may have had early, prolonged exposure to violence (such as child abuse), which increases their sensitivity to slights and maltreatment. Oversensitivity to rejection by their peers is a continuation of sensitivity to rejection by their parents.[127] Violence becomes a stable behavior because the scripts that emphasize aggressive responses are repeatedly rehearsed as the child matures.

Information-processing theory has been used to explain the occurrence of date rape. For example, when their dates refuse sexual advances, sexually violent males believe that the women are really playing games and actually want to be taken forcefully.[128]

The various psychological theories of crime are set out in Concept Summary 5.2.

Personality and Crime

Personality can be defined as the reasonably stable patterns of behavior, including thoughts and emotions, that distinguish one person from another.[129] One's personality reflects a characteristic way of adapting to life's demands and problems. The way we behave is a function of how our personality enables us to interpret life events and make appropriate behavioral choices. Can the cause of crime be linked to personality?

Several research efforts have attempted to identify criminal personality traits.[130] Suspected traits include impulsivity, hostility, and aggression.[131] For example, Hans Eysenck's PEN model associates two personality traits, extroversion and introversion, with antisocial behavior. Extreme introverts are overaroused and avoid sources of stimulation; extreme extroverts are underaroused and seek sensation. Introverts are slow to learn and conditioned; extroverts are impulsive individuals who lack the ability to examine their

personality
The reasonably stable patterns of behavior, including thoughts and emotions, that distinguish one person from another.

own motives and behaviors. Extroverts who are also unstable, a condition that Eysenck calls neuroticism, are anxious, tense, and emotionally unstable.[132] People who are both neurotic and extroverted lack self-insight and are impulsive and emotionally unstable; they are unlikely to have reasoned judgments of life events. Whereas extroverted neurotics may act self-destructively, for example, by abusing drugs, more stable people will be able to reason that such behavior is ultimately harmful. They are the type of offenders who will repeat their criminal activity over and over.[133]

Psychopathic Personality   Some people lack affect, cannot empathize with others, and are short-sighted and hedonistic. These traits make them prone to problems ranging from psychopathology to drug abuse, sexual promiscuity, and violence.[134] As a group, people who share these traits are believed to have a character defect referred to as sociopathic, psychopathic, or **antisocial personality.** Although these terms are often used interchangeably, some psychologists distinguish between sociopaths and psychopaths by suggesting that the former are a product of a destructive home environment, whereas the latter are a product of a defect or aberration within themselves.[135]

Studies of the antisocial personality have been conducted worldwide.[136] There is evidence that offenders with an antisocial personality are crime prone, respond to frustrating events with strong negative emotions, feel stressed and harassed, and are adversarial in their interpersonal relationships. They maintain "negative emotionality"—a tendency to experience aversive affective states such as anger, anxiety, and irritability. They also are predisposed to weak personal constraints and have difficulty controlling impulsive behavior urges. Because they are both impulsive and aggressive, crime-prone people are quick to act against perceived threats.

A number of factors are believed to contribute to the development of a criminal personality.[137] Some factors are related to improper socialization and include having a psychopathic parent, parental rejection and lack of love during childhood, and inconsistent discipline. Some psychologists believe the cause is related to neurological or brain dysfunction. They suspect that psychopaths suffer from a low level of arousal as measured by the activity of their autonomic nervous system. It is possible, therefore, that psychopaths are thrill-seekers who engage in high-risk antisocial activities to raise their general neurological arousal level. In one recent study, Kent Kiehl and his associates performed functional magnetic resonance imaging (fMRI) scans on eight psychopathic criminals, eight nonpsychopathic criminals, and eight noncriminal controls and found that psychopathic criminals could be identified by the way their brain reacted to negative stimuli. These findings suggest that psychopaths may have brain-related physical anomalies that cause them to process emotional input differently from nonpsychopaths.[138]

Evidence that personality traits predict crime and violence suggests that the root cause of crime can be found in the forces that influence early human development. If these results are valid, rather than focus on job creation and neighborhood improvement, crime control efforts might be better focused on helping families raise reasoned, reflective children who enjoy a safe environment.

Intelligence and Crime

Early criminologists maintained that many delinquents and criminals have below-average intelligence and that low IQ causes their criminality. Criminals were believed to have inherently substandard intelligence and thus seemed naturally inclined to commit more crimes than more intelligent persons. Furthermore, it was thought that if authorities could determine which

antisocial personality
Combination of traits, such as hyperactivity, impulsivity, hedonism, and inability to empathize with others, that make a person prone to deviant behavior and violence; also referred to as sociopathic or psychopathic personality.

individuals had low IQs, they might identify potential criminals before they committed socially harmful acts. These ideas led to the nature versus nurture controversy that continues to rage today.

Nature Theory   Proponents of **nature theory** argue that intelligence is largely determined genetically, that ancestry determines IQ, and that low intelligence, as demonstrated by low IQ, is linked to criminal behavior. When newly developed IQ tests were administered to inmates of prisons and juvenile training schools in the first decades of the twentieth century, the nature position gained support because most of the inmates scored low on the tests.[139] In 1926, William Healy and Augusta Bronner tested groups of delinquent boys in Chicago and Boston and found that 37 percent were subnormal in intelligence. They concluded that delinquents were 5 to 10 times more likely to be mentally deficient than normal boys.[140] These and other early studies were embraced as proof that low IQ scores indicated potentially delinquent children and that a correlation existed between innate low intelligence and deviant behavior. IQ tests were believed to measure the inborn genetic makeup of individuals, and many criminologists accepted the idea that individuals with substandard IQs were predisposed toward delinquency and adult criminality.

Nurture Theory   Proponents of **nurture theory** argue that intelligence is not inherited and that low-IQ parents do not necessarily produce low-IQ children.[141] Intelligence must be viewed as partly biological but primarily sociological. Nurture theorists discredit the notion that persons commit crimes because they have low IQs. Instead, they postulate that environmental stimulation from parents, relatives, social contacts, schools, peer groups, and innumerable others account for a child's IQ level and that low IQs may result from an environment that also encourages delinquent and criminal behavior. Thus, if low IQ scores are recorded among criminals, these scores may reflect the criminals' cultural background, not their mental ability.

In 1931, Edwin Sutherland evaluated IQ studies of criminals and delinquents and questioned whether criminals in fact have low IQs.[142] Sutherland's research all but put an end to the belief that crime was caused by feeblemindedness; the IQ–crime link was almost forgotten in criminological literature.

IQ and Criminality   Although the alleged IQ–crime link was dismissed by mainstream criminologists, it once again became an important area of study when respected criminologists Travis Hirschi and Michael Hindelang published a widely read 1977 article linking the two variables.[143] They proposed the idea that low IQ increases the likelihood of criminal behavior through its effect on school performance. That is, youths with low IQs do poorly in school, and school failure and academic incompetence are highly related to delinquency and later to adult criminality.

Hirschi and Hindelang's inferences have been supported by both U.S. and international research.[144] In their influential book *Crime and Human Nature,* James Q. Wilson and Richard Herrnstein also agreed that the IQ–crime link is indirect: Low intelligence leads to poor school performance, which enhances the chances of criminality.[145] They conclude, "A child who chronically loses standing in the competition of the classroom may feel justified in settling the score outside, by violence, theft, and other forms of defiant illegality."[146]

IQ and Crime Reconsidered   In their controversial 1994 book *The Bell Curve,* Richard Herrnstein and Charles Murray firmly advocate an IQ–crime link. Their extensive review of the available literature shows that adolescents with low IQs are more likely to commit crime, get caught, and be sent to

nature theory
The view that intelligence is largely determined genetically and that low intelligence is linked to criminal behavior.

nurture theory
The view that intelligence is not inherited but is largely a product of environment. Low IQ scores do not cause crime but may result from the same environmental factors.

prison. Conversely, at-risk kids with higher IQs seem to be protected from becoming criminals by their superior ability to succeed in school and in social relationships. Herrnstein and Murray conclude that criminal offenders have an average IQ of 92, about 8 points below the mean; chronic offenders score even lower than the average criminal. To those who suggest that the IQ–crime relationship can be explained by the fact that only low-IQ criminals get caught, they counter with data showing little difference in IQ scores between self-reported and official criminals.[147] This means that even criminals whose activities go undetected have lower IQs than the general public; the IQ–crime relationship cannot be explained away by the fact that slow-witted criminals are the ones most likely to be apprehended.

Although Herrnstein and Murray's review of the literature was extensive, a number of recent studies have found that IQ has negligible influence on criminal behavior.[148] Also, a recent evaluation of research on intelligence conducted by the American Psychological Association concludes that the strength of an IQ–crime link is "very low."[149]

It is unlikely that the IQ–criminality debate will be settled soon. Measurement is beset by many methodological problems. The well-documented criticisms suggesting that IQ tests are race- and class-biased would certainly influence the testing of the criminal population, which is besieged with a multitude of social and economic problems. Even if it can be shown that known offenders have lower IQs than the general population, it is difficult to explain many patterns in the crime rate: Why are there more male than female criminals? Why do crime rates vary by region, time of year, and even weather patterns? Why does aging out occur? IQ does not increase with age, so why should crime rates fall? ✔ Checkpoints

Social Policy Implications

For most of the twentieth century, biological and psychological views of criminality have influenced crime control and prevention policy. The result has been front-end or **primary prevention programs** that seek to treat personal problems before they manifest themselves as crime. To this end, thousands of family therapy organizations, substance abuse clinics, and mental health associations operate throughout the United States. Teachers, employers, courts, welfare agencies, and others make referrals to these facilities. These services are based on the premise that if a person's problems can be treated before they become overwhelming, some future crimes will be prevented. **Secondary prevention programs** provide treatment such as psychological counseling to youths and adults after they have violated the law. Attendance at such programs may be a requirement of a probation order, part of a diversionary sentence, or aftercare at the end of a prison sentence.

Biologically oriented therapy is also being used in the criminal justice system. Programs have altered diets, changed lighting, compensated for learning disabilities, treated allergies, and so on.[150] More controversial has been the use of mood-altering chemicals, such as lithium, pemoline, imipramine, phenytoin, and benzodiazepines, to control behavior. Another practice that has elicited concern is the use of psychosurgery (brain surgery) to control antisocial behavior. Surgical procedures have been used to alter the brain structure of convicted sex offenders in an effort to eliminate or control their sex drives. Results are still preliminary, but some critics argue that these procedures are without scientific merit.[151]

Numerous psychologically based treatment methods range from individual counseling to behavior modification. For example, treatment based on how people process information takes into account that people are more likely to respond aggressively to provocation if thoughts intensify the insult or otherwise stir feelings of anger. Cognitive therapists attempt to teach explosive people to control aggressive impulses by viewing social provocations as problems demanding a solution rather than retaliation. Programs are aimed at

primary prevention programs
Programs, such as substance abuse clinics and mental health associations, that seek to treat personal problems before they manifest themselves as crime.

secondary prevention programs
Programs that provide treatment such as psychological counseling to youths and adults after they have violated the law.

teaching problem-solving skills that may include self-disclosure, role playing, listening, following instructions, joining in, and using self-control.[152] Therapeutic interventions designed to make people better problem solvers may involve measures that enhance

- Coping and problem-solving skills.
- Relationships with peers, parents, and other adults.
- Conflict resolution and communication skills, and methods for resisting peer pressure related to drug use and violence.
- Consequential thinking and decision-making abilities.
- Prosocial behaviors, including cooperation with others, self-responsibility, respecting others, and public speaking efficacy.
- Empathy.[153]

Summary

- The earliest positivist criminologists were biologists.

- Led by Cesare Lombroso, these early researchers believed that some people manifested primitive traits that made them born criminals.

- Today their research is debunked because of poor methodology, testing, and logic.

- Biological views fell out of favor in the early twentieth century. In the 1970s, spurred by the publication of Edmund O. Wilson's *Sociobiology,* several criminologists again turned to study of the biological basis of criminality. For the most part, the effort has focused on the cause of violent crime.

- One area of interest is biochemical factors, such as diet, allergies, hormonal imbalances, and environmental contaminants (such as lead). The conclusion is that crime, especially violence, is a function of diet, vitamin intake, hormonal imbalance, or food allergies.

- Neurophysiological factors, such as brain disorders, ADHD, EEG abnormalities, tumors, and head injuries have been linked to crime. Criminals and delinquents often suffer brain impairment, as measured by the EEG. Attention deficit hyperactivity disorder and minimal brain dysfunction are related to antisocial behavior.

- Some biocriminologists believe that the tendency to commit violent acts is inherited. Research has been conducted with twin pairs and adopted children to determine whether genes are related to behaviors.

- An evolutionary branch holds that changes in the human condition, which have taken millions of years to evolve, may help explain crime rate differences. As the human race evolved, traits and characteristics have become ingrained.

- The psychodynamic view, developed by Sigmund Freud, links aggressive behavior to personality conflicts arising from childhood.

- The development of the unconscious personality early in childhood influences behavior for the rest of a person's life. Criminals have weak egos and damaged personalities.

- According to some psychoanalysts, psychotics are aggressive, unstable people who can easily become involved in crime.

- Cognitive psychology is concerned with human development and how people perceive the world. Criminality is viewed as a function of improper information processing. Individual reasoning processes influence behavior. Reasoning is influenced by the way people perceive their environment.

- Behavioral and social learning theorists see criminality as a learned behavior. Children who are exposed to violence and see it rewarded may become violent as adults. People commit crime when they model their behavior after others they see being rewarded for the same acts. Behavior is reinforced by rewards and extinguished by punishment.

- Psychological traits such as personality and intelligence have been linked to criminality. One important area of study has been the antisocial personality, a person who lacks emotion and concern for others.

- The controversial issue of the relationship of IQ to criminality has been resurrected once again with the publication of research studies purporting to show that criminals have lower IQs than noncriminals.

Thinking Like a Criminologist

Fourteen-year-old Daphne A. is a product of Boston's best private schools; she lives with her wealthy family on Beacon Hill. Her father is an executive at a local financial services conglomerate and makes close to $1 million per year. Daphne, however, has a hidden, darker side. She is always in trouble at school, and teachers report that she is impulsive and has poor self-control. At times, she can be kind and warm, but on other occasions she is obnoxious, unpredictable, insecure, and craves attention. She is overly self-conscious about her body and has a drinking problem. Daphne attends AA meetings and is on the waiting list at High Cliff Village, a residential substance abuse treatment program. Her parents seem intimidated by her and confused by her complexities; her father even filed a harassment complaint against her once, saying she had slapped him.

Despite repeated promises to get her life together, Daphne likes to hang out most nights in the Public Gardens and drink with neighborhood kids. On more than one occasion she went to the park with her friend and confidant Christopher G., a quiet boy who had his own set of personal problems. His parents had separated and subsequently he began to suffer severe anxiety attacks. He stayed home from school and was diagnosed with depression for which he took two drugs—Zoloft, an antidepressant, and Lorazepam, a sedative.

One night Daphne and Chris met up with Michael M., a 44-year-old man with a long history of alcohol problems. After a night of drinking, a fight broke out and Michael was stabbed, his throat cut, and his body dumped in the pond. Daphne was quickly arrested when soon after the attack she placed a 911 call to police, telling them that a friend had "jumped in the lake and didn't come out." Police searched the area and found Michael's slashed and stabbed body in the water; he had been disemboweled by Chris and Daphne in an attempt to sink the body.

At a waiver hearing, Daphne admitted that she had participated in the killing but could not articulate what caused her to get involved. She had been drinking and remembers little of the events. She said she was flirting with Michael, and Chris stabbed him in a jealous rage. She speaks in a flat hollow voice and shows little remorse for her actions. It was a spur of the moment thing, she claims, and after all it was Chris who had the knife and not her. Later, Chris testifies, and claims that Daphne instigated the fight and egged him on, taunting him that he was too scared to kill someone. Chris says that Daphne, while drunk, often talked of killing an adult because she hated older people, especially her parents.

Daphne's parents claim that while she has been a burden with her mood swings and volatile behavior she is still a child and can be helped with proper treatment. They are willing to supplement any state intervention with privately funded psychiatrists. Given that this is her first real offense and because of her age (14), the parents believe home confinement with intense treatment is the best course.

The district attorney wants Daphne treated as an adult and waived to adult court where, if she is found guilty, she can receive a 25-year sentence on second degree murder; there is little question of her legal culpability.

As a criminologist, you are asked by a juvenile court judge to help her make a suitable disposition of this case. Would you conclude that Daphne's crime was a function of some abnormal trait or condition that is amenable to treatment? Or is she a calculating criminal who should be locked away in prison?

Go to the Criminology: The Core 2e Web site to review the content of this chapter.

Doing Research on the Web

For an up-to-date list of URLs, go to

http://www.cj.wadsworth.com/siegel_crimcore2e

This vignette was based on an actual case, which you can read about at:

http://www.echonyc.com/~hearst/otr/ma/archive/featherstone2.html

http://www.meandmymouse.com/web_site_networker/archive/0697/060897killers.html

http://www.news-star.com/stories/040398/new_forgive.html

http://www.nynewsday.com/entertainment/nyc-
centralcrime,0,6359569.photogallery?index=10

To read about antisocial personality disorder, go to:

http://www.mentalhealth.com/dis/p20-pe04.html

Pro/Con discussions and Viewpoint Essays on some of the topics in this chapter may be found at the Opposing Viewpoints Resource Center:

http://www.gale.com/OpposingViewpoints

Key Terms

trait theory 97
sociobiology 98
equipotentiality 98
hypoglycemia 100
androgens 100
testosterone 102
premenstrual syndrome (PMS) 102
neurophysiology 103
minimal brain dysfunction (MBD) 103
attention deficit hyperactivity disorder (ADHD) 103
neurotransmitters 104

arousal theory 105
monozygotic (MZ) twins 107
dizygotic (DZ) twins 107
cheater theory 109
psychodynamic (psychoanalytic) 111
id 111
ego 112
superego 112
neurotic 112
psychotic 112
disorder 112
schizophrenia 112
bipolar disorder 113

behavior theory 114
social learning theory 114
behavior modeling 114
cognitive theory 116
information-processing theory 116
personality 117
antisocial personality 118
nature theory 119
nurture theory 119
primary prevention programs 120
secondary prevention programs 120

Critical Thinking Questions

1. If research could show that the tendency to commit crime is inherited, what should be done with the young children of violence-prone criminals?

2. Would you recommend that young children be forbidden to view films with violent content?

3. Knowing what you do about trends and patterns in crime, how would you counteract the assertion that people who commit crime are physically or mentally abnormal?

4. Aside from becoming a criminal, what other career paths are open to psychopaths?

5. Should sugar be banned from school lunches?

6. Can gender differences in the crime rate be explained by evolutionary factors? Do you agree that male aggression is linked to mating patterns developed millions of years ago?

CHAPTER 6

Social Structure Theory: Because They're Poor

Chapter Objectives

1. Be familiar with the concept of social structure.
2. Have knowledge of the socioeconomic structure of American society.
3. Be able to discuss the concept of social disorganization.
4. Be familiar with the works of Shaw and McKay.
5. Know what is meant by concentric zone theory.
6. Know the various elements of ecological theory.
7. Be able to discuss the association between collective efficacy and crime.
8. Be familiar with the concept of strain.
9. Know what is meant by the term *anomie*.
10. Understand the concept of cultural deviance.

EEN GANGS HAVE BECOME AN
EVER-PRESENT FIXTURE OF
THE AMERICAN URBAN EXPE-
RIENCE. THE MOST RECENT
federally sponsored surveys of gang activity now estimates that youth gangs
are active in over 2,300 cities. More than
90 percent of the largest cities (over
100,000 population) reported gang activity.[1] There are now an estimated 24,000
active gangs containing about 750,000 gang
members who are active in the United States.[2]

CNN. View the CNN video clip of this story and answer related critical thinking questions on your Criminology: The Core 2e CD.

Gang members are heavily armed, dangerous, and more violent than nonmembers. Gang kids are
about ten times more likely to carry handguns than non-gang members and gun toting gang members commit about ten times more violent crimes than nonmembers. Nowhere is the gang problem
more serious than Los Angeles. The 18th Street gang, considered the largest gang in Los Angeles
County, alone has 20,000. There are over 600 active Hispanic gangs in Los Angeles County; the Asian
gang population numbers approximately 20,000 members, and LA is the home of the nation's most
notorious African American gangs, the Crips and Bloods.

Many criminologists believe that it should come as no surprise that gangs develop in poor, deteriorated urban neighborhoods. Many kids in these areas grow up hopeless and alienated, believing
that they have little chance of being part of the "American Dream."[3]

any criminologists have observed that crime and violence are common in poor, deteriorated neighborhoods. Because these neighborhoods have substantially higher crime rates than more affluent
areas, the majority of criminologists believe it would be a mistake to
ignore social and environmental factors in trying to understand the
cause of criminal behavior.[4] Most criminals are indigent and desperate, not calculating or evil. Many were raised in deteriorated parts of
town and lack the social support and economic resources familiar to
more affluent members of society. Understanding criminal behavior,
then, requires analyzing the influence of these destructive social
forces on human behavior.

Criminologists have long attempted to discover why certain
neighborhoods and geographic locations are more prone to criminal
activity than others. Explanations of crime as an individual-level
phenomenon, with its locus in either destructive personal choices or
deviant traits, fail to account for these consistent crime rate patterns.
If violence, as some criminologists suggest, is related to chemical or
chromosome abnormality, then how can ecological differences in
crime rates be explained? It is unlikely that all people with physical
anomalies live in one section of town or in one area of the country.

125

There has been a heated national debate over the effects of violent TV shows on adolescent aggression. Yet adolescents in cities and towns with widely disparate crime rates may all watch the same shows and movies; so how can crime rate differences in these areas be explained? If violence has a biological or psychological origin, should it not be distributed more evenly throughout the social structure rather than concentrated in certain areas?

Because of these issues, many criminologists believe that understanding the dynamics of interactions between individuals and important social institutions, such as families, peers, schools, jobs, and criminal justice agencies, is important for understanding the cause of crime.[5] The relationship of one social class or group to another or to the power structure that controls the nation's legal and economic system may also be closely related to criminality. It seems logical that people on the lowest rung of the economic ladder will have the greatest incentive to commit crime. They may be either enraged by their lack of economic success or simply financially desperate and disillusioned. In either case, crime, despite its inherent dangers, may be an attractive alternative to a life of indigence.

Economic Structure and Crime

People in the United States live in a **stratified society**. Social strata are created by unequal distribution of wealth, power, and prestige. **Social classes** are segments of the population whose members have a relatively similar portion of desirable things and who share attitudes, values, norms, and an identifiable lifestyle. In U.S. society, it is common to identify people as upper, middle, or lower class, with a broad range of economic variations within each group. The upper-upper class consists of a small number of exceptionally well-to-do families who control enormous financial and social resources. In the United States about 2 million people have at least $1 million in assets. In 2002, there were 7.3 million high-net-worth individuals worldwide. Combined, they controlled $27.2 trillion in assets (Table 6.1).

In contrast, the indigent have scant, if any, resources and suffer socially and economically as a result. Although the proportion of indigent Americans has been declining, the most recent federal data indicate that poverty rose and income levels declined in 2002 (Figure 6.1). The poverty rate in 2002 was 12.1 percent, and nearly 34.6 million people lived in poverty—about 1.7 million more than the previous year. Median household income declined 1.1 percent between 2001 and 2002 to $42,409, after accounting for inflation. That means half of all households earned more than that amount, and half earned less.[6]

Minority Group Poverty

The burdens of underclass life are most often felt by minority group members. Although poverty has actually been declining faster among minorities than among European Americans, 24 percent of African Americans and 21 percent

stratified society
People grouped according to economic or social class; characterized by the unequal distribution of wealth, power, and prestige.

social class
Segment of the population whose members are at a relatively similar economic level and who share attitudes, values, norms, and an identifiable lifestyle.

TABLE 6.1 Distribution of Wealth Worldwide, 2002	
WEALTH	NUMBER OF PEOPLE
$1 million to $5 million	6.5 million
$5 million to $10 million	446,000
$10 million to $20 million	166,000
$20 million to $30 million	44,000
More than $30 million	58,000

SOURCE: *World Wealth Report 2003*, Merrill Lynch/Cap Gemini Ernst & Young.

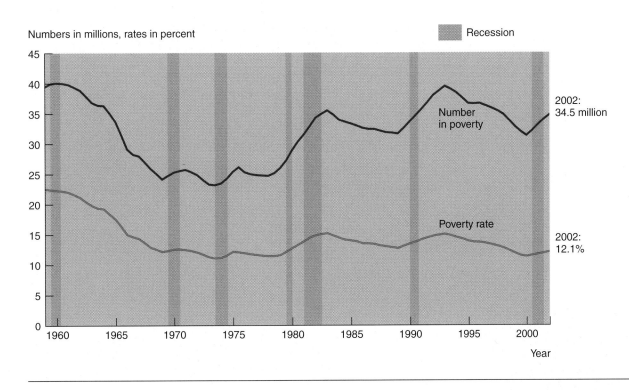

Numbers in millions, rates in percent

Recession

Figure 6.1

Number in Poverty and Poverty Rate, 1959–2002

Note: The data points represent the midpoints of the respective years.

SOURCE: U.S. Census Bureau, *Current Population Survey, 1960–2003,* Annual Social and Economic Supplements.

of Hispanic Americans still live in poverty, compared to about 9 percent of European Americans. According to the U.S. Census Bureau, the median family income of Hispanic and African Americans is only two-thirds that of European Americans.[7]

A 2003 study by the UCLA Center for Health Policy Research highlights some of the fallout from these differences in poverty levels. After examining the health, access to health care, and well-being of young children in the state of California, the UCLA researchers found that Latino children and those in low-income families are four times less likely to have health insurance as other kids. The study concluded that Latino children in California begin life with significant social and educational deficits.[8]

Economic disparity continually haunts members of the minority underclass and their children. Even if they value education and other middle-class norms, their desperate life circumstances (including high unemployment and nontraditional family structures) may prevent them from developing the skills, habits, and styles that lead first to educational success and later to success in the workplace; these factors have been linked to crime and drug abuse.[9] Interracial differences in the crime rate could be significantly reduced by improving levels of education, lowering levels of poverty, and reducing the extent of male unemployment among minority populations.[10] The issue of minority poverty is explored further in the Race, Culture, Gender, and Criminology feature.

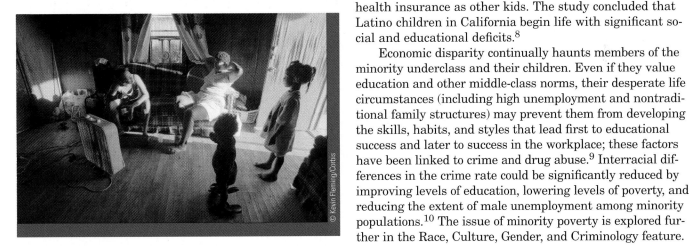

■ About 25 percent of the children in the United States live in poverty. These children are less likely to achieve in school or complete their education. They are more likely to have health problems and to receive inadequate health care. Children living in poverty suffer a variety of social and physical ills, ranging from low birth weight to dropping out of school or becoming teenage parents.

Child Poverty

The timing of poverty also seems to be relevant. Findings suggest that poverty during early childhood may have a more severe impact than poverty during adolescence and adulthood.[11] This is particularly important because, as Figure 6.2 on page 130 shows, children have a higher poverty rate than any other age group.

Hundreds of studies have documented the association between family poverty and children's health, achievement, and behavior impairments.[12]

RACE, CULTURE, GENDER, AND CRIMINOLOGY

Bridging the Racial Divide

illiam Julius Wilson, one of the nation's most prominent sociologists, has produced an impressive body of work detailing racial problems and racial politics in American society. In 1987 he described the plight of the lowest levels of the underclass, which he labeled the **truly disadvantaged.** Wilson portrayed members of this group as socially isolated people who dwell in urban inner cities, occupy the bottom rung of the social ladder, and are the victims of discrimination. They live in areas in which the basic institutions of society—family, schools, housing—have long since declined. Their decline triggers similar breakdowns in the strengths of inner-city areas, including the loss of community cohesion and the ability of people living in the area to control the flow of drugs and criminal activity. For example, in a more affluent area, neighbors might complain to parents that their children were acting out. In distressed areas, this element of informal social control may be absent because parents are under stress or all too often are absent. These effects magnify the isolation of the underclass from mainstream society and promote a ghetto culture and behavior.

Since the truly disadvantaged rarely come into contact with the actual source of their oppression, they direct their anger and aggression at those with whom they are in close and intimate contact, such as neighbors, business people, and landlords. Members of this group, plagued by under- or unemployment, begin to lose self-confidence, a feeling supported by the plight of kin and friendship groups who also experience extreme economic marginality. Self-doubt is a neighborhood norm, overwhelming those forced to live in areas of concentrated poverty.

In his important book *When Work Disappears,* Wilson assesses the effect of joblessness and underemployment on residents in poor neighborhoods on Chicago's south side. He argues that for the first time in the twentieth century, most adults in inner-city ghetto neighborhoods are not working during a typical week. He finds that inner-city life is only marginally affected by the surge in the nation's economy, which has been brought about by new industrial growth connected with technological development. Poverty in these inner-city areas is eternal and unchanging and, if anything, worsening as residents are further shut out of the economic mainstream.

Wilson focuses on the plight of the African American community, which had enjoyed periods of relative prosper-ity in the 1950s and 1960s. He suggests that as difficult as life was for African Americans in the 1940s and 1950s, they at least had a reasonable hope of steady work. Now, because of the globalization of the economy, those opportunities have evaporated. Though in the past racial segregation had limited opportunity, growth in the manufacturing sector fueled upward mobility and provided the foundation of today's African American middle class. Those opportunities no longer exist as manufacturing plants have moved to inaccessible rural and overseas locations where the cost of doing business is lower. With manufacturing opportunities all but obsolete in the United States, service and retail establishments, which depended on blue-collar spending, have similarly disappeared, leaving behind an economy based on welfare and government supports. In less than 20 years, formerly active African American communities have become crime-infested slums.

The hardships faced by residents on Chicago's south side are not unique to that community. Beyond sustaining inner-city poverty, the absence of employment opportunities has torn at the social fabric of the nation's inner-city neighborhoods. Jobs help socialize young people into the wider society, instilling in them such desirable values

FIND IT ON INFOTRAC
College Edition

Did you know that although income per capita in the United States is among the world's highest, so is its rate of child poverty? To read more about this, use "poverty" and "children" as key words.

truly disadvantaged
The lowest level of the underclass; urban, inner-city, socially isolated people who occupy the bottom rung of the social ladder and are the victims of discrimination.

Children who grow up in low-income homes are less likely to achieve in school and are less likely to complete their schooling than children with more affluent parents.[13] Poor children are also more likely to suffer from health problems and to receive inadequate health care. The number of U.S. children covered by health insurance is declining and will continue to do so for the foreseeable future.[14] Without health benefits or the means to afford medical care, these children are likely to have health problems that impede their long-term development. Children who live in extreme poverty or who remain poor for multiple years appear to suffer the worst outcomes.

Besides their increased chance of physical illness, poor children are much more likely than wealthy children to suffer various social and physical ills, ranging from low birth weight to a limited chance of earning a college degree. Many live in substandard housing—high-rise, multiple-family dwellings—that can have a negative influence on their long-term psychological health.[15]

The social problems found in lower-class slum areas have been described as an "epidemic" that spreads like a contagious disease, destroying the inner workings that enable neighborhoods to survive; they become "hollowed out."[16]

as hard work, caring, and respect for others. When work becomes scarce, however, the discipline and structure it provides are absent. Community-wide underemployment destroys social cohesion, increasing the presence of neighborhood social problems ranging from drug use to educational failure. Schools in these areas are unable to teach basic skills, and because desirable employment is lacking, there are few adults to serve as role models. In contrast to more affluent suburban households where daily life is organized around job and career demands, children in inner-city areas are not socialized in the workings of the mainstream economy.

In a recent book, *The Bridge over the Racial Divide: Rising Inequality and Coalition Politics,* Wilson expands further on his views of race in contemporary society. He argues that despite economic gains there is a growing inequality in American society, and ordinary families, of all races and ethnic origins, are suffering. Whites, Latinos, African Americans, Asians, and Native Americans must therefore begin to put aside their differences and concentrate more on what they have in common—their aspirations, problems, and hopes. Mutual cooperation across racial lines is essential.

One reason for this set of mutual problems is that the government tends to aggravate rather than ease the financial stress being placed on ordinary families. Monetary policy, trade policy, and tax policy are harmful to working class families. A multiracial citizen's coalition could pressure national public officials to focus on the interests of ordinary people. As long as middle- and working-class groups are fragmented along racial lines, such pressure is impossible.

Wilson finds that racism is becoming more subtle and harder to detect. Whites believe African Americans are responsible for their own inferior economic status because of their cultural traits. Because even affluent whites fear corporate downsizing, they are unwilling to vote for governmental assistance to the poor. Whites are continuing to be suburban dwellers, further isolating poor minorities in central cities and making their problems distant and unimportant. Wilson continues to believe that the changing marketplace, with its reliance on sophisticated computer technologies, continually decreases demand for low-skilled workers, which has a larger negative impact on African Americans than on other, better educated and affluent groups.

Wilson argues for a cross-race, class-based alliance of working- and middle-class Americans to pursue policies that will benefit them rather than the affluent. These include full employment, programs to help families and workers in their private lives, and a reconstructed "affirmative opportunity" program that benefits African Americans without antagonizing whites.

Critical Thinking

1. Is it unrealistic to assume that a government sponsored public works program can provide needed jobs in this era of budget cutbacks?

2. What are some of the hidden costs of unemployment in a community setting?

3. How would a biocriminologist explain Wilson's findings?

InfoTrac College Edition Research

For more on Wilson's view of poverty, unemployment, and crime, check out: Gunnar Almgren, Avery Guest, George Immerwahr, and Michael Spittel, "Joblessness, Family Disruption, and Violent Death in Chicago, 1970–90," *Social Forces* June 1998 v76 n4 p1465 William Julius Wilson, "Inner-City Dislocations," *Society,* Jan–Feb 1998 v35 n2 p270

SOURCES: William Julius Wilson, *The Truly Disadvantaged* (Chicago: University of Chicago Press, 1987); *When Work Disappears, The World of the Urban Poor* (New York: Alfred Knopf, 1996); *The Bridge over the Racial Divide: Rising Inequality and Coalition Politics,* Wildavsky Forum Series, 2 (Berkeley: University of California Press, 1999).

As neighborhood quality decreases, the probability that residents will develop problems sharply increases. Adolescents in the worst neighborhoods have the greatest risks of dropping out of school and of becoming teenage parents.

Lower-Class Culture

culture of poverty
A separate lower-class culture, characterized by apathy, cynicism, helplessness, and mistrust of social institutions such as schools, government agencies, and the police that is passed from one generation to the next.

underclass
The lowest social stratum in any country, whose members lack the education and skills needed to function successfully in modern society.

In 1966 sociologist Oscar Lewis argued that the crushing lifestyle of slum areas produces a **culture of poverty** that is passed from one generation to the next.[17] Apathy, cynicism, helplessness, and mistrust of social institutions, such as schools, government agencies, and the police, mark the culture of poverty. This mistrust prevents the inner-city poor from taking advantage of the meager opportunities available to them. Lewis's work was the first of a group of studies that described the plight of at-risk children and adults. In 1970 Swedish economist Gunnar Myrdal described a worldwide **underclass** that was cut off from society, its members lacking the education and skills needed to function successfully in modern society.[18]

Today, lower-class areas are scenes of inadequate housing and health care, disrupted family lives, underemployment, and despair. Members of the

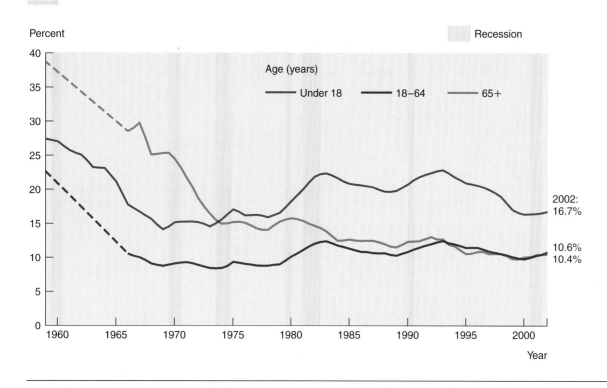

Figure 6.2
Poverty Rates by Age, 1959–2002

Note: The data points represent the midpoints of the respective years. Data for people 18 to 64 and 65 and older are not available from 1960 to 1965.

SOURCE: U.S. Census Bureau, *Current Population Survey, 1960–2003,* Annual Social and Economic Supplements.

lower class also suffer in other ways. They are more prone to depression, less likely to have achievement motivation, and less likely to put off immediate gratification for future gain. For example, they may be less willing to stay in school because the rewards for educational achievement are in the distant future. Because they lack ties to the mainstream culture, some lower-class people are driven to desperate measures, such as crime and substance abuse, to cope with their economic plight.[19]

Social Structure Theories

Many criminologists view disadvantaged economic class position as a primary cause of crime. This view is referred to as **social structure theory.** As a group, social structure theories suggest that social and economic forces operating in deteriorated lower-class areas push many of their residents into criminal behavior patterns. These theories consider the existence of unsupervised teenage gangs, high crime rates, and social disorder in poor inner-city areas as major social problems. Because crime rates are higher in lower-class urban centers than in middle-class suburbs, social forces must influence or control behavior.[20]

The social structure perspective encompasses three independent yet overlapping branches: social disorganization theory, strain theory, and cultural deviance theory. These three branches are summarized in Figure 6.3.

Social disorganization theory focuses on the urban conditions that affect crime rates. A disorganized area is one in which institutions of social control, such as the family, commercial establishments, and schools, have broken down and can no longer perform their expected or stated functions. Indicators of social disorganization include high unemployment and school dropout rates, deteriorated housing, low income levels, and large numbers of single-parent households. Residents in these areas experience conflict and despair, and, as a result, antisocial behavior flourishes.

Strain theory holds that crime is a function of the conflict between people's goals and the means they can use to obtain them. Strain theorists argue that although social and economic goals are common to people in all economic strata, the ability to obtain these goals is class-dependent. Most people in the United States desire wealth, material possessions, power, pres-

social structure theory
The view that disadvantaged economic class position is a primary cause of crime.

social disorganization theory
Branch of social structure theory that focuses on the breakdown of institutions such as the family, school, and employment in inner-city neighborhoods.

strain theory
Branch of social structure theory that sees crime as a function of the conflict between people's goals and the means available to obtain them.

FIND IT ON INFOTRAC
College Edition

To learn more about the extent of poverty in the United States and its impact on the nation's poorest citizens, read:

John A. Bishop, John P. Formby, and Buhong Zheng, "Extent of Material Hardship and Poverty in the United States: Comment," *Review of Social Economy*, September 1999 v57 i3 p388(1)

Figure 6.3
The Three Branches of Social Structure Theory

Social disorganization theory focuses on conditions in the environment:
- Deteriorated neighborhoods
- Inadequate social control
- Law-violating gangs and groups
- Conflicting social values

Cultural deviance theory combines these two:
- Development of subcultures as a result of disorganization and stress
- Subcultural values in opposition to conventional values

CRIME

Strain theory focuses on conflict between goals and means:
- Unequal distribution of wealth and power
- Frustration
- Alternative methods of achievement

✔ Checkpoints

✔ Because crime rates are higher in lower-class areas, many criminologists believe that the causes of crime are rooted in socioeconomic factors.

✔ Despite economic headway, there are still more than 30 million indigent Americans. Minority groups are more likely than the white majority to be poor.

✔ Some criminologists believe that destructive social forces in poverty areas are responsible for high crime rates.

✔ The strain and frustration caused by poverty is a suspected cause of crime.

✔ Indigents may become involved in a deviant subculture that sustains and supports criminality.

To quiz yourself on this material, go to questions 6.1–6.5 on the Criminology: The Core 2e Web site.

tige, and other life comforts. Members of the lower class are unable to achieve these symbols of success through conventional means. Consequently, they feel anger, frustration, and resentment, referred to collectively as **strain.** Lower-class citizens can either accept their condition and live as socially responsible if unrewarded citizens, or they can choose an alternative means of achieving success, such as theft, violence, or drug trafficking.

Cultural deviance theory combines elements of both strain and social disorganization theories. According to this view, because of strain and social isolation, a unique lower-class culture develops in disorganized neighborhoods. These independent **subcultures** maintain unique values and beliefs that conflict with conventional social norms. Criminal behavior is an expression of conformity to lower-class subcultural values and traditions, not a rebellion from conventional society. Subcultural values are handed down from one generation to the next in a process called **cultural transmission.**

Although each of these theories is distinct in critical aspects, each approach has at its core the view that socially isolated people, living in disorganized neighborhoods, are likely to experience crime-producing social forces. In the remainder of this chapter, each branch of social structure theory will be discussed in some detail. **✔ Checkpoints**

Social Disorganization Theory

strain
The anger, frustration, and resentment experienced by people who believe they cannot achieve their goals through legitimate means.

cultural deviance theory
Branch of social structure theory that sees strain and social disorganization together resulting in a unique lower-class culture that conflicts with conventional social norms.

Social disorganization theory links crime rates to neighborhood ecological characteristics. Crime rates are elevated in highly transient, mixed-use (where residential and commercial property exist side by side), and changing neighborhoods in which the fabric of social life has become frayed. These localities are unable to provide essential services, such as education, health care, and proper housing, and, as a result, they experience significant levels of unemployment, single-parent families, and families on welfare.

Social disorganization theory views crime-ridden neighborhoods as those in which residents are trying to leave at the earliest opportunity. Residents are uninterested in community matters, so the common sources of control—the family, school, business community, social service agencies—are weak and disorganized. Personal relationships are strained because neighbors are constantly moving. Constant resident turnover weakens communications and blocks attempts at solving neighborhood problems or establishing common goals (see Figure 6.4).[21]

Figure 6.4
Social Disorganization Theory

Poverty
- Development of isolated slums
- Lack of conventional social opportunities
- Racial and ethnic discrimination

Social disorganization
- Breakdown of social institutions and organizations such as school and family
- Lack of informal social control

Breakdown of social control
- Development of gangs, groups
- Peer group replaces family and social institutions

Criminal areas
- Neighborhood becomes crime prone
- Stable pockets of delinquency develop
- Lack of external support and investment

Cultural transmission
Older youths pass norms (focal concerns) to younger generation, creating stable slum culture.

Criminal careers
Most youths "age out" of delinquency, marry, and raise families, but some remain in life of crime.

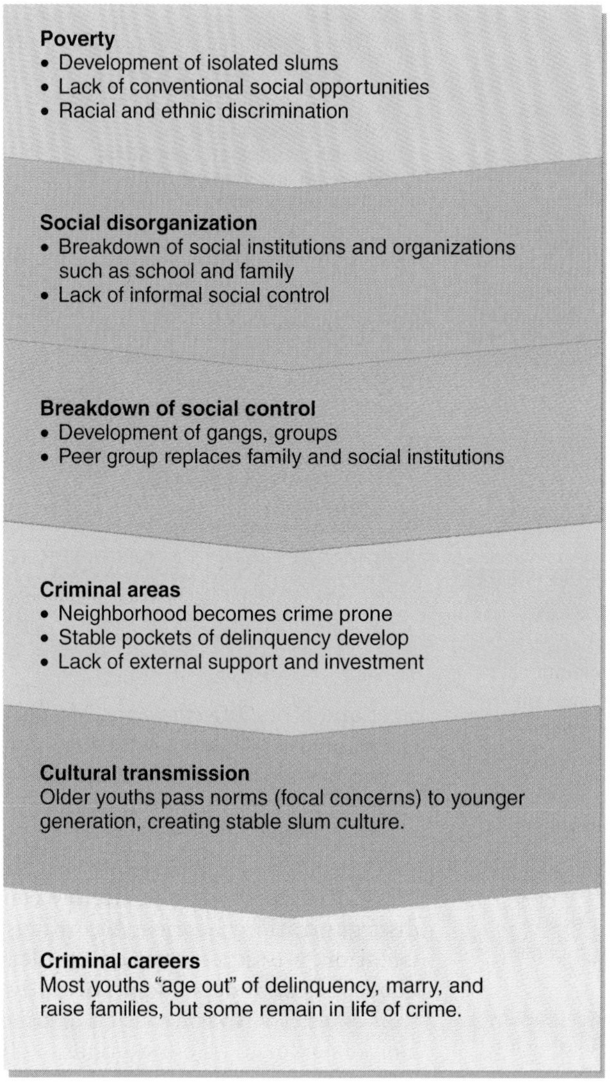

Connections
If social disorganization causes crime, why are most low-income people law-abiding? To explain this anomaly, some sociologists have devised theoretical models suggesting that individual socialization experiences mediate environmental influences. These theories will be discussed in Chapter 7.

subculture
A set of values, beliefs, and traditions unique to a particular social class or group within a larger society.

cultural transmission
Process whereby values, beliefs, and traditions are handed down from one generation to the next.

transitional neighborhood
An area undergoing a shift in population and structure, usually from middle-class residential to lower-class mixed use.

The Work of Shaw and McKay

Social disorganization theory was popularized by the work of two Chicago sociologists, Clifford R. Shaw and Henry McKay, who linked life in transitional slum areas to the inclination to commit crime. Shaw and McKay began their pioneering work on Chicago crime during the early 1920s while working as researchers for a state-supported social service agency.[22]

Shaw and McKay explained crime and delinquency within the context of the changing urban environment and ecological development of the city. They saw that Chicago had developed into distinct neighborhoods (natural areas), some affluent and others wracked by extreme poverty. These poverty-ridden **transitional neighborhoods** suffered high rates of population turnover and were incapable of inducing residents to remain and defend the neighborhoods against criminal groups.

In transitional areas, successive changes in population composition, disintegration of traditional cultures, diffusion of divergent cultural standards, and gradual industrialization dissolve neighborhood culture and organization. The continuity of conventional neighborhood traditions and institutions is broken, leaving children feeling displaced and without a strong or definitive set of values.

Concentric Zones   Shaw and McKay identified the areas in Chicago that had excessive crime rates. They noted that distinct ecological areas had devel-

Figure 6.5
Shaw and McKay's Concentric Zones Map of Chicago

Note: Arabic numerals represent the rate of male delinquency.

SOURCE: Clifford R. Shaw et al., *Delinquency Areas* (Chicago: University of Chicago Press, 1929), p. 99. Reprinted with permission. Copyright 1929 by the University of Chicago. All rights reserved.

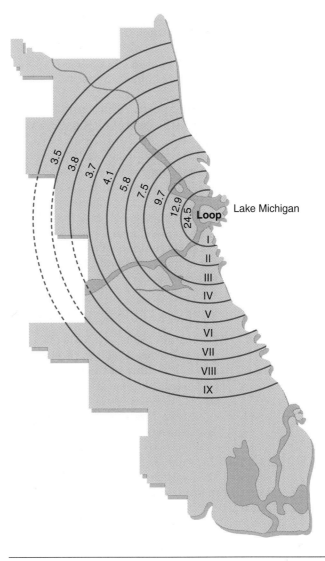

oped in the city, forming a series of nine concentric circles, or zones, and that there were stable and significant interzone differences in crime rates (see Figure 6.5). The areas of heaviest crime concentration appeared to be the transitional inner-city zones, where large numbers of foreign-born citizens had recently settled.[23] The zones farthest from the city's center had correspondingly lower crime rates.

Analysis of these data indicated a surprisingly stable pattern of criminal activity in the nine ecological zones over 65 years. Shaw and McKay concluded that multiple cultures and diverse values, both conventional and deviant, coexist in the transitional neighborhoods. Children growing up in the street culture often find that adults who have adopted a deviant lifestyle (gamblers, pimps, drug dealers) are the most financially successful people in the neighborhood. Forced to choose between conventional and deviant lifestyles, many slum kids opt for the latter. They join other like-minded youths and form law-violating gangs and cliques. The development of teenage law-violating groups is an essential element of youthful misbehavior in slum areas. The values that slum youths adopt often conflict with existing middle-class norms, which demand strict obedience to the legal code. Consequently, a value conflict further separates the delinquent youth and his or her peer group from conventional society; the result is a more solid embrace of deviant goals and behavior. To further justify their choice of goals, these youths seek support for their choice by recruiting new members and passing on the delinquent tradition.

Shaw and McKay's statistical analysis confirmed that even though crime rates changed, the highest rates were always in Zones I and II (the central city and a transitional area). The areas with the highest crime rates retained high rates even when their ethnic composition changed (the areas Shaw and McKay examined shifted from German and Irish to Italian and Polish).[24]

The Legacy of Shaw and McKay Social disorganization concepts articulated by Shaw and McKay have remained prominent within criminology for more than 75 years. Although cultural and social conditions have changed over time and today we live in a much more heterogeneous, mobile society, the most important of Shaw and McKay's findings—crime rates correspond to neighborhood structure—still holds up.[25]

Their research supported their belief that crime is a constant fixture in areas of poverty, regardless of residents' racial or ethnic identity. Because the basis of their theory was that neighborhood disintegration is the primary cause of criminal behavior, Shaw and McKay paved the way for many of the community action and treatment programs that have been developed in the last half-century.

The Social Ecology School

During the 1970s, criminologists were influenced by several critical analyses of social disorganization theory that challenged its validity.[26] The criminological literature of the period was dominated by theories with a social-psychological orientation, stressing offender socialization within the family, school, and peer group.

In the 1980s, a group of criminologists continued studying ecological conditions, reviving concern about the effects of social disorganization.[27] These contemporary social ecologists developed a purer form of structural theory that emphasizes the association of community deterioration and economic decline with criminality but places less emphasis on value conflict. The following sections discuss some of the more recent social ecological research.

Community Disorganization Crime rates and the need for police services are associated with community deterioration: disorder, poverty, alienation, disassociation, and fear of crime.[28] Even in rural areas, which normally have low crime rates, increased levels of crime and violence are associated with indicators of social disorganization such as residential instability (a large number of people moving in and out), family disruption, and changing ethnic composition.[29]

In larger cities, neighborhoods with a high percentage of deserted houses and apartments experience high crime rates; abandoned buildings serve as a "magnet for crime."[30] Areas in which houses are in poor repair, boarded up, and burned out, whose owners are best described as slumlords, are also the location of the highest violence rates and gun crime.[31] These neighborhoods, in which retail establishments often go bankrupt, are abandoned and deteriorate physically.[32]

Poverty and Unemployment Economically disadvantaged neighborhoods have high rates of serious crimes such as homicide.[33] For example, the percentage of people living in poverty and the percentage of broken homes are strongly related to neighborhood crime rates.[34] Violent crime rates are associated with such variables as the percentage of the neighborhood living below the poverty line, the lack of mortgage investment in a neighborhood, the unemployment rate, and the influx of new immigrants; these factors are usually found in disorganized areas.[35] The influence of these economic disadvantages is felt by both male and female residents. Though female crime rates may be lower than male rates, women living in deteriorated areas also feel the effects of poverty.[36]

Shaw and McKay claimed that areas continually wracked by poverty also experience social disorganization.[37] Research indicates that neighborhoods with few employment opportunities for youth and adults are the most vulnerable to predatory crime such as armed robbery and mugging.[38] Unemployment destabilizes households, and unstable families are likely to breed children who use violence and aggression to deal with limited opportunity. This lack of opportunity perpetuates higher crime rates, especially when large groups or cohorts of people of the same age compete for relatively scant resources.[39]

Limited employment opportunities also reduce the stabilizing influence of parents and other adults, who may once have counteracted the allure of youth gangs. Sociologist Elijah Anderson's analysis of Philadelphia neighborhood life found that "old heads" (respected neighborhood residents), who at one time played an important role in socializing youth, have been displaced by younger street hustlers and drug dealers. Although the old heads may complain that these newcomers have not earned or worked for their fortunes in the old-fashioned way, the old heads admire and envy these young people whose gold chains and luxury cars advertise their wealth amid poverty.[40] So while the old heads may disdain the violent manner in which they are acquired, they admire the fruits of crime.

Residents in disorganized neighborhoods suffer social and physical isolation and experience a great deal of fear. People dread leaving their homes at night and withdraw from community life. Those who have already been victimized are more fearful of the future than those who have escaped crime.

Community Fear In neighborhoods where people help each other out, residents are less likely to fear crime or to be afraid of becoming a crime victim.[41] In disorganized neighborhoods that suffer social and physical incivilities, residents experience rowdy youth, trash and litter, graffiti, abandoned storefronts, burned-out buildings, littered lots, strangers, drunks, vagabonds, loiterers, prostitutes, noise, congestion, angry words, dirt, and stench. Having parks and playgrounds where teens hang out and loiter may contribute to fear.[42] The presence of such incivilities makes residents of disorganized areas believe that their neighborhood is dangerous and that they face a considerable chance of becoming crime victims. Therefore, when crime rates are actually high in these disorganized areas, fear levels increase dramatically.[43] Perceptions of crime and victimization produce neighborhood fear.[44]

Fear can be contagious. People tell others when they have been victimized, thus spreading the word that the neighborhood is getting dangerous and that the chance of future victimization is high.[45] As a result, people dread leaving their homes at night and withdraw from community life. Not surprisingly, people who have already been victimized fear the future more than those who have escaped crime.[46]

Siege Mentality People who live in neighborhoods that experience high levels of crime and civil disorder become suspicious and mistrusting.[47] They develop a sense of powerlessness, which increases levels of mistrust. Some residents become so suspicious of authority that they develop a "siege mentality," in which the outside world is considered the enemy out to destroy the neighborhood.

Siege mentality often results in an expanding mistrust of critical social institutions, including business, government, and schools. Government officials seem arrogant and haughty. The police are believed to ignore crime, and when they do take action, to use excessive force. Residents' fears may not be misplaced; research does show that police are more likely to use higher levels of force when suspects are encountered in high-crime, disadvantaged neighborhoods regardless of the suspects' behaviors or reactions.[48] When police ignore crime in poor areas or, conversely, when they are violent and corrupt, anger flares, and people take to the streets and react in violent ways.

Community Change Communities undergoing rapid structural changes in racial and economic composition also seem to experience the greatest change in crime rates. Recent studies recognize that change, not stability, is the hallmark of inner-city areas. A neighborhood's residents, wealth, density, and purpose are constantly evolving. Even disorganized neighborhoods acquire new identifying features. Some may become multiracial and others racially homogeneous. Some areas become stable and family-oriented, whereas in others, mobile, never-married people predominate.[49]

As areas decline, residents flee to safer, more stable locales. Those who cannot afford to leave for more affluent communities face an increased risk of victimization. Because of racial differences in economic well-being, those left behind are often minority citizens.[50] Those who cannot move find themselves surrounded by new residents. High population turnover can devastate community culture because it thwarts communication and information flow.[51] In response to this turnover, a culture may develop that dictates to neighborhood youth standards of dress, language, and behavior that are opposite to those of conventional society.[52] The breakdown of neighborhood culture undermines its ability to exert informal social control and contributes to elevated crime rates.[53]

As communities change, neighborhood deterioration precedes increasing rates of crime and delinquency.[54] Neighborhoods most at risk for increased crime contain large numbers of single-parent families and unrelated people living together, have changed from owner-occupied to renter-occupied units, and have lost semiskilled and unskilled jobs (indicating a growing residue of discouraged workers who are no longer seeking employment).[55] These ecological disruptions strain existing social control mechanisms and inhibit their ability to control crime and delinquency.

Poverty Concentration One aspect of community change may be the concentration of poverty in deteriorated urban neighborhoods. William Julius Wilson describes how working- and middle-class families flee inner-city poverty areas, resulting in a **concentration effect** in which the most disadvantaged population is consolidated in the most disorganized urban neighborhoods. As the working and middle classes move out, they take with them their financial and institutional resources and support. Businesses are disinclined to locate in poverty areas; banks become reluctant to lend money for new housing or businesses.[56] Minority group members living in these areas also suffer race-based inequality such as income inequality and institutional racism.[57] Urban areas marked by concentrated poverty become isolated and insulated from the social mainstream and more prone to criminal activity, violence, and homicide.[58] Gangs also concentrate in these areas, bringing with them a significant increase in criminal activity.[59]

Collective Efficacy Cohesive communities with high levels of social control and social integration, where people know one another and develop interpersonal ties, may also develop **collective efficacy**: mutual trust, a willingness to intervene in the supervision of children, and the maintenance of public order.[60] It is the cohesion among neighborhood residents combined with shared expectations for informal social control of public space that promotes collective efficacy.[61] In contrast, socially disorganized neighborhoods find that efforts at social control are weak and attenuated. When community social

concentration effect
As working- and middle-class families flee inner-city poverty areas, the most disadvantaged population is consolidated in urban ghettos.

collective efficacy
Social control exerted by cohesive communities, based on mutual trust, including intervention in the supervision of children and maintenance of public order.

control efforts are blunted, crime rates increase, further weakening neighbor-hood cohesiveness.[62] This suggests that there are spillover effects that extend beyond the geographic boundaries of a single neighborhood.

There are three forms of collective efficacy—informal social control, institutional social control, and public social control—and all three contribute to community stability.

1. **Informal Social Control.** Some elements of collective efficacy operate on the primary or private level and involve peers, families, and relatives. These sources exert informal control by either awarding or withholding approval, respect, and admiration. Informal control mechanisms include direct criticism, ridicule, ostracism, desertion, and physical punishment.[63]

The most important wielder of informal social control is the family, which may keep at-risk kids in check through such mechanisms as corporal punishment, withholding privileges, or ridiculing lazy or disrespectful behavior. The informal social control provided by the family takes on greater importance in neighborhoods with few social ties among adults and limited collective efficacy. In these areas parents cannot call upon neighborhood resources to take up the burden of controlling children; family members face the burden of providing adequate supervision.[64]

In some neighborhoods, neighbors are willing to practice informal social control through surveillance practices, for example, by keeping an "eye out" for intruders when their neighbors go out of town. Informal surveillance has been found to reduce the levels of some crimes such as street robberies; however, if robbery rates remain high, surveillance may be terminated because people become fearful for their safety.[65]

2. **Institutional Social Control.** Social institutions such as schools and churches cannot work effectively in a climate of alienation and mistrust. Unsupervised peer groups and gangs, which flourish in disorganized areas, disrupt the influence of those neighborhood control agents that do exist.[66] Children who reside in these neighborhoods find that involvement with conventional social institutions, such as schools and afternoon programs, is blocked; they are instead at risk for recruitment into gangs and law-violating groups.[67] As crime flourishes, neighborhood fear increases, which in turn decreases a community's cohesion and thwarts the ability of its institutions to exert social control over its residents.[68]

To combat these influences, communities that have collective efficacy attempt to utilize their local institutions to control crime. Sources of institutional social control include businesses, stores, schools, churches, and social service and volunteer organizations.[69] When these institutions are effective, rates for some crimes such as burglary decline.[70] Some institutions, such as recreation centers for teens, have been found to lower crime rates because they exert a positive effect; others, such as taverns and bars, can help destabilize neighborhoods and increase the rate of violent crimes such as rape and robbery.[71]

3. **Public Social Control.** Stable neighborhoods are also able to arrange for external sources of social control. If they can draw on outside help and secure external resources—a process referred to as public social control—they are better able to reduce the effects of disorganization and maintain lower levels of crime and victimization.[72]

The level of policing, one of the primary sources of public social control, may vary between neighborhoods. The police presence is typically greatest when community organizations and local leaders have sufficient political clout to get funding for additional law enforcement personnel. The presence of police sends a message that the area will not tolerate deviant behavior. Because they can respond vigorously to crime, they prevent criminal groups from gaining a toehold in the neighborhood.[73] Criminals and drug dealers avoid such areas and relocate to easier and more appealing "targets."[74]

In more disorganized areas, the absence of political power brokers limits access to external funding and protection. Without money from the outside, the neighborhood lacks the ability to "get back on its feet."[75] In these areas there are fewer police, and those that do patrol the area are less motivated and their resources are stretched more tightly. These communities cannot mount an effective social control effort because as neighborhood disadvantage increases the level of informal social control decreases.[76]

The ramifications of having adequate controls are critical. In areas where collective efficacy remains high, children are less likely to become involved with deviant peers and engage in problem behaviors.[77] In disorganized areas, however, the population is transient, so interpersonal relationships remain superficial. And even when an attempt is made to revitalize a disorganized neighborhood by creating institutional support programs such as community centers and better schools, the effort may be countered by the ongoing drain of deep-rooted economic and social deprivation.[78]

Social Support/Altruism   Neighborhoods that can provide strong social supports for their members can help young people cope with life's stressors. Sometimes this is organized on the block level where neighbors meet face-to-face to deal with problems. Crime rates may be lower on blocks where people are committed to preserving their immediate environment by confronting destablizing forces such as teen gangs and encouraging others to do so also.[79] By helping neighbors to become more resilient and self-confident, adults in these areas can provide the external support systems that enable youth to desist from criminality. For example, residents can teach one another that they have moral and social obligations to their fellow citizens; children can learn to be sensitive to the rights of others and respect differences. They may form neighborhood associations and self-help groups. In contrast, less altruistic areas stress individualism and self-interest.

Areas that place a greater stress on caring for fellow citizens are less crime prone than those that emphasize self-reliance. Even in the cities' poorest areas, if people are generous and caring, their neighborhoods are also relatively crime free. **Social altruism** (indications of generosity, such as the ratio of contributions given to the United Way charity by area income levels) has been found to be inversely related to crime rates.[80] This relationship can be interpreted in one of two ways: (a) crime rates are lower in altruistic areas because of the overall positive social climate, or (b) well-funded charities in these areas help lower crime rates by providing a secure safety net for at-risk families.

The government can also be a force for social altruism by providing economic and social supports through publicly funded programs. Though welfare programs are often criticized by conservative politicians as being "government handouts," there is evidence showing that government assistance may help lower crime rates.[81] Government assistance may help people improve their social status by providing them with the financial resources to clothe, feed, and educate their children while at the same time reducing stress, frustration, and anger.

It is also possible that people living in disorganized areas are able to draw on resources from their neighbors in more affluent surrounding communities, thereby helping to keep crime rates down.[82] This phenomenon may help to explain, in part, why violence rates are high in poor African American neighborhoods that are cut off from outside areas for support.[83]

Concept Summary 6.1 lists some of the basic concepts and theories of the social disorganization view. ✔ Checkpoints

✔ Checkpoints

✔ Social disorganization theory holds that destructive social forces present in inner-city areas control human behavior and promote crime.

✔ Shaw and McKay first identified the concepts central to social disorganization. They found stable patterns of crime in the central city.

✔ The social ecology school associates community deterioration and economic decline with crime rates.

✔ Ecological factors such as community deterioration, changing neighborhoods, fear, lack of employment opportunities, incivility, poverty, and deterioration produce high crime rates.

✔ Collective efficacy and social altruism can reduce neighborhood crime rates.

To quiz yourself on this material, go to questions 6.6–6.8 on the Criminology: The Core 2e Web site.

social altruism
Voluntary mutual support systems, such as neighborhood associations and self-help groups, that reinforce moral and social obligations.

CONCEPT SUMMARY	6.1 Social Disorganization Theories		
THEORY	**MAJOR PREMISE**	**STRENGTHS**	**RESEARCH FOCUS**
Shaw and McKay's concentric zones theory	Crime is a product of transitional neighborhoods that manifest social disorganization and value conflict.	Identifies why crime rates are highest in slum areas. Points out the factors that produce crime. Suggests programs to help reduce crime.	Poverty; disorganization
Social ecology theory	The conflicts and problems of urban social life and communities, including fear, unemployment, deterioration, and siege mentality, influence crime rates.	Accounts for urban crime rates and trends.	Social control; fear; collective efficacy; unemployment

Strain Theories

Inhabitants of a disorganized inner-city area feel isolated, frustrated, ostracized from the economic mainstream, hopeless, and eventually angry. How do these feelings affect criminal activities?

Strain theorists view crime as a direct result of lower-class frustration and anger. Although most people share similar values and goals, the ability to achieve personal goals is stratified by socioeconomic class. Strain is limited in affluent areas because educational and vocational opportunities are available. In disorganized areas, strain occurs because legitimate avenues for success are all but closed. To relieve strain, indigent people may achieve their goals through deviant methods, such as theft or drug trafficking, or they may reject socially accepted goals and substitute more deviant goals, such as being tough and aggressive (see Figure 6.6).

Theory of Anomie

Sociologist Robert Merton applied the sociological concepts first identified by Durkheim to criminology in his theory of **anomie**.[84] He found that two elements of culture interact to produce potentially anomic conditions: culturally defined goals and socially approved means for obtaining them. For example, U.S. society stresses the goals of acquiring wealth, success, and power. Socially permissible means include hard work, education, and thrift.

Merton argues that in the United States legitimate means to acquire wealth are stratified across class and status lines. Those with little formal education and few economic resources soon find that they are denied the ability to legally acquire wealth—the preeminent success symbol. When socially mandated goals are uniform throughout society and access to legitimate means is bound by class and status, the resulting strain produces anomie among those who are locked out of the legitimate opportunity structure. Consequently, they may develop criminal or delinquent solutions to the problem of attaining goals.

Social Adaptations   Merton argues that each person has his or her own concept of society's goals and means to attain them. Some people have inadequate means of attaining success; others who have the means reject societal goals. The result is a variety of social adaptations.

1. **Conformity.** Conformity occurs when individuals embrace conventional social goals and also have the means to attain them. They remain law-abiding.

Connections

As you may recall from Chapter 1, the roots of strain theories can be traced to Émile Durkheim's notion of anomie (from the Greek *a nomos,* without norms). According to Durkheim, an anomic society is one in which rules of behavior (the norms) have broken down or become inoperative during periods of rapid social change or social crisis such as war or famine.

anomie
A lack of norms or clear social standards. Because of rapidly shifting moral values, the individual has few guides to what is socially acceptable.

Figure 6.6
The Basic Concepts of Strain Theory

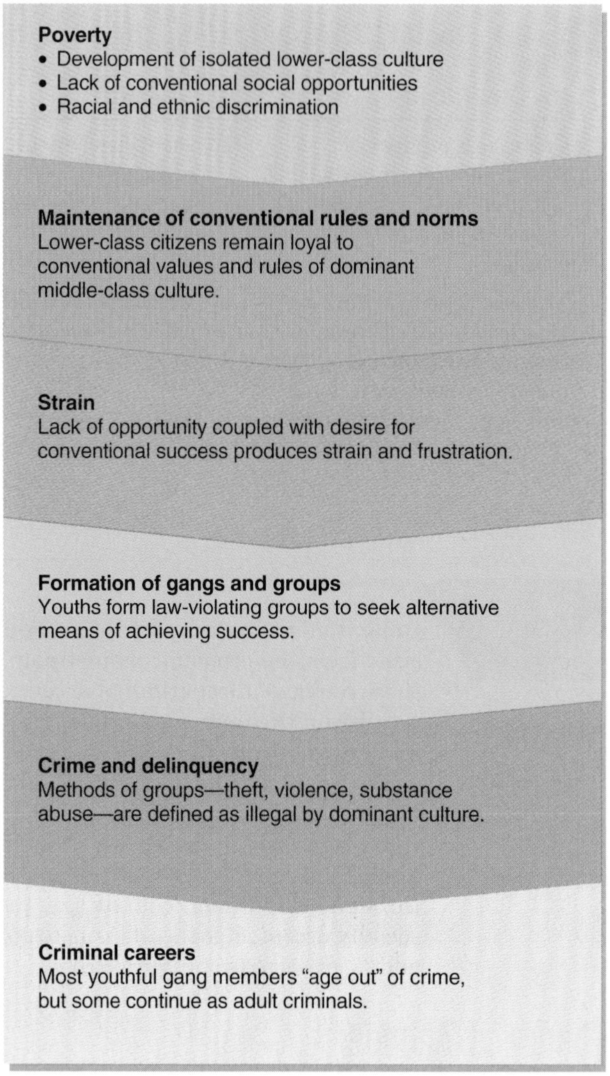

Poverty
- Development of isolated lower-class culture
- Lack of conventional social opportunities
- Racial and ethnic discrimination

Maintenance of conventional rules and norms
Lower-class citizens remain loyal to conventional values and rules of dominant middle-class culture.

Strain
Lack of opportunity coupled with desire for conventional success produces strain and frustration.

Formation of gangs and groups
Youths form law-violating groups to seek alternative means of achieving success.

Crime and delinquency
Methods of groups—theft, violence, substance abuse—are defined as illegal by dominant culture.

Criminal careers
Most youthful gang members "age out" of crime, but some continue as adult criminals.

FIND IT ON INFOTRAC
College Edition

Anomie theory suggests that American culture prescribes material success as the prime goal while at the same time maintaining social structural arrangements that preclude many people from realistic access to means for legitimately achieving that goal. To read what he and others have to say, use "anomie" as a key word.

2. **Innovation.** Innovation occurs when individuals accept the goals of society but are unable or unwilling to attain them through legitimate means. The resulting conflict forces them to adopt innovative solutions to their dilemma: they steal, sell drugs, or extort money. Of the five adaptations, innovation is most closely associated with criminal behavior.

3. **Ritualism.** Ritualists gain pleasure from practicing traditional ceremonies, regardless of whether they have a real purpose or goal. The strict customs in religious orders, feudal societies, clubs, and college fraternities encourage and appeal to ritualists.

4. **Retreatism.** Retreatists reject both the goals and the means of society. They attempt to escape their lack of success by withdrawing, either mentally or physically, by taking drugs or becoming drifters.

5. **Rebellion.** Rebellion involves substituting an alternative set of goals and means for conventional ones. Revolutionaries who wish to promote radical change in the existing social structure and who call for alternative lifestyles, goals, and beliefs are engaging in rebellion. Rebellion may be a reaction against a corrupt, hated government or an effort to create alternative opportunities and lifestyles within the existing system.

Evaluation of Anomie Theory   According to **anomie theory,** social inequality leads to perceptions of anomie. To resolve the goals–means conflict and relieve their sense of strain, some people innovate by stealing or extorting money; others retreat into drugs and alcohol; some rebel by joining revolutionary groups; and still others get involved in ritualistic behavior by joining a religious cult.

Merton's view of anomie has been one of the most enduring and influential sociological theories of criminality. By linking deviant behavior to the success goals that control social behavior, anomie theory attempts to pinpoint the cause of the conflict that produces personal frustration and consequent criminality. By acknowledging that society unfairly distributes the legitimate means to achieving success, anomie theory helps explain the existence of high-crime areas and the apparent predominance of delinquent and criminal behavior in the lower class. By suggesting that social conditions, not individual personalities, produce crime, Merton greatly influenced the directions taken to reduce and control criminality during the latter half of the twentieth century.

A number of questions are left unanswered by anomie theory.[85] Merton does not explain why people choose to commit certain types of crime. For example, why does one anomic person become a mugger while another deals drugs? Anomie may explain differences in crime rates, but it cannot explain why most young criminals desist from crime as adults. Does this mean that perceptions of anomie dwindle with age? Is anomie short-lived?

Institutional Anomie Theory

Steven Messner and Richard Rosenfeld's **institutional anomie theory** is an updating of Merton's work.[86] Messner and Rosenfeld agree with Merton that the success goal is pervasive in American culture. For them, the **American Dream** refers to both a goal and a process. As a goal, the American Dream involves accumulating material goods and wealth via open individual competition. As a process, it involves both being socialized to pursue material success and believing that prosperity is achievable in American culture. Anomic conditions arise because the desire to succeed at any cost drives people apart, weakens the collective sense of community, fosters ambition, and restricts the desire to achieve anything other than material wealth. Achieving respect, for example, is not sufficient.

Why does anomie pervade American culture? According to Messner and Rosenfeld, it is because institutions that might otherwise control the exaggerated emphasis on financial success, such as religious or charitable institutions, have been rendered powerless or obsolete. These social institutions have been undermined in three ways:

1. Noneconomic functions and roles have been devalued. Performance in other institutional settings—the family, school, or community—is assigned a lower priority than the goal of financial success.

2. When conflicts emerge, noneconomic roles become subordinate to and must accommodate economic roles. The schedules, routines, and demands of the workplace take priority over those of the home, the school, the community, and other aspects of social life.

3. Economic language, standards, and norms penetrate into noneconomic realms. Economic terms become part of the common vernacular: People want to get to the "bottom line." Spouses view themselves as "partners" who "manage" the household. Retired people say they want to "downsize" their household. We "outsource" home repairs instead of doing them ourselves. Corporate leaders run for public office promising to "run the country like a business."

---

anomie theory
View that anomie results when socially defined goals (such as wealth and power) are universally mandated but access to legitimate means (such as education and job opportunities) is stratified by class and status.

institutional anomie theory
The view that anomie pervades U.S. culture because the drive for material wealth dominates and undermines social and community values.

American Dream
The goal of accumulating material goods and wealth through individual competition; the process of being socialized to pursue material success and to believe it is achievable.

According to Messner and Rosenfeld, the relatively high American crime rates can be explained by the interrelationship of culture and institutions. At the cultural level, the dominance of the American Dream mythology ensures that many people will develop desires for material goods that cannot be satisfied by legitimate means. Anomie becomes a norm, and extralegal means become a strategy for attaining material wealth. At the institutional level, the dominance of economic concerns weakens the informal social control exerted by family, church, and school. These institutions have lost their ability to regulate behavior and have instead become a conduit for promoting material success. For example, schools are evaluated not for imparting knowledge but for their ability to train students to get high-paying jobs. Social conditions reinforce each other: culture determines institutions, and institutional change influences culture.[87] Crime rates may rise in a healthy economy because national prosperity heightens the attractiveness of monetary rewards, encouraging people to gain financial success by any means possible, including illegal ones. In this culture of competition, self-interest prevails and generates amorality, acceptance of inequality, and disdain for the less fortunate.[88]

Relative Deprivation Theory

There is ample evidence that neighborhood-level income inequality is a significant predictor of neighborhood crime rates.[89] Sharp divisions between the rich and the poor create an atmosphere of envy and mistrust. Criminal motivation is fueled both by perceived humiliation and the perceived right to humiliate a victim in return.[90] Psychologists warn that under these circumstances young males will begin to fear and envy "winners" who are doing very well at their expense. If they fail to take risky aggressive tactics, they are surely going to lose out in social competition and have little chance of future success.[91] These generalized feelings of **relative deprivation** are precursors to high crime rates.[92]

The concept of relative deprivation was proposed by sociologists Judith Blau and Peter Blau, who combined concepts from anomie theory with those found in social disorganization models.[93] According to the Blaus, lower-class people may feel both deprived and embittered when they compare their life circumstances to those of the more affluent. People who feel deprived because of their race or economic class eventually develop a sense of injustice and dis-

■ Sharp divisions between the rich and poor create an atmosphere of envy and mistrust. Criminal motivation is fueled both by perceived humiliation and the perceived right to humiliate a victim in return. People living in poverty may become enraged when they compare their social position and circumstances to the more affluent and powerful.

relative deprivation
Envy, mistrust, and aggression resulting from perceptions of economic and social inequality.

FIND IT ON INFOTRAC
College Edition

To read more about this topic, use "relative deprivation" as a subject guide.

Connections

Can relative deprivation concepts be applied to white-collar crime? Perhaps some of the individuals involved in the savings and loan scandals or Wall Street stock fraud cases felt relatively deprived and socially frustrated when they compared the paltry few millions they had already accumulated with the hundreds of millions held by wealthier people whom they envied. For more on this issue, see discussions of the savings and loan scandal and the causes of white-collar crime in Chapter 12.

Connections

The GST is not solely a cultural deviance theory because it recognizes non-class-related sources of strain. In this regard it is similar to the social process theories discussed in Chapter 7. It is included here because it incorporates the view that social class position can be an important source of strain, thus following in the tradition of Merton's theory of anomie.

general strain theory (GST)
The view that multiple sources of strain interact with an individual's emotional traits and responses to produce criminality.

negative affective states
Anger, frustration, and adverse emotions produced by a variety of sources of strain.

content. The less fortunate begin to distrust the society that has nurtured social inequality and obstructed their chances of progressing by legitimate means. The constant frustration that results from these feelings of inadequacy produces pent-up aggression and hostility, eventually leading to violence and crime. The effect of inequality may be greatest when the impoverished believe that they are becoming less able to compete in a society whose balance of economic and social power is shifting further toward the already affluent. Under these conditions, the relatively poor are increasingly likely to choose illegitimate life-enhancing activities. Crime rates may then spiral upward even if the relative size of the poor population does not increase.[94]

Relative deprivation is felt most acutely by African American youths because they consistently suffer racial discrimination and economic deprivation that place them in a lower status than other urban residents.[95] Wage inequality may motivate young African American males to enter the drug trade, an enterprise that increases the likelihood that they will become involved in violent crimes.[96]

In sum, according to the relative deprivation concept, people who perceive themselves as economically deprived relative to people they know, as well as to society in general, may begin to form negative self-feelings and hostility, which motivate them to engage in deviant and criminal behaviors.[97]

General Strain Theory (GST)

Sociologist Robert Agnew's **general strain theory (GST)** helps identify the micro- or individual-level influences of strain. Whereas Merton and Messner and Rosenfeld try to explain social class differences in the crime rate, Agnew tries to explain why individuals who feel stress and strain are likely to commit crimes. Agnew also offers a more general explanation of criminal activity among all elements of society rather than restricting his views to lower-class crime.[98]

Multiple Sources of Strain   Agnew suggests that criminality is the direct result of **negative affective states**—the anger, frustration, and adverse emotions that emerge in the wake of destructive social relationships. He finds that negative affective states are produced by a variety of sources of strain (see Figure 6.7):

■ **Failure to achieve positively valued goals.** This cause of strain, similar to what Merton speaks of in his theory of anomie, is a result of the disjunction between aspirations and expectations. This type of strain occurs when a youth aspires to wealth and fame but, lacking financial and educational resources, assumes that such goals are impossible to achieve; he then turns to crime and drug dealing.

■ **Disjunction of expectations and achievements.** Strain can also be produced by a disjunction between expectations and achievements. When people compare themselves to peers who seem to be doing a lot better financially or socially (such as making more money or getting better grades), even those doing relatively well feel strain. For example, when a high school senior is accepted at a good college but not a prestige school, like some of her friends, she will feel strain. Perhaps she is not being treated fairly because the playing field is tilted against her: "Other kids have connections," she may say. Perceptions of inequity may result in many adverse reactions, ranging from running away from its source to lowering others' benefits through physical attacks or property vandalism.

■ **Removal of positively valued stimuli.** Strain may occur because of the actual or anticipated loss of positively valued stimuli.[99] For example, the loss of a girl- or boyfriend can produce strain, as can the death of a loved one, moving to a new neighborhood or school, or the divorce or separation of paren

Figure 6.7
Elements of General Strain Theory
(GST)

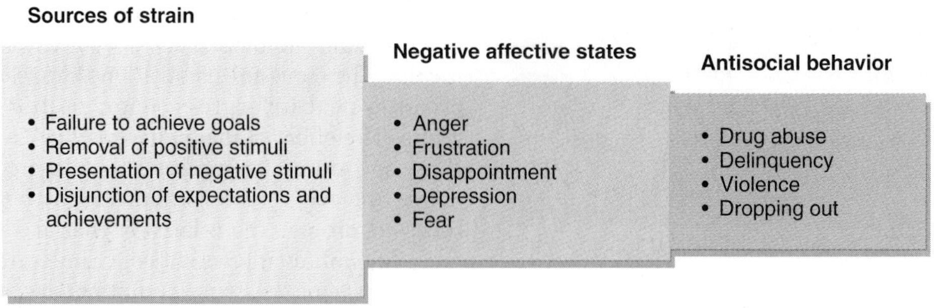

Sources of strain

- Failure to achieve goals
- Removal of positive stimuli
- Presentation of negative stimuli
- Disjunction of expectations and achievements

Negative affective states

- Anger
- Frustration
- Disappointment
- Depression
- Fear

Antisocial behavior

- Drug abuse
- Delinquency
- Violence
- Dropping out

The loss of positive stimuli may lead to delinquency as the adolescent tries to prevent the loss, retrieve what has been lost, obtain substitutes, or seek revenge against those responsible for the loss.

■ **Presentation of negative stimuli.** Strain may also be caused by negative or noxious stimuli, such as child abuse or neglect, crime victimization, physical punishment, family or peer conflict, school failure, or stressful life events ranging from verbal threats to air pollution. For example, adolescent delinquency has been linked to maltreatment through the rage and anger it generates. Children who are abused at home may take out their rage on younger children at school or become involved in violent delinquency.[100]

Although these sources of strain are independent of one another, they may overlap. For example, if a teacher insults a student, it may be viewed as an unfair application of negative stimuli that interferes with a student's academic aspirations. The greater the intensity and frequency of strain experiences, the greater their impact and the more likely they are to cause delinquency.

The Consequences of Strain   According to Agnew, each type of strain increases the likelihood of experiencing such negative emotions as disappointment, depression, fear, and most importantly, anger. Anger increases perceptions of injury and of being wronged. It produces a desire for revenge, energizes individuals to take action, and lowers inhibitions. Violence and aggression seem justified if you have been wronged and are righteously angry. Because it produces these emotions, chronic, repetitive strain can be considered a predisposing factor for delinquency when it creates a hostile, suspicious, aggressive attitude. Individual strain episodes may trigger delinquency, such as when a particularly stressful event ignites a violent reaction.

Kids who report feelings of stress and anger are more likely to interact with delinquent peers and engage in criminal behaviors.[101] They may join deviant groups and gangs whose law-violating activities produce even more strain and pressure to commit even more crime. For example, the angry youngster who gets involved with substance abusing peers may feel forced to go on unwanted shoplifting sprees to pay for drugs.[102]

Coping with Strain   Not all people who experience strain eventually resort to criminality. Some are able to marshal their emotional, mental, and behavioral resources to cope with the anger and frustration produced by strain. Some individuals may be able to rationalize frustrating circumstances: Getting a good job is "just not that important"; they may be poor, but the "next guy is worse off"; if things didn't work out, they "got what they deserved." Others seek behavioral solutions, running away from adverse conditions or seeking revenge against those who caused the strain. Some try to regain emotional equilibrium with techniques ranging from physical exercise to drug abuse.

However, some people cannot cope with strain because they have traits that make them particularly sensitive to strain. Juveniles high in negative emotionality and low in constraint will be more likely to react to strain with

FIND IT ON INFOTRAC
College Edition

To read about how strain influences teen suicide, see:

Toni Terling Watt and Susan Sharp, "Gender Differences in Strains Associated with Suicidal Behavior among Adolescents," *Journal of Youth and Adolescence* June 2001 v30 i3 p333–18

✔ Checkpoints

✔ Strain theories hold that economic deprivation causes frustration, which leads to crime.

✔ According to Merton's anomie theory, many people who desire material goods and other forms of economic success lack the means to achieve their goals. Some may turn to crime.

✔ Messner and Rosenfeld's institutional anomie theory argues that the goal of success at all costs has invaded every aspect of American life.

✔ Agnew's general theory of strain suggests that there is more than one source of anomie.

To quiz yourself on this material, go to questions 6.9–6.11 on the Criminology: The Core 2e Web site.

antisocial behaviors.[103] Kids with a tendency toward depression, anxiety, and poor reaction to stress, who have an explosive temperament, low tolerance for adversity, poor problem-solving skills, and who are overly sensitive or emotional are less likely to cope well with strain.

Although these traits, which are linked to aggressive, antisocial behavior, seem to be stable over the life cycle, they may peak during adolescence.[104] This is a period of social stress caused by weakening parental supervision and the development of relationships with a diverse peer group. Many adolescents going through the trauma of family breakup and frequent changes in family structure feel a high degree of strain. They may react by becoming involved in precocious sexuality or by turning to substance abuse to mask the strain.[105]

As children mature, their expectations increase. Some are unable to meet academic and social demands. Adolescents are very concerned about their standing with peers. Teenagers who are deficient in these areas may find they are social outcasts, another source of strain. In adulthood, crime rates may drop because these sources of strain are reduced. New sources of self-esteem emerge, and adults seem more likely to align their goals with reality.

Evaluating GST Agnew's important work both clarifies the concept of strain and directs future research agendas. It also adds to the body of literature describing how social and life history events influence offending patterns. Because sources of strain vary over the life course, so too do crime rates.

There is also empirical support for GST.[106] Some research efforts have shown that indicators of strain—family breakup, unemployment, moving, feelings of dissatisfaction with friends and school, dropping out of school—are positively related to criminality.[107] As predicted by GST, people who report feelings of stress and anger are more likely to interact with delinquent peers and to engage in criminal behaviors.[108] Lashing out at others may reduce feelings of strain, as may stealing or vandalizing property.[109] There is also evidence that, as predicted by the GST, people who fail to meet success goals are more likely to engage in criminal activities.[110] Agnew himself has recently found evidence that experiencing violent victimization and anticipating future victimization are associated with antisocial behavior.[111] This finding indicates that not only is strain produced by actual experiences but it may result from anticipated ones as well.

Concept Summary 6.2 reviews major concepts and theories of the strain perspective. ✔ Checkpoints

CONCEPT SUMMARY 6.2 Strain Theories

THEORY	MAJOR PREMISE	STRENGTHS	RESEARCH FOCUS
Anomie theory	People who adopt the goals of society but lack the means to attain them seek alternatives, such as crime.	Points out how competition for success creates conflict and crime. Suggests that social conditions and not personality can account for crime. Explains high lower-class crime rates.	Frustration; anomie; effects of failure to achieve goals
Institutional anomie theory	Material goods pervade all aspects of American life.	Explains why crime rates are so high in American culture.	Frustration; effects of materialism
Relative deprivation theory	Crime occurs when the wealthy and poor live close to one another.	Explains high crime rates in deteriorated inner-city areas located near more affluent neighborhoods.	Relative deprivation
General strain theory	Strain has a variety of sources. Strain causes crime in the absence of adequate coping mechanisms.	Identifies the complexities of strain in modern society. Expands on anomie theory. Shows the influence of social events on behavior over the life course. Explains middle-class crimes.	Strain; inequality; negative affective states; influence of negative and positive stimuli

Cultural Deviance Theory

The third branch of social structure theory combines the effects of social disorganization and strain to explain how people living in deteriorated neighborhoods react to social isolation and economic deprivation. Because their lifestyle is draining, frustrating, and dispiriting, members of the lower class create an independent subculture with its own set of rules and values. Whereas middle-class culture stresses hard work, delayed gratification, formal education, and being cautious, the lower-class subculture stresses excitement, toughness, taking risks, fearlessness, immediate gratification, and street smarts.

The lower-class subculture is an attractive alternative because the urban poor find it impossible to meet the behavioral demands of middle-class society. However, subcultural norms often clash with conventional values. Urban dwellers are forced to violate the law because they obey the rules of the deviant culture with which they are in immediate contact (see Figure 6.8).

More than 40 years ago, sociologist Walter Miller identified the unique conduct norms that help define lower-class culture.[112] Miller referred to them as **focal concerns,** values that have evolved specifically to fit conditions in lower-class environments. The major lower-class focal concerns are set out in Exhibit 6.1.[113]

Figure 6.8
Elements of Cultural Deviance Theory

Poverty
- Lack of opportunity
- Feeling of oppression

Socialization
Lower-class youths are socialized to value middle-class goals and ideas. However, their environment inhibits proper socialization and attainment of goals.

Subculture
Blocked opportunities prompt formation of groups with alternative lifestyles and values.

Gang formation
Gangs provide alternative methods of gaining success for some, venting anger for others.

Crime and delinquency
New methods of gaining success involve law-violating behavior.

Criminal careers
Some gang boys can parlay their status into criminal careers; others become drug users or violent assaulters.

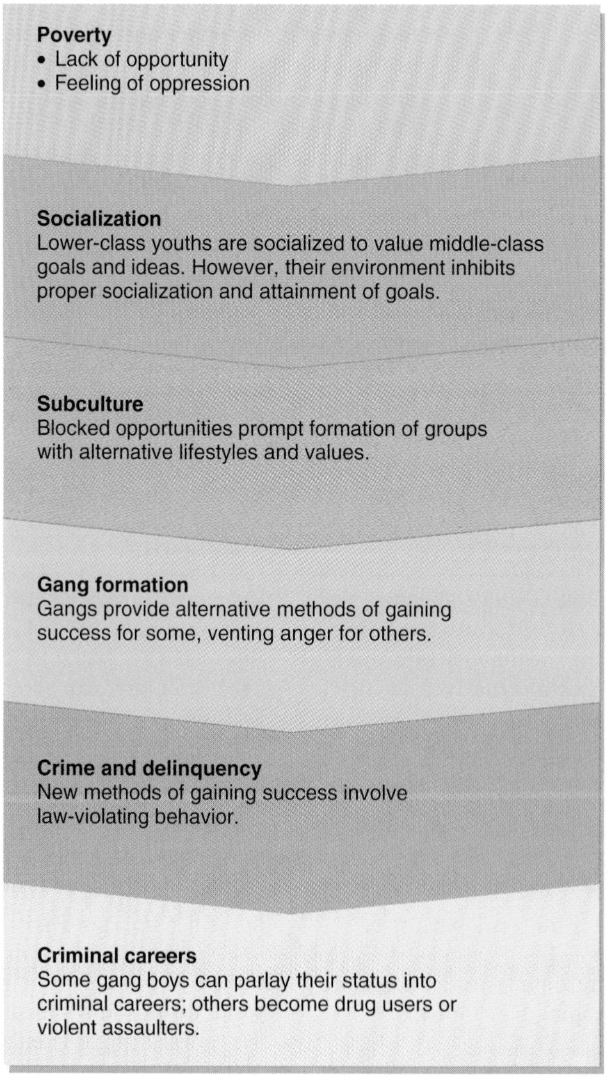

focal concerns
Values, such as toughness and street smarts, that have evolved specifically to fit conditions in lower-class environments.

EXHIBIT	6.1 Miller's Lower-Class Focal Concerns
Trouble	In lower-class communities, people are evaluated by their actual or potential involvement in making trouble. Getting into trouble includes such behaviors as fighting, drinking, and sexual misconduct. Dealing with trouble can confer prestige—for example, when a man establishes a reputation for being able to handle himself well in a fight. Not being able to handle trouble, and having to pay the consequences, can make a person look foolish and incompetent.
Toughness	Lower-class males want local recognition of their physical and spiritual toughness. They refuse to be sentimental or soft and instead value physical strength, fighting ability, and athletic skill. Those who cannot meet these standards risk getting a reputation for being weak, inept, and effeminate.
Smartness	Members of the lower-class culture want to maintain an image of being streetwise and savvy, using their street smarts, and having the ability to outfox and out-con the opponent. Although formal education is not admired, knowing essential survival techniques, such as gambling, conning, and outsmarting the law, is a requirement.
Excitement	Members of the lower class search for fun and excitement to enliven an otherwise drab existence. The search for excitement may lead to gambling, fighting, getting drunk, and sexual adventures. In between, the lower-class citizen may simply "hang out" and "be cool."
Fate	Lower-class citizens believe their lives are in the hands of strong spiritual forces that guide their destinies. Getting lucky, finding good fortune, and hitting the jackpot are all slum dwellers' daily dreams.
Autonomy	Being independent of authority figures, such as the police, teachers, and parents, is required; losing control is an unacceptable weakness, incompatible with toughness.

SOURCE: Walter Miller, "Lower-Class Culture as a Generating Milieu of Gang Delinquency," *Journal of Social Issues* 14 (1958): 5–19.

According to Miller, clinging to lower-class focal concerns promotes illegal or violent behavior. Toughness may mean displaying fighting prowess; street smarts may lead to drug deals; excitement may result in drinking, gambling, or drug abuse.[114] To illustrate, consider a recent study of violent young men in New York. Sociologist Jeffrey Fagan found that the most compelling function that violence served was to develop status as a "tough," an identity that helps young men acquire social power while at the same time insulating them from becoming victims. Violence was also seen as a means to acquire the trappings of wealth (such as nice clothes, flashy cars, or access to clubs), control or humiliate another person, defy authority, settle drug-related disputes, attain retribution, satisfy the need for thrills or risk taking, and respond to challenges to one's manhood.[115] Lower-class focal concerns seem as relevant today as when they were first identified by Miller more than 40 years ago!

Theory of Delinquent Subcultures

Albert Cohen first articulated the theory of **delinquent subcultures** in his classic 1955 book, *Delinquent Boys*.[116] Cohen's central position was that delinquent behavior of lower-class youths is actually a protest against the norms and values of middle-class U.S. culture. Because social conditions prevent them from achieving success legitimately, lower-class youths experience a form of culture conflict that Cohen labels **status frustration**.[117] As a result, many of them join gangs and engage in behavior that is "non-utilitarian, malicious, and negativistic."[118]

Cohen viewed the delinquent gang as a separate subculture, possessing a value system directly opposed to that of the larger society. He described the subculture as one that "takes its norms from the larger culture, but turns them upside down. The delinquent's conduct is right by the standards of his subculture precisely because it is wrong by the norms of the larger culture."[119]

According to Cohen, the development of the delinquent subculture is a consequence of socialization practices in lower-class environments. Here children lack the basic skills necessary to achieve social and economic success, including a proper education, which renders them incapable of developing

delinquent subculture
A value system adopted by lower-class youths that is directly opposed to that of the larger society.

status frustration
A form of culture conflict experienced by lower-class youths because social conditions prevent them from achieving success as defined by the larger society.

skills to succeed in society. Lower-class parents are incapable of teaching children the necessary techniques for entering the dominant middle-class culture. The consequences of this deprivation include developmental handicaps, poor speech and communication skills, and inability to delay gratification.

Middle-Class Measuring Rods   One significant handicap that lower-class children face is the inability to positively impress authority figures, such as teachers, employers, or supervisors. In U.S. society, these positions tend to be held by members of the middle class, who have difficulty relating to the lower-class youngster. Cohen calls the standards set by these authority figures **middle-class measuring rods.**

The conflict and frustration lower-class youths experience when they fail to meet these standards is a primary cause of delinquency. They may find themselves prejudged by others and not measuring up in the final analysis. Negative evaluations become part of a permanent file that follows an individual for the rest of his or her life. When the individual wants to improve, evidence of prior failures is used to discourage advancement.

The Formation of Deviant Subcultures   Cohen believes that lower-class boys rejected by middle-class decision makers usually join one of three existing subcultures: the corner boy, the college boy, or the delinquent boy.

The *corner boy* role is the most common response to middle-class rejection. The corner boy is not a chronic delinquent but may be a truant who engages in petty or status offenses, such as precocious sex and recreational drug abuse. His main loyalty is to his peer group, on which he depends for support, motivation, and interest. His values, therefore, are those of the group with which he is in close contact. The corner boy, well aware of his failure to achieve the standards of the American Dream, retreats into the comforting world of his lower-class peers and eventually becomes a stable member of his neighborhood, holding a menial job, marrying, and remaining in the community.

The *college boy* embraces the cultural and social values of the middle class. Rather than scorning middle-class measuring rods, he actively strives to succeed by those standards. Cohen views this type of youth as one who is embarking on an almost hopeless path because he is ill-equipped academically, socially, and linguistically to achieve the rewards of middle-class life.

The *delinquent boy* adopts a set of norms and principles that directly oppose middle-class values. He engages in short-run hedonism, living for today and letting "tomorrow take care of itself."[120] Delinquent boys strive for group autonomy. They resist efforts by family, school, or other sources of authority to control their behavior. Frustrated by their inability to succeed, these boys resort to a process Cohen calls **reaction formation,** including overly intense responses that seem disproportionate to the stimuli that trigger them. For the delinquent boy, this takes the form of irrational, malicious, and unaccountable hostility to the enemy, which in this case is "the norms of respectable middle-class society."[121]

Cohen's approach skillfully integrates strain and social disorganization theories and has become an enduring element of criminological literature.

Theory of Differential Opportunity

In their classic work *Delinquency and Opportunity,* written more than 40 years ago, Richard Cloward and Lloyd Ohlin combined strain and social disorganization principles to portray a gang-sustaining criminal subculture.[122]

The centerpiece of the Cloward and Ohlin theory is the concept of **differential opportunity.** According to this concept, people in all strata of society share the same success goals; however, those in the lower class have limited means of achieving them. People who perceive themselves as failures within conventional society will seek alternative or innovative ways to succeed. People who conclude that there is little hope for legitimate advancement may join like-minded peers to form a gang, which can provide them with emo-

middle-class measuring rods
The standards by which authority figures, such as teachers and employers, evaluate lower-class youngsters and often prejudge them negatively.

reaction formation
Irrational hostility evidenced by young delinquents, who adopt norms directly opposed to middle-class goals and standards that seem impossible to achieve.

differential opportunity
The view that lower-class youths, whose legitimate opportunities are limited, join gangs and pursue criminal careers as alternative means to achieve universal success goals.

tional support. The youth who is considered a failure at school and is qualified for only a menial job at a minimum wage can earn thousands of dollars plus the respect of his or her peers by joining a gang and engaging in drug deals or armed robberies.

Cloward and Ohlin recognize that the opportunity for success in both conventional and criminal careers is limited. In stable areas, adolescents may be recruited by professional criminals, drug traffickers, or organized crime groups. Unstable areas, however, cannot support flourishing criminal opportunities. In these socially disorganized neighborhoods, adult role models are absent, and young criminals have few opportunities to join established gangs or learn the fine points of professional crime. Their most important finding, then, is that all opportunities for success, both illegal and conventional, are closed for the most disadvantaged youths.

Because of differential opportunity, young people are likely to join one of three types of gangs.

1. **Criminal gangs.** Criminal gangs exist in stable neighborhoods where close connections among adolescent, young adult, and adult offenders create an environment for successful criminal enterprise.[123] Youths are recruited into established criminal gangs that provide training for a successful criminal career. Gang membership is a learning experience in which the knowledge and skills needed for success in crime are acquired. During this apprenticeship, older, more experienced members of the criminal subculture hold youthful trainees on tight reins, limiting activities that might jeopardize the gang's profits (for example, engaging in nonfunctional, irrational violence).

2. **Conflict gangs.** Conflict gangs develop in communities unable to provide either legitimate or illegitimate opportunities.[124] These gangs attract tough adolescents who fight with weapons to win respect from rivals and engage in unpredictable and destructive assaults on people and property. Conflict gang members must be ready to fight to protect their own and their gang's integrity and honor. By doing so, they acquire a "rep," which gains admiration from their peers and consequently helps them develop their self-image.

3. **Retreatist gangs.** Retreatists are double failures, unable to gain success through legitimate means and unwilling to do so through illegal ones. Members of the retreatist subculture constantly search for ways of getting high—alcohol, pot, heroin, unusual sexual experiences, music. To feed their habits, retreatists develop a "hustle"—pimping, conning, selling drugs, or committing petty crimes. Personal status in the retreatist subculture is derived from peer approval.

Cloward and Ohlin's theory integrates cultural deviance and social disorganization variables and recognizes different modes of criminal adaptation. The fact that criminal cultures can be supportive, rational, and profitable seems to more realistically reflect the actual world of the delinquent than Cohen's original view of purely negativistic, destructive delinquent youths who oppose all social values.

Concept Summary 6.3 reviews the major concepts of cultural deviance theory. ✔ Checkpoints

✔ Checkpoints

✔ Cultural deviance theory shows how subcultures develop with norms in opposition to the general society.

✔ Walter Miller describes the focal concerns that shape this subculture.

✔ Albert Cohen analyzes the lifestyle of delinquent boys, revealing how they obey an independent social code with its own values.

✔ Cohen shows how members of the lower class fail when they are judged by "middle class measuring rods."

✔ Cloward and Ohlin find that deviant subcultures form when people believe that their legitimate opportunities are blocked or impaired.

✔ Crime prevention efforts have been aimed at increasing the conventional options for success open to members of the lower class.

To quiz yourself on this material, go to questions 6.12–6.15 on the Criminology: The Core 2e Web site.

Social Structure Theory and Public Policy

Social structure theory has significantly influenced public policy. If the cause of criminality is viewed as a schism between lower-class individuals and conventional goals, norms, and rules, it seems logical that alternatives to criminal behavior can be provided by giving inner-city youth opportunities to share in the rewards of conventional society.

One approach is to give indigent people direct financial aid through public assistance or welfare. Although welfare has been curtailed under the Federal Welfare Reform Act of 1996, research shows that crime rates decrease

CONCEPT SUMMARY **6.3 Cultural Deviance Theories**

THEORY	MAJOR PREMISE	STRENGTHS	RESEARCH FOCUS
Miller's focal concern theory	Citizens who obey the street rules of lower-class life (focal concerns) find themselves in conflict with the dominant culture.	Identifies the core values of lower-class culture and shows their association to crime.	Cultural norms; focal concerns
Cohen's theory of delinquent gangs	Status frustration of lower-class boys, created by their failure to achieve middle-class success, causes them to join gangs.	Shows how the conditions of lower-class life produce crime. Explains violence and destructive acts. Identifies conflict of lower class with middle class.	Gangs; culture conflict; middle-class measuring rods; reaction formation
Cloward and Ohlin's theory of opportunity	Blockage of conventional opportunities causes lower-class youths to join criminal, conflict, or retreatist gangs.	Shows that even illegal opportunities are structured in society. Indicates why people become involved in a particular type of criminal activity. Presents a way of preventing crime.	Gangs; cultural norms; culture conflict; effects of blocked opportunity

when families receive supplemental income through public assistance payments.[125]

Efforts have also been made to reduce crime by improving the community structure in inner-city high-crime areas. Crime prevention efforts based on social structure precepts can be traced back to the Chicago Area Project supervised by Clifford R. Shaw. This program attempted to organize existing community structures to develop social stability in otherwise disorganized slums. The project sponsored recreation programs for neighborhood children, including summer camping. It campaigned for community improvements in such areas as education, sanitation, traffic safety, resource conservation, and law enforcement. Project members also worked with police and court agencies to supervise and treat gang youth and adult offenders.

■ According to structural theories, social programs may help reduce crime rates. However, there must be a major commitment of funds and resources if they are to be successful.

FIND IT ON INFOTRAC
College Edition

To find out more about Operation
Weed and Seed, use it in a key
word search.

Social structure concepts, especially Cloward and Ohlin's views, were a critical ingredient in the Kennedy and Johnson administrations' War on Poverty, begun in the early 1960s. War on Poverty programs—Head Start, Neighborhood Legal Services, and the Community Action Program—have continued to help people. Today the Weed and Seed program is a descendant of the social structure approach to crime prevention.

Summary

- Sociology has been the main orientation of criminologists because they know that crime rates vary among elements of the social structure, that society goes through changes that affect crime, and that social interaction relates to criminality.

- Social structure theories suggest that people's place in the socioeconomic structure influences their chances of becoming criminals.

- Poor people are more likely to commit crimes because they are unable to achieve monetary or social success in any other way.

- Social structure theory includes three schools of thought: social disorganization, strain, and cultural deviance theories.

- Social disorganization theory suggests that the urban poor violate the law because they live in areas in which social control has broken down. The origin of social disorganization theory can be traced to the work of Clifford R. Shaw and Henry D. McKay. Shaw and McKay concluded that disorganized areas, marked by divergent values and transitional populations, produce criminality. Modern social ecology theory looks at such issues as community fear, unemployment, and deterioration.

- Strain theories view crime as resulting from the anger people experience over their inability to achieve legitimate social and economic success.

- Strain theories hold that most people share common values and beliefs, but the ability to achieve them is differentiated by the social structure.

- The best-known strain theory is Robert Merton's theory of anomie, which describes what happens when people have inadequate means to satisfy their goals.

- Steven Messner and Richard Rosenfeld show that the core values of American culture produces strain.

- Robert Agnew suggests that strain has multiple sources and is linked to anger and frustration that people endure when their goals and aspirations are frustrated or when they lose something they value.

- Cultural deviance theories hold that a unique value system develops in lower-class areas. Lower-class values approve of behaviors such as being tough, never showing fear, and defying authority. People perceiving strain will bond together in their own groups or subcultures for support and recognition.

- Albert Cohen links the formation of subcultures to the failure of lower-class citizens to achieve recognition from middle-class decision makers, such as teachers, employers, and police officers.

- Richard Cloward and Lloyd Ohlin have argued that crime results from lower-class people's perception that their opportunity for success is limited. Consequently, youths in low-income areas may join criminal, conflict, or retreatist gangs.

Thinking Like a Criminologist

You have accepted a position in Washington as an assistant to the undersecretary of urban affairs. The secretary informs you that he wants to initiate a demonstration project in a major city to show that government can reduce poverty, crime, and drug abuse.

The area he has chosen is a large inner-city neighborhood in a Midwestern city of more than 3 million people. It suffers disorganized community structure, poverty, and hopelessness. Predatory delinquent gangs run free, terrorizing local merchants and citizens. The school system has failed to provide opportunities and educational experiences sufficient to dampen enthusiasm for gang recruitment. Stores, homes, and public buildings are deteriorated and decayed. Commercial enterprise has fled the area, and civil servants are reluctant to enter the neighborhood. There is an uneasy truce among the varied ethnic and racial groups that populate the area. Residents feel that little can be done to bring the neighborhood back to life. Merchants are afraid to open stores, and there is little outside development from major retailers or manufacturers. People who want to start their own businesses find that banks will not lend them money.

One of the biggest problems has been the large housing projects built in the 1960s. These are now overcrowded and deteriorated. Police are actually afraid to enter the buildings unless they arrive with a SWAT team. Each building is controlled by a gang whose members demand tribute from the residents.

You are asked to propose an urban redevelopment program to revitalize the area and eventually bring down the crime rate. You can bring any public or private element to bear on this overwhelming problem. You can also ask private industry to help in the struggle, promising them tax breaks for their participation. What programs would you recommend to break the cycle of urban poverty?

Go to the Criminology: The Core 2e Web site to review the content of this chapter.

Doing Research on the Web

For an up-to-date list of URLs, go to

http://www.cj.wadsworth.com/siegel_crimcore2e

Here are a few sites that can help you design your program. To read about what some communities have done to reduce their crime rates, go to the Operation Weed and Seed Home page and look at their publications:

http://www.ojp.usdoj.gov/eows/

The Design Out Crime program was used in Los Angeles to reduce crime by changing the design of buildings and public spaces. Read about it:

http://www.lapdonline.org/bldg_safer_comms/ design_out_crime.htm

New York State Division of Housing and Community Renewal also has information on this:

http://www.dhcr.state.ny.us/ohm/progs/antidrug/ ohmprgan.htm

Pro/Con discussions and Viewpoint Essays on some of the topics in this chapter may be found at the Opposing Viewpoints Resource Center:

http://www.gale.com/OpposingViewpoints

Key Terms

stratified society 126
social class 126
truly disadvantaged 128
culture of poverty 129
underclass 129
social structure theory 130
social disorganization theory 130
strain theory 130
strain 131
cultural deviance theory 131

subculture 132
cultural transmission 132
transitional neighborhood 132
concentration effect 136
collective efficacy 136
social altruism 138
anomie 139
anomie theory 141
institutional anomie theory 141
American Dream 141

relative deprivation 142
general strain theory (GST) 143
negative affective states 143
focal concerns 146
delinquent subculture 147
status frustration 147
middle-class measuring rods 148
reaction formation 148
differential opportunity 148

Critical Thinking Questions

1. Is there a "transitional" area in your town or city? Does the crime rate remain constant there, regardless of who moves in or out?

2. Is it possible that a distinct lower-class culture exists? Do you know anyone who has the focal concerns Miller talks about? Were there "focal concerns" in your high school or college experience?

3. Have you ever perceived anomie? What causes anomie? Is there more than one cause of strain?

4. How would Merton explain middle-class crime? How would Agnew?

5. Could "relative deprivation" produce crime among college-educated white-collar workers?

CHAPTER 7

Social Process Theories: Socialized to Crime

Chapter Objectives

1. Be familiar with the concept of socialization.
2. Discuss the effect of schools, family, and friends on crime.
3. Be able to discuss the differences between learning, control, and reaction.
4. Be familiar with the concept of differential association.
5. Be able to discuss what is meant by a definition toward criminality.
6. Understand the concept of neutralization.
7. Be able to discuss the relationship between self-concept and crime.
8. Know the elements of the social bond.
9. Describe the labeling process.
10. Be familiar with the concepts of primary and secondary deviance.
11. Show how the process of labeling leads to criminal careers.

NDER THE ALASKA SEX OF-
FENDER REGISTRATION ACT,
AN INCARCERATED SEX OF-
FENDER OR CHILD KIDNAPPER

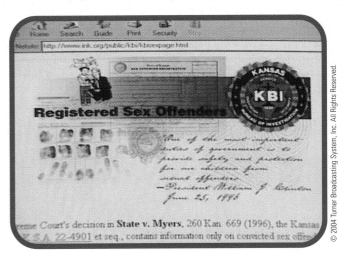

must register with the Department
of Corrections within 30 days before
release. The law requires that the
offender's name, aliases, address,
photograph, and physical description
be published on the Internet. Both
the Act's registration and notification
requirements were made retroactive

CNN. View the CNN video clip of this story and answer
related critical thinking questions on your
Criminology: The Core 2e CD.

to previously convicted offenders. In a recent case, *Smith v. Doe,* the Supreme Court upheld
the Alaska Sex Offender Registration Act's requirement that offenders who had been incarcerated prior to its passage be made to conform to its provisions.[1] Reasoning that the law
was nonpunitive, the Court ruled that the Alaska legislature's intent was to protect the public from
sex offenders.

While some lawmakers may view sex offender registration as an effective method of
alerting citizens to the presence of dangerous predators in their community, such methods
may also have their downside. Sex registration stigmatizes people who have already
paid their debt to society and labels them as a continuing threat despite the fact that
correctional authorities have ordered their release. Is it possible that such drastic measures,
which turn former offenders into social outcasts, might actually encourage rather than deter
deviant behaviors?

o some criminologists, an individual's relationship with critical elements of the social process is the key to understanding the onset and
continuation of criminal behaviors. They believe that criminality is a
function of individual socialization and the interactions people have
with various organizations, institutions, and processes of society.
Most people are influenced by their family relationships, peer group
associations, educational experiences, and interactions with authority figures, including teachers, employers, and agents of the justice
system.

Socialization and Crime

Some criminologists focus their attention on social-psychological processes and interactions common to people in all segments of the social structure, not just the lower class. They believe criminality is a function of individual **socialization** and the interactions people have with various organizations, institutions, and processes of society. Most people are influenced by their family relationships, peer group associations, educational experiences, and interactions with authority figures, including teachers, employers, and agents of the justice system. If these relationships are positive and supportive, people can succeed within the rules of society; if these relationships are dysfunctional and destructive, conventional success may be impossible, and criminal solutions may become a feasible alternative. Taken together, this view of crime is referred to as **social process theory.**

Social process theories share one basic concept: All people, regardless of their race, class, or gender, have the potential to become delinquents or criminals. Although members of the lower class may have the added burdens of poverty, racism, poor schools, and disrupted family lives, these social forces can be counteracted by positive peer relations, a supportive family, and educational success. In contrast, even the most affluent members of society may turn to antisocial behavior if their life experiences are intolerable or destructive.

Social process theories have endured because the relationship between social class and crime is still uncertain. Most residents of inner-city areas refrain from criminal activity, and few of those that commit crimes persist into adulthood. If poverty were the sole cause of crime, then indigent adults would be as criminal as indigent teenagers. But we know that, regardless of class position, most people age out of crime. The association between economic status and crime is problematic because class position alone cannot explain crime rates.[2] Simply living in a violent neighborhood does not produce violent children; research shows that family, peer, and individual characteristics play a large role in predicting violence in childhood.[3]

Criminologists have long studied the critical elements of socialization to determine how they contribute to a burgeoning criminal career. Prominent among these elements are family, peer group, school, and church.

Connections

Chapter 2's analysis of the class–crime relationship showed why this relationship is still a hotly debated topic. Although serious criminals may be found disproportionately in lower-class areas, self-report studies show that criminality cuts across class lines. Middle class use and abuse of recreational drugs, discussed in Chapter 13, suggests that law violators are not necessarily economically motivated.

Family Relations

Family relationships are considered a major determinant of behavior.[4] In fact, parenting factors, such as the ability to communicate and provide proper discipline, may play a critical role in determining whether people misbehave as children and even later as adults. The family–crime relationship is significant across racial, ethnic, and gender lines and is one of the most replicated findings in the criminological literature.[5]

Parents who are supportive and effectively control their children in a noncoercive fashion are more likely to raise children who refrain from delinquency; this is referred to as **parental efficacy.**[6] Delinquency will be reduced if parents provide the type of structure that integrates children into families while giving them the ability to assert their individuality and regulate their own behavior.[7] Children who have warm and affectionate ties to their parents report greater levels of self-esteem beginning in adolescence and extending into their adulthood; high self-esteem is inversely related to criminal behavior.[8]

Other family factors that have predictive value include the following:

1. Inconsistent discipline, poor supervision, and the lack of a warm, loving, supportive parent–child relationship are all associated with delinquency.[9]

socialization
Process of human development and enculturation. Socialization is influenced by key social processes and institutions.

social process theory
The view that criminality is a function of people's interactions with various organizations, institutions, and processes in society.

parental efficacy
Parents who are supportive and effectively control their children in a noncoercive fashion.

FIND IT ON INFOTRAC
College Edition

What values are being transmitted as children are being socialized in the home? Do kids really understand their parents? To find out, read:

Ariel Knafo and Shalom Schwartz, "Parenting and Adolescents' Accuracy in Perceiving Parental Values," *Child Development*, 74 (2003): 595–611

■ According to social process theories, a positive educational experience helps protect at-risk kids from crime. Ruth Esparza, 28, poses with her daughter, Fancy Zaldivar, in East Wenatchee, Washington, February 15, 2003. Esparza, who was a Wenatchee High School dropout, has gone back to school and is now a first-year student at Gonzaga Law School in Spokane, Washington. Esparza, a single mother, went back to school in 1997 because she had her daughter. "I knew I didn't want my daughter to have an ignorant mom," Esparza said. "She's my motivation."

Connections

As you may recall from Chapter 2, most juveniles age out of crime and do not become adult offenders. Having delinquent friends may help to retard this process. According to the social process view, a chronic offender may have learned a delinquent way of life from his or her peer group members.

2. Adolescents who do not receive affection from their parents during childhood are more likely to use illicit drugs and be more aggressive as they mature.[10]

3. Children growing up in homes where a parent suffers mental impairment are also at risk for delinquency.[11]

4. Children whose parents abuse drugs are more likely to become persistent substance abusers than the children of nonabusers.[12]

5. Children who experience abuse, neglect, or sexual abuse are believed to be more crime prone.[13]

6. Children who grow up in homes where parents use severe discipline yet lack warmth and involvement in their lives are prone to antisocial behavior.[14] Links have been found among corporal punishment, delinquency, anger, spousal abuse, depression, and adult crime.[15]

Educational Experience

The educational process and adolescent school achievement have been linked to criminality. Children who do poorly in school, lack educational motivation, and feel alienated are the most likely to engage in criminal acts.[16] Children who fail in school offend more frequently than those who succeed. These children commit more serious and violent offenses and persist in crime into adulthood.[17]

Schools contribute to criminality by labeling problem youths, which sets them apart from conventional society. One way in which they perpetuate this stigmatization is through the track system, which identifies some students as college-bound and others as academic underachievers or potential dropouts.[18] Research findings over the past two decades indicate that many school dropouts, especially those who have been expelled, face a significant chance of entering a criminal career.[19]

Peer Relations

Psychologists have long recognized that peer groups powerfully affect human conduct and can dramatically influence decision making and behavior choices.[20] Children who are rejected by their peers are more likely to display aggressive behavior and to disrupt group activities through bickering, bullying, or other antisocial behavior.[21] Research shows that adolescents who report inadequate or strained peer relations, and who say they are not popular with the opposite sex, are most likely to become delinquent.[22]

Because delinquent friends tend to be, as criminologist Mark Warr puts it, "sticky" (once acquired, they are not easily lost), peer influence may continue through the life span.[23] The more antisocial the peer group, the more likely its members are to engage in delinquency. Nondelinquent friends help to moderate delinquency.[24] People who maintain close relations with antisocial peers will sustain their own criminal behavior into adulthood. If peer influence diminishes, so too does criminal activity.[25]

Religious Belief

Logic would dictate that people who hold high moral values and beliefs, who have learned to distinguish right from wrong, and who regularly attend religious services should also eschew crime and other antisocial behaviors.

Religion binds people together and forces them to confront the consequences of their behavior. Committing crimes would violate the principles of all organized religions.

Recent research findings suggest that attending religious services does in fact have a significant negative impact on crime.[26] For example, kids living in disorganized high-crime areas who attend religious services are better able to resist illegal drug use than nonreligious youth.[27] Interestingly, participation seems to be a more significant inhibitor of crime than merely having religious beliefs and values. That is, actually attending religious services has a more dramatic effect on behavior than merely holding religious beliefs.[28]

The Effects of Socialization on Crime

According to the social process view, socialization is the key element in the formation of a criminal career. People living in even the most deteriorated urban areas can successfully resist inducements to crime if they have a positive self-image, strong moral values, and support from their parents, peers, teachers, and neighbors. The more social problems encountered during the socialization process, the greater the likelihood that youths will encounter difficulties and obstacles as they mature, such as being unemployed or becoming teenage parents.

The social process approach has several independent branches (see Figure 7.1). The first branch, **social learning theory,** suggests that people learn the techniques and attitudes of crime from close relationships with criminal peers: Crime is a learned behavior. The second branch, **social control theory,** maintains that everyone has the potential to become a criminal,

Figure 7.1

The Complex Web of Social Processes That Controls Human Behavior

social learning theory
The view that people learn to be aggressive by observing others acting aggressively to achieve some goal or being rewarded for violent acts.

social control theory
The view that people commit crime when the forces binding them to society are weakened or broken.

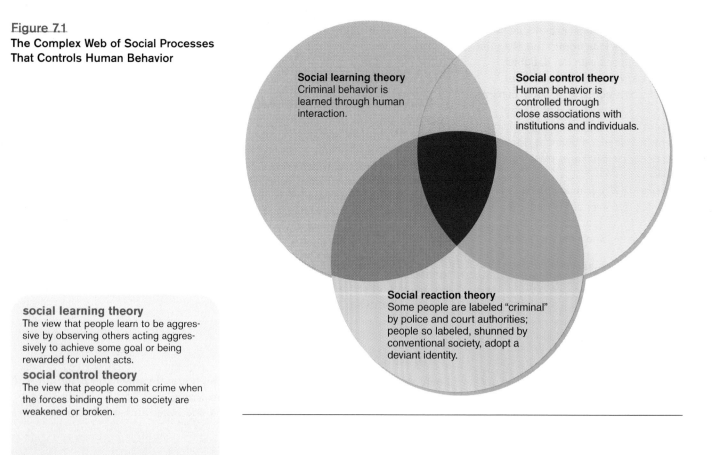

Social learning theory
Criminal behavior is learned through human interaction.

Social control theory
Human behavior is controlled through close associations with institutions and individuals.

Social reaction theory
Some people are labeled "criminal" by police and court authorities; people so labeled, shunned by conventional society, adopt a deviant identity.

but most people are controlled by their bonds to society. Crime occurs when the forces that bind people to society are weakened or broken. The third branch, **social reaction (labeling) theory,** says that people become criminals when significant members of society label them as such and they accept those labels as a personal identity.

Put another way, social learning theories assume that people are born good and learn to be bad; social control theory assumes that people are born bad and must be controlled in order to be good; and social reaction theory assumes that whether good or bad, people are controlled by the evaluations of others. Each of these independent branches will be discussed separately. ✔ Checkpoints

Social Learning Theories

Social learning theorists believe that crime is a product of learning the norms, values, and behaviors associated with criminal activity. Social learning can involve the actual techniques of crime (how to hot-wire a car or roll a joint) as well as the psychological aspects of criminality (how to deal with the guilt or shame associated with illegal activities). This section briefly reviews two of the most prominent forms of social learning theory: differential association theory and neutralization theory.

Differential Association Theory

One of the most prominent social learning theories is Edwin H. Sutherland's **differential association theory.** Often considered the preeminent U.S. criminologist, Sutherland first put forth his theory in 1939 in *Principles of Criminology.*[29] The final version of the theory appeared in 1947. When Sutherland died in 1950, his longtime associate Donald Cressey continued his work until his own death in 1987.

Sutherland's research on white-collar crime, professional theft, and intelligence led him to dispute the notion that crime was a function of the inadequacy of people in the lower classes.[30] He believed crime was a function of a learning process that could affect any individual in any culture. Acquiring a behavior is a socialization process, not a political or legal process. Skills and motives conducive to crime are learned as a result of contact with pro-crime values, attitudes, and definitions and other patterns of criminal behavior.

Principles of Differential Association Sutherland and Cressey explain the basic principles of differential association as follows:[31]

1. **Criminal behavior is learned.** This statement differentiates Sutherland's theory from prior attempts to classify criminal behavior as an inherent characteristic of criminals. Sutherland implies that criminality is learned in the same manner as any other learned behavior, such as writing, painting, or reading.

2. **Criminal behavior is learned as a by-product of interacting with others.** An individual does not start violating the law simply by living in a crimogenic environment or by manifesting personal characteristics associated with criminality, such as low IQ or family problems. People actively learn as they are socialized and interact with other individuals who serve as teachers and guides to crime. Thus, criminality cannot occur without the aid of others.

3. **Learning criminal behavior occurs within intimate personal groups.** People's contacts with their most intimate social companions—family, friends, peers—have the greatest influence on their deviant behavior and attitude development. Relationships with these influential individuals color and control the way individuals interpret everyday events. For example,

social reaction (labeling) theory
The view that people become criminals when labeled as such and when they accept the label as a personal identity.

differential association theory
The view that people commit crime when their social learning leads them to perceive more definitions favoring crime than favoring conventional behavior.

■ According to differential association theory, becoming a criminal is a learning process. Conversely, it may be possible to help troubled youth forgo criminality if they are taught prosocial behavior and attitudes. Here, brothers Hans (with daughter Jamile) and Ivan Hageman are shown outside the East Harlem School at Exodus House. The brothers gave up lucrative careers to run the school at the site of a former drug rehabilitation center. It has been described as a "nugget of hope within a neighborhood of despair."

children who grow up in homes where parents abuse alcohol are more likely to view drinking as socially and physically beneficial.[32]

4. **Learning criminal behavior involves assimilating the techniques of committing crime, including motives, drives, rationalizations, and attitudes.** Young delinquents learn from their associates the proper way to pick a lock, shoplift, and obtain and use narcotics. In addition, novice criminals learn the proper terminology for their acts and acquire approved reactions to law violations. Criminals must learn how to react properly to their illegal acts, such as when to defend them, rationalize them, or show remorse for them.

5. **The specific direction of motives and drives is learned from perceptions of various aspects of the legal code as favorable or unfavorable.** Because the reaction to social rules and laws is not uniform across society, people constantly meet others who hold different views on the utility of obeying the legal code. Some people they admire may openly disdain or flout the law or ignore its substance. People experience what Sutherland calls **culture conflict** when they are exposed to opposing attitudes toward right and wrong or moral and immoral. The conflict of social attitudes and cultural norms is the basis for the concept of differential association.

6. **A person becomes a criminal when he or she perceives more favorable than unfavorable consequences to violating the law.** According to Sutherland's theory, individuals become law violators when they are in contact with persons, groups, or events that produce an excess of definitions favorable toward criminality and are isolated from counteracting forces (see Figure 7.2). A definition favorable toward criminality occurs, for example, when a person hears friends talking about the virtues of getting high on drugs. A definition unfavorable toward crime occurs when friends or parents demonstrate their disapproval of crime.

7. **Differential associations may vary in frequency, duration, priority, and intensity.** Whether a person learns to obey the law or to disregard it is influenced by the quality of social interactions. Those of lasting duration have greater influence than those that are brief. Similarly, frequent contacts have greater effect than rare, haphazard contacts. *Priority* means the age of children when they first encounter definitions of criminality. Contacts made early in life probably have more influence than those developed later on. Finally, *intensity* is generally interpreted to mean the importance and prestige attrib-

culture conflict
Result of exposure to opposing norms, attitudes, and definitions of right and wrong, moral and immoral.

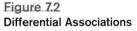
Figure 7.2
Differential Associations
Differential association theory suggests that criminal behavior will occur when the definitions favorable toward crime outweigh the unfavorable definitions.

uted to the individual or groups from whom the definitions are learned. For example, the influence of a father, mother, or trusted friend far outweighs the effect of more socially distant figures.

8. **The process of learning criminal behavior by association with criminal and anticriminal patterns involves all of the mechanisms that are involved in any other learning process.** Learning criminal behavior patterns is similar to learning nearly all other patterns and is not a matter of mere imitation.

9. **Although criminal behavior expresses general needs and values, it is not excused by those general needs and values because noncriminal behavior also expresses the same needs and values.** This principle suggests that the motives for criminal behavior cannot logically be the same as those for conventional behavior. Sutherland rules out such motives as desire to accumulate money or social status, personal frustration, or low self-concept as causes of crime because they are just as likely to produce noncriminal behavior, such as getting a better education or working harder on a job. Only the learning of deviant norms through contact with an excess of definitions favorable toward criminality produces illegal behavior.

In sum, differential association theory holds that people learn criminal attitudes and behavior during their adolescence from close, trusted friends or relatives. A criminal career develops if learned antisocial values and behaviors are not matched or exceeded by conventional attitudes and behaviors. Criminal behavior, then, is learned in a process that is similar to learning any other human behavior.

Testing Differential Association Theory Despite the importance of differential association theory, research devoted to testing its assumptions has been relatively sparse. It has proven difficult to conceptualize the principles

FIND IT ON INFOTRAC
College Edition

Use "differential association" as a subject guide to review some of the latest studies that test Sutherland's basic assumptions about human nature.

of the theory in a way that can be tested empirically. For example, social scientists find it difficult to evaluate such vague concepts as "definition favorable toward criminality." It is also difficult to follow people over time, establish precisely when definitions favorable toward criminality begin to outweigh prosocial definitions, and determine if this imbalance produces criminal behavior.

Despite these limitations, several notable research efforts have supported the core principles of this theory.[33] For example, family relations have been linked to criminality. Crime appears to be intergenerational: Kids whose parents are deviant and criminal are more likely to become criminal themselves and eventually produce criminal children.[34]

Peer relations is another cornerstone of differential association theory. Research shows that even at an early age kids who associate and presumably learn from aggressive peers are more likely to behave aggressively themselves.[35] As they mature, having delinquent friends who support criminal attitudes and behavior is strongly related to developing criminal careers.[36] Maintaining deviant peer relations and exposure to pro-crime definitions have been found to predict crimes ranging from computer offenses to drug trafficking.[37] Even kids who hold after-school jobs are at risk. They find that rather than being a "character building" experience as some believe, after-school employment exposes them to peers who drink and take drugs, factors that facilitate their own substance abuse.[38] These deviant peers interfere with the natural process of aging out of crime by helping provide the support that keeps kids in criminal careers.[39]

Analysis of Differential Association Theory   Differential association theory is important because it does not specify that criminals come from a disorganized area or are members of the lower class. Outwardly law-abiding, middle-class parents can encourage delinquent behavior by their own drinking, drug use, or family violence. The influence of differential associations is affected by social class; deviant learning experiences can affect youths in all classes.[40]

There are, however, a number of valid criticisms of Sutherland's work.[41] It fails to account for the origin of criminal definitions. How did the first "teacher" learn criminal attitudes and definitions in order to pass them on? Another criticism of differential association theory is that it assumes criminal and delinquent acts to be rational and systematic. This ignores spontaneous, wanton acts of violence and damage that appear to have little utility or purpose, such as the isolated psychopathic killing that is virtually unsolvable because of the killer's anonymity and lack of delinquent associations.

Some critics suggest that the theory is tautological: How can we know when a person has experienced an excess of definitions favorable toward criminality? When he or she commits a crime! Why do people commit crime? When they are exposed to an excess of criminal definitions!

Neutralization Theory

neutralization theory
The view that law violators learn to neutralize conventional values and attitudes, enabling them to drift back and forth between criminal and conventional behavior.

drift
Movement in and out of delinquency, shifting between conventional and deviant values.

neutralization techniques
Methods of rationalizing deviant behavior, such as denying responsibility or blaming the victim.

Neutralization theory is identified with the writings of David Matza and his associate Gresham Sykes.[42] These criminologists also view the process of becoming a criminal as a learning experience. They theorize that law violators must learn and master techniques that enable them to neutralize conventional values and attitudes, thus allowing them to drift back and forth between illegitimate and conventional behavior.

Neutralization theory points out that even the most committed criminals and delinquents are not involved in criminality all the time; they also attend schools, family functions, and religious services. Thus, their behavior falls along a continuum between total freedom and total restraint. This process of **drift,** or movement from one extreme to another, produces behavior that is sometimes unconventional or deviant and at other times constrained and sober.[43] Learning **neutralization techniques** allows a person to temporarily drift away from conventional behavior and become involved in antisocial behaviors, including crime and drug abuse.[44]

Neutralization Techniques Sykes and Matza suggest that people develop a distinct set of justifications for their law-violating behavior. They base their theoretical model on several observations:[45]

1. **Criminals sometimes voice guilt over their illegal acts.** If they truly embraced criminal or antisocial values, criminals would probably not exhibit remorse for their acts, other than regret at being apprehended.
2. **Offenders frequently respect and admire honest, law-abiding persons.** Those admired may include entertainers, sports figures, priests and other clergy, parents, teachers, and neighbors.
3. **Criminals define whom they can victimize.** Members of similar ethnic groups, churches, or neighborhoods are often off-limits. This practice implies that criminals are aware of the wrongfulness of their acts.
4. **Criminals are not immune to the demands of conformity.** Most criminals frequently participate in the same social functions as law-abiding people—for example, school, church, and family activities.

Sykes and Matza conclude that criminals must first neutralize accepted social values before they are free to commit crimes; they do so by learning a set of techniques that allow them to counteract the moral dilemmas posed by illegal behavior.[46]

Through their research, Sykes and Matza have identified the following techniques of neutralization:

- **Denial of responsibility.** Young offenders sometimes claim that their unlawful acts are not their fault—that they result from forces beyond their control or are accidents.

- **Denial of injury.** By denying the injury caused by their acts, criminals neutralize illegal behavior. For example, stealing is viewed as borrowing; vandalism is considered mischief that has gotten out of hand. Offenders may find that their parents and friends support their denial of injury. In fact, they may claim that the behavior was merely a prank, helping affirm the offender's perception that crime can be socially acceptable.

- **Denial of the victim.** Criminals sometimes neutralize wrongdoing by maintaining that the crime victim "had it coming." Vandalism may be directed against a disliked teacher or neighbor, or a gang may beat up homosexuals because their behavior is considered offensive.

- **Condemnation of the condemners.** An offender views the world as a corrupt place with a dog-eat-dog code. Because police and judges are on the take, teachers show favoritism, and parents take out their frustrations on their children, offenders claim it is ironic and unfair for these authorities to condemn criminal misconduct. By shifting the blame to others, criminals repress the feeling that their own acts are wrong.

- **Appeal to higher loyalties.** Novice criminals often argue that they are caught in the dilemma of being loyal to their peer group while attempting to abide by the rules of society. The needs of the group take precedence because group demands are immediate and localized (see Figure 7.3).

In sum, neutralization theory states that people neutralize conventional norms and values by using excuses that allow them to drift into crime.

Testing Neutralization Theory Attempts have been made to verify neutralization theory empirically, but the results have been inconclusive.[47] One area of research has been directed at determining whether law violators really need to neutralize moral constraints. The thinking behind this research

Connections

Denial of the victim may help explain hate crimes, in which people are victimized simply because they belong to the "wrong" race, religion, or ethnic group or because of their sexual orientation. Hate crimes are discussed in Chapter 10.

Figure 7.3
Techniques of Neutralization

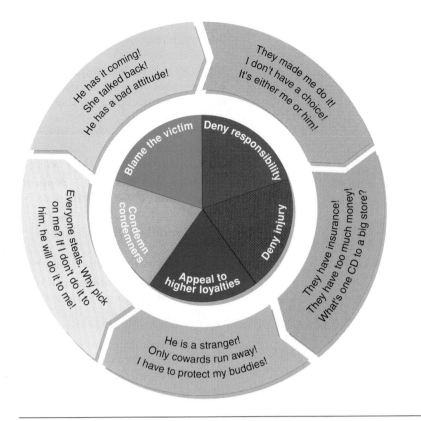

is that if criminals hold values in opposition to accepted social norms, then there is really no need to neutralize. So far, the evidence is mixed. Some studies show that law violators approve of criminal behavior such as theft and violence, whereas others find evidence that even though they may be active participants themselves, criminals voice disapproval of illegal behavior.[48] Some studies indicate that law violators approve of social values such as honesty and fairness; others come to the opposite conclusion.[49]

Although the existing research findings are ambiguous, the weight of the evidence shows that most adolescents generally disapprove of deviant behaviors such as violence, and that neutralizations do in fact enable youths to engage in socially disapproved behavior.[50] And, as Matza predicted, people seem to drift in and out of antisocial behavior rather than being committed solely to a criminal way of life.[51]

Are Learning Theories Valid?

Learning theories contribute significantly to our understanding of the onset of criminal behavior. Nonetheless, the general learning model has been criticized. One complaint is that learning theorists fail to account for the origin of criminal definitions. How did the first criminal learn the necessary techniques and definitions? Who came up with the original neutralization technique?

Learning theories imply that people systematically learn techniques that allow them to be active, successful criminals. However, they fail to adequately explain spontaneous, wanton acts of violence, damage, and other expressive crimes that appear to have little utility or purpose. Although principles of differential association can easily explain shoplifting, is it possible that a random shooting is caused by excessive deviant definitions? It is estimated that about 70 percent of all arrestees were under the influence of drugs and alcohol when they committed their crime. Do "crack heads" pause to neutralize their moral inhibitions before mugging a victim? Do drug-involved kids stop to consider what they have learned about moral values?[52]

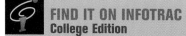

FIND IT ON INFOTRAC
College Edition

Do delinquents neutralize some
moral values more than others?
To find out, read:

J. A. Landsheer, H. T. Hart, and W. Kox,
"Delinquent Values and Victim Damage:
Exploring the Limits of Neutralization Theory,"
British Journal of Criminology, 34 (1994):
44–53

Little evidence exists that people learn the techniques that enable them to become criminals before they actually commit criminal acts. It is equally plausible that people who are already deviant seek others with similar lifestyles to learn from. Early onset of deviant behavior is now considered a key determinant of criminal careers. It is difficult to see how extremely young children have had the opportunity to learn criminal behavior and attitudes within a peer group setting.

Despite these criticisms, learning theories have an important place in the study of delinquent and criminal behavior. They help explain the important role that peers, family, and education play in shaping criminal and conventional behaviors. If crime were a matter of personal traits alone, it would be unlikely that these elements of socialization would play as important a role in determining human behavior as they do. And unlike social structure theories, learning theories are not limited to explaining a single facet of antisocial activity; they explain criminality across all class structures. Even corporate executives may be exposed to pro-criminal definitions and learn to neutralize moral constraints. Learning theories can thus be applied to a wide assortment of criminal activity.

Social Control Theory

Social control theorists maintain that all people have the potential to violate the law and that modern society presents many opportunities for illegal activity. Criminal activities, such as drug abuse and car theft, are often exciting pastimes that hold the promise of immediate reward and gratification.

Considering the attractions of crime, social control theorists question why people obey the rules of society. They argue that people obey the law because behavior and passions are controlled by internal and external forces. Some individuals have **self-control**—a strong moral sense that renders them incapable of hurting others and violating social norms.

Other people have been socialized to have a **commitment to conformity.** They have developed a real, present, and logical reason to obey the rules of society, and they instinctively avoid behavior that will jeopardize their reputation and achievements.[53] The stronger people's commitment to conventional institutions, individuals, and processes, the less likely they are to commit crime. If that commitment is absent, there is little to lose, and people are free to violate the law.[54]

Connections

The association of self-control and crime will be discussed more fully in Chapter 9 in the context of human development.

Self-Concept and Crime

Early versions of control theory speculated that criminality was a product of weak self-concept and poor self-esteem. Youths who are socialized to feel good about themselves and who maintain a positive attitude are able to control their own behavior and resist the temptations of the streets.

As early as 1951, sociologist Albert Reiss described delinquents as having weak egos and lacking the self-control to produce conforming behavior.[55] Scott Briar and Irving Piliavin noted that youths who believe criminal activity will damage their self-image and their relationships with others are likely to conform to social rules; in contrast, those less concerned about their social standing are free to violate the law.[56] Pioneering control theorist Walter Reckless argued that a strong self-image insulates a youth from the pressures of crimogenic influences in the environment.[57] In studies conducted within the school setting, Reckless and his colleagues found that students who were able to maintain a positive self-image were insulated from delinquency.[58]

These early works suggested that people who have a weak self-image and damaged ego are crime prone. They are immune from efforts to apply social control: Why obey the rules of society when you have no stake in the future and little to lose?

self-control
A strong moral sense that renders a person incapable of hurting others or violating social norms.

commitment to conformity
A strong personal investment in conventional institutions, individuals, and processes that prevents people from engaging in behavior that might jeopardize their reputation and achievements.

Contemporary Social Control Theory

The version of control theory articulated by Travis Hirschi in his influential 1969 book, *Causes of Delinquency,* is today the dominant version of control theories.[59] Hirschi links the onset of criminality to the weakening of the ties that bind people to society. He assumes that all individuals are potential law violators, but most are kept under control because they fear that illegal behavior will damage their relationships with friends, family, neighbors, teachers, and employers. Without these **social bonds** or ties, a person is free to commit criminal acts. Among all ethnic, religious, racial, and social groups, people whose bond to society is weak may fall prey to crimogenic behavior patterns.

Hirschi argues that the social bond a person maintains with society is divided into four main elements: attachment, commitment, involvement, and belief (see Figure 7.4).

1. **Attachment.** Attachment refers to a person's sensitivity to and interest in others.[60] Hirschi views parents, peers, and schools as the important social institutions with which a person should maintain ties. Attachment to parents is the most important. Even if a family is shattered by divorce or separation, a child must retain a strong attachment to one or both parents. Without this attachment, it is unlikely that respect for other authorities will develop.

2. **Commitment.** Commitment involves the time, energy, and effort expended in conventional actions such as getting an education and saving money for the future. If people build a strong commitment to conventional society, they will be less likely to engage in acts that jeopardize their hard-won position. Conversely, the lack of commitment to conventional values may foreshadow a condition in which risk-taking behavior, such as crime, becomes a reasonable behavior alternative.

Figure 7.4
Elements of the Social Bond

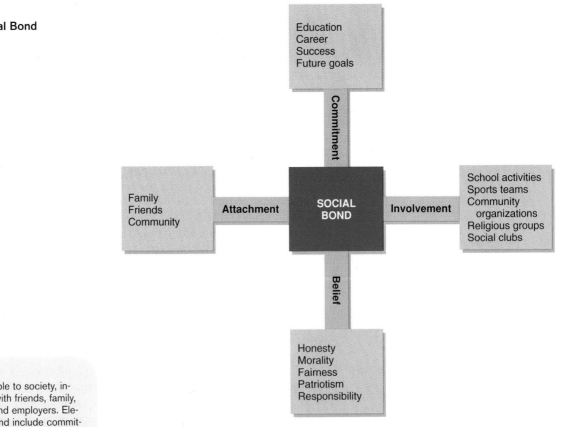

social bonds
The ties that bind people to society, including relationships with friends, family, neighbors, teachers, and employers. Elements of the social bond include commitment, attachment, involvement, and belief.

3. **Involvement.** Heavy involvement in conventional activities leaves little time for illegal behavior. Hirschi believes that involvement in school, recreation, and family insulates people from the potential lure of criminal behavior. Idleness, on the other hand, enhances that lure.

4. **Belief.** People who live in the same social setting often share common moral beliefs; they may adhere to such values as sharing, sensitivity to the rights of others, and admiration for the legal code. If these beliefs are absent or weakened, individuals are more likely to participate in antisocial or illegal acts.

Hirschi further suggests that the interrelationship of social bond elements controls subsequent behavior. For example, people who feel kinship and sensitivity to parents and friends should be more likely to adopt and work toward legitimate goals. A person who rejects such social relationships is more likely to lack commitment to conventional goals. Similarly, people who are highly committed to conventional acts and beliefs are more likely to be involved in conventional activities.

Testing Social Control Theory

One of Hirschi's most significant contributions was his attempt to test the principal hypotheses of social control theory. He administered a detailed self-report survey to a sample of more than 4,000 junior and senior high school students in Contra Costa County, California.[61] In a detailed analysis of the data, Hirschi found considerable evidence to support the control theory model. Among Hirschi's more important findings are the following:

- Youths who were strongly attached to their parents were less likely to commit criminal acts.
- Youths involved in conventional activity, such as homework, were less likely to engage in criminal behavior.
- Youths involved in unconventional behavior, such as smoking and drinking, were more prone to delinquency.
- Youths who maintained weak, distant relationships with people tended toward delinquency.
- Those who shunned unconventional acts were attached to their peers.
- Delinquents and nondelinquents shared similar beliefs about society.

Hirschi's data gave important support to the validity of social control theory. Even when the statistical significance of his findings was less than he expected, the direction of his research data was notably consistent. Only rarely did his findings contradict the theory's most critical assumptions.

Supporting Research   Hirschi's version of social control theory has been corroborated by numerous research studies showing that delinquent youths often feel detached from society.[62] Supporting research indicates that both male and female delinquents experience attachments to the family, peer group, and school that are strained and weakened whereas those who are able to maintain nurturing social relationships remain crime free.[63] For example, children who are raised in homes that are warm and supportive, whose parents are knowledgeable about their activities, are much less likely to engage in crime than those whose parents are distant, uninformed, and withdrawn.[64] Adolescents are less likely to engage in delinquent behavior if they are closely monitored and supervised by their parents.[65] Youths who fail at school and are detached from the educational experience are at risk of criminality.[66] In contrast, those who are committed to school are less likely to engage in delinquent acts.[67] Recent research shows that these influences may be interrelated. For example, elements of early family relationship (closeness, monitoring, and conflict) are related to later school success factors (grades, homework time, educational aspirations, and commitment). Attachment and commitment to both of these social institutions wielded a significant influence on deviant behaviors.[68] Similarly, family functioning is related to subsequent peer group involvement. Kids who are raised in a functional and close-knit family are less likely to get involved in a deviant peer group and consequently less likely to engage in criminal activities.[69]

Opposing Views Although there is a great deal of supportive research, a number of questions have been raised about the validity of control theory:

■ **Friendship.** One significant criticism concerns Hirschi's contention that delinquents are detached loners whose bond to family and friends has been broken. In fact, delinquents seem not to be "lone wolves" whose only personal relationships are exploitative; their friendship patterns seem quite close to those of conventional youth.[70] Some types of offenders, such as drug abusers, may maintain even more intimate relations with their peers than nonabusers.[71] Hirschi would counter that what appears to be a close friendship is really a relationship of convenience.

■ **Failure to achieve.** Hirschi argues that commitment to career and economic advancement reduces criminal involvement. However, research indicates that people who are committed to success but fail to achieve it may be crime prone.[72]

■ **Involvement negates supervision.** Adolescents who report high levels of involvement, which Hirschi suggests should reduce delinquency, actually report high levels of criminal behavior. Perhaps adolescents who are involved in activities outside the home have less contact with parental supervision and greater opportunity to commit crime.[73]

■ **Deviant peers and parents.** Hirschi's conclusion that any form of social attachment is beneficial, even to deviant peers and parents, has also been disputed. Rather than deter delinquency, attachment to deviant peers may support and nurture antisocial behavior.[74] A number of research efforts have found that youths attached to drug-abusing parents are more likely to use drugs themselves.[75] Attachment to deviant family members, peers, and associates may help motivate youths to commit crime and facilitate their antisocial acts.[76]

■ **Mistaken causal order.** Hirschi's theory proposes that a weakened bond leads to delinquency, but Robert Agnew suggests that the chain of events may flow in the opposite direction: Perhaps youngsters who break the law find that their bonds to parents, schools, and society eventually become weak. Other studies have also found that criminal behavior weakens social bonds and not vice versa.[77]

These criticisms are important, but Hirschi's views still constitute one of the preeminent theories in criminology.[78] Many criminologists consider social control theory the most important way of understanding the onset of youthful misbehavior. ✔ Checkpoints

Connections

Hirschi, along with Michael Gottfredson, has restructured his concept of control by integrating biosocial, psychological, and rational choice theory ideas into a general theory of crime. Because this new theory is essentially developmental, it will be discussed more fully in Chapter 9.

✔ Checkpoints

✔ Social control theories maintain that behavior is a function of the attachment that people feel toward society. People who have a weak commitment to conformity are free to commit crime.

✔ A strong self-image may insulate people from crime.

✔ According to Hirschi, social control is measured by a person's attachment, commitment, involvement, and belief.

✔ Significant research supports Hirschi's theory, but a number of criminologists question its validity.

To quiz yourself on this material, go to questions 7.4–7.13 on the Criminology: The Core 2e Web site.

Social Reaction (Labeling) Theory

Social reaction theory, or labeling theory (the two terms are used interchangeably here), explains criminal careers in terms of destructive social interactions and stigma-producing encounters.

According to this view, people are given a variety of symbolic labels that help define not just one trait but the whole person. Valued labels, such as "smart," "honest," and "hardworking," suggest overall competence. Sometimes the labels are symbolic, such as being named "most likely to succeed" or class valedictorian. People who hold these titles are automatically assumed to be leaders who are well on their way to success. Without meeting them, we know

FIND IT ON INFOTRAC
College Edition

To read more about the labeling approach, use "labeling theory" in a key word search.

that they are hardworking, industrious, and bright. These positive labels can improve self-image and social standing. Research shows that people who are labeled with one positive trait, such as being physically attractive, are assumed to have other positive traits, such as being intelligent and competent.[79]

In contrast, some people are given negative labels, such as "troublemaker," "mentally ill," and "stupid," that **stigmatize** them and reduce their self-image. For example, people labeled "insane" are also assumed to be dangerous, dishonest, unstable, violent, strange, and otherwise unsound.

Both positive and negative labels involve subjective interpretation of behavior: A "troublemaker" is merely someone whom people label as "troublesome." In a famous statement, Howard Becker sums up the importance of the audience's reaction:

> Social groups create deviance by making rules whose infractions constitute deviance, and by applying those rules to particular people and labeling them as outsiders. From this point of view, deviance is not a quality of the act a person commits, but rather a consequence of the application by others of rules and sanctions to an "offender." The deviant is one to whom the label has successfully been applied; deviant behavior is behavior that people so label.[80]

In its purest form, social reaction theory argues that even such crimes as murder, rape, and assault are only bad or evil because people label them as such. After all, the difference between an excusable act and a criminal one is often a matter of changing legal definition. Acts such as performing an abortion, using marijuana, possessing a handgun, and gambling have been legal at some times and places and illegal at others.

Even if some acts are labeled as bad or evil, those who participate in them can be spared a negative label. For example, it is possible to take another person's life but not be considered a "murderer" because the killing was considered self-defense or even an accident. Acts have negative consequences only when labeled by others as being wrong or evil.

A social reaction theorist views crime as a subjective concept whose definition depends entirely on the viewing audience. An act that is considered criminal by one person may be perfectly acceptable behavior to another. Because crime is defined by those in power, the shape of criminal law is defined by the values of those who rule, not an objective standard of moral conduct. Howard Becker refers to people who create rules as **moral entrepreneurs.** An example of a moral entrepreneur today might be a member of an ultra-orthodox religious group who targets the gay lifestyle and campaigns to prevent gays from adopting children or marrying their same-sex partners.[81]

Consequences of Labeling

stigmatize
To apply negative labeling with enduring effects on a person's self-image and social interactions.

moral entrepreneur
A person who creates moral rules that reflect the values of those in power rather than any objective, universal standards of right and wrong.

Although a label may be a function of rumor, innuendo, or unfounded suspicion, its adverse impact can be immense. If a devalued status is conferred by a significant other—a teacher, police officer, parent, or valued peer—the negative label may permanently harm the target. The degree to which a person is perceived as a social deviant may affect his or her treatment at home, at work, at school, and in other social situations. Children may find that their parents consider them a bad influence on younger brothers and sisters. School officials may limit them to classes reserved for people with behavioral problems. Likewise, when adults are labeled as "criminal," "ex-con," or "drug addict," they may find their eligibility for employment severely restricted. If the label is bestowed as the result of conviction for a criminal offense, the labeled person may also be subjected to official sanctions ranging from a mild reprimand to incarceration. The simultaneous effects of labels and sanctions reinforce feelings of isolation and detachment.

Public denunciation plays an important part in the labeling process. Condemnation is often carried out in "ceremonies" in which the individual's identity is officially transformed. Examples of such reidentification ceremonies are

**Initial
criminal act**
People commit
crimes for a
number of reasons.

**Detection by the
justice system**
Arrest is influenced by
racial, economic, and
power relations.

**Decision
to label**
Some are labeled "official"
criminals by police and
court authorities.

**Creation of a
new identity**
Those labeled are known
as troublemakers, crim-
inals, etc., and shunned
by conventional society.

**Acceptance
of labels**
Labeled people begin to
see themselves as
outsiders (secondary
deviance, self-labeling).

**Deviance
amplification**
Stigmatized offenders
are now locked into
criminal careers.

Figure 7.5
The Labeling Process

**successful degradation
ceremony**
A course of action or ritual in which
someone's identity is publicly redefined
and destroyed and they are thereafter
viewed as socially unacceptable.

retrospective reading
The reassessment of a person's past to fit
a current generalized label.

primary deviance
A norm violation or crime with little or no
long-term influence on the violator.

a competency hearing in which a person is declared to be "mentally ill" or a public trial in which a person is found to be a "rapist" or "child molester." During the process, a permanent record is produced, such as an arrest or conviction record, so that the denounced person is ritually separated from a place in the legitimate order and placed outside the world occupied by citizens of good standing. Harold Garfinkle has called transactions that produce irreversible, permanent labels **successful degradation ceremonies.**[82]

Self-Labeling According to labeling theory, depending on the visibility of the label and the manner and severity with which it is applied, negatively labeled individuals will become increasingly committed to a deviant career. Labeled persons may find themselves turning to others similarly stigmatized for support and companionship.

Isolated from conventional society, labeled people may identify themselves as members of an outcast group and become locked into deviance. Kids who view themselves as delinquents after being labeled as such are giving an inner voice to their perceptions of how parents, teachers, peers, and neighbors view them. When they believe that others view them as antisocial or troublemakers, they take on attitudes and roles that reflect this assumption; they expect to become suspects and then to be rejected.[83]

Joining Deviant Cliques People who are labeled as deviant may join with similarly outcast peers who facilitate their behavior. Eventually, antisocial behavior becomes habitual and automatic.[84] The desire to join deviant cliques and groups may stem from self-rejecting attitudes ("At times, I think I am no good at all") that eventually weaken commitment to conventional values and behaviors. In turn, stigmatized individuals may acquire motives to deviate from social norms because they now share a common bond with similarly labeled social outcasts.[85] They may join cliques like the "Trenchcoat Mafia" whose members were involved in the 1999 Littleton, Colorado, school massacre. Membership in a deviant subculture often involves conforming to group norms that conflict with those of conventional society, further enhancing the effects of the labeling process.

Retrospective Reading Beyond any immediate results, labels tend to redefine the whole person. For example, the label "ex-con" may create in people's imaginations a whole series of behavior descriptions—tough, mean, dangerous, aggressive, dishonest, sneaky—that may or may not apply to a person who has been in prison. People react to the label description and what it signifies instead of reacting to the actual behavior of the person who bears it. The labeled person's past is reviewed and reevaluated to fit his or her current status—a process known as **retrospective reading.** For example, boyhood friends of an assassin or serial killer, interviewed by the media, report that the suspect was withdrawn, suspicious, and negativistic as a youth; they were always suspicious but never thought to report their concerns to the authorities. According to this retrospective reading, we can now understand what prompted his current behavior; therefore, the label must be accurate.[86]

Labels, then, become the basis of personal identity. As the negative feedback of law enforcement agencies, parents, friends, teachers, and other figures amplifies the force of the original label, stigmatized offenders may begin to reevaluate their own identities (see Figure 7.5). If they are not really evil or bad, they may ask themselves, "Why is everyone making such a fuss?" This process has been referred to as the "dramatization of evil."[87]

Primary and Secondary Deviance

One of the better-known views of the labeling process is Edwin Lemert's concept of primary deviance and secondary deviance.[88] According to Lemert, **primary deviance** involves norm violations or crimes that have little influence

Figure 7.6
Secondary Deviance: The Labeling Process

Fear of stigma has prompted efforts to reduce the impact of criminal labels through such programs as pretrial diversion and community treatment. In addition, some criminologists have called for noncoercive "peacemaking" solutions to interpersonal conflict. This peacemaking or restorative justice movement is reviewed in Chapter 8.

secondary deviance
A norm violation or crime that comes to the attention of significant others or social control agents, who apply a negative label with long-term consequences for the violator's self-identity and social interactions.

deviance amplification
Process whereby secondary deviance pushes offenders out of mainstream of society and locks them into an escalating cycle of deviance, apprehension, labeling, and criminal self-identity.

on the actor and can be quickly forgotten. For example, a college student successfully steals a textbook at the campus bookstore, gets an A in the course, graduates, is admitted to law school, and later becomes a famous judge. Because his shoplifting goes unnoticed, it is a relatively unimportant event that has little bearing on his future life.

In contrast, **secondary deviance** occurs when a deviant event comes to the attention of significant others or social control agents, who apply a negative label. The newly labeled offender then reorganizes his or her behavior and personality around the consequences of the deviant act. The shoplifting student is caught by a security guard and expelled from college. With his law school dreams dashed and his future cloudy, his options are limited; people say he lacks character, and he begins to share their opinion. He eventually becomes a drug dealer and winds up in prison (see Figure 7.6).

Secondary deviance involves resocialization into a deviant role. The labeled person is transformed into one who, according to Lemert, "employs his behavior or a role based upon it as a means of defense, attack, or adjustment to the overt and covert problems created by the consequent social reaction to him."[89] Secondary deviance produces a **deviance amplification** effect: Offenders feel isolated from the mainstream of society and become locked within their deviant role. They may seek others similarly labeled to form deviant groups. Ever more firmly enmeshed in their deviant role, they are trapped in an escalating cycle of deviance, apprehension, more powerful labels, and identity transformation. Lemert's concept of secondary deviance expresses the core of social reaction theory: Deviance is a process in which one's identity is transformed. Efforts to control offenders, whether by treatment or punishment, simply help to lock them in their deviant role.

Crime and Labeling Theory

Because the process of becoming stigmatized is essentially interactive, labeling theorists blame the establishment of criminal careers on the social agencies originally designed for crime control, such as police, courts, and correctional agencies. It is these institutions, labeling theorists claim, that produce the stigma that harms the people they are trying to help, treat, or correct. As a result, they actually help to maintain and amplify criminal behavior.

Because crime and deviance are defined by the social audience's reaction to people and their behavior and the subsequent effects of that reaction, these institutions form the audience that helps define behavior as evil or wrong, locking people into deviant identities.

Differential Enforcement

An important principle of social reaction theory is that the law is differentially applied, benefiting those who hold economic and social power and penalizing the powerless. The probability of being brought under the control of legal authority is a function of a person's race, wealth, gender, and social standing. A core concept of social reaction theory is that police officers are more likely to formally arrest males, minority group members, and those in the lower class, and to use their discretionary powers to give beneficial treatment to more favored groups.[90] Minorities and the poor are more likely to be prosecuted for criminal offenses and to receive harsher punishments when convicted.[91] Judges may sympathize with white defendants and help them avoid criminal labels, especially if they seem to come from "good families," whereas minority youths are not afforded that luxury.[92] This helps to explain the significant racial and economic differences in the crime rate.

In sum, a major premise of social reaction theory is that the law is differentially constructed and applied, depending on the offender. It favors powerful members of society, who direct its content, and penalizes people whose actions threaten those in control, such as minority group members and the poor who demand equal rights.[93]

Research on Social Reaction Theory

Research on social reaction theory can be classified into two distinct categories. The first focuses on the characteristics of those offenders who are chosen for labeling. The theory predicts that they will be relatively powerless people who are unable to defend themselves against the negative labeling. The second type of research attempts to discover the effects of being labeled. Labeling theorists predict that people who are negatively labeled will view themselves as deviant and commit increasing amounts of crime.

Targets of Labeling   There is evidence that, as predicted by labeling theory, poor and powerless people are victimized by the law and justice system. Labels are not equally distributed across class and racial lines. From the police officer's decision on whom to arrest, to the prosecutor's decisions on whom to charge and how many and what kinds of charges to bring, to the court's decision on whom to release or grant bail, to the grand jury's decision on indictment, to the judge's decision on sentence length, discretion works to the detriment of minorities.[94]

Effects of Labeling   Empirical evidence shows that negative labels may dramatically influence the self-image of offenders. Although the effects of labeling by the justice system may have a lesser impact than previously believed, considerable evidence indicates social sanctions lead to self-labeling and deviance amplification.[95] For example, children negatively labeled by their parents routinely suffer a variety of problems, including antisocial behavior and school failure.[96] This process has been observed in the United States and abroad, indicating that the labeling process is universal, especially in nations in which a brush with the law brings personal dishonor, such as China and Japan.[97]

This labeling process is important because once they are stigmatized as troublemakers, adolescents begin to reassess their self-image. Parents who label their children as troublemakers promote deviance amplification. Labeling alienates parents from their children, and negative labels reduce children's self-image and increase delinquency; this process is referred to as **reflected appraisals**.[98] Parental labeling is extremely damaging because it may cause adolescents to seek out deviant peers whose behavior amplifies the effect of the labeling.[99]

As they mature, children are in danger of receiving repeated, intensive, official labeling, which has been shown to produce self-labeling and to damage identities.[100] Kids who perceive that they have been negatively labeled by significant others such as peers and teachers are also more likely to self-report delinquent behavior and to adopt a deviant self-concept.[101]

Youngsters labeled as troublemakers in school are the most likely to drop out; dropping out has been linked to delinquent behavior.[102] Even in adults, the labeling process can take its toll. Male drug users labeled as addicts by social control agencies eventually become self-labeled and increase their drug use.[103] People arrested in domestic violence cases, especially those with a low stake in conformity (for example, those who are jobless and unmarried), increase offending after being given official labels.[104]

Empirical evidence supports the view that labeling plays an important role in persistent offending.[105] Although labels may not cause adolescents to initiate criminal behaviors, experienced delinquents are significantly more likely to continue offending if they believe their parents and peers view them in a negative light.[106] Labeling, then, may help sustain criminality over time.

reflected appraisal
When parents are alienated from their children, their negative labeling reduces their children's self-image and increases delinquency.

FIND IT ON INFOTRAC
College Edition

To learn more about the process of reflected appraisals and how it reflects gender differences, read:

Dawn Jeglum Bartusch and Ross L. Matsueda, "Gender, Reflected Appraisals, and Labeling: A Cross-Group Test of an Interactionist Theory of Delinquency," *Social Forces*, 75 (1996): 145–176

✔ Checkpoints

✔ According to labeling theory, stigma helps lock people into deviant careers.

✔ Labels amplify deviant behavior rather than deter future criminality.

✔ Primary deviants view themselves as good people who have done a bad thing; secondary deviants accept a negative label as an identity.

✔ Labels are bestowed in a biased fashion. The poor and minority group members are more likely to receive labels.

To quiz yourself on this material, go to questions 7.14–7.15 on the Criminology: The Core 2e Web site.

Is Labeling Theory Valid?

Criminologists Raymond Paternoster and Leeann Iovanni have identified features of the labeling perspective that are important contributions to the study of criminality:[107]

- The labeling perspective identifies the role played by social control agents in crime causation. Criminal behavior cannot be fully understood if the agencies and individuals empowered to control and treat it are neglected.
- Labeling theory recognizes that criminality is not a disease or pathological behavior. It focuses attention on the social interactions and reactions that shape individuals and their behavior.
- Labeling theory distinguishes between criminal acts (primary deviance) and criminal careers (secondary deviance) and shows that these concepts must be interpreted and treated differently.

Labeling theory is also important because of its focus on interaction as well as the situation surrounding the crime. Rather than viewing the criminal as a robot-like creature whose actions are predetermined, it recognizes that crime often results from complex interactions and processes. The decision to commit crime involves actions of a variety of people, including peers, victim, police, and other key characters. Labels may foster crime by guiding the actions of all parties involved in these criminal interactions. Actions deemed innocent when performed by one person are considered provocative when engaged in by someone who has been labeled as deviant. Similarly, labeled people may be quick to judge, take offense, or misinterpret others' behavior because of past experience. ✔ Checkpoints

Social Process Theory and Public Policy

Social process theories have had a major influence on public policy since the 1950s. Learning theories have greatly influenced the way criminal offenders are treated. The effect of these theories has been felt mainly by young offenders, who are viewed as being more salvageable than hardened criminals. Advocates of the social learning approach argue that if people become criminal by learning definitions and attitudes favoring criminality, they can unlearn them by being exposed to definitions favoring conventional behavior.

■ According to social process theories, programs that aid a child's socialization also help protect them from crime-producing influences in the environment. Here, as part of the Ex-Cite/Head Start program, a retired professor spends time in the classroom with elementary students, teaching the colors of the rainbow, reading stories, tying dangling shoelaces, and giggling over games.

POLICY AND PRACTICE IN CRIMINOLOGY

Head Start

Head Start is probably the best-known effort to help lower-class youths achieve proper socialization and, in so doing, reduce their potential for future criminality. Head Start programs were instituted in the 1960s as part of President Johnson's War on Poverty. In the beginning, Head Start was a 2-month summer program for children who were about to enter school that was aimed at embracing the "whole child." In embracing the whole child, the school offered comprehensive programming that helped improve physical health, enhance mental processes, and improve social and emotional development, self-image, and interpersonal relationships. Preschoolers were provided with an enriched educational environment to develop their learning and cognitive skills. They were given the opportunity to use pegs and pegboards, puzzles, toy animals, dolls, letters and numbers, and other materials that middle-class children take for granted. These opportunities provided the children a leg up in the educational process. The program is divided into four segments:

- **Education.** Head Start's educational program is designed to meet the needs of each child, the community served, and its ethnic and cultural characteristics. Every child receives a variety of learning experiences to foster intellectual, social, and emotional growth.

- **Health.** Head Start emphasizes the importance of the early identification of health problems. Every child is involved in a comprehensive health program, which includes immunizations, medical, dental, mental health, and nutritional services.

- **Parent Involvement.** An essential part of Head Start is the involvement of parents in parent education, program planning, and operating activities.

- **Social Services.** Specific services are geared to each family including community outreach, referrals, family need assessments, recruitment and enrollment of children, and emergency assistance and crisis intervention.

Today, with annual funding approaching $6.5 billion, the Head Start program is administered by the Head Start Bureau, the Administration on Children, Youth, and Families (ACFY), the Administration for Children and Families (ACF), and the Department of Health and Human Services (DHHS). Head Start teachers strive to provide a variety of learning experiences appropriate to the child's age and development. These experiences encourage the child to read books, to understand cultural diversity, to express feelings, and to play with and relate to peers in an appropriate fashion. Students are guided in developing gross and fine motor skills and self-confidence. Health care is also an issue, and most children

enrolled in the program receive comprehensive health screening, physical and dental examinations, and appropriate follow-up. Many programs provide meals, and in so doing help children receive proper nourishment.

Head Start programs now serve parents in addition to their preschoolers. Some programs allow parents to enroll in classes, which cover parenting, literacy, nutrition/weight loss, domestic violence prevention, and other social issues; social services, health, nutrition, and educational services are also available.

Considerable controversy has surrounded the success of the Head Start program. In 1970, the Westinghouse Learning Corporation issued an evaluation of the Head Start effort and concluded that there was no evidence of lasting cognitive gains on the part of the participating children. While disappointing, this evaluation focused on IQ levels and gave short shrift to improvement in social competence and other survival skills. More recent research has produced dramatically different results. One report found that, by age 5, children who experienced the enriched day care offered by Head Start averaged more than 10 points higher on their IQ scores than their peers who did not participate in the program. Other research that carefully compared Head Start children to similar youngsters who did not attend the program found that the former made significant intellectual gains. Head Start children were less likely to have been retained

This philosophy has been used in numerous treatment facilities based in part on two early, pioneering efforts: the Highfields Project in New Jersey and the Silverlake Program in Los Angeles. These residential treatment programs, geared toward young male offenders, used group interaction sessions to attack criminal behavior orientations while promoting conventional lines of behavior. It is common today for residential and nonresidential programs to offer similar treatment, teaching children and adolescents to refuse drugs, to forgo delinquent behavior, and to stay in school. It is even common for celebrities to return to their old neighborhoods to urge young people to stay in school or off drugs. If learning did not affect behavior, such exercises would be futile.

Control theories have also influenced criminal justice and other social policies. Programs have been developed to increase people's commitment to conventional lines of action. Some work at creating and strengthening bonds early in life before the onset of criminality. The educational system has hosted

in a grade or placed in classes for slow learners; they outperformed peers on achievement tests; and they were more likely to graduate from high school.

Head Start kids also made strides in nonacademic areas: they appear to have better health, immunization rates, nutrition, and enhanced emotional characteristics after leaving the program. Research also shows that the Head Start program can have important psychological benefits for the mothers of participants, such as decreasing depression and anxiety and increasing feelings of life satisfaction. The best available evidence suggests that:

- Head Start is associated with short-term gains in cognitive skills as well as longer-term gains in school completion, and even greater gains are possible if children receive good follow-up in the early grades.

- Head Start may be focused too heavily on social supports at the expense of language and literacy training.

- Although Head Start centers vary in quality, on average they are better than privately run child care centers, have achieved short-term benefits, and would pay for themselves if they produced even a fraction of the long-term benefits associated with model programs. For this reason, they merit some expansion and greater attention paid to their quality.

If, as many experts believe, there is a close link between school performance, family life, and crime, programs such as Head Start can help some potentially criminal youths avoid prob-

TABLE	Head Start, 2002–2003	
Students		912,000
Number of Classrooms		49,800
Number of Centers		18,865
Average Cost per Child		$6,934
Paid Staff		198,000
Volunteers		1,450,000

lems with the law. Head Start's mission is to help low-income children start school ready to learn by providing early childhood education, child development, and comprehensive health and social services. By implication, their success indicates that programs that help socialize youngsters can be used to combat urban criminality.

Since 1965, local Head Start programs across the country have served more than 21 million children and built strong partnerships with parents and families. The table above illustrates the size of this vast program.

At the time of this writing, there is a great deal of controversy over President George Bush's plan to give control of Head Start to the states, a move some critics fear might conflict with the ability to fund both Head Start and local preschool programs. States would have to maintain current Head Start funding levels for at least 5 years under Bush's

plan, but states have ignored such federal requirements in the past.

Critical Thinking

1. If crime is a matter of human traits, as some criminologists suggest, would a program such as Head Start help kids avoid criminal careers?

2. Are there any other types of programs that you might suggest that would help parents or children avoid involvement in drugs or crime?

3. Were you in Head Start? If so, did it help you attain your current academic success?

InfoTrac College Edition Research

To learn more about the Head Start program and its current status, use "Head Start" as a subject guide.

SOURCES: Head Start Statistics can be accessed at the Head Start Bureau Web site http://www.acf.hhs.gov/programs/hsb/research/2003.htm (accessed October 5, 2003); Janet Currie, *A Fresh Start for Head Start?* (Washington, D.C.: Brookings Institute, March 2001); Statement by Wade F. Horn, Assistant Secretary for Children and Families on Head Start and Child Care in the Context of Early Learning before the House Committee on Appropriations, Subcommittee on Labor, Health, and Human Services, and Education April 17, 2002; Edward Zigler and Sally Styfco, "Head start, criticisms in a constructive context," *American Psychologist* 49:127–132 (1994); Nancy Kassebaum, "Head start, only the best for America's children," *American Psychologist* 49 (1994): 123–126; Faith Lamb Parker, Chaya Piorkowski, and Lenore Peay, "Head start as social support for mothers: the psychological benefits of involvement," *American Journal of Orthopsychiatry* 57 (1987): 220–233.

numerous programs designed to improve basic skills and create an atmosphere in which youths will develop a bond to their schools. The Policy and Practice in Criminology feature discusses the Head Start program, perhaps the largest and most successful attempt to solidify social bonds.

Control theory's focus on the family has played a key role in programs designed to strengthen the bond between parent and child. Others attempt to repair bonds that have been broken and frayed. Examples of this approach are the career, work furlough, and educational opportunity programs being developed in the nation's prisons. These programs are designed to help inmates maintain a stake in society so they will be less willing to resort to criminal activity after their release.

Labeling theorists caution against too much intervention. Rather than ask social agencies to attempt to rehabilitate people having problems with the law, they argue that less is better. Put another way, the more institutions try

CONCEPT SUMMARY 7.1 Social Process Theories

THEORY	MAJOR PREMISE	STRENGTHS	RESEARCH FOCUS
Social Learning Theories			
Differential association theory	People learn to commit crime from exposure to antisocial definitions.	Explains onset of criminality. Explains the presence of crime in all elements of social structure. Explains why some people in high-crime areas refrain from criminality. Can apply to adults and juveniles.	Measuring definitions toward crime; influence of deviant peers and parents
Neutralization theory	Youths learn ways of neutralizing moral restraints and periodically drift in and out of criminal behavior patterns.	Explains why many delinquents do not become adult criminals. Explains why youthful law violators can participate in conventional behavior.	Do people who use neutralizations commit more crimes? Beliefs, values, and crime
Social Control Theory			
Hirschi's control theory	A person's bond to society prevents him or her from violating social rules. If the bond weakens, the person is free to commit crime.	Explains the onset of crime; can apply to both middle- and lower-class crime. Explains its theoretical constructs adequately so they can be measured. Has been empirically tested.	The association between commitment, attachment, involvement, belief, and crime
Social Reaction Theory			
Labeling theory	People enter into law-violating careers when they are labeled for their acts and organize their personalities around the labels.	Explains the role of society in creating deviance. Explains why some juvenile offenders do not become adult criminals. Develops concepts of criminal careers.	Self-concept and crime; differential application of labels; effect of stigma

to help people, the more these people will be stigmatized and labeled. For example, a special education program designed to help problem readers may cause them to label themselves and others as slow or stupid. Similarly, a mental health rehabilitation program created with the best intentions may cause clients to be labeled as crazy or dangerous.

The influence of labeling theory can be seen in diversion and restitution programs. **Diversion programs** remove both juvenile and adult offenders from the normal channels of the criminal justice process by placing them in rehabilitation programs. For example, a college student whose drunken driving hurts a pedestrian may, before trial, be placed for 6 months in an alcohol treatment program. If he successfully completes the program, charges against him will be dismissed; thus he avoids the stigma of a criminal label. Such programs are common throughout the United States. Often they offer counseling, medical advice, and vocational, educational, and family services.

Another popular label-avoiding innovation is **restitution.** Rather than face the stigma of a formal trial, an offender is asked either to pay back the victim of the crime for any loss incurred or to do some useful work in the community in lieu of receiving a court-ordered sentence.

Despite their good intentions, stigma-reducing programs have not met with great success. Critics charge that they substitute one kind of stigma for another—for instance, attending a mental health program in lieu of a criminal trial. In addition, diversion and restitution programs usually screen out violent and repeat offenders. Finally, there is little hard evidence that these alternative programs improve recidivism rates.

Concept Summary 7.1 outlines the major concepts of social process theories.

diversion programs
Programs of rehabilitation that remove offenders from the normal channels of the criminal justice process, thus avoiding the stigma of a criminal label.

restitution
Permitting an offender to repay the victim or do useful work in the community rather than face the stigma of a formal trial and a court-ordered sentence.

Summary

- Social process theories view criminality as a function of people's interaction with various organizations, institutions, and processes in society.

- People in all walks of life have the potential to become criminals if they maintain destructive social relationships. Improper socialization is a key component of crime.

- Social process theory has three main branches. Social learning theory stresses that people learn how to commit crimes. Social control theory analyzes the failure of society to control criminal tendencies. Labeling theory maintains that negative labels produce criminal careers.

- Social learning theory suggests that people learn criminal behaviors much as they learn conventional behavior.

- Differential association theory, formulated by Edwin Sutherland, holds that criminality is a result of a person's perceiving an excess of definitions in favor of crime over definitions that uphold conventional values.

- Sykes and Matza's theory of neutralization stresses that youths learn behavior rationalizations that enable them to overcome societal values and norms and break the law.

- Control theory maintains that all people have the potential to become criminals, but their bonds to conventional society prevent them from violating the law. This view suggests that a person's self-concept aids his or her commitment to conventional action.

- Travis Hirschi's social control theory describes the social bond as containing elements of attachment, commitment, involvement, and belief. Weakened bonds allow youths to behave antisocially.

- Social reaction or labeling theory holds that criminality is promoted by becoming negatively labeled by significant others. Such labels as "criminal," "ex-con," and "junkie" isolate people from society and lock them into lives of crime.

- Labels create expectations that the labeled person will act in a certain way; labeled people are always watched and suspected. Eventually these people begin to accept their labels as personal identities, locking them further into lives of crime and deviance.

- Edwin Lemert suggests that people who accept labels are involved in secondary deviance while primary deviants are able to maintain an undamaged identity.

- Unfortunately, research on labeling has not supported its major premises. Consequently, critics have charged that it lacks credibility as a description of crime causation.

- Social process theories have greatly influenced social policy. They have controlled treatment orientations as well as community action policies.

Thinking Like a Criminologist

The state legislature is considering a bill that requires the names of people convicted of certain offenses, such as vandalism, soliciting a prostitute, or nonpayment of child support, to be posted in local newspapers under the heading "The Rogues Gallery." Those who favor the bill cite similar practices elsewhere: In Boston, men arrested for soliciting prostitutes are forced to clean streets. In Dallas, shoplifters are made to stand outside stores with signs stating their misdeeds.

Members of the state Civil Liberties Union have opposed the bill, stating, "It's simply needless humiliation of the individual." They argue that public shaming is inhumane and further alienates criminals who already have little stake in society, further ostracizing them from the mainstream. According to civil liberties attorneys, applying stigma helps criminals acquire a damaged reputation, which further locks them into criminal behavior patterns.

This "liberal" position is challenged by those who believe that convicted lawbreakers have no right to conceal their crimes from the public. Shaming penalties seem attractive as cost-effective alternatives to imprisonment. These critics ask what could be wrong with requiring a teenage vandal to personally apologize at the school he or she defaced and to wear a shirt with a big "V" on it while cleaning up the mess. If you do something wrong, they argue, you should have to face the consequences.

You have been asked to address a legislative committee on the issue of whether shaming could deter crime. What would you say?

Go to the Criminology: The Core 2e Web site to review the content of this chapter.

Doing Research on the Web

For an up-to-date list of URLs, go to

http://www.cj.wadsworth.com/siegel_crimcore2e

To conduct research on the effects of stigma, check out this site:

http://agetaboo.org/info/stigma.htm

You might also go to the home page of Howard Becker, one of the pioneers of labeling theory:

http://home.earthlink.net/~hsbecker/ http://home.earthlink.net/~hsbecker/

To see how labeling impacts on the mentally ill, go to these sites:

http://www.mentalhealthworks.ca/facts/sheets/stigma.asp

http://www.stigma.org/

Pro/Con discussions and Viewpoint Essays on some of the topics in this chapter may be found at the Opposing Viewpoints Resource Center:

http://www.gale.com/OpposingViewpoints

Key Terms

socialization 156
social process theory 156
parental efficacy 156
social learning theory 158
social control theory 158
social reaction (labeling) theory 159
differential association theory 159
culture conflict 160
neutralization theory 162

drift 162
neutralization techniques 162
self-control 165
commitment to conformity 165
social bond 166
stigmatize 169
moral entrepreneur 169
successful degradation ceremony 170
retrospective reading 170

primary deviance 170
secondary deviance 171
deviance amplification 171
reflected appraisal 172
diversion programs 176
restitution 176

Critical Thinking Questions

1. If criminal behavior is learned, who taught the first criminal? Are such behaviors as vandalism and bullying actually learned?

2. Children who do well in school are less likely to commit criminal acts than those who are school failures. Which element of Hirschi's theory is supported by the school failure–delinquency link?

3. Have you ever been given a negative label, and, if so, did it cause you social harm? How did you lose the label, or did it become a permanent marker that still troubles you today?

4. If negative labels are damaging, do positive ones help insulate children from crime-producing forces in their environment?

5. How would a social process theorist explain the fact that many children begin offending at an early age and then desist as they mature?

CHAPTER 8

Social Conflict Theory: It's a Class Thing

Chapter Objectives

1. Be familiar with the concept of social conflict and how it shapes behavior.
2. Be able to discuss elements of conflict in the justice system.
3. Be familiar with the idea of critical criminology.
4. Be able to discuss the difference between structural and instrumental Marxism.
5. Know the various techniques of critical research.
6. Be able to discuss the term *left realism.*
7. Understand the concept of patriarchy.
8. Know what is meant by feminist criminology.
9. Be able to discuss peacemaking.
10. Understand the concept of restorative justice.

URING THE MONTHS OF FEB-
RUARY AND MARCH 2003,
SOMEWHERE BETWEEN SIX
AND TEN MILLION PEOPLE IN
up to 60 countries are thought to have
marched against the American involvement in Iraq. They were the largest anti-
war demonstrations since the Vietnam
War. In London, organizers claimed that
more than two million people protested
(police estimates were a more modest
750,000), while in Barcelona, Spanish police
estimated that up to 1.3 million people marched. Europeans were not alone in venting their anger
against U.S. military operations; there were also widespread demonstrations on American soil, including a large march in New York City where around 100,000 people marched filling 20 city blocks.

CNN View the CNN video clip of this story and answer
related critical thinking questions on your
Criminology: The Core 2e CD.

It would be unusual to pick up the morning paper and not see headlines loudly proclaiming renewed strife between the United States and its overseas adversaries, between union negotiators and
management attorneys, between citizens and police authorities, or between feminists and reac-
tionary males protecting their turf. The world is filled with conflict. Conflict can be destructive when
it leads to war, violence, and death; it can be functional when it results in positive social change.

This chapter reviews criminological theories that allege that criminal
behavior is a function of conflict, a reaction to the unfair distribution
of wealth and power in society. The social conflict perspective has several independent branches. One, generally referred to as conflict theory, maintains that intergroup conflict and rivalry cause crime in any
society, regardless of its economic structure. A second branch, **critical
criminology,** focuses on the crime-producing traits of capitalist society; it is sometimes referred to as radical or Marxist criminology.[1] Finally, emerging forms of social conflict theory include feminist, left
realism, peacemaking, and postmodern thought (see Figure 8.1).

The Conflict Theory of Crime

Conflict theory tries to explain crime within economic and social
contexts and to express the connection between social class, crime,
and social control.[2] Conflict theorists are concerned with issues such
as these:

- The role government plays in creating a crimogenic
  environment.
- The relationship between personal or group power and the
  shaping of criminal law.

critical criminology
The view that crime is a product of the capitalist system.

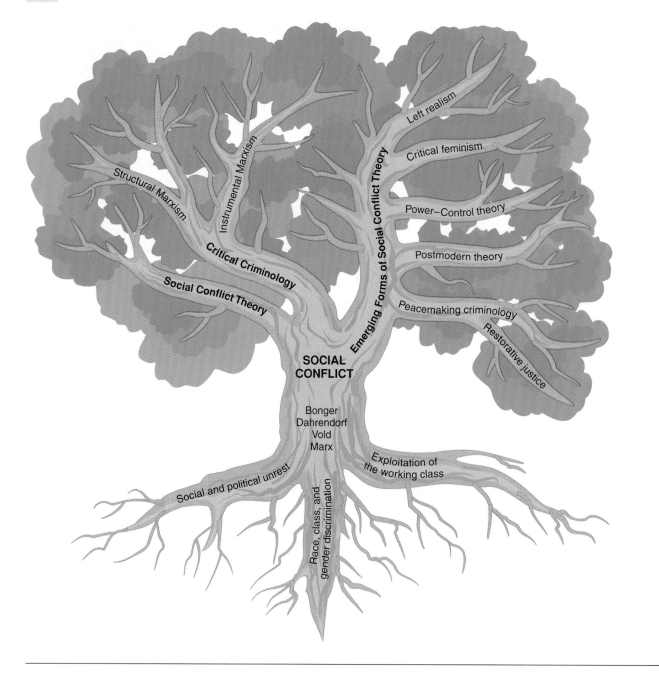

Figure 8.1
The Branches of Social Conflict Theory

- The prevalence of bias in justice system operations.
- The relationship between a capitalist, free enterprise economy and crime rates.

Conflict promotes crime by creating a social atmosphere in which the law is a mechanism for controlling dissatisfied, have-not members of society while the wealthy maintain their power. This is why crimes that are the province of the wealthy, such as illegal corporate activities, are sanctioned much more leniently than those, such as burglary, that are considered lower-class activities. Conflict theory came into criminological prominence during the 1960s, when self-report studies began to yield data suggesting that the class–crime correlation found in official crime data was spurious. The self-reports showed that crime and delinquency were distributed much more evenly throughout the social structure than indicated by official statistics, which reported more crime in lower-class environments.[3] If these self-reports were accurate,

conflict theory
The view that crime is a function of class conflict and power relations. Laws are created and enforced by those in power to protect their own interests.

middle-class participation in crime was going unrecorded while the lower class was subjected to discriminatory law enforcement practices.[4]

The theme that dominated much of this scholarship was the contention that criminal legislation was determined by the relative power of groups determined to use criminal law to advance their own special interests or to impose their own moral preferences on others.[5] This movement was aided by the widespread social and political upheaval of the late 1960s and early 1970s. These social forces included anti–Vietnam War demonstrations, counterculture movements, and various forms of political protest. Conflict theory flourished within this framework because it provided a systematic basis for challenging the legitimacy of the government's creation and application of law. The federal government's crackdown on political dissidents and prosecution of draft resisters seemed designed to maintain control in the hands of political power brokers.

Power Relations

As conflict theory began to influence criminological study, several influential scholars embraced its ideas. William Chambliss and Robert Seidman wrote the well-respected treatise *Law, Order and Power,* which documented how the justice system protects the rich and powerful.[6] Some common objectives of conflict criminology that appear in Chambliss and Seidman's writing include the following:

- Describing how control of the political and economic system affects the way criminal justice is administered
- Showing how definitions of crime favor those who control the justice system
- Analyzing the role of conflict in contemporary society

In another influential work, *The Social Reality of Crime,* Richard Quinney spelled out the conflict view of law and crime.[7] According to Quinney, criminal definitions (law) represent the interests of those who hold power in society. Where there is conflict between social groups—for example, the wealthy and the poor—those who hold power will create laws that benefit themselves and hold rivals in check. Law is not an abstract body of rules that represents an absolute moral code; rather, law is an integral part of society, a force that represents a way of life and a method of doing things. Crime is a function of power relations and an inevitable result of social conflict. Criminals are not simply social misfits but people who have come up short in the struggle for success and are seeking alternative means of achieving wealth, status, or even survival.

This scholarship reflects a major objective of conflict theory—to show how U.S. justice is skewed. According to the conflict view, crime is defined by those in power. **Power** refers to the ability of persons and groups to determine and control the behavior of others and to shape public opinion to meet their personal interests. Because those in power shape the content of the law, it comes as no surprise that their behavior is often exempt from legal sanctions. Those who deserve the most severe sanctions (wealthy white-collar criminals whose crimes cost society millions of dollars) usually receive lenient punishments while those whose relatively minor crimes are committed out of economic necessity (petty thieves and drug dealers) receive stricter penalties, especially if they are minority group members who lack social and economic power.[8]

Research on Conflict Theory

One area of conflict-oriented research involves examining the criminal justice system to see if it operates as an instrument of class oppression or as a fair, even-handed social control agency. Some conflict researchers have found

Connections

The enforcement of laws against illegal business activities such as price fixing, restraint of trade, environmental crimes, and false advertising is discussed in Chapter 12. Although some people are sent to prison for these white-collar offenses, many offenders are still punished with a fine or economic sanction.

power
The ability of persons and groups to control the behavior of others, to shape public opinion, and to define deviance.

FIND IT ON INFOTRAC
College Edition

Research shows that African Americans are sent to prison on drug charges at 27 to 50 times the rate of European Americans. To read more about the effects of racial discrimination, use the term "race discrimination" as a subject guide.

✔ Checkpoints

✔ Social conflict theory is aimed at identifying "real" crimes in U.S. society, such as profiteering, sexism, and racism.

✔ It seeks to evaluate how criminal law is used as a mechanism of social control.

✔ It describes how power relations create inequities in U.S. society.

✔ The idea of the social reality of crime is that those who hold power in society define those who oppose their values as criminals.

✔ Racism and classism pervade the U.S. justice system and shape crime rates.

To quiz yourself on this material, go to questions 8.1–8.4 on the Criminology: The Core 2e Web site.

evidence of class bias. Legal jurisdictions with significant levels of economic disparity are also the most likely to have large numbers of people killed by police officers. Police may act more forcefully in areas where class conflict creates the perception that extreme forms of social control are needed to maintain order.[9]

Research also shows, as predicted by conflict theory, that a suspect's race is an important factor in shaping police discretion and decision making. Using data from a national survey, Ronald Weitzer and Steven Tuch found that about 40 percent of African American respondents claimed they were stopped by police because of their race as compared to just 5 percent of whites; almost 75 percent of young African American men, ages 18 to 34, said they were victims of profiling.[10] Recent research by Albert Meehan and Michael Ponder found that police are more likely to use racial profiling to stop black motorists as they travel further into the boundaries of predominantly white neighborhoods: Black motorists driving in an all white neighborhood set up a red flag because they are "out of place."[11] It is not surprising to conflict theorists that police brutality complaints are highest in minority neighborhoods, especially those that experience relative deprivation (African American residents earn significantly less money than the European American majority).[12]

Criminal courts are also more likely to dole out harsh punishments to members of powerless, disenfranchised groups.[13] Both white and black offenders have been found to receive stricter sentences if their personal characteristics (single, young, urban, male) show them to be members of the "dangerous classes."[14] Unemployed racial minorities may be perceived as "social dynamite" who present a real threat to society and must be controlled and incapacitated.[15] Race also plays a role in prosecution and punishment. African American defendants are more likely to be prosecuted under habitual offender statutes if they commit crimes where there is a greater likelihood of a white victim, for example, larceny and burglary, than if they commit violent crimes that are largely intraracial; where there is a perceived "racial threat," punishment is enhanced.[16]

Considering these examples of how conflict controls the justice process, it is not surprising when analysis of national population trends and imprisonment rates shows that as the percentage of minority group members increases in a population, the imprisonment rate does likewise.[17] Similarly, states with a substantial minority population have a much higher imprisonment rate than those with predominantly white populations.[18] ✔ Checkpoints

Critical Criminology

As you may recall (Chapter 1), Karl Marx identified the economic structures in society that control all human relations. In so doing, he planted the seeds of critical criminology. Those criminologists who gain their inspiration from Marx reject the notion that law is designed to maintain a tranquil, fair society and that criminals are malevolent people who wish to trample the rights of others. Critical theorists consider acts of racism, sexism, imperialism, unsafe working conditions, inadequate child care, substandard housing, pollution of the environment, and war-making as a tool of foreign policy to be "true crimes." The crimes of the helpless—burglary, robbery, and assault—are more expressions of rage over unjust conditions than actual crimes.[19] By focusing on how the capitalist state uses law to control the lower classes, Marxist thought serves as the basis for critical theory.

Origins of Critical Criminology

In the 1960s, theories that focused on the relationship between crime and conflict in any society began to be supplanted by more radical, Marxist-oriented theories that examined the specific role of capitalism in law and criminality. In 1968, a group of British sociologists formed the National Deviancy Conference (NDC). With about 300 members, this organization sponsored several national symposiums and dialogues. Members came from all walks of life, but at its core was a group of academics who were critical of the positivist criminology being taught in British and American universities. More specifically, they rejected the conservative stance of criminologists and their close financial relationship with government funding agencies.

The NDC was not conceived as a Marxist-oriented group; rather, it investigated the concept of deviance from a labeling perspective. It called attention to ways in which social control might actually cause deviance rather than just respond to antisocial behavior. Many conference members became concerned about the political nature of social control. In time, a schism developed within the NDC, with one group clinging to the interactionist/labeling perspective, while the second embraced Marxist thought.

In 1973, critical theory was given a powerful academic boost when British scholars Ian Taylor, Paul Walton, and Jock Young published *The New Criminology*.[20] This brilliant, thorough, and well-constructed critique of existing concepts in criminology called for the development of new methods of criminological analysis and critique. *The New Criminology* became the standard resource for scholars critical of both the field of criminology and the existing legal process.

During the same period, a small group of scholars in the United States also began to follow a new, radical approach to criminology. The locus of the radical school was the criminology program at the University of California at Berkeley. The most noted Marxist scholars at that institution were Anthony Platt, Paul Takagi, Herman Schwendinger, and Julia Schwendinger. Radical scholars at other U.S. academic institutions included Richard Quinney, William Chambliss, Steven Spitzer, and Barry Krisberg.

The U.S. scholars were influenced by the widespread social ferment during the late 1960s and early 1970s. The war in Vietnam, prison struggles, and the civil rights and feminist movements produced a climate in which criticism of the ruling class seemed a natural by-product. Mainstream, positivist criminology was criticized as being overtly conservative, pro-government, and antihuman. Critical criminologists scoffed when their fellow scholars used statistical analysis of computerized data to describe criminal and delinquent behavior.

In the early 1980s, the left realism school was started by scholars affiliated with the Middlesex Polytechnic and the University of Edinburgh in Great Britain. In the United States, scholars influenced in part by the pioneering work of Dennis Sullivan and Larry Tifft laid the foundation for what eventually became known as the peacemaking movement, which calls for a humanist vision of justice.[21] At the same time, feminist scholars began to critically analyze the relationship between gender, power, and criminality.

Since the 1980s critical criminologists have been deeply concerned with the conservative trend in American politics and the creation of what they consider to be an American Empire. The conservative agenda, initiated by Ronald Reagan, called for lowering labor costs through union busting, welfare limitations, tax cuts that favor the wealthy, ending affirmative action, and reducing environmental control and regulation. While spending was cut on social programs, spending on the military expanded. The rapid buildup of the prison system and passage of draconian criminal laws that threatened civil rights and liberties (for example, three strikes laws and the USA Patriot Act) are other elements of the conservative agenda. Critical criminologists believe that they are responsible for informing the public about the dangers of these developments.[22]

Critical criminologists have turned their attention to the threat competitive capitalism presents to the working class. In addition to perpetuating male supremacy and racialism, they believe that modern global capitalism helps destroy the lives of workers in less developed countries. For example, capitalists hailed China's entry into the World Trade Organization in 2001 as a significant economic event. However, critical thinkers point out that the economic boom has significant costs: the average manufacturing wage in China is 20 to 25 cents per hour; during the first half of 2001, 47,000 workers were killed at work; during the first 6 months of 2001, 35.2 million Chinese workers were permanently or temporarily disabled.[23]

Defining Crime Critical theorists use the conflict definition of crime: Crime is a political concept designed to protect the power and position of the upper classes at the expense of the poor. Some, but not all, Marxists would include in a list of "real" crimes such acts as violations of human rights due to racism, sexism, and imperialism and other violations of human dignity and physical needs and necessities. Part of the critical agenda, argues criminologist Robert Bohm, is to make the public aware that these behaviors "are crimes just as much as burglary and robbery."[24]

The nature of a society controls the direction of its criminality; criminals are not social misfits but products of the society and its economic system. "Capitalism," claims Bohm, "as a mode of production, has always produced a relatively high level of crime and violence."[25] According to Michael Lynch and W. Byron Groves, three implications follow from this view:

1. Each society produces its own types and amounts of crime.
2. Each society has its own distinctive ways of dealing with criminal behavior.
3. Each society gets the amount and type of crime that it deserves.[26]

This analysis tells us that criminals are not a group of outsiders who can be controlled by increased law enforcement. Criminality, instead, is a function of social and economic organization. To control crime and reduce criminality, societies must remove the social conditions that promote crime.

Fundamentals of Critical Criminology

Critical criminologists view crime as a function of the capitalist mode of production. Capitalism produces haves and have-nots, each engaging in a particular branch of criminality.[27] The mode of production shapes social life. Because economic competitiveness is the essence of capitalism, conflict increases and eventually destabilizes social institutions and the individuals within them.[28]

In a capitalist society, those with economic and political power control the definition of crime and the manner in which the criminal justice system enforces the law.[29] Consequently, the only crimes available to the poor, or proletariat, are the severely sanctioned "street crimes": rape, murder, theft, and mugging. Members of the middle class, or petite bourgeoisie, cheat on their taxes and engage in petty corporate crime (employee theft), acts that generate social disapproval but are rarely punished severely. The wealthy bourgeoisie are involved in acts that should be described as crimes but are not, such as racism, sexism, and profiteering. Although regulatory laws control illegal business activities, these are rarely enforced, and violations are lightly punished. One reason is that an essential feature of capitalism is the need to expand business and create new markets. This goal often comes in conflict with laws designed to protect the environment and creates clashes with those who seek their enforcement. In advanced capitalist society the need for expansion usually triumphs. For example, corporate spokespeople and their political allies will brand environmentalists as "tree huggers" who stand in the way of jobs and prosperity.[30]

The rich are insulated from street crimes because they live in areas far removed from crime. Those in power use the fear of crime as a tool to maintain their control over society. The poor are controlled through incarceration, and the middle class is diverted from caring about the crimes of the powerful by their fear of the crimes of the powerless.[31] Ironically, they may have more

FIND IT ON INFOTRAC
College Edition

Did you know that at one time Karl Marx was a reporter for the *New York Tribune*? To read more about Marx's life, use his name as a subject guide and check out the encyclopedia reference. Then read some of the many periodical selections devoted to his thought and philosophy.

to lose from the economic crimes committed by the rich than the street crimes of the poor. Stock market swindles and savings and loan scams cost the public billions of dollars but are typically settled with fines and probationary sentences.

Because private ownership of property is the true measure of success in capitalism (as opposed to being, say, a worthy person), the state becomes an ally of the wealthy in protecting their property interests. As a result, theft-related crimes are often punished more severely than are acts of violence because although the former may be interclass the latter are typically intraclass.

This vision creates a dilemma: How can a critical thinker explain the fact that society does in fact punish many wealthy people and sends corporate criminals to prison for such crimes as insider trading and stock market manipulation? The answer may be found in the distinction between the concepts of structural and instrumental Marxism.

Instrumental Marxism   **Instrumental Marxism** views criminal law and the criminal justice system solely as instruments for controlling the poor, have-not members of society. It views the state as the tool of capitalists.

According to the instrumental view, capitalist justice serves the powerful and rich and enables them to impose their morality and standards of behavior on the entire society. Under capitalism, those who wield economic power are able to extend their self-serving definition of illegal or criminal behavior to encompass those who might threaten the status quo or interfere with their quest for ever-increasing profits.[32] For example, the concentration of economic assets in the nation's largest industrial firms translates into the political power needed to control tax laws to limit the firms' tax liabilities.[33] Some have the economic clout to hire top attorneys to defend them against antitrust actions, making them almost immune to regulation.

The poor, according to this branch of Marxist theory, may or may not commit more crimes than the rich, but they certainly are arrested and punished more often. Under the capitalist system, the poor are driven to crime because a natural frustration exists in a society in which affluence is well publicized but unattainable. When class conflict becomes unbearable, frustration can spill out in riots, such as the one that occurred in Los Angeles on April 29, 1992, which was described as a "class rebellion of the underprivileged against the privileged."[34] Because of class conflict, a deep-rooted hostility is generated among members of the lower class toward a social order they are not allowed to shape and whose benefits are unobtainable.[35]

Instrumental Marxists consider it essential to **demystify** law and justice—that is, to unmask its true purpose. Criminological theories that focus on family structure, intelligence, peer relations, and school performance keep the lower classes servile by showing why they are more criminal, less intelligent, and more prone to school failure and family problems than the middle class. Demystification involves identifying the destructive intent of capitalist inspired and funded criminology. Instrumental Marxists' goal for criminology is to show how capitalist law preserves ruling-class power.[36]

Structural Marxism   **Structural Marxism** disagrees with the view that the relationship between law and capitalism is unidirectional, always working for the rich and against the poor.[37] Law is not the exclusive domain of the rich; rather, it is used to maintain the long-term interests of the capitalist system and to control members of any class who threaten its existence. If law and justice were purely instruments of the capitalist class, why would laws controlling corporate crimes, such as price-fixing, false advertising, and illegal restraint of trade, have been created and enforced?

To a structuralist, the law is designed to keep the capitalist system operating efficiently, and anyone, capitalist or proletarian, who rocks the boat is targeted for sanction. For example, antitrust legislation is designed to prevent any single capitalist from dominating the system. If the capitalist system is to function, no single person can become too powerful at the expense of the economic

instrumental Marxist
One who sees criminal law and the criminal justice system as capitalist instruments for controlling the lower class.

demystify
To unmask the true purpose of law, justice, or other social institutions.

structural Marxism
Based on the belief that criminal law and the criminal justice system area means of defending and preserving the capitalist system.

system as a whole. Structuralists would regard the efforts of the U.S. government to break up Microsoft as an example of capitalists controlling capitalists to keep the system on an even keel. The long prison sentences given to corporate executives who engage in insider trading is a warning to capitalists that they must play by the rules.

Economic Structure and Surplus Value   Regardless of whether they take an instrumental or structural view, critical thinkers believe that the key crime-producing element of capitalism is **surplus value**—the profits produced by the laboring classes that are accrued by business owners. Surplus value can be either reinvested or used to enrich the owners. To increase the rate of surplus value, workers can be made to work harder for less pay, be made more efficient, or be replaced by machines or technology. Therefore, economic growth does not benefit all elements of the population, and in the long run it may produce the same effect as a depression or recession.

As the rate of surplus value increases, more people are displaced from productive relationships, and the size of the marginal population swells. As corporations downsize to increase profits, high-paying labor and managerial jobs are lost to computer-driven machinery. Displaced workers are forced into service jobs at minimum wage. Many become temporary employees without benefits or a secure position.

As more people are thrust outside the economic mainstream, a condition referred to as **marginalization,** a larger portion of the population is forced to live in areas conducive to crime. Once people are marginalized, commitment to the system declines, producing another crimogenic force: a weakened bond to society.[38] This process is illustrated in Figure 8.2.

■ According to Marxist theory, the need to create surplus value involves the exploitation of the working classes. Here, protesters clash with undercover police in Miami on November 20, 2003, during a march against the Free Trade Act, which they consider an instrument of worker oppression.

The government may be quick to respond during periods of economic decline because those in power assume that poor economic conditions breed crime and social disorder. When unemployment is increasing, public officials assume the worst and devote greater attention to the criminal justice system, perhaps building new prisons to prepare for the coming "crime wave."[39] Empirical research confirms that economic downturns are indeed linked to both crime rate increases and government activities such as passing anticrime legislation.[40] For example, as the level of surplus value increases, so too do police expenditures, most likely because of the perceived or real need for the state to control those on the economic margin.[41]

Globalization   The new global economy is a particular vexing development for critical theorists and their use of the concept of surplus value. **Globalization,** which usually refers to the process of creating transnational markets and political and legal systems, has shifted the focus of critical inquiry to a world perspective.

Globalization began when large companies decided to establish themselves in foreign markets by adapting their products or services to the local culture. The process took off with the fall of the Soviet Union, which opened new European markets. The development of China into a super industrial power encouraged foreign investors to take advantage of China's huge supply of workers. As the Internet and communication revolution unfolded, companies were able to establish instant communications with their far-flung corporate empires, a technological breakthrough that further aided trade and foreign investments. A series of transnational corporate mergers (such as Daimler Chrysler) and takeovers (such as Ford and Volvo) produced ever-larger transnational corporations.

Some experts believe globalization can improve the standard of living in third world nations by providing jobs and training, but critical theorists ques-

surplus value
The difference between what workers produce and what they are paid, which goes to business owners as profits.

marginalization
Displacement of workers, pushing them outside the economic and social mainstream.

globalization
The process of creating a global economy through transnational markets and political and legal systems.

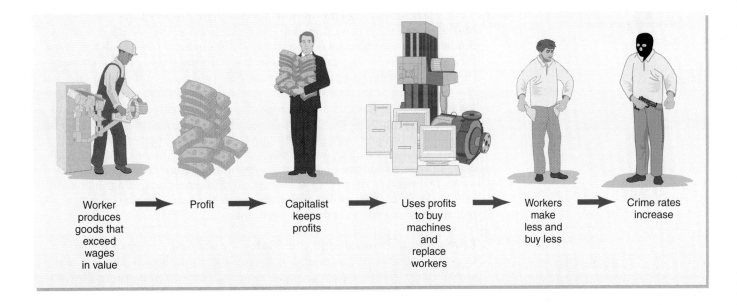

Figure 8.2
Surplus Value and Crime

tion the altruism of multinational corporations. Their motives are exploiting natural resources, avoiding regulation, and taking advantage of desperate workers. When these giant corporations set up a factory in a developing nation, it is not to help the local population but to get around environmental laws and take advantage of needy workers who may be forced to labor in substandard conditions. Globalization has replaced imperialism and colonization as a new form of economic domination and oppression.

Conflict thinkers David Friedrichs and Jessica Friedrichs warn that globalization presents a four-pronged threat to the world economy:

1. Growing global dominance and the reach of the free-market capitalist system, which disproportionately benefits wealthy and powerful organizations and individuals.
2. Increasing vulnerability of indigenous people with a traditional way of life to the forces of globalized capitalism.
3. Growing influence and impact of international financial institutions (such as the World Bank) and the related relative decline of power of local or state-based institutions.
4. Nondemocratic operation of international financial institutions.[42]

Globalization may have a profound influence on the concept of surplus value. Workers in the United States may be replaced in high-paying manufacturing jobs not by machines but by foreign workers. Instant communication via the Internet and global communications, a development that Marx could not have foreseen, will speed the effect immeasurably. Globalization will have a profound effect on both the economy and eventually on crime rates.

Research on Critical Criminology

Marxist criminologists rarely use standard social science methodologies to test their views because many believe the traditional approach of measuring research subjects is antihuman and insensitive.[43] Marxists believe that the research conducted by mainstream liberal and positivist criminologists is designed to unmask weak, powerless members of society so they can be better dealt with by the legal system. They are particularly offended by purely empirical studies, such as those designed to show that minority group members have lower IQs than whites or that the inner city is the site of the most serious crime whereas middle-class areas are relatively crime free.

Empirical research, however, is not considered totally incompatible with Marxist criminology, and there have been some important efforts to test its fundamental assumptions quantitatively.[44] For example, research has shown that the property crime rate reflects a change in the level of surplus value; the capitalist system's emphasis on excessive profits accounts for the need of the working class to commit property crime.[45] Nonetheless, critical research tends to be historical and analytical, not quantitative and empirical. Social trends are interpreted with regard to how capitalism has affected human interaction. Research focuses on both macro-level issues, such as how the accumulation of wealth affects crime rates, and micro-level issues, such as the effect of criminal interactions on the lives of individuals living in a capitalist society. Of particular importance to critical thinkers is analyzing the historical development of capitalist social control institutions, such as criminal law, police agencies, courts, and prison systems.

Crime, the Individual, and the State   Critical criminologists devote considerable attention to the relationships among crime, victims, the criminal, and the state. Two common themes emerge: (1) crime and its control are a function of capitalism, and (2) the justice system is biased against the working class and favors upper-class interests.

Critical analysis of the criminal justice system is designed to identify the often-hidden processes that control people's lives. It takes into account how conditions, processes, and structures evolved into what they are today. One issue considered is the process by which deviant behavior is defined as criminal or delinquent in U.S. society.[46] Another issue is the degree to which class affects the justice system's decision-making process.[47] Also subject to analysis is how power relationships help undermine any benefit the lower class receives from sentencing reforms.[48]

In general, critical research efforts have yielded evidence linking operations of the justice system to class bias.[49] In addition, some researchers have attempted to show how capitalism intervenes across the entire spectrum of crime-related phenomena. In addition to conducting studies showing the relationship between crime and the state, some critical researchers have attempted to show how capitalism influences the distribution of punishment. Robert Weis found that the expansion of the prison population is linked to the need for capitalists to acquire a captive and low-paid labor force to compete with overseas laborers and domestic immigrant labor. Employing immigrants has its political downside because it displaces "American" workers and antagonizes their legal representatives. In contrast, using prison labor can be viewed as a humanitarian gesture. Weiss also observes that an ever-increasing prison population is politically attractive because it masks unemployment rates. Many inmates were chronically unemployed before their imprisonment; incarcerating the chronically unemployed allows politicians to claim they have lowered unemployment. When the millions of people who are on probation and parole and who must maintain jobs are added to the mix, the correctional system is now playing an ever-more important role in suppressing wages and maintaining the profitability of capitalism.[50]

This type of research does not set out to prove statistically that capitalism causes crime but rather to show that it creates an environment in which crime is inevitable. Critical research is humanistic, situational, descriptive, and analytical rather than statistical, rigid, and methodological.

Critical theorists argue that there must be a thorough rethinking of the role and purpose of the criminal justice system, giving the powerless a greater voice to express their needs and concerns, if these inequities are to be addressed.[51]

Historical Analysis   Another type of critical research focuses on the historical background of commonly held institutional beliefs and practices. One goal is to show how changes in criminal law correspond to the development of the capitalist economy. The second goal is to investigate the development of modern police agencies.

To examine the changes in criminal law, historian Michael Rustigan analyzed historical records to show that law reform in nineteenth-century England was largely a response to pressure from the business community to increase punishment for property law violations to protect their rapidly increasing wealth.[52] Other research has focused on topics such as how the relationship between convict work and capitalism evolved during the nineteenth century. During this period, prisons became a profitable method of centralized state control over lower-class criminals, whose labor was exploited by commercial concerns. These criminals were forced to labor to pay off wardens and correctional administrators.[53]

Critique of Critical Criminology

Critical criminology has been sharply criticized by some members of the criminological mainstream, who charge that its contribution has been "hot air, heat, but no real light."[54] In turn, critical thinkers have accused mainstream criminologists of being culprits in developing state control over individual lives and selling out their ideals for the chance to receive government funding.

Mainstream criminologists have also attacked the substance of critical thought. Some argue that critical theory simply rehashes the old tradition of helping the underdog, in which the poor steal from the rich to survive.[55] In reality, most theft is for luxury, not survival. While the wealthy do commit their share of illegal acts, these are nonviolent and leave no permanent injuries.[56] People do not live in fear of corrupt businessmen and stock traders; they fear muggers and rapists.

Other critics suggest that critical theorists unfairly neglect the capitalist system's efforts to regulate itself—for example, by instituting antitrust regulations and putting violators in jail. Similarly, they ignore efforts to institute social reforms aimed at helping the poor.[57] There seems to be no logic in condemning a system that helps the poor and empowers them to take on corporate interests in a court of law. Even inherently conservative institutions such as police departments have made attempts at self-regulation when they become aware of class- and race-based inequality such as the use of racial profiling in making traffic stops.[58]

Some argue that critical thinkers refuse to address the problems and conflicts that exist in socialist countries, such as the gulags and purges of the Soviet Union under Stalin. Similarly, they fail to explain why some highly capitalist countries, such as Japan, have extremely low crime rates. Critical criminologists are too quick to blame capitalism for every human vice without adequate explanation or regard for other social and environmental factors.[59] In so doing, they ignore objective reality and refuse to acknowledge that members of the lower classes tend to victimize one another. They ignore the plight of the lower classes, who must live in crime-ridden neighborhoods, while condemning the capitalist system from the security of the "ivory tower." ✔ Checkpoints

✔ Checkpoints

✔ Critical criminology tries to explain how the workings of the capitalist system produce inequality and crime.

✔ In this view, the state serves the interests of the ruling capitalist class. Criminal law is an instrument of economic oppression. Capitalism demands that the subordinate classes remain oppressed.

✔ Instrumental Marxists believe that the legal system supports the owners at the expense of the workers.

✔ Structural Marxists believe that the law also ensures that no capitalist becomes too powerful. The law is used to maintain the long-term interests of the capitalist system.

✔ The concept of surplus value means that capitalists exploit workers and keep the excess profits from workers' labors.

✔ Globalization has meant that capitalists can exploit foreign workers for labor and acquire foreign natural resources to maximize their profits.

✔ Critical research is designed to show how capitalism creates large groups of people who turn to crime for survival.

To quiz yourself on this material, go to questions 8.5–8.9 on the Criminology: The Core 2e Web site.

Emerging Forms of Social Conflict Theory

Social conflict thinkers are now exploring new avenues of inquiry which fall outside the traditional models of conflict and critical theories. The following sections discuss in detail some recent developments in the conflict approach to crime.

Left Realism

Some conflict scholars are now addressing the need for the left wing to respond to the increasing power of right-wing conservatives. They are troubled by the emergence of a strict "law and order" philosophy, which has as its centerpiece a policy of punishing juveniles severely in adult court. At the same time, they find the focus of most left-wing scholarship—the abuse of power by the ruling elite—too narrow. It is wrong, they argue, to ignore inner-city gang crime and violence, which often target indigent people.[60] The approach of scholars who share these concerns is referred to as **left realism**.[61]

Left realism is most often connected to the writings of British scholars John Lea and Jock Young. In their well-respected 1984 work, *What Is to Be Done about Law and Order?*, they reject the utopian views of "idealistic" Marxists who portray street criminals as revolutionaries.[62] They take the more "realistic" approach that street criminals prey on the poor and disenfranchised, thus making the poor doubly abused, first by the capitalist system and then by members of their own class.

Lea and Young's view of crime causation borrows from conventional sociological theory and closely resembles the relative deprivation approach, which posits that experiencing poverty in the midst of plenty creates discontent and breeds crime. As they put it, "The equation is simple: relative deprivation equals discontent; discontent plus lack of political solution equals crime."[63]

In a more recent book, *Crime in Context: A Critical Criminology of Market Societies* (1999), Ian Taylor recognizes that anyone who expects an instant socialist revolution to take place is simply engaging in wishful thinking.[64] He uses data from both Europe and North America to show that the world is currently in the midst of multiple crises, which are shaping all human interaction including criminality. These crises include lack of job creation, social inequality, social fear, political incompetence and failure, gender conflict, and family and parenting issues. These crises have led to a society in which the government seems incapable of creating positive social change: people have become more fearful and isolated from one another and some are excluded from the mainstream because of racism and discrimination; manufacturing jobs have been exported overseas to nations that pay extremely low wages; and fiscal constraints inhibit the possibility of reform. These problems often fall squarely on the shoulders of young black men, who suffer from exclusion and poverty and who now feel the economic burden created by the erosion of manufacturing jobs due to the globalization of the economy. In response, they engage in a form of hypermasculinity, which helps increase their crime rates.[65]

■ Preemptive deterrence is an approach that seeks to reduce crime before police involvement is required. Here, Acting Chief of Police Deborah Barrows, of Hartford, Connecticut, speaks at a news conference about a federally funded gun buyback program, as HUD Assistant Secretary Cardell Cooper listens. The HUD-funded program will give a voucher worth $100 for each gun turned in to the Hartford Police Department, no questions asked.

left realism
Approach that sees crime as a function of relative deprivation under capitalism and favors pragmatic, community-based crime prevention and control.

preemptive deterrence
Efforts to prevent crime through community organization and youth involvement.

Crime Protection   Left realists argue that crime victims in all classes need and deserve protection; crime control reflects community needs. They do not view police and the courts as inherently evil tools of capitalism whose tough tactics alienate the lower classes. In fact, they recognize that these institutions offer life-saving public services. The left realists wish, however, that police would reduce their use of force and increase their sensitivity to the public.[66]

Preemptive deterrence is an approach in which community organization efforts eliminate or reduce crime before police involvement becomes necessary. The reasoning behind this approach is that if the number of marginalized youths (those who feel they are not part of society and have nothing to lose by committing crime) could be reduced, then delinquency rates would decline.[67]

Although implementing a socialist economy might help eliminate the crime problem, left realists recognize that something must be done to control crime under the existing capitalist system. To develop crime control policies, left realists not only welcome critical ideas but also build on the work of strain theorists, social ecologists, and other mainstream views. Community-based efforts seem to hold the greatest promise of crime control.

Left realism has been criticized by critical thinkers as legitimizing the existing power structure: By supporting existing definitions of law and justice, it suggests that the "deviant" and not the capitalist system causes society's problems. Critics question whether left realists advocate the very institutions that "currently imprison us and our patterns of thought and action."[68] In rebuttal, left realists say that it is unrealistic to speak of a socialist state lacking a police force or a system of laws and justice. They believe the criminal code does, in fact, represent public opinion.

Critical Feminist Theory

Like so many theories in criminology, most of the efforts of critical theorists have been devoted to explaining male criminality.[69] To remedy this theoretical lapse, a number of feminist writers have attempted to explain the cause of crime, gender differences in crime rates, and the exploitation of female victims from a critical perspective.

Critical feminism views gender inequality as stemming from the unequal power of men and women in a capitalist society, which leads to the exploitation of women by fathers and husbands. Under this system, women are considered a commodity worth possessing, like land or money.[70]

The origin of gender differences can be traced to the development of private property and male domination of the laws of inheritance, which led to male control over property and power.[71] A **patriarchal** system developed in which men's work was valued and women's work was devalued. As capitalism prevailed, the division of labor by gender made women responsible for the unpaid maintenance and reproduction of the current and future labor force, which was derisively called "domestic work." Although this unpaid work done by women is crucial and profitable for capitalists, who reap these free benefits, such labor is exploitative and oppressive for women.[72] Even when women gained the right to work for pay, they were exploited as cheap labor. The dual exploitation of women within the household and in the labor market means that women produce far greater surplus value for capitalists than men.

Patriarchy, or male supremacy, has been and continues to be supported by capitalists. This system sustains female oppression at home and in the workplace.[73] Although the number of traditional patriarchal families is in steep decline, in those that still exist, a wife's economic dependence ties men more securely to wage-earning jobs, further serving the interests of capitalists by undermining potential rebellion against the system.

Patriarchy and Crime   Critical feminists link criminal behavior patterns to the gender conflict created by the economic and social struggles common in postindustrial societies. In *Capitalism, Patriarchy, and Crime,* James Messerschmidt argues that capitalist society is marked by both patriarchy and class conflict. Capitalists control the labor of workers, and men control women both economically and biologically.[74] This "double marginality" explains why females in a capitalist society commit fewer crimes than males. Because they are isolated in the family, they have fewer opportunities to engage in elite deviance (white-collar and economic crimes). Although powerful females as well as males will commit white-collar crimes, the female crime rate is restricted because of the patriarchal nature of the capitalist system.[75] Women are also denied access to male-dominated street crimes. Because capitalism renders lower-class women powerless, they are forced to commit less serious, nonviolent, self-destructive crimes, such as abusing drugs.

Powerlessness also increases the likelihood that women will become targets of violent acts.[76] When lower-class males are shut out of the economic opportunity structure, they try to build their self-image through acts of machismo; such acts may involve violent abuse of women. This type of

Critical feminism
Approach that explains both victimization and criminality among women in terms of gender inequality, patriarchy, and the exploitation of women under capitalism.

patriarchal
Male-dominated.

■ Critical feminists view gender inequality as a function of female exploitation by men. Women have become a "commodity" worth possessing, like land or money. The origin of gender differences can be traced to the development of private property and male domination over the laws of inheritance, which led to their control over property and power. Are these teen prostitutes—shown here waiting to be booked at the Maricopa, Arizona, jail—a by-product of this view of women as commodities, which was engendered by the capitalist system?

reaction accounts for a significant percentage of female victims who are attacked by a spouse or intimate partner.

In *Masculinities and Crime,* Messerschmidt expands on these themes.[77] He suggests that in every culture males try to emulate "ideal" masculine behaviors. In Western culture, this means being authoritative, in charge, combative, and controlling. Failure to adopt these roles leaves men feeling effeminate and unmanly. Their struggle to dominate women in order to prove their manliness is called "doing gender." Crime is a vehicle for men to "do gender" because it separates them from the weak and allows them to demonstrate physical bravery. Violence directed toward women is an especially economical way to demonstrate manhood. Would a weak, effeminate male ever attack a woman?

Feminist writers have supported this view by maintaining that in contemporary society men achieve masculinity at the expense of women. In the best-case scenario, men must convince others that in no way are they feminine or have female qualities. For example, they are sloppy and don't cook or do house work because these are "female" activities. More ominously, men may work at excluding, hurting, denigrating, exploiting, or otherwise abusing actual women. Even in all-male groups men often prove their manhood by treating the weakest member of the group as "woman-like" and abusing him accordingly. Men need to defend themselves at all costs from being contaminated with femininity, and these efforts begin in children's play groups and continue into adulthood and marriage.[78]

Exploitation and Criminality   Feminists also focus on the social forces that shape women's lives and experiences to explain female criminality.[79] For example, they attempt to show how the sexual victimization of girls is a function of male socialization because so many young males learn to be aggressive and to exploit women. Males seek out same-sex peer groups for social support; these groups encourage members to exploit and sexually abuse women. On college campuses, peers encourage sexual violence against women who are considered "teasers," "bar pickups," or "loose women." These derogatory labels allow the males to justify their actions; a code of secrecy then protects the aggressors from retribution.[80]

According to the critical feminist view, exploitation triggers the onset of female delinquent and deviant behavior. When female victims run away and abuse substances, they may be reacting to abuse they have suffered at home or at school. Their attempts at survival are labeled as deviant or delinquent behavior.[81] In a sense, the female criminal is herself a victim.

Power–Control Theory

John Hagan and his associates have created a critical feminist model that uses gender differences to explain the onset of criminality.[82] Hagan's view is that crime and delinquency rates are a function of two factors: (1) class position (power) and (2) family functions (control).[83] The link between these two variables is that, within the family, parents reproduce the power relationships they hold in the workplace; a position of dominance at work is equated with control in the household. As a result, parents' work experiences and class position influence the criminality of children.[84]

In **paternalistic families,** fathers assume the traditional role of bread-winners, while mothers tend to have menial jobs or remain at home to supervise domestic matters. Within the paternalistic home, mothers are expected to control the behavior of their daughters while granting greater freedom to sons. In such a home, the parent–daughter relationship can be viewed as a preparation for the "cult of domesticity," which makes girls' involvement in delinquency unlikely, whereas boys are freer to deviate because they are not subject to maternal control. Girls growing up in patriarchal families are socialized to fear legal sanctions more than are males; consequently, boys in these families exhibit more delinquent behavior than their sisters. The result is that boys not only engage in more antisocial behaviors but have greater access to legitimate adult behaviors, such as working at part-time jobs or possessing their own transportation. In contrast, without these legitimate behavioral outlets, girls who are unhappy or dissatisfied with their status are forced to seek out risky **role exit behaviors,** including such desperate measures as running away and contemplating suicide.

In **egalitarian families**—those in which the husband and wife share similar positions of power at home and in the workplace—daughters gain a kind of freedom that reflects reduced parental control. These families produce daughters whose law-violating behavior mirrors their brothers'. In an egalitarian family, girls may have greater opportunity to engage in legitimate adult status behaviors and less need to enact deviant role exits.[85]

Ironically, these relationships also occur in female-headed households with absent fathers. Hagan and his associates found that when fathers and mothers hold equally valued managerial positions, the similarity between the rates of their daughters' and sons' delinquency is greatest. By implication, middle-class girls are the most likely to violate the law because they are less closely controlled than their lower-class counterparts. In homes in which both parents hold positions of power, girls are more likely to have the same expectations of career success as their brothers. Consequently, siblings of both sexes will be socialized to take risks and engage in other behavior related to delinquency.

Evaluating Power–Control This **power–control theory** has received a great deal of attention in the criminological community because it encourages a new approach to the study of criminality, one that includes gender differences, class position, and the structure of the family. Empirical analysis of its premises has generally been supportive. For example, Brenda Sims Blackwell's research supports a key element of power–control theory: Females in paternalistic households have learned to fear legal sanctions more than have their brothers.[86]

Not all research is as supportive.[87] Some critics have questioned its core assumption that power and control variables can explain crime.[88] More specifically, critics fail to replicate the finding that upper-class kids are more likely to deviate than their lower-class peers or that class and power interact

paternalistic families
Father is breadwinner and rule maker; mother has menial job or is homemaker only. Sons are granted greater freedom than daughters.

role exit behaviors
Strategies such as running away or contemplating suicide used by young girls unhappy with their status in the family.

egalitarian families
Husband and wife share similar positions of power at home and in the workplace. Sons and daughters have equal freedom.

power–control theory
The view that gender differences in crime are a function of economic power (class position, one- versus two-earner families) and parental control (paternalistic versus egalitarian families).

FIND IT ON INFOTRAC
College Edition

Use "semiotics" as a key word to learn more about this complex concept.

to produce delinquency.[89] Some researchers have found few gender-based supervision and behavior differences in worker-, manager-, or owner-dominated households.[90] It is possible that the concept of class employed by Hagan may have to be reconsidered. Moreover, power–control theory must now consider the multitude of power and control relationships that are emerging in postmodern society: blended families, and families where mothers hold managerial positions and fathers are blue-collar workers, and so forth.[91]

Postmodern Theory

A number of critical thinkers, referred to as postmodernists or deconstructionists, have embraced semiotics as a method of understanding all human relations, including criminal behavior. **Semiotics** refers to the use of language elements as signs or symbols beyond their literal meaning. Thus, **deconstructionists** critically analyze communication and language in legal codes to determine whether they contain language and content that institutionalize racism or sexism.[92]

Postmodernists rely on semiotics to conduct their research efforts. For example, the term *special needs children* is designed to describe these youngsters' learning needs, but it may also characterize the children themselves as mentally challenged, dangerous, or uncontrollable. Postmodernists believe that value-laden language can promote inequities. Truth, identity, justice, and power are all concepts whose meaning is derived from the language dictated by those in power.[93] Laws, legal skill, and justice are commodities that can be bought and sold like any other service or product.[94] For example, the O. J. Simpson case is vivid proof that the affluent can purchase a different brand of justice than the indigent.[95]

Postmodernists assert that there are different languages and ways of knowing. Those in power can use their own language to define crime and law while excluding or dismissing those who oppose their control, such as prisoners and the poor. By dismissing these oppositional languages, certain versions of how to think, feel, or act are devalued and excluded. This exclusion is seen as the source of conflict in society.[96]

Peacemaking Criminology

To members of the **peacemaking** movement, the main purpose of criminology is to promote a peaceful, just society. Rather than standing on empirical analysis of data, peacemaking draws its inspiration from religious and philosophical teachings ranging from Quakerism to Zen.[97]

Peacemakers view the efforts of the state to punish and control as crime-encouraging rather than crime-discouraging. These views were first articulated in a series of books with an anarchist theme written by criminologists Larry Tifft and Dennis Sullivan in 1980.[98] Tifft argues, "The violent punishing acts of the state and its controlling professions are of the same genre as the violent acts of individuals. In each instance these acts reflect an attempt to monopolize human interaction."[99]

Sullivan stresses the futility of correcting and punishing criminals in the context of our conflict-ridden society: "The reality we must grasp is that we live in a culture of severed relationships, where every available institution provides a form of banishment but no place or means for people to become connected, to be responsible to and for each other."[100] Sullivan suggests that mutual aid rather than coercive punishment is the key to a harmonious society. In their newest volume, *Restorative Justice* (2001), Sullivan and Tifft reaffirm their belief that society must seek humanitarian forms of justice without resorting to brutal punishments:

✔ **Checkpoints**

✔ Left realists are conflict scholars who believe the lower classes must be protected from predatory criminals until the social system changes and makes crime obsolete.

✔ Critical feminists study patriarchy and the oppression of women. They link female criminality to gender inequality.

✔ Power–control theory shows how family structure, women's economic status, and gender inequity interact to produce male/female differences in crime rates.

✔ Postmodernists think language controls thought and behavior.

✔ Peacemaking criminologists seek nonviolent, humane alternatives to coercive punishment.

To quiz yourself on this material, go to questions 8.10–8.15 on the Criminology: The Core 2e Web site.

semiotics
The use of language elements as signs or symbols beyond their literal meaning.

deconstructionist
Approach that focuses on the use of language by those in power to define crime based on their own values and biases; also called postmodernist.

postmodernist
Approach that focuses on the use of language by those in power to define crime based on their own values and biases; also called deconstructionist.

peacemaking
Approach that considers punitive crime control strategies to be counterproductive and favors the use of humanistic conflict resolution to prevent and control crime.

Peacemakers believe in restoration and not revenge, even for the most heinous of crimes. They are firmly against the death penalty. Here, Scott Langley, Chris Banner, and Virginia Flodges sing together for death row inmates at the U.S. Federal Penitentiary in Terre Haute, Indiana. The three participated in an 80-mile march from Indianapolis to Terre Haute in protest of the death penalty.

© 2000 AP/Wide World Photos

By allowing feelings of vengeance or retribution to narrow our focus on the harmful event and the person responsible for it—as others might focus solely on a sin committed and the "sinner"—we tell ourselves we are taking steps to free ourselves from the effects of the harm or the sin in question. But, in fact, we are putting ourselves in a servile position with respect to life, human growth, and the further enjoyment of relationships with others.[101]

Today, advocates of the peacemaking movement, such as Harold Pepinsky and Richard Quinney (who has shifted his theoretical orientation from conflict theory to Marxism and now to peacemaking), try to find humanist solutions to crime and other social problems.[102] Rather than punishment and prison, they advocate such policies as mediation and conflict resolution.[103]

Concept Summary 8.1 summarizes the various emerging forms of critical criminology. ✔ Checkpoints

CONCEPT SUMMARY 8.1 Emerging Forms of Critical Criminology

THEORY	MAJOR PREMISE	STRENGTHS	RESEARCH FOCUS
Left realism	Crime is a function of relative deprivation; criminals prey on the poor.	Represents a compromise between conflict and traditional criminology.	Deterrence; protection
Critical feminist theory	The capitalist system creates patriarchy, which oppresses women.	Explains gender bias, violence against women, and repression.	Gender inequality; oppression; patriarchy
Power–control theory	Girls are controlled more closely than boys in traditional male-dominated households. There is gender equity in contemporary egalitarian homes.	Explains gender differences in the crime rate as a function of class and gender conflict.	Power and control; gender differences; domesticity
Postmodern theory	Language controls the meaning and use of the law.	Provides a critical analysis of meaning.	Language; gesture; interpretation
Peacemaking criminology	Peace and humanism can reduce crime; conflict resolution strategies can work.	Offers a new approach to crime control through mediation.	Punishment; nonviolence; mediation

Social Conflict Theory and Public Policy

Connections

Contrast this approach with the crime control–deterrence policies advocated by rational choice theorists in Chapter 4.

At the core of all the varying branches of social conflict theory is the fact that conflict causes crime. If conflict and competition in society could somehow be reduced, it is possible that crime rates would fall. Some critical theorists believe this goal can only be accomplished by thoroughly reordering society so that capitalism is destroyed and a socialist state is created. Others call for a more "practical" application of conflict principles. Nowhere has this been more successful than in applying peacemaking principles in the criminal justice system.

There has been an ongoing effort to reduce the conflict created by the criminal justice system when it hands out harsh punishments to offenders, many of whom are powerless social outcasts. Conflict theorists argue that the "old methods" of punishment are a failure and that upwards of two-thirds of all prison inmates recidivate soon after their release. They scoff at claims that the crime rate has dropped because the number of people in prison is at an all time high, countering these claims with studies showing that imprisonment rates are not at all related to crime rates; there is no consistent finding that locking people up helps reduce crimes.[104]

Rather than cast them aside, peacemakers have found a way to bring them back to the community. This peacemaking movement has adopted nonviolent methods and applied them to what is known as **restorative justice.** Springing both from academia and justice system personnel, the restorative approach relies on nonpunitive strategies for crime prevention and control.[105] The next sections discuss the foundation and principles of restorative justice.

The Concept of Restorative Justice

The term *restorative justice* is often hard to define because it encompasses a variety of programs and practices. According to a leading restorative justice scholar, Howard Zehr, restorative justice requires that society address victims' harms and needs, hold offenders accountable to put right those harms, and involve victims, offenders, and communities in the process of healing. Zehr maintains that the core value of the restoration process can be translated into respect for all, even those who are different from us, even those who seem to be our enemies. At its core, Zehr argues, restorative justice is a set of principles, a philosophy, an alternate set of guiding questions that provide an alternative framework for thinking about wrongdoing.[106]

Restorative justice has grown out of a belief that the traditional justice system has done little to involve the community in the process of dealing with crime and wrongdoing. What has developed is a system of coercive punishments, administered by bureaucrats, that are inherently harmful to offenders and reduce the likelihood offenders will ever become productive members of society. This system relies on punishment, stigma, and disgrace. In his controversial book, *The Executed God: The Way of the Cross in Lockdown America*, theology professor Mark Lewis Taylor discusses the similarities between this contemporary, coercive justice system and that which existed in imperial Rome when Jesus and many of his followers were executed because they were an inspiration to the poor and slave populations. They represented a threat to the ruling Roman power structure. So, too, is our modern justice system designed to keep the downtrodden in their place. Taylor suggests that there should be a movement to reduce such coercive elements of justice as police brutality and the death penalty before our "lockdown society" becomes the model used around the globe.[107]

Advocates of restorative justice argue that rather than today's "lockdown" mentality, what is needed is a justice policy that repairs the harm caused by crime and that includes all parties who have suffered from that harm: the victim, the community, and the offender. The principles of this approach are set out in Exhibit 8.1.

restorative justice
Using humanistic, nonpunitive strategies to right wrongs and restore social harmony.

EXHIBIT **8.1 The Basic Principles of Restorative Justice**

- Crime is an offense against human relationships.
- Victims and the community are central to justice processes.
- The first priority of justice processes is to assist victims.
- The second priority is to restore the community, to the degree possible.
- The offender has personal responsibility to victims and to the community for crimes committed.
- The offender will develop improved competency and understanding as a result of the restorative justice experience.
- Stakeholders share responsibilities for restorative justice through partnerships for action.

SOURCE: Anne Seymour, "Restorative Justice/Community Justice," in *National Victim Assistance Academy Textbook* (Washington, D.C.: National Victim Assistance Academy, 2001).

The Process of Restoration

The restoration process begins by redefining crime in terms of a conflict among the offender, the victim, and affected constituencies (families, schools, workplaces, and so forth). Therefore, it is vitally important that the resolution take place within the context in which the conflict originally occurred rather than being transferred to a specialized institution that has no social connection to the community or group from which the conflict originated. In other words, most conflicts are better settled in the community than in a court.

By maintaining "ownership" or jurisdiction over the conflict, the community is able to express its shared outrage about the offense. Shared community outrage is directly communicated to the offender. The victim is also given a chance to voice his or her story, and the offender can directly communicate his or her need for social reintegration and treatment.

All restoration programs involve an understanding between all the parties involved in a criminal act: the victim, the offender, and community. Although processes differ in structure and style, they generally include these elements:

1. The offender is asked to recognize that he or she caused injury to personal and social relations along with a determination and acceptance of responsibility (ideally accompanied by a statement of remorse). Only then can the offender be restored as a productive member of the community.

2. Restoration involves turning the justice system into a "healing" process rather than being a distributor of retribution and revenge.

3. Reconciliation is a big part of the restorative approach. Most people involved in offender–victim relationships actually know one another or were related in some way before the criminal incident took place. Instead of treating one of the involved parties as a victim deserving of sympathy and the other as a criminal deserving of punishment, it is more productive to address the issues that produced conflict between these people.[108]

4. The effectiveness of justice ultimately depends on the stake a person has in the community (or a particular social group). If a person does not value his or her membership in the group, the person will be unlikely to accept responsibility, show remorse, or repair the injuries caused by his or her actions. In contrast, people who have a stake in the community and its principle institutions, such as work, home, and school, find that their involvement enhances their personal and familial well-being.[109]

FIND IT ON INFOTRAC
College Edition

To read about restorative justice in practice, go to:

Mary Steiner and Matt Johnson, "Using Restorative Practices in Group Treatment," *Reclaiming Children and Youth*, 12 (2003): 53–57

5. A commitment to both material (monetary) restitution and symbolic reparation (an apology).

6. A determination of community support and assistance for both victim and offender.

The intended result of the process is to repair injuries suffered by the victim and the community while assuring reintegration of the offender.

Restoration Programs

Negotiation, mediation, consensus-building ,and peacemaking have been part of the dispute resolution process in European and Asian communities for centuries.[110] Native American and Native Canadian people have long used the type of community participation in the adjudication process (for example, sentencing circles, sentencing panels, elders panels) that restorative justice advocates are now embracing.[111]

In some Native American communities, people accused of breaking the law meet with community members, victims, if any, village elders, and agents of the justice system in a **sentencing circle.** Each member of the circle expresses his or her feelings about the act that was committed and raises questions or concerns. The accused can express regret about his or her actions and a desire to change the harmful behavior. People may suggest ways the offender can make things up to the community and those he or she harmed. A treatment program, such as Alcoholics Anonymous, can be suggested, if appropriate.

Restorative justice is now being embraced on many levels within our society and the justice system:

■ **Community.** Communities that isolate people and have few mechanisms for interpersonal interaction encourage and sustain crime. Those that implement forms of community dialogue to identify problems and plan tactics for their elimination, guided by restorative justice practices and principles, may create a climate in which violent crime is less likely to occur.[112]

■ **Schools.** Some schools have embraced restorative justice practices to deal with students who are involved in drug and alcohol abuse without having to resort to more punitive measures such as expulsion. Schools in Minnesota, Colorado, and elsewhere are now trying to involve students in "relational rehabilitation" programs that strive to improve individuals' relationships with key figures in the community who may have been harmed by their actions.[113]

■ **Police.** Restorative justice has also been implemented by police when crime is first encountered. The new community policing models discussed in Chapter 4 are an attempt to bring restorative concepts into law enforcement. Restorative justice relies on the fact that criminal justice policymakers need to listen and respond to the needs of those who are to be affected by their actions, and community policing relies on policies established with input and exchanges between officers and citizens.[114]

■ **Courts.** Restorative programs in the courts typically involve diverting the formal court process. These programs encourage meeting and reconciling the conflicts between offenders and victims via victim advocacy, mediation programs, and sentencing circles, in which crime victims and their families are brought together with offenders and their families in an effort to formulate a sanction that addresses the needs of each party. Victims are given a chance to voice their stories, and offenders can help compensate them financially or provide some service (for example, fixing damaged property).[115] The goal is to enable offenders to appreciate the damage they have caused, to make amends, and to be reintegrated back into society.

The Policy and Practice in Criminology feature discusses some recent innovative community programs based on the principles of restorative justice.

sentencing circle
A peacemaking technique in which offenders, victims, and other community members are brought together in an effort to formulate a sanction that addresses the needs of all.

POLICY AND PRACTICE IN CRIMINOLOGY

Practicing Restorative Justice

A number of new and innovative community programs based on restorative justice principles, four of which are discussed here, are being tested around the nation and the world.

South Africa

After 50 years of oppressive white rule in South Africa, the race-dividing apartheid policy was abolished in the early 1990s, and in 1994 Nelson Mandela, leader of the African National Congress, was elected president. Some black leaders wanted revenge for the political murders carried out during the apartheid era, but Mandela established The Truth and Reconciliation Commission. Rather than seeking vengeance for the crimes, this government agency investigated the atrocities with the mandate of granting amnesty to those individuals who confessed their roles in the violence and could prove that their actions served some political motive rather than being based on personal factors such as greed or jealousy.

Supporters of the commission believe that this approach will help heal the nation's wounds and prevent years of racial and ethnic strife. Mandela, who had been unjustly jailed for 27 years by the regime, had reason to desire vengeance. Yet he wanted to move the country forward after the truth of what happened in the past had been established. Though many South Africans, including some ANC members, believe the commission is too lenient, Mandela's attempts at reconciliation have prevailed. The commission is a model of restoration over revenge.

Minnesota

Minnesota has been a groundbreaker in restorative justice. Its Department of Corrections created the Restorative Justice Initiative in 1992, hiring Kay Pranis as a full-time restorative justice planner in 1994—the first such position in the country. The initiative offers training in restorative justice principles and practices, provides technical assistance to communities in designing and implementing practices, and creates networks of professionals and ac-

tivists to share knowledge and provide support.

Besides promoting victim–offender mediation, family group conferencing, and neighborhood conferencing, the department has introduced sentencing circles. Citizen volunteers and criminal justice officials from Minnesota have participated in training in the Yukon Territory, Canada, where peacemaking circles have been held since the late 1980s. In Minnesota the circle process is used by the Mille Lacs Indian Reservation and in other communities in several counties. The circle process usually has several phases. First, the Community Justice Committee conducts an intake interview with offenders who want to participate. Then, separate healing circles are held for the victim (and others who feel harmed) and the offender. The committee tries to cultivate a close personal relationship with victims and offenders and to create support networks for them. In the end, a sentencing circle, open to the community, meets to work out a sentencing plan.

Vermont

A pilot reparative probation program began in Vermont in 1994, and the first cases were heard by a reparative citizen board the following year. Three features distinguish this restorative justice initiative from most others in the United States: the Department of Corrections designed the program, it is implemented statewide, and it involves a sizable number of volunteer citizens. The process is straightforward. Following an adjudication of guilt, the judge sentences the offender to probation, with the sentence suspended and only two conditions imposed: the offender will commit no more crimes and will complete the reparative program. The volunteer board members meet with the offender and the victim and together discuss the offense, its effects on victim and community, and the life situations of victim and offender. All participants must agree on a contract to be fulfilled by the offender. It is based on five goals: the victim is restored and healed, the community is restored, the offender understands the effects of the crime, the

offender learns ways to avoid reoffending, and the community offers reintegration to the offender. Since reparative probation targets minor crimes, it is not meant as a prison diversion program. In 1998 the 44 boards handled 1,200 cases, accounting for more than one-third of the probation caseload. More than 300 trained volunteers serve as board members. Ten coordinators handle case management and organization for the boards. The goal is to have the boards handle about 70 percent of the targeted probation cases. That only about 17 percent of offenders fail to complete their agreements or attend follow-up board meetings is a measure of the program's success. These offenders are referred back to the courts.

Critical Thinking

Restorative justice may be the model that best serves alternative sanctions. How can this essentially humanistic approach be sold to the general public that now supports more punitive sanctions? For example, would it be feasible that using restorative justice with nonviolent offenders could free up resources for the relatively few dangerous people in the criminal population? Explain.

InfoTrac College Edition Research

To learn more about the restorative justice approach, see:

Gordon Bazemore, "Restorative Justice and Earned Redemption: Communities, Victims, and Offender Reintegration," *American Behavioral Scientist* 41 (1998): 768

Tag Evers, "A Healing Approach to Crime," *The Progressive* 62 (1998): 30

Carol La Prairie, "The Impact of Aboriginal Justice Research on Policy: A Marginal Past and an Even More Uncertain Future," *Canadian Journal of Criminology* 41 (1999): 249

SOURCES: Leena Kurki, *Incorporating Restorative and Community Justice into American Sentencing and Corrections* (Washington, D.C.: National Institute of Justice, 1999); Deborah Posel and Graeme Simpson, *Commissioning the Past: Understanding South Africa's Truth and Reconciliation Commission* (Johannesburg, South Africa: Witwatersrand University Press, 2003).

FIND IT ON INFOTRAC
College Edition

To read a critique of the approach, go to:

"Really Really Sorry; Restorative Justice," *The Economist (US)*, August 2, 2003 v368 p54

The Challenge of Restorative Justice

Restorative justice holds great promise, but there are also some concerns. For example, on a philosophical level, as John Braithwaite warns, there is tension when restorative justice advocates warn of the uneven exercise of state power and view it as a social movement designed to work at the lowest levels of the justice system and the fact that its philosophical fundamentals require it to exercise power albeit in a fair and even manner.[116]

Restorative justice programs must be wary of the cultural and social differences that can be found throughout our heterogeneous society. What may be considered "restorative" in one subculture may be considered insulting and damaging in another.[117] Similarly, so many diverse programs call themselves "restorative" that it is difficult to evaluate them since each one may be pursuing a unique objective. In other words, there is still no single definition of what constitutes restorative justice.[118]

Possibly the greatest challenge to restorative justice is the difficult task of balancing the needs of offenders with those of their victims. If programs focus solely on victims' needs, they may risk ignoring the offenders' needs and increased the likelihood of re-offending. Sharon Levrant and her colleagues suggest that restorative justice programs that feature short-term interactions with victims fail to help offenders learn pro-social ways of behaving. Restorative justice advocates may falsely assume that relatively brief interludes of public shaming will change deeply rooted criminal predispositions.[119]

In contrast, programs that focus on the offender may turn off victims and their advocates. Some victim advocacy groups have voiced concerns about the focus of restorative justice programs (see Exhibit 8.2).

EXHIBIT 8.2 Victim Concerns about Restorative Justice

- Restorative justice processes can cast victims as little more than props in a psychodrama focused on the offender, to restore him and thereby render him less likely to offend again.

- A victim, supported by family and intimates while engaged in restorative conferencing, and feeling genuinely free to speak directly to the offender, may press a blaming rather than restorative shaming agenda.

- The victims' movement has focused for years on a perceived imbalance of "rights." Criminal defendants enjoy the presumption of innocence, the right to proof beyond a reasonable doubt, the right not to have to testify, and lenient treatment when found guilty of crime. Victims were extended no rights at all in the legal process. Is restorative justice another legal giveaway to criminals?

- Victims' rights are threatened by some features of the restorative justice process, such as respectful listening to the offender's story and consensual dispositions. These features seem affronts to a victim's claim of the right to be seen as a victim, to insist on the offender being branded a criminal, to blame the offender, and not to be "victimized all over again by the process."

- Many victims do want an apology, if it is heartfelt and easy to get, but some want, even more, to put the traumatic incident behind them; to retrieve stolen property being held for use at trial; to be assured that the offender will receive treatment he is thought to need if he is not to victimize someone else. For victims such as these, restorative justice processes can seem unnecessary at best.

- Restorative processes depend, case by case, on victims' active participation in a role more emotionally demanding than that of complaining witness in a conventional criminal prosecution, which is itself a role avoided by many, perhaps most, victims.

SOURCE: Michael E. Smith, *What Future for "Public Safety" and "Restorative Justice" in Community Corrections?* (Washington, D.C.: National Institute of Justice, 2001).

These are a few of the obstacles that restorative justice programs must overcome to be successful and productive. Yet because the method holds so much promise, criminologists are now conducting numerous demonstration projects to find the most effective means of returning the ownership of justice to the people and the community.

Summary

- Social conflict theorists view crime as a function of the conflict that exists in society.

- Conflict theorists suggest that crime in any society is caused by class conflict. Laws are created by those in power to protect their rights and interests.

- All criminal acts have political undertones. Richard Quinney has called this concept "the social reality of crime."

- One of conflict theory's most important premises is that the justice system is biased and designed to protect the wealthy.

- Marxist criminology views the competitive nature of the capitalist system as a major cause of crime. The poor commit crimes because of their frustration, anger, and need. The wealthy engage in illegal acts because they are used to competition and because they must do so to keep their positions in society.

- Marxist scholars have attempted to show that the law is designed to protect the wealthy and powerful and to control the poor, have-not members of society.

- Among the branches of critical theory are instrumental Marxism and structural Marxism. The former holds that those in power wield their authority to control society and keep the lower classes in check. The latter maintains that the justice system is designed to maintain the status quo and is used to punish the wealthy if they bend the rules governing capitalism.

- Research on critical theory focuses on how the system of justice was designed and how it operates to further class interests. Quite often, this research uses historical analysis to show how the capitalist classes have exerted control over the police, courts, and correctional agencies.

- Both critical and conflict criminology have been heavily criticized by consensus criminologists, who suggest that social conflict theories make fundamental errors in their concepts of ownership and class interest.

- New forms of social conflict theory have been emerging.

- Critical feminist writers draw attention to the influence of patriarchal society on crime.

- According to power–control theory, gender differences in the crime rate can be explained by the structure of the family in a capitalist society.

- Left realism takes a centrist position on crime by showing its rational and destructive nature; the justice system is necessary to protect the lower classes until a socialist society can be developed, which will end crime.

- Postmodern theory looks at the symbolic meaning of law and culture.

- Peacemaking criminology brings a call for humanism to criminology.

- Conflict principles have been used to develop the restorative justice model. This holds that reconciliation rather than retribution should be used to prevent and control crime.

Thinking Like a Criminologist

An interim evaluation of Restoration House's New Hope for Families program, a community-based residential treatment program for women with dependent children, shows that 70 percent of women who complete follow-up interviews 6 months after treatment have maintained abstinence or reduced their drug use. The other 30 percent, however, lapse back into their old habits.

The program relies on restorative justice techniques in which community people meet with the women to discuss the harm drug use can cause and how it can damage both them and their children. The community members show their support and help the women find a niche in the community.

Women who complete the Restoration House program improve their employment, reduce parenting stress, retain custody of their children, and restore their physical, mental, and emotional health. The program focuses not only on reducing drug and alcohol use but also on increasing health, safety, self-sufficiency, and positive attitudes.

As a criminologist, would you consider this program a success? What questions would have to be answered before it gets your approval? How do you think the program should handle women who do not succeed in the program? Are there any other approaches you would try with these women? If so, explain.

Go to the Criminology: The Core 2e Web site to review the content of this chapter.

Doing Research on the Web

For an up-to-date list of URLs, go to

http://www.cj.wadsworth.com/siegel_crimcore2e

Before you formulate your answer, you may want to refer to the Center for Restorative Justice & Peacemaking, which provides links and information on the ideals of restoration and programs based on its principles:

http://ssw.che.umn.edu/rjp/default.html

Restorative Justice Online is a service of the Prison Fellowship International. More information on PFI can be found on Restorative Justice Online, which is a credible, nonpartisan source of information on restorative justice:

http://www.restorativejustice.org/rj3/
about_default.htm

The Balanced and Restorative Justice project (BARJ) is a nonprofit restorative justice training program funded by the United States Office of Juvenile Justice Delinquency Prevention and housed at the Community Justice Institute, Florida Atlantic University, Ft. Lauderdale Florida. BARJ provides training, technical assistance, system leadership development, and community support to those interested in implementing restorative justice initiatives in their agencies or local communities. Their site has a lot of important sources and information:

http://barjproject.org/index.html

Pro/Con discussions and Viewpoint Essays on some of the topics in this chapter may be found at the Opposing Viewpoints Resource Center:

http://www.gale.com/OpposingViewpoints

Key Terms

critical criminology 181
conflict theory 182
power 183
instrumental Marxist 187
demystify 187
structural Marxism 187
surplus value 188
marginalization 188
globalization 188
left realism 192
preemptive deterrence 192
critical feminism 193
patriarchal 193
paternalistic families 195
role exit behaviors 195
egalitarian families 195
power–control theory 195
semiotics 196
deconstructionist 196
postmodernist 196
peacemaking 196
restorative justice 198
sentencing circle 200

Critical Thinking Questions

1. How would a conservative reply to a call for more restorative justice? How would a restorative justice advocate respond to a conservative call for more prisons?

2. Considering recent changes in American culture, how would a power–control theorist explain recent drops in the U.S. crime rate?

3. Is conflict inevitable in all cultures? If not, what can be done to reduce the level of conflict in our own society?

4. If Marx were alive today, what would he think about the prosperity enjoyed by the working class in industrial societies? Might he alter his vision of the capitalist system?

Developmental Theories: Things Change

Chapter Objectives

1. Be familiar with the concept of developmental theory.
2. Know what is meant by a latent trait.
3. Be able to discuss Gottfredson and Hirschi's general theory of crime.
4. Be familiar with the concepts of impulsivity and self-control.
5. Know the factors that influence the life course.
6. Recognize that there are different pathways to crime.
7. Be able to discuss the social development model.
8. Describe what is meant by interactional theory.
9. Be familiar with the "turning points in crime."
10. Be able to discuss the influence of social capital on crime.

WILLIAM JANKLOW, A MAJOR FORCE IN SOUTH DAKOTA POLITICS, SERVED TERMS AS ATTORNEY GENERAL, governor, and then congressman. On August 16, 2003, Congressman Janklow ran a stop sign and hit Randy Scott, killing the motorcyclist. Despite his political prominence, the 64-year-old Janklow was charged with manslaughter, reckless driving, running a stop sign, and speeding. At his trial the defense argued that at the time of the crash Janklow, a diabetic, was suffering the effects of low blood sugar but did not know it because the symptoms were masked by heart medication. Witnesses rebuked that defense and testified that Janklow was driving in a reckless fashion and plowed through a stop sign at more than 70 miles per hour.

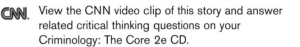

View the CNN video clip of this story and answer related critical thinking questions on your *Criminology: The Core 2e* CD.

The prosecution wanted to enter evidence of Janklow's prior behavior, but the trial judge prohibited mention of his 12 prior speeding tickets and three accidents. Yet most South Dakotans knew that Janklow had a long history of roaring down the road and flouting the speed limit. He bragged about his reckless driving in speeches and, as the state's attorney general and governor, had his car equipped with a siren and a flashing red light. On December 18, 2003, Janklow was found guilty on all four charges.

How can the chronic, risk-taking behavior of William Janklow be explained? Certainly his antisocial acts were not the product of a deprived background or a troubled childhood. What could trigger such reckless and impulsive behavior?

Some experts believe antisocial behavior is a function of a personal trait, such as a low IQ or impulsive personality, which is present at birth or soon afterward. Yet, if the onset of crime is explained by abnormally low intelligence or a defective personality, why is it that most people *desist* or age out of crime as they mature? It seems unlikely that intelligence increases as young offenders mature or that personality flaws disappear. Even if the onset of criminality can be explained by a single biological or personal trait, some other factor must explain its change, development, and continuance or termination.

Concern over these critical issues has prompted the development of some contemporary visions of criminality referred to here as

Connections

Chapter 2 addresses both chronic offending and aging out. These two issues are the cornerstones of contemporary criminological theories.

Latent trait theory

- Master trait
  - Personality
  - Intelligence
  - Genetic makeup
- People do not change, criminal opportunities change; maturity brings fewer opportunities
- Early social control and proper parenting can reduce criminal propensity

- Criminal careers are a passage
- Personal and structural factors influence crime
- Change affects crime
- Personal vs. situational

Life course theory

- Multiple traits: social, psychological, economic
- People change over the life course
- Family, job, peers influence behavior

Figure 9.1
Latent Trait versus Life Course Theories

developmental theory
The view that criminality is a dynamic process, influenced by social experiences as well as individual characteristics.

latent trait theory
The view that criminal behavior is controlled by a "master trait," present at birth or soon after, that remains stable and unchanging throughout a person's lifetime.

life course theory
Theory that focuses on changes in criminality over the life course; developmental theory.

latent trait
A stable feature, characteristic, property, or condition, such as defective intelligence or impulsive personality, that makes some people crime prone over the life course.

developmental theories. They seek to identify, describe, and understand the developmental factors that explain the onset and continuation of a criminal career. Rather than look at a single factor, such as poverty or low intelligence, and suggest that people who maintain this trait are predisposed to crime, developmental theories attempt to provide a more global vision of a criminal career encompassing its onset, continuation, and termination. It is not uncommon for developmental theories to intertwine *personal factors* such as personality and intelligence, *social factors* such as income and neighborhood, *socialization factors* such as marriage and military service, *cognitive factors* such as information processing and attention/perception, and *situational factors* such as criminal opportunity, effective guardianship, and apprehension risk into complex multifactor explanations of human behavior. As a group, they do not ask the relatively simple question: Why do people commit crime? Instead, they focus on more complex issues: Why do some offenders persist in criminal careers while others desist from or alter their criminal activity as they mature?[1] Why do some people continually escalate their criminal involvement while others slow down and turn their lives around? Are all criminals similar in their offending patterns, or are their different types of offenders and paths to offending? Developmental theorists want to know not only why people enter a criminal way of life but why, once they do, they are able to alter the trajectory of their criminal involvement.

Developmental theories fall into two distinct groups: latent trait and life course theories. **Latent trait theories** hold that human development is controlled by a "master trait" present at birth or soon after. Some criminologists believe this master trait remains stable and unchanging throughout a person's lifetime; others suggest it can be altered or influenced or changed by experience. In either event, as people travel through their life course, this trait is always present, directing their behavior. Because this master trait is enduring, the ebb and flow of criminal behavior is directed by the impact of external forces such as criminal opportunity and the reaction of others.

In contrast to this view, the **life course** branch views criminality as a dynamic process, influenced by a multitude of individual characteristics, traits, and social experiences. As people travel through the life course, they are constantly bombarded by changing perceptions and experiences, and as a result, their behavior changes directions, sometimes for the better and sometimes for the worse (see Figure 9.1). Each of these positions is discussed in detail in the following sections.

Latent Trait Theories

In a popular 1985 book, *Crime and Human Nature,* two prominent social scientists, James Q. Wilson and Richard Herrnstein, argued that personal traits, such as genetic makeup, intelligence, and body build, operate in tandem with social variables such as poverty and family function. Together these factors influence people to "choose crime" over noncriminal behavioral alternatives.[2]

Following their lead, David Rowe, D. Wayne Osgood, and W. Alan Nicewander proposed the concept of **latent traits.** Their model assumes that a number of people in the population have a personal attribute or characteristic that controls their inclination or propensity to commit crimes.[3] This disposition, or latent trait, is either present at birth or established early in life, and it remains stable over time. Suspected latent traits include defective intelligence, impulsive personality, genetic abnormalities, the physical-chemical functioning of the brain, and environmental influences on brain function such as drugs, chemicals, and injuries.[4] Those who carry one of these latent traits are in danger of becoming career criminals; those who lack the traits have a much lower risk. Latent traits should affect the behavioral choices of all people equally, regardless of their gender or personal characteristics.[5]

FIND IT ON INFOTRAC
College Edition

To learn more, use the term *general theory of crime* in a key word search.

Impulsive personality
• Physical
• Insensitive
• Risk-taking
• Short-sighted
• Nonverbal

Low self-control
• Poor parenting
• Deviant parents
• Lack of supervision
• Active
• Self-centered

Weakening of social bonds
• Attachment
• Involvement
• Commitment
• Belief

Criminal opportunity
• Gangs
• Free time
• Drugs
• Suitable targets

Crime and deviance
• Delinquency
• Smoking
• Drinking
• Sex
• Crime

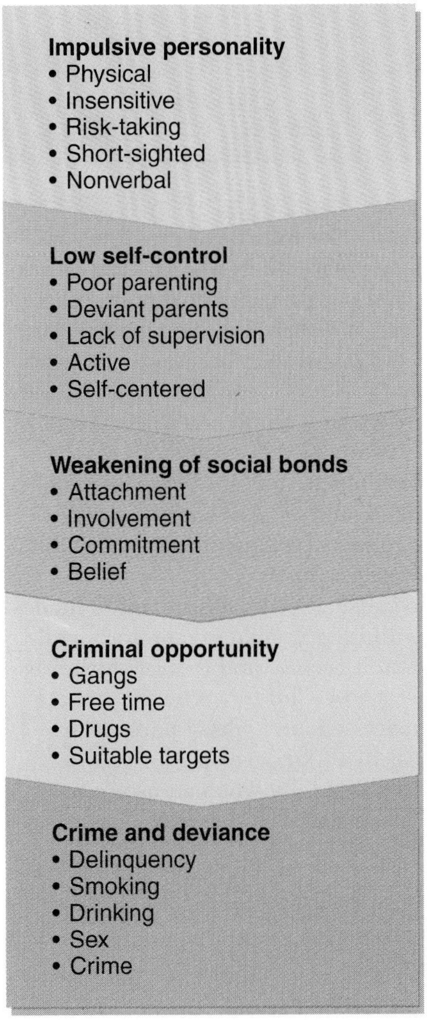

Figure 9.2
The General Theory of Crime

general theory of crime (GTC)
A developmental theory that modifies social control theory by integrating concepts from biosocial, psychological, routine activities, and rational choice theories.

According to this view, the *propensity* to commit crime is stable, but the *opportunity* to commit crime fluctuates over time. People age out of crime as they mature because there are simply fewer opportunities to commit crime and greater inducements to remain "straight." They may marry, have children, and obtain jobs. The former delinquents' newfound adult responsibilities leave them little time to hang with their friends, abuse substances, and get into scrapes with the law.

Assume, for example, that a stable latent trait such as low IQ causes some people to commit crime. Teenagers have more opportunity to commit crime than adults, so at every level of intelligence, adolescent crime rates will be higher. As they mature, however, teens with both high and low IQs will commit less crime because their adult responsibilities provide them with fewer criminal opportunities. Thus, latent trait theories integrate concepts usually associated with trait theories (such as personality and temperament) and concepts associated with rational choice theories (such as criminal opportunity and suitable targets).

General Theory of Crime

Michael Gottfredson and Travis Hirschi's **general theory of crime (GTC)** modifies and redefines some of the principles articulated in Hirschi's social control theory (Chapter 7) by integrating the concepts of control with those of biosocial, psychological, routine activities, and rational choice theories.[6]

The Act and the Offender   In their general theory of crime, Gottfredson and Hirschi consider the criminal offender and the criminal act as separate concepts. Criminal acts, such as robberies or burglaries, are illegal events or deeds that people engage in when they perceive them to be advantageous. For example, burglaries are typically committed by young males looking for cash, liquor, and entertainment; the crime provides "easy, short-term gratification."[7] Crime is rational and predictable: People commit crime when it promises rewards with minimal threat of pain. The threat of punishment can deter crime, and if targets are well guarded, crime rates diminish.

Criminal offenders are individuals predisposed to commit crimes. Given the same set of criminal opportunities, such as having a lot of free time for mischief and living in a neighborhood with unguarded homes containing valuable merchandise, crime-prone people have a much higher probability of violating the law than do noncriminals. The propensity to commit crimes remains stable throughout a person's life. Change in the frequency of criminal activity is purely a function of change in criminal opportunity.

By recognizing that there are stable differences in people's propensity to commit crime, the GTC adds a biosocial element to the concept of social control. The biological and psychological factors that make people impulsive and crime prone may be inherited or may develop through incompetent or absent parenting.

What Makes People Crime Prone?   Gottfredson and Hirschi attribute the tendency to commit crimes to a person's level of self-control. People with limited self-control tend to be impulsive; they are insensitive to other people's feelings, physical (rather than mental), risk takers, shortsighted, and nonverbal.[8] They have a here-and-now orientation and refuse to work for distant goals; they lack diligence, tenacity, and persistence. People lacking self-control tend to be adventuresome, active, physical, and self-centered. As they mature, they often have unstable marriages, jobs, and friendships.[9] People lacking self-control are less likely to feel shame if they engage in deviant acts and are more likely to find them pleasurable.[10] They are also more likely to engage in dangerous behaviors such as drinking, smoking, and reckless driving; all of these behaviors are associated with criminality[11] (see Figure 9.2).

■ According to Gottfredson and Hirschi, people with limited self-control who have impulsive personalities, and are insensitive to other people's feelings, are the ones most likely to commit crime. Here Robert Chambers, the notorious "Preppie Killer," is shown as he is released from prison on February 14, 2003, after serving 17 years for strangling Jennifer Levin, a young college girl, in New York's Central Park.

Connections

In his original version of control theory, discussed in Chapter 7, Hirschi focused on the social controls that attach people to conventional society and insulate them from criminality. In this newer work, he concentrates on self-control as a stabilizing force. The two views are connected, however, because both social control (or social bonds) and self-control are acquired through early experiences with effective parenting.

FIND IT ON INFOTRAC
College Edition

To find out more about the relationship between child-rearing techniques and social development of children, read:

Bruce Bower, "Raising Trust," *Science News*, July 1, 2000 v158 i1 p8

Because those with low self-control enjoy risky, exciting, or thrilling behaviors with immediate gratification, they are more likely to enjoy criminal acts, which require stealth, agility, speed, and power, than conventional acts, which demand long-term study and cognitive and verbal skills. Because they enjoy taking risks, they are more likely to get involved in accidents and suffer injuries than people who maintain self-control.[12] As Gottfredson and Hirschi put it, they derive satisfaction from "money without work, sex without courtship, revenge without court delays."[13] Many of these individuals who have a propensity for committing crime also engage in other behaviors such as smoking, drinking, gambling, and illicit sexuality.[14] Although these acts are not illegal, they too provide immediate, short-term gratification. Exhibit 9.1 lists the elements of impulsivity, or low self-control.

Gottfredson and Hirschi trace the root cause of poor self-control to inadequate child-rearing practices. Parents unwilling or unable to monitor a child's behavior, to recognize deviant behavior when it occurs, and to punish that behavior will produce children who lack self-control. Children who are not attached to their parents, who are poorly supervised, and whose parents are criminal or deviant themselves are the most likely to develop poor self-control. In a sense, lack of self-control occurs naturally when steps are not taken to stop its development.[15] It comes as no shock to life course theorists

EXHIBIT **9.1 The Elements of Impulsivity: Signs That a Person Has Low Self-Control**

- Insensitive
- Physical
- Shortsighted
- Nonverbal
- Here-and-now orientation
- Unstable social relations
- Enjoys deviant behaviors
- Risk taker
- Refuses to work for distant goals

- Lacks diligence
- Lacks tenacity
- Adventuresome
- Self-centered
- Shameless
- Imprudent
- Lacks cognitive and verbal skills
- Enjoys danger and excitement

when research shows that criminality runs in families and that having criminal relatives is a significant predictor of future misbehaviors.[16] Low self-control develops early in life and remains stable into and through adulthood.[17]

Self-Control and Crime Gottfredson and Hirschi claim that the principles of self-control theory can explain all varieties of criminal behavior and all the social and behavioral correlates of crime. That is, such widely disparate crimes as burglary, robbery, embezzlement, drug dealing, murder, rape, and insider trading all stem from a deficiency of self-control. Likewise, gender, racial, and ecological differences in crime rates can be explained by discrepancies in self-control. Put another way, the male crime rate is higher than the female crime rate because males have lower levels of self-control.

Unlike other theoretical models that explain only narrow segments of criminal behavior (such as theories of teenage gang formation), Gottfredson and Hirschi argue that self-control applies equally to all crimes, ranging from murder to corporate theft. For example, Gottfredson and Hirschi maintain that white-collar crime rates remain low because people who lack self-control rarely attain the positions necessary to commit those crimes. However, the relatively few white-collar criminals lack self-control to the same degree and in the same manner as criminals such as rapists and burglars. Although the criminal activity of individuals with low self-control also declines as those individuals mature, they maintain an offense rate that remains consistently higher than those with strong self-control.

Connections

As you may recall from Chapter 2, the Philadelphia cohort studies conducted by Wolfgang and his associates identified a relatively small group of chronic offenders who committed a significant amount of all serious crimes and persisted in criminal careers into their adulthood.

Evaluating the GTC Following the publication of *A General Theory of Crime,* dozens of research efforts tested the validity of Gottfredson and Hirschi's theoretical views. One approach involved identifying indicators of impulsiveness and self-control to determine whether scales measuring these factors correlate with measures of criminal activity. A number of studies conducted both in the United States and abroad have successfully showed this type of association.[18] Some of the most important findings are summarized in Exhibit 9.2.

Although the general theory seems persuasive, several questions and criticisms remain unanswered. Among the most important are the following:

1. **Tautological.** Some critics argue that the theory is tautological—that is, it involves circular reasoning. How do we know when people are impulsive? When they commit crimes. Are all criminals impulsive? Of course, or else they would not have broken the law![19]

2. **Personality disorder.** It is possible that a lack of self-control is merely a symptom of some broader, underlying personality disorder, such as an antisocial personality, which produces crime, and therefore, self-control cannot stand alone as a predictor of criminality.[20] Other personality traits such as low self-direction (the tendency or lack thereof to act for one's long-term benefit) may be a better predictor of criminality than impulsivity or lack of self-control.[21]

3. **Ecological/individual differences.** The GTC also fails to address individual and ecological patterns in the crime rate. For example, if crime rates are higher in Los Angeles than in Albany, New York, can it be assumed that residents of Los Angeles are more impulsive than residents of Albany?

4. **Racial and gender differences.** Although distinct gender differences in the crime rate exist, there is little evidence that males are more impulsive than females (although females and males differ in many other personality traits).[22] Similarly, Gottfredson and Hirschi explain racial differences in the crime rate as a failure of child-rearing practices in the African American community.[23] In so doing, they overlook issues of institutional racism, poverty, and relative deprivation, which have been shown to have a significant impact on crime rate differentials.

EXHIBIT 9.2 **Empirical Evidence Supporting the General Theory of Crime**

- Novice offenders, lacking in self-control, commit a garden variety of criminal acts.[1]
- More mature and experienced criminals become more specialized in their choice of crime (for example, robbers, burglars, drug dealers).[2]
- Male and female drunk drivers are impulsive individuals who manifest low self-control.[3]
- Repeat violent offenders are more impulsive than their less violent peers.[4]
- Incarcerated youth enjoy risk-taking behavior and hold values and attitudes that suggest impulsivity.[5]
- Kids who take drugs and commit crime are impulsive and enjoy engaging in risky behaviors.[6]
- Measures of self-control can predict deviant and antisocial behavior across age groups ranging from teens to adults age 50.[7]
- People who commit white-collar and workplace crime have lower levels of self-control than nonoffenders.[8]
- Gang members have lower levels of self-control than the general population; gang members report lower levels of parental management, a factor associated with lower self-control.[9]
- Low self-control shapes perceptions of criminal opportunity and consequently conditions the decision to commit crimes.[10]
- People who lack self-control expect to commit crime in the future.[11]
- Kids whose problems develop early in life are the most resistant to change in treatment and rehabilitation programs.[12]
- Gender differences in self-control are responsible for crime rate differences. Females who lack self-control are as crime prone as males with similar personalities.[13]
- Parents who manage their children's behavior increase their self-control, which helps reduce their delinquent activities.[14]
- Having parents (or guardians) available to control behavior may reduce the opportunity to commit crime.[15]
- Victims have lower self-control than nonvictims. Impulsivity predicts both the likelihood that a person will engage in criminal behavior and the likelihood that the person will become a victim of crime.[16]

Notes: (1) Xiaogang Deng and Lening Zhang, "Correlates of Self-Control: An Empirical Test of Self-Control Theory," *Journal of Crime and Justice* 21 (1998): 89–103. (2) Alex Piquero, Raymond Paternoster, Paul Mazeroole, Robert Brame, and Charles Dean, "Onset Age and Offense Specialization," *Journal of Research in Crime and Delinquency* 36 (1999): 275–299. (3) Carl Keane, Paul Maxim, and James Teevan, "Drinking and Driving, Self-Control, and Gender: Testing a General Theory of Crime," *Journal of Research in Crime and Delinquency* 30 (1993): 30–46. (4) Judith DeJong, Matti Virkkunen, and Marku Linnoila, "Factors Associated with Recidivism in a Criminal Population," *Journal of Nervous and Mental Disease* 180 (1992): 543–550. (5) David Cantor, "Drug Involvement and Offending among Incarcerated Juveniles," paper presented at the annual meeting of the American Society of Criminology, Boston, November 1995. (6) David Brownfield and Ann Marie Sorenson, "Self-Control and Juvenile Delinquency: Theoretical Issues and an Empirical Assessment of Selected Elements of a General Theory of Crime," *Deviant Behavior* 14 (1993): 243–264; John Cochran, Peter Wood, and Bruce Arneklev, "Is the Religiosity–Delinquency Relationship Spurious? A Test of Arousal and Social Control Theories," *Journal of Research in Crime and Delinquency* 31 (1994): 92–123. (7) Velmer Burton, T. David Evans, Francis Cullen, Kathleen Olivares, and R. Gregory Dunaway, "Age, Self-Control, and Adults' Offending Behaviors: A Research Note Assessing a General Theory of Crime," *Journal of Criminal Justice* 27 (1999): 45–54; John Gibbs and Dennis Giever, "Self-Control and Its Manifestations among University Students: An Empirical Test of Gottfredson and Hirschi's General Theory," *Justice Quarterly* 12 (1995): 231–255. (8) Carey Herbert, "The Implications of Self-Control Theory for Workplace Offending," paper presented at the annual meeting of the American Society of Criminology, San Diego, 1997. (9) Dennis Giever, Dana Lynskey, and Danette Monnet, "Gottfredson and Hirschi's General Theory of Crime and Youth Gangs: An Empirical Test on a Sample of Middle School Youth," paper presented at the annual meeting of the American Society of Criminology, San Diego, 1997. (10) Douglas Longshore, Susan Turner, and Judith Stein, "Self-Control in a Criminal Sample: An Examination of Construct Validity," *Criminology* 34 (1996): 209–228. (11) Deng and Zhang, "Correlates of Self-Control: An Empirical Test of Self-Control Theory." (12) Linda Pagani, Richard Tremblay, Frank Vitaro, and Sophie Parent, "Does Preschool Help Prevent Delinquency in Boys with a History of Perinatal Complications?" *Criminology* 36 (1998): 245–268. (13) Velmer Burton, Francis Cullen, T. David Evans, Leanne Fiftal Alarid, and R. Gregory Dunaway, "Gender, Self-Control, and Crime," *Journal of Research in Crime and Delinquency* 35 (1998): 123–147. (14) John Gibbs, Dennis Giever, and Jamie Martin, "Parental Management and Self-Control: An Empirical Test of Gottfredson and Hirschi's General Theory," *Journal of Research in Crime and Delinquency* 35 (1998): 40–70. (15) Vic Bumphus and James Anderson, "Family Structure and Race in a Sample of Offenders," *Journal of Criminal Justice* 27 (1999): 309–320. (16) Christopher Schreck, "Criminal Victimization and Low Self-Control: An Extension and Test of a General Theory of Crime," *Justice Quarterly* 16 (1999): 633–654.

5. **People change.** The general theory assumes that criminal propensity does not change; opportunities change. A number of research efforts show that factors that help control criminal behavior, such as peer relations and school performance, vary over time. Social influences, which are dominant in early adolescence, may fade and be replaced by others in adulthood.[24] This finding contradicts the GTC, which suggests that the influence of friends should be stable and unchanging.

Gottfredson and Hirschi assume that low self-control varies little with age and that low self-control is almost exclusively a product of early childhood rearing; but research shows that self-control may vary with age. As some people mature, they may be better able to control their impulsive behavior; the GTC seems to work better with some age groups than with others.[25] These findings contradict the GTC, which assumes that levels of self-control and therefore criminal propensity are constant and independent of personal relationships. However, it is uncertain whether life changes affect the propensity to commit crime or merely the opportunity, as Gottfredson and Hirschi suggest.

6. **Modest relationship.** Some research results support the proposition that self-control is a causal factor in criminal and other forms of deviant behavior, but that the association is quite modest.[26] This would indicate that other forces influence criminal behavior and that low self-control alone cannot predict the onset of a criminal or deviant career.

7. **Cross-cultural differences.** There is some evidence that criminals in other countries do not lack self-control, indicating that the GTC may be culturally limited.[27] Behavior that may be considered imprudent in one culture may be socially acceptable in another and therefore cannot be viewed as "lack of self-control."[28] In an important recent study, Alexander Vazsonyi and his associates analyzed self-control and deviant behavior with samples drawn from four different countries (Hungary, Switzerland, the Netherlands, and the United States).[29] Their findings indicate that, as predicted by Gottfredson and Hirschi, low self-control is significantly related to antisocial behavior and that the association can be seen regardless of culture or national setting.

Although questions like these remain, the strength of the general theory lies in its scope and breadth; it attempts to explain all forms of crime and deviance, from lower-class gang delinquency to sexual harassment in the business community.[30] By integrating concepts of criminal choice, criminal opportunity, socialization, and personality, Gottfredson and Hirschi make a plausible argument that all deviant behaviors may originate at the same source. Continued efforts are needed to test the GTC and establish the validity of its core concepts. It remains one of the key developments of modern criminological theory. ✔ Checkpoints

The Life Course Perspective

The second developmental view that has emerged is life course theories. According to this view, even as toddlers people begin relationships and behaviors that will determine their adult life course. At first they must learn to conform to social rules and function effectively in society. Later they are expected to begin thinking about careers, leave their parental homes, find permanent relationships, and eventually marry and begin their own families.[31] These transitions are expected to take place in order, beginning with finishing school, then entering the workforce, getting married, and having children.

Some individuals, however, are incapable of maturing in a reasonable and timely fashion because of family, environmental, or personal problems. In some cases transitions can occur too early—for example, when adolescents engage in precocious sex. In other cases transitions may occur too late, as when a student fails to graduate on time because of bad grades or too many incompletes. Sometimes disruption of one trajectory can harm another. For example, teenage childbirth will most likely disrupt educational and career development.

Disruptions in life's major transitions can be destructive and ultimately can promote criminality. Those who are already at risk because of socioeconomic problems or family dysfunction are the most susceptible to these awkward transitions. The cumulative impact of these disruptions sustains criminality from childhood into adulthood.

Because a transition from one stage of life to another can be a bumpy ride, the propensity to commit crimes is neither stable nor constant; it is a developmental process. A positive life experience may help some criminals desist from crime for a while, whereas a negative one may cause them to resume their activities. Criminal careers are also said to be interactional because people are influenced by the behavior of those around them and, in turn, influence others' behavior. For example, a youth's antisocial behavior may turn his or her more conventional friends against him; their rejection solidifies and escalates his antisocial behavior.

Life course theories also recognize that as people mature the factors that influence their behavior change.[32] At first, family relations may be most influential; in later adolescence, school and peer relations predominate; in adulthood, vocational achievement and marital relations may be the most critical influences. For example, some antisocial children who are in trouble throughout their adolescence may manage to find stable work and maintain intact marriages as adults; these life events help them desist from crime. In contrast, the less fortunate adolescents who develop arrest records and get involved with the wrong crowd may find themselves limited to menial jobs and at risk for criminal careers.

Life course theories are inherently multidimensional, suggesting that criminality has multiple roots, including maladaptive personality traits, educational failure, and dysfunctional family relations. Criminality, according to this view, cannot be attributed to a single cause, nor does it represent a single underlying tendency.[33] People are influenced by different factors as they mature. Consequently, a factor that may have an important influence at one stage of life (such as delinquent peers) may have little influence later on.[34]

The Glueck Research

One of the cornerstones of recent life course theories has been a renewed interest in the research efforts of Sheldon and Eleanor Glueck. While at Harvard University in the 1930s, the Gluecks popularized research on the life cycle of delinquent careers. In a series of longitudinal research studies, they followed the careers of known delinquents to determine the factors that predicted persistent offending.[35] The Gluecks made extensive use of interviews and records in their elaborate comparisons of delinquents and nondelinquents.[36]

The Gluecks' research focused on early onset of delinquency as a harbinger of a criminal career: "The deeper the roots of childhood maladjustment, the smaller the chance of adult adjustment."[37] They also noted the stability of offending careers: Children who are antisocial early in life are the most likely to continue their offending careers into adulthood.

They identified a number of personal and social factors related to persistent offending. The most important of these factors was family relations, considered in terms of quality of discipline and emotional ties with parents. The adolescent raised in a large, single-parent family of limited economic means and educational achievement was the most vulnerable to delinquency.

The Gluecks did not restrict their analysis to social variables. When they measured such biological and psychological traits as body type, intelligence, and personality, they found that physical and mental factors also played a role in determining behavior. Children with low intelligence, a background of mental disease, and a powerful (mesomorph) physique were the most likely to become persistent offenders.

Life Course Concepts

A 1990 review paper (revised in 1998) by Rolf Loeber and Marc LeBlanc was an important event in popularizing life course theory.[38] They proposed that criminologists should devote time and effort to understanding some basic questions about the evolution of criminal careers: Why do people begin committing antisocial acts? Why do some stop while others continue? Why do some escalate the severity of their criminality (that is, go from shoplifting to drug dealing to armed robbery) while others de-escalate and commit less serious crime as they mature? If some terminate their criminal activity, what, if anything, causes them to begin again? Why do some criminals specialize in certain types of crime, whereas others are generalists engaging in a variety of antisocial behaviors?

According to Loeber and LeBlanc's developmental view, criminologists must pay attention to how a criminal career unfolds. In this section, we review some of the more important concepts associated with the life course perspective. In the remainder of the section, we discuss some prominent life course concepts.

Age of Onset   Most life course theories assume that the seeds of a criminal career are planted early in life and that early onset of deviance strongly predicts later and more serious criminality.[39] Research supports this by showing that children who will later become delinquents begin their deviant careers at a very early (preschool) age and that the earlier the onset of criminality the more frequent, varied, and sustained the criminal career.[40] Early onset criminals typically have a history of disruptive behavior beginning in early childhood with truancy, cruelty to animals, lying, and theft.[41]

But not all persistent offenders begin at an early age. Some are precocious, beginning their criminal careers early and persisting into adulthood.[42] Others stay out of trouble in adolescence and do not violate the law until their teenage years. There are even offenders who begin their offending career in adulthood, most often when they face persistent employment problems.[43] Some offenders may peak at an early age, whereas others persist into adulthood. Some youth maximize their offending rates at a relatively early age and then reduce their criminal activity; others persist into their twenties as they enter "emerging adulthood."[44] Some are high-rate offenders; others offend at relatively low rates.[45]

According to psychologist Terrie Moffitt, although the prevalence and frequency of antisocial behavior peak in adolescence and then diminish for most offenders (she labels these **adolescent-limiteds**), a small group of **life course persisters** offends well into adulthood.[46] Life course persisters combine family dysfunction with severe neurological problems that predispose them to antisocial behavior patterns. These problems can be the result of maternal drug abuse, poor nutrition, or exposure to toxic agents such as lead. Life course persisters may have lower verbal ability, which inhibits reasoning skills, learning ability, and school achievement. They seem to mature faster and to engage in early sexuality and drug use, referred to as **pseudomaturity**.[47] There may be more than one subset of life course persisters. One group begins acting out during the preschool years; these children show signs of ADHD and do not outgrow the levels of disobedience typical of the preschool years. The second group show few symptoms of ADHD but, from an early age, are aggressive, underhanded, and in constant opposition to authority.[48]

Adolescent-limited delinquents mimic the behavior of these more troubled teens but reduce the frequency of their offending as they mature to around age 18.[49] They are deeply influenced by the misbehavior of their friends and peers up to around age 16; when peer group deviance begins to decline, they reduce their criminal activities.[50] These kids may be considered "typical teenagers" who get into minor scrapes and engage in what might be considered rebellious teenage behavior with their friends such as recreational drug use.[51]

Why do some people enter a "path to crime" later rather than sooner? Early starters, who begin offending before age 14, follow a path from (1) poor parenting to (2) deviant behaviors and then to (3) involvement with delinquent groups. Late starters, who begin offending after age 14, follow a somewhat different path: (1) Poor parenting leads to (2) identification with delinquent groups and then to (3) deviant behaviors. By implication, adolescents who suffer poor parenting and are at risk for deviant careers can avoid criminality if they can bypass involvement with delinquent peers.[52]

Problem Behavior Syndrome   The life course view is that criminality can best be understood as one of many social problems faced by at-risk youth. Crime is just one among a group of antisocial behaviors that cluster together, referred to collectively as **problem behavior syndrome (PBS).** PBS typically involves family dysfunction, substance abuse, smoking, precocious sexuality and early pregnancy, educational underachievement, suicide attempts, sensation seeking, and unemployment (see Exhibit 9.3).[53]

adolescent-limited
Offender who follows the most common criminal trajectory, in which antisocial behavior peaks in adolescence and then diminishes.

life course persister
One of the small group of offenders whose criminal career continues well into adulthood.

pseudomaturity
Characteristic of life course persisters, who tend to engage is early sexuality and drug use.

problem behavior syndrome (PBS)
A cluster of antisocial behaviors that may include family dysfunction, substance abuse, smoking, precocious sexuality and early pregnancy, educational underachievement, suicide attempts, sensation seeking, and unemployment, as well as crime.

■ Adolescents with multiple problems present a significant challenge for the justice system. What can be done to help them avoid more serious anti-social behavior? Some jurisdictions have developed special programs for multiple offenders. Here, Joey Anderson, 18, thanks his mother, Mary Sanchez, for supporting him during the Juvenile DWI/Drug Court program in Albuquerque. Anderson was placed under the no-nonsense supervision of the Drug Court team led by Children's Court Judge Geraldine Rivera. Teens qualifying for this program have had several run-ins with the law.

Connections

Social process theories lay the foundation for assuming that problems with peer, family, educational, and other relations, which vary over the life course, influence behaviors. See the first few sections of Chapter 7 for a review of these issues.

People who suffer from one of these conditions typically exhibit many symptoms of the others.[54] For example, a recent study of adolescent offending patterns found these relationships:

■ Youths who drink in the late elementary school years, who are aggressive, and who have attention problems are more likely to be offenders during adolescence.

■ Youths who are less attached to their parents are more likely to be offenders.

■ Youths who have antisocial friends are more likely to be offenders.

■ Youths who are less attached to school are more likely to be offenders.

■ Youths from neighborhoods where drugs are easily available are more likely to be offenders during adolescence.[55]

All varieties of criminal behavior, including violence, theft, and drug offenses, may be part of a generalized PBS, indicating that all forms of antisocial behavior have similar developmental patterns.[56]

Those who exhibit PBS are prone to more difficulties than the general population.[57] They face a range of personal dilemmas ranging from drug abuse, to being accident prone, to requiring more health care and hospitalization, to becoming teenage parents. PBS has been linked to personality prob-

EXHIBIT 9.3 Problem Behaviors

Social
■ Family dysfunction
■ Unemployment
■ Educational underachievement
■ School misconduct

Environmental
■ High-crime area
■ Disorganized area
■ Racism
■ Exposure to poverty

Personal
■ Substance abuse
■ Suicide attempts
■ Early sexuality
■ Sensation seeking
■ Early parenthood
■ Accident-proneness
■ Medical problems
■ Mental disease
■ Anxiety
■ Eating disorders (bulimia, anorexia)

✔ **Checkpoints**

✔ Pioneering criminologists Sheldon and Eleanor Glueck tracked the onset and termination of criminal careers.

✔ Life course theories look at such issues as the onset of crime, escalation of offenses, continuity of crime, and desistance from crime.

✔ The concept of a problem behavior syndrome suggests that criminality may be just one of a cluster of social, psychological, and physical problems.

✔ There is more than one pathway to crime.

✔ Adolescent-limited offenders begin offending late and age out of crime. Life course persisters exhibit early onset of crime that persists into adulthood.

To quiz yourself on this material, go to questions 9.7–9.11 on the Criminology: The Core 2e Web site.

authority conflict pathway
Pathway to criminal deviance that begins at an early age with stubborn behavior and leads to defiance and then to authority avoidance.

covert pathway
Pathway to a criminal career that begins with minor underhanded behavior, leads to property damage, and eventually escalates to more serious forms of theft and fraud.

overt pathway
Pathway to a criminal career that begins with minor aggression, leads to physical fighting, and eventually escalates to violent crime.

lems (such as rebelliousness and low ego), family problems (such as intrafamily conflict and parental mental disorder), and educational failure.[58] Multisite research has shown that PBS is not unique to any single area of the country and that children who exhibit PBS, including drug use, delinquency, and precocious sexuality, display symptoms at an early age.[59]

Multiple Pathways to Crime   Life course theorists recognize that career criminals may travel more than a single road. Some are chronic offenders, others rarely but persistently commit crime, some increase their activities as they age, and others de-escalate their antisocial behaviors.[60] Some may specialize in violence and extortion; some may be involved in theft and fraud; others may engage in a variety of criminal acts. Some offenders may begin their careers early in life, whereas others are late bloomers who begin committing crime when most people desist.

Are there different pathways to crime? Using data from a longitudinal cohort study conducted in Pittsburgh, Rolf Loeber and his associates have identified three distinct paths to a criminal career (see Figure 9.3):[61]

1. The **authority conflict pathway** begins at an early age with stubborn behavior. This leads to defiance (doing things one's own way, disobedience) and then to authority avoidance (staying out late, truancy, running away).

2. The **covert pathway** begins with minor, underhanded behavior (lying, shoplifting) that leads to property damage (setting nuisance fires, damaging property). This behavior eventually escalates to more serious forms of criminality, ranging from joyriding, pocket picking, larceny, and fencing to passing bad checks, using stolen credit cards, stealing cars, dealing drugs, and breaking and entering.

3. The **overt pathway** escalates to aggressive acts beginning with aggression (annoying others, bullying), leading to physical (and gang) fighting, and then to violence (attacking someone, forced theft).

The Loeber research indicates that each of these paths may lead to a sustained deviant career. Some people enter two or even three paths simultaneously: They are stubborn, lie to teachers and parents, are bullies, and commit petty thefts. These adolescents are the most likely to become persistent offenders. Although some persistent offenders may specialize in one type of behavior, others engage in varied criminal acts and antisocial behaviors as they mature. For example, they cheat on tests, bully others in the schoolyard, take drugs, commit burglary, steal a car, and then shoplift from a store.

Continuity of Crime   Another aspect of life course theory is the continuity of crime: The best predictor of future criminality is past criminality. Children who are repeatedly in trouble during early adolescence will generally still be antisocial in their middle and late teens and as adults.[62] Early criminal activity is likely to be sustained because these offenders seem to lack the social survival skills necessary to find work or to develop the interpersonal relationships needed to allow them to drop out of crime.[63]

One explanation for this phenomenon suggests that criminal propensity may be "contagious." Children at risk to commit crime may be located in families and neighborhoods in which they are constantly exposed to deviant behavior. As they mature, having brothers, fathers, neighbors, and friends who engage in and support their activities reinforces their deviance.[64]

The discovery that people begin their criminal careers at different ages and follow different criminal paths and trajectories provides strong support for life course theory. If all criminals possessed a singular latent trait that made them crime prone, it would be unlikely that these variations in criminal careers would be observed. It is difficult to explain such concepts as late-onset and adolescent-limited behavior from the perspective of latent trait theory. ✔ **Checkpoints**

Figure 9.3
Loeber's Pathways to Crime

SOURCE: Barbara Tatem Kelley, Rolf Loeber, Kate Keenan, and Mary DeLamatre, "Developmental Pathways in Boys' Disruptive and Delinquent Behavior," *Juvenile Justice Bulletin* (November 1997), p. 3.

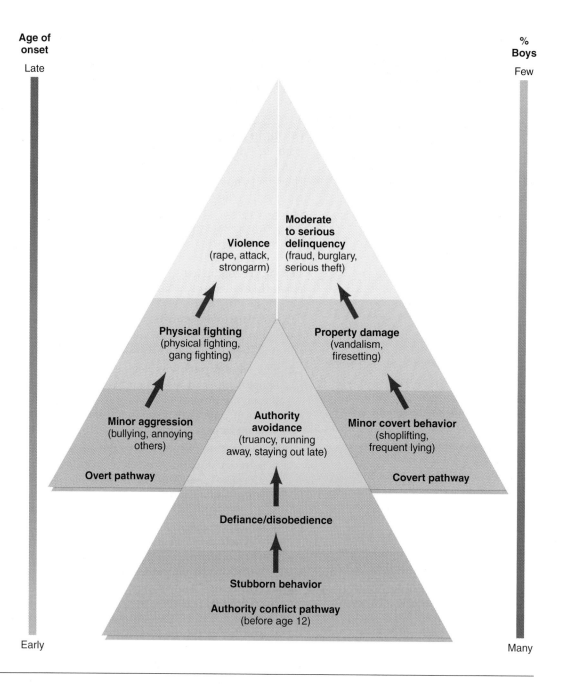

Age of onset: Late / Early

% Boys: Few / Many

Violence (rape, attack, strongarm)

Moderate to serious delinquency (fraud, burglary, serious theft)

Physical fighting (physical fighting, gang fighting)

Property damage (vandalism, firesetting)

Minor aggression (bullying, annoying others)

Authority avoidance (truancy, running away, staying out late)

Minor covert behavior (shoplifting, frequent lying)

Overt pathway

Covert pathway

Defiance/disobedience

Stubborn behavior

Authority conflict pathway (before age 12)

Life Course Theories

An ongoing effort has been made to track persistent offenders over their life course.[65] The early data seem to support what is already known about delinquent and criminal career patterns: Juvenile offenders are likely to become adult criminals; early onset predicts more lasting crime; and chronic offenders commit a significant portion of all crimes.[66] Based on these findings, criminologists have formulated several systematic theories that account for the onset, continuance, and desistance from crime.

The Social Development Model

social development model (SDM)
A developmental theory that attributes criminal behavior patterns to childhood socialization and pro- or antisocial attachments over the life course.

In their **social development model (SDM),** Joseph Weis, Richard Catalano, J. David Hawkins, and their associates show how different factors affecting a child's social development over the life course influence criminal behavior patterns.[67] As children mature within their environment, elements of socialization control their developmental process. Children are socialized and develop

■ According to interactional theory, the onset of crime can be traced to a deterioration of the social bond during adolescence, marked by weakened attachment to parents, commitment to school, and belief in conventional values and institutions. To combat crime, social programs may try to help children maintain these ties and attachments. Here, "Join the Circus" campers apply clown makeup at the Hispanic Outreach "El Verano" camp run by the Girl Scout Council of the Nation's Capital in Dale City, Virginia.

prosocial bonds
Socialized attachment to conventional institutions, activities, and beliefs.

interactional theory
A developmental theory that attributes criminal trajectories to mutual reinforcement between delinquents and significant others over the life course—family in early adolescence, school and friends in mid-adolescence, and social peers and one's own nuclear family in adulthood.

bonds to their families through four distinct interactions and processes:

1. Perceived opportunities for involvement in activities and interactions with others
2. The degree of involvement and interaction with parents
3. The children's ability to participate in these interactions
4. The reinforcement (such as feedback) they perceive for their participation

To control the risk of antisocial behavior, a child must maintain **prosocial bonds.** These are developed within the context of family life, which not only provides prosocial opportunities but reinforces them by consistent, positive feedback. Parental attachment affects a child's behavior for life, determining both school experiences and personal beliefs and values. For those with strong family relationships, school will be a meaningful experience marked by academic success and commitment to education. Young people in this category are likely to develop conventional beliefs and values, become committed to conventional activities, and form attachments to conventional others. Kids who learn deviant attitudes and behaviors and who also have weak ties to conventional institutions are the most likely to engage in criminal behaviors. Kids who maintain antisocial opportunities and involvement and who also perceive that it is easy to get away with antisocial behaviors and who see them as "cool" and rewarding are also the ones most likely to engage in antisocial activities.[68]

Children's antisocial behavior also depends on the quality of their attachments to parents and other influential relations. If they remain unattached or develop attachments to deviant others, their behavior may become deviant as well. Unlike Hirschi's control theory, which assumes that all attachments are beneficial, the SDM suggests that interaction with antisocial peers and adults promotes participation in delinquency and substance abuse.[69]

As Figure 9.4 shows, the SDM differs from Hirschi's vision of how the social bond develops. Whereas Hirschi maintains that early family attachments are the key determinant of future behavior, the SDM suggests that later involvement in prosocial or antisocial behavior determines the quality of attachments. Adolescents who perceive opportunities and rewards for antisocial behavior will form deep attachments to deviant peers and will become committed to a delinquent way of life. In contrast, those who perceive opportunities for prosocial behavior will take a different path, getting involved in conventional activities and forming attachments to others who share their conventional lifestyle.

The SDM holds that commitment and attachment to conventional institutions, activities, and beliefs insulate youths from the crimogenic influences of their environment. The prosocial path inhibits deviance by strengthening bonds to prosocial others and activities. Without the proper level of bonding, adolescents can succumb to the influence of deviant others. The path predicted by the SDM seems an accurate picture of the onset and continuation of violent and antisocial behavior both for early-onset offenders who engage in antisocial acts in childhood and later-onset offenders who begin offending in their teens.[70]

Interactional Theory

Terence Thornberry has proposed an age-graded view of crime that he calls **interactional theory** (see Figure 9.5).[71] He too finds that the onset of crime can be traced to a deterioration of the social bond during adolescence, marked by weakened attachment to parents, commitment to school, and belief in conventional values.

Interactional theory holds that seriously delinquent youths form belief systems that are consistent with their deviant lifestyle. They seek out the company

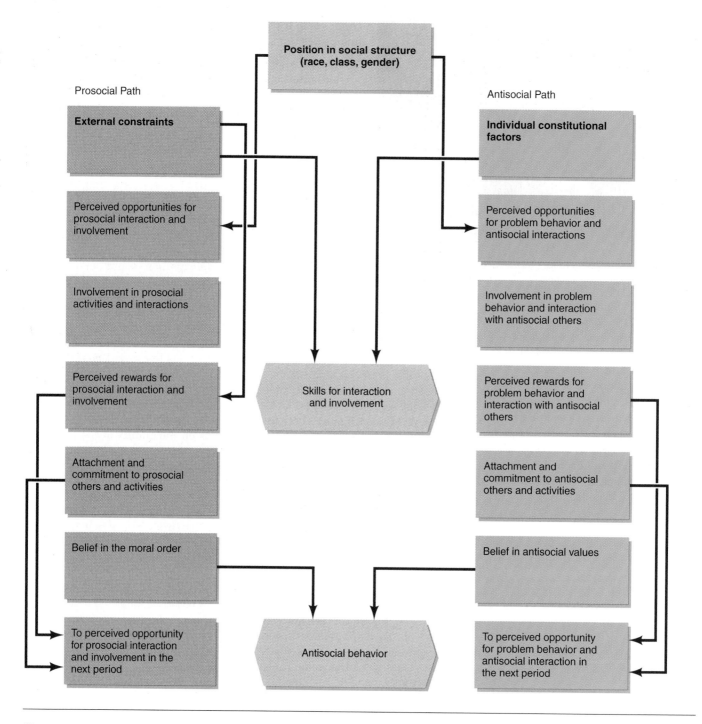

Figure 9.4
The Social Development Model of Antisocial Behavior

SOURCE: Adapted from Seattle Social Development Project.

of other adolescents who share their interests and who are likely to reinforce their beliefs about the world and support their delinquent behavior. According to interactional theory, delinquents find a criminal peer group in the same way that chess buffs look for others who share their passion for the game; hanging out with other chess players helps improve their game. Similarly, deviant peers do not turn an otherwise innocent boy into a delinquent; they support and amplify the behavior of those who have already accepted a delinquent way of life.[72]

Thornberry suggests that criminality is a developmental process that takes on different meanings and forms as a person matures. According to Thornberry, the causal process is dynamic and develops over a person's life.[73] During early adolescence, attachment to the family is the single most important determinant of whether a youth will adjust to conventional society and be shielded from delinquency. By midadolescence, the influence of the family is replaced by the "world of friends, school and youth culture."[74] In adulthood,

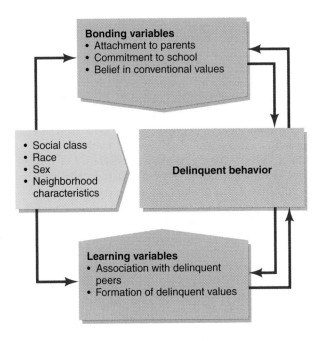

Bonding variables
• Attachment to parents
• Commitment to school
• Belief in conventional values

• Social class
• Race
• Sex
• Neighborhood characteristics

Delinquent behavior

Learning variables
• Association with delinquent peers
• Formation of delinquent values

Figure 9.5

Overview of the Interactional Theory of Delinquency

SOURCE: Terence Thornberry, Margaret Farnworth, Alan Lizotte, and Susan Stern, "A Longitudinal Examination of the Causes and Correlates of Delinquency," working paper No. 1, Rochester Youth Development Study (Albany, NY: Hindelang Criminal Justice Research Center, 1987), p. 11.

a person's behavioral choices are shaped by his or her place in conventional society and his or her own nuclear family.

The key idea here is that causal influences are *bi-directional.* Weak bonds lead children to develop friendships with deviant peers and get involved in delinquency; frequent delinquency involvement further weakens bonds and makes it difficult to reestablish conventional ones. Early and persistent involvement in antisocial behavior generates consequences that are hard to shake. Kids who are in trouble with the law find it hard to establish social bonds and develop social capital. Their social deficits increase the likelihood that they will get involved in deviant networks and belief systems. By shutting offenders out of a conventional lifestyle, early criminality helps entrap them in a deviant lifestyle.[75] These delinquency-promoting factors tend to reinforce one another and sustain a chronic criminal career. Recent research by Kee Jeong Kim and his associates supports this view. They found that in a sample of 451 adolescents, those who suffer stressful life events such as a family financial crises, death of a parent, parents' divorce, physical illness, breaking up with a boyfriend or girlfriend, changing schools, and getting into trouble with classmates at school were more likely to later get involved in antisocial behaviors and vice versa. Stressful life events at one point significantly predicted delinquent behaviors one year later, and delinquent involvements significantly predicted stressful life events one year later.[76]

Nor does the social deficits–criminality link end in a single generation. It is unlikely that an offender in trouble with the law in adolescence will later develop the skills to become a nurturing parent. The lack of parental efficacy renders his or her own children susceptible to antisocial behaviors. It is not surprising then that delinquency seems to be intergenerational: criminal fathers produce criminal sons who in turn produce criminal grandsons.[77]

In sum, interactional theory suggests that criminality is part of a dynamic social process and not just an outcome of that process. Although crime is influenced by social forces, it also influences these processes and associations to create behavioral trajectories toward increasing law violations for some people.[78] Interactional theory integrates elements of social disorganization, social control, social learning, and cognitive theories into a powerful model of the development of a criminal career.

Age-Graded Theory

If there are various pathways to crime and delinquency, are there trails back to conformity? In an important 1993 work, *Crime in the Making,* Robert Sampson and John Laub identify **turning points** in a criminal career.[79] Reanalyzing the original Glueck data, they found that the stability of delinquent behavior can be affected by events that occur later in life, even after a chronic delinquent career has been established. They agree with Hirschi and Gottfredson that formal and informal social controls restrict criminality and that crime begins early in life and continues over the life course; they disagree that once this course is set, nothing can impede its progress.

Turning Points Sampson and Laub's most important contribution is identifying the life events that enable adult offenders to desist from crime. Two critical turning points are career and marriage. Adolescents who are at risk for crime can live conventional lives if they can find good jobs or achieve successful careers. Their success may hinge on a lucky break. Even those who have been in trouble with the law may turn from crime if employers are willing to give them a chance despite their records.

Adolescents who have had significant problems with the law are also able to desist from crime if, as adults, they become attached to a spouse who

turning points
Critical life events, such as career and marriage, that may enable adult offenders to desist from crime.

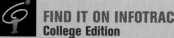

FIND IT ON INFOTRAC
College Edition

The concept of social capital is quite complex. Use it as a subject guide and find out what it actually entails.

supports and sustains them even when the spouse knows they have been in trouble in the past. Happy marriages are life-sustaining, and marital quality improves over time (as people work less and have fewer parental responsibilities).[80] Spending time in marital and family activities also reduces exposure to deviant peers, which in turn reduces the opportunity to become involved in delinquent activities.[81] People who cannot sustain secure marital relations are less likely to desist from crime.

Sampson and Laub's age-graded theory is supported by research that shows that children who grow up in two-parent families are more likely to have happier marriages than children whose parents were divorced or never married.[82] This finding suggests that the marriage–crime association may be intergenerational: If people with marital problems are more crime prone, their children will also suffer a greater long-term risk of marital failure and antisocial activity.

Social Capital   Social scientists recognize that people build **social capital**—positive relations with individuals and institutions that are life-sustaining. Social capital, which includes the resources accessed through interpersonal connections and relationships, is as critical as **human capital,** or what a person or organization actually possesses, to individuals, social groups, organizations, and communities in obtaining their objectives.[83]

In the same manner that building financial capital improves the chances for economic success, building social capital supports conventional behavior and inhibits deviant behavior. A successful marriage creates social capital when it improves a person's stature, creates feelings of self-worth, and encourages others to trust the person. A successful career inhibits crime by creating a stake in conformity: Why commit crime when you are doing well at your job? The relationship is reciprocal. If people are chosen to be employees, they return the favor by doing the best job possible; if they are chosen as spouses, they blossom into devoted partners. In contrast, moving to a new city reduces social capital by closing people off from long-term relationships.[84]

Sampson and Laub's research indicates that building social capital and strong social bonds reduces the likelihood of long-term deviance. This finding suggests that, in contrast to latent trait theories, events that occur in later adolescence and adulthood do, in fact, influence the direction of delinquent and criminal careers. Life events can help either terminate or sustain deviant careers. For example, getting arrested and punished may have little direct effect on future criminality, but it can help sustain a criminal career because it reduces the chances of employment and job stability, two factors that are directly related to crime (see Figure 9.6).[85]

The Marriage Factor   People who maintain a successful marriage and become parents are the most likely to mature out of crime.[86] Marriage stabilizes people and helps them build social capital, it also may discourage crime by reducing contact with criminal peers. As Mark Warr states:

> For many individuals, it seems, marriage marks a transition from heavy peer involvement to a preoccupation with one's spouse. That transition is likely to reduce interaction with former friends and accomplices and thereby reduce the opportunities as well as the motivation to engage in crime.[87]

Even people with a history of criminal activity who have been convicted of serious offenses reduce the frequency of their offending if they live with spouses and maintain employment when they are in the community.[88] The marriage benefit may also be intergenerational: children who grow up in two-parent families are more likely to later have happier marriages themselves than children who are the product of divorced or never-married parents.[89] If people with marital problems are more crime prone, their children will also suffer a greater long-term risk of marital failure and antisocial activity.

One important new research study further confirms the benefits of marriage as a crime reducing social event. Researchers Alex Piquero, Karen

social capital
Positive relations with individuals and institutions, as in a successful marriage or a successful career, that support conventional behavior and inhibit deviant behavior.

human capital
What a person or organization actually possesses.

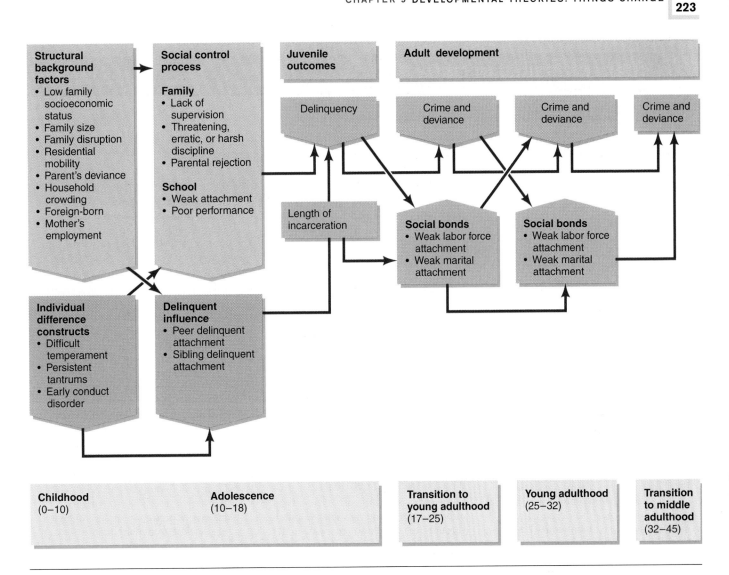

Figure 9.6
Sampson and Laub's Age-Graded Theory

SOURCE: Robert Sampson and John Laub, *Crime in the Making: Pathways and Turning Points Through Life* (Cambridge, MA: Harvard University Press, 1993), pp. 244–245.

Parker, and John MacDonald tracked each of 524 men in their late teens and early twenties for a seven-year period after they were paroled from the California Youth Authority during the 1970s and 1980s. The sample of men, who had been incarcerated for lengthy periods of time, was 48.5 percent white, 33 percent black, 16.6 percent Hispanic, and 1.9 percent other races.[90] The research team found former offenders were far less likely to return to crime if they settled down into the routine of a solid marriage. Common-law marriages or living with a partner did not have the same crime-reducing effect as did traditional marriages in which the knot is tied, the union is registered at the courthouse, and there is a general expectation to lead a steady life. Among people of color, parolees cohabiting without the benefit of marriage actually increased their recidivism rates.

Piquero explains his findings by suggesting that "people who are married often have schedules where they work 9-to-5 jobs, come home for dinner, take care of children if they have them, watch television, go to bed and repeat that cycle over and over again, people who are not married have a lot of free rein to do a lot of what they want, especially if they are not employed. There's something about crossing the line of getting married that helps these men stay away from crime. If they don't cross that line, they can continue their lifestyles, which are pretty erratic."[91]

While the Piquero research is persuasive, some important questions still need to be answered: Why do some people enter strong marriages while others fail? Does the influence of marriage have an equal effect on men and women? Some recent research by Ronald Simons and his associates found

CURRENT ISSUES IN CRIME

Tracking Down the 500 Delinquent Boys in the New Millennium

Why are some delinquents destined to become persistent criminals as adults? John Laub and Robert Sampson have conducted a follow-up to their reanalysis of Sheldon and Eleanor Glueck's study that matched 500 delinquent boys with 500 nondelinquents. The individuals in the original sample were re-interviewed by the Gluecks at ages 25 and 32. Now Sampson and Laub have located the survivors of the delinquent sample, the oldest being 70 years old and the youngest 62, and they are re-interviewing this cohort.

Persistence and Desistance

Laub and Sampson find that delinquency and other forms of antisocial conduct in childhood are strongly related to adult crime and drug and alcohol abuse. Former delinquents also suffer consequences in other areas of social life, such as school, work, and family life. For example, delinquents are far less likely to finish high school than are nondelinquents and subsequently more likely to be unemployed, receive welfare, and experience separation or divorce as adults.

In their latest research, Laub and Sampson address one of the key questions posed by life course theories: Is it possible for former delinquents to turn their lives around as adults? They find that most antisocial children do not remain antisocial as adults. For example, of men in the study cohort who survived to age 50, 24 percent had no arrests for crimes of violence and property after age 17 (6 percent had no arrests for total crime); 48 percent had no arrests for these predatory crime after age 25 (19 percent for total crime); 60 percent had no arrests for predatory crime after age 31 (33 percent for total crime); and 79 percent had no arrests for predatory crime after age 40 (57 percent for total crime). They conclude that desistance from crime is the norm and that most, if not all, serious delinquents desist from crime.

Why Do Delinquents Desist?

Laub and Sampson's earlier research indicated that building social capital through marriage and jobs were key components of desistance from crime. In this new round of research, they were able to find out more about long-term desistance by interviewing 52 men as they approached age 70. Drawing on the men's own words, they find that one important element for "going straight"

is the "knifing off" of individuals from their immediate environment and offering them a new script for the future. Joining the military can provide this knifing-off effect, as does marriage, or changing one's residence. One former delinquent (age 69) told them this:

I'd say the turning point was, number one, the Army. You get into an outfit, you had a sense of belonging, you made your friends. I think I became a pretty good judge of character. In the Army, you met some good ones, you met some foul balls. Then I met the wife. I'd say probably that would be the turning point. Got married, then naturally, kids come. So now you got to get a better job, you got to make more money. And that's how I got to the Navy Yard and tried to improve myself.

Former delinquents who "went straight" were able to put structure into their lives. Structure often led the men to disassociate from delinquent peers, reducing the opportunity to get into trouble. Getting married, for example, may limit the number of nights men can "hang with the guys." As one wife of a former delinquent said, "It is not how many beers you have, it's who you drink with." Even multiple offenders who did

that marriage significantly improves a woman's life chances but has less impact on men.[92] However, Simons found that, for both males and females, having an antisocial romantic partner as a young adult increased the likelihood of later criminal behavior, a finding that supports Laub and Sampson's work.

Testing Age-Graded Theory   Several indicators support the validity of age-graded theory.[93] Evidence now shows that once begun criminal career trajectories can be reversed if life conditions improve, an outcome predicted by age-graded theory.[94] For example, employment status affects behavior. Men who are unemployed or underemployed report higher criminal participation rates than employed men. Similarly, men released from prison on parole who obtain jobs are less likely to recidivate than those who lack or lose employment.[95] When justice expert Shadd Maruna interviewed a group of serious criminals in order to understand how they were able to reform their lives, he found that going straight was a long process, not an instantaneous event.[96] Those who leave a life of crime begin to feel a sense of fulfillment in engaging in productive behaviors and in so doing become agents of their own

time in prison were able to desist with the help of a stabilizing marriage.

Former delinquents who can turn their life around, who have acquired a degree of maturity by taking on family and work responsibilities, and who have forged new commitments are the ones most likely to make a fresh start and find new direction and meaning in life. It seems that men who desisted changed their identity as well, and this, in turn, affected their outlook and sense of maturity and responsibility. The ability to change did not reflect crime "specialty": violent offenders followed the same path as property offenders.

Early Death

In a follow-up analysis (conducted with George Vaillant), Laub found that many former delinquents who desisted from crime still faced the risk of an early and untimely death. Following two matched samples of delinquents and nondelinquents until they reached age 65, Laub found that 13 percent (N = 62) of the delinquent as compared to only 6 percent (N = 28) of the nondelinquent subjects died unnatural deaths such as violence, cirrhosis of the liver caused by alcoholism, poor self-care, suicide, and so forth. By age 65, 29 percent (N = 139) of the delinquent subjects and 21 percent (N = 95) of the nondelinquent subjects had died from natural causes. Frequent delinquent involvement in adolescence and alcohol abuse were the

strongest predictors of an early and unnatural death. So, even though many troubled youth are able to reform, their early excesses may haunt them across their life span.

Policy Implications

Laub and Sampson find that youth problems—delinquency, substance abuse, violence, dropping out, teen pregnancy—often share common risk characteristics. Intervention strategies, therefore, should consider a broad array of antisocial, criminal, and deviant behaviors, and not limit the focus to just one subgroup or crime type. Because criminality and other social problems are linked, early prevention efforts that reduce crime will probably also reduce alcohol abuse, drunk driving, drug abuse, sexual promiscuity, and family violence. The best way to achieve these goals is through four significant life-changing events: marriage, joining the military, getting a job, and changing one's environment or neighborhood. What appears to be important about these processes is that they all involve, to varying degrees, the following items: a knifing off of the past from the present; new situations that provide both supervision and monitoring as well as new opportunities of social support and growth; and new situations that provide the opportunity for transforming identity. Prevention of crime must be a policy at all times and at all stages of life.

Critical Thinking

Do you believe the factors that influenced the men in the original Glueck sample are still relevant for change, for example, a military career? Would it be possible for men such as these to join the military today? Do you think some sort of universal service program might be beneficial and help people turn their lives around?

InfoTrac College Edition Research

To learn more about the concept of social capital, use it as a key word. Then read a review of Laub and Sampson's *Crime in the Making*:
Roland Chilton, "Crime in the Making: Pathways and Turning Points Through Life," *Social Forces,* Sept 1995 v74 n1 p357(2)

SOURCES: John Laub and Robert Sampson, *Shared beginnings, divergent lives: Delinquent boys to age 70* (Cambridge, MA: Harvard University Press, 2004); John Laub and Robert Sampson, "Understanding desistance from crime," in *Crime and Justice, An Annual Review of Research,* Vol. 28, Michael Tonry, ed. (Chicago: University of Chicago Press, 2001): 1–71; John Laub, "Crime over the life course," *Poverty Research News,* The Newsletter of the Northwestern University/University of Chicago Joint Center for Poverty Research, vol. 4, no. 3, May–June 2000; John Laub and George Vaillant, "Delinquency and mortality: A 50-year follow-up study of 1,000 delinquent and nondelinquent boys," *American Journal of Psychiatry,* 157 (2000): 96–102.

change. They start feeling in control of their future and have a newfound purpose in life. Importantly, rather than running from their past, they view their prior history as a learning experience, finding a silver lining in an otherwise awful situation. Maruna's research indicates that even experienced criminals can change if they acquire social capital.

Research has been directed at identifying the sources of social capital and determining whether and how it is related to crime. Youths who accumulate social capital in childhood (for example, by doing well in school or having a tightly knit family) are also the most likely to maintain steady work as adults; employment may help insulate them from crime.[97]

As predicted by age-graded theory, delinquent youth who enter the military, serve overseas, and receive veterans' benefits enhance their occupational status (social capital) while reducing criminal involvement.[98] In contrast, research shows that people who are self-centered and present-oriented are less likely to accumulate social capital and more prone to commit criminal acts.[99]

Laub and Sampson are now conducting an important follow-up to their original research, and their findings are discussed in the Current Issues in Crime feature.

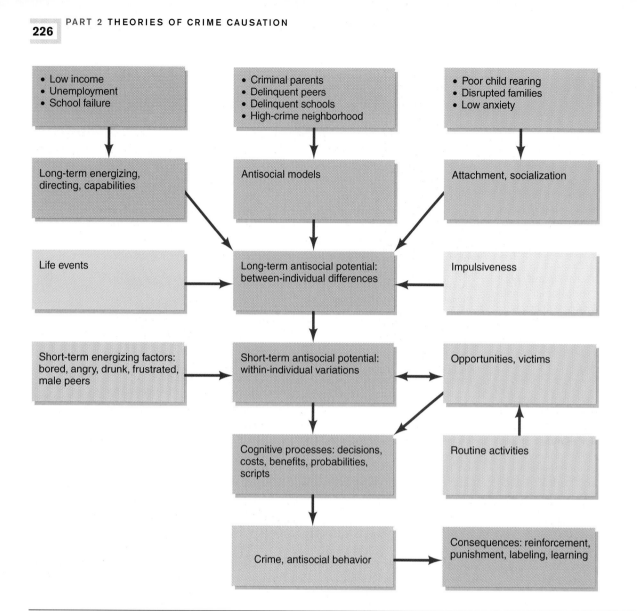

Figure 9.7
Integrated Cognitive Antisocial Potential (ICAP) Theory

SOURCE: David Farrington, "Developmental and Life-Course Criminology: Key Theoretical and Empirical Issues," Sutherland Award address at the American Society of Criminology meeting in Chicago, November 2002 (revised March 2003).

Integrated Cognitive Antisocial Potential Theory (ICAP)

David Farrington, a distinguished criminologist, has formulated a new life course theory with the rather elaborate title "integrated cognitive antisocial potential," or ICAP for short.[100] Farrington's model is set out in Figure 9.7.

The key element of Farrington's model is what he calls **antisocial potential (AP),** which refers to the potential to commit antisocial acts. AP can be viewed as both a long- and short-term phenomenon.

Long-Term AP Farrington believes antisocial potential falls along a continuum ranging from low to high AP. Those with high levels of AP are at risk for offending over the life course; those with low AP levels live more conventional lives. Because relatively few people experience very high levels of AP, the number of chronic offenders in the population is limited. People with high AP are more likely to commit many different types of antisocial acts including crimes. Though AP levels are fairly consistent over time, they peak in the teenage years because of the effects of maturational factors such as peer influence and a decrease in family influences.

Farrington finds that long-term AP increases when people desire material goods, want to increase their status among intimates, and seek excitement and sexual satisfaction yet lack legitimate means for their attainment. Here

antisocial potential (AP)
An individual's potential to commit antisocial acts.

CHAPTER 9 DEVELOPMENTAL THEORIES: THINGS CHANGE **227**

■ According to the ICAP theory people with long-term antisocial potential are doomed to repeat their criminal offending. An assistant U.S. marshal, right, escorts James Justin Sledge, a man once tied to the 1997 Pearl High School shootings, from the federal courthouse in Jackson, Mississippi, April 29, 2003, after being sentenced on a gun charge. Sledge pleaded guilty in February to possessing an unregistered machine gun ordered over the Internet. Sledge was sentenced to four months in federal prison, four months of house arrest and three years of probation, and a $100 fine.

Farrington seems to be borrowing from strain theories. A person's potential for antisocial behavior increases when he or she becomes frustrated and despondent because of the absence of legitimate opportunities and means. However, the responses to strain depend on physical capabilities and behavioral skills; for example, a 5-year-old would have difficulty stealing a car.

Farrington also believes that long-term AP depends on attachment and socialization. Hence, AP will be low if parents consistently reward good behavior and punish bad behavior. AP will be high if children are not attached to parents, or if their parents are cold and rejecting. Disrupted families (broken homes) may impair both attachment and socialization processes. Families are not the only behavioral influence on long-term AP. People are exposed to and influenced by other antisocial models, such as criminal parents, delinquent siblings, and delinquent peers.

There may also be some biological elements to high AP. Long-term AP is high for impulsive people because they tend to act without thinking about the consequences. The children of criminal parents could have high AP partly because of genetic transmission, school failure could depend partly on low intelligence, and high impulsiveness and low anxiety could both reflect biological factors.

Can high long-term AP be reduced? Farrington believes changing life events can lower AP. For example, AP decreases after people get married or move out of high-crime areas, and it increases after separation from a partner. There may also be interaction effects between the influences on long-term AP. For example, people who experience strain or poor socialization may be disproportionately antisocial if they are also exposed to antisocial models or live in high-crime areas.

Short-Term AP Farrington also recognizes that a person may be influenced by situational inducements to crime. He calls this short-term AP. Immediate life events may increase antisocial potential so that, in the immediate moment, individuals may increase their location on the AP continuum. For example, a person with a relatively low long-term AP may suffer a temporary amplification if he is bored, angry, drunk, or frustrated. Short-term AP may be experienced within a group context such as when deviant behavior is encouraged or demanded by a group of male peers.

Short-term AP also reflects criminal opportunities and the availability of victims. The effects may be reciprocal: Encountering a tempting opportunity or victim may cause a short-term increase in AP; short-term increases in AP may motivate a person to seek out criminal opportunities and victims.

AP and Crime According to the ICAP theory, the commission of offenses and other types of antisocial acts depends on the interaction between the individual (with his immediate level of AP) and the social environment (especially criminal opportunities and victims). Whether a person with a certain level of AP commits a crime in a given situation depends on cognitive processes, including considering the subjective benefits, costs, and probabilities of the different outcomes, and stored behavioral repertoires or scripts (based on previous experiences). The subjective benefits and costs include immediate situational factors such as the material goods that can be stolen and the likelihood and consequences of being caught by the police. They also include social factors such as likely disapproval by parents or female partners, and encouragement or reinforcement from peers. In general, people tend to make decisions that seem rational to them, but those with low levels of AP will not commit offenses even when it appears rational to do so. Equally, high short-term levels of AP (caused by anger or drunkenness, for example) may induce people to commit offenses when it is not rational for them to do so. Here Farrington integrates rational choice theory into his model.

As a result of a learning process, the consequences of offending may lead to changes in long-term AP and in future cognitive decision-making processes. This is especially likely if the consequences are reinforcing (gaining material goods or peer approval) or punishing (receiving legal sanctions or parental disapproval). Also, if the consequences involve labeling or stigmatizing the offender, this may make it more difficult for him to achieve his aims legally and may lead to an increase in AP.

Why Do People Start or Stop Offending?   According to ICAP theory, long-term offending patterns result when people with relatively high AP also experience increases in their long-term motivation (for example, desires for material goods, status, sex, or excitement), increases in physical capabilities and skills, and changes in socialization influences (decreasing importance of parents, increasing importance of peers).

People begin to stop offending because of decreasing long-term motivation, decreasing impulsiveness, a greater ability to satisfy needs legally, decreasing physical capabilities, changes in socialization influences (decreasing importance of peers, increasing importance of female partners and children), and life events such as getting married, having children, moving home, and getting a steady job.

In contrast, short-term offending is caused by increasing short-term motivation (for example, bored, angry, drunk, or frustrated) and increasing opportunities for offending because of changes in routine activities (such as going out more). Short-term AP is decreased by a reduction in short-term energizing factors (less bored, angry, drunk, frustrated) and decreasing opportunities for offending because of changes in routine activities (such as going out less with male peers).

Farrington's theory is an important addition to the developmental model of criminality. It is unique because it distinguishes between long- and short-term propensity to commit crime. It occupies a middle ground between latent trait and life course theories because it proposes a master trait (AP) that controls behavior but one that can be influenced by long- and short-term life events. ✔ Checkpoints

Evaluating Developmental Theories

Although the differences between the views presented in this chapter may seem irreconcilable, they in fact share some common ground. They indicate that a criminal career must be understood as a passage along which people travel, that it has a beginning and an end, and that events and life circumstances influence the journey. The factors that affect a criminal career may include structural factors, such as income and status; socialization factors, such as family and peer relations; biological factors, such as size and strength; psychological factors, including intelligence and personality; and opportunity factors, such as free time, inadequate police protection, and a supply of easily stolen merchandise.

Life course theories emphasize the influence of changing interpersonal and structural factors (that is, people change along with the world they live in). Latent trait theories place more emphasis on the fact that behavior is linked less to personal change than to changes in the surrounding world.

These perspectives differ in their view of human development (see Concept Summary 9.1 for a comparison). Do people constantly change, as life course theories suggest, or are they more stable, constant, and changeless, as the latent trait view indicates? Are the factors that produce criminality different at each stage of life, as the life course view suggests, or does a master

CONCEPT SUMMARY 9.1 Developmental Theories

THEORY	MAJOR PREMISE	STRENGTHS	RESEARCH FOCUS
Latent Trait Theories	A master trait controls human development	Explains the continuity of crime and chronic offending	Identify the master trait that produces crime
General theory of crime	Crime and criminality are separate concepts. People choose to commit crime when they lack self-control. People lacking self-control will seize criminal opportunities.	Integrates choice and social control concepts. Identifies the difference between crime and criminality.	Measure association between impulsivity, low self-control, and criminal behaviors
Life Course Theories	As people go through the life course, social and personal traits undergo change and influence behavior.	Explains why some at-risk children desist from crime.	Identify critical moments in a person's life course that produce crime
Social development model (SDM)	Weak social controls produce crime. A person's place in the structure influences his or her bond to society.	Combines elements of social structural and social process theories. Accounts for variations in the crime rate.	Show how different factors affecting a child's social development over the life course influence criminal behavior patterns
Interactional theory	Criminals go through lifestyle changes during their offending career.	Combines sociological and psychological theories.	Identify crime-producing interpersonal interactions and their reciprocal effects
Age-graded theory	As people mature, the factors that influence their propensity to commit crime change. In childhood, family factors are critical; in adulthood, marital and job factors are key.	Shows how crime is a developmental process that shifts in direction over the life course.	Identify critical points in the life course that produce crime; analyze the association between social capital and crime
Integrated cognitive antisocial potential theory (ICAP)	People with antisocial potential (AP) are at risk to commit antisocial acts. AP can be viewed as both a long- and short-term phenomenon.	Identifies different types of criminal propensity and shows how they may influence behavior in both the short and long term.	Identify the components of long- and short-term AP

trait such as impulsivity or lack of self-control steer the course of human behavior?

It is also possible that these two positions are not mutually exclusive and each may make a notable contribution to understanding the onset and continuity of a criminal career. For example, recent research by Bradley Entner Wright and his associates found evidence supporting both latent trait and life course theories.[101] Their research, conducted with subjects in New Zealand, indicates that low self-control in childhood predicts disrupted social bonds and criminal offending later in life, a finding that supports latent trait theory. They also found that maintaining positive social bonds helps reduce criminality and that maintaining prosocial bonds could even counteract the effect of low self-control. Latent traits are an important influence on crime, but Wright's findings indicate that social relationships that form later in life appear to influence criminal behavior "above and beyond" individuals' preexisting characteristics.[102] This finding may reflect the fact that there are two classes of criminals: a less serious group who are influenced by life events, and a more chronic group whose latent traits insulate them from any positive prosocial relationships.[103]

Summary

- Latent trait theories hold that some underlying condition present at birth or soon after controls behavior. Suspect traits include low IQ, impulsivity, and personality structure. This underlying trait explains the continuity of offending because, once present, it remains with a person throughout his or her life.

- The general theory of crime, developed by Gottfredson and Hirschi, integrates choice theory concepts. People with latent traits choose crime over noncrime; the opportunity for crime mediates their choice.

- Life course theories argue that events that take place over the life course influence criminal choices.

- The cause of crime constantly changes as people mature. At first, the nuclear family influences behavior; during adolescence, the peer group dominates; in adulthood, marriage and career are critical.

- There are a variety of pathways to crime: some kids are sneaky, others hostile, and still others defiant.

- Crime may be part of a variety of social problems, including health, physical, and interpersonal troubles.

- The social development model finds that living in a disorganized area helps weaken social bonds and sets people off on a delinquent path.

- According to interactional theory, crime influences social relations, which in turn influences crime; the relationship is interactive. The sources of crime evolve over time.

- Sampson and Laub's age-graded theory holds that the social sources of behavior change over the life course. People who develop social capital are best able to avoid antisocial entanglements. Important life events or turning points enable adult offenders to desist from crime. Among the most important are getting married and serving in the military.

- According to David Farrington's ICAP theory, people with antisocial potential (AP) stand a greater chance of engaging in criminal offenses and remaining in a life of crime.

Thinking Like a Criminologist

Luis Francisco is the leader of the Almighty Latin Kings and Queens Nation. He was convicted of murder in 1998 and sentenced to life imprisonment plus 45 years. Francisco's life has been filled with displacement, poverty, and chronic predatory crime. The son of a prostitute in Havana, at the age of 9 he was sent to prison for robbery. He had trouble in school, and teachers described him as having attention problems; he dropped out in the seventh grade. On his nineteenth birthday in 1980, he immigrated to the United States and soon after became a gang member in Chicago, where he joined the Latin Kings. After moving to the Bronx, he shot and killed his girlfriend in 1981. He fled to Chicago and was not apprehended until 1984. Sentenced to nine years for second-degree manslaughter, Francisco ended up in a New York prison, where he started a New York prison chapter of the Latin Kings. As King Blood, Inka, First Supreme Crown, Francisco ruled the 2,000 Latin Kings in and out of prison. Disciplinary troubles erupted when some Kings were found stealing from the organization. Infuriated, King Blood wrote to his street lieutenants and ordered their termination. Federal authorities, who had been monitoring Francisco's mail, arrested 35 Latin Kings. The other 34 pled guilty; only Francisco insisted on a trial, where he was found guilty of conspiracy to commit murder.

Explain Luis Francisco's behavior patterns from a developmental perspective. How would a latent trait theorist explain his escalating criminal activities?

Go to the Criminology: The Core 2e Web site to review the content of this chapter.

Doing Research on the Web

For an up-to-date list of URLs, go to
http://www.cj.wadsworth.com/siegel_crimcore2e

Before you comment on Francisco, it may help to read Rebecca S. Katz's attempt to explain the relationship between developmental theories. "Building the Foundation for a Side-by-Side Explanatory Model: A General Theory of Crime, the Age-Graded Life Course Theory, and Attachment Theory" can be found at:

http://wcr.sonoma.edu/v1n2/katz.html

You may also want to check out the Web site of the Social Development Model project:

http://depts.washington.edu/ssdp/

And the Life History Studies Program at the University of Pittsburgh:

http://www.wpic.pitt.edu/research/famhist/

Pro/Con discussions and Viewpoint Essays on some of the topics in this chapter may be found at the Opposing Viewpoints Resource Center:

http://www.gale.com/OpposingViewpoints

Key Terms

developmental theory 208
latent trait theory 208
life course theory 208
latent trait 208
general theory of crime (GTC) 209
adolescent-limited 215
life course persister 215

pseudomaturity 215
problem behavior syndrome (PBS) 215
authority conflict pathway 217
covert pathway 217
overt pathway 217
social development model (SDM) 218

prosocial bonds 219
interactional theory 219
turning points 221
social capital 222
human capital 222
antisocial potential (AP) 226

Critical Thinking Questions

1. Do you consider yourself the holder of social capital? If so, what form does it take?

2. A person gets a 1600 on the SAT. Without knowing this person, what personal, family, and social characteristics must he or she have? Another person becomes a serial killer. Without knowing this person, what personal, family, and social characteristics must he or she have? If "bad behavior" is explained by multiple problems, is "good behavior" explained by multiple strengths?

3. Do you believe there is a latent trait that makes a person crime prone, or is crime a function of environment and socialization?

4. Do you agree with Loeber's multiple pathway model? Do you know people who have traveled down those paths?

part 3

Crime Typologies

Criminologists have sought to study criminal behaviors in groupings or typologies so they may be more easily understood and conceptualized. In this section, crime patterns are clustered into four typologies: violent crime (Chapter 10); economic crimes involving common theft offenses (Chapter 11); economic crimes involving white-collar criminals, cyber criminals, or criminal organizations (Chapter 12); and public order crimes, such as prostitution and drug abuse (Chapter 13). This format groups criminal behaviors by their focus and consequence: bringing physical harm to others; misappropriating other people's property; and violating laws designed to protect public morals.

Violent Crime

Chapter Objectives

1. Be familiar with the various causes of violent crime.
2. Know the concept of the brutalization process.
3. Be able to discuss the history of rape.
4. Be familiar with the different types of rape.
5. Be able to discuss the legal issues in rape prosecution.
6. Recognize that there are different types of murder.
7. Be able to discuss the differences between serial killing, mass murder, and spree killing.
8. Be familiar with the nature of assault in the home.
9. Understand the careers of armed robbers.
10. Be able to discuss newly emerging forms of violence such as stalking, hate crimes, and workplace violence.
11. Understand the different types of terrorism and what is being done today to combat terrorist activities.

N OCTOBER OF 2002, A MYSTE-
RIOUS AND DEADLY SNIPER
TERRORIZED RESIDENTS IN
THE WASHINGTON, D.C. AREA.[1]
The attacks began on October 2, 2002,
in the northern Washington suburbs
around Montgomery County, where six
victims were killed, each with a single
shot, during a two-day period. Afterward,
the sniper circled through areas in suburbs to the east, south, and west, cutting
down individuals with a single shot. At a

CNN. View the CNN video clip of this story and answer related critical thinking questions on your Criminology: The Core 2e CD.

shooting scene on October 7, the sniper reportedly left a tarot death card inscribed: "Dear Policeman, I am God." As the investigation proceeded, rumors were rampant: the sniper was part of a terrorist cell; he was a psychopath influenced by the release of the popular serial killer film *Red Dragon*.

The sniper attacks were unique. Unlike most mass murderers, he did not kill his victims in a single violent outburst; unlike most serial killers, he did not touch, interact, or get close to his victims. Nor did the sniper seek out a specific class of victims; his casualties included the young and old, African Americans and whites, men and women. When the sniper contacted police, his crime spree began to unravel. He felt his early calls were not being given the proper attention. To give himself more credibility, the sniper called a local priest and bragged about a robbery and killing in Montgomery, Alabama; he hoped the priest would act as a go-between. Instead, the priest told authorities about the strange phone call. When authorities investigated the Alabama case, they were able to obtain a crime scene fingerprint and identify the suspect as John Lee Malvo, 17, a Jamaican citizen. Malvo was known as the unofficial stepson and traveling companion of John Allen Muhammad, 41, an Army veteran with an expert's rating in marksmanship.[2] In 2004, Muhammad was sentenced to death, and Malvo to life in prison.

The sniper attacks galvanized the public and were the subject of vast media coverage. They show why many people believe the United States is still an extremely violent nation despite the fact the UCR tells us that the violence rate has been in a recent decline. Though people report that they feel somewhat safer than they did a decade ago, surveys indicate that more than half of all women are still afraid to walk alone in their neighborhood at night.[3]

The sniper attacks also show how understanding and controlling violence can be quite complex. Muhammad had a history of violence and domestic abuse, yet he was still able to buy a lethal weapon with a sniper scope. The sniper attacks again raised questions about the utility of gun control and creating a national database to track weapons and ammunition, a plan opposed by the National Rifle Association.

World Report on Violence

The danger from various forms of violent behavior has become a worldwide epidemic. In fact, a comprehensive report by the United Nation's World Health Organization issued in 2002 views violence as a global public health problem.

According to the WHO report, violence kills more than 1.6 million people every year. Yet this staggering number may only be the tip of the iceberg because many violent acts, especially domestic violence, go unreported. In addition to the deaths, millions of people are left injured as a result of violence and suffer from physical, sexual, reproductive, and mental health problems.

According to the WHO report, violence is among the leading causes of death for people aged 15 to 44 years of age, accounting for 14 percent of deaths among males and 7 percent of deaths among females around the world. Almost every minute of the day someone is murdered, an average of 1,424 daily murders; adding to this number is an almost equal number of daily suicides. About 35 people are killed every hour as a direct result of armed conflict. During the twentieth century, nearly 200 million people were killed during warfare, more than half of them civilians.

Youth Violence

The WHO report collected data on specific types of violence including youth violence, which is defined as homicide and nonfatal attacks perpetrated by or against a person aged 10 to 29 years of age. Youth violence can be committed by gangs or by young people on the streets or in schools, and it can involve physical fights, bullying, and weapon-carrying.

The data show that youth homicide rates have increased in many parts of the world and that fighting and bullying are common among young people. The report found that in a single year (2000) more than one-third of the deaths around the globe due to interpersonal violence occurred among young adults aged 15 to 29 years of age. The rate for this age range is more than triple the percentage for youths 10 to14 years of age, indicating that risks become greater as adolescents mature. Homicide rates for 10- to 29-year-olds vary significantly by region: from 0.9 percent in the high-income regions of Europe and parts of Asia and the Western Pacific to 36.4 percent in Latin America. Male youth homicide rates are substantially higher than female youth homicide rates: for the 15- to 29-year-old group, for example, the male rate was 19.4 percent, compared to 4.4 percent for females.

Sexual Violence

The World Report on Violence and Health found that at least one in five women may experience sexual violence by an intimate partner in their lifetime. Studies on sexual violence conducted in Canada, Finland, Switzerland, Great Britain, and the United States found that between 2 and 13 percent of women report being the victim of either an attempted or completed rape by a partner. In smaller population-based studies, for example, in London, England, Guadalajara, Mexico, and the Midland Province in Zimbabwe, the reported rate is higher at about 25 percent.

For many women, sexual violence starts in childhood and adolescence and may occur in the home, the school, and the community. Studies conducted in a wide variety of nations ranging from Cameroon to New Zealand found high rates of reported forced sexual initiation. In some nations, as high as 46 percent of adolescent women and 20 percent of adolescent men report sexual coercion at the hands of family members, teachers, boyfriends, or strangers.

Critical Thinking

Risk factors at all levels of social and personal life contribute to youth violence. But kids in all nations who experience economic inequalities, rapid social change, and the easy availability of firearms, alcohol, and drugs seem the most likely to get involved in violence. Can anything be done to help alleviate these social problems?

InfoTrac College Edition Research

To find out more about violence around the world, use "violence Europe," "violence Asia," and "violence Africa" as key words.

SOURCE: Etienne Krug, Linda Dahlberg, James Mercy, Anthony Zwi, and Rafael Lozano, *World report on violence and health.* Geneva: World Health Organization, 2002.

Some experts argued that Muhammad and Malvo's violent outburst was really motivated by their dislike of the United States government. If it were, criminologists would categorize their outburst as **expressive violence,** acts that vent rage, anger, or frustration. It has also been suggested that the snipers' motives were more personal and part of an elaborate, albeit deadly, extortion scheme in which they hoped to gain $10 million. This would make their violence **instrumental:** designed to improve the financial or social position of the criminal, for example, through an armed robbery or murder for hire.

While U.S. violence rates have been on the decline, violence rates are on the upswing elsewhere around the world. You can learn more about this in the Race, Culture, Gender, and Criminology feature.

expressive violence
Acts that vent rage, anger, or frustration.
instrumental violence
Acts designed to improve the financial or social position of the criminal.

Figure 10.1
Sources of Violence

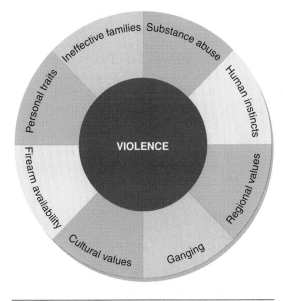

The Causes of Violence

Connections

As you may recall from Chapter 5, biosocial theorists link violence to a number biological irregularities, including but not limited to genetic influences and inheritance, the action of hormones, the functioning of neurotransmitters, brain structure, and diet. Psychologists link violent behavior to observational learning from violent TV shows, traumatic childhood experiences, low intelligence, mental illness, impaired cognitive processes, and abnormal (psychopathic) personality structure.

FIND IT ON INFOTRAC
College Edition

To read an interview with Dorothy Otnow Lewis in which she discusses how the problems in an aggressive boy's life should be evaluated and how appropriate treatment should be provided, go to:

Rena Large, "New Path for Aggressive Boys," *NEA Today* Oct 1998 v17 n2 p29(1)

What sets off a violent person? Some experts suggest that a small number of inherently violence-prone individuals may themselves have been the victims of physical or psychological abnormalities. Another view is that violence and aggression are inherently human traits that can affect any person at any time. There may be violence-prone subcultures within society whose members value force, routinely carry weapons, and consider violence to have an acceptable place in social interaction.[4] A few of the most prominent factors discussed here are illustrated in Figure 10.1.

Personal Traits

On March 13, 1995, an ex–Boy Scout leader named Thomas Hamilton took four high-powered rifles into the primary school of the peaceful Scottish town of Dunblane and slaughtered 16 children and their teacher. This horrific crime shocked the British Isles into implementing strict controls on all guns.[5] Bizarre outbursts such as Hamilton's support a link between violence and personal traits.

Psychologist Dorothy Otnow Lewis and her associates found that murderous youths suffer signs of major neurological impairment (such as abnormal EEGs, multiple psychomotor impairments, and severe seizures), low intelligence as measured on standard IQ tests, psychotic close relatives, and psychotic symptoms such as paranoia, illogical thinking, and hallucinations.[6] In her book *Guilty by Reason of Insanity*, Lewis finds that death row inmates have a history of mental impairment and intellectual dysfunction.[7] Abnormal personality structures, including such traits as depression, impulsivity, aggression, dishonesty, pathological lying, lack of remorse, borderline personality syndrome, and psychopathology, have been associated with various forms of violence.[8] It comes as no surprise then that many murderers kill themselves shortly after committing their crime.[9] Although this evidence indicates that violent offenders are more prone to psychosis than other people, no single clinical diagnosis can characterize their behavior.[10]

Ineffective Families

Absent or deviant parents, inconsistent discipline, physical abuse, and lack of supervision have all been linked to persistent violent offending.[11] Although infants demonstrate individual temperaments, who they become may have a

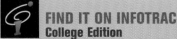
lot to do with how they are treated during their early years. Some children are less easy to soothe than others; in some cases, difficult infant temperament has been associated with later aggression and behavioral problems.[12] Parents who fail to set adequate limits or to use proper, consistent discipline reinforce a child's coercive behavior.[13] The effects of inadequate parenting and early rejection may affect violent behavior throughout life.[14]

Abuse may have the greatest effect if it is persistent and extends from childhood to adolescence.[15] Children who are physically punished by their parents are likely to physically abuse a sibling and later engage in spouse abuse and other forms of criminal violence.[16] There is evidence that batterers receive significantly less love and more punishment from their mothers than did men in a general population comparison group. Abusive childhood experiences may be a key factor in the later development of relationship aggression.[17]

Evolutionary Factors/Human Instinct

Perhaps violent responses and emotions are actually inherent in all humans, and the right spark can trigger them. Sigmund Freud believed that human aggression and violence are produced by instinctual drives.[18] Freud maintained that humans possess two opposing instinctual drives that interact to control behavior: **eros,** the life instinct, which drives people toward self-fulfillment and enjoyment; and **thanatos,** the death instinct, which produces self-destruction. Thanatos can be expressed externally (as violence and sadism) or internally (as suicide, alcoholism, or other self-destructive habits). Because aggression is instinctual, Freud saw little hope for its treatment.

A number of biologists and anthropologists have also speculated that instinctual violence-promoting traits may be common in the human species. One view is that aggression and violence are the result of instincts inborn in all animals, including human beings.[19] However, unlike other animals, humans lack the inhibition against killing members of their own species, which protects animals from self-extinction, and are capable of killing their own kind in war or as a result of interpersonal conflicts.

Exposure to Violence

Kids who are constantly exposed to violence at home, at school, or in the environment may adopt violent methods themselves. Wade Myers, a psychiatrist, studied juvenile rapist/murderers and found that almost all had grown up in dysfunctional families and had early and frequent exposures to abuse and violence.[20]

Exposure to violence can also occur at the neighborhood level when people are forced to live in violent, dangerous neighborhoods. Children living in areas marked by extreme violence may eventually become desensitized to the persistent neighborhood brutality and conflict they witness, eventually succumbing to violent behaviors themselves.[21] And, not surprisingly, those children who are exposed to violence in the home and also live in neighborhoods with high violence rates are the ones most likely to engage in violence crime themselves.[22]

Substance Abuse

It has become common to link violence to substance abuse. In fact, substance abuse influences violence in three ways:[23]

1. A **psychopharmacological relationship** may be the direct consequence of ingesting mood-altering substances. For example, alcohol abuse has long been associated with all forms of violence because drinking reduces cognitive ability, making miscommunication more likely while

eros
The life instinct, which drives people toward self-fulfillment and enjoyment.

thanatos
The death instinct, which produces self-destruction.

psychopharmacological relationship
The direct consequence of ingesting mood-altering substances.

Connections

Although it seems logical that banning the sale and ownership of firearms might help reduce violence, those in favor of gun ownership, as discussed in a feature on gun control in Chapter 2, do not agree. Some experts believe taking guns away from citizens might endanger them against armed criminals.

Connections

Delinquent subcultures were discussed in some detail in Chapter 6. Recall that subculture theorists portray delinquents not as rebels from the normative culture but rather as people who are in accord with the informal rules and values of their immediate culture. By adhering to cultural norms, they violate the law.

■ Violence rates are highest in urban areas where subcultural values support teenage gangs. Youths in gangs are more likely to own guns and other weapons than non–gang members, as well as have peers who are gun owners. They are also more likely to carry guns outside the home.

economic compulsive behavior
Drug users who resort to violence to support their habit.

systemic link
A link that occurs when drug dealers turn violent in their competition with rival gangs.

subculture of violence
Violence has become legitimized by the custom and norms of that group.

at the same time limiting the capacity for rational dialogue and compromise.[24]

2. Drug ingestion may also cause **economic compulsive behavior,** in which drug users resort to violence to support their habit.

3. A **systemic link** between drugs and violence occurs when drug dealers turn violent in their competition with rival gangs.[25]

Recent research by Kenneth Tardiff and his associates affirms the substance abuse–violence link and indicates that the pharmacological link is actually the most significant.[26]

Firearm Availability

Although firearm availability alone does not cause violence, it may be a facilitating factor. A petty argument can escalate into a fatal encounter if one party has a handgun. The nation has also been rocked by the use of firearms in schools and the resulting slew of well-publicized school shootings. Research indicates that a significant number of kids routinely carry guns to school; those who have been the victims of crime themselves and who hang with peers who carry weapons are the ones most likely to bring guns to school.[27]

The Uniform Crime Report (UCR) indicates that two-thirds of all murders and about two-fifths of all robberies involve firearms.[28] Handguns kill two-thirds of all police who die in the line of duty. The presence of firearms in the home also significantly increases the risk of suicide among adolescents, regardless of how carefully the guns are secured or stored.[29]

Cultural Values

Areas that experience violence seem to cluster together.[30] To explain this phenomenon, criminologists Marvin Wolfgang and Franco Ferracuti formulated the famous concept that some areas contain an independent **subculture of violence.**[31]

The subculture's norms are separate from society's central, dominant value system. In this subculture, a potent theme of violence influences lifestyles, the socialization process, and interpersonal relationships. Even

though the subculture's members share some of the dominant culture's values, they expect that violence will be used to solve social conflicts and dilemmas. In some cultural subgroups, then, violence has become legitimized by custom and norms. It is considered appropriate behavior within culturally defined conflict situations in which an individual who has been offended by a negative outcome in a dispute seeks reparations through violent means (disputatiousness).[32] For example, when Charis Kubrin and Ronald Weitzer studied homicide in St. Louis, Missouri, they discovered that a certain type of killing they refer to as "cultural retaliatory homicide" is common in some neighborhoods that suffer economic disadvantage, pro-violence cultural codes, and less than adequate policing. In these areas, residents often resolve interpersonal conflicts informally—without calling the police—even if it means killing their opponent; these killings are accepted by neighborhood values, which support retaliatory killing.[33]

Empirical evidence shows that violence rates are highest in urban areas where subcultural values support teenage gangs, whose members typically embrace the use of violence. Gang boys are more likely to own guns and other weapons than non–gang members. They are also more likely to have peers who are gun owners and are more likely to carry guns outside the home.[34] The association between gang membership and violence has a number of roots. It can result from drug trafficking activities and turf protection but also stems from personal vendettas and a perceived need for self-protection.[35] Violence is a core value of gang membership.[36]

Each of these factors is believed to influence violent crime, including both traditional common-law crimes, such as rape, murder, assault, and robbery, and newly recognized problems, such as workplace violence, hate crimes, and political violence. Each of these forms of violent behavior is discussed in some detail later in this chapter. ✔ Checkpoints

Forcible Rape

Rape (from the Latin *rapere,* to take by force) is defined in common law as "the carnal knowledge of a female forcibly and against her will."[37] It is one of the most loathed, misunderstood, and frightening crimes. Under traditional common-law definitions, rape involves nonconsensual sexual intercourse with a female by a male. There are, of course, other forms of sexual assault, including male on male and female on male sexual assaults (some studies estimate that up to 25 percent of males have been the target of unwanted sexual advances by women), but these are not considered here within the traditional concept of rape.[38]

Rape was often viewed as a sexual offense in the traditional criminological literature. It was presented as a crime that involved overwhelming lust, driving a man to force his attentions on a woman. Criminologists now consider rape a violent, coercive act of aggression, not a forceful expression of sexuality. There has been a national campaign to alert the public to the seriousness of rape, offer help to victims, and change legal definitions to facilitate the prosecution of rape offenders. Such efforts have been only marginally effective in reducing rape rates, but there has been significant progress in overhauling rape laws and developing a vast social service network to aid victims.

History of Rape

Rape has been a recognized crime throughout history. It has been the subject of art, literature, film, and theater. Paintings such as the *Rape of the Sabine Women* by Nicolas Poussin, novels such as *Clarissa* by Samuel Richardson, poems such as *The Rape of Lucrece* by William Shakespeare, and films such as *The Accused* and *Thelma and Louise* have sexual violence as their central theme.

rape
The carnal knowledge of a female forcibly and against her will.

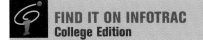

FIND IT ON INFOTRAC
College Edition

Use the term *rape* as a subject guide to search for more information on this topic.

In early civilization rape was common. Men staked a claim of ownership on women by forcibly abducting and raping them.[39] Under Babylonian and Hebraic law, the rape of a virgin was a crime punishable by death. However, if the victim was married, then both she and her attacker were considered equally to blame, and unless her husband intervened, both were put to death.

During the Middle Ages, it was common for ambitious men to abduct and rape wealthy women in an effort to force them into marriage. The practice of "heiress stealing" illustrates how feudal law gave little thought or protection to women and equated them with property.[40] Only in the late fifteenth century, after a monetary economy developed, was forcible sex outlawed and then only if the victim was of the nobility. Peasant women and married women were not considered rape victims until well into the sixteenth century.

Incidence of Rape

According to the most recent UCR data, about 94,000 rapes or attempted rapes were reported to U.S. police in 2002, a rate of about 32 per 100,000 inhabitants or, more relevantly, 62 per 100,000 females.[41] Like other violent crimes, the rape rate has been in a decade-long decline, and the 2002 totals are significantly below 1992 levels when 84 women per 100,000 were rape victims.

Population density influences the rape rate. Metropolitan areas today have rape rates significantly higher than rural areas; nonetheless, urban areas have experienced a much greater drop in rape reports than rural areas. The police make arrests in slightly more than half of all reported rape offenses. Of the offenders arrested, about 45 percent were under 25 years of age, and 63 percent were white. The racial and age pattern of rape arrests has been fairly consistent for some time. Finally, rape is a warm-weather crime—most incidents occur during July and August, with the lowest rates occurring during December, January, and February.

These data must be interpreted with caution. According to the National Crime Victimization Survey (NCVS), rape is frequently underreported. For example, in 2002 the NCVS estimates that about 248,000 rapes and attempted rapes took place, suggesting that almost two-thirds of rape incidents are not reported to police.[42] Many people fail to report rapes because they are embarrassed, believe nothing can be done, or blame themselves. Some victims of sexual assaults may even question whether they have really been "raped"; research indicates that when the assault involved a boyfriend, or if the woman was severely impaired by alcohol or drugs, or if the act involved oral or digital sex, the women were unlikely to label their situations as being a "real" rape.[43]

Because other victim surveys indicate that at least 20 percent of adult women, 15 percent of college-aged women, and 12 percent of adolescent girls have experienced sexual abuse or assault at some time during their lives, it is evident that both official and victimization statistics significantly undercount rape.[44] However, like the UCR, the NCVS indicates that the number of rapes have been in a sharp decline, falling 56 percent between 1993 and 2002.

Types of Rapists

Some rapes are planned, others are spontaneous; some focus on a particular victim, whereas others occur almost as an afterthought during the commission of another crime, such as a burglary. Some rapists commit a single crime, whereas others are multiple offenders; some attack alone, and others engage in group or gang rapes.[45] Because there is no single type of rape or rapist, criminologists have attempted to define and categorize the vast variety of rape situations.

Criminologists now recognize that there are numerous motivations for rape and as a result various types of rapists. One of the best-known attempts

EXHIBIT 10.1 Varieties of Forcible Rape

Anger rape occurs when sexuality becomes a means of expressing and discharging pent-up anger and rage. The rapist uses far more brutality than would have been necessary if his real objective had been simply to have sex with his victim. His aim is to hurt his victim as much as possible; the sexual aspect of rape may be an afterthought. Often the anger rapist acts on the spur of the moment after an upsetting incident has caused him conflict, irritation, or aggravation. Surprisingly, anger rapes are less psychologically traumatic for the victim than might be expected. Because a woman is usually physically beaten during an anger rape, she is more likely to receive sympathy from her peers, relatives, and the justice system and consequently be immune from any suggestion that she complied with the attack.

Power rape involves an attacker who does not want to harm his victim as much as he wants to possess her sexually. His goal is sexual conquest, and he uses only the amount of force necessary to achieve his objective. The power rapist wants to be in control, to be able to dominate women and have them at his mercy. Yet it is not sexual gratification that drives the power rapist; in fact, he often has a consenting relationship with his wife or girlfriend. Rape is instead a way of putting personal insecurities to rest, asserting heterosexuality, and preserving a sense of manhood. The power rapist's victim usually is a woman equal in age to or younger than the rapist. The lack of physical violence may reduce the support given the victim by family and friends. Therefore, the victim's personal guilt over her rape experience is increased—perhaps, she thinks, she could have done something to get away.

Sadistic rape involves both sexuality and aggression. The sadistic rapist is bound up in ritual—he may torment his victim, bind her, or torture her. Victims are usually related, in the rapist's view, to a personal characteristic that he wants to harm or destroy. The rape experience is intensely exciting to the sadist; he gets satisfaction from abusing, degrading, or humiliating his captive. This type of rape is particularly traumatic for the victim. Victims of such crimes need psychiatric care long after their physical wounds have healed.

SOURCE: A. Nicholas Groth and Jean Birnbaum, *Men Who Rape* (New York: Plenum Press, 1979).

to classify the personalities of rapists was made by psychologist A. Nicholas Groth, an expert on classifying and treating sex offenders. According to Groth, every rape encounter contains at least one of these three elements: anger, power, or sadism.[46] Consequently, rapists can be classified according to one of the three dimensions described in Exhibit 10.1. In treating rape offenders, Groth found that about 55 percent were of the power type; about 40 percent, the anger type; and about 5 percent, the sadistic type. Groth's major contribution has been his recognition that rape is generally a crime of violence, not a sexual act. In all of these circumstances, rape involves a violent criminal offense in which a predatory criminal chooses to attack a victim.[47]

Types of Rapes

In addition to there being a variety of types of rapists, there are also different categories of rapes.

Date Rape   One disturbing trend of rape involves people who are in some form of courting relationship known as **date rape.** There is no single form of date rape. Some occur on first dates, others after a relationship has been developing, and still others occur after the couple has been involved for some time. In long-term or close relationships, the male partner may feel he has invested so much time and money in his partner that he is owed sexual relations or that sexual intimacy is an expression that the involvement is progressing.[48] Date rape is believed to be frequent on college campuses. It has been estimated that 15 to 20 percent of all college women are victims of rape or attempted rape. Despite their seriousness and prevalence, fewer than 1 in 10 date rapes may be reported to police.[49] Some victims do not report because they do not view their experience as a "real rape," which, they believe, involves a strange man "jumping out of the bushes." Other victims are embarrassed and frightened. Many tell their friends about their rape while refusing to let authorities know what happened; reporting is most common in the most

date rape
A rape that involves people who are in some form of courting relationship.

FIND IT ON INFOTRAC
College Edition

Does watching films that degrade women influence the commission of a date rape? To find out, read:

Michael Milburn, Roxanne Mather, and Sheree D. Conrad, "The Effects of Viewing R-Rated Movie Scenes That Objectify Women on Perceptions of Date Rape," *Sex Roles: A Journal of Research,* Nov 2000 p645

serious cases, for example, when a weapon is used; it is less common when drugs or alcohol are involved.[50]

Marital Rape   Traditionally, a legally married husband could not be charged with raping his wife; this was referred to as the **marital exemption.** However, research indicates that many women are raped each year by their husbands as part of an overall pattern of spousal abuse, and they deserve the protection of the law. Many spousal rapes are accompanied by brutal, sadistic beatings and have little to do with normal sexual interests.[51] Not surprisingly, the marital exemption has undergone significant revision. In 1980, only three states had laws against marital rape; today almost every state recognizes marital rape as a crime.[52]

Statutory Rape   The term **statutory rape** refers to sexual relations between an underage minor female and an adult male. Although the sex is not forced or coerced, the law says that young girls are incapable of giving informed consent, so the act is legally considered nonconsensual. Typically a state's law will define an age of consent above which there can be no criminal prosecution for sexual relations.[53]

The Causes of Rape

What factors predispose some men to commit rape? Criminologists' responses to this question are almost as varied as the crime itself. However, most explanations can be grouped into a few consistent categories.

Evolutionary, Biological Factors   One explanation for rape focuses on the evolutionary, biological aspects of the male sexual drive. This perspective suggests that rape may be instinctual, developed over the ages as a means of perpetuating the species. In more primitive times, forcible sexual contact may have helped spread genes and maximize offspring. Some believe that these prehistoric drives remain: males still have a natural sexual drive that encourages them to have intimate relations with as many women as possible.[54] The evolutionary view is that the sexual urge corresponds to the unconscious need to preserve the species by spreading one's genes as widely as possible. Men who are sexually aggressive will have a reproductive edge over their more passive peers.[55]

Male Socialization   In contrast to the evolutionary biological view, some researchers argue that rape is a function of socialization. Some men have been socialized to be aggressive with women and believe that the use of violence or force is legitimate if their sexual advances are rebuffed ("women like to play hard to get and expect to be forced to have sex"). Those who have been socialized to believe that "no means yes" are more likely to be sexually aggressive.[56] The use of sexual violence is aggravated if pro-force socialization is reinforced by peers who share similar values.[57]

Diana Russell describes the **virility mystique**—the belief that males must separate their sexual feelings from needs for love, respect, and affection. She believes men are socialized to be the aggressors and expect to be sexually active with many women; consequently, male virginity and sexual inexperience are shameful. Similarly, sexually aggressive women frighten some men and cause them to doubt their own masculinity. Sexual insecurity may lead some men to commit rape to bolster their self-image and masculine identity.[58]

Psychological Abnormality   Rapists may suffer from some type of personality disorder or mental illness. Research shows that a significant percentage of incarcerated rapists exhibit psychotic tendencies, and many others have hostile, sadistic feelings toward women.[59] A high proportion of serial rapists

marital exemption
Traditionally, a legally married husband could not be charged with raping his wife.

statutory rape
Sexual relations between an underage minor female and an adult male.

virility mystique
The belief that males must separate their sexual feelings from needs for love, respect, and affection.

Connections

This view will be explored further in Chapter 13 when the issue of pornography and violence is analyzed in greater detail. Most research does not show that watching pornography is directly linked to sexual violence, but there may be a link between sexual aggression and viewing movies with sexual violence as their theme.

and repeat sexual offenders exhibit psychopathic personality structures.[60] There is evidence linking rape proclivity with **narcissistic personality disorder,** a pattern of traits and behaviors that indicate infatuation and fixation with one's self to the exclusion of all others and the egotistic and ruthless pursuit of one's gratification, dominance, and ambition.[61]

Social Learning   This perspective submits that men learn to commit rapes much as they learn any other behavior. For example, sexual aggression may be learned through interaction with peers who articulate attitudes supportive of sexual violence.[62] Nicholas Groth found that 40 percent of the rapists he studied were sexually victimized as adolescents.[63] A growing body of literature links personal sexual trauma with the desire to inflict sexual trauma on others.[64] Watching violent or pornographic films featuring women who are beaten, raped, or tortured has been linked to sexually aggressive behavior in men.[65]

Sexual Motivation   Most criminologists believe rape is a violent act that is not sexually motivated. Yet it might be premature to dismiss the sexual motive from all rapes.[66] NCVS data reveal that rape victims tend to be young and that rapists prefer younger, presumably more attractive, victims. Data show an association between the ages of rapists and their victims, indicating that men choose rape targets of approximately the same age as consensual sex partners. And, despite the fact that younger criminals are usually the most violent, older rapists tend to harm their victims more than younger rapists. This pattern indicates that older criminals may rape for motives of power and control, whereas younger offenders may be seeking sexual gratification. Victims may, therefore, suffer less harm from severe beatings and so forth from younger attackers.

Rape and the Law

Of all violent crimes, none has created such conflict in the legal system as rape. Even if women choose to report sexual assaults to police, they are often initially reluctant because of the sexist fashion in which rape victims are treated by police, prosecutors, and court personnel and the legal technicalities that authorize invasion of women's privacy when a rape case is tried in court. Police officers may be hesitant to make arrests and testify in court when the alleged assaults do not yield obvious signs of violence or struggle (presumably showing the victim strenuously resisted the attack). Police are also loath to testify on the victim's behalf if she had previously known or dated her attacker. Some state laws have made rape so difficult to prove that women believe the slim chance that their attacker will be convicted is not sufficient to warrant their participation in the legal process. However, police and courts are now becoming more sensitive to the plight of rape victims and are just as likely to investigate acquaintance rapes as they are **aggravated rapes** involving multiple offenders, weapons, and victim injuries. In some jurisdictions, the justice system takes all rape cases seriously and does not ignore those in which victim and attacker have had a prior relationship or those that did not involve serious injury.[67]

Proving Rape   Proving guilt in a rape case is extremely challenging for prosecutors. Some judges also fear that women may charge men with rape because of jealousy, false marriage proposals, or pregnancy. There is also evidence that juries may consider the race of the victim and offender in their decision making, for example, believing victims and convicting in interracial rapes more often than they do in intrarace rapes.[68] Although the law does not recognize it, jurors are sometimes swayed by the insinuation that the rape was victim-precipitated; thus, the blame is shifted from rapist to victim. To get a conviction, prosecutors must establish that the act was forced and violent and that no question of voluntary compliance exists. They may be reluc-

narcissistic personality disorder
A pattern of traits and behaviors that indicate infatuation and fixation with one's self to the exclusion of all others and the egotistic and ruthless pursuit of one's gratification, dominance, and ambition.

aggravated rape
Rape involving multiple offenders, weapons, and victim injuries.

tant to prosecute cases where they have questions about the victim's moral character or if they believe the victim's demeanor and attitude will turn off the jury and undermine the chance of conviction.[69] And there is always fear that a frightened and traumatized victim may later identify the wrong man, which happened in the case of Dennis Maher, a Massachusetts man freed in 2003 after spending more than 19 years in prison for rapes he did not commit. Though three victims provided eyewitness identification at trial, DNA testing proved that Maher could not have been the rapist.[70]

Consent Rape represents a major legal challenge to the criminal justice system for a number of reasons.[71] One issue involves the concept of **consent.** It is essential to prove that the attack was forced and that the victim did not give voluntary consent to her attacker. In a sense, the burden of proof is on the victim to show that her character is beyond question and that she in no way encouraged, enticed, or misled the accused rapist. Proving victim dissent is not a requirement in any other violent crime. For example, robbery victims do not have to prove they did not entice their attackers by flaunting expensive jewelry; yet the defense counsel in a rape case can create reasonable doubt about the woman's credibility. A common defense tactic is to introduce suspicion in the minds of the jury that the woman may have consented to the sexual act and later regretted her decision. Conversely, it is difficult for a prosecuting attorney to establish that a woman's character is so impeccable that the absence of consent is a certainty. Research shows that even when a defendant is found guilty in a sexual assault case his punishment is significantly reduced if the victim is believed to have negative personal characteristics such as being a transient, hitchhiker, alone in a bar, or a drug and alcohol abuser.[72]

Legal Reform Because of the difficulty rape victims have in obtaining justice, rape laws have been changing around the country. Reform efforts include changing the language of statutes, dropping the condition of victim resistance, and changing the requirement of use of force to include the threat of force or injury.[73] Most states and the federal government have developed **shield laws,** which protect women from being questioned about their sexual history unless it directly bears on the case. In some instances these laws are quite restrictive, whereas in others they grant the trial judge considerable discretion to admit prior sexual conduct in evidence if it is deemed relevant for the defense. In an important 1991 case, *Michigan v. Lucas,* the U.S. Supreme Court upheld the validity of shield laws and ruled that excluding evidence of a prior sexual relationship between the parties did not violate the defendant's right to a fair trial.[74]

In addition to requiring evidence that consent was not given, the common law of rape required corroboration that the crime of rape actually took place. This involved the need for independent evidence from police officers, physicians, and witnesses that the accused was actually the person who committed the crime, that sexual penetration took place, and that force was present and consent absent. This requirement shielded rapists from prosecution in cases where the victim delayed reporting the crime or in which physical evidence had been compromised or lost. Corroboration is no longer required except under extraordinary circumstances, such as when the victim is too young to understand the crime, has had a previous sexual relationship with the defendant, or gives a version of events that is improbable and self-contradictory.[75]

The federal government may have given rape victims another source of redress when it passed the Violence Against Women Act in 1994. This statute allows rape victims to sue in federal court on the grounds that sexual violence violates their civil rights; so far the provisions of this act have been upheld by appellate courts.[76] Despite these reform efforts, prosecutors may be influenced in their decision to bring charges by the circumstances of a crime.[77]

consent
The victim of rape must prove that she in no way encouraged, enticed, or misled the accused rapist.

shield laws
Laws that protect women from being questioned about their sexual history unless it directly bears on the case.

Murder and Homicide

Murder is defined in common law as "the unlawful killing of a human being with malice aforethought."[78] It is the most serious of all common-law crimes and the only one that can still be punished by death. Western society's abhorrence of murderers is illustrated by the fact that there is no statute of limitations in murder cases. Whereas state laws limit prosecution of other crimes to a fixed period, usually 7 to 10 years, accused killers can be brought to justice at any time after their crimes were committed.

To legally prove that a murder has taken place, most state jurisdictions require prosecutors to show that the accused maliciously intended to kill the victim. "Express or actual malice" is the state of mind assumed to exist when someone kills another person in the absence of any apparent provocation. "Implied or constructive malice" is considered to exist when a death results from negligent or unthinking behavior. In these cases, even though the perpetrator did not wish to kill the victim, the killing resulted from an inherently dangerous act and therefore is considered murder. An unusual example of this concept is the attempted murder conviction of Ignacio Perea, an AIDS-infected Miami man who kidnapped and raped an 11-year-old boy. Perea was sentenced to up to 25 years in prison when the jury agreed with the prosecutor's contention that the AIDS virus is a deadly weapon.[79]

Degrees of Murder

There are different levels or degrees of homicide.[80] **First-degree murder** occurs when a person kills another after premeditation and deliberation. **Premeditation** means that the killing was considered beforehand and suggests that it was motivated by more than a simple desire to engage in an act of violence. **Deliberation** means the killing was planned after careful thought rather than carried out on impulse: "To constitute a deliberate and premeditated killing, the slayer must weigh and consider the question of killing and the reasons for and against such a choice; having in mind the consequences, he decides to and does kill."[81] The planning implied by this definition need not be a long process; it may be an almost instantaneous decision to take another's life. Also, a killing accompanying a felony, such as robbery or rape, usually constitutes first-degree murder (**felony murder**).

Second-degree murder requires the killer to have malice aforethought but not premeditation or deliberation. A second-degree murder occurs when a person's wanton disregard for the victim's life and his or her desire to inflict serious bodily harm on the victim result in the victim's death.

Homicide without malice is called **manslaughter** and is usually punished by anywhere from 1 to 15 years in prison. **Voluntary or nonnegligent manslaughter** refers to a killing committed in the heat of passion or during a sudden quarrel that provoked violence. Although intent may be present, malice is not. **Involuntary or negligent manslaughter** refers to a killing that occurs when a person's acts are negligent and without regard for the harm they may cause others. Most involuntary manslaughter cases involve motor vehicle deaths—for example, when a drunk driver kills a pedestrian. However, one can be held criminally liable for the death of another in any instance where disregard of safety kills. One of the most famous cases illustrating the difference between murder and manslaughter occurred on January 26, 2001, when Diane Whipple, a San Francisco woman, died after two large presa canario dogs attacked her in the hallway of her apartment building. The dogs' owners/keepers, Marjorie Knoller and her husband, Robert Noel, were charged with second-degree murder and involuntary manslaughter respectively. (Ms. Knoller faced the more severe charge of second-degree murder because she was present during the attack.) After the couple's conviction on March 21, 2002, Judge James Warren overturned the murder conviction of Marjorie Knoller and instituted one of manslaughter. He stated that Knoller could not have known that her two dogs would fatally attack Whipple and therefore the

murder
The unlawful killing of a human being with malice aforethought.

first-degree murder
Killing a person after premeditation and deliberation.

premeditation
Considering the criminal act beforehand, which suggests that it was motivated by more than a simple desire to engage in an act of violence.

deliberation
Planning a criminal act after careful thought rather than carrying it out on impulse.

felony murder
A killing accompanying a felony, such as robbery or rape.

second-degree murder
A person's wanton disregard for the victim's life and his or her desire to inflict serious bodily harm on the victim, which results in the victim's death.

manslaughter
Homicide without malice.

voluntary or nonnegligent manslaughter
A killing committed in the heat of passion or during a sudden quarrel that provoked violence.

involuntary or negligent manslaughter
A killing that occurs when a person's acts are negligent and without regard for the harm they may cause others.

© 2003 AP/Wide World Photos

■ While murder rates have declined, passion, greed, and conflict insure that people will continue to take the lives of others. Sherry Dukette, in red, reacts to the sentence of 25 years in prison being read in Hillsboro County Superior Court on September 3, 2003, for the stabbing death in 1998 of her boyfriend, Shawn Howard. Dukette claimed she had been abused for years by Howard and was acting in self-defense. Prosecutors said she killed him because she wanted custody of their child and she was seeing another man, Rocky Brooks.

Connections

Is it possible that the recent decline in the murder rate is linked to a relatively mundane factor such as improved health care? Read about Anthony Harris's study on the effects of improved health care on the murder rate in the Current Issues in Crime feature, "Explaining Crime Trends," in Chapter 2.

infanticide
A murder involving a very young child.

eldercide
A murder involving a senior citizen.

facts did not support the charge of second-degree murder.[82] Nonetheless, the case involved manslaughter because the couple knew the dogs were dangerous and did not exercise the proper precautions to ensure that they would not attack people.

The Nature and Extent of Murder

It is possible to track U.S. murder rate trends from 1900 to the present with the aid of coroners' reports and UCR data. The murder rate peaked in 1933, a time of high unemployment and lawlessness, and then fell until 1958. The homicide rate doubled from the mid-1960s to the late 1970s and then peaked at 10.2 per 100,000 population in 1980. After a brief decline, the murder rate rose again in the late 1980s and early 1990s to a peak of 9.8 per 100,000 in 1991. Since then, the rate has declined, to about 5.7 per 100,000 in 2002: a decline of about 33 percent between 1993 and 2002. Although this is a welcome development, about 16,000 citizens were killed in 2002, and the murder rate actually increased slightly from the 2001 rate.

What else do official crime statistics tell us about murder today? Murder tends to be an urban crime. More than half of the homicides occur in cities with a population of 100,000 or more.[83] Almost one-quarter of homicides occur in cities with a population of more than 1 million. Not surprisingly, large cities are much more commonly the site of drug-related killings, gang-related murders, and relatively less likely the location of family-related homicides, including murders of intimates.

Murder victims and offenders tend to be males. Males represent 75 percent of homicide victims and nearly 90 percent of offenders. In terms of rates per 100,000, males are three times more likely to be killed and eight times more likely to commit homicide than are females. Approximately one-third of murder victims and almost half the offenders are under the age of 25. For both victims and offenders, the rate per 100,000 peaks in the 18- to 24-year-old age group.

About 49 percent of all victims are African Americans, and another 49 percent are white (including Hispanic and other races). Compared to their portion of the population, African Americans are disproportionately represented as both homicide victims and offenders. Murder, like rape, tends to be an intraracial crime; about 90 percent of victims are slain by members of their own race. Similarly, people arrested for murder are generally young (under 35) and male, a pattern that has proved consistent over time.

Some murders involve very young children, a crime referred to as **infanticide,** and others involve senior citizens, referred to as **eldercide.**[84] The UCR indicates that about 500 children under 4 years of age are murdered each year. The younger the child, the greater the risk for infanticide. At the opposite end of the age spectrum, less than 5 percent of all homicides involve people age 65 or older. Males age 65 or older are more likely than females of the same age to be homicide victims. Although most of the offenders who committed eldercide were age 50 or younger, elderly females were more likely than elderly males to be killed by an elderly offender.[85]

Today few would deny that some relationship exists between social and ecological factors and murder. The following section explores some of the more important issues related to these factors.

Murderous Relations

One factor that has received a great deal of attention from criminologists is the relationship between the murderer and the victim.[86] Most criminologists generally agree that murders can be separated into those involving strangers and those involving people who were acquainted with one another. Stranger homicides typically occur during commission of a felony such as a robbery or

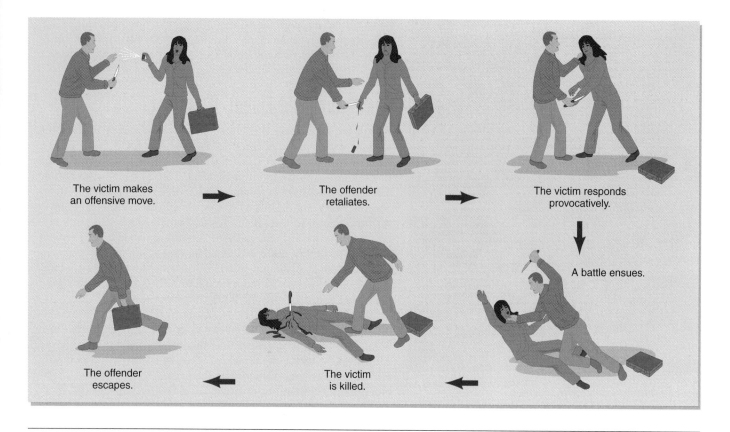

The victim makes an offensive move.

The offender retaliates.

The victim responds provocatively.

A battle ensues.

The offender escapes.

The victim is killed.

Figure 10.2
Murder Transactions

drug deal. However, some criminologists fear that the number of stranger killings may increase because tough new sentencing laws, such as the "three strikes and your out" laws used in California and other habitual criminal statutes, mandate that a "three time loser" be given a life sentence if convicted of multiple felonies. It is possible that these laws may encourage experienced criminals to kill while committing burglaries and robberies: Why hesitate to kill now because, if caught, they will receive a life sentence anyway?[87]

In contrast, acquaintance homicides involve disputes between family, friends, and acquaintances.[88] Although on the surface acquaintance homicides may seem senseless, they are often the result of a long-simmering dispute motivated by revenge, dispute resolution, jealousy, drug deals, racial bias, or threats to identity or status.[89] For example, a prior act of violence, motivated by profit or greed, may generate revenge killing, such as when a buyer robs his dealer during a drug transaction.

How do these murderous relations develop between two people who may have had little prior conflict? In a classic study, David Luckenbill studied murder transactions to determine whether particular patterns of behavior are common between the killer and the victim.[90] He found that many homicides follow a sequential pattern. First, the victim makes what the offender considers an offensive move. The offender typically retaliates verbally or physically. An agreement to end things violently is forged with the victim's provocative response. The battle ensues, leaving the victim dead or dying. The offender's escape is shaped by his or her relationship to the victim or the reaction of the audience, if any (Figure 10.2).

School Relations

Though relatively rare events, the recent spate of deadly school shootings has captured significant media attention. They seem to straddle the divide between acquaintance and stranger murder: the killers may have known some but not all of the victims.

One recent study examined all school-related shootings occurring between July 1, 1994, and June 30, 1999.[91] The study found that a total of 220 incidents on or near school grounds had resulted in 253 deaths. Of these, 202 involved a single victim, and 18 had multiple victims. Although highly publicized in the media, the average annual incidence is very small, 0.068 per 100,000 students. Between 1992 and 1999, the rate of single-victim student homicides decreased significantly while multiple-victim incidents increased significantly.

The research found that most shooting incidents occur around the start of the school day, the lunch period, or the end of the school day. In most of the shootings (55 percent), a note, threat, or other action indicating risk for violence occurred prior to the event. Shooters were also likely to have expressed some form of suicidal behavior and to have been bullied by their peers. Kids who have been the victims of crime themselves are the ones most likely to bring guns to school.[92]

Serial and Mass Murder

According to Colombian police, Luis Alfredo Garavito is a glib predator and a "solitary sadist" who stands accused as one of the world's worst **serial killers.**[93] In 1999, Garavito, a 42-year-old drifter, confessed to the slayings of at least 140 boys between the ages of 8 and 16 during a five-year killing spree. Garavito would befriend the children and take them on long walks until they were tired. Then he would tie them up with nylon rope, slit their throats or behead them, and then bury their bodies. Most of Garavito's victims were street children, children from poor families, or children separated from their parents by poverty or political violence. Authorities said it was because there was no one to notice that the children were missing or to inquire about their whereabouts that Garavito was able to go on killing for so long without being detected.

Some serial murderers, such as the American Theodore Bundy, roam the country killing at random.[94] Other serial killers terrorize a city, such as the Los Angeles–based Night Stalker and the Hillside Stranglers, Kenneth Bianchi and Angelo Buono, who tortured and killed 10 women in the Los Angeles area.[95] A third type of serial murderer, such as Garavito and Milwaukee cannibal Jeffrey Dahmer, kills so cunningly that many victims are dispatched before the authorities even realize the deaths can be attributed to a single perpetrator.[96]

■ According to Colombian police, Luis Alfredo Garavito is one of the world's worst serial killers. In 1999 Garavito confessed to the slayings of at least 140 boys between the ages of 8 and 16 during a five-year killing spree. This monument in Pereira, Colombia, was constructed to commemorate his victims.

serial killer
A person who kills more than one victim over a period of time.

FIND IT ON INFOTRAC
College Edition

Multiple murders by serial killers
are not a recent phenomenon. To
read about the history of such
gruesome acts, read:

Bernard Capp, "Serial Killers in 17th-Century
England," *History Today*, March 1996 v46 n3
p21

There is more than one type of serial killer, and experts have attempted to classify them based on their motivations and offense patterns.[97] According to serial murder experts James A. Fox and Jack Levin, there are three different types of serial killers:[98]

1. *Thrill killers* strive for either sexual sadism or dominance. This is the most common form of serial murderer.
2. *Mission killers* want to reform the world or have a vision that drives them to kill.
3. *Expedience killers* are out for profit or want to protect themselves from a perceived threat.

Why do serial murderers kill? They kill for fun. They enjoy the thrill, the sexual gratification, and the dominance they achieve over the lives of their victims. The serial killer rarely uses a gun because this method is too quick and would deprive him of his greatest pleasure, exalting in his victim's suffering. Serial killers are not insane; according to Fox and Levin, they are more cruel than crazy.

Serial killers operate over a long period and can be distinguished from **mass murderers,** who kill many victims in a single, violent outburst. Fox and Levin define four types of mass murderers:

1. *Revenge killers* seek to get even with individuals or society at large. Their typical target is an estranged wife and "her" children or an employer and "his" employees.
2. *Love killers* are motivated by a warped sense of devotion. They are often despondent people who commit suicide and take others, such as a wife and children, with them.
3. *Profit killers* are usually trying to cover up a crime, eliminate witnesses, and carry out a criminal conspiracy.
4. *Terrorist killers* are trying to send a message. Gang killings tell rivals to watch out; cult killers may actually leave a message behind to warn society about impending doom.[99]

The Washington-area sniper presented a new type or category of multiple killer, the **spree killer:** killer of multiple victims whose murders occur over a relatively short span of time and follow no discernible pattern. Concept Summary 10.1 compares the various types of multiple murderers.

Female Serial Killers An estimated 10 to 15 percent of serial killers are women. A recent study by criminologists Belea Keeney and Kathleen Heide investigated the characteristics of a sample of 14 female serial killers and found some striking differences between the way male and female killers carried out their crimes.[100] Males were much more likely than females to use extreme violence and torture. Whereas males used a "hands-on" approach, including beating, bludgeoning, and strangling their victims, females were more likely to poison or smother their victims. Men tracked or stalked their victims, but women were more likely to lure victims to their death.

There were also gender-based personality and behavior characteristics. Female killers, somewhat older than their male counterparts, abused both alcohol and drugs; males were not likely to be substance abusers. Women were diagnosed as having histrionic, manic-depressive, borderline, dissociative, and antisocial personality disorders; men were more often diagnosed as having antisocial personalities.

The profile of the female serial killer that emerges is a person who smothers or poisons someone she knows. During childhood she suffered from an abusive relationship in a disrupted family. Female killers' education levels are below average, and if they hold jobs, they are in low-status positions.

mass murderer
A person who kills many victims in a single, violent outburst.

spree killer
A killer of multiple victims whose murders occur over a relatively short span of time and follow no discernible pattern.

CONCEPT SUMMARY **10.1 Explanations for Multiple Murders**

MOTIVATION	SERIAL KILLER	MASS MURDERER	SPREE KILLER
Power	Inspired by sadistic fantasies, a man tortures and kills a series of strangers to satisfy his need for control and dominance.	A pseudo-commando, dressed in battle fatigues and armed with a semiautomatic, turns a shopping mall into a "war zone."	A zealot guns down people over a period of weeks because he considers them weak or inferior.
Revenge	Grossly mistreated as a child, a man avenges his past by slaying women who remind him of his mother.	After being fired from his job, a gunman returns to the worksite and opens fire on his former boss and coworkers.	A woman kills the three men who raped her.
Loyalty	A team of killers turns murder into a ritual for proving their dedication and commitment to one another.	A depressed husband/father kills his entire family and himself to remove them from their miserable existence to a better life in the hereafter.	A gang member shoots followers of a rival group to prove his loyalty.
Profit	A woman poisons to death a series of husbands so she can collect on their life insurance.	A band of armed robbers execute the employees of a store to eliminate all witnesses to their crime.	A gunman shoots strangers and demands money to stop the killing spree.
Terror	A profoundly paranoid man commits a series of bombings to warn the world of impending doom.	A group of antigovernment extremists blow up a train to send a political message.	Terrorists shoot civilians to frighten the population.

Assault and Battery

Although many people mistakenly believe *assault and battery* refers to a single act, they are actually two separate crimes. **Battery** requires offensive touching, such as slapping, hitting, or punching a victim. **Assault** requires no actual touching but involves either attempted battery or intentionally frightening the victim by word or deed. Although common law originally intended these twin crimes to be misdemeanors, most jurisdictions now upgrade them to felonies either when a weapon is used or when they occur during the commission of a felony (for example, when a person is assaulted during a robbery).[101]

Under common law, battery required bodily injury, such as broken limbs or wounds. However, under modern law, an assault and battery occurs if the victim suffers a temporarily painful blow, even if no injury results. Battery can also involve offensive touching, such as if a man kisses a woman against her will or puts his hands on her body.

Nature and Extent of Assault

The pattern of criminal assault is quite similar to that of homicide; one could say that the only difference between the two is that the victim survives.[102] Assaults may be common in our society simply because of common life stresses. Motorists who assault each other have become such a familiar occurrence that the term **road rage** has been coined. There have even been frequent incidents of violent assault among frustrated airline passengers who lose control while traveling.[103]

In 2002 the FBI recorded slightly less than 900,000 assaults, a rate of about 300 per 100,000 inhabitants. Like other violent crimes, the number of assaults has been in decline, down more than 28 percent from 1992.

People arrested for assault and those identified by victims are usually young, male (80 percent), and white, although the number of African Americans arrested for assault (34 percent) is disproportionate to their representation in

battery
Offensive touching, such as slapping, hitting, or punching a victim.

assault
Does not require actual touching but involves either attempted battery or intentionally frightening the victim by word or deed.

road rage
Violent assault by a motorist who loses control while driving.

the population. Assault victims tend to be male, but women also face a significant danger. Assault rates are highest in urban areas, during summer, and in southern and western regions. The most common weapons used in assaults are blunt instruments and hands and feet.

The NCVS indicates that only about half of all serious assaults are reported to the police. Victims reported about 990,000 aggravated assaults in 2002 and 3.5 million simple or weaponless assaults. Like other violent crimes, the NCVS indicates that the number of assaults has been in steep decline, down 52 percent since 1993.

Assault in the Home

Violent attacks in the home are one of the most frightening types of assault. Criminologists recognize that intrafamily violence is an enduring social problem in the United States and abroad.

Child Abuse   One area of intrafamily violence that has received a great deal of media attention is **child abuse.** This term describes any physical or emotional trauma to a child for which no reasonable explanation, such as an accident or ordinary disciplinary practices, can be found.[104] Child abuse can result from actual physical beatings administered to a child by hands, feet, weapons, belts, sticks, burning, and so on. Another form of abuse results from **neglect**—not providing a child with the care and shelter to which he or she is entitled.

It is difficult to estimate the actual number of child abuse cases because many incidents are never reported to the police. Nonetheless, child abuse and neglect appear to be serious social problems. According to the latest surveys conducted by the National Child Abuse and Neglect Data System (NCANDS), a reporting system developed by the Children's Bureau of the U.S. Department of Human Services, approximately 903,000 children were victims of abuse and neglect during 2001, or 12.4 children for every 1,000 children in the population. Approximately 1,300 children died of abuse or neglect during 2001, a rate of 1.81 children per 100,000 children in the population. The youngest children were the most vulnerable: Children younger than one year old accounted for 41 percent of child fatalities, and 85 percent of child fatalities were younger than six years of age.[105] However, as Figure 10.3 shows, maltreatment rates are lower today than they were a decade ago.

Child Sexual Abuse   Another aspect of the abuse syndrome is **child sexual abuse**—the exploitation of children through rape, incest, and molestation by parents or other adults. It is difficult to estimate the incidence of sexual abuse, but a number of attempts have been made to gauge the extent of the problem. In a classic study, Diana Russell's survey of women in the San Francisco area found that 38 percent had experienced intra- or extrafamilial sexual abuse by the time they reached age 18.[106] Others have estimated that at least 20 percent of females suffer some form of sexual violence; that is, at least one in five girls suffers sexual abuse.[107]

Although sexual abuse is still quite prevalent, the number of reported cases has been in significant decline. Research by Lisa Jones and David Finkelhor of the University of New Hampshire's Crimes Against Children Research Center shows that after a 15-year increase substantiated child sexual abuse cases in the United States dropped 31 percent between 1992 and 1998. Most states (36 out of the 47 they reviewed) showed declines of at least 30 percent.[108] These data could mean that the actual number of cases is truly in decline because of the effectiveness of prevention programs, increased prosecution, and public awareness campaigns. It could also mean that more cases are overlooked because of (1) increased evidentiary requirements to substantiate cases, (2) increased caseworker caution due to new legal rights for caregivers, and (3) increasing limitations on the types of cases that agencies accept for investigation.[109]

child abuse
Any physical or emotional trauma to a child for which no reasonable explanation, such as an accident or ordinary disciplinary practices, can be found.

neglect
Not providing a child with the care and shelter to which he or she is entitled.

child sexual abuse
The exploitation of children through rape, incest, and molestation by parents or other adults.

Figure 10.3
Child Maltreatment Rates, 1990–2001

SOURCE: Department of Health and Human Services

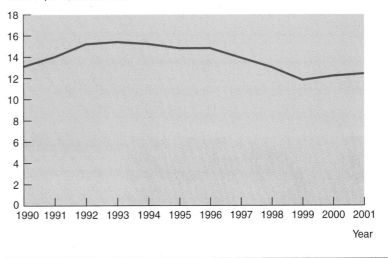

Victims per 1,000 children

Sexual abuse is of particular concern because children who have been abused experience a long list of symptoms, including fear, posttraumatic stress disorder, behavior problems, sexualized behavior, and poor self-esteem. Women who were abused as children are also at greater risk to be re-abused as adults than those who escaped childhood victimization.[110] The amount of force used during the abuse, its duration, and its frequency are all related to the extent of the long-term effects and the length of time needed for recovery.

Causes of Child Abuse   Why do parents physically assault their children? Such maltreatment is a highly complex problem with neither a single cause nor a readily available solution. It cuts across ethnic, religious, and socioeconomic lines. Abusive parents cannot be categorized by sex, age, or educational level; they come from all walks of life.[111]

A number of factors have been commonly linked to abuse and neglect:

- Family violence seems to be perpetuated from one generation to another within families.
- The behavior of abusive parents can often be traced to negative experiences in their own childhood—physical abuse, lack of love, emotional neglect, incest, and so on.
- Blended families, which include children living with an unrelated adult such as a stepparent or another unrelated co-resident, have also been linked to abuse. For example, children who live with a mother's boyfriend are at much greater risk for abuse than children living with two genetic parents. Some stepparents do not have strong emotional ties to their nongenetic children, nor do they reap emotional benefits from the parent–child relationship.[112]
- Parents may also become abusive if they are isolated from friends, neighbors, or relatives who can help in times of crisis. Potentially abusive parents are often alienated from society; they have carried the concept of the shrinking nuclear family to its most extreme form and are cut off from ties of kinship and contact with other people in the neighborhood.[113]

Parental Abuse   Parents are sometimes the target of abuse from their own children. Researchers Arina Ulman and Murray Straus found these factors in child-to-parent violence (CPV):

- The younger the child, the higher the rate of CPV.
- At all ages, more children were violent to mothers than to fathers.

- Both boys and girls hit mothers more than fathers.
- At all ages, slightly more boys than girls hit parents.

Ulman and Straus found that child-to-parent violence was associated with some form of violence by parents, which could either be husband-to-wife, wife-to-husband, corporal punishment of children, or physical abuse. If the use of physical punishment could be eliminated or curtailed, they suggest that child-to-parent violence would similarly decline.[114]

■ While it is difficult to estimate the extent of spousal abuse, it appears to remain a significant problem. Here former Hollywood madam Heidi Fleiss sobs on the witness stand as she describes to the jury the abuse she suffered from actor Thomas Sizemore while living with him, during testimony at Los Angeles County Superior Court, August 5, 2003.

Spousal Abuse Spousal abuse has occurred throughout recorded history. By the mid-nineteenth century, severe wife beating fell into disfavor, and accused wife beaters were subject to public ridicule. Nonetheless, limited chastisement was still the rule. These ideas form the foundation of men's traditional physical control of women and have led to severe cases of spousal assault.

It is difficult to estimate how widespread spousal abuse is today; however, some statistics indicate the extent of the problem. In their classic study of family violence, Richard Gelles and Murray Straus found that 16 percent of surveyed families had experienced husband–wife assaults.[115] Nor is violence restricted to marriage: national surveys indicate that between 20 and 40 percent of females experience violence while dating.[116] According to a recently released survey conducted by researchers from the Harvard School of Public Health, one in five high school girls suffered sexual or physical abuse from a boyfriend. The study found that teen girls who had been abused by their boyfriends also were much more likely to use drugs or alcohol, to have unsafe sex, and to acquire eating disorders among other social problems.[117]

In some instances spousal abuse tragically leads to the death of the intimate partner. Factors that predict a lethal conclusion to domestic violence include the perpetrator's access to a gun and previous threat with a weapon, having a stepchild living in the home, estrangement, especially from a controlling partner, and subsequent involvement with another partner[118] (see Exhibit 10.2).

Robbery

robbery
Taking or attempting to take anything of value from the care, custody, or control of a person or persons by force or threat of force or violence and/or by putting the victim in fear.

The common-law definition of **robbery** (and the one used by the FBI) is "the taking or attempting to take anything of value from the care, custody or control of a person or persons by force or threat of force or violence and/or by putting the victim in fear."[119] A robbery is considered a violent crime because it involves the use of force to obtain money or goods. Robbery is punished severely because the victim's life is put in jeopardy. In fact, the severity of punishment is based on the amount of force used during the crime, not the value of the items taken.

In 2002 the FBI recorded about 418,000 robberies, a rate of 148 per 100,000 population. As with other violent crimes, there was a significant reduction in the robbery rate during the 1990s; the robbery rate is down more than 44 percent since 1992.

The ecological pattern for robbery is similar to that of other violent crimes, with one significant exception: northeastern states have the highest robbery rates by far. According to the NCVS, about 512,000 robberies were committed or attempted in 2002, a decline of about 200,000 in a single year. Like other violent crimes, there has been a decade-long drop in the robbery rate, from 6 percent in 1993 to about 2.2 percent today, a decline of 63 percent!

EXHIBIT 10.2 Factors That Predict Spousal Abuse

Presence of alcohol. Excessive alcohol use may turn otherwise docile husbands into wife abusers.

Hostility toward dependency. Some husbands who appear docile and passive may resent their dependence on their wives and react with rage and violence; this reaction has been linked to sexual inadequacy.

Excessive brooding. Obsession with a wife's behavior, however trivial, can result in violent assaults.

Social approval. Some husbands believe society approves of wife abuse and use these beliefs to justify their violent behavior.

Socioeconomic factors. Men who fail as providers and are under economic stress may take their frustrations out on their wives.

Flashes of anger. Research shows that a significant amount of family violence results from a sudden burst of anger after a verbal dispute.

Military service. Spouse abuse among men who have served in the military service is extremely high. Similarly, those serving in the military are more likely to assault their wives than civilian husbands. The reasons for this phenomenon may be the violence promoted by military training and the close proximity in which military families live to one another.

Having been battered as children. Husbands who assault their wives were generally battered as children.

Unpredictableness. Batterers are unpredictable, unable to be influenced by their wives, and impossible to prevent from battering once an argument has begun. Batterers can be classified into two distinct types: men whose temper slowly simmers until it suddenly erupts into violence, and those who strike out immediately.

SOURCE: Neil Jacobson and John Mordechai Gottman, *When Men Batter Women: New Insights into Ending Abusive Relationships* (New York: Simon and Schuster, 1998); Kenneth Leonard and Brian Quigley, "Drinking and Marital Aggression in Newlyweds: An Event-Based Analysis of Drinking and the Occurrence of Husband Marital Aggression," *Journal of Studies on Alcohol* 60 (1999): 537–541; Graeme Newman, *Understanding Violence* (New York: Lippincott, 1979).

The Armed Robber

The typical armed robber is unlikely to be a professional who carefully studies targets while planning a crime. People walking along the street, convenience stores, and gas stations are much more likely robbery targets than banks or other highly secure environments. Robbers, therefore, seem to be diverted by modest defensive measures, such as having more than one clerk in a store or locating stores in strip malls; they are more likely to try an isolated store.[120] Most robbers may be opportunistic rather than professional, but the patterns of robbery suggest that it is not merely a random act committed by an alcoholic or drug abuser. Though most crime rates are higher in the summer, robberies seem to peak during the winter months. One reason may be that the cold weather allows for greater disguise; another reason is that robbers may be attracted to the high amounts of cash people and merchants carry during the Christmas shopping season.[121] Robbers may also be attracted to the winter because days are shorter, affording them greater concealment in the dark.

Robbers also choose vulnerable victims. According to research by criminologist Jody Miller, female armed robbers are likely to choose female targets, reasoning that they will be more vulnerable and offer less resistance.[122] When robbing males, women "set them up" to catch them off guard; some feign sexual interest or prostitution to gain the upper hand.[123] As you may recall (Chapter 3), some robbers specialize in attacking drug dealers, recognizing

■ Robbers use force to steal, an undertaking that can lead to tragic outcomes. Here a bank robbery suspect carrying a handgun came out of a house and pointed his gun at police officers. He was shot up to 20 times and died at the scene.

© 2003 AP/Wide World Photos

acquaintance robbery
A robber whose victims are people he or she knows.

that they have a lot of cash on hand and are unlikely to call the police. Of course, it is hard to view drug dealers as "vulnerable"; they are likely to seek vengeance if they can to repair their damaged reputation (not to mention recovering their drug money!).[124]

Acquaintance Robbery

One type of robber may focus on people they know, a phenomenon referred to as **acquaintance robbery.** This seems puzzling because victims can easily identify their attackers and report them to the police. However, despite this threat, acquaintance robbery may be attractive for a number of rational reasons:[125]

■ Victims may be reluctant to report these crimes because they do not want to get involved with the police: they may be involved in crime themselves (drug dealers, for example), or they may fear retaliation if they report the crime. Some victims may be reluctant to gain the label of "rat" or "fink" if they go to the police.

■ Some robberies are motivated by street justice. The robber has a grievance against the victim and settles the dispute by stealing the victim's property. In this instance, robbery may be considered a substitute for an assault: the robber wants retribution and revenge rather than remuneration.[126]

■ Because the robber knows the victim personally, the robber has inside information that there will be a "good take." Offenders may target people they know to be carrying a large amount of cash or who just purchased expensive jewelry.

■ When a person in desperate need for immediate cash runs out of money, the individual may target people in close proximity simply because they are convenient targets.

When Richard Felson and his associates studied acquaintance robbery, they found that victims were more likely to be injured in acquaintance robberies than in stranger robberies, indicating that revenge rather than reward was the primary motive.[127] Similarly, robberies of family members were more likely to have a bigger pay-off than stranger robberies, an indication that the offender was aware that the target had a large amount of cash on hand.

In an important book, Scott Decker and Richard Wright interviewed active robbers in St. Louis, Missouri.[128] Their findings, presented in the Current Issues in Crime feature, also suggest that robbers are rational decision makers. **✔ Checkpoints**

CURRENT ISSUES IN CRIME

Armed Robbers in Action

Criminologists Richard Wright and Scott Decker identified and interviewed a sample of 86 active armed robbers in St. Louis, Missouri. Their sample, primarily young African American men, helped provide an in-depth view of armed robbery that had been missing from the criminological literature.

Wright and Decker found that most armed robberies are motivated by a pressing need for cash. Many robbers careen from one financial crisis to the next, prompted by their endless quest for stimulation and thrills. Interviewees told of how they partied, gambled, drank, and abused substances until they were broke. Their partying not only provided excitement, but it helped generate a street reputation as a "hip" guy who can "make things happen." Robbers had a "here-and-now" mentality and required a constant supply of cash to fuel their appetites. Those interviewed showed little long-range planning or commitment to the future. Because of their street hustler mentality, few if any of the robbers were able to obtain or keep legitimate employment, even if it was available.

Armed robbery also provided a psychic thrill. It was a chance to hurt or humiliate victims, or to get even with someone who may have wronged them in the past. As one robber explained, "This might sound stupid, but I [also] like to see a person get scared, be scared of the pistol. . . . You got power. I come in here with a big old pistol and I ain't playing."

Robbers show evidence of being highly rational offenders. Many choose victims who themselves are involved in illegal behavior, most often drug dealers. Ripping off a dealer kills three birds with one stone, providing both money and drugs while at the same time targeting victims who are quite unlikely to call the police. Another ideal target is a married man who is looking for illicit sexual adventures. He also is disinclined to call the police and bring attention to himself. One told them why he chose to be a robber:

> I feel more safer doing a robbery because doing a burglary, I got a fear

of breaking into somebody's house not knowing who might be up in there. . . . On robbery I can select my victims, I can select my place of business. I can watch and see who all work in there or I can rob a person and pull them around in the alley or push them up in a doorway and rob them. (p. 52)

Others target noncriminal victims. They like to stay in their own neighborhood, relying on their intimate knowledge of streets and alleys to avoid detection. Although some range far afield seeking affluent victims, others believe that residents in the city's poorest areas are more likely to carry cash (wealthy people carry checks and credit cards). Because they realize that the risk of detection and punishment is the same whether the victim is carrying a load of cash or is penniless, experienced robbers use discretion in selecting targets. People whose clothing, jewelry, and demeanor mark them as carrying substantial amounts of cash make suitable targets; people who look like they can fight back are avoided. Some station themselves at cash machines to spot targets who are flashing rolls of money.

Robbers have racial, gender, and age preferences in their selection of targets. Some African American robbers prefer white targets because they believe they are too afraid to fight back. Others concentrate on African American victims, who are more likely to carry cash than credit cards. As one interviewee revealed, "White guys can be so paranoid [that] they just want to get away. . . . They're not . . . gonna argue with you." Likewise, intoxicated victims in no condition to fight back were favored targets. Some robbers tend to target women because they feel they are easy subjects; however, others avoid them because they believe they will get emotionally upset and bring unwanted attention. Most agree that the elderly are less likely to put up a fuss than younger, stronger targets.

Some robbers choose commercial targets, such as convenience stores or markets that are cash businesses open late at night. Gas stations are a favorite victim. Security is of little consequence to

experienced robbers, who may bring an accomplice to subdue guards.

Once they choose their targets, robbers carefully orchestrate the criminal incidents. They immediately impose their will on their chosen victims, leaving little room for the victims to maneuver and making sure the victims feel threatened enough to offer no resistance. Some approach from behind so they cannot be identified, and others approach victims head-on, showing that they are tough and bold. By convincing the victims of their impending death, the robber takes control.

Critical Thinking

1. It is unlikely that the threat of punishment can deter robbery (most robbers refuse to think about apprehension and punishment), but Wright and Decker suggest that eliminating cash and relying on debit and credit cards may be the most productive method to reduce the incidence of robbery. Although this seems far-fetched, our society is becoming progressively more cashless; it is now possible to buy both gas and groceries with credit cards. Would a cashless society end the threat of robbery, or would innovative robbers find new targets?

2. Based on what you know about how robbers target victims, how can you better protect yourself from robbery?

InfoTrac College Edition Research

To learn more about robbery, read: Peter J. van Koppen and Robert W. J. Jansen, "The Road to the Robbery: Travel Patterns in Commercial Robberies," *British Journal of Criminology*. Spring 1998 v38 n2 p230
D. J. Pyle and D. F. Deadman, "Crime and the Business Cycle in Post-War Britain," *British Journal of Criminology*, Summer 1994 34 n3 p339–357

SOURCE: Richard Wright and Scott Decker, *Armed Robbers in Action, Stickups and Street Culture* (Boston, Mass.: Northeastern University Press, 1997).

Emerging Forms of Interpersonal Violence

Assault, rape, robbery, and murder are traditional forms of interpersonal violence. As more data become available, criminologists have recognized relatively new subcategories within these crime types, such as serial murder and date rape. Additional new categories of interpersonal violence are now receiving attention in criminological literature; the next sections describe three of these forms of violent crime.

Hate Crimes

In the fall of 1998 Matthew Shepard, a gay college student, was kidnapped and severely beaten. He died five days after he was found unconscious on a Wyoming ranch, where he had been left tied to a fence for 18 hours in near freezing temperatures.[129] His two killers, Aaron J. McKinney and Russell A. Henderson, both 22, were sentenced to life in prison after the Shepard family granted them mercy.

Hate crimes or **bias crimes** are violent acts directed toward a particular person or members of a group merely because the targets share a discernible racial, ethnic, religious, or gender characteristic.[130] Hate crimes can include the desecration of a house of worship or cemetery, harassment of a minority group family that has moved into a previously all-white neighborhood, or a racially motivated murder.

Hate crimes usually involve convenient, vulnerable targets who are incapable of fighting back. For example, there have been numerous reported incidents of teenagers attacking vagrants and the homeless in an effort to rid their town or neighborhood of people they consider undesirable.[131] Another group targeted for hate crimes is gay men and women: gay bashing has become common in U.S. cities.

Racial and ethnic minorities have also been the targets of attack. In California, Mexican laborers have been attacked and killed; in New Jersey, Indian immigrants have been the targets of racial hatred; people of Arab descent have been attacked in the aftermath of the 9/11 terror attack. The factors that precipitate hate crimes are listed in Exhibit 10.3.

The Roots of Hate   Why do people commit bias crimes? In a series of research studies Jack McDevitt, Jack Levin, and Susan Bennet identify four motivations for hate crimes:[132]

- **Thrill-seeking hate crimes.** In the same way some kids like to get together to shoot hoops, hate-mongers join forces to have fun by bashing mi-

---

hate or bias crimes
Violent acts directed toward a particular person or members of a group merely because the targets share a discernible racial, ethnic, religious, or gender characteristic.

> **EXHIBIT 10.3 Factors That Produce Hate Crimes**
>
> - Poor or uncertain economic conditions
> - Racial stereotypes in films and on television
> - Hate-filled discourse on talk shows or in political advertisements
> - The use of racial code language such as "welfare mothers" and "inner-city thugs"
> - An individual's personal experiences with members of particular minority groups
> - Scapegoating—blaming a minority group for the misfortunes of society as a whole
>
> SOURCE: "A Policymaker's Guide to Hate Crimes," *Bureau of Justice Assistance Monograph* (Washington, D.C.: Bureau of Justice Assistance, 1997).

norities or destroying property. Inflicting pain on others gives them a sadistic thrill.

- **Reactive (defensive) hate crimes**. Perpetrators of these crimes rationalize their behavior as a defensive stand taken against outsiders whom they believe threaten their community or way of life. A gang of teens that attacks a new family in the neighborhood because they are the "wrong" race is committing a reactive hate crime.

- **Mission hate crimes**. Some disturbed individuals see it as their duty to rid the world of evil. Those on a "mission," like Skinheads, the Ku Klux Klan (KKK), and white supremacist groups, may seek to eliminate people who threaten their religious beliefs because they are members of a different faith or threaten "racial purity" because they are of a different race.

- **Retaliatory hate crimes**. These offenses are committed in response to a hate crime, whether real or perceived; whether the original incident actually occurred is irrelevant. Sometimes a rumor of an incident may cause a group of offenders to take vengeance, even if the original information was unfounded or inaccurate; the hate crimes occur before anyone has had a chance to verify the accuracy of the original rumor. Attacks based on revenge tend to have the greatest potential for fueling and refueling additional hate offenses.

Their research indicates that most hate crimes can be classified as thrill motivated (66 percent) followed by defensive (25 percent) and retaliation (8 percent); few, if any, cases had mission-oriented offenders.

Nature and Extent of Hate Crime   During 2002, about 7,300 offenders were involved in 7,462 hate crime incidents that resulted in 8,832 offenses. Racial bias accounted for 48.8 percent of the incidents, religious bias motivated 19.1 percent of the incidents, sexual-orientation bias motivated 16.7 percent, and bias against an ethnicity or national origin motivated 14.8 percent. Bias against a physical or mental disability was the basis for 0.6 percent of the single-bias incidents. In all there were 9,222 victims of hate crimes in 2002 (including individuals, businesses, government, religious organizations, and society); 11 of the hate crime victims were murdered.[133]

A recent analysis of 3,000 hate crime cases reported to the police found that about 60 percent of hate crimes involved a violent act, most commonly intimidation or simple assault, and 40 percent of the incidents involved property crimes, most commonly damage, destruction, or vandalism of property.[134] Most crimes are motivated by race, and to a lesser degree religion (most often anti-Semitism), sexual orientation, ethnicity, and about 1 percent by victim disability. Vandalism and property crimes were the products of hate crimes motivated by religion. However, criminals were more likely to turn to violent acts when race, ethnicity, and sexual orientation were the motivation. Most targets of hate crimes, especially the violent variety, were young white men. More than half of victims of violence were age 24 or under, and nearly a third were under 18. Similarly, the majority of known hate crime offenders were young: 31 percent of violent offenders and 46 percent of property offenders were under age 18.

In crimes where victims could actually identify the culprits, most victims reported that they were acquainted with their attackers or that their attackers were actually friends, coworkers, neighbors, or relatives.[135] Younger victims were more likely to be victimized by persons known to them. Hate crimes can occur in many settings but most are perpetrated in public settings.

Controlling Hate Crimes

Because of the extent and seriousness of the problem, a number of legal jurisdictions have made a special effort to control the spread of hate crimes. Boston maintains the Community Disorders Unit, and the New York City police department formed the Bias Incident Investigating Unit in 1980. When a crime anywhere in the city is suspected of being motivated by bias, the unit initiates an investigation. The unit also assists victims and works with concerned organizations such as the Commission on Human Rights and the Gay and Lesbian Task Force. These agencies deal with noncriminal bias incidents through mediation, education, and other forms of prevention.[136]

Specific hate crime laws originated after the Civil War and were designed to protect the rights of freed slaves.[137] Today, almost every state jurisdiction has enacted some form of legislation designed to combat hate crimes: 39 states have enacted laws against bias-motivated violence and intimidation; 19 states have statutes that specifically mandate the collection of hate crime data.

Legal Controls Should symbolic acts of hate such as drawing a Swastika or burning a cross be banned, or are they protected by the Free Speech clause of the First Amendment? The United States Supreme Court helped answer this question in the case of *Virginia v. Black* (2003) when it upheld a Virginia statute that makes it a felony "for any person . . . , with the intent of intimidating any person or group . . . , to burn . . . a cross on the property of another, a highway or other public place," and specifies that "[a]ny such burning . . . shall be prima facie evidence of an intent to intimidate a person or group." In its decision, the Court upheld Virginia's law, which criminalized cross burning. The Court ruled that cross burning was intertwined with the Ku Klux Klan and its reign of terror throughout the South. The Court has long held that statements in which the speaker intends to communicate intent to commit an act of unlawful violence to a particular individual or group of individuals is not protected free speech and can be criminalized; the speaker need not actually intend to carry out the threat.[138]

Workplace Violence

Workplace violence is now considered the third leading cause of occupational injury or death.[139] Who engages in workplace violence? The typical offender is a middle-aged white male who faces termination in a worsening economy. The fear of economic ruin is especially strong in agencies such as the U.S. Postal Service, where long-term employees fear job loss because of automation and reorganization. In contrast, younger workers usually kill while committing a robbery or another felony.

A number of factors precipitate workplace violence. One suspected cause is a management style that appears cold and insensitive to workers. As corporations cut their staffs because of an economic downturn or workers are summarily replaced with cost-effective technology, long-term employees may become irate and irrational; their unexpected layoff can lead to violent reactions.[140]

Not all workplace violence is triggered by management-induced injustice. In some incidents coworkers have been killed because they refused romantic relationships with the assailants or reported them for sexual harassment. Others have been killed because they got a job the assailant coveted. Irate clients and customers have also killed because of poor service or perceived slights.[141]

These provocations have resulted in a significant number of violent incidents. Each year more than 2 million U.S. residents become victims of violent crime while they work. The most common type of victimization is assault, with an estimated 1.5 million simple assaults and 396,000 aggravated assaults reported annually. Each year sees 84,000 robberies, about 51,000 rapes or sexual assaults, and more than 1,000 workplace homicides.[142]

Stalking

In Wes Craven's popular movies *Scream 1–3,* the heroine Sydney (played by Neve Campbell) is stalked by a mysterious adversary who scares her half to death while killing off most of her peer group. Although obviously extreme

---

Connections

Does the fact that sales clerks and police officers have the highest injury risk support routine activities theory? People in high-risk jobs who are out late at night and, in the case of sales clerks, do business in cash seem to have the greatest risk of injury on the job. See Chapter 3 for more on routine activities and crime.

---

workplace violence
Violence such as assault, rape, or murder committed at the workplace.

Connections

The Fisher research found that the likelihood of becoming stalked may be related to the victim's lifestyle and routine activities. Female students who are the victims of stalking tend to date more, go out at night to bars and parties, and live alone. Their lifestyle both brings them into contact with potential stalkers and makes them vulnerable to stalking. For more on routine activities, go to Chapter 3.

even by Hollywood standards, the *Scream* movies focus on a newly recognized form of long-term and repeat victimization: **stalking.**[143]

Stalking can be defined as a course of conduct directed at a specific person that involves repeated physical or visual proximity, nonconsensual communication, or verbal, written, or implied threats sufficient to cause fear in a reasonable person. According to a leading government survey, it is a problem that affects an estimated 1.4 million victims annually.[144] Recent research by Bonnie Fisher and her associates suggests that even that substantial figure may undercount the actual problem. They found that about 13 percent of the women in a nationally drawn sample of more than 4,000 college women were victims of stalking. Considering that there are more than 6.5 million women attending college in the United States, about 700,000 women are being stalked each year on college campuses alone.[145] Though students are more likely to have a lifestyle that increases the risk of stalking compared to women in the general population, these data make it clear that stalking is a very widespread phenomenon.

Although stalking usually stops within one to two years, victims experience its social and psychological consequences long afterward. About one-third seek psychological treatment, and about one-fifth lose time from work; some never return to work.

Though stalking is a serious problem, research indicates that many cases are dropped by the courts despite the fact that stalkers often have extensive criminal histories and are frequently the subject of protective orders. A lenient response may be misplaced considering that there is evidence that stalkers repeat their criminal activity within a short time after the lodging of a stalking charge with police authorities.[146]

Terrorism

Despite its long history, it is often difficult to precisely define terrorism and to separate terrorist acts from interpersonal crimes of violence. For example, if a group robs a bank to obtain funds for its revolutionary struggles, should the act be treated as terrorism or as a common bank robbery? In this instance, defining a crime as terrorism depends on the kind of legal response the act evokes from those in power. To be considered terrorism, which is a political crime, an act must carry with it the intent to disrupt and change the government and must not be merely a common-law crime committed for greed or egotism.

Because of its complexity, an all-encompassing definition of terrorism is difficult to formulate, although most experts agree that it generally involves the illegal use of force against innocent people to achieve a political objective. According to the U.S. State Department, the term **terrorism** means premeditated, politically motivated violence perpetrated against noncombatant targets by subnational groups or clandestine agents, usually intended to influence an audience. The term **international terrorism** means terrorism involving citizens or the territory of more than one country. A **terrorist group** is any group practicing, or that has significant subgroups that practice, international terrorism.[147]

Terrorism usually involves a type of political crime that emphasizes violence as a mechanism to promote change. Whereas some political criminals may demonstrate, counterfeit, sell secrets, spy, and the like, terrorists systematically murder and destroy or threaten such violence to terrorize individuals, groups, communities, or governments into conceding to the terrorists' political demands.[148] However, it may be erroneous to equate terrorism with political goals because not all terrorist actions are aimed at political change. Some terrorists may try to bring about what they consider to be economic or social reform—for example, by attacking women wearing fur coats or sabotaging property during a labor dispute. Terrorism must also be distinguished from conventional warfare because it requires secrecy and clandestine operations to exert social control over large populations.[149]

stalking
A course of conduct directed at a specific person that involves repeated physical or visual proximity, nonconsensual communication, or verbal, written, or implied threats sufficient to cause fear in a reasonable person.

terrorism
Premeditated, politically motivated violence perpetrated against noncombatant targets by subnational groups or clandestine agents, usually intended to influence an audience.

international terrorism
Terrorism involving citizens or the territory of more than one country.

terrorist group
Any group practicing, or that has significant subgroups that practice, international terrorism.

Contemporary Forms of Terrorism

Today the term *terrorism* encompasses many different behaviors and goals. Some of the more common forms are briefly described here.

Revolutionary Terrorism   Revolutionary terrorists use violence to frighten those in power and their supporters in order to replace the existing government with a regime that holds acceptable political or religious views. Terrorist actions such as kidnapping, assassination, and bombing are designed to draw repressive responses from governments trying to defend themselves. These responses help revolutionaries expose the government's inhumane nature through their skilled use of media coverage. The original reason for the government's harsh response may be lost as the effects of counterterrorist activities are felt by uninvolved people. For example, on October 12, 2002, a powerful bomb exploded in a nightclub on the Indonesian island of Bali, killing more than 180 foreign tourists. In the aftermath of the attack, the Indonesian government declared that the attack was the work of the fundamentalist Islamic group Jemaah Islamiyah, which is a terrorist organization aligned with al-Qaeda. Jemaah Islamiyah is believed to be intent on driving away foreign tourists and ruining the nation's economy so that they can set up a Pan-Islamic nation in Indonesia and neighboring Malaysia.[150]

Political Terrorism   Political terrorism is directed at people or groups who oppose the terrorists' political or religious ideology or whom the terrorists define as "outsiders" who must be destroyed. Political terrorists may not want to replace the existing government but shape it so that it accepts their views.

U.S. political terrorists tend to be heavily armed groups organized around such themes as white supremacy, militant tax resistance, and religious revisionism. Identified groups have included the Aryan Republican Army, the Aryan Nation, the Posse Comitatus, and the Ku Klux Klan. Although unlikely to topple the government, these individualistic acts of terror are difficult to predict or control. For example, antiabortion groups have demonstrated at abortion clinics, and some members have attacked clients, bombed offices, and killed doctors who perform abortions. On October 23, 1998, Dr. Barnett Slepian was shot by a sniper and killed in his Buffalo, New York, home; he was one of a growing number of abortion providers believed to be the victims of terrorists who ironically claim to be "pro-life." On April 19, 1995, 168 people were killed during the Oklahoma City bombing. This is the most severe example of political terrorism in the United States.

Nationalist Terrorism   Nationalist terrorism promotes the interests of a minority ethnic or religious group that believes it has been persecuted under majority rule and wishes to carve out its own independent homeland.

In the Middle East, terrorist activities have been linked to the Palestinians' desire to wrest their former homeland from Israel. The leading group, the Palestinian Liberation Organization (PLO), had directed terrorist activities against Israel. Although the PLO now has political control over the West Bank and the Gaza Strip, splinter groups have broken from the PLO. These groups, Hamas and the Iranian-backed Hizballah, are perpetuating the conflict that Israel and the PLO sought to resolve and are behind a spate of suicide bombings and terrorist attacks designed to elicit a sharp response from Israel and set back any chance for peace in the region. In the first half of 2003, hundreds on both sides of the conflict were killed during terrorist attacks and reprisals.

Cause-Based Terrorism   Some terrorists, such as bin Laden's al-Qaeda organization, direct their terrorist activities against individuals or governments to whom they object. They espouse a particular social or religious cause and use violence to attract followers to their standard. They do not wish to set up their own homeland or topple a government; rather, they want to impose their social and religious code on the world.

In 1995 members of Aum Shinrikyo, a Japanese religious cult, released deadly sarin nerve gas into the Tokyo subway system, killing 12 people and sending more than 5,000 others to hospitals. The objective was to kill as many policemen as possible because Aum Shinrikyo feared that the Tokyo police planned to conduct raids against cult facilities.

Environmental Terrorism   On August 22, 2003, members of the extremist environmental group Earth Liberation Front (ELF) claimed responsibility for fires that destroyed several SUVs at a Chevrolet dealership in West Covina, California.[151] This is not the first attack by the group. On October 19, 1998, ELF members set fires atop Vail Mountain, claiming that the ski resort was expanding into animal habitats (especially that of the mountain lynx). More than 1,500 terrorist acts have been committed by environmental terrorists during the past two decades in an effort to slow down developers who they believe are threatening the environment or harming animals. Fires have also been set in government labs where animal research is conducted. Spikes are driven into trees to prevent logging in fragile areas. Members of such groups as the Animal Liberation Front (ALF) and Earth First! take responsibility for these attacks; they have also raided turkey farms before Thanksgiving and rabbit farms before Easter. ELF has been active for several years in the United States and abroad. In addition to its raid on the SUV dealer and ski resort developers, members have conducted arson attacks on property ranging from a sport utility vehicles sales lot in Eugene, Oregon, to a Nike shop in a mall north of Minneapolis, and to new homes on Long Island, New York.[152]

State-Sponsored Terrorism   State-sponsored terrorism occurs when a repressive government regime forces its citizens into obedience, oppresses minorities, and stifles political dissent. **Death squads** and the use of government troops to destroy political opposition parties are often associated with Latin American political terrorism. Much of what we know about state-sponsored terrorism comes from the efforts of human rights groups. London-based Amnesty International maintains that tens of thousands of people continue to become victims of security operations that result in disappearances and executions. Political prisoners are now being tortured in about 100 countries; people have disappeared or are being held in secret detention in about 20 countries; and government-sponsored death squads have been operating in more than 35 countries. Countries known for encouraging violent control of dissidents include Brazil, Colombia, Guatemala, Honduras, Peru, Iraq, and the Sudan.

Criminal Terrorism   Sometimes terrorist groups become involved in common-law crimes such as drug dealing and kidnapping, even selling nuclear materials. According to terrorism expert Chris Dishman, these illegal activities may on occasion become so profitable that they replace the group's original focus. Burmese insurgents continue to actively cultivate, refine, and traffic opium and heroin out of the Golden Triangle (the border between Burma, Thailand, and Laos), and some have even moved into the methamphetamine market.

What Motivates Terrorists?

In the aftermath of the September 11, 2001, destruction of the World Trade Center in New York City, many Americans asked themselves the same simple question: Why? What could motivate someone like Osama bin Laden to order the deaths of thousands of innocent people? How could someone who had never been to the United States or suffered personally at its hands develop such lethal hatred?

One view is that terrorists are emotionally disturbed individuals who act out their psychosis within the confines of violent groups. According to this

death squads
The use of government troops to destroy political opposition parties.

USA Patriot Act (USAPA)
An act that gives sweeping new powers to domestic law enforcement and international intelligence agencies in an effort to fight terrorism, to expand the definition of terrorist activities, and to alter sanctions for violent terrorism.

view, "terrorist" violence is not so much a political instrument as an end in itself; it is the result of compulsion or psychopathology. Terrorists do what they do because of a garden variety of emotional problems, including but not limited to self-destructive urges, disturbed emotions combined with problems with authority, and inconsistent and troubled parenting.[153]

Another view is that terrorists hold extreme ideological beliefs that prompt their behavior. At first they have heightened perceptions of oppressive conditions, believing that they are being victimized by some group or by the government. Once these potential terrorists recognize that these conditions can be changed by an active governmental reform effort that has not happened, they conclude that they must resort to violence to encourage change. Ironically, many terrorists appear to be educated members of the upper class. Osama bin Laden is a multimillionaire and at least some of his followers are highly educated and trained. The acts of the modern terrorist—using the Internet, logistically complex and expensive assaults, and writing and disseminating formal critiques, manifestos, and theories—require the training and education of the social elite, not the poor and the oppressed.

Responses to Terrorism

In the wake of the 9/11 attacks, the United States Congress moved quickly to pass the **USA Patriot Act (USAPA)**,[154] giving law enforcement agencies a freer hand to investigate and apprehend suspected terrorists. The bill, more than 342 pages long, created new laws and made changes to more than 15 different existing statutes. Its aim was to give sweeping new powers to domestic law enforcement and international intelligence agencies in an effort to fight terrorism, to expand the definition of terrorist activities, and to alter sanctions for violent terrorism. Among its provisions, USAPA expands all four traditional tools of surveillance—wiretaps, search warrants, pen/trap orders (installing devices that record phone calls), and subpoenas. The Foreign Intelligence Surveillance Act (FISA), which allows domestic operations by intelligence agencies, was also expanded. USAPA gave greater power to the FBI to check and monitor phone, Internet, and computer records without first needing to demonstrate that they were being used by a suspect or were a target of a court order. Under USAPA, the government does not need to show a court that the information or communication is relevant to a criminal investigation, nor do they have to report where they served the order or what information they received.

Law Enforcement Responses The FBI is currently expanding its force of agents, and hired approximately 1,000 more between 2002 and 2003. In addition to recruiting candidates with the more traditional background of law enforcement, law, and accounting, the bureau is concentrating on hiring agents with scientific and technological skills as well as foreign language proficiency in priority areas, such as Arabic, Farsi, Pashtu, and Urdu, all dialects of Chinese, Japanese, Korean, Russian, Spanish, and Vietnamese, and other priority backgrounds such as foreign counterintelligence, counterterrorism, and military intelligence. In addition to helping in counterterrorism activities, these agents will help staff the new Cyber Division, which was created in 2001 to coordinate, oversee, and facilitate FBI investigations in which the Internet, online services, and computer systems and networks are the principal instruments or targets of terrorists.

In addition to the FBI, the Department of Homeland Security has been assigned the following mission:

- Prevent terrorist attacks within the United States.
- Reduce America's vulnerability to terrorism.
- Minimize the damage and recovery from attacks that do occur.

FIND IT ON INFOTRAC
College Edition

What can be done to prevent terrorism in the new millennium? Can technology hold the key? Find out by reading:

Richard K. Betts, "Fixing Intelligence," *Foreign Affairs*, Jan–Feb 2002 v81 i1 p43

The DHS now has five independent branches:

1. Border and Transportation Security (BTS): responsible for maintaining the security of our nation's borders and transportation systems.
2. Emergency Preparedness and Response (EPR): ensures that our nation is prepared for, and able to recover from, terrorist attacks and natural disasters.
3. Science and Technology (S & T): coordinates efforts in research and development, including preparing for and responding to the full range of terrorist threats involving weapons of mass destruction.
4. Information Analysis and Infrastructure Protection (IAIP): merges the capability to identify and assess intelligence information concerning threats to the homeland under one roof, issue timely warnings, and take appropriate preventive and protective action.
5. Management: responsible for budget, management, and personnel issues in DHS.

✔ **Checkpoints**

Summary

- Violence has become an all too common aspect of modern life.

- Among the various explanations for violent crimes are the availability of firearms, human traits, a subculture of violence that stresses violent solutions to interpersonal problems, and family conflict.

- Rape, the carnal knowledge of a female forcibly and against her will, has been known throughout history, but society's view of rape has evolved.

- At present, close to 100,000 rapes are reported to U.S. police each year; the actual number of rapes is probably much higher. However, like other violent crimes, the rape rate is in decline.

- There are numerous forms of rape including statutory, acquaintance, and date rape.

- Rape is an extremely difficult charge to prove in court. The victim's lack of consent must be proven; therefore, it almost seems that the victim is on trial. Consequently, changes are being made in rape law and procedure.

- Rape shield laws have been developed to protect victims from having their personal life placed on trial.

- Murder is defined as killing a human being with malice aforethought. There are different degrees of murder, and punishments vary accordingly.

- Like rape, the murder rate and the number of annual murders is in decline.

- Murder can involve a single victim or be a serial killing, mass murder, or spree killing that involves multiple victims.

- One important characteristic of murder is that the victim and criminal often know each other.

- Murder often involves an interpersonal transaction in which a hostile action by the victim precipitates a murderous relationship.

- Assault, another serious interpersonal violent crime, often occurs in the home, including child abuse and spouse abuse. There also appears to be a trend toward violence between dating couples.

- Robbery involves theft by force, usually in a public place. Robbery is considered a violent crime because it can and often does involve violence.

- Newly emerging forms of violent crime include hate crimes, stalking, and workplace violence.

- Terrorism is a significant form of violence. Many terrorist groups exist at both the national and international levels.

- There are a variety of terrorist goals including political change, nationalism, causes, criminality, and environmental protection.

- Terrorists may be motivated by criminal gain, psychosis, grievance against the state, or ideology.

- The FBI and the Department of Homeland Security have been assigned the task of protecting the nation from terrorist attacks. The USA Patriot Act was passed to provide them with greater powers.

Thinking Like a Criminologist

The state legislature has asked you to prepare a report on statutory rape because of the growing number of underage girls who have been impregnated by adult men. Studies reveal that many teenage pregnancies result from affairs that underage girls have with older men, with age gaps ranging from 7 to 10 years. For example, the typical relationship that is prosecuted in California involves a 13-year-old girl and a 22-year-old male partner. Some outraged parents adamantly support a law that provides state grants to counties to prosecute statutory rape. These grants would allow more vigorous enforcement of the law and could result in the conviction of more than 1,500 offenders annually.

However, some critics suggest that implementing statutory rape laws to punish males who have relationships with minor girls does not solve the problems of teenage pregnancies and out-of-wedlock births. Liberals dislike the idea of using criminal law to solve social problems because it does not provide for the girls and their young children and focuses only on punishing offenders. In contrast, conservatives fear that such laws give the state power to prosecute people for victimless crimes, thereby adding to the government's ability to control people's private lives. Not all cases involve much older men, and critics ask whether we should criminalize the behavior of 17-year-old boys and their 15-year-old girlfriends. As a criminologist with expertise on rape and its effects, what would you recommend regarding implementation of the law?

Go to the Criminology: The Core 2e Web site to review the content of this chapter.

Doing Research on the Web

For an up-to-date list of URLs, go to

http://www.cj.wadsworth.com/siegel_crimcore2e

Go to this family planning site to get more insight on this issue:

http://www.agi-usa.org/pubs/journals/2903097.html

Also, check out the Violence Against Women Web site:

http://www.vaw.umn.edu/documents/stateleg/stateleg.html

Pro/Con discussions and Viewpoint Essays on some of the topics in this chapter may be found at the Opposing Viewpoints Resource Center:

http://www.gale.com/OpposingViewpoints

Key Terms

expressive violence 236
instrumental violence 236
eros 238

thanatos 238
psychopharmacological relationship 238

economic compulsive behavior 239
systemic link 239
subculture of violence 239

Critical Thinking Questions

1. Should different types of rape receive different legal sanctions? For example, should someone who rapes a stranger be punished more severely than someone who is convicted of marital rape or date rape? If your answer is "yes," then do you think someone who kills a stranger should be punished more severely than someone who kills a spouse or a friend?

2. Is there a subculture of violence in your home city or town? If so, how would you describe its environment and values?

3. There have been significant changes in rape law involving issues such as corroboration and shield laws.

What other measures would you take to protect victims of rape when they are forced to testify in court?

4. Should hate crimes be punished more severely than crimes motivated by greed, anger, or revenge? Why should crimes be distinguished by the motivations of the perpetrator? Is hate a more heinous motivation than revenge?

5. In light of the 9/11 attacks, should acts of terrorism be treated differently from other common-law violent crimes? For example, should terrorists be executed for attempting to commit violence even if no one is killed during their attack?

CHAPTER 11

Property Crimes

Chapter Objectives

1. Be familiar with the history of theft offenses.
2. Recognize the differences between professional and amateur thieves.
3. Know the similarities and differences between the different types of larceny.
4. Understand the different forms of shoplifting.
5. Be able to discuss the concept of fraud.
6. Know what is meant by a confidence game.
7. Understand what it means to burgle a home.
8. Know what it takes to be a good burglar.
9. Understand the concept of arson.
10. Be able to discuss why people commit arson for profit.

N DECEMBER 12, 2001, AC-
TRESS WINONA RYDER WAS
APPREHENDED BY SAKS FIFTH
AVENUE STORE DETECTIVES
as she attempted to leave the premises
with clothes, socks, hats, hair acces-
sories, and handbags worth some $5,500.
Store detectives found her in possession
of designer tops and handbags, all bearing holes where security tags had been removed. Store detectives later found the
security tags in the pocket of a coat in a sec-

CNN View the CNN video clip of this story and answer
related critical thinking questions on your
Criminology: The Core 2e CD.

tion that Ryder had been seen to visit while in the store. Three of them contained material that
matched holes in two handbags and a hair bow allegedly stolen by Ryder. During her trial on
shoplifting charges in the fall of 2002, prosecutors alleged that she went to the store equipped with
scissors and tissue paper with intent to steal. Jury members were shown a store security tape of
Ryder being detained on a dark street after she left the store weighed down with bags. The store's security manager testified that Ryder told him she was researching for a role in an upcoming movie
and that the director had told her to shoplift in preparation for the role. Her attorney told jurors that
Saks had Ryder's credit card and that she had told them to keep her account open on that day. Movie
stars routinely take stock and are billed later; perhaps she assumed that her account would be
charged. On November 6, 2002, Ms. Ryder was found guilty of grand theft and vandalism and sentenced to probation.[1]

inona Ryder's arrest made headlines because of her celebrity status,
but her crime is by no means unique. Each year millions of people
shoplift, costing retail establishments billions in losses. Shoplifting is
one of many different types of property crimes. As a group, these
theft offenses can be defined as acts that violate criminal law and are
designed to bring financial reward to an offender. The range and
scope of U.S. criminal activity motivated by financial gain are
tremendous. Self-report studies show that property crime is widespread among the young in every social class. National surveys of
criminal behavior indicate that almost 30 million personal and
household thefts occur annually; corporate and other white-collar
crimes are accepted as commonplace; and political scandals, ranging
from Watergate to Whitewater, indicate that even high government
officials may be suspected of criminal acts.

This chapter is the first of two that review the nature and extent of economic crime in the United States. It begins with some background information on the history and nature of theft as a crime. It then discusses larceny/theft and related offenses, including shoplifting, forgery, credit card theft, auto theft, fraud, confidence games, and embezzlement. Next the discussion turns to a more serious form of theft, burglary, which involves forcible entry into a person's home or workplace for the purpose of theft. Finally, the crime of arson is discussed briefly. Chapter 12 is devoted to white-collar crimes, cyber crimes, and economic crimes that involve criminal organizations.

History of Theft

Theft is not unique to modern times; the theft of personal property has been known throughout recorded history. The Crusades of the eleventh century inspired peasants and downtrodden noblemen to leave the shelter of their estates to prey upon passing pilgrims.[2] Crusaders felt it within their rights to appropriate the possessions of any infidels—Greeks, Jews, or Muslims—they happened to encounter during their travels. By the thirteenth century, returning pilgrims, not content to live as serfs on feudal estates, gathered in the forests of England and the Continent to poach game that was the rightful property of their lord or king and, when possible, to steal from passing strangers. By the fourteenth century, many such highwaymen and poachers were full-time livestock thieves, stealing great numbers of cattle and sheep.[3]

The fifteenth and sixteenth centuries brought hostilities between England and France in the Hundred Years' War. Foreign mercenary troops fighting for both sides roamed the countryside; loot and pillage were viewed as a rightful part of their pay. As cities developed and a permanent class of propertyless urban poor[4] was established, theft became more professional. By the eighteenth century, three separate groups of property criminals were active:

- *Skilled thieves* typically worked in the larger cities, such as London and Paris. This group included pickpockets, forgers, and counterfeiters, who operated freely. They congregated in flash houses—public meeting places, often taverns, that served as headquarters for gangs. Here, deals were made, crimes were plotted, and the sale of stolen goods was negotiated.[5]

- *Smugglers* moved freely in sparsely populated areas and transported goods, such as spirits, gems, gold, and spices, without paying tax or duty.

- *Poachers* typically lived in the country and supplemented their diet and income with game that belonged to a landlord.

■ Property crimes have a long history. This painting illustrates fourteenth-century thieves plundering a home in Paris.

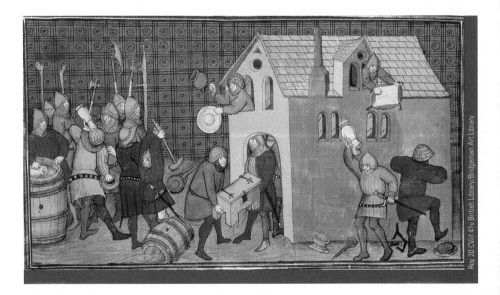

By the eighteenth century, professional thieves in the larger cities had banded together into gangs to protect themselves, increase the scope of their activities, and help dispose of stolen goods. Jack Wild, perhaps London's most famous thief, perfected the process of buying and selling stolen goods and gave himself the title of "Thief Taker General of Great Britain and Ireland." Before he was hanged, Wild controlled numerous gangs and dealt harshly with any thief who violated his strict code of conduct.[6] During this period, individual theft-related crimes began to be defined by common law. The most important of these categories are still used today.

Contemporary Thieves

Of the millions of property and theft-related crimes that occur each year, most are committed by **occasional criminals** who do not define themselves by a criminal role or view themselves as committed career criminals. Other thefts are committed by skilled professional criminals.

Criminologists suspect that most economic crimes are the work of amateur occasional criminals, whose decision to steal is spontaneous and whose acts are unskilled, unplanned, and haphazard. Millions of thefts occur each year, and most are not reported to police agencies. Many of these theft offenses are committed by school-age youths who are unlikely to enter criminal careers and who drift between conventional and criminal behavior. Added to the pool of amateur thieves are the millions of adults whose behavior may occasionally violate the law—shoplifters, pilferers, tax cheats—but whose main source of income is conventional and whose self-identity is noncriminal. Added together, their behaviors form the bulk of theft crimes.

Occasional property crime occurs when there is an opportunity or **situational inducement** to commit crime.[7] Members of the upper class have the opportunity to engage in lucrative business-related crimes such as price-fixing, bribery, and embezzlement; lower-class individuals, lacking such opportunities, are overrepresented in street crime. Situational inducements are short-term influences on a person's behavior that increase risk-taking. They include psychological factors, such as financial problems, and social factors, such as peer pressure.

Occasional criminals may deny their criminality and instead view their transgressions as out of character. For example, they were only "borrowing" the car the police caught them with; they were going to pay for the merchandise they stole from the store—eventually. Because of their lack of commitment to a criminal lifestyle, occasional offenders may be the most likely to respond to the general deterrent effect of the law.

In contrast to occasional criminals, **professional criminals** make a significant portion of their income from crime. Professionals do not delude themselves with the belief that their acts are impulsive, one-time efforts, nor do they use elaborate rationalizations to excuse the harmfulness of their actions ("shoplifting doesn't really hurt anyone"). Consequently, professionals pursue their craft with vigor, attempting to learn from older, experienced criminals the techniques that will earn the most money with the least risk. Although their numbers are relatively few, professionals engage in crimes that produce the greater losses to society and perhaps cause the more significant social harm.

Professional theft traditionally refers to nonviolent forms of criminal behavior that are undertaken with a high degree of skill for monetary gain and that maximize financial opportunities and minimize the possibilities of apprehension. The most typical forms include pocket picking, burglary, shoplifting, forgery, counterfeiting, extortion, sneak theft, and confidence swindling (see Figure 11.1).[8]

The following sections discuss some of the more important contemporary theft categories in some detail. ✔ Checkpoints

✔ Checkpoints

✔ Theft offenses have been common throughout recorded history.

✔ During the Middle Ages, poachers stole game, smugglers avoided taxes, and thieves worked as pickpockets and forgers.

✔ Occasional thieves are opportunistic amateurs who steal because of situational inducements.

✔ Professional thieves learn their trade and develop skills that help them avoid capture.

To quiz yourself on this material, go to questions 11.1–11.2 on the Criminology: The Core 2e Web site.

occasional criminals
Offenders who do not define themselves by a criminal role or view themselves as committed career criminals.

situational inducement
Short-term influence on a person's behavior, such as financial problems or peer pressure, that increases risk-taking.

professional criminals
Offenders who make a significant portion of their income from crime.

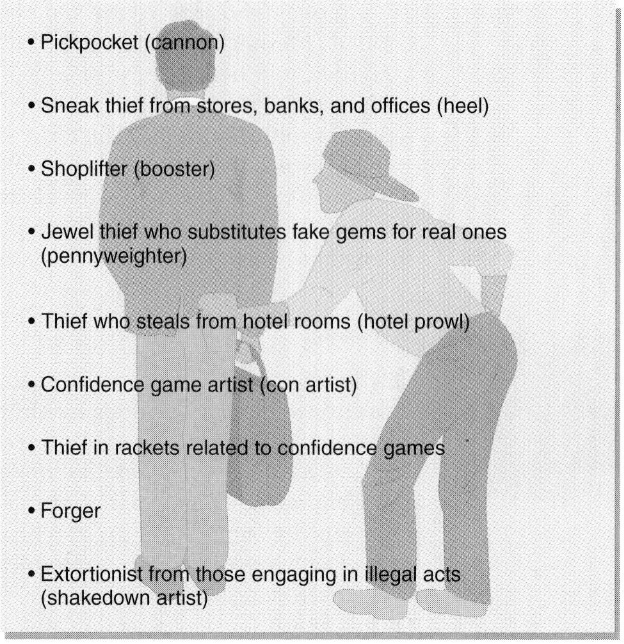

Figure 11.1
Categories of Professional Theft

SOURCE: Edwin Sutherland and Chic Conwell, *The Professional Thief* (Chicago: University of Chicago Press, 1937).

- Pickpocket (cannon)

- Sneak thief from stores, banks, and offices (heel)

- Shoplifter (booster)

- Jewel thief who substitutes fake gems for real ones (pennyweighter)

- Thief who steals from hotel rooms (hotel prowl)

- Confidence game artist (con artist)

- Thief in rackets related to confidence games

- Forger

- Extortionist from those engaging in illegal acts (shakedown artist)

Larceny/Theft

Theft, or **larceny,** was one of the earliest common-law crimes created by English judges to define acts in which one person took for his or her own use the property of another.[9] According to common law, larceny was defined as "the trespassory taking and carrying away of the personal property of another with intent to steal."[10] Most U.S. states have incorporated the common-law crime of larceny in their legal codes. Contemporary definitions of larceny often include such familiar acts as shoplifting, passing bad checks, and other theft offenses that do not involve using force or threats on the victim or forcibly breaking into a person's home or workplace. (The former is robbery; the latter, burglary.)

As originally construed, larceny involved taking property that was in the possession of the rightful owner. For example, it would have been considered larceny for someone to sneak into a farmer's field and steal a cow. Thus, the original common-law definition required a "trespass in the taking"; that is, for an act to be considered larceny, goods must have been taken from the physical possession of the rightful owner. In creating this definition of larceny, English judges were more concerned with disturbance of the peace than with theft itself. They reasoned that if someone tried to steal property from another's possession, the act could eventually lead to a physical confrontation and possibly the death of one party or the other. Consequently, the original definition of larceny did not include crimes in which the thief had taken the property by trickery or deceit. For example, if someone entrusted with another person's property decided to keep it, it was not considered larceny.

The growth of manufacturing and the development of the free enterprise system required greater protection for private property. The pursuit of commercial enterprise often required that one person's legal property be entrusted to a second party; therefore, larceny evolved to include the theft of goods that had come into the thief's possession through legitimate means.

To get around the element of "trespass in the taking," English judges created the concept of **constructive possession.** This legal fiction applies to situations in which persons voluntarily, temporarily give up custody of their property but still believe that the property is legally theirs. For example, if a person gives a jeweler her watch for repair, she still believes she owns the watch, although she has handed it over to the jeweler. Similarly, when a person misplaces his wallet and someone else finds it and keeps it (although

larceny
Taking for one's own use the property of another, by means other than force or threats on the victim or forcibly breaking into a person's home or workplace; theft.

constructive possession
A legal fiction that applies to situations in which persons voluntarily give up physical custody of their property but still retain legal ownership.

identification of the owner can be plainly seen), the concept of constructive possession makes the person who has kept the wallet guilty of larceny.

Most U.S. state criminal codes separate larceny into **petit** (or **petty**) **larceny** and **grand larceny.** The former involves small amounts of money or property and is punished as a misdemeanor. Grand larceny, involving merchandise of greater value, is a felony punished by a sentence in the state prison. Each state sets its own boundary between grand larceny and petty larceny, but $50 to $100 is not unusual.

Larceny/theft is probably the most common of all crimes. Self-report studies indicate that a significant number of youths have engaged in theft. The FBI recorded about 7 million acts of larceny in 2002, a rate of almost 2,500 per 100,000 persons. Larceny rates declined about 20 percent between 1992 and 2002.[11]

There are many different varieties of larceny. Some involve small items of little value. Many of these go unreported, especially if the victims are business owners who do not want to take the time to get involved with police; they simply write off losses as a cost of doing business. For example, hotel owners estimate that each year guests filch $100 million worth of towels, bathrobes, ashtrays, bedspreads, showerheads, flatware, and even television sets and wall paintings.[12] Another favorite is car parts, which can be taken from stolen autos or simply ripped off on the street. Among the most attractive targets are these parts:

Head lights. Blue-white, high-intensity discharge headlights. New ones go for $500 and up per light, sometimes $3,000 per car.

Air bags. About 10 percent of all theft claims involve an air bag. The driver's side bag, mounted in the steering wheel, is the easiest to remove and costs $500 to $1,000 to replace.

Wheels. Custom rims are attractive to thieves, especially the "spinners" that keep revolving when the car is stopped. They go from $100 each up to $15,000 for a set of super-deluxe models.[13]

Shoplifting

Shoplifting is a common form of larceny/theft involving the taking of goods from retail stores. Usually shoplifters try to snatch goods—such as jewelry, clothes, records, and appliances—when store personnel are otherwise occupied and hide the goods on their bodies. The "five-finger discount" is an extremely common crime, and retailers lose an estimated $30 billion annually to inventory shrinkage; on average, stores small and large lose at least 2 percent of total sales to thieves.[14] Retail security measures add to the already high cost of this crime, all of which is passed on to the consumer. Shoplifting incidents have increased dramatically in the past 20 years, and retailers now expect an annual increase of from 10 to 15 percent. Some studies estimate that about one in every nine shoppers steals from department stores. Moreover, the increasingly popular discount stores, such as Kmart, Wal-Mart, and Target, have minimal sales help and depend on highly visible merchandise displays to attract purchasers, all of which makes them particularly vulnerable to shoplifters.

The Shoplifter   In the early 1960s, Mary Owen Cameron conducted a classic study of shoplifting.[15] In her pioneering effort, Cameron found that about 10 percent of all shoplifters were professionals who derived the majority of their income from shoplifting. Sometimes called **boosters,** or heels, professional shoplifters steal with the intention of reselling stolen merchandise to pawnshops or **fences** (people who buy stolen property), usually at half the original price.[16]

Cameron found that the majority of shoplifters are amateur pilferers, called **snitches** in thieves' argot. Snitches are otherwise respectable persons who do not conceive of themselves as thieves but systematically steal merchandise for their own use. They are not simply taken by an uncontrollable

petit (petty) larceny
Theft of a small amount of money or property, punished as a misdemeanor.

grand larceny
Theft of money or property of substantial value, punished as a felony.

shoplifting
The taking of goods from retail stores.

booster
Professional shoplifter who steals with the intention of reselling stolen merchandise.

fence
A receiver of stolen goods.

snitch
Amateur shoplifter who does not self-identify as a thief but who systematically steals merchandise for personal use.

urge to snatch something that attracts them; they come equipped to steal. Snitches who are arrested usually have never been apprehended before. For the most part, they lack the kinds of criminal experience that suggest extensive association with a criminal subculture.

Criminologists view shoplifters as people who are likely to reform if apprehended. Cameron reasoned that because snitches are not part of a criminal subculture and do not think of themselves as criminals, they are deterred by initial contact with the law. Getting arrested traumatizes them, and they will not risk a second offense.[17] Although this argument seems plausible, some criminologists suggest that apprehension may in fact have a labeling effect that inhibits deterrence and results in repeated offending.[18]

Controlling Shoplifting Fewer than 10 percent of shoplifting incidents are detected by store employees; customers who notice boosters are unwilling to report even serious cases to managers.[19]

To encourage the arrest of shoplifters, a number of states have passed **merchant privilege laws** that are designed to protect retailers and their employees from lawsuits stemming from improper or false arrests of suspected shoplifters.[20] These laws require that arrests be made on reasonable grounds or probable cause, that detention be short, and that store employees or security guards conduct themselves reasonably.

Retail stores are now initiating a number of strategies designed to reduce or eliminate shoplifting. **Target removal strategies** involve displaying dummy or disabled goods while the "real" merchandise is locked up. For example, audio equipment is displayed with parts missing, and only after items are purchased are the necessary components installed. Some stores sell from catalogs, keeping the merchandise in stockrooms.

Target hardening strategies involve locking goods into place or having them monitored by electronic systems. Clothing stores may use racks designed to prevent large quantities of garments from being slipped off easily. Store owners also rely on electronic article surveillance (EAS) systems, featuring tags with small electronic sensors that trip alarms if not removed by employees before the item leaves the store; these are used on highly desired yet small items such as Gillette's Mach3 razorblades.[21]

Security systems now feature source tagging, a process by which manufacturers embed the tag in the packaging or in the product itself. Thieves have trouble removing or defeating such tags, and retailers save on the time and labor needed to attach the tags at the store[22] (see Figure 11.2).

While these methods may control shoplifting, stores must be wary of becoming overzealous in their enforcement policies. Those falsely accused have won significant judgments when they filed civil actions. For example, a woman accused of shoplifting at a J. C. Penney Co. Inc. store in Media, Pennsylvania, was awarded $250,000 in 2003, charging false confinement and malicious prosecution after she was mistakenly taken for a shoplifter.[23]

Steps recommended by retail insurers to reduce the incidence of shoplifting:

- Train employees to watch for suspicious behavior, such as a shopper loitering over a trivial item. Have them keep an eye out for shoppers wearing baggy clothes, carrying their own bag, or using some other method to conceal products taken from the shelf.

- Develop a call code. When employees suspect that a customer is shoplifting, they can use the call to bring store management or security to the area.

- Because products on lower floors face the greatest risk, relocate the most tempting targets to upper floors.

- Use smaller exits and avoid placing the most expensive merchandise near these exits.

- Design routes within stores to make theft less tempting and funnel customers toward cashiers.

- Place service departments (credit and packaging) near areas where shoplifters are likely to stash goods. Extra supervision reduces the problem.

- Avoid creating corners with no supervision sight lines in areas of stores favored by young males. Restrict and supervise areas where electronic tags can be removed.

Figure 11.2
How to Stop Shoplifting

SOURCE: Marcus Felson, "Preventing Retail Theft: An Application of Environmental Criminology," *Security Journal* 7 (1996): 71–75; Marc Brandeberry, "$15 Billion Lost to Shoplifting," *Today's Coverage*, a newsletter of the Grocers Insurance Group, Portland, Oregon, 1997.

merchant privilege laws
Legislation that protects retailers and their employees from lawsuits if they arrest and detain a suspected shoplifter on reasonable grounds.

target removal strategy
Displaying dummy or disabled goods as a means of preventing shoplifting.

target hardening strategy
Locking goods into place or using electronic tags and sensing devices as means of preventing shoplifting.

Bad Checks

Another form of larceny is cashing bad checks to obtain money or property. The checks are intentionally drawn on a nonexistent or underfunded bank account. In general, for a person to be guilty of passing a bad check, the bank the check is drawn on must refuse payment and the check casher must fail to make the check good within 10 days after finding out the check was not honored.

Connections

Situational crime prevention measures, discussed in Chapter 4, are designed to make it more difficult to commit crimes. Some stores are now using these methods—for example, placing the most valuable goods in the least vulnerable places, posting warning signs to deter potential thieves, and using closed-circuit cameras.

Edwin Lemert conducted the best-known study of check forgers more than 40 years ago.[24] Lemert found that the majority of check forgers—he calls them **naive check forgers**—are amateurs who do not believe their actions will hurt anyone. Most naive check forgers come from middle-class backgrounds and have little identification with a criminal subculture. They cash bad checks because of a financial crisis that demands an immediate resolution—perhaps they have lost money at the horse track and have some pressing bills to pay. Naive check forgers are often socially isolated people who have been unsuccessful in their personal relationships. They are risk prone when faced with a situation that is unusually stressful for them. The willingness of stores and other commercial establishments to cash checks with a minimum of fuss to promote business encourages the check forger to risk committing a criminal act.

Lemert found that a few professionals, whom he calls **systematic forgers,** make a substantial living passing bad checks. It is difficult to estimate the number of such forgeries committed each year or the amounts involved. Stores and banks may choose not to press charges because the effort to collect the money due them is often not worth their while. It is also difficult to separate the true check forger from the neglectful shopper.

Credit Card Theft

The use of stolen credit cards has become a major problem in the United States. Estimates are that about $1.8 billion per year is lost to stolen or faked credit cards.[25] Most credit card abuse is the work of amateurs who acquire stolen cards through theft or mugging and then use them for two or three days. However, professional credit card rings may be getting into the act. International credit card theft rings now buy cards from street thieves and pickpockets and offer stolen card numbers on the Internet. A card stolen in Amsterdam can be used to make bogus online purchases in Prague within hours. Largely run by former Soviet Union residents, these international cartels cost the financial system billions each year.[26]

To combat individual losses from credit card theft, in 1971 Congress limited a cardholder's liability to $50 per stolen card. Similarly, some states, such as California, have passed laws making it a misdemeanor to obtain property or services by means of cards that have been stolen, forged, canceled, or revoked, or whose use is for any reason unauthorized.[27] However, while the public is protected, merchants may have to foot the bill. For example, Website Billing.com Inc., a Hollywood, Florida-based Web company that processes payments for merchants, was required to pay the Visa credit card company $15 for each fraudulent transaction that it processed. But because fraudulent purchases exceeded 5 percent of all its international transactions, Visa assessed an additional $100 penalty for each fraudulent transaction; in 2001, Website Billing paid Visa more than $1 million in fees. Merchants argue that these fees—which generate an estimated $500 million in revenue for the card industry each year—eliminate much of the card companies' incentive to pursue credit card fraud.[28]

The problem of credit card misuse is being compounded by thieves who set up bogus Internet sites to trick people into giving them their credit card numbers, which they then use for their own gain. This problem is growing so rapidly that a number of new technologies are being prepared to combat credit card number theft over the Internet. One method incorporates digital signatures into computer operating systems, which can be accessed with a digital key that comes with each computer. Owners of new systems can present three forms of identification to a notary public and trade a notarized copy of their key for a program that will sign files. The basis of the digital signature is a digital certificate, a small block of data that contains a person's "public key." This certificate is signed, in turn, by a certificate authority. The digital certificate acts like a credit card with a hologram and a photograph; it identifies the user to the distant Web site.[29]

Connections

Similar frauds are conducted over the Internet. These are discussed in Chapter 12.

naive check forgers
Amateurs who cash bad checks because of some financial crisis but have little identification with a criminal subculture.

systematic forgers
Professionals who make a living by passing bad checks.

Auto Theft

Motor vehicle theft is another common larceny offense. Because of its frequency and seriousness, it is treated as a separate category in the Uniform Crime Report (UCR). The FBI recorded slightly more than 1.2 million auto thefts in 2002, accounting for a total loss of more than $8 billion. UCR projections on auto theft are similar to the projections of the National Crime Victim Survey (NCVS), probably because almost every state requires owners to insure their vehicles, and auto theft is one of the most highly reported of all major crimes (75 percent of all auto thefts are reported to police).

Which Cars Are Taken Most?   According to the National Insurance Crime Bureau, the Toyota Camry and Honda Accord are the cars most often stolen (2002), followed in popularity by the Honda Civic, Oldsmobile Cutlass, Jeep Cherokee/Grand Cherokee, Chevrolet full size C/K pickup, Toyota Corolla, Ford Taurus, Chevy Caprice, and Ford F150 pickup. The NICB also found that American cars were more attractive to thieves in cities such as Chicago, and pickups were more frequently stolen in Dallas. In the Los Angeles area, thieves preferred Japanese models.[30]

According to the NICB, thieves typically choose these vehicles because of their high profit potential when the cars are stripped of their component parts, which are then sold on the black market. These vehicles are popular overseas and, once taken, organized theft rings illegally export them to foreign destinations. Many of the highly desired cars are never recovered because they are immediately trans-shipped abroad where they command prices three times higher than U.S. sticker prices.[31]

Types of Auto Theft   A number of attempts have been made to categorize the various forms of auto theft. Typically, distinctions are made between theft for temporary personal use, for resale, and for chopping or stripping cars for parts:[32]

1. *Joyriding.* Many car thefts are motivated by teenagers' desire to acquire the power, prestige, sexual potency, and recognition associated with an automobile. Joyriders steal cars not for profit or gain but to experience, even briefly, the benefits associated with owning an automobile.

■ Suspect Jose Valadez remains inside a stolen van as Beloit, Wisconsin, police officer Mike Crall, right, and firefighters work to free him from the wreckage after a high-speed chase.

2. *Short-term transportation.* Auto theft for short-term transportation is similar to joyriding. It involves the theft of a car simply to go from one place to another. In more serious cases, the thief may drive to another city or state and then steal another car to continue the journey.

3. *Long-term transportation.* Thieves who steal cars for long-term transportation intend to keep the cars for their personal use. Usually older than joyriders and from a lower-class background, these auto thieves may repaint and otherwise disguise cars to avoid detection.

4. *Profit.* Auto theft for profit is motivated by the hope of monetary gain. At one extreme are highly organized professionals who resell expensive cars after altering their identification numbers and falsifying their registration papers. At the other end of the scale are amateur auto strippers who steal batteries, tires, and wheel covers to sell or to reequip their own cars.

5. *Commission of another crime.* A few auto thieves steal cars to use in other crimes, such as robberies and thefts. This type of auto thief desires both mobility and anonymity.

At one time, joyriding was the predominant motive for auto theft, and most cars were taken by relatively affluent, white, middle-class teenagers looking for excitement.[33] There appears to be a change in this pattern: Fewer cars are being taken today, and fewer stolen cars are being recovered. Part of the reason is that there has been an increase in professional car thieves who are linked to chop shops, export rings, or both. Exporting stolen vehicles has become a global problem, and the emergence of capitalism in Eastern Europe has increased the demand for U.S-made cars.[34]

Combating Auto Theft There has been an ongoing effort to reduce the number of auto thefts by using situational crime prevention techniques. One approach has been to increase the risks of apprehension. Information hot lines offer rewards for information leading to the arrest of car thieves. A Michigan-based program, Operation HEAT (Help Eliminate Auto Theft), is credited with recovering more than 900 vehicles, worth $11 million, and resulting in the arrest of 647 people. Another approach has been to place fluorescent decals on windows indicating that the car is never used between 1:00 A.M. and 5:00 A.M.; if police spot a car with the decal being operated during this period, they know it is stolen.

The Lojack system installs a hidden tracking device in cars; the device gives off a signal enabling the police to pinpoint its location. Research evaluating the effectiveness of this device finds that it significantly reduces crime.[35] Other prevention efforts involve making it more difficult to steal cars. Publicity campaigns have been directed at encouraging people to lock their cars. Parking lots have been equipped with theft-deterring closed-circuit TV cameras and barriers. Manufacturers have installed more sophisticated steering-column locking devices and other security systems that complicate theft.

A study by the Highway Loss Data Institute (HLDI) found that most car theft prevention methods, especially alarms, have little effect on theft rates. The most effective methods appear to be devices that immobilize a vehicle by cutting off the electrical power needed to start the engine when a theft is detected.[36]

False Pretenses/Fraud

The crime of **false pretenses,** or **fraud,** involves misrepresenting a fact in a way that causes a victim to willingly give his or her property to the wrongdoer, who then keeps it.[37] In 1757, the English Parliament defined false pretenses to cover an area of law left untouched by larceny statutes. The first false pretenses law punished people who "knowingly and designedly by false pretense or pretenses, [obtained] from any person or persons, money, goods, wares or merchandise with intent to cheat or defraud any person or persons of the same."[38]

false pretenses or fraud
Misrepresenting a fact in a way that causes a deceived victim to give money or property to the offender.

False pretense differs from traditional larceny because the victims willingly give their possessions to the offender, and the crime does not, as does larceny, involve a "trespass in the taking." An example of false pretenses would be an unscrupulous merchant selling someone a chair by claiming it was an antique, knowing all the while that it was a cheap copy. Another example would be a phony healer selling a victim a bottle of colored sugar water as an "elixir" that would cure a disease.

Confidence Games

Confidence games are run by swindlers who aspire to separate a victim from his or her hard-earned money. These con games usually involve getting a mark (target) interested in some get-rich-quick scheme, which may have illegal overtones. The criminal's hope is that when victims lose their money, they will be either too embarrassed or too afraid to call the police. There are hundreds of varieties of con games.

Contemporary confidence games have gone high-tech. Corrupt telemarketers contact people, typically elderly victims, over the phone in order to bilk them out of their savings. The FBI estimates that illicit telephone pitches cost Americans some $40 billion a year.[39] In one scam, a salesman tried to get $500 out of a 78-year-old woman by telling her the money was needed as a deposit to make sure she would get $50,000 she had supposedly won in a contest. In another scheme, a Las Vegas–based telephone con game used the name Feed America Inc. to defraud people out of more than $1.3 million by soliciting donations for various causes, including families of those killed in the Oklahoma City bombing. With the growth of direct-mail marketing and "900" telephone numbers that charge callers more than $2.50 per minute for conversations with what are promised to be beautiful, willing sex partners, a flood of new confidence games may be about to descend on the U.S. public. Here are some common confidence games:

- Con artists read the obituary column and then send a surviving spouse bills supposedly owed by the person deceased. Or they deliver an item, such as a Bible, that they say the deceased relative ordered just before he died.

- A swindler, posing as a bank employee, stops a customer as he or she is about to enter the bank. The swindler claims to be an investigator who is trying to catch a dishonest teller. He asks the customer to withdraw cash to see if he or she got the right amount. After the cash is withdrawn, the swindler asks that it be turned over to him so he can check the serial numbers.

- Pyramid schemes involve selling phony franchises. The investor buys a franchise to sell golf clubs or some other commodity, paying thousands of dollars. The investor is asked to recruit some friends to buy more franchises and is promised a percentage of the sales of every new franchisee he recruits. Eventually there are hundreds of distributors, few customers, and the merchandise is typically unavailable. Those at the top make lots of money before the pyramid collapses, leaving individual investors without their cash.

- Shady contractors offer unusually low prices for expensive jobs such as driveway repair and then use old motor oil rather than asphalt to make the repairs. The first rain brings disaster. Some offer a low rate but conduct a "free" inspection that turns up several expensive repairs that are actually bogus.

- A business office receives a mailing that looks like an invoice with a self-addressed envelope that makes it look like it comes from the phone company (walking fingers on a yellow background). It appears to be a contract for an ad in the yellow pages. On the back, in small print, will be written, "By returning this confirmation, you're signing a contract to be an advertiser in the upcoming, and all subsequent, issues." If the invoice is returned, the business soon finds that it has agreed to a long-term contract to advertise in some private publication that is not widely distributed.

confidence game
A swindle, usually involving a get-rich-quick scheme, often with illegal overtones, so that the victim will be afraid or embarrassed to call the police.

✔ Checkpoints

✔ Larceny is the taking and carrying away of the constructive possessions of another.

✔ Shoplifting involves theft from a retail establishment by stealth and deception. Some shoplifters are impulsive; others are professionals who use elaborate means and devices.

✔ Passing bad checks without adequate funds is a form of larceny.

✔ The use of stolen credit cards and account numbers results in annual losses of more than $1 billion.

✔ Auto theft adds up to more than $8 billion each year.

✔ Embezzlement occurs when trusted persons or employees take someone else's property for their own use.

To quiz yourself on this material, go to questions 11.3–11.13 on the Criminology: The Core 2e Web site.

Embezzlement

Embezzlement goes back at least to ancient Greece; the writings of Aristotle allude to theft by road commissioners and other government officials.[40] The crime of embezzlement was first codified into law by the English Parliament during the sixteenth century.[41] Until then, to be guilty of theft, a person had to take goods from the physical possession of another (trespass in the taking). In everyday commerce, store clerks, bank tellers, brokers, and merchants gain lawful possession but not legal ownership of other people's money. Embezzlement occurs when someone who is trusted with property fraudulently converts it—that is, keeps it for his or her own use or for the use of others. Most U.S. courts require a serious breach of trust before a person can be convicted of embezzlement. The mere act of moving property without the owner's consent, using it, or damaging it is not considered embezzlement. However, using it up, selling it, pledging it, giving it away, and holding it against the owner's will are all considered embezzlement.[42]

Although it is impossible to know how many embezzlement incidents occur annually, the FBI found that only 20,000 people were arrested for embezzlement in 2001—probably an extremely small percentage of all embezzlers. However, the number of people arrested for embezzlement has actually increased in the past two decades, indicating that (1) more employees are willing to steal from their employers, (2) more employers are willing to report instances of embezzlement, or (3) law enforcement officials are more willing to prosecute embezzlers. ✔ Checkpoints

Burglary

Common law defines the crime of **burglary** as "the breaking and entering of a dwelling house of another in the nighttime with the intent to commit a felony within."[43] Burglary is considered a much more serious crime than larceny/theft because it involves entering another's home, which threatens occupants. Even though the home may be unoccupied at the time of the burglary, the potential for harm to the occupants is so significant that most state jurisdictions punish burglary as a felony.

The legal definition of burglary has undergone considerable change since its common-law origins. When first created by English judges during the late Middle Ages, laws against burglary were designed to protect people whose home might be set upon by wandering criminals. Including the phrase "breaking and entering" in the definition protected people from unwarranted intrusions; if an invited guest stole something, it would not be considered a burglary. Similarly, the requirement that the crime be committed at nighttime was added because evening was considered the time when honest people might fall prey to criminals.[44]

More recent U.S. state laws have changed the requirements of burglary, and most have discarded the necessity of forced entry. Entry through deceit (for example, by posing as a deliveryman), through threat, or through conspiracy with others such as guests or servants is deemed legally equivalent to breaking and is called "constructive breaking." Many states now protect all structures, not just dwelling houses. A majority of states have also removed the nighttime element from burglary definitions. States commonly enact laws creating different degrees of burglary. The more serious, heavily punished crimes involve nighttime forced entry into the home; the least serious involve daytime entry into a nonresidential structure by an unarmed offender. Several legal gradations may be found between these extremes.

The Nature and Extent of Burglary

The FBI's definition of burglary is not restricted to burglary from a person's home; it includes any unlawful entry of a structure to commit a theft or felony. Burglary is further categorized into three subclasses: forcible entry, unlawful entry where no force is used, and attempted forcible entry.

embezzlement
Taking and keeping the property of others, such as clients or employers, with which one has been entrusted.

burglary
Entering a home by force, threat, or deception with intent to commit a crime.

© 2000 AP/Wide World Photos

■ Professional burglars develop technical competence, personal integrity, specialization in burglary, financial success, and the ability to avoid prison sentences. But everyone gets caught sometime. Here Darryl English, whom prosecutors have called the "premier burglar of Rockingham County" is flanked by public defender Larissa Kiers during his sentencing in Brentwood, New Hampshire. English was sentenced to spend 20–40 years in state prison.

Connections

According to the rational choice approach discussed in Chapter 4, burglars make rational and calculating decisions before committing crimes. If circumstances and culture dictate their activities, their decisions must be considered a matter of choice.

FIND IT ON INFOTRAC
College Edition

To learn more about the definition of burglary, use it as a key word. You can also find articles on steps that can be taken to limit the risk of becoming a burglary victim.

According to the UCR, about 2.1 million burglaries occurred in 2002. Though there was a slight increase between 2001 and 2002, the burglary rate has dropped by more than 35 percent since 1992. Both residential and commercial burglaries underwent steep declines during the 1990s; residential crimes committed at night declined more than residential daytime burglaries. Overall, the average loss for a burglary was about $1,500 per victim, for a total of about $3 billion.

The NCVS reports that about 3 million residential burglaries were either attempted or completed in 2002. Similar to the UCR, the NCVS indicates that the number of burglaries has declined significantly, dropping from 5.8 million in 1992. According to the NCVS, those most likely to be burglarized are relatively poor Hispanic and African American families (annual income under $7,500). Owner-occupied and single-family residences had lower burglary rates than renter-occupied and multiple-family dwellings.

Types of Burglaries

Because it involves planning, risk, and skill, burglary has long been associated with professional thieves who carefully learn their craft.[45] Burglars must master the skills of their trade, learning to spot environmental cues that nonprofessionals fail to notice.[46] In an important book called *Burglars on the Job,* Richard Wright and Scott Decker describe the working conditions of active burglars.[47] Most are motivated by the need for cash in order to get high; they want to enjoy the good life, "keep the party going," without having to work. They approach their job in a rational, businesslike fashion; still, their lives are controlled by their culture and environment. Unskilled and uneducated, urban burglars choose crime because they have few conventional opportunities for success (see Figure 11.3).

Residential Burglary   Experienced burglars learn to avoid areas of the city in which most residents are renters and not home owners, reasoning that renters are less likely to be suitable targets than the homes of more affluent owners.[48] Because it involves planning, risk, and skill, burglary has been a crime long associated with professional thieves who carefully learn their "craft." For example, Francis Hoheimer, an experienced professional burglar, has described how he learned the "craft of burglary" from a fellow inmate, Oklahoma Smith, when the two were serving time in the Illinois State Penitentiary. Smith recommended the following:

> Never wear deodorant or shaving lotion; the strange scent might wake someone up. The more people there are in a house, the safer you are. If someone hears you moving around, they will think it's someone else.... If they call, answer in a muffled sleepy voice.... Never be afraid of dogs, they can sense fear. Most dogs are friendly, snap your finger, they come right to you.[49]

Despite his elaborate preparations, Hoheimer spent many years in confinement.

Burglars must "master" the skills of their "trade," learning to spot environmental cues "nonprofessionals" fail to notice.[50] For example, they must learn which targets contain valuables worth stealing and which are most likely to prove to be dry holes. Research shows that burglary rates for student-occupied apartments are actually much lower than the rate for other residences in the same neighborhoods; burglars appear to have learned which apartments to avoid![51]

Commercial Burglars   Some burglars prefer to victimize commercial property rather than private homes, and a growing amount of research indicates

According to active burglars:

- Targets are often acquaintances.

- Drug dealers are favored targets because they tend to have a lot of cash and drugs, and victims aren't going to call police!

- Tipsters help them select attractive targets.

- Some stake out residences to learn occupants' routine.

- Many approach a target masquerading as workmen such as carpenters or house painters.

- Most avoid occupied residences, considering them high-risk targets.

- Most are not deterred by alarms and elaborate locks; in fact, these devices tell them there is something inside worth stealing.

- Some call occupants from a pay phone, and if the phone is still ringing when they arrive, they know no one is home.

- After entering a residence, anxiety turns to calm as they first turn to the master bedroom for money and drugs. They also search kitchens believing that some people keep money in the mayonnaise jar!

- Most work in groups, one serving as a lookout while the other(s) ransacks the place.

- Some dispose of goods through a professional fence; others try to pawn the goods. Some exchange goods for drugs; some sell them to friends and relatives; and a few keep the stolen items for themselves, especially guns and jewelry.

Figure 11.3
How Burglars Approach Their "Job"

SOURCE: Richard Wright and Scott Decker, *Burglars on the Job: Streetlife and Residential Break-ins* (Boston: Northeastern University Press, 1994).

that business premises have a higher risk of experiencing crimes such as burglary than households.[52]

Of all business establishments, retail stores are the favorite target. Because they display merchandise, burglars know exactly what to look for, where it can be found, and, because the prices are also displayed, how much they can hope to gain from resale to a fence. Burglars can legitimately enter a retail store during business hours and see what the store contains and where it is stored; they can also check for security alarms and devices. Commercial burglars perceive retail establishments as ready sources of merchandise that can be easily sold.[53]

Other commercial establishments, such as service centers, warehouses, and factories, are less attractive targets because it is more difficult to gain legitimate access to plan the theft. The burglar must use guile to scope out these places, perhaps posing as a delivery person. In addition, the merchandise is more likely to be used or more difficult to fence at a premium price. If burglars choose to attack factories, warehouses, or service centers, the most vulnerable properties are those located far from major roads and away from pedestrian traffic. In remote areas, burglar alarms are less effective because it takes police longer to respond than on more heavily patrolled thoroughfares, and an alarm is less likely to be heard by a pedestrian who would be able to call for help. Even in the most remote areas, however, burglars are wary of alarms, though their presence suggests that there is something worth stealing.

Repeat Burglars Whether residential or commercial, some burglars strike the same victim more than once.[54] Graham Farrell, Coretta Phillips, and Ken Pease suggest some reasons burglars might want to hit the same target more than once:

- It takes less effort to burgle a home or apartment known to be a suitable target than an unknown or unsuitable one.
- The burglar is already aware of the target's layout.
- The ease of entry of the target has probably not changed, and escape routes are known.
- The lack of protective measures and the absence of nosy neighbors, which made the first burglary a success, have probably not changed.
- Goods have been observed that could not be taken out the first time.[55]

It is also likely that since burgled items are both indispensable (such as televisions and VCRs) and covered by insurance it is safe to assume they will be quickly replaced, encouraging a second round of burglary![56]

The repeat burglary phenomenon should mean that homes in close proximity to a burgled dwelling should have an increased burglary risk, especially if they are quite similar in structure to the initial target. When this hypothesis was recently tested by Michael Townsley and his colleagues in Brisbane, Australia, they found the opposite to be true: little or no diversity in the physical construction and general appearance of dwellings serves to restrict the extent of repeat victimization. Townsley reasons that housing diversity allows offenders a choice of targets, and favored targets will be "revisited" by burglars. If houses are identical, there is no motive for an offender to favor one property over another and therefore the risk of repeat victimization is limited.[57]

Careers in Burglary

Some criminals make burglary their career and continually develop new specialized skills. Neal Shover has studied the careers of professional burglars and uncovered the existence of a particularly successful type—the "good burglar."[58] Characteristics of the good burglar include technical competence, personal integrity, specialization in burglary, financial success, and the ability to avoid prison sentences. Shover found that to receive recognition as good burglars, novices must develop four key requirements of the trade:

1. They must learn the many skills needed to commit lucrative burglaries. These skills may include gaining entry into homes and apartment houses; selecting targets with high potential payoffs; choosing items with a high resale value; opening safes properly without damaging their contents; and using the proper equipment, including cutting torches, electric saws, explosives, and metal bars.

2. The good burglar must be able to team up to form a criminal gang. Choosing trustworthy companions is essential if the obstacles to completing a successful job—police, alarms, secure safes—are to be overcome.

3. The good burglar must have inside information. Without knowledge of what awaits them inside, burglars can spend a tremendous amount of time and effort on empty safes and jewelry boxes.

4. The good burglar must cultivate fences or buyers for stolen wares. Once the burglar gains access to people who buy and sell stolen goods, he or she must also learn how to successfully sell these goods for a reasonable profit.

Evidence of these skills was discovered in a recent study of more than 200 career burglars in Australia. Burglars reported that they had developed a number of relatively safe methods for disposing of their loot. Some traded stolen goods directly for drugs; others used fences, legitimate businesses, pawnbrokers, and secondhand dealers as trading partners. Surprisingly, many sold their illegal gains to family or friends. Burglars report that disposing of stolen goods was actually low risk and more efficient than expected. One reason was that in many cases fences and shady businesspeople put in a request for particular items and the ready-made market allowed the stolen merchandise to be disposed of quickly, often in less than one hour. Though the typical markdown was about 67 to 75 percent of the price of the goods, most reported they could still earn a good living, averaging AUS$2,000 per week (about $1,000 in U.S. dollars). Those who benefit most from these transactions are the receivers of stolen property, who make considerable profits and are unlikely to get caught.[59]

According to Shover, an older burglar teaches the novice how to handle such requirements of the trade as dealing with defense attorneys, bail bond agents, and other agents of the justice system. Apprentices must be known to have the appropriate character before they are accepted for training. Usually the opportunity to learn burglary comes as a reward for being a highly respected juvenile gang member; from knowing someone in the neighborhood who has made a living at burglary; or, more often, from having built a reputation for being solid while serving time in prison. Consequently, the opportunity to become a good burglar is not open to everyone.

The "good burglar" concept is supported by the interviews Paul Cromwell, James Olson, and D'Aunn Wester Avary conducted with 30 active burglars in Texas. They found that burglars go through stages of career development, beginning as young novices who learn the trade from older, more experienced burglars, frequently siblings or relatives. Novices continue to get this tutoring as long as they can develop their own markets (fences) for stolen goods. After their education is over, novices enter the journeyman stage, characterized by forays in search of lucrative targets and by careful planning. At this point they develop reputations as experienced, reliable

Connections

Shover finds that the process of becoming a professional burglar is similar to the process described in Sutherland's theory of differential association in Chapter 7.

✔ Checkpoints

✔ Burglary is the breaking and entering of a structure in order to commit a felony, typically theft.

✔ Some burglars specialize in residential theft; others steal from commercial establishments.

✔ Some burglars repeatedly attack the same target, mainly because they are familiar with the layout and protective measures.

✔ Professional burglars have careers in which they learn the tricks of the trade from older, more experienced pros.

To quiz yourself on this material, go to question 11.14 on the Criminology: The Core 2e Web site.

N OCTOBER 15, 2002, DR. SAMUEL WAKSAL, FOUNDER OF IMCLONE SYSTEMS, A BIOTECH COMPANY, PLEADED guilty to charges of securities fraud, perjury, and obstruction of justice. The charges were a result of an investigation into the dumping of ImClone stock by Waksal and his friends and family shortly before the company announced that its application for approval of a cancer drug had been rejected by the Food and Drug

CNN View the CNN video clip of this story and answer related critical thinking questions on your Criminology: The Core 2e CD.

Administration. The fraud charge involved, among other acts, the sale of nearly 40,000 ImClone shares by Waksal's daughter Aliza, whom he called the day before the failure was made public, advising her to sell all her stock so that she would have cash to buy an apartment. Another player in the ImClone case was decorating guru Martha Stewart, who dumped her shares just prior to the negative announcement. Stewart quickly became the target of a government probe and in 2004 was convicted on securities related charges. "I have made terrible mistakes," Waksal, 55, told reporters after his courtroom appearance. "I deeply regret what has happened. I was wrong."[1] Ironically, in June 2003, clinical trials of ImClone's drug Erbitux proved positive, and the stock boomed at about the same time Waksal was sentenced to seven years in prison. At the time of this writing, Stewart, who resigned from her company, was awaiting sentencing.

t has become routine in our free-enterprise, global economy for people such as Martha Stewart and Sam Waksal to use illegal tactics to make a profit. We refer to these crimes of the marketplace as **enterprise crimes.** In this chapter we divide these crimes of illicit entrepreneurship into three distinct categories: white-collar crime, cyber crime, and organized crime. **White-collar crime** involves illegal activities of people and institutions whose acknowledged purpose is profit through legitimate business transactions. **Cyber crime** involves people using the instruments of modern technology for criminal purposes. **Organized crime** involves illegal activities of people and organizations whose acknowledged purpose is profit through illegitimate business enterprise.

Cyber crime, organized crime, and white-collar crime are linked together here because the three often overlap and in each category offenders twist the legal rules of commercial enterprise for criminal purposes (see Figure 12.1). Organized criminals may use the Internet to conduct fraud schemes and then seek legitimate enterprises to launder money, diversify their source of income, increase their power and influence, and gain and enhance respectability.[2] Otherwise legitimate businesspeople may turn to organized criminals to help them

enterprise crimes
Crimes of illicit entrepreneurship.

white-collar crime
Illegal activities of people and institutions whose acknowledged purpose is profit through legitimate business transactions.

cyber crime
Illegal activities using the instruments of modern technology for criminal purposes.

organized crime
Illegal activities of people and organizations whose acknowledged purpose is profit through illegitimate business enterprise.

Figure 12.1
Enterprise Crimes: The Linkage between White-Collar Crime, Cyber Crime, and Organized Crime

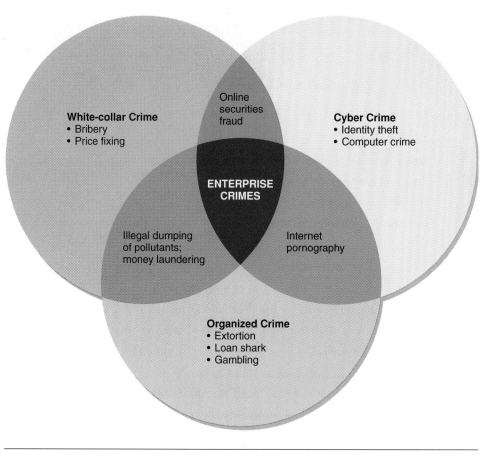

White-collar Crime
• Bribery
• Price fixing

Online securities fraud

Cyber Crime
• Identity theft
• Computer crime

ENTERPRISE CRIMES

Illegal dumping of pollutants; money laundering

Internet pornography

Organized Crime
• Extortion
• Loan shark
• Gambling

✔ Checkpoints

✔ Enterprise crimes involve illicit entrepreneurship and commerce.

✔ White-collar crime involves the illegal distribution of legal material.

✔ Cyber crime involves using technology to commit crime.

✔ Organized crime involves the illegal distribution of illegal material.

✔ White-collar crime, cyber crime, and organized crime are linked together because they involve entrepreneurship.

✔ Losses from enterprise crime may far outstrip any other type of crime.

---

with economic problems (such as breaking up a strike or dumping hazardous waste products), stifle or threaten competition, and increase their influence.[3] Whereas some corporate executives cheat to improve their company's position in the business world, others are motivated purely by personal gain, acting more like organized criminals than indiscreet businesspeople.[4]

These organizational crimes taint and corrupt the free-market system. They mix and match illegal and legal methods and legal and illegal products in all phases of commercial activity. Organized criminals often use illegal marketing techniques (threat, extortion, and smuggling) to distribute otherwise legal products and services (lending money, union activities, selling securities); they also engage in the distribution of products and services (drugs, sex, gambling, and prostitution) that have been outlawed. White-collar criminals use illegal business practices (embezzlement, price-fixing, bribery, and so on) to merchandise what are normally legitimate commercial products (securities, medical care, online auctions). Cyber criminals use their technical expertise for criminal misappropriations (Internet fraud).[5]

Surprisingly to some, all three forms of enterprise crime can involve violence. Although the use of force and coercion by organized crime members has been popularized in the media and therefore comes as no shock, that white-collar and cyber criminals may inflict pain and suffering seems astonishing. ✔ **Checkpoints**

White-Collar Crime

In the late 1930s, the distinguished criminologist Edwin Sutherland first used the phrase "white-collar crime" to describe the criminal activities of the rich and powerful. He defined white-collar crime as "a crime committed by a person of respectability and high social status in the course of his occupation."[6] Sutherland believed that the great majority of white-collar criminals did not become the subject of criminological study because most cases were handled in civil courts. Yet the cost of white-collar crime is probably several times greater than common theft offenses such as burglaries, and white-collar offenses breed distrust in economic and social institutions, lower public morale, and undermine faith in business and government.[7]

Contemporary definitions of white-collar crime are typically much broader and include both middle-income Americans and corporate titans who use the marketplace for their criminal activity.[8] Included within recent views of white-collar crime are such acts as income tax evasion, credit card fraud, and bankruptcy fraud. Other white-collar criminals use their positions of trust in business or government to commit crimes. Their activities might include pilfering, soliciting bribes or kickbacks, and embezzlement. Some white-collar criminals set up business for the sole purpose of victimizing the general public. They engage in land swindles (for example, representing swamps as choice building sites), securities theft, medical fraud, and so on. And, in addition to acting as individuals, some white-collar criminals become involved in criminal conspiracies designed to improve the market share or profitability of their corporations. This type of white-collar crime, which includes antitrust violations, price-fixing, and false advertising, is known as corporate crime.

It is difficult to estimate the extent and influence of white-collar crime on victims because all too often those who suffer the consequences of white-collar crime are ignored by victimologists.[9] Some experts place its total monetary value in the hundreds of billions of dollars, far outstripping the expense of any other type of crime. Nor is it likely that the full extent of white-collar crime will ever be known because victims believe that reporting these white-collar crimes is pointless and achieves nothing.[10]

Beyond their monetary cost, white-collar crimes often damage property and kill people. Violations of safety standards, pollution of the environment, and industrial accidents due to negligence can be classified as corporate violence. White-collar crime also destroys confidence, saps the integrity of commercial life, and has the potential for devastating destruction. Think of the possible results if nuclear regulatory rules are flouted or if toxic wastes are dumped into a community's drinking water supply.

White-collar crimes today represent a range of behaviors involving individuals acting alone and within the context of a business structure. The victims of white-collar crime can be the general public, the organization that employs the offender, or a competing organization.[11]

Stings and Swindles

For more than a decade the Gold Club in Atlanta was the hottest spot in town, the destination for conventioneers and businessmen looking for a rowdy night on the town filled with good cigars, strong drinks, and nude dancers.[12] It became the home away from home for well-known professional athletes who stopped by to receive sexual favors from the girls who worked at the club. In 2001, the federal government filed charges claiming that the Gold Club manager, Steven Kaplan, was in cahoots with the Gambino organized-crime family of New York in a scheme to overcharge and double-billed credit cards of unsuspecting customers. The club owners were also charged with ordering women in their employ to provide sexual services to professional athletes and celebrities to encourage their presence at the club. The government won its case when Mr. Kaplan pleaded guilty and received a three- to five-year prison sentence and a $5 million fine. Ironically, as part of the deal, the federal government took over the Gold Club, making it the manager of one of the largest strip clubs in the nation!

Mr. Kaplan and his co-conspirators were found guilty of engaging in a **sting** or **swindle,** a white-collar crime in which people use their institutional or business position to bilk people out of their money. Offenses in this category range from fraud involving the door-to-door sale of faulty merchandise to passing millions of dollars in counterfeit stock certificates to an established

sting or **swindle**
A white-collar crime in which people use their institutional or business position to bilk others out of their money.

■ **Stings and swindles** are a white-collar crime in which people use their institutional or business position to bilk people out of their money. Here Jules "Dr. Feelgood" Lusman (left) and his attorney appear in court at the Airport Courthouse July 29, 2003, in Los Angeles, California. Lusman, a medical doctor whose license was revoked in December 2002, is accused of performing unlicensed cosmetic procedures on two women in his home.

churning
Repeated, excessive, and unnecessary buying and selling of a client's stock.

front running
Brokers place personal orders ahead of a large customer's order to profit from the market effects of the trade.

bucketing
Skimming customer trading profits by falsifying trade information.

insider trading
Using one's position of trust to profit from inside business information.

brokerage firm. If caught, white-collar swindlers are usually charged with common-law crimes such as embezzlement or fraud.

Swindlers often choose targets they consider to be the most vulnerable. The elderly and religious are considered easy pickings, and it is estimated that fake religious organizations bilk thousands of people out of more than $100 million per year.[13] How do religious swindlers operate? Some create fraudulent charitable organizations and convince devout people to contribute to their seemingly worthwhile cause. Some use religious television and radio shows to sell their products. Others place verses from the scriptures on their promotional literature to comfort hesitant investors.

Chiseling

Chiseling involves cheating an organization, its consumers, or both on a regular basis. Chiselers may be individuals looking to make quick profits in their own businesses or employees of large organizations who decide to cheat on obligations to their own company or its clients by doing something contrary to either the law or company policy. Chiseling can involve charging for bogus auto repairs, cheating customers on home repairs, or short-weighting (intentionally tampering with the accuracy of scales used to weigh products) in supermarkets or dairies. In some cases, workers use their position in an organization to conduct illegal schemes or help others benefit illegally. Chiseling may even involve illegal use of information about company policies that have not been disclosed to the public. The secret information can be sold to speculators or used to make money in the stock market. Use of the information violates the obligation to keep company policy secret.

Professional Chiseling It is not uncommon for professionals to use their positions to chisel clients. Pharmacists have been known to alter prescriptions or to substitute low-cost generic drugs for more expensive name brands.[14] In one case that made national headlines in 2001, Kansas City pharmacist Robert R. Courtney was charged with fraud when it was discovered that he had been selling diluted mixtures of the cancer medications Taxol, Gemzar, Paraplatin, and Platinol, which are used to treat a variety of illnesses including pancreatic and lung cancer.[15] After he pleaded guilty, Courtney told authorities his criminal activities had actually begun in 1992 or even earlier, affected the patients of 400 doctors, involved 98,000 prescriptions, and harmed approximately 4,200 patients.[16] There is no telling how many people died or suffered serious medical complications because of Courtney's criminal conduct.

Securities Fraud A great deal of chiseling takes place on the commodity and stock markets, where individuals engage in deceptive practices that are prohibited by federal law. Some brokers use their positions to cheat individual clients: for example, **churning** the client's account by repeated, excessive, and unnecessary buying and selling of stock.[17] Other broker fraud includes **front running,** in which brokers place personal orders ahead of a large customer's order to profit from the market effects of the trade; and **bucketing,** which is skimming customer trading profits by falsifying trade information.[18] Securities chiseling can also involve using one's position of trust to profit from inside business information, referred to as **insider trading.** The information can then be used to buy and sell securities, giving the trader an unfair advantage over the general public, which lacks this inside information.

Connections

In Chapter 11 fraud was described as a common theft offense in which one person uses illegal methods to bilk another person out of money; white-collar fraud involves a person using his or her institutional or business position to reach the same goal. Common-law fraud is typically a short-term transaction, whereas white-collar fraud involves a long-term criminal conspiracy. Although the ends are similar, the means are somewhat different.

Connections

The case of Sam Waksal described at the beginning of the chapter is a notorious example of insider trading.

When the stock market collapsed in 2000, securities fraud became a major national issue. Leading market analysts have been accused of providing false and misleading information to pump up the price of stocks in an effort to secure business for their firms. On April 28, 2003, the Securities and Exchange Commission announced a settlement in which leading Wall Street brokerage firms including Salomon Smith Barney, CSFB (Credit Suisse First Boston), Morgan Stanley, Goldman Sachs, Bear Stearns, J. P. Morgan, Lehman Brothers, UBS Warburg, and U.S. Bancorp Piper Jaffray paid a $1.4 billion fine.[19] Some leading analysts were fined millions of dollars and barred from the security industry for life.

Individual Exploitation of Institutional Position

Another type of white-collar crime involves individuals' exploiting their power or position in organizations to take advantage of other individuals who have an interest in how that power is used. For example, a fire inspector who demands that the owner of a restaurant pay him to be granted an operating license is abusing his institutional position. This type of offense occurs when the victim has a clear right to expect a service and the offender threatens to withhold the service unless an additional payment or bribe is forthcoming.

Influence Peddling and Bribery

Sometimes individuals holding important institutional positions sell power, influence, and information to outsiders who have an interest in influencing or predicting the activities of the institution. Offenses within this category include government employees' taking kickbacks from contractors in return for awarding them contracts they could not have won on merit, or outsiders' bribing government officials who might sell information about future government activities. Political leaders have been convicted of accepting bribes to rig elections that enable their party to control state politics.[20]

One major difference distinguishes **influence peddling** from the previously discussed types of exploitation. Exploitation involves forcing victims to pay for services *to which they have a clear right*. In contrast, influence peddlers and bribe takers use their institutional positions to grant favors and sell information to which their *co-conspirators are not entitled*. In sum, in crimes of institutional exploitation, the victim is threatened and forced to pay, whereas the victim of influence peddling is the organization compromised by its employees for their own interests.

Influence Peddling in Government   It has become all too common for legislators and other state officials to be forced to resign or even to be jailed for accepting bribes to use their influence. For example, in 2003 Manhattan prosecutors began an investigation into whether lobbyists for the Correctional Services Corp., a firm that builds and runs private prison facilities, failed to follow state laws in their efforts to gain favor with legislators. The investigation focused on whether "gifts" to state lawmakers exceeded the legal limit and whether the lobbyists accurately reported, or reported at all, gifts they had given. One state assemblywoman resigned after admitting that she accepted free transportation from the company in return for helping it obtain state contracts.[21] The state's Lobbying Commission fined the company a record $300,000 for failing to report free transportation, meals, and other gifts it had given to legislators in an effort to keep millions of dollars in state contracts; the $300,000 fine is the largest that the state has ever imposed on a single company for breaking its lobbying laws.[22]

Influence Peddling in Business   Politicians and government officials are not the only ones accused of bribery; business has had its share of scandals. The 1970s witnessed revelations that multinational corporations regularly made payoffs to foreign officials and businesspeople to secure business contracts.

influence peddling
Using one's institutional position to grant favors and sell information to which one's co-conspirators are not entitled.

Gulf Oil executives admitted paying $4 million to the South Korean ruling party; Burroughs Corporation admitted paying $1.5 million to foreign officials; and Lockheed Aircraft admitted paying $202 million. McDonnell-Douglas Aircraft Corporation was indicted for paying $1 million in bribes to officials of Pakistani International Airlines to secure orders.[23]

In response to these revelations, in 1977 Congress passed the Foreign Corrupt Practices Act (FCPA), which makes it a criminal offense to bribe foreign officials or to make other questionable overseas payments. Violations of the FCPA draw strict penalties for both the defendant company and its officers.[24] Moreover, all fines imposed on corporate officers are paid by them, not absorbed by the company. For example, for violating the antibribery provisions of the FCPA, a domestic corporation can be fined up to $1 million. Company officers, employees, or stockholders who are convicted of bribery may have to serve a prison sentence of up to five years and pay a $10,000 fine.

Embezzlement and Employee Fraud

The fifth type of white-collar crime involves individuals' use of their positions to embezzle company funds or appropriate company property for themselves. Here the company or organization that employs the criminal, rather than an outsider, is the victim of white-collar crime. For example, in 2001 the FBI uncovered a scheme by eight McDonald's employees to steal $13 million worth of McDonald's game prizes from its Monopoly game promotion, which offered a top prize of $1 million. Those involved in the scam were in a position to obtain winning game pieces, which they distributed to friends and associates who acted as recruiters. These recruiters then solicited individuals who falsely and fraudulently represented that they were the legitimate winners of the McDonald's games.[25]

Blue-Collar Fraud   In 2002, three employees and a friend of theirs allegedly stole moon rocks from a NASA laboratory in Houston. FBI agents arrested them after they tried to sell the contraband to an undercover agent in Orlando, Florida. The would-be seller reportedly asked $2,000 per gram for the rocks initially, but later bumped the price to $8,000 per gram.[26] Although the theft of moon rocks does not happen too often, employees have been involved in systematic theft of other types of company property, commonly called **pilferage**.[27]

Employee theft is most accurately explained by factors relevant to the work setting, such as job dissatisfaction and the workers' belief that they are being exploited by employers or supervisors; economic problems play a relatively small role in the decision to pilfer. So, although employers attribute employee fraud to economic conditions and declining personal values, workers themselves say they steal because of strain and conflict.

It is difficult to determine the value of goods taken by employees, but some recent surveys indicate it is substantial. A recent poll among 30 of Britain's top retailers found they lost an estimated $5 billion to theft by employees in a single year (2001); shrinkage cost the European economy $29 billion, more than the losses due to car theft and domestic burglary.[28] A recent study co-sponsored by the National Food Service Security Council found the average restaurant worker now (2002) steals $204 in cash or merchandise per year, up from $96 in 1998 when the economy was in better shape.[29] However, these figures may underestimate the problem because they rely on employee self-reporting; experts believe employees now take $1,500 each year![30]

Management Fraud   Blue-collar workers are not the only employees who commit corporate theft. Management-level fraud is also quite common. Such acts include (1) converting company assets for personal benefit, (2) fraudulently receiving increases in compensation (such as raises or bonuses), (3) fraudulently increasing personal holdings of company stock, (4) retaining

pilferage
Systematic theft of company property.

one's present position within the company by manipulating accounts, and (5) concealing unacceptable performance from stockholders.[31]

There have been numerous cases of management fraud since 2000, perhaps the most notorious involving the demise of the oil and natural gas trading company Enron, the aggressive energy company that sought to transform itself into the world's biggest energy trader.[32] At one time Enron was, by stock market value, the seventh largest U.S. company. But its share price collapsed when word got out that the company had been setting up shell companies and limited partnerships to conceal debts. Enron executives lied about profits and conducted a range of shady dealings, including concealing debts so they didn't show up in the company's accounts.[33]

The Enron case is not unique. Executives as WorldCom Inc., parent of long-distance carrier MCI, were charged with misappropriating more than $7 billion including more than $1 billion in questionable loans to the firm's former chief.[34] Similar charges have been leveled at L. Dennis Kozlowski, former chief executive, and Mark Swartz, former chief financial officer of Tyco International who, at the time of this writing, are on trial on charges of misappropriating some $600 million from Tyco.[35]

Client Fraud

A sixth component of white-collar crime is theft by an economic client from an organization that advances credit to its clients or reimburses them for services rendered. These offenses are linked together because they involve cheating an organization (such as a government agency or insurance company) with many individual clients that the organization supports financially (such as welfare clients), reimburses for services provided (such as health care providers), covers losses of (such as insurance policyholders), or extends credit to (such as bank clients or taxpayers). Included in this category are insurance fraud, credit card fraud, fraud related to welfare and Medicare programs, and tax evasion. For example, some critics suggest that welfare recipients cheat the federal government out of billions each year. As eligibility for public assistance becomes more limited, recipients are resorting to a number of schemes to maintain their status. Some women collect government checks while working on the side or living illegally with boyfriends or husbands. Some young mothers tell children to answer exam questions incorrectly to be classified as disabled and receive government assistance.[36]

Health Care Fraud It is also common for doctors to violate their ethical vows and engage in fraud in obtaining patients and administering their treatment. An extreme instance occurred in 2001 when 172 people in New Jersey—including a medical doctor, a lawyer, and two chiropractors—were charged with staging 19 automobile accidents and filing false medical claims totaling more than $5 million. They recruited participants who were paid up to $2,500 to claim they were injured in an accident. The ringleaders coached them about the types of injuries to fake. The medical professionals would then file claims with the drivers' insurance companies for services never rendered.[37]

Abusive and deceptive health care practices include such techniques as "ping-ponging" (referring patients to other physicians in the same office), "gang visits" (billing for multiple services), and "steering" (directing patients to particular pharmacies). Doctors who abuse their Medicaid or Medicare patients in this way are liable to civil suits and even criminal penalties.

In light of these and other health care scandals, the government has attempted to tighten control over the industry. New regulations restrict the opportunity for physicians to commit fraud. Health care companies providing services to federal health care programs are also regulated by federal laws that prohibit kickbacks and self-referrals. For example, it is a crime, punishable by up to five years in prison, to provide anything of value, money or otherwise, directly or indirectly, with the intent to induce a referral of a patient

■ Tax evasion is a type of fraud in which the victim is the government that is cheated by one of its clients, the errant taxpayer, to whom it extended credit by allowing the taxpayer to delay paying taxes on money he or she had already earned. Here, Tyco CEO Dennis Kozlowski leaves the New York Supreme Court on June 4, 2002, after his arraignment on charges that he avoided more than $1 million in sales tax on paintings he purchased. State and federal prosecutors have turned up the heat on the art industry by going after dealers and buyers, who authorities say arrange with each other to avoid sales taxes.

or a health care service. Federal law also prohibits physicians and other health care providers from referring beneficiaries in federal health care programs to clinics or other facilities in which the physician or health care provider has a financial interest. For example, it would be illegal for a doctor to refer all of her patients to a blood testing lab she secretly owns. These practices—kickbacks and self-referrals—are prohibited under federal law because they would compromise medical professionals' independent judgment. Federal law prohibits arrangements that tend to corrupt medical judgment and put the provider's bottom line ahead of the patient's well-being.[38]

Bank Fraud   Bank fraud can encompass such diverse schemes as check kiting, check forgery, false statements on loan applications, sale of stolen checks, bank credit card fraud, unauthorized use of automatic teller machines (ATMs), auto title fraud, and illegal transactions with offshore banks.[39] To be found guilty of bank fraud, one must knowingly execute or attempt to execute a scheme to fraudulently obtain money or property from a financial institution. For example, a car dealer would commit bank fraud by securing loans on titles to cars it no longer owned. A real estate owner would be guilty of bank fraud if he or she obtained a false appraisal on a piece of property with the intention of obtaining a bank loan in excess of the property's real worth. Penalties for bank fraud include a maximum fine of $1 million and up to 30 years in prison.

Tax Evasion   Another important aspect of client fraud is tax evasion. Here the victim is the government that is cheated by one of its clients, the errant taxpayer to whom it extended credit by allowing the taxpayer to delay paying taxes on money he or she had already earned. Tax fraud is a particularly challenging area for criminological study because (1) so many U.S. citizens regularly underreport their income, and (2) it is often difficult to separate honest error from deliberate tax evasion.

The basic law on tax evasion is contained in the U.S. Internal Revenue Code, section 7201, which states:

> Any person who willfully attempts in any manner to evade or defeat any tax imposed by this title or the payment thereof shall, in addition to other penalties provided by law, be guilty of a felony and, upon conviction thereof, shall be fined not more than $100,000 or imprisoned not more than five years, or both, together with the costs of prosecution.

To prove tax fraud, the government must find that the taxpayer either underreported his or her income or did not report taxable income. No minimum dollar amount is stated before fraud exists, but the government can take legal action when there is a "substantial underpayment of tax." A second element of tax fraud is "willfulness" on the part of the tax evader. In the major case on this issue, willfulness was defined as a "voluntary, intentional violation of a known legal duty and not the careless disregard for the truth."[40] Finally, to prove tax fraud, the government must show that the taxpayer has purposely attempted to evade or defeat a tax payment. If the offender is guilty of passive neglect, the offense is a misdemeanor. Passive neglect means simply not paying taxes, not reporting income, or not paying taxes when due. On the other hand, affirmative tax evasion, such as keeping double books, making false entries, destroying books or records, concealing assets, or covering up sources of income, constitutes a felony.

Tax cheating is a serious crime, but the great majority of major tax cheats are not prosecuted because the IRS lacks the money to enforce the law.[41] Today, the IRS has a budget that amounts to only 41 cents per tax return, 10 percent less, after adjusting for inflation, than in 1997. In addition, because most IRS resources are devoted to processing tax returns, there is less money for audits, investigations, and collections than there was a decade ago.

The problem of tax fraud is significant, and honest taxpayers are forced to bear the cost, which may run into the hundreds of billions of dollars. For example, the IRS must process each year more than 13 million cases in which financial documents from business partnerships do not match up with reports on individual tax returns. But the agency has the resources to pursue only a fifth of these cases. The losses from the failure to report income from partnerships alone could be as high as $64 billion per year. Another loophole in the tax law is the use of offshore accounts to evade taxes. Interest earned in these accounts often goes unreported as income on U.S. tax returns, costing the federal government an estimated $70 billion annually. And though the IRS has identified thousands of people currently using this type of scheme to defraud the government, budget restraints mean that it can only investigate about 20 percent of the cases.[42]

Corporate Crime

The final component of white-collar crime involves situations in which powerful institutions or their representatives willfully violate the laws that restrain these institutions from doing social harm or require them to do social good. This is also known as **corporate** or **organizational crime.**

Interest in corporate crime first emerged in the early 1900s, when a group of writers, known as the muckrakers, targeted the unscrupulous business practices of John D. Rockefeller, Andrew Carnegie, J. P. Morgan, and other corporate business leaders. In a 1907 article, sociologist E. A. Ross described the "criminaloid": a business leader who while enjoying immunity from the law victimized an unsuspecting public.[43] Edwin Sutherland focused theoretical attention on corporate crime when he began his research on the subject in the 1940s; corporate crime was probably what he had in mind when he coined the phrase white-collar crime.[44]

Corporate crimes are socially injurious acts committed by people who control companies to further their business interests. The target of their crimes can be the general public, the environment, or even their companies' workers. What makes these crimes unique is that the perpetrator is a legal fiction—a corporation—and not an individual. In reality, it is company employees or owners who commit corporate crimes and who ultimately benefit through career advancement or greater profits. For a corporation to be held criminally liable, the employee committing the crime must be acting within the scope of his employment and must have actual or apparent authority to engage in the particular act in question. **Actual authority** occurs when a corporation knowingly gives authority to an employee; **apparent authority** is satisfied if a third party, like a customer, reasonably believes the agent has the authority to perform the act in question. Courts have ruled that actual authority may occur even when the illegal behavior is not condoned by the corporation but is nonetheless within the scope of the employee's authority.[45]

Some of the acts included within corporate crime are price-fixing and illegal restraint of trade, false advertising, and the use of company practices that violate environmental protection statutes. The variety of crimes contained within this category are great, and they cause vast damage. The following subsections examine some of the most important offenses.

Illegal Restraint of Trade and Price-Fixing   A restraint of trade involves a contract or conspiracy designed to stifle competition, create a monopoly, artificially maintain prices, or otherwise interfere with free-market competition.

corporate or organizational crime
Powerful institutions or their representatives willfully violate the laws that restrain these institutions from doing social harm or require them to do social good.

actual authority
When a corporation knowingly gives authority to an employee.

apparent authority
If a third party, such as a customer, reasonably believes the agent has the authority to perform the act in question.

The control of restraint of trade violations has its legal basis in the **Sherman Antitrust Act,** which subjects to criminal or civil sanctions any person "who shall make any contract or engage in any combination or conspiracy" in restraint of interstate commerce.[46] For violations of its provisions, this federal law created criminal penalties of up to three years' imprisonment and $100,000 in fines for individuals and $10 million in fines for corporations.[47] The act outlaws conspiracies between corporations designed to control the marketplace.

In most instances, the act lets the presiding court judge whether corporations have conspired to "unreasonably restrain competition." However, these four types of market conditions are considered so inherently anticompetitive that federal courts, through the Sherman Antitrust Act, have defined them as illegal per se, without regard to the facts or circumstances of the case:

- **Division of markets:** firms divide a region into territories, and each firm agrees not to compete in the others' territories.
- **Tying arrangement:** a corporation requires customers of one of its services to use other services it offers. For example, it would be an illegal restraint of trade if a railroad required that companies doing business with it or supplying it with materials ship all goods they produce on trains owned by the rail line.[48]
- **Group boycott:** an organization or company boycotts retail stores that do not comply with its rules or desires.
- **Price-fixing:** a conspiracy to set and control the price of a necessary commodity is considered an absolute violation of the act.

Deceptive Pricing   Another type of corporate crime, deceptive pricing, occurs when contractors provide the government or other corporations with incomplete or misleading information on how much it will actually cost to fulfill the contracts they are bidding on or use mischarges once the contracts are signed.[49] For example, defense contractors have been prosecuted for charging the government for costs incurred on work they are doing for private firms or shifting the costs on fixed-price contracts to ones in which the government reimburses the contractor for all expenses ("cost-plus" contracts).

False Claims and Advertising   Executives in even the largest corporations sometimes face stockholders' expectations of ever-increasing company profits that seem to demand that sales be increased at any cost. At times executives respond to this challenge by making claims about their products that cannot be justified by actual performance. However, the line between clever, aggressive sales techniques and fraudulent claims is fine. It is traditional to show a product in its best light, even if that involves resorting to fantasy. It is not fraudulent to show a delivery service vehicle taking off into outer space or to imply that taking one sip of iced tea will make people feel they have just jumped into a swimming pool. However, it is illegal to knowingly and purposely advertise a product as possessing qualities that the manufacturer realizes it does not have.

An interesting twist on this concept, using false claims to solicit charitable contributions, was dealt with by the United States Supreme Court in the case of *Illinois Ex Rel. Madigan, Attorney General of Illinois v. Telemarketing Associates, Inc., et al.* (2003).[50] Telemarketing Associates, a for-profit fund-raising corporation, was retained by a charity to solicit donations to aid Vietnam veterans in the state of Illinois. Though donors were told that a significant portion of the money would go to the vets, Telemarketing actually retained 85 percent of all the money collected. The Illinois attorney general filed a complaint in state court, alleging that such representations were knowingly deceptive and materially false. Telemarketing said they were exercising their First Amendment free speech rights when they made their pitch for money. The Supreme Court disagreed and found that states may charge

Sherman Antitrust Act
Subjects to criminal or civil sanctions any person "who shall make any contract or engage in any combination or conspiracy" in restraint of interstate commerce.

division of markets
Firms divide a region into territories, and each firm agrees not to compete in the others' territories.

tying arrangement
A corporation requires customers of one of its services to use other services it offers.

group boycott
An organization or company boycotts retail stores that do not comply with its rules or desires.

price-fixing
A conspiracy to set and control the price of a necessary commodity.

fraud when fundraisers make false or misleading representations designed to deceive donors about how their donations will be used. The Court held that it is false and misleading for a solicitor to fool potential donors into believing that a substantial portion of their contributions would fund specific programs or services, knowing full well that was not the case.

Worker Safety/Environmental Crimes   Much attention has been paid to intentional or negligent environmental pollution caused by many large corporations. The numerous allegations in this area involve almost every aspect of U.S. business. There are many different types of environmental crimes. Some corporations have endangered the lives of their own workers by maintaining unsafe conditions in their plants and mines. It has been estimated that more than 20 million workers have been exposed to hazardous materials while on the job. Some industries have been hit particularly hard by complaints and allegations. The control of workers' safety has been the province of the Occupational Safety and Health Administration (OSHA). OSHA sets industry standards for the proper use of such chemicals as benzene, arsenic, lead, and coke. Intentional violation of OSHA standards can result in criminal penalties.

The major enforcement arm against environmental crimes is the Environmental Protection Agency, which was given full law enforcement authority in 1988. The EPA has successfully prosecuted significant violations across all major environmental statutes, including data fraud cases (private laboratories submitting false environmental data to state and federal environmental agencies); indiscriminate hazardous waste dumping that resulted in serious injuries and death; industry-wide ocean dumping by cruise ships; oil spills that caused significant damage to waterways, wetlands, and beaches; international smuggling of CFC refrigerants that damage the ozone layer and increase skin cancer risk; and illegal handling of hazardous substances such as pesticides and asbestos that exposed children, the poor, and other especially vulnerable groups to potentially serious illness.[51] Its Criminal Investigation Division (EPA CID) investigates allegations of criminal wrongdoing prohibited by various environmental statutes. Such investigations involve, but are not limited to:

- Illegal disposal of hazardous waste
- Export of hazardous waste without the permission of the receiving country
- Illegal discharge of pollutants to a water of the United States
- Removal and disposal of regulated asbestos containing materials in a manner inconsistent with the law and regulations
- Illegal importation of certain restricted or regulated chemicals into the United States
- Tampering with a drinking water supply
- Mail fraud
- Wire fraud
- Conspiracy and money laundering relating to environmental criminal activities

✔ Checkpoints

✔ Checkpoints

✔ White-collar crime has a number of different subcategories.

✔ Stings and swindles involve long-term efforts to cheat people out of their money.

✔ Chiseling involves regular cheating of an organization or its customers.

✔ People who engage in exploitation demand that victims pay for services they are entitled to by threatening consequences if they refuse. The victim here is the client.

✔ Influence peddling and bribery occur when a person in authority demands payment for a service to which the payer is clearly not entitled. The victim here is the organization.

✔ Embezzlement and employee fraud occur when a person uses a position of trust to steal from an organization.

✔ Client fraud involves theft from an organization that advances credit, covers losses, or reimburses for services.

✔ Corporate crime involves various illegal business practices such as price-fixing, restraint of trade, and false advertising.

To quiz yourself on this material, go to questions 12.1–12.8 on the Criminology: The Core 2e Web site.

Causes of White-Collar Crime

When Ivan Boesky pleaded guilty to one count of securities fraud, he agreed to pay a civil fine of $100 million, the largest at that time in SEC history. Boesky's fine was later surpassed by financier Michael Milken's fine of more than $1 billion. How, people asked, can someone with so much disposable wealth get involved in a risky scheme to produce even more? There probably are as many explanations for white-collar crime as there are white-collar crimes. Many offenders feel free to engage in business crime because they can easily rationalize its effects. Some convince themselves that their actions are not really crimes because the acts involved do not resemble street crimes. For example, a banker who uses his position of trust to lend his institution's assets to a company he secretly controls may see himself as a shrewd businessman, not as a criminal. Or a pharmacist who chisels customers on prescription drugs may rationalize her behavior by telling herself that it does not really hurt anyone. Further, some businesspeople feel justified in committing white-collar crimes because they believe government regulators do not really understand the business world or the problems of competing in the free-enterprise system. Even when caught, many white-collar criminals cannot see the error of their ways. For example, one offender who was convicted in an electrical industry price-fixing conspiracy categorically denied the illegality of his actions. "We did not fix prices," he said; "I am telling you that all we did was recover costs."[52] Some white-collar criminals believe that everyone violates business laws, so it is not so bad if they do so themselves. Rationalizing greed is a common trait of white-collar criminals.

Greedy or Needy?

When Kansas City pharmacist Robert Courtney was asked after his arrest why he substituted improper doses of drugs instead of what doctors had prescribed, he told investigators he cut the drugs' strength "out of greed."[53]

Greed is not the only motivation for white-collar crime; need also plays an important role. Executives may tamper with company books because they feel the need to keep or improve their jobs, satisfy their egos, or support their children. Blue-collar workers may pilfer because they need to keep pace with inflation or buy a new car. Kathleen Daly's analysis of convictions in seven federal district courts indicate that many white-collar crimes involve relatively trivial amounts. Women convicted of white-collar crime typically work in lower-echelon positions, and their acts seem motivated more by economic survival than by greed and power.[54]

A well-known study of embezzlers by Donald Cressey illustrates the important role need plays in white-collar crime. According to Cressey, embezzlement is caused by what he calls a "nonshareable financial problem." This condition may be the result of offenders' living beyond their means, perhaps piling up gambling debts; offenders feel they cannot let anyone know about such financial problems without ruining their reputations. Cressey claims that the door to solving personal financial problems through criminal means is opened by the rationalizations society has developed for white-collar crime: "Some of our most respectable citizens got their start in life by using other people's money temporarily"; "in the real estate business, there is nothing wrong about using deposits before the deal is closed"; "all people steal when they get in a tight spot."[55] Offenders use these and other rationalizations to resolve the conflict they experience over engaging in illegal behavior. Rationalizations allow offenders' financial needs to be met without compromising their values.

There are a number of more formal theories of white-collar crime. The next sections describe two of the more prominent theories.

Corporate Culture Theory

The corporate culture view is that some business organizations promote white-collar criminality in the same way that lower-class culture encourages the development of juvenile gangs and street crime. According to the corporate culture view, some business enterprises cause crime by placing excessive demands on employees while at the same time maintaining a business climate tolerant of employee deviance. New employees learn the attitudes and techniques needed to commit white-collar crime from their business peers.

The corporate culture theory can be used to explain the collapse of Enron. A new CEO had been brought in to revitalize the company, and he wanted to

Connections

The view that white-collar crime is a learning process seems reminiscent of Edwin Sutherland's description of how gang boys learn the techniques of drug dealing and burglary from older youths through differential association. See Chapter 7 for a description of this process.

become part of the "new economy" based on the Internet. Layers of management were wiped out, and hundreds of outsiders were recruited. Huge cash bonuses and stock options were granted to top performers. Young managers were given authority to make $5 million decisions without higher approval. It became common for executives to change jobs two or three times in an effort to maximize bonuses and pay. Seminars were conducted showing executives how to hide profits and avoid taxes.[56]

Those holding the corporate culture view point to the Enron scandal as a prime example of what happens when people work in organizations whose cultural values stress profit over fair play, in which government scrutiny is limited and regulators are viewed as the enemy, and in which senior members encourage newcomers to believe that "greed is good."

The Self-Control View

Not all criminologists agree with the corporate culture theory. Travis Hirschi and Michael Gottfredson take exception to the hypothesis that white-collar crime is a product of corporate culture.[57] If that were true, there would be much more white-collar crime than actually exists, and white-collar criminals would not be embarrassed by their misdeeds, as most seem to be. Instead, Hirschi and Gottfredson maintain that the motives that produce white-collar crimes—quick benefits with minimal effort—are the same as those that produce any other criminal behaviors.

Connections

As you may recall from Chapter 9, Hirschi and Gottfredson's general theory of crime holds that criminals lack self-control. Since Gottfredson and Hirschi believe all crime has a similar basis, the motivation and pressure to commit white-collar crime is the same as for any other form of crime.

White-collar criminals have low self-control and are inclined to follow momentary impulses without considering the long-term costs of such behavior.[58] White-collar crime is relatively rare because, as a matter of course, business executives tend to hire people with self-control, thereby limiting the number of potential white-collar criminals. Hirschi and Gottfredson have collected data showing that the demographic distribution of white-collar crime is similar to other crimes. For example, gender, race, and age ratios are the same for crimes such as embezzlement and fraud as they are for street crimes such as burglary and robbery.

White-Collar Law Enforcement Systems

On the federal level, detection of white-collar crime is primarily in the hands of administrative departments and agencies.[59] The decision to pursue criminal rather than civil violations usually is based on the seriousness of the case and the perpetrator's intent, actions to conceal the violation, and prior record. Any evidence of criminal activity is then sent to the Department of Justice or the FBI for investigation. Some other federal agencies, such as the Securities and Exchange Commission and the U.S. Postal Service, have their own investigative arms. Investigations are carried out by the various federal agencies and the FBI. If criminal prosecution is called for, the case will be handled by attorneys from the criminal, tax, antitrust, or civil rights divisions of the Justice Department. If insufficient evidence is available to warrant a criminal prosecution, the case will be handled civilly or administratively by some other federal agency. For example, the Federal Trade Commission can issue a cease and desist order in antitrust or merchandising fraud cases.

On the state and local levels, law enforcement officials have made progress in a number of areas, such as controlling consumer fraud. For example, the Environmental Crimes Strike Force in Los Angeles County, California, is considered a model for the control of illegal dumping and pollution.[60] Some of the more common environmental offenses investigated and prosecuted by the task force include:

- The illegal transportation, treatment, storage or disposal of hazardous waste
- Oil spills
- Fraudulent certification of automobile smog tests[61]

The number of state-funded technical assistance offices to help local prosecutors has increased significantly; more than 40 states offer such services.

Controlling White-Collar Crime

The prevailing wisdom is that, unlike lower-class street criminals, white-collar criminals are rarely prosecuted and, when convicted, receive relatively light sentences. In years past, it was rare for a corporate or white-collar criminal to receive a serious criminal penalty.[62] White-collar criminals are often considered nondangerous offenders because they usually are respectable, older citizens who have families to support. These "pillars of the community" are not seen in the same light as a teenager who breaks into a drugstore to steal a few dollars. Their public humiliation at being caught is usually deemed punishment enough; a prison sentence seems unnecessarily cruel.

What efforts have been made to bring violators of the public trust to justice? White-collar criminal enforcement typically involves two strategies designed to control organizational deviance: compliance and deterrence.[63]

Compliance Strategies   Compliance strategies aim for law conformity without the necessity of detecting, processing, or penalizing individual violators. At a minimum, they ask for cooperation and self-policing among the business community. Compliance systems attempt to create conformity by giving companies economic incentives to obey the law. They rely on administrative efforts to prevent unwanted conditions before they occur. Compliance systems depend on the threat of economic sanctions or civil penalties to control corporate violators.

One method of compliance is to set up administrative agencies to oversee business activity. For example, the Securities and Exchange Commission regulates Wall Street activities, and the Food and Drug Administration regulates drugs, cosmetics, medical devices, meats, and other foods. The legislation creating these agencies usually spells out the penalties for violating regulatory standards. This approach has been used to control environmental crimes, for example, by levying heavy fines based on the quantity and quality of pollution released into the environment.[64] It is easier and less costly to be in compliance, the theory goes, than to pay costly fines and risk criminal prosecution for repeat violations. Moreover, the federal government bars people and businesses from receiving government contracts if they have engaged in repeated business law violations.

It seems that enforcing compliance with civil penalties is on the upswing. For example, the antitrust division of the U.S. Department of Justice reports that between 1997 and 2002 more than $2 billion in criminal fines were levied on business violators, an amount equal to more than all the money collected for violations of the Sherman Antitrust Act between 1890 and 1997! In the 10 years prior to 1997, the antitrust division obtained, on average, $29 million in criminal fines annually; by 2001, fines amounted to more than $280 million.[65]

In sum, compliance strategies attempt to create a marketplace incentive to obey the law; for example, the more a company pollutes, the more costly and unprofitable that pollution becomes. Compliance strategies also avoid stigmatizing and shaming businesspeople by focusing on the act, rather than the actor, in white-collar crime.[66]

Deterrence Strategies   Deterrence strategies involve detecting criminal violations, determining who is responsible, and penalizing the offenders to deter future violations. Deterrence systems are oriented toward apprehending violators and punishing them rather than creating conditions that induce conformity to the law.

Deterrence strategies should work—and they have—because white-collar crime by its nature is a rational act whose perpetrators are extremely sensitive to the threat of criminal sanctions. Perceptions of detection and punishment for white-collar crimes appear to be a powerful deterrent to future law violations. Although deterrence strategies may prove effective, federal agencies have traditionally been reluctant to throw corporate executives in jail. For example, the courts have not hesitated to enforce the Sherman Antitrust Act in civil actions, but they have limited application of the criminal sanctions. Similarly, the government seeks criminal indictments in corporate violations only in "instances of outrageous conduct of undoubted illegality," such as price-fixing.[67] The government has also been lenient with companies and individuals that cooperate voluntarily after an investigation has begun.[68]

Is the Tide Turning?

Despite years of neglect, there is growing evidence that white-collar crime deterrence strategies have become normative. Deterrence policies are now being aided because the federal government has created sentencing guidelines that control punishment for convicted criminals. Prosecutors can now control the length and type of sentence through their handling of the charging process. The guidelines also create mandatory minimum prison sentences that must be served for some crimes; judicial clemency can no longer be counted on.[69]

This new get-tough deterrence approach appears to be affecting all classes of white-collar criminals. Although many people believe affluent corporate executives usually avoid serious punishment, public displeasure with such highly publicized white-collar crimes may be producing a backlash that is resulting in more frequent use of prison sentences.[70] With the Enron scandal depriving so many people of their life savings, the general public has become educated about the damage caused by white-collar criminals and now considers white-collar crimes as more serious offenses than common-law theft offenses.[71]

Some commentators now argue that the government may actually be going overboard in its efforts to punish white-collar criminals, especially for crimes that are the result of negligent business practices rather than intentional criminal conspiracy.[72] For example, in April 2001 the United States Sentencing Commission voted to increase penalties for high-dollar fraud and theft offenses.[73] Whereas the Sherman Antitrust Act caps fines at $10 million, the United States Sentencing Guidelines penalties are far more severe. Under the Guidelines, corporations convicted of antitrust felonies may result in fines equal to the greater of twice the corporation's illegal financial gain or twice the victim's loss. Both fines and penalties have been increasing and in one case a food company executive was sentenced to serve more than five years in prison for his role in a bid-rigging scheme; it was the longest single prison sentence ever obtained for an antitrust violation.[74] Sam Waksal's seven-year sentence for insider trading may become the norm for serious business crimes. **✔ Checkpoints**

✔ Checkpoints

✔ There are numerous explanations for white-collar crime.

✔ Some offenders are motivated by greed; others offend due to personal problems.

✔ Corporate culture theory suggests that some businesses actually encourage employees to cheat or cut corners.

✔ The self-control view is that white-collar criminals are like any other law violators: impulsive people who lack self-control.

✔ White-collar enforcement may encourage self-regulation. Organizations that violate the law are given civil fines.

✔ Deterrence systems punish individuals with prison sentences.

To quiz yourself on this material, go to questions 12.9–12.11 on the Criminology: The Core 2e Web site.

Cyber Crime

Cyber crimes are a new breed of enterprise crimes that can be singular or ongoing and typically involve the use of computers to illegally take possession of information, resources, or funds. Cyber criminals use emerging forms of technology to commit criminal acts. In some instances, they involve the use of technology to commit common-law crimes such as fraud and theft. In other instances, the technology itself is the target, for example, illegal copying and sale of computer software.

Cyber crimes cost consumers billions of dollars each year and will most likely increase dramatically in the years to come. Let's look at some emerging forms of this new version of criminal enterprise crime.

FIND IT ON INFOTRAC
College Edition

Use "cyber crime" in a key word search to learn more about this newer form of enterprise crime.

Internet Crimes

Millions of people use the Internet daily in the United States and Canada alone, and the number entering cyber space is growing rapidly. Criminal entrepreneurs view this vast pool as a target for cyber crimes. For example, consumer surveys have shown that each year more than $700 million in online sales were lost to fraud, or about 1.14 percent of total annual online sales of $61.8 billion.[75] The Internet Fraud Complaint Center (IFCC) reports that the total dollar loss from all referred fraud cases was $54 million in 2002, up from $17 million in 2001.[76] More than 75 percent of employers now claim to detect employee abuse of Internet access privileges (for example, downloading pirated software or inappropriate use of email systems). More than 33 percent find that employees engage in unauthorized access or misuse on their Web sites, and 25 percent of those acknowledging attacks reported from 2 to 5 incidents; 39 percent reported 10 or more incidents.[77]

It is likely that these losses are only the tip of the iceberg: With the continuing growth of e-commerce, it is now estimated that Internet credit card fraud alone will increase worldwide from $1.6 billion in 2000 to $15.5 billion by 2005.[78] Nor is Internet fraud unique to the United States. The European Commission reported that in 2000 payment-card fraud in the European Union rose by 50 percent to $553 million in fraudulent transactions; the International Chamber of Commerce reported that nearly 66 percent of all cases it handled in 2000 involved online fraud.[79] Here are some other forms Internet fraud takes.[80]

Internet Securities Fraud Some criminals make use of Internet chat rooms in their fraudulent schemes. In one famous case, 15-year-old Jonathan Lebed was charged with securities fraud by the SEC after he repeatedly bought low-cost, thinly traded stocks and then spread hundreds of false and misleading messages concerning them—generally baseless price predictions. When their values were artificially inflated, Lebed sold the securities at an inflated price. Lebed agreed to findings of fraud but later questioned whether he had done anything wrong.[81]

Though he might not agree, young Lebed's actions are considered Internet fraud because they involve using the Internet to intentionally manipulate the securities marketplace for profit. There are actually three major types of Internet securities fraud today:

Market manipulation: Stock market manipulation occurs when an individual tries to control the price of a stock by interfering with the natural forces of supply and demand either by "pump and dump" or "cyber smear." In a pump and dump scheme, erroneous and deceptive information is posted online to get unsuspecting investors to become interested in a stock while those spreading the information sell previously purchased stock at an inflated price. The cyber smear is a reverse pump and dump: negative information is spread online about a stock, driving down its price and enabling people to buy it at an artificially low price before rebuttals by the company's officers reinflate the price.[82]

Fraudulent offerings of securities: Some cyber criminals create Web sites specifically designed to fraudulently sell securities. To make the offerings look more attractive than they are, assets may be inflated, expected returns overstated, or risks understated.

Illegal touting: This crime occurs when individuals make securities recommendations and fail to disclose that they are being paid to

■ Internet crime has become a multibillion dollar problem. This image shows famed "hacker" Kevin Mitnick, who has turned into an author of books on computer crime. Though terms of his probation prevent him from using computers for security transactions, he was allowed to use one to type his book *The Art of Deception.*

© 2003 AP/Wide World Photos

Connections

The use of the Internet in the sex industry is discussed more fully in Chapter 13. Needless to say, being able to access pornographic material over the Internet has helped expand the sale of sexually related material. However, the federal government has recently cracked down on this type of offense, resulting in hundreds of arrests.

EXHIBIT   **12.1 Common Internet Fraud Schemes**

Online Auction/Retail The fraud attributable to the misrepresentation of a product advertised for sale through an Internet auction site or the nondelivery of merchandise or goods purchased through an Internet auction site.

Business Opportunity/"Work at Home" The offering of a phony job opportunity, often with associated charges such as "processing" or "application" fees. Perpetrators frequently forge the name of a computer service or Internet service provider.

Financial Institution Fraud Misrepresentation of the truth or concealment of a material fact by a person to induce a business, organization, or other entity that manages money, credit, or capital to perform a fraudulent activity.

Credit Card Theft/Fraud The unauthorized use of a credit/debt card or credit/debt card number to fraudulently obtain money or property. Credit/debt card numbers can be stolen from unsecured Web sites.

Ponzi/Pyramid Schemes An investment scheme in which investors are promised abnormally high profits on their investments. No investment is actually made. Early investors are paid returns with the investment money received from the later investors. The system usually collapses, and the later investors do not receive dividends and lose their initial investment. For example, the Tri-West Investment Company solicited investments in "prime bank notes" from 1999 to 2001. Visitors to their Web site were promised an annualized rate of return of 120 percent plus return of their principal at the end of a year, as well as substantial referral fees of 15 percent of all referred investments. The Web site, which contained alleged testimonials describing instant wealth from early investors, also told investors that their investments were "guaranteed." Investors contributed $60 million in funds to Tri-West, and some "dividends" were paid. However, no money was actually invested, the dividends were paid from new investments, and most of the cash was siphoned off by the schemers.

Nondelivery of Goods/Services The nondelivery of goods or services that were purchased or contracted remotely through the Internet, independent of an Internet auction.

SOURCES: Department of Justice Press Release, "Alleged Leaders of $60 Million Internet Scam Indicted on Fraud and Money Laundering Charges Massive Internet Investment Fraud Case Involves 15,000 Investors from 60 Countries," January 3, 2003; FBI, *Common Internet Fraud Schemes* (Washington, D.C.: Author, 2001).

FIND IT ON INFOTRAC
College Edition

Internet information theft and access violations threaten companies worldwide. To read how business leaders are fighting back, read this article:

Luis Ramiro Hernandez, "Integrated Risk Management in the Internet Age," *Risk Management* June 2000 v47 i6 p29

disseminate their favorable opinions. Section 17(b) of the Securities Act of 1933 requires that paid touters disclose the nature, source, and amount of their compensation. If those who tout stocks fail to disclose their relationship with the company, information misleads investors into believing that the speaker is objective and credible rather than bought and paid for.

Identity Theft Identity theft occurs when a person uses the Internet to steal someone's identity or to impersonate someone to open a new credit card account or conduct some other financial transaction. Identity information can be gathered easily from confederates because people routinely share their name, address, phone numbers, personal information, credit card account numbers, and Social Security number (SSN) when making purchases over the Internet or in stores. An identity thief appropriates personal information to commit fraud or theft. For example, they can fill out change of address cards at the post office and obtain people's credit card bills and bank statements. They may then call the credit card issuer and, pretending to be the victim, ask for a change in address on the account. They can then charge numerous items over the Internet and have the merchandise sent to the new address. It may take months for the victim to realize the fraud because they are not getting bills from the credit card company. Some other common Internet crimes are listed in Exhibit 12.1.

Computer Crimes

Computer crime has also reached epidemic proportions. The 2002 Computer Crime and Security Survey found a significant amount of criminal activity directed at computer services. Of the large companies and government agencies they surveyed,

- 85 percent detected computer viruses.
- 90 percent of respondents detected computer security breaches within the last 12 months.
- 80 percent acknowledged financial losses due to computer breaches.
- 44 percent were willing and/or able to quantify their financial losses; these 223 respondents reported $455,848,000 in financial losses.

As in previous years, the most serious financial losses occurred through theft of proprietary information (26 respondents reported $170,827,000) and financial fraud (25 respondents reported $115,753,000).

Types of Computer Crime Computer crimes generally fall into one of five categories:[83]

1. Theft of services, in which the criminal uses the computer for unauthorized purposes or an unauthorized user penetrates the computer system. Included within this category is the theft of processing time and services not entitled to an employee.
2. Use of data in a computer system for personal gain.
3. Unauthorized use of computers employed for various types of financial processing to obtain assets.
4. Theft of property by computer for personal use or conversion to profit. For example, using a computer to illegally copy and sell software. This is a significant problem; it is estimated that $11 billion or more is lost each year to the unauthorized use of software.[84]
5. Making the computer itself the subject of a crime—for example, when a virus is placed in it to destroy data.

Although most of these types of crimes involve using computers for personal gain, the last category typically involves activities that are motivated more by malice than by profit. When computers themselves are the target, criminals are typically motivated by revenge for some perceived wrong; a need to exhibit their technical prowess and superiority; a wish to highlight the vulnerability of computer security systems; a desire to spy on other people's private financial and personal information ("computer voyeurism"); or a philosophy of open access to all systems and programs.[85]

Committing Computer Crimes Several common techniques are used by computer criminals. In fact, computer theft has become so common that experts have created their own jargon to describe theft styles and methods:

The Trojan horse: One computer is used to reprogram another for illicit purposes. In one incident, two high school–age computer users reprogrammed the computer at DePaul University, preventing that institution from using its own processing facilities. The youths were convicted of a misdemeanor.

The salami slice: An employee sets up a dummy account in the company's computerized records. A small amount—even a few pennies—is subtracted from customers' accounts and added to the account of the thief. Even if they detect the loss, customers don't complain because a few cents is an insignificant amount to them. The pennies picked up here and there eventually amount to thousands of dollars in losses.

Super-zapping: Most computer programs used in business have built-in antitheft safeguards. However, employees can use a repair or maintenance program to supersede the antitheft program. Some tinkering with the program is required, but the "super-zapper" is soon able to order the system to issue checks to his or her private account.

The logic bomb: A program is secretly attached to the company's computer system. The new program monitors the company's work and waits for a sign of error to appear, some illogic that was designed for the computer to follow. Illogic causes the logic bomb to kick into action and exploit the weakness. The way the thief exploits the situation depends on his or her original intent—theft of money or defense secrets, sabotage, or the like.

Impersonation: An unauthorized person uses the identity of an authorized computer user to access the computer system.

Data leakage: A person illegally obtains data from a computer system by leaking it out in small amounts.

Computer virus: Installing a virus in a program that disrupts or destroys existing programs and networks, causing them to perform the task for which the virus was designed.[86] The virus is then spread from one computer to another when a user sends out an infected file by email, through a network, or by sending a disk. (Worms are similar to viruses, but they use computer networks or the Internet to self-replicate and "send themselves" to other users, generally via email, without the aid of the operator.)

Controlling Cyber Crime

✔ Checkpoints

✔ Cyber crimes use technology to commit crime.

✔ Billions are lost each year on Internet fraud schemes.

✔ Computer criminals use a variety of techniques to steal data, damage equipment, or steal funds from business enterprises.

✔ There has been an ongoing effort to control cyber crimes.

To quiz yourself on this material, go to question 12.12 on the Criminology: The Core 2e Web site.

The proliferation of cyber crimes has created the need for new laws and enforcement processes specifically aimed at controlling its new and emerging formulations. Because technology evolves so rapidly, enforcement presents challenges that are particularly vexing. Numerous organizations provide training and support for law enforcement agents. In addition, new federal and state laws have been aimed at particular areas of cyber crimes. For example, Congress has treated computer-related crimes as distinct federal offenses since the passage of the Counterfeit Access Device and Computer Fraud and Abuse Law in 1984.[87] The 1984 act protected classified United States defense and foreign relations information, financial institution and consumer reporting agency files, and access to computers operated for the government. The act was supplemented in 1996 by the National Information Infrastructure Protection Act (NIIPA), which significantly broadens the scope of the law.[88] Among its other provisions, NIPPA makes it a crime to access computer files without authorization or in excess of authorization, and subsequently to transmit classified government information. Other methods of controlling cyber crimes are discussed in the Policy and Practice feature. These measures may now be paying off. Many business enterprises are installing antivirus software and other protections to prevent outsiders from tampering with their computer systems. In addition, anti-intrusion detection technology has been vastly improved. There are indications that these measures are having a significant impact and that the financial losses due to cyber crime have somewhat abated.[89] ✔ Checkpoints

Organized Crime

The third branch of enterprise criminality involves organized crime—ongoing criminal enterprise groups whose ultimate purpose is personal economic gain through illegitimate means. Here a structured enterprise system is set up to continually supply consumers with merchandise and services banned by criminal law but for which a ready market exists: prostitution, pornography, gambling, and narcotics. The system may resemble a legitimate business run by an ambitious chief executive officer, his or her assistants, staff attorneys, and accountants, with thorough, efficient accounts receivable and complaint departments.[90]

Because of its secrecy, power, and fabulous wealth, a great mystique has grown up about organized crime. Its legendary leaders—Al Capone, Meyer

POLICY AND PRACTICE IN CRIMINOLOGY

Controlling Cyber Crime

What is now being done to control the newest forms of cyber crime that use technology and the Internet for criminal pursuits?

Controlling Internet Crime

1. Because cyber crime is so new, existing laws are sometimes inadequate to address the problem. Therefore, new legislation must be drafted to protect the public from this new breed of cyber criminals. For example, before October 30, 1998, when the Identity Theft and Assumption Act of 1998 became law, there was no federal statute that made identity theft a crime. Today, federal prosecutors are making substantial use of the statute and have prosecuted more than 90 cases of identity theft.

2. The federal government is now operating a number of organizations that are coordinating efforts to control cyber fraud. One approach is to create working groups that coordinate the activities of numerous agencies involved in investigating cyber crime. For example, the Interagency Telemarketing and Internet Fraud Working Group brings together representatives of numerous United States attorneys' offices, the FBI, the Secret Service, the Postal Inspection Service, the Federal Trade Commission, the Securities and Exchange Commission, and other law enforcement and regulatory agencies to share information about trends and patterns in Internet fraud schemes.

3. Specialized enforcement agencies are being created. The Internet Fraud Complaint Center, based in Fairmont, West Virginia, is run by the FBI and the National White-Collar Crime Center. It brings together about 1,000 state and local law enforcement officials and regulators who analyze fraud-related complaints for patterns, develop additional information on particular cases, and send investigative packages to law enforcement authorities in the jurisdiction that appears likely to have the greatest investigative interest in the matter. In the first year of its operation, the center received 36,000 complaints, the majority involving auction fraud. Law enforcement has made remarkable strides in dealing with identity theft as a crime problem over the last two years.

4. Some private security companies now offer services to counter Internet criminals. For example, the Equifax Corporation has launched a credit-monitoring service that alerts clients by email whenever an inquiry is made of their credit file or a new account is opened under their name. Other firms already sell credit-monitoring services, and several of them offer daily alerts.

Controlling Computer Crime

In the wake of the 9/11 attacks, the NIPPA has been amended by sections of the USA Patriot Act to make it easier to enforce attacks by terrorists and other organized enemies against the nation's computer systems. Subsection 1030(a)(5)(A)(i) of the act criminalizes knowingly causing the transmission of a program, code, or command, and as a result, intentionally causing damage to a protected computer. This section applies regardless of whether the user had authorization to access the protected computer; company insiders and authorized users can be culpable for intentional damage to a protected computer. The act also prohibits intentional access without authorization that results in damage, but does not require intent to damage; the attacker can merely be negligent or reckless.

In addition to these main acts, computer-related crimes can also be charged under at least 40 different federal statutes. These include the Copyright Act and Digital Millennium Copyright Act, the National Stolen Property Act, the mail and wire fraud statutes, the Electronic Communications Privacy Act, the Communications Decency Act of 1996, the Child Online Protection Act, the Child Pornography Prevention Act of 1996, and the Internet False Identification Prevention Act of 2000.

Critical Thinking

1. How far should the government go in protecting consumers from Internet crime? Might aggressive efforts inhibit the development of this new technology?

2. Considering the complexity of this task, should a new law enforcement agency be developed devoted solely to investigating cyber crimes? This agency would recruit people who are computer/Internet literate but who may not be able to fire guns.

InfoTrac College Edition Research

Use "Internet crime" as a key word to learn more about this contemporary crime problem.

SOURCES: Heather Jacobson and Rebecca Green, "Computer crime," *American Criminal Law Review,* 39 (2002): 273–326; Identity Theft and Assumption Act of 1998 (18 U.S.C. 1028(a)(7)); Bruce Swartz, Deputy Assistant General, Criminal Division, Justice Department Internet Fraud Testimony Before the House Energy and Commerce Committee, May 23, 2001; Comprehensive Crime Control Act of 1984, PL 98–473, 2101–03, 98 Stat. 1837, 2190 (1984), adding 18 USC 1030 (1984); Counterfeit Active Device and Computer Fraud and Abuse Act Amended by PL 99–474, 100 Stat. 1213 (1986) codified at 18 U.S.C. 1030 (Supp. V 1987); Computer Abuse Amendments Act 18 U.S.C. section 1030 (1994); Copyright Infringement Act 17 U.S.C. section 506(a) 1994; Electronic Communications Privacy Act of 198618 U.S.C. 2510–2520 (1988 and Supp. II 1990).

Lansky, Lucky Luciano—have been the subjects of books and films. The famous *Godfather* films popularized and humanized organized crime figures; the media often glamorize organized crime figures.[91] Watching the exploits of Tony Soprano and his family life has become a national craze.

Most citizens believe organized criminals are capable of taking over legitimate business enterprises if given the opportunity. Almost everyone is famil-

■ Former Latin Kings gang member "Rey" testifies about organized crime before the New Jersey State Commission of Investigation during a hearing at the Statehouse in Trenton, New Jersey, April 29, 2003. The Commission opened a two-day inquiry on organized crime by examining the emergence of nontraditional gangs into criminal areas once controlled by the Mafia.

iar with such terms as *mob, underworld, Mafia, wise guys, syndicate,* or *La Cosa Nostra,* which refer to organized crime. Although most of us have neither met nor seen members of organized crime families, we feel sure that they exist, and we fear them. This section briefly defines organized crime, reviews its history, and discusses its economic effect and control.

Characteristics of Organized Crime

A precise description of the characteristics of organized crime is difficult to formulate, but here are some of its general traits:[92]

■ Organized crime is a conspiratorial activity involving the coordination of numerous persons in the planning and execution of illegal acts or in the pursuit of a legitimate objective by unlawful means (for example, threatening a legitimate business to get a stake in it). Organized crime involves continuous commitment by primary members, although individuals with specialized skills may be brought in as needed. Organized crime is usually structured along hierarchical lines—a chieftain supported by close advisers, lower subordinates, and so on.

■ Organized crime has economic gain as its primary goal, although power and status may also be motivating factors. Economic gain is achieved through maintenance of a near-monopoly on illegal goods and services, including drugs, gambling, pornography, and prostitution.

■ Organized crime activities are not limited to providing illicit services. They include such sophisticated activities as laundering illegal money through legitimate businesses, land fraud, and computer crimes.

■ Organized crime employs predatory tactics, such as intimidation, violence, and corruption. It appeals to greed to accomplish its objectives and preserve its gains.

■ By experience, custom, and practice, organized crime's conspiratorial groups are usually very quick and effective in controlling and disciplining their members, associates, and victims. The individuals involved know that any deviation from the rules of the organization will evoke a prompt response from the other participants. This response may range from a reduction in rank and responsibility to a death sentence.

■ Organized crime is not synonymous with the Mafia, the most experienced, most diversified, and possibly best-disciplined of these groups. The Mafia is actually a common stereotype of organized crime. Although several families in the organization called the Mafia are important components of organized crime activities, they do not hold a monopoly on underworld activities.

■ Organized crime does not include terrorists dedicated to political change. Although violent acts are a major tactic of organized crime, the use of violence does not mean that a group is part of a confederacy of organized criminals.

Activities of Organized Crime

What are the main activities of organized crime? The traditional sources of income are derived from providing illicit materials and using force to enter into and maximize profits in legitimate businesses.[93] Most organized crime income comes from narcotics distribution, loan sharking (lending money at illegal rates), and prostitution. However, additional billions come from gambling, theft rings, pornography, and other illegal enterprises. Organized criminals have infiltrated labor unions and taken control of their pension funds and dues.[94] Hijacking shipments and cargo theft are other **sources of income**. Underworld figures fence high-value items and maintain **international sales territories**. In recent years they have branched into **computer crime** and other white-collar activities. Organized crime figures **have also kept up** with the information age by using computers and the **Internet to sell illegal material** such as pornography.

In recent years, organized crime figures have entered the **high-tech world of Internet crime** and stock market manipulation. The FBI notes **that organized crime groups** are now targeting "small-cap" or "micro-cap" **stocks, over-the-counter stocks**, and other types of thinly traded stocks that **can be easily manipulated** and sold to elderly or inexperienced investors. The **conspirators use offshore bank accounts** to conceal their participation in the **fraud scheme and to launder** the illegal proceeds to avoid paying income tax.[95]

The Concept of Organized Crime

The term *organized crime* conjures up images of strong men in **dark suits, machine gun–toting bodyguards**, rituals of allegiance to secret **organizations, professional** "gangland" killings, and meetings of "family" **leaders who chart the course** of crime much as the board members at General **Motors decide on the country's** transportation needs. These images have become **part of what criminologists** refer to as the **alien conspiracy theory** concept **of organized crime**. This is the belief, adhered to by the federal government **and many respected criminologists**, that organized crime is a direct offshoot **of a criminal society**—the **Mafia**—that first originated in Italy and Sicily and **now controls racketeering** in major U.S. cities. A major premise of the alien **conspiracy theory** is that the Mafia is centrally coordinated by a national **committee that settles disputes**, dictates policy, and assigns territory.[96] Not all **criminologists believe** in this narrow concept of organized crime, and many **view the alien conspiracy theory** as a figment of the media's imagination.[97] **Their view depicts organized crime** as a group of ethnically diverse gangs or **groups who compete for profit** in the sale of illegal goods and services or **who use force and violence** to extort money from legitimate enterprises. These **groups are not bound** by a central national organization but act independently **on their own turf**. We will now examine these perspectives in some detail.

Alien Conspiracy Theory According to the alien conspiracy **theory, organized crime** is made up of a national syndicate of 25 or so Italian-**dominated crime families** that call themselves **La Cosa Nostra**. The major **families have a total membership** of about 1,700 "made men," who have been **inducted into organized crime** families, and another 17,000 "associates," who **are criminally involved** with syndicate members. The families control crime in **distinct geographic areas**. New York City alone, the most important organized **crime area**, contains five families—the Gambino, Columbo (formerly **Profaci**), Lucchese, Bonnano, and Genovese families—named after their founding "**godfathers**"; in contrast, Chicago contains a single mob organization **called the** "outfit," which also influences racketeering in such cities as **Milwaukee, Kansas City**, and Phoenix.[98] The families are believed to be ruled by a "**commission**" made up of the heads of the five New York families **and bosses from Detroit, Buffalo, Chicago**, and Philadelphia, which settles personal **problems and jurisdictional** conflicts and enforces rules that allow members **to gain huge profits** through the manufacture and sale of illegal goods **and services**.

In sum, the alien conspiracy theory sees organized crime **as being run by** an ordered group of ethnocentric (primarily of Italian origin) **criminal syndicates**, maintaining unified leadership and shared values. These **syndicates communicate** closely with other groups and obey the decisions **of a national commission** charged with settling disputes and creating crime **policy**.

Contemporary Organized Crime Groups Even such devoted alien conspiracy advocates now view organized crime as a loose confederation of ethnic

alien conspiracy theory
The belief, adhered to by the federal government and many respected criminologists, that organized crime is a direct offshoot of a criminal society.

Mafia
A criminal society that first originated in Italy and Sicily and now controls racketeering in major U.S. cities.

La Cosa Nostra
A national syndicate of 25 or so Italian-dominated crime families.

FIND IT ON INFOTRAC
College Edition

To find out more, use "Russian organized crime" as a subject guide.
Also, read this article:

Sherry Ricchiardi, "The Best Investigative
Reporter You've Never Heard Of," *American
Journalism Review* Jan 2000 v22 i1 p44

and regional crime groups, bound together by a commonality of economic and
political objectives.[99] Some of these groups are located in fixed geographical
areas. Chicano crime families are found in areas with significant Hispanic
populations, such as California and Arizona. White-ethnic crime organizations are found across the nation. Some Italian and Cuban groups operate in-
ternationally. Some have preserved their past identity, whereas others are
constantly changing organizations.

One important recent change in organized crime is the interweaving of
ethnic groups into the traditional structure. African American, Hispanic, and
Asian racketeers now compete with the more traditional groups, overseeing
the distribution of drugs, prostitution, and gambling in a symbiotic relationship with old-line racketeers.

Eastern European Crime Groups   Eastern Europe has been the scene of
a massive buildup in organized crime since the fall of the Soviet Union. Trading in illegal arms, narcotics, pornography, and prostitution, they operate a
multibillion-dollar transnational crime cartel. For example, organized groups
prey on women in the poorest areas of Europe—Romania, the Ukraine,
Bosnia—and sell them into virtual sexual slavery. Many of these women are
transported as prostitutes around the world, some finding themselves in the
United States. In September of 2002, an intensive European enforcement operation conducted with U.S. assistance to eliminate some of the major players
in the international sex trade resulted in the arrest of 293 traffickers. It is estimated that 700,000 women are transported, mostly involuntarily, over international borders each year for the sex trade. One reason for the difficulty in
creating effective enforcement is the complicity of local authorities with criminal organizations. For example, during the 2002 raids, the United Nations
Mission in Sarajevo dismissed 11 Bosnian police officers, including members
of the antitrafficking squad, after they were apprehended visiting brothels
and abusing prostitutes.[100]

Since 1970, Russian and other Eastern European groups have been operating on U.S. soil. Some groups are formed by immigrants from former satel-
lites of the Soviet Union. For example, in 1998 the FBI established the
Yugoslavian/Albanian/Croatian/Serbian (YACS) Crime Group initiative as a
response to the increasing threat of criminal activity by people originating
from these areas. YACS gangs focus on highly organized and specialized
thefts from ATM machines in the New York City area.[101]

Some experts believe Russian crime families, thanks to their control of
gasoline terminals and distributorships in the New York metropolitan area,
evade as much as $5 billion a year in state and federal taxes. Some of that
money then goes to pay off their allies, the Italian Mafia.

In addition, as many as 2,500 Russian immigrants are believed to be involved in criminal activity, primarily in Russian enclaves in New York City.
Beyond extortion from immigrants, Russian organized crime groups have co-
operated with Mafia families in narcotics trafficking, fencing stolen property,
money laundering, and other traditional organized crime schemes.[102] Some of
these gangs have engaged in wide-ranging multinational conspiracies. The
Race, Culture, Gender, and Criminology feature provides more information
about Russian organized crime.

Controlling Organized Crime

George Vold has argued that the development of organized crime parallels
early capitalist enterprises. Organized crime employs ruthless monopolistic
tactics to maximize profits; it is also secretive, protective of its operations,
and defensive against any outside intrusion.[103] Consequently, controlling its
activities is extremely difficult.

Federal and state governments actually did little to combat organized
crime until fairly recently. One of the first measures aimed directly at organized crime was the Interstate and Foreign Travel or Transportation in Aid

RACE, CULTURE, GENDER, AND CRIMINOLOGY

Russian Organized Crime

In the decade since the collapse of the Soviet Union, criminal organizations in Russia and other former Soviet republics such as Ukraine have engaged in a variety of crimes; illegal drugs, arms trafficking, stolen automobiles, trafficking in women and children, and money laundering are among the most prevalent. No area of the world seems immune to this menace, especially not the United States. America is the land of opportunity for unloading criminal goods and laundering dirty money.

Unlike Colombian, Italian, Mexican, or other well-known forms of organized crime, Soviet organized crime is not primarily based on ethnic or family structures. Instead, Russian organized crime is based on economic necessity, which was nurtured by the oppressive Soviet regime. A professional criminal class developed in Soviet prisons during the Stalinist period that began in 1924—the era of the gulag. These criminals adopted behaviors, rules, values, and sanctions that bound them together in what was called the thieves' world, led by the elite *vory v zakone,* criminals who lived according to the "thieves' law." This thieves' world, and particularly the *vory,* created and maintained the bonds and climate of trust necessary for carrying out organized crime.

Here are some specific characteristics of Russian organized crime in the post-Soviet era:

- Russian criminals make extensive use of the state governmental apparatus to protect and promote their criminal activities. For example, most businesses in Russia—legal, quasi-legal, and illegal—must operate with the protection of a *krysha* (roof). Protection is often provided by police or security officials employed outside their "official" capacities for this purpose. In other cases, officials are "silent partners" in criminal enterprises that they, in turn, protect.

- The criminalization of the privatization process has resulted in the massive use of state funds for criminal gain. Valuable properties are purchased through insider deals for

much less than their true value and then resold for lucrative profits.

- Criminals have been able to directly influence the state's domestic and foreign policy to promote the interests of organized crime, either by attaining public office themselves or by buying public officials.

Beyond these particular features, organized crime in Russia shares other characteristics that are common to organized crime elsewhere in the world:

- Systematic use of violence, including both the threat and the use of force

- Hierarchical structure

- Limited or exclusive membership

- Specialization in types of crime and a division of labor

- Military-style discipline, with strict rules and regulations for the organization as a whole

- Possession of high-tech equipment, including military weapons, threats, blackmail, and violence used to penetrate business management and assume control of commercial enterprises, or in some instances, to found their own enterprises with money from their criminal activities

As a result of these activities:

- Russia has high rates of homicide that are now more than 20 times those in Western Europe and approximately 3 times the rates recorded in the United States. The rates more closely resemble those of a country in civil war or in conflict than those of a country 10 years into a transition.

- Corruption and organized crime are globalized. Russian organized crime is active in Europe, Africa, Asia, and North and South America.

- Massive money laundering is now common, allowing Russian and foreign organized crime to flourish. In some cases, it is tied to terrorist funding.

The organized crime threat to Russia's national security is now becoming

a global threat. They are operating both on their own and in cooperation with foreign groups. The latter cooperation often comes in the form of joint money laundering ventures. Russian criminals have become involved in killings for hire in Central and Western Europe, Israel, Canada, and the United States. However, in the United States, with the exception of extortion and money laundering, Russians have had little or no involvement in some of the more traditional types of organized crime, such as drug trafficking, gambling, and loan sharking. Instead, these criminal groups are extensively engaged in a broad array of frauds and scams, including health care fraud, insurance scams, stock frauds, antiquities swindles, forgery, and fuel tax evasion schemes. Recently, for example, Russians have become the main purveyors of credit card fraud in the United States. Legitimate businesses such as the movie business and textile industry have become targets of criminals from the former Soviet Union, and they are often used for money laundering.

Critical Thinking

The influence of new immigrant groups in organized crimes seems to suggest that illegal enterprise is a common practice among "new Americans." Do you believe some aspect of American culture causes immigrants to choose a criminal lifestyle? Or does our open culture encourage criminal activities that may have been incubated in their native lands?

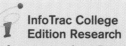

InfoTrac College Edition Research

To learn more about Russian organized crime, read: Scott O'Neal, "Russian Organized Crime," *FBI Law Enforcement Bulletin* May 2000 v69 i5 p1

SOURCES: Louise I. Shelley, "Crime and corruption: enduring problems of post-Soviet development," *Demokratizatsiya,* 11 (2003): 110–114; James O. Finckenauer and Yuri A. Voronin, *The threat of Russian organized crime* (Washington, D.C.: National Institute of Justice, 2001).

✔ Checkpoints

✔ Organized crime is an ongoing criminal enterprise that employees illegal methods for personal gain.

✔ In some instances, organized crime involves the sale and distribution of illegal merchandise, such as drugs and pornography, while in other cases it uses illegitimate means to market legal services, such as lending money (loan sharking) or selling stocks (market manipulation).

✔ Traditional, organized crime families were Italian-dominated and called *La Cosa Nostra*.

✔ Contemporary gangs are multicultural and multinational.

✔ Russian gangs are becoming more common.

✔ The government has used the Racketeer Influenced and Corrupt Organization Act (RICO) to go after gangs.

To quiz yourself on this material, go to questions 12.13–12.15 on the Criminology: The Core 2e Web site.

Racketeer Influenced and Corrupt Organization Act (RICO)
An act that created new categories of offenses in racketeering activity, which it defined as involvement in two or more acts prohibited by 24 existing federal and 8 state statutes.

enterprise theory of investigation (ETI)
Model that focuses on criminal enterprise and investigation attacks on the structure of the criminal enterprise rather than on criminal acts viewed as isolated incidents.

of Racketeering Enterprises Act (Travel Act).[104] The Travel Act prohibits travel in interstate commerce or use of interstate facilities with the intent to promote, manage, establish, carry on, or facilitate an unlawful activity; it also prohibits the actual or attempted engagement in these activities. In 1970 Congress passed the Organized Crime Control Act. Title IX of the act, probably its most effective measure, has been called the **Racketeer Influenced and Corrupt Organization Act (RICO)**.[105]

RICO did not create new categories of crimes but rather new categories of offenses in racketeering activity, which it defined as involvement in two or more acts prohibited by 24 existing federal and 8 state statutes. The offenses listed in RICO include state-defined crimes, such as murder, kidnapping, gambling, arson, robbery, bribery, extortion, and narcotic violations; and federally defined crimes, such as bribery, counterfeiting, transmission of gambling information, prostitution, and mail fraud. RICO is designed to limit patterns of organized criminal activity by prohibiting involvement in acts intended to

- Derive income from racketeering or the unlawful collection of debts and use or invest such income.
- Acquire through racketeering an interest in or control over any enterprise engaged in interstate or foreign commerce.
- Conduct business through a pattern of racketeering.
- Conspire to use racketeering as a means of making income, collecting loans, or conducting business.

An individual convicted under RICO is subject to 20 years in prison and a $25,000 fine. Additionally, the accused must forfeit to the U.S. government any interest in a business in violation of RICO. These penalties are much more potent than simple conviction and imprisonment.

RICO's success has shaped the way the FBI attacks organized crime groups. They now use the **enterprise theory of investigation (ETI)** model as their standard investigative tool. Rather than investigate crimes after they are committed, under the ETI model the focus is on criminal enterprise and investigation attacks on the structure of the criminal enterprise rather than on criminal acts viewed as isolated incidents.[106] For example, a drug trafficking organization must get involved in such processes as transportation and distribution of narcotics, finance such as money laundering, and communication with clients and dealers. The ETI identifies and then targets each of these areas simultaneously, focusing on the subsystems that are considered the most vulnerable. **✔ Checkpoints**

Summary

- Enterprise crimes involve criminal acts that twist the legal rules of commercial enterprise for criminal purposes.

- Enterprise crimes can be divided into three independent yet overlapping categories: white-collar crime, cyber crimes, and organized crime (see Concept Summary 12.1).

- White-collar crime involves illegal activities of people and institutions whose acknowledged purpose is profit through legitimate business transactions.

- Cyber crime involves people using the instruments of modern technology for criminal purpose.

- Organized crime involves illegal activities of people and organizations whose acknowledged purpose is profit through illegitimate business enterprise.

CONCEPT SUMMARY **12.1 Criminal Enterprise Crimes**

CRIME	GOALS	OVERLAP	EXAMPLES
White-collar crime	Using illegal means to make profits in the marketplace	Businesspeople use organized criminals to bust up unions. Organized criminals launder money in commercial banks.	Chiseling Bribery Insider trading Price-fixing
Cyber crime	Using technology for criminal gain; using illegal means to misappropriate technology	Cyber criminals drive up the price of securities to benefit businesspeople.	Identity theft Computer crimes Internet fraud
Organized crime	Using illegal means to market illegal goods; using illegal means to market legal goods	Organized criminals launder money for cyber criminals.	Loan-sharking Gambling Extortion

■ White-collar crimes include stings and swindles involving the use of deception to bilk people out of their money and chiseling customers, businesses, or the government. Surprisingly, many professionals engage in chiseling offenses. Other white-collar criminals use their positions in business and the marketplace to commit economic crimes, including exploitation of position in a company or the government to secure illegal payments, embezzlement and employee pilferage and fraud, client fraud, and influence peddling and bribery. Further, corporate officers sometimes violate the law to improve the position and profitability of their businesses. Their crimes include price-fixing, false advertising, and environmental offenses.

■ So far, little has been done to combat white-collar crimes. Most offenders do not view themselves as criminals and therefore do not seem to be deterred by criminal statutes. Although thousands of white-collar criminals are prosecuted each year, their numbers are insignificant compared with the magnitude of the problem.

■ The government has used various law enforcement strategies to combat white-collar crime. Some involve deterrence, which uses punishment to frighten potential abusers. Others involve economic or compliance strategies, which create economic incentives to obey the law.

■ Cyber criminals use emerging forms of technology to commit criminal acts. In some instances, they involve the use of technology to commit common-law crimes such as fraud and theft. In other instances, the technology itself is the target, for example, illegal copying and sale of computer software. Law enforcement officials fear that the incidence of cyber crime will explode in the future.

■ Organized crime supplies alcohol, gambling, drugs, prostitutes, and pornography to the public. It is immune from prosecution because of public apathy and because of its own strong political connections.

■ Organized criminals used to be white ethnics—Jews, Italians, and Irish—but today African Americans, Hispanics, and other groups have become involved in organized crime activities. The old-line "families" are now more likely to use their criminal wealth and power to buy into legitimate businesses.

■ There is debate over the control of organized crime. Some experts believe a national crime cartel controls all activities. Others view organized crime as a group of disorganized, competing gangs dedicated to extortion or to providing illegal goods and services. Efforts to control organized crime have been stepped up. The federal government has used antiracketeering statutes to arrest syndicate leaders. But as long as huge profits can be made, illegal enterprises will continue to flourish.

Thinking Like a Criminologist

People who commit computer crime are found in every segment of society. They range in age from 10 to 60, and their skill level runs from novice to professional. They are otherwise average people, not supercriminals possessing unique abilities and talents. Any person of any age with even a little skill is a potential computer criminal.

Most studies indicate that employees represent the greatest threat; almost 90 percent of computer crimes against businesses are inside jobs. Ironically, as advances continue in remote data processing, the threat from external sources will probably increase. With the networking of systems and the adoption of more user-friendly software, the sociological profile of the computer offender may change. For example, computer criminals may soon be members of organized crime syndicates. They will use computer systems to monitor law enforcement activities. To become a made man in the twenty-first-century organized crime family, the recruit will have to develop knowledge of the equipment used for audio surveillance of law enforcement communications: computers with sound card or microphone, modems, and software programs for the remote operation of the systems.

Which theories of criminal behavior best explain the actions of computer criminals, and which ones fail to account for computer crime?

Go to the Criminology: The Core 2e Web site to review the content of this chapter.

Doing Research on the Web

For an up-to-date list of URLs, go to

http://www.cj.wadsworth.com/siegel_crimcore2e

To help you in your research, check out these sites:

http://www.cybercrime.gov/

http://www.crime-research.org/eng/

Pro/Con discussions and Viewpoint Essays on some of the topics in this chapter may be found at the Opposing Viewpoints Resource Center:

http://www.gale.com/OpposingViewpoints

Key Terms

enterprise crimes 289
white-collar crime 289
cyber crime 289
organized crime 289
sting or swindle 291
churning 292
front running 292
bucketing 292
insider trading 292

influence peddling 293
pilferage 294
corporate or organizational crime 297
actual authority 297
apparent authority 297
Sherman Antitrust Act 298
division of markets 298
tying arrangement 298
group boycott 298

price-fixing 298
alien conspiracy theory 310
Mafia 310
La Cosa Nostra 310
Racketeer Influenced and Corrupt Organization Act (RICO) 313
enterprise theory of investigation (ETI) 313

Critical Thinking Questions

1. How would you punish a corporate executive whose product killed people if the executive had no knowledge that the product was potentially lethal? What if the executive did know?

2. Is organized crime inevitable as long as immigrant groups seek to become part of the "American Dream"?

3. Does the media glamorize organized crime? Does it paint an inaccurate picture of noble crime lords fighting to protect their families?

4. Apply traditional theories of criminal behavior to white-collar and organized crime. Which one seems to best predict why someone would engage in these behaviors?

CHAPTER 13

Public Order Crimes

Chapter Objectives

1. Be familiar with the association between law and morality.
2. Know what is meant by the terms *moral crusade* and *moral entrepreneur.*
3. Be able to discuss the legal problems faced by gay people.
4. Know the constitutional cases that define gay rights.
5. Be able to discuss what is meant by "obscenity."
6. Know the various techniques being used to control pornography.
7. Be able to discuss the various types of prostitution.
8. Know what is meant by the term *paraphilias.*
9. Discuss the history of drug abuse.
10. Be able to discuss the cause of substance abuse.
11. Identify the various drug control strategies.

HE ISSUE OF GAY MARRIAGE HAS PROVEN QUITE CONTROVERSIAL. ON JANUARY 16, 1997, PRESIDENT CLINTON SIGNED the federal Defense of Marriage Act, which both defined marriage as involving a man and a woman and also allowed states to not recognize same-sex marriages performed in other states. Today more than 37 states have Defense of Marriage Acts that define marriage as a union exclusively between one man and one

CNN. View the CNN video clip of this story and answer related critical thinking questions on your Criminology: The Core 2e CD.

woman. However, gay marriage received a boost on June 10, 2003, when an appeals court in the Canadian province of Ontario struck down a ban on same-sex marriage. It said that Canada's marriage laws were unconstitutional and redefined them as "the voluntary union for life of two persons to the exclusion of others." Because there is no mention of gender, the decision allows any two persons who are committed to each other to marry, regardless of their sex. Then on November 18, 2003, the highest court of Massachusetts ruled that same-sex couples are legally entitled to wed under the state constitution.[1] The Supreme Judicial Court said the state of Massachusetts may not "deny the protections, benefits and obligations conferred by civil marriage to two individuals of the same sex who wish to marry." At the time of this writing, it is still uncertain how this decision will influence national policy and practices. The debate rages on: Is it fair to prevent one group of loyal tax-paying citizens from engaging in a behavior that is allowed to others who do not share that status or orientation? Are there objective standards of morality, or should society respect people's differences? How far should the law go in curbing human behaviors that do not cause social harm?

ocieties have long banned or limited behaviors that are believed to run contrary to social norms, customs, and values. These behaviors are often referred to as **public order crimes** or victimless crimes, although the latter term can be misleading.[2] Public order crimes involve acts that interfere with the operations of society and the ability of people to function efficiently. Put another way, whereas such common-law crimes as rape or robbery are considered inherently wrong and damaging, other behaviors are outlawed because they conflict with social policy, prevailing moral rules, and current public opinion.

Statutes designed to uphold public order usually prohibit the manufacture and distribution of morally questionable goods and services such as erotic material, commercial sex, and mood-altering drugs. They may also ban acts that a few people holding political power consider morally tinged, such as homosexual contact. Statutes

public order crime
Behavior that is outlawed because it threatens the general well-being of society and challenges its accepted moral principles.

317

like these are controversial in part because millions of otherwise law-abiding citizens often engage in these outlawed activities and consequently become criminals. These statutes are also controversial because they selectively prohibit desired goods, services, and behaviors; in other words, they outlaw sin and vice.

This chapter covers these public order crimes. It first briefly discusses the relationship between law and morality. Next the chapter addresses public order crimes of a sexual nature: pornography, prostitution, deviant sex, and homosexual acts. The chapter concludes by focusing on the abuse of drugs and alcohol.

Law and Morality

Legislation of moral issues has continually frustrated lawmakers. There is little debate that the purpose of criminal law is to protect society and reduce social harm. When a store is robbed or a child assaulted, it is relatively easy to see and condemn the harm done the victim. It is, however, more difficult to sympathize with or even identify the victims of immoral acts, such as pornography or prostitution, where the parties involved may be willing participants. If there is no victim, can there be a crime? Should acts be made illegal merely because they violate prevailing moral standards? If so, who defines morality?

To answer these questions, we might first consider whether there is actually a victim in so-called **victimless crimes.** Some participants may have been coerced into their acts; if so, then they are victims. Opponents of pornography, such as Andrea Dworkin, charge that women involved in adult films, far from being highly paid stars, are "dehumanized—turned into objects and commodities."[3] Although taking drugs may be a matter of personal choice, it too has serious consequences. One study of 171 crack cocaine-using women found that since initiating crack use, 62 percent of the women reported suffering a physical attack and 32 percent suffered rape; more than half were forced to seek medical care for their injuries.[4]

Some scholars argue that pornography, prostitution, and drug use erode the moral fabric of society and therefore should be prohibited and punished. They are crimes, according to the great legal scholar Morris Cohen, because "it is one of the functions of the criminal law to give expression to the collective feeling of revulsion toward certain acts, even when they are not very dangerous."[5]

According to this view, so-called victimless crimes are prohibited because one of the functions of criminal law is to express a shared sense of public morality.[6] However, basing criminal definitions on moral beliefs is often an impossible task. Who defines morality? Are we not punishing differences rather than social harm? As U.S. Supreme Court Justice William O. Douglas so succinctly put it, "What may be trash to me may be prized by others."[7] Would not any attempt to control or limit "objectionable" material eventually lead to the suppression of free speech and political dissent? Is this not a veiled form of censorship? Not so, according to social commentator Irving Kristol:

> If we start censoring pornography and obscenity, shall we not inevitably end up censoring political opinion? A lot of people seem to think this would be the case—which only shows the power of doctrinaire thinking over reality. We had censorship of pornography and obscenity for 150 years, until almost yesterday, and I am not aware that freedom of opinion in this country was in any way diminished as a consequence of this fact.[8]

Criminal or Immoral?

victimless crime
Public order crime that violates the moral order but has no specific victim other than society as a whole.

Acts that most of us deem highly immoral are not criminal. There is no law against lust, gluttony, avarice, spite, anger, or envy, although they are characterized as the "seven deadly sins." Nor is it a crime in most jurisdictions to ignore the pleas of a drowning person, even though such callous behavior is surely immoral.

Some acts that seem both well-intentioned and moral are nonetheless considered criminal. It is a crime (euthanasia) to kill a loved one who is suffering from an incurable disease to spare him or her further pain. Stealing a rich person's money to feed a poor family is considered larceny. Marrying more than one woman is considered a crime (bigamy), even though multiple marriage may conform to religious beliefs.[9] As legal experts Wayne LaFave and Austin Scott Jr. state, "A good motive will not normally prevent what is otherwise criminal from being a crime."[10]

Generally, immoral acts can be distinguished from crimes on the basis of the social harm they cause: Acts that harm the public are usually outlawed. Yet this perspective does not always hold sway. Some acts that cause enormous amounts of social harm are perfectly legal. All of us are aware of the illness and death associated with the consumption of tobacco and alcohol, but they remain legal to produce and sell. Manufacturers continue to sell sports cars and motorcycles that can accelerate to more than 100 mph, although the legal speed limit is usually 65. More people die each year from alcohol-, tobacco-, and auto-related deaths than from all illegal drugs combined. Should drugs be legalized and fast cars outlawed?

And sometimes even "social harm" is hard to define. For example, the recent scandals involving the sexual activities of some Roman Catholic priests have been shocking. Most Americans would agree that sexuality and children never mix. It is not surprising then that Judith Levine caused a commotion in 2002 with her book *Harmful to Minors: The Perils of Protecting Children from Sex*.[11] In this controversial book, Levine took American culture to task for attempting to control, monitor, and suppress children's knowledge of sex and their sexual expression. Levine argued that children were more likely to be harmed by efforts to shield and protect them then they are in danger from information about sexuality. She hinted that in some instances kids were not damaged by relations with older people and that some sexual relations between adults and minors could have a positive outcome. As a result, *Harmful to Minors* was rejected by many publishing houses and when finally published by the University of Minnesota press became the target of a campaign by social conservatives to have it taken out of publication. Is Levine correct? Has American society become overly protective of adolescents and in denial that they may have sexual feelings?

Moral Crusaders

moral entrepreneur
A person who creates moral rules, which thus reflect the values of those in power rather than any objective, universal standards of right and wrong.

Public order crimes often trace their origin to moral crusaders who seek to shape the law toward their own way of thinking; Howard Becker calls them **moral entrepreneurs.** These rule creators, argues Becker, operate with an absolute certainty that their way is right and that any means are justified to get their way: "the crusader is fervent and righteous, often self-righteous."[12] Today's moral crusaders take on such issues as prayer in school, the right to legal abortions, and the distribution of sexually explicit books and magazines.

Moral crusades are often directed against people clearly defined as evil by one segment of the population, even though they may be admired by others. For example, antismut campaigns may attempt to ban the books of a popular author from the school library or prevent a controversial figure from speaking at the local college. One way for moral crusaders to accomplish their goal is to prove to all who will listen that some unseen or hidden trait makes their target truly evil and unworthy of a public audience—for example, the Bible condemns their behavior. This polarization of good and evil creates a climate where those categorized as "good" are deified while the "bad" are demonized and become objects suitable for control.

Sometimes moral crusaders justify their actions by claiming that the very structure of our institutions and beliefs is in danger because of immorality. For example, Andrea Friedman's analysis of antiobscenity campaigns during the Cold War era (post–World War II) found that the politics of the times led to an image of aggressive, even violent males being used in comic books and pornography. Moral crusaders argued that this depiction threatened family values, which led them to advocate a ban on violent comics and porn magazines.[13] The public order crimes discussed in this chapter are divided into two broad areas. The first relates to what conventional society considers deviant sexual practices: homosexual acts, paraphilias, prostitution, and pornography. The second area concerns the use of substances that have been outlawed or controlled because of the alleged harm they cause: drugs and alcohol. ✔ Checkpoints

Homosexuality

It may be surprising that a section on homosexuality is still included in a criminology text, but even in this new millennium, homosexuals not only face archaic legal restrictions but are targeted for so many violent hate crimes that a specific term, **gay bashing,** has been coined to describe violent acts directed at people because of their sexual orientation.

Homosexuality (the word derives from the Greek *homos,* meaning "same") refers to erotic interest in members of one's own sex, one "who is motivated in adult life by a definite preferential erotic attraction to members of the same sex and who usually (but not necessarily) engages in overt sexual relations with them."[14]

Attitudes Toward Homosexuality

Homosexual behavior has existed in most societies. Records of it can be found in prehistoric art and hieroglyphics.[15] Nonetheless, throughout much of Western history, homosexuals have been subject to discrimination, sanction, and violence. The Bible implies that God destroyed the ancient cities of Sodom and Gomorrah because of their residents' deviant behavior, presumably homosexuality; Sodom is the source of the term **sodomy** (deviant intercourse). The Bible expressly forbids homosexuality—in Leviticus in the Old Testament; Paul's Epistles, Romans, and Corinthians in the New Testament—and this prohibition has been the basis for repressing homosexual behavior.[16] Gays were brutalized and killed by the ancient Hebrews, a practice continued by the Christians who ruled Western Europe. Laws providing the death penalty for homosexuals existed until 1791 in France, until 1861 in England, and until 1889 in Scotland. Until the Revolution, some American colonies punished homosexuality with death. In Hitler's Germany, 50,000 homosexuals were put in concentration camps; up to 400,000 more from occupied countries were killed. In 1996, conservative Christian groups in the United States began a national campaign aimed at counteracting legislative victories won by gay rights groups in the area of discrimination and civil rights.[17] Some groups have taken out ads in local newspapers showing "former homosexuals" who "overcame" their sexual orientation through prayer and the help of Christian "ex-gay ministries." Nor is intolerance unique to the United States. In 2002 three men in Saudi Arabia were beheaded in front of the public in the southwestern mountain resort town of Abha because they had "committed acts of sodomy, married each other, seduced young men, and attacked those who rebuked them."[18] Gay bashing remains a common occurrence around the world.[19]

Today, many reasons are given for the extremely negative overreaction to homosexuals referred to as **homophobia.**[20] Some ultra-religious people believe that the Bible condemns same-sex relations and that this behavior is therefore a sin. Others are ignorant about the lifestyle of gays and fear that homosexuality is a contagious disease or that homosexuals will seduce their children.[21] Research shows that some males who express homophobic attitudes are also likely to become aroused by erotic images of homosexual behavior. Homophobia, then, may be associated with homosexual arousal that the homophobe is either unaware of or denies.[22]

✔ Checkpoints

✔ Societies can ban behaviors that lawmakers consider offensive. Critics question whether this amounts to censorship.

✔ The line between behaviors that are merely immoral and those that are criminal is often blurred.

✔ Immoral acts are considered crimes when they cause social harm.

✔ Though sometimes called victimless crimes, critics argue that there really are victims in seemingly voluntary crimes such as pornography or prostitution.

✔ People who seek to control or criminalize deviant behaviors are called moral entrepreneurs. They often go on moral crusades.

To quiz yourself on this material, go to questions 13.1–13.2 on the Criminology: The Core 2e Web site.

Connections

As you may recall from Chapter 10, gay men and women are still subject to thousands of incidents of violence and other hate crimes each year.

gay bashing
Violent hate crimes directed toward people because of their sexual orientation.

homosexuality
Erotic interest in members of one's own sex.

sodomy
Deviant forms of sexual intercourse.

homophobia
Extremely negative overreaction to homosexuals.

FIND IT ON INFOTRAC
College Edition

Like other crimes, assaults on homosexuals are adjudicated in the
criminal courts. How have victims
fared when they seek damages in
civil courts? To find out, read:

Lisa Gelhaus, "Gay-Bashing Victims
Overcome Prejudice to Win Civil
Settlements," *Trial*, February 1999 v35 i2
p14(1)

Legal Liabilities

Homosexuality, considered a legal and moral crime throughout most of Western history, is no longer a crime in the United States. In the case of *Robinson v. California,* the U.S. Supreme Court determined that people could not be criminally prosecuted because of their status (such as drug addict or homosexual).[23] Despite this protection, most states and the federal government criminalize the lifestyle and activities of homosexuals. For example, aside from Vermont (which has civil unions), no state or locality allows any form of same-sex marriage, and homosexuals cannot obtain a marriage license to legitimize their relationship. In 1996, Congress passed the Defense of Marriage Act, which declared that states are not obligated to recognize same-sex marriages performed in other states. Individual states have adopted similar provisions in their legal codes. For example, on May 27, 2003, Texas created its own Defense of Marriage Act prohibiting same-sex unions.[24]

The U.S. military bans openly gay people from serving but has compromised with a "don't ask, don't tell" policy. The military does not ask about sexual orientation, and gay people can serve as long as their sexuality remains secret. In 1996, the U.S. Supreme Court tacitly approved this policy by declining to hear a case brought by Navy Lieutenant Paul Thomasson, who was discharged in 1994 for openly declaring himself homosexual.[25] In January 1998, a federal judge barred the U.S. Navy from dismissing Chief Petty Officer Timothy McVeigh, who had posted sexually oriented material on the Internet. The judge ruled that the Navy had violated McVeigh's privacy when it asked America Online to divulge his identity; in so doing, the Navy violated the spirit of the "don't ask, don't tell" policy.[26] Gays have also lost custody of their children because of their sexual orientation, although more courts are now refusing to consider a gay lifestyle alone as evidence of parental unfitness.[27] And in an important 2000 case, *Dale v. Boy Scouts of America,* the Supreme Court ruled that the Boy Scouts are entitled to exclude openly gay scouts and scout leaders.[28] In their decision, the Court recognized that employing an openly gay scout leader would significantly burden the organization's right to oppose or disfavor homosexual conduct.

Is the Tide Turning?

Although the unenlightened may still hold negative attitudes toward gays and gays still face legal burdens, there seems to be a long overdue increase in social tolerance. Surveys shows that a significant majority of Americans now support gays in the military and equality in employment, housing, inheritance rights, and social security benefits for same-sex couples.[29] Changing public attitudes are reflected in legal change. In 1998, more than 20 years after one of the country's first gay rights ordinances was repealed in Miami, Florida, the Miami–Dade County commission voted again to ban discrimination based on sexual orientation, a position adopted in more than 136 other cities nationwide.[30]

Two recent Supreme Court cases illustrate changing attitudes toward the gay lifestyle. In a 1996 Colorado case, *Romer v. Evans,* the U.S. Supreme Court ruled 6 to 3 that Colorado's Amendment 2, which prohibited state and local governments from protecting the civil rights of gay people, was unconstitutional. The Court ruled that the state is not entitled to distinguish a group of people for the single purpose of treating them differently from everyone else. In essence, the *Romer* decision said that gay people cannot be stripped of legal protection and made "strangers to the law."[31]

Then in 2003 the Court rendered an historic decision in *Lawrence v. Texas* that made it impermissible for states to criminalize oral and anal sex and all other forms of intercourse that are not heterosexual under statutes prohibiting sodomy, deviant sexuality, or buggery.[32] In so doing it overruled its 1986 decision in the *Bowers v. Hardwick* case, which had upheld a Georgia statute making it a crime to engage in consensual sodomy, even within one's own home.[33] The *Lawrence* case involved two gay men who had been arrested in 1998 for having sex in the privacy of their Houston home. In overturning their convictions, the Court said:

> Although the laws involved...here...do not more than prohibit a particular sexual act, their penalties and purposes have more far-reaching consequences, touching upon the most private human conduct, sexual behavior, and in the most private of places, the home. They seek to control a personal relationship that, whether or not entitled to formal recognition in the law, is within the liberty of persons to choose without being punished as criminals. The liberty protected by the Constitution allows homosexual persons the right to choose to enter upon relationships in the confines of their homes and their own private lives and still retain their dignity as free persons.

As a result of the decision, all sodomy laws in the United States are now unconstitutional and unenforceable. The *Romer* and *Lawrence* decisions have heralded a new era of legal and civil rights for homosexual men and women. The same-sex marriage issue is the last major legal hurdle facing gay men and women.

Paraphilias

During the past few years, the Catholic Church has been rocked by allegations that numerous priests had been involved in sexually molesting children. Nowhere did the scandal take on greater proportion than in Boston where Cardinal Bernard Law was forced to step down as leader of the diocese. Among the most notorious offenders was Father James Porter, accused of molesting at least 125 children of both sexes over a 30-year period reaching back to the early 1960s. Porter was eventually sentenced to an 18- to 20-year prison term.

Porter's behavior is an extreme example of sexual abnormality referred to as **paraphilia,** from the Greek *para,* "to the side of," and *philos,* "loving." Paraphilias are bizarre or abnormal sexual practices involving recurrent sexual urges focused on (1) nonhuman objects (such as underwear, shoes, or leather), (2) humiliation or the experience of receiving or giving pain (as in sadomasochism or bondage), or (3) children or others who cannot grant consent.[34] Paraphilias have existed and been recorded for thousands of years. Buddhist texts more than 2,000 years old contain references to sexually deviant behaviors among monastic communities, including sexual activity with animals and sexual interest in corpses. Richard von Krafft-Ebing's *Psychopathia Sexualis,* first published in 1887, was the first text to discuss such paraphilias as sadism, bestiality, and incest.[35]

Some paraphilias, such as wearing clothes normally worn by the opposite sex (transvestite fetishism), can be engaged in by adults in the privacy of their homes and do not involve a third party; these relatively harmless escapades are outside the law's reach. Others, however, risk social harm and are subject to criminal penalties. This group of outlawed sexual behavior includes the following acts:

- *Frotteurism*: rubbing against or touching a nonconsenting person in a crowd, elevator, or other public area.
- *Voyeurism*: obtaining sexual pleasure from spying on a stranger while he or she disrobes or engages in sexual behavior with another.
- *Exhibitionism*: deriving sexual pleasure from exposing the genitals to surprise or shock a stranger.
- *Sadomasochism*: deriving pleasure from receiving pain or inflicting pain on another.
- *Pedophilia*: attaining sexual pleasure through sexual activity with prepubescent children.

paraphilia
Bizarre or abnormal sexual practices that may involve nonhuman objects, humiliation, or children.

■ Some of the most notorious cases of pedophilia concern Catholic priests who abused young children in their parishes. Here Carol McCormick, of Chelford, Massachusetts, looks on as Fred Paine, of Warwick, Rhode Island, a victim of Rev. James Porter, pauses during a July 26, 2003, panel discussion on their experiences with settling civil suits against the Church, in Wellesley, Massachusetts.

Research indicates that more than 20 percent of males report sexual attraction to at least one child, although the rate of sexual fantasies and the potential for sexual contacts are much lower.[36]

Prostitution

Prostitution has been known for thousands of years. The term derives from the Latin *prostituere,* which means "to cause to stand in front of." The prostitute is viewed as publicly offering his or her body for sale. The earliest record of prostitution appears in ancient Mesopotamia, where priests engaged in sex to promote fertility in the community. All women were required to do temple duty, and passing strangers were expected to make donations to the temple after enjoying their services.[37]

Modern commercial sex appears to have its roots in ancient Greece, where Solon established licensed brothels in 500 B.C. The earnings of Greek prostitutes helped pay for the temple of Aphrodite. Famous men openly went to prostitutes to enjoy intellectual, aesthetic, and sexual stimulation; prostitutes, however, were prevented from marrying.[38]

Today **prostitution** can be defined as granting nonmarital sexual access, established by mutual agreement of the prostitutes, their clients, and their employers, for remuneration. This definition is sexually neutral because prostitutes can be straight or gay and male or female. A recent analysis has amplified the definition of prostitution by describing the conditions usually present in a commercial sexual transaction:

■ *Activity that has sexual significance for the customer.* This includes the entire range of sexual behavior, from sexual intercourse to exhibitionism, sadomasochism, oral sex, and so on.

■ *Economic transaction.* Something of economic value, not necessarily money, is exchanged for the activity.

■ *Emotional indifference.* The sexual exchange is simply for economic consideration. Although the participants may know one another, their interaction has nothing to do with affection for one another.[39]

prostitution
The granting of nonmarital sexual access for remuneration.

Incidence of Prostitution

It is difficult to assess the number of prostitutes operating in the United States. Fifty years ago, about two-thirds of non–college educated men and one-quarter of college educated men had visited a prostitute.[40] It is likely that the number of men who hire prostitutes has declined sharply since then.

How can these changes be accounted for? Changing sexual mores, brought about by the so-called sexual revolution, have liberalized sexuality. Men are less likely to use prostitutes because legitimate alternatives for sexuality are more open to them. In addition, the prevalence of sexually transmitted diseases has caused many men to avoid visiting prostitutes for fear of irreversible health hazards.[41] Why do men still employ prostitutes? When interviewing a prostitute's clients, sociologist Monica Prasad found that while their decision to employ a prostitute was shaped by sexuality, it was also influenced by pressure from friends to try something different and exciting, the wish for a sexual exchange free from obligations, and curiosity about the world of prostitution. Prasad found that most customers who became "regulars" began to view prostitution as a service occupation not different from other service occupations.[42]

Despite such changes, the Uniform Crime Report (UCR) indicates that about 80,000 prostitution arrests are made annually, with the gender ratio being about 2:1 female to male. The number of prostitution arrests has been trending downward for some time; for example, about 100,000 arrests were made in 1995. It is possible that (a) fewer people are seeking the services of prostitutes, (b) police are reluctant to make arrests in prostitution cases, or (c) more sophisticated prostitutes using the Internet or other forms of technology to "make dates" are better able to avoid detection by police.

International Sex Trade

Although prostitution arrests are down in the United States, there is a troubling overseas trade in prostitution in which men from wealthy countries frequent semiregulated sex areas in needy nation's such as Thailand to procure young girls forced or sold into prostitution, a phenomenon known as "sex tourism." There has also been a soaring demand for pornography, strip clubs, lap dancing, escorts, telephone sex, and "sex tours" in developing countries.[43]

In addition, every year, hundreds of thousands of women and children—primarily from Southeast Asia and Eastern Europe—are lured by the promise of good jobs and then end up forced into brothels or as circuit travelers in labor camps. It is believed that traffickers import up to 50,000 women and children every year into the United States despite legal prohibitions (in addition to prostitution, some are brought in to work in sweat shops).[44] The international trade in prostitution is the subject of the Race, Culture, Gender, and Criminology feature.

Types of Prostitutes

Several different types of prostitutes operate in the United States.

Streetwalkers   Prostitutes who work the streets in plain sight of police, citizens, and customers are referred to as hustlers, hookers, or streetwalkers. Although glamorized by the Julia Roberts character in the film *Pretty Woman* (who winds up with multimillionaire Richard Gere), streetwalkers are considered the least attractive, lowest paid, most vulnerable men and women in the profession. Streetwalkers wear bright clothing, makeup, and jewelry to attract customers; they take their customers to hotels. The term *hooker,* however, is not derived from the ability of streetwalkers to hook clients on their charms. It actually stems from the popular name given women who followed Union General "Fighting Joe" Hooker's army during the Civil War.[45] Studies

RACE, CULTURE, GENDER, AND CRIMINOLOGY

The Natasha Trade: International Trafficking in Prostitution

Trafficking in women and girls for the purpose of sexual exploitation is market-valued at US$7 billion annually. Trafficking may be the result of force, coercion, manipulation, deception, abuse of authority, initial consent, family pressure, past and present family and community violence, economic deprivation, or other conditions of inequality for women and children. Women are trafficked to, from, and through every region in the world. Exact numbers are unknown, but international agencies and governmental bodies estimate that each year more than 1 million women and girls are trafficked for sexual exploitation in sex industries.

The U.S. State Department estimates that 50,000 to 100,000 women and children are trafficked into the United States each year for labor or sexual exploitation. The moneymakers are transnational networks of traffickers and pimps who prey on women seeking employment and opportunities. These illegal activities and related crimes not only harm the women involved but also undermine the social, political, and economic fabric of the nations where they occur.

Countries with large sex industries create the demand for women; countries where traffickers easily recruit women provide the supply. For decades, the primary sending countries were in Asia, but the collapse of the Soviet Union opened up a pool of millions of women from which traffickers can recruit. Former Soviet republics such as Belarus, Latvia, Moldova, Russia, and Ukraine have become major suppliers of women to sex industries all over the world.

In the sex industry today, the most popular and valuable women are from Russia and Ukraine. Authorities in the Ukraine estimate that more than 100,000 women were trafficked during the previous decade. Popular destination countries include Canada, the Czech Republic, Germany, Greece, Hungary, the Netherlands, Turkey, the

United Arab Emirates, the United States, and Yugoslavia. Large numbers of Ukrainian women are trafficked into Korea to be used as prostitutes near military bases.

Migration from the former Soviet republics has aided trafficking. Members of organized crime rings establish contacts with collaborators in overseas communities and work within migrating populations to build criminal networks. Increased migration also serves as a cover for traffickers transporting women. Computer technologies also have enabled the increased volume and complexity of international financial transactions, increasing opportunities for transnational crime and decreasing the probability of detection.

Recruiting Women

Recruiters, traffickers, and pimps have developed common operating methods. One strategy is advertisements in newspapers offering lucrative job opportunities in foreign countries for low-skilled jobs, such as waitresses and nannies. Another method of recruitment is through "marriage agencies," sometimes called mail-order bride agencies or international introduction services. But the most common way for women to be recruited is through a friend or acquaintance who gains the woman's confidence. "Second wave" recruiting occurs when a trafficked woman returns home to draft other women. Once a woman has been trafficked and trapped in the sex industry, she has few options. One of the few means of escaping the brutality of being forced to have sex with multiple men each day is to move from victim to perpetrator.

Once they reach the destination country, travel documents are confiscated, and they are subjected to violence and threats to harm their family members. They are told they owe thousands in travel costs and must pay them off through prostitution. The women get to keep little, if any, of the money. Women must repay their pur-

chase price and travel and other expenses before they are allowed to leave. They can expect little help from law enforcement authorities who are either ambivalent or working with the traffickers.

Combating Trafficking

Recently, the United States made stopping the trafficking of women a top priority. In 1998, a Memorandum on Steps to Combat Violence against Women and the Trafficking of Women and Girls was issued that directed the Secretary of State, the Attorney General, and the President's Interagency Council on Women to expand their work against violence against women to include work against the trafficking of women.

In the former Soviet Union, prevention education projects are aimed at potential victims of trafficking, and nongovernmental organizations have established hotlines for victims or women seeking information about the risks of accepting job offers abroad.

Critical Thinking

1. If put in charge, what would you do to slow or end the "Natasha Trade"? Before, you answer, remember the saying that prostitution is the "oldest profession," which implies that curbing it may prove quite difficult.

2. Should men who hire prostitutes be punished very severely to deter them from getting involved in the exploitation of these vulnerable young women?

InfoTrac College Edition Research

Brenda Platt, "Commercial Sexual Exploitation of Children: A Global Problem Requiring Global Action," *Sexual Health Exchange,* Summer 2002 v2002 i3 p10(2

SOURCE: Donna Hughes, "The 'Natasha' Trade: Transnational Sex Trafficking," *National Institute of Justice Journal* (January 2001).

indicate they are most likely to be impoverished members of ethnic or racial minorities. Many are young runaways who gravitate to major cities to find a new, exciting life and escape from sexual and physical abuse at home.[46] Of all prostitutes, streetwalkers have the highest incidence of drug abuse.[47]

Bar Girls   B-girls, as they are also called, spend their time in bars, drinking and waiting to be picked up by customers. Although alcoholism may be a problem, B-girls usually work out an arrangement with the bartender so they are served diluted drinks or water colored with dye or tea, for which the customer is charged an exorbitant price. In some bars, the B-girl is given a credit for each drink she gets the customer to buy. It is common to find B-girls in towns with military bases and large transient populations.[48]

Brothel Prostitutes   Also called bordellos, cathouses, sporting houses, and houses of ill repute, brothels flourished in the nineteenth and early twentieth centuries. They were large establishments, usually run by madams, that housed several prostitutes. A madam is a woman who employs prostitutes, supervises their behavior, and receives a fee for her services; her cut is usually 40 to 60 percent of the prostitutes' earnings. The madam's role may include recruiting women into prostitution and socializing them in the trade.[49]

Brothels declined in importance following World War II. The closing of the last brothel in Texas is chronicled in the play and movie *The Best Little Whorehouse in Texas*. Today the best-known brothels exist in Nevada, where prostitution is legal outside large population centers.

Call Girls   The aristocrats of prostitution are call girls. They charge customers up to $1,500 per night and may net more than $100,000 per year. Some gain clients through employment in escort services; others develop independent customer lists. Many call girls come from middle-class backgrounds and service upper-class customers. Attempting to dispel the notion that their service is simply sex for money, they concentrate on making their clients feel important and attractive. Working exclusively via telephone "dates," call girls get their clients by word of mouth or by making arrangements with bellhops, cab drivers, and so on. They either entertain clients in their own apartments or visit clients' hotels and apartments. Upon retiring, a call girl can sell her date book listing client names and sexual preferences for thousands of dollars. Despite the lucrative nature of their business, call girls suffer considerable risk by being alone and unprotected with strangers. They often request the business cards of their clients to make sure they are dealing with "upstanding citizens."

Escort Services/Call Houses   Some escort services are fronts for prostitution rings. Both male and female sex workers can be sent out after the client calls an ad in the yellow pages. How common are adult sexual services? In 2003 Las Vegas, Nevada, alone had 561 listings for adult services in the yellow pages; New York City had 135.

A relatively new phenomenon, the call house combines elements of the brothel and call girl rings. A madam receives a call from a prospective customer, and if she finds the client acceptable, she arranges a meeting between the caller and a prostitute in her service. The madam maintains a list of prostitutes who are on call rather than living together in a house. The call house insulates the madam from arrest because she never meets the client or receives direct payment.[50]

Circuit Travelers   Prostitutes known as circuit travelers move around in groups of two or three to lumber, labor, and agricultural camps. They ask the foreman for permission to ply their trade, service the whole crew in an evening, and then move on. Some circuit travelers seek clients at truck stops and rest areas.

Sometimes young girls are forced to become circuit travelers by unscrupulous pimps who force them to work for months as prostitutes in agricultural migrant camps. The young women are lured from developing countries such as Mexico with offers of jobs in landscaping, health care, housecleaning, and restaurants. When they arrive in the United States they are told that they owe their captors thousands of dollars and must work as prostitutes to pay it off. The young women are raped and beaten if they complain or try to escape.[51]

Cyber Prostitutes The technological revolution has begun to alter the world of prostitution. "Cyber prostitutes" set up personal Web sites or put listings on Web boards such as "Adult Friendfinder" that carry personals. They may use loaded phrases such as "looking for generous older man" in their self-descriptions. When contacted, they ask to exchange emails, chat online, or make voice calls with prospective clients. They may even exchange pictures. This allows them to select who they want to be with and avoid clients who may be threatening or dangerous. Some cyber prostitution rings offer customers the opportunity to choose women from their Internet page and then have them flown in from around the country.

Becoming a Prostitute

Why does someone turn to prostitution? Both male and female prostitutes often come from troubled homes marked by extreme conflict and hostility and from poor urban areas or rural communities. Divorce, separation, or death splits the family; most prostitutes grew up in homes without fathers.[52] Many prostitutes were initiated into sex by family members at ages as young as 10 to 12 years; they have long histories of sexual exploitation and abuse.[53] The early experiences with sex help teach them that their bodies have value and that sexual encounters can be used to obtain affection, power, or money. In a detailed study of child sexual exploitation in North America, Richard J. Estes and Neil Alan Weiner found that the problem of child sexual abuse is much more widespread than previously had been believed or documented.[54] Their research shows that each year in the United States 25,000 children are subjected to some form of sexual exploitation, which often begins with sexual assaults by relatives and acquaintances, such as a teacher, a coach, or a neighbor.

Lower-class girls who get into "the life" report conflict with school authorities, poor grades, and an overly regimented school experience.[55] Drug abuse, including heroin and cocaine addiction, is often a factor in the prostitute's life.[56] However, there is no actual evidence that people become prostitutes because of psychological problems or personality disturbances. Money, drugs, and survival seem to be greater motivations.

Controlling Prostitution

In the late nineteenth and early twentieth century efforts were made to regulate prostitution in the United States through medical supervision and licensing and zoning brothels in districts outside residential neighborhoods.[57] After World War I, prostitution became associated with disease and the desire to protect young servicemen from harm helped to end almost all experiments with legalization in the United States.[58] Some reformers attempted to paint pimps and procurers as immigrants who used their foreign ways to snare unsuspecting American girls into prostitution. Such fears prompted passage of the federal Mann Act (1925) prohibited bringing women into the country or transporting them across state lines for the purposes of prostitution. Often called the "white slave act," it carried a $5,000 fine, five years in prison, or both.[59]

Today, prostitution is considered a misdemeanor, punishable by a fine or a short jail sentence. In practice, most law enforcement is uneven and aims at

■ While some people believe that prostitution should be legalized, others view prostitution as a serious social problem that can cause significant social harm to prostitutes, their clients, and society in general. It is not surprising, then, that most police departments continue to enforce laws prohibiting prostitution. Here, Officer Laura Nopurski poses as a prostitute during a sting operation in Duluth, Minnesota.

confining illegal activities to particular areas in the city.[60] Prostitution is illegal in all states except Nevada (except in the counties in which Las Vegas and Reno are located) where it is a highly regulated business enterprise.

Legalize Prostitution?

Feminists have staked out conflicting views of prostitution. One position is that women must become emancipated from male oppression and reach sexual equality. The sexual equality view considers the prostitute a victim of male dominance. In patriarchal societies, male power is predicated on female subjugation, and prostitution is a clear example of this gender exploitation.[61] In contrast, for some feminists, the fight for equality depends on controlling all attempts by men or women to impose their will on women. The free choice view is that prostitution, if freely chosen, expresses women's equality and is not a symptom of subjugation.[62]

Advocates of both positions argue that the penalties for prostitution should be reduced (decriminalized), but neither side advocates outright legalization. Decriminalization would relieve already desperate women of the additional burden of severe legal punishment. However, legalization might be coupled with regulation by male-dominated justice agencies. For example, required medical examinations would mean increased male control over women's bodies.

Should prostitution be legalized in the United States? In a recent book *Brothel* by Alexa Albert, a Harvard-trained physician who interviewed young women working at a legal brothel in Nevada makes a compelling case for legalization. She found that the women remained HIV-free and felt safer working in a secure environment than alone on city streets. Despite long hours and rules that gave too much profit to the owners, the women actually took "pride" in their work. Besides the security, most earn between $300 and $1,500 per day.[63]

Pornography

pornography
Sexually explicit books, magazines, films, or tapes intended to provide sexual titillation and excitement for paying customers.

obscenity
Material that violates community standards of morality or decency and has no redeeming social value.

The term **pornography** derives from the Greek *porne,* meaning "prostitute," and *graphein,* meaning "to write." In the heart of many major cities are stores that display and sell books, magazines, and films explicitly depicting every imaginable sex act. Suburban video stores also rent and sell sexually explicit tapes, which make up 15 to 30 percent of the home rental market. The purpose of this material is to provide sexual titillation and excitement for paying customers. Although material depicting nudity and sex is typically legal, protected by the First Amendment's provision limiting government control of speech, most criminal codes prohibit the production, display, and sale of obscene material.

Obscenity, derived from the Latin *caenum* for "filth," is defined by Webster's dictionary as "deeply offensive to morality or decency . . . designed to incite to lust or depravity."[64] The problem of controlling pornography centers on this definition of obscenity. Police and law enforcement officials can legally seize only material that is judged obscene. "But who," critics ask, "is to judge what is obscene?" At one time, such novels as *Tropic of Cancer* by Henry Miller, *Ulysses* by James Joyce, and *Lady Chatterley's Lover* by D. H. Lawrence were prohibited because they were considered obscene; today they are considered works of great literary value. Thus, what is obscene today may be considered socially acceptable at a future time. After all, *Playboy* and other "men's magazines," sold openly in most bookstores, display nude models in all kinds of sexually explicit poses. The uncertainty surrounding this issue is illustrated by Supreme Court Justice Potter Stewart's famous 1964 statement

FIND IT ON INFOTRAC
College Edition

Prior to the nineteenth century, pornography essentially involved the written word. During the 1880s and 1890s, the photographic image began to replace older forms of pornography. The content stayed remarkably similar: visual pornography continued to focus on women as the objects of sexual desire. To learn more about the history of pornography, read:

Lisa Z. Sigel, "Filth in the Wrong People's Hands: Postcards and the Expansion of Pornography in Britain and the Atlantic World, 1880–1914," *Journal of Social History,* Summer 2000 v33 i4 p859

on how he defined obscenity: "I know it when I see it." Because of this legal and moral ambiguity, the sex trade is booming around the United States.

Is Pornography Harmful?

Opponents of pornography argue that it degrades both the people who are photographed and members of the public who are sometimes forced to see obscene material. Pornographers exploit their models, who often include underage children. The Attorney General's Commission on Pornography, set up by the Reagan administration to review the sale and distribution of sexually explicit material, concluded that many performers and models are victims of physical and psychological coercion.[65]

One uncontested danger of pornography is "kiddie porn." Each year more than a million children are believed to be used in pornography or prostitution, many of them runaways whose plight is exploited by adults. Sexual exploitation by these rings can devastate the child victims. Exploited children are prone to such acting-out behavior as setting fires and becoming sexually focused in the use of language, dress, and mannerisms; they also may suffer physical problems ranging from headaches and loss of appetite to genital soreness, vomiting, and urinary tract infections and psychological problems including mood swings, withdrawal, edginess, and nervousness. In his recent book, *Beyond Tolerance: Child Pornography on the Internet* (2001), sociologist Philip Jenkins argues that activists are focused on stamping out Internet pornography but have not focused on kiddie porn, which is a bigger problem. Jenkins suggests that kiddie porn is best combated by more effective law enforcement; instead of focusing on users, enforcement should be directed against the suppliers. He also suggests that newsgroups and bulletin boards that advertise or discuss kiddie porn be criminalized.[66] Jenkins's warnings may have had an effect: research indicates that the amount of Web-based kiddie porn is now in decline.[67]

Does Pornography Cause Violence?

An issue critical to the debate over pornography is whether viewing it produces sexual violence or assaultive behavior. This debate was given added interest when serial killer Ted Bundy claimed his murderous rampage was fueled by reading pornography.

The scientific evidence linking sexually explicit material to violence is definitely mixed. Most national reviews have found little conclusive evidence.[68] Some research has found that viewing erotic material may act as a safety valve for those whose impulses might otherwise lead them to violence.[69] Viewing obscene material may have the unintended side effect of satisfying erotic impulses that otherwise might result in more sexually aggressive behavior. It is not surprising to some skeptics that convicted rapists and sex offenders report less exposure to pornography than control groups of nonoffenders.[70]

This issue is far from settled. Although there is little or no documentation of a correlation between pornography and violent crime, there is stronger evidence that people exposed to material that portrays violence, sadism, and women enjoying being raped and degraded are likely to be sexually aggressive toward female victims.[71] Laboratory experiments conducted by a number of leading authorities have found that men exposed to violent pornography are more likely to act aggressively toward women.[72] The evidence suggests that violence and sexual aggression are not linked to erotic or pornographic films per se but that erotic films depicting violence, rape, brutality, and aggression may evoke similar feelings in viewers. This finding is especially distressing because it is common for adult books and films to have sexually violent themes such as rape, bondage, and mutilation.[73] One of the leading critics of pornography, Diana Russell, contends that hatred of women is a principal theme in pornography and is often coupled with racism. Her research provides strong evidence linking pornography to misogyny (the hatred of women), an emotional response that leads to rape.[74]

Pornography and the Law

The First Amendment of the U.S. Constitution protects free speech and prohibits police agencies from limiting the public's right of free expression. However, the Supreme Court held in the twin cases of *Roth v. United States* and *Alberts v. California* that although the First Amendment protects all "ideas with even the slightest redeeming social importance—unorthodox ideas, controversial ideas, even ideas hateful to the prevailing climate of opinion . . . implicit in the history of the First Amendment is the rejection of obscenity as utterly without redeeming social importance."[75] These decisions left unclear how obscenity is defined. If a highly erotic movie tells a "moral tale," must it be judged legal even if 95 percent of its content is objectionable? A spate of movies made after the *Roth* decision claimed that they were educational or warned the viewer about sexual depravity, so they could not be said to lack redeeming social importance. Many state obscenity cases were appealed to federal courts so judges could decide whether the films totally lacked redeeming social importance. To rectify the situation, the Supreme Court redefined its concept of obscenity in the case of *Miller v. California:*

> The basic guidelines for the trier of fact must be (a) whether the average person applying contemporary community standards would find that the work taken as a whole appeals to the prurient interest; (b) whether the work depicts or describes, in a patently offensive way, sexual conduct specifically defined by the applicable state law, and (c) whether the work, taken as a whole, lacks serious literary, artistic, political or scientific value.[76]

To convict a person of obscenity under the *Miller* doctrine, the state or local jurisdiction must specifically define obscene conduct in its statute, and the pornographer must engage in that behavior. The Court gave some examples of what is considered obscene: "patently offensive representations or descriptions of masturbation, excretory functions and lewd exhibition of the genitals."[77] Obviously a plebiscite cannot be held to determine the commu-

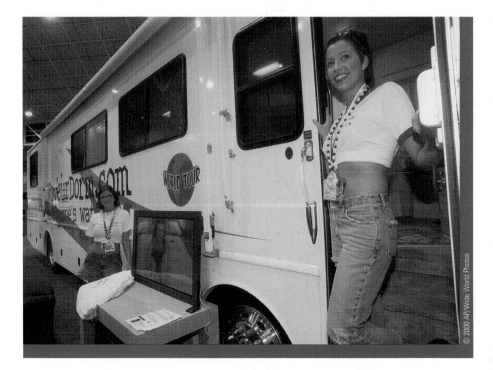

■ The technological revolution represented by the Internet poses a major obstacle for people who want to control or limit sex-related entertainment. Here, Ashley West, one of the roommates on the VoyeurDorm.com Web site, poses in front of a new recreational vehicle owned by the site while Faith Gardner demonstrates the real-time video being shot inside. Clients pay a monthly fee to watch the girls 24 hours a day. Should such activities be criminalized? Or are they legitimate and harmless business transactions between consenting adults?

nity's attitude for every trial concerning the sale of pornography. Works that are considered obscene in Omaha might be considered routine in New York, but how can we be sure? To resolve this dilemma, the Supreme Court in *Pope v. Illinois* articulated a reasonableness doctrine: A work is obscene if a reasonable person applying objective (national) standards would find the material lacking in any social value.[78]

Despite these cases, the First Amendment right to free speech makes legal control of pornography, even kiddie porn, quite difficult. For example, Congress attempted to control the growth of Internet porn when it passed the Child Pornography Prevention Act of 1996 (CPPA). This act expanded the federal prohibition on child pornography to include not only pornographic images made using actual children but also "any visual depiction, including any photograph, film, video, picture, or computer or computer-generated image or picture" that "is, or appears to be, of a minor engaging in sexually explicit conduct," and any sexually explicit image that is "advertised, promoted, presented, described, or distributed in such a manner that conveys the impression" it depicts "a minor engaging in sexually explicit conduct." This language was used in order to ban "virtual child pornography," which appears to depict minors but is produced by means other than using real children, such as through the use of youthful-looking adults or computer-imaging technology. It also bans Web postings of material deemed "harmful to minors."[79] However, in 2002, the U.S. Supreme Court struck down some sections of the CPPA as being unconstitutionally deficient, especially those that ban "virtual porn":

> Finally, the First Amendment is turned upside down by the argument that, because it is difficult to distinguish between images made using real children and those produced by computer imaging, both kinds of images must be prohibited. The overbreadth doctrine prohibits the Government from banning unprotected speech if a substantial amount of protected speech is prohibited or chilled in the process.[80]

Since the Court's ruling, the act has not been enforced.

Can Pornography Be Controlled?

The legal difficulties encountered by the CPPA illustrate the difficulty society has controlling the distribution of sexually related materials. Recent reports indicate that the sex business is currently booming and now amounts to $10 billion per year.[81]

Although politically appealing, law enforcement crusades may not necessarily obtain the desired effect. A get-tough policy could make sex-related goods and services scarce, driving up prices and making their sale even more desirable and profitable. Going after national distributors may help decentralize the adult movie and photo business and encourage local rings to expand their activities, for example, by making and marketing videos as well as still photos or distributing them through computer networks.

An alternative approach has been to restrict the sale of pornography within acceptable boundaries. For example, New York City has enacted zoning that seeks to break up the concentration of peep shows, topless bars, and X-rated businesses in several neighborhoods, particularly in Times Square.[82] The law forbids sex-oriented businesses within 500 feet of residential zones, schools, churches, or day care centers. Sex shops cannot be located within 500 feet of each other, so concentrated "red light" districts must be dispersed. Rather than close their doors, sex shops got around the law by adding products such as luggage, cameras, T-shirts, and classic films. The courts have upheld the law, ruling that stores can stay in business if no more than 40 percent of their floor space and inventory are dedicated to adult entertainment.[83]

The biggest challenge to those seeking to control the sex-for-profit industry has been the technological change in the industry. Adult movie theaters are closing as people are able to buy or rent tapes in their local video stores

✔ Checkpoints

✔ It is illegal to engage in homosexual acts in about half the U.S. states. Many organizations, including the Boy Scouts and the U.S. military, limit gay participation.

✔ Paraphilias are deviant sexual acts such as exhibitionism and voyeurism. Many are considered crimes.

✔ Prostitution has been common throughout recorded history. There are many kinds of prostitutes, including streetwalkers, bar girls, call girls, brothel prostitutes, and circuit travelers.

✔ It is feared that some girls are forced or tricked into prostitution against their will.

✔ A multibillion dollar international sex trade involves tricking young girls from Eastern Europe and Asia into becoming prostitutes.

✔ Pornography is a billion dollar industry that is growing through technological advances such as the Internet.

✔ There is great debate whether obscene materials are harmful and are related to violence.

(continued)

and play them in the privacy of their homes. Adult CD-ROMs are now a staple of the computer industry. Internet sex services include live, interactive stripping and sexual activities.

To control the spread of Internet pornography, Congress passed the Communications Decency Act (CDA), which made all Internet service providers, commercial online services, bulletin board systems, and electronic mail providers criminally liable whenever their services are used to transmit any material considered "obscene, lewd, lascivious, filthy, or indecent" (S 314, 1996). However, in *Reno v. ACLU* (1997), the Supreme Court ruled that the CDA unconstitutionally restricted free speech, once again illustrating the difficulty law enforcement has when trying to balance the need to control obscenity with the First Amendment.[84] ✔ Checkpoints

Substance Abuse

The problem of substance abuse stretches across the United States. Large urban areas are beset by drug-dealing gangs, drug users who engage in crime to support their habits, and alcohol-related violence. Rural areas are important staging centers for the shipment of drugs across the country and are often the production sites for synthetic drugs and marijuana farming.[85]

Another indication of the concern about drugs has been the increasing number of drug-related visits to hospital emergency rooms. For example, marijuana-related visits to hospital emergency departments have risen from an estimated 16,000 visits in 1991 to about 120,000 in 2002. Heroin-related visits increased from about 35,000 in 1991 to more than 93,000 in 2002. Cocaine continues to be the illicit drug responsible for the most emergency department visits, accounting for more than 199,000 visits in 2002.[86] In all 670,000 people went to emergency rooms with drug-related problems in 2002 and more than 1.2 million mentioned drugs as a problem during their visit.

Despite the scope of the drug problem, some still view it as another type of victimless public order crime. There is great debate over the legalization of drugs and the control of alcohol. Some consider drug use a private matter and drug control another example of government intrusion into people's private lives. Furthermore, legalization could reduce the profit of selling illegal substances and drive suppliers out of the market.[87] Others see these substances as dangerous, believing that the criminal activity of users makes the term "victimless" nonsensical. Still another position is that the possession and use of all drugs and alcohol should be legalized but that the sale and distribution of drugs should be heavily penalized. This would punish those profiting from drugs while enabling users to be helped without fear of criminal punishment.

When Did Drug Use Begin?

The use of chemical substances to change reality and provide stimulation, relief, or relaxation has gone on for thousands of years. Mesopotamian writings indicate that opium was used 4,000 years ago—it was known as the "plant of joy."[88] The ancient Greeks knew and understood the problem of drug use. At the time of the Crusades, the Arabs were using marijuana. In the Western Hemisphere, natives of Mexico and South America chewed coca leaves and used "magic mushrooms" in their religious ceremonies.[89] Drug use was also accepted in Europe well into the twentieth century. Recently uncovered pharmacy records circa 1900 to 1920 showed sales of cocaine and heroin solutions to members of the British royal family; records from 1912 show that Winston Churchill, then a member of Parliament, was sold a cocaine solution while staying in Scotland.[90]

In the early years of the United States, opium and its derivatives were easily obtained. Opium-based drugs were used in various patent medicine cure-alls. Morphine was used extensively to relieve the pain of wounded soldiers in the Civil War. By the turn of the century, an estimated 1 million U.S. citizens were opiate users.[91]

Alcohol and Its Prohibition

The history of alcohol and the law in the United States has also been controversial and dramatic. At the turn of the century, a drive was mustered to prohibit the sale of alcohol. This **temperance movement** was fueled by the belief that the purity of the U.S. agrarian culture was being destroyed by the growth of cities. Urbanism was viewed as a threat to the lifestyle of the majority of the nation's population, then living on farms and in villages. The forces behind the temperance movement were such lobbying groups as the Anti-Saloon League led by Carrie Nation, the Women's Temperance Union, and the Protestant clergy of the Baptist, Methodist, and Congregationalist faiths.[92] They viewed the growing city, filled with newly arriving Irish, Italian, and Eastern European immigrants, as centers of degradation and wickedness. Ratification of the Eighteenth Amendment in 1919, prohibiting the sale of alcoholic beverages, was viewed as a triumph of the morality of middle- and upper-class Americans over the threat posed to their culture by the "new Americans."[93]

Prohibition failed. It was enforced by the Volstead Act, which defined intoxicating beverages as those containing one-half of 1 percent, or more, alcohol.[94] What doomed Prohibition? One factor was the use of organized crime to supply illicit liquor. Also, the law made it illegal only to sell alcohol, not to purchase it, which reduced the deterrent effect. Finally, despite the work of Elliot Ness and his "Untouchables," law enforcement agencies were inadequate, and officials were likely to be corrupted by wealthy bootleggers.[95] In 1933, the Twenty-First Amendment to the Constitution repealed Prohibition, signaling the end of the "noble experiment."

The Extent of Substance Abuse

Despite continuing efforts at control, the use of mood-altering substances persists in the United States. What is the extent of the substance abuse problem today?

A number of national surveys attempt to chart trends in drug abuse in the general population. One important source of information on drug use is the annual Monitoring the Future self-report survey of drug abuse among high school students conducted by the Institute of Social Research (ISR) at the University of Michigan.[96] This survey is based on the self-report responses of about 17,000 high school seniors, 15,500 10th graders, and 18,800 8th graders in hundreds of schools around the United States. As Figure 13.1 shows, drug use declined from a high point late in the 1970s until 1990, when it began to increase once again. More than 40 percent of all high school seniors report using an illicit substance during the past 12 months.

Another drug use survey, the National Household Survey on Drug Abuse and Health sponsored by the federal government, also shows that drug use, which had been on the decline, may now be increasing. The 2002 survey of more than 65,000 people found that 19.5 million Americans ages 12 or older, or 8.3 percent of the population, used an illicit drug in the month preceding the interview; in 2001 the survey estimate was 15.9 million Americans, or 7.1 percent of the population. Among youths ages 12 to 17, in 2002 11.6 percent were current (past month) illicit drug users compared to 10.8 percent in 2001. The most recent report found that 22 million Americans, or 9.4 percent of the total population ages 12 or older, were classified with substance dependence or abuse.[97]

How can the trends in drug use be explained? These data indicate that although general usage is lower than it was 20 years ago, the drug problem has been on the rise, and the use of some drugs, such as Ecstasy, may be increasing among high school youth. Why has drug use remained a major social problem? When drug use declined between 1970 and 1992, one reason may have been changing perceptions about the harmfulness of drugs such as cocaine and marijuana; as people come to view these drugs as harmful, they

temperance movement
The drive to prohibit the sale of alcohol in the United States, culminating in ratification of the Eighteenth Amendment in 1919.

Prohibition
The period from 1919 until 1933, when the Eighteenth Amendment to the U.S. Constitution outlawed the sale of alcohol; also known as the "noble experiment."

Figure 13.1

Monitoring the Future: Annual Trends in Prevalence of Illicit Drug Use for 8th, 10th, and 12th Graders

SOURCE: Monitoring the Future (Ann Arbor, Mich.: Institute for Social Research, 2003).

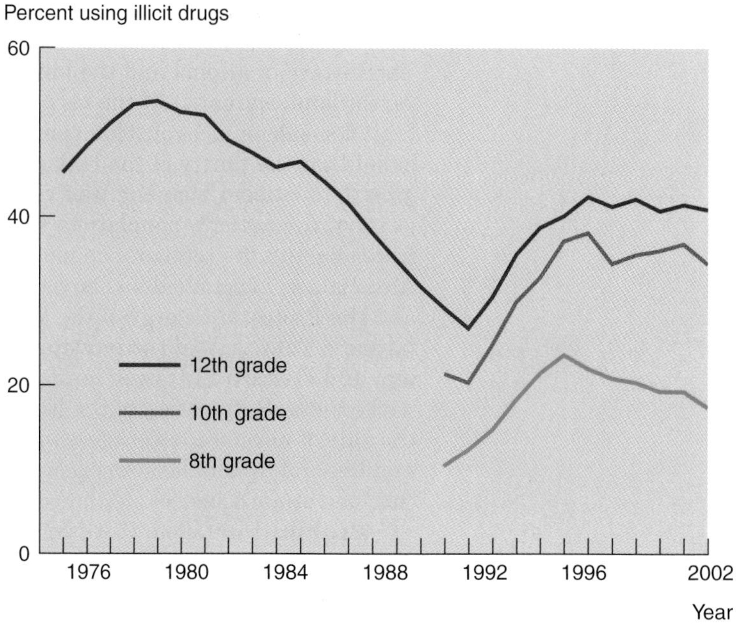

Percent using illicit drugs

tend to use them less. Because of widespread publicity linking drug use, needle sharing, and the AIDS virus, people began to see drug taking as dangerous and risky. Today, the perceived risk of drugs has declined. For example, the ISR reports that 80 percent of high school seniors in 1991 thought they ran a great risk if they were regular marijuana users; today only about 60 percent view regular marijuana use as risky.

In addition, when drug use declined, youths reported greater disapproval of drug use among their friends, and peer pressure may help account for lower use rates. The number of youths disapproving of drugs has declined significantly in the past decade (although a majority still disapproves); with lower disapproval has come increased usage.

It also appears that it is easier to obtain drugs, especially for younger adolescents. For example, the ISR survey found that in 1992 about 42 percent of 8th graders said it was easy to obtain pot; today about half say that it is easy to get that drug. So, despite a decade-long "war on drugs," it may be easier to get drugs today than 10 years ago. Finally, parents may now be unwilling or reluctant to educate their children about the dangers of substance abuse because as baby boomers they were drug abusers themselves in the 1960s and 1970s.

There also appears to be a trend for alcohol abuse to begin at an early age and remain an extremely serious problem over the life course. According to research conducted at the National Center on Addiction and Substance Abuse at Columbia University, children under the age of 21 drink about 19 percent of the alcohol consumed in the United States. More than 5 million high school students (31.5 percent) admit to binge drinking at least once a month. The age at which children begin drinking is dropping: since 1975, the proportion of children who begin drinking in the 8th grade or earlier has jumped by almost a third, from 27 percent to 36 percent.[98]

The Causes of Substance Abuse

What causes people to abuse substances? Although there are many different views on the cause of drug use, most can be characterized as seeing the onset of an addictive career as either an environmental or a personal matter.

Subcultural View Those who view drug abuse as having an environmental basis concentrate on lower-class addiction. Because a disproportionate number of drug abusers are poor, the onset of drug use can be tied to such factors as racial prejudice, devalued identities, low self-esteem, poor socioeconomic status, and the high level of mistrust, negativism, and defiance found in impoverished areas.

Residing in a deteriorated inner-city area is often correlated with entry into a drug subculture. Youths living in these depressed areas, where feelings of alienation and hopelessness run high, often meet established drug users who teach them that narcotics provide an answer to their feelings of personal inadequacy and stress.[99] The youths may join peers to learn the techniques of drug use and receive social support for their habit. Research shows that peer influence is a significant predictor of drug careers that actually grows stronger as people mature.[100] Shared feelings and a sense of intimacy lead the youths to become fully enmeshed in what has been described as the "drug-use subculture."[101] Some join gangs and enter into a career of using and distributing illegal substances while also committing property and violent crimes.[102]

Psychological View Not all drug abusers reside in lower-class slum areas; the problem of middle-class substance abuse is very real. Consequently, some experts have linked substance abuse to psychological deficits such as impaired cognitive functioning, personality disturbance, and emotional problems that can strike people in any economic class.[103] For example, a young teen may resort to drug abuse to remain dependent on an overprotective mother, to reduce the emotional turmoil of adolescence, or to cope with troubling impulses.[104]

Personality testing of known users suggests that a significant percentage suffer from psychotic disorders, including various levels of schizophrenia. Surveys show that youngsters with serious behavioral problems were more than seven times as likely as those with less serious problems to report that they were dependent on alcohol or illicit drugs. Youths with serious emotional problems were nearly four times more likely to report dependence on drugs than those without such issues.[105]

Genetic Factors It is also possible that substance abuse may have a genetic basis. For example, the biological children of alcoholics reared by nonalcoholic adoptive parents develop alcohol problems more often than the biological children of the adoptive parents.[106] In a similar vein, a number of studies comparing alcoholism among identical twins and fraternal twins have found that the degree of concordance (both siblings behaving identically) is twice as high among the identical twin groups. These inferences are still inconclusive because identical twins are more likely to be treated similarly than fraternal twins and are therefore more likely to be influenced by environmental conditions. Nonetheless, most children of abusing parents do not become drug dependent themselves, suggesting that even if drug abuse is heritable, environment and socialization must play some role in the onset of abuse.[107]

Social Learning Social psychologists suggest that drug abuse may also result from observing parental drug use. Parental drug abuse begins to have a damaging effect on children as young as 2 years old, especially when parents manifest drug-related personality problems such as depression or poor impulse control.[108] Children whose parents abuse drugs are more likely to have persistent abuse problems than the children of nonabusers.[109]

People who learn that drugs provide pleasurable sensations may be the most likely to experiment with illegal substances; a habit may develop if the user experiences lower anxiety, fear, and tension levels.[110] Having a history of family drug and alcohol abuse has been found to be a characteristic of violent teenage sexual abusers.[111] Heroin abusers report an unhappy childhood that included harsh physical punishment and parental neglect and rejection.[112]

According to the social learning view, drug involvement begins with using tobacco and drinking alcohol at an early age, which progresses to experimentation with marijuana and hashish and finally to cocaine and even heroin.

Although most recreational users do not progress to "hard stuff," few addicts begin their involvement with narcotics without first experimenting with recreational drugs. By implication, if teen smoking and drinking could be reduced, the gateway to hard drugs would be narrowed. For example, one 2003 research study found that a 50 percent reduction in the number of teens who smoke cigarettes can cut marijuana use by 16 to 28 percent.[113]

Problem Behavior Syndrome (PBS) For many people, substance abuse is just one of many problem behaviors. Longitudinal studies show that drug abusers are maladjusted, alienated, and emotionally distressed and that their drug use is one among many social problems.[114] Having a deviant lifestyle begins early in life and is punctuated with criminal relationships, family history of substance abuse, educational failure, and alienation. People who abuse drugs lack commitment to religious values, disdain education, spend most of their time in peer activities, engage in precocious sexual behavior, and experience school failure, family conflict, and other similar social problems.[115]

Rational Choice Not all people who abuse drugs do so because of personal pathology. Some may use drugs and alcohol because they want to enjoy their effects: get high, relax, improve creativity, escape reality, and increase sexual responsiveness. Research indicates that adolescent alcohol abusers believe that getting high will make them powerful, increase their sexual performance, and facilitate their social behavior; they care little about negative future consequences.[116]

Substance abuse, then, may be a function of the rational but mistaken belief that drugs can benefit the user. The decision to use drugs involves evaluations of personal consequences (such as addiction, disease, and legal punishment) and the expected benefits of drug use (such as peer approval, positive affective states, heightened awareness, and relaxation). Adolescents may begin using drugs because they believe their peers expect them to do so.[117]

Is There a Single "Cause" of Drug Abuse? There are many different views of why people take drugs, and no one theory has proved adequate to explain all forms of substance abuse. Recent research efforts show that drug users suffer a variety of family and socialization difficulties, have addiction-prone personalities, and are generally at risk for many other social problems.[118] One long-held assumption is that addicts progress along a continuum from using so-called gateway drugs such as alcohol and marijuana to using ever more potent substances, such as cocaine and heroin.[119] That view may also be misleading. Research by Andrew Golub and Bruce Johnson shows that many hard-core drug abusers have never smoked or used alcohol. And while many American youths have tried marijuana, few actually progress to crack or heroin abuse.[120] In sum, there may be no single cause of substance abuse.

Drugs and Crime

One of the main reasons for the criminalization of particular substances is the significant association believed to exist between drug abuse and crime. Research suggests that many criminal offenders have extensive experience with alcohol and drug use and that abusers commit an enormous amount of crime.[121] Substance abuse appears to be an important precipitating factor in domestic assault, armed robbery, and homicide cases.[122]

Although the drug–crime connection is powerful, the relationship is still uncertain because many users had a history of criminal activity before the onset of their substance abuse.[123] Nonetheless, if drug use does not turn otherwise law-abiding citizens into criminals, it certainly amplifies the extent of their criminal activities.[124] And as addiction levels increase, so do the frequency and seriousness of criminality.[125]

A number of data sources provide powerful evidence of a drug–crime linkage. The federally sponsored Arrestee Drug Abuse Monitoring Program

Connections

Chapter 10 provides an analysis of the drugs–violence relationship, which rests on three factors: (1) psychopharmacological relationship, which is a direct consequence of ingesting mood-altering substances; (2) economic compulsive behavior, which occurs when drug users resort to violence to support their habit; and (3) a systemic link, which occurs when drug dealers battle for territories.

(ADAM) conducts urinalysis testing for drug usage among arrestees in major cities around the country.[126] The most recent ADAM survey found that a significant portion of all male arrestees drank heavily a short time before their arrest. Depending on the city being tested, between 35 and 70 percent reported having had five or more drinks on at least one occasion in the month before their arrest. The heaviest drinkers were also likely to have used illicit drugs; 71 percent of them had used at least one drug in the month before their arrest. Between about one-fourth and one-half of all adult male arrestees were found to have been at risk for dependence on drugs. The ADAM testing also revealed that a large percentage of women arrestees had used drugs, cocaine being the most widely used, with marijuana coming in second. Of the women arrestees who used drugs or alcohol, about half were found at risk for drug dependence.

It is of course possible that most criminals are not actually drug users but that police are more likely to apprehend muddle-headed substance abusers than clear-thinking abstainers. Although this is plausible, data from the National Crime Victimization Survey helps support the drug–crime link because it asks victims of violence to describe whether they perceived the offender who attacked them to have been drinking or using drugs. The most recent (2002) survey found that:

- About 29 percent of the victims of violence reported that the offender was using drugs, alone or in combination with alcohol.
- About 1 million violent crimes occurred each year in which victims were certain that the offender had been drinking. For about one in five of these violent victimizations involving alcohol use by the offender, victims believed the offender was also using drugs at the time of the offense (see Figure 13.2).

The NCVS data indicate that a significant number of criminals are in fact substance abusers, even those who have not been apprehended by the authorities.

What causes this linkage? Drug use interferes with maturation and socialization. Drug abusers are more likely to drop out of school, be underemployed, engage in premarital sex, and become unmarried parents. These factors have been linked to a weakening of the social bond that leads to antisocial behaviors.[127]

Figure 13.2
Victims' Perception of the Use of Alcohol and Drugs by Violent Offenders, 2002

SOURCE: *National Crime Victimization Survey,* 2002

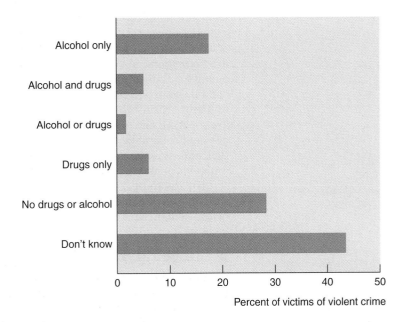

✔ **Checkpoints**

✔ Substance abuse is an ancient practice dating back more than 4,000 years.

✔ A wide variety of drugs are in use today; alcohol is a major problem.

✔ Drug use in the general population has increased during the past decade; about half of all high school seniors have tried illegal drugs at least once.

✔ There is no single cause of substance abuse. Some people may use drugs because they are predisposed to abuse.

✔ There is a strong link between drug abuse and crime. People who become addicts may increase their illegal activities to support their habits. Others engage in violence as part of their drug-dealing activities.

To quiz yourself on this material, go to questions 13.12–13.14 on the Criminology: The Core 2e Web site.

In sum, research testing both the criminality of known narcotics users and the narcotics use of known criminals produces a very strong association between drug use and crime. Even if the crime rate of drug users were actually half that reported in the research literature, users would be responsible for a significant portion of the total criminal activity in the United States. ✔ Checkpoints

Drugs and the Law

The federal government first initiated legal action to curtail the use of some drugs early in the twentieth century.[128] In 1906, the Pure Food and Drug Act required manufacturers to list the amounts of habit-forming drugs in products on the labels but did not restrict their use. However, the act prohibited the importation and sale of opiates except for medicinal purposes. In 1914, the Harrison Narcotics Act restricted the importation, manufacture, sale, and dispensing of narcotics. It defined **narcotic** as any drug that produces sleep and relieves pain, such as heroin, morphine, and opium. The act was revised in 1922 to allow importation of opium and coca (cocaine) leaves for qualified medical practitioners. The Marijuana Tax Act of 1937 required registration and payment of a tax by all persons who imported, sold, or manufactured marijuana. Because marijuana was classified as a narcotic, those registering would also be subject to criminal penalty.

In later years, other federal laws were passed to clarify existing drug statutes and revise penalties. For example, the Boggs Act of 1951 provided mandatory sentences for violating federal drug laws. The Durham–Humphrey Act of 1951 made it illegal to dispense barbiturates and amphetamines without a prescription. The Narcotic Control Act of 1956 increased penalties for drug offenders. In 1965, the Drug Abuse Control Act set up stringent guidelines for the legal use and sale of mood-modifying drugs, such as barbiturates, amphetamines, LSD, and any other "dangerous drugs," except narcotics prescribed by doctors and pharmacists. Illegal possession was punished as a misdemeanor and manufacture or sale as a felony. And in 1970, the Comprehensive Drug Abuse Prevention and Control Act set up unified categories of illegal drugs and attached specific penalties to their sale, manufacture, or possession. The law gave the U.S. attorney general discretion to decide in which category to place any new drug.

Since then, various federal laws have attempted to increase penalties imposed on drug smugglers and limit the manufacture and sale of newly developed substances. For example, the 1984 Controlled Substances Act set new, stringent penalties for drug dealers and created five categories of narcotic and non-narcotic substances subject to federal laws.[129] The Anti–Drug Abuse Act of 1986 again set new standards for minimum and maximum sentences for drug offenders, increased penalties for most offenses, and created a new drug penalty classification for large-scale offenses (such as trafficking in more than one kilogram of heroin), for which the penalty for a first offense was 10 years to life in prison.[130] With then-President George Bush's endorsement, Congress passed the Anti–Drug Abuse Act of 1988, which created a coordinated national drug policy under a "drug czar," set treatment and prevention priorities, and, symbolizing the government's hard-line stance against drug dealing, imposed the death penalty for drug-related killings.[131]

For the most part, state laws mirror federal statutes. Some apply extremely heavy penalties for selling or distributing dangerous drugs, involving prison sentences of up to 25 years.

Drug Control Strategies

Substance abuse remains a major social problem in the United States. Politicians looking for a safe campaign issue can take advantage of the public's fear of drug addiction by calling for a war on drugs. These wars have been de-

narcotic
A drug that produces sleep and relieves pain, such as heroin, morphine, and opium; a habit-forming drug.

clared even when drug usage is stable or in decline.[132] Can these efforts pay off? Can illegal drug use be eliminated or controlled?

A number of different drug control strategies have been tried, with varying degrees of success. Some aim to deter drug use by stopping the flow of drugs into the country, apprehending and punishing dealers, and cracking down on street-level drug deals. Others focus on preventing drug use by educating potential users to the dangers of substance abuse (convincing them to "say no to drugs") and by organizing community groups to work with the at-risk population in their area. Still another approach is to treat known users so they can control their addictions. Some of these efforts are discussed next.

Source Control One approach to drug control is to deter the sale and importation of drugs through the systematic apprehension of large-volume drug dealers, coupled with the enforcement of strict drug laws that carry heavy penalties. This approach is designed to capture and punish known international drug dealers and deter those who are considering entering the drug trade. A major effort has been made to cut off supplies of drugs by destroying overseas crops and arresting members of drug cartels in Central and South America, Asia, and the Middle East, where many drugs are grown and manufactured. The federal government has been in the vanguard of encouraging exporting nations to step up efforts to destroy drug crops and prosecute dealers. Three South American nations, Peru, Bolivia, and Colombia, have agreed with the United States to coordinate control efforts. However, translating words into deeds is a formidable task. Drug lords are willing and able to fight back through intimidation, violence, and corruption when necessary. The Colombian drug cartels do not hesitate to use violence and assassination to protect their interests.

The amount of narcotics grown each year is so vast that even if three-quarters of the opium crop were destroyed, the U.S. market would still require only 10 percent of the remainder to sustain the drug trade. Adding to control problems is the fact that the drug trade is an important source of foreign revenue for third world nations, and destroying the drug trade undermines their economies. More than 1 million people in Peru, Bolivia, Colombia, Thailand, Laos, and other developing nations depend on the cultivating and processing of illegal substances. The federal government estimates that U.S. citizens spend more than $40 billion annually on illegal drugs, and much of this money is funneled overseas. Even if the government of one nation were willing to cooperate in vigorous drug suppression efforts, suppliers in other nations, eager to cash in on the seller's market, would be encouraged to turn more acreage over to coca or poppy production. For example, enforcement efforts in Peru and Bolivia have been so successful that they altered cocaine cultivation patterns. As a consequence, Colombia became the premier coca-cultivating country because the local drug cartels encouraged local growers to cultivate coca plants. When the Colombian government mounted an effective eradication campaign in the traditional growing areas, the cartels linked up with rebel groups in remote parts of the country for their drug supply.[133]

Interdiction Strategies Law enforcement efforts have also been directed at intercepting drug supplies as they enter the country. Border patrols and military personnel using sophisticated hardware have been involved in massive interdiction efforts; many impressive multimillion-dollar seizures have been made. Yet the U.S. borders are so vast and unprotected that meaningful interdiction is impossible. And even if all importation were shut down, home-grown marijuana and laboratory-made drugs, such as Ecstasy, LSD, and PCP, could become the drugs of choice. Even now, their easy availability and relatively low cost are increasing their popularity among the at-risk population.

Law Enforcement Strategies Local, state, and federal law enforcement agencies have been actively fighting against drugs. One approach is to direct efforts at large-scale drug rings. The long-term consequence has been to de-centralize drug dealing and encourage young independent dealers to become major suppliers. Ironically, it has proven easier for federal agents to infiltrate and prosecute traditional organized crime groups than to take on drug-dealing gangs. Consequently, some nontraditional groups have broken into the drug trade. Police can also target, intimidate, and arrest street-level deal-ers and users in an effort to make drug use so much of a hassle that con-sumption is cut back and the crime rate reduced. Approaches that have been tried include reverse stings, in which undercover agents pose as dealers to ar-rest users who approach them for a buy. Police have attacked fortified crack houses with heavy equipment to breach their defenses. They have used rack-eteering laws to seize the assets of known dealers. Special task forces of local and state police have used undercover operations and drug sweeps to discour-age both dealers and users.[134]

Although some street-level enforcement efforts have succeeded, others are considered failures. Drug sweeps have clogged courts and correctional facilities with petty offenders while draining police resources. There are also suspicions that a displacement effect occurs; stepped-up efforts to curb drug dealing in one area or city simply encourage dealers to seek out friendlier territory.[135]

Punishment Strategies   Even if law enforcement efforts cannot produce a general deterrent effect, the courts may achieve the required result by se-verely punishing known drug dealers and traffickers. A number of initiatives have made the prosecution and punishment of drug offenders a top priority. State prosecutors have expanded their investigations into drug importation and distribution and created special prosecutors to focus on drug dealers. The fact that drugs such as crack are considered a serious problem may have con-vinced judges and prosecutors to expedite substance abuse cases.

However, these efforts often have their downside. Defense attorneys con-sider delay tactics sound legal maneuvering in drug-related cases. Courts are so backlogged that prosecutors are anxious to plea-bargain. The conse-quence of this legal maneuvering is that many people convicted on federal drug charges are granted probation or some other form of community release. Even so, prisons have become jammed with inmates, many of whom were in-volved in drug-related cases. Many drug offenders sent to prison do not serve their entire sentences because they are released in an effort to relieve prison overcrowding.[136]

Community Strategies   Another type of drug control effort relies on the involvement of local community groups to lead the fight against drugs. Repre-sentatives of various local government agencies, churches, civic organizations, and similar institutions are being brought together to create drug prevention and awareness programs.

Citizen-sponsored programs attempt to restore a sense of community in drug-infested areas, reduce fear, and promote conventional norms and val-ues.[137] These efforts can be classified into one of four distinct categories.[138] The first involves law enforcement aid type efforts, which may include block watches, cooperative police–community efforts, and citizen patrols. These citi-zen groups are nonconfrontational: They simply observe or photograph deal-ers, write down their license plate numbers, and then notify police.

A second tactic is to use the civil justice system to harass offenders. Land-lords have been sued for owning properties that house drug dealers; neigh-borhood groups have scrutinized drug houses for building code violations. Information acquired from these various sources is turned over to local au-thorities, such as police and housing agencies, for more formal action.

A third approach is through community-based treatment efforts in which citizen volunteers participate in self-help support programs, such as Narcotics Anonymous or Cocaine Anonymous, which have more than 1,000 chapters na-tionally. Other programs provide youths with martial arts training, dancing, and social events as alternatives to the drug life.

A fourth type of community-level drug prevention effort is designed to enhance the quality of life, improve interpersonal relationships, and upgrade the neighborhood's physical environment. Activities might include the creation of drug-free school zones (which encourage police to keep drug dealers away from the vicinity of schools). Consciousness-raising efforts include demonstrations and marches to publicize the drug problem and build solidarity among participants.

Drug Education and Prevention Strategies   Prevention strategies are aimed at convincing youths not to get involved in drug abuse; heavy reliance is placed on educational programs that teach kids to say no to drugs. The most widely used program is Drug Abuse Resistance Education (DARE), an elementary school course designed to give students the skills for resisting peer pressure to experiment with tobacco, drugs, and alcohol. It is unique in that it employs uniformed police officers to carry the antidrug message to the students before they enter junior high school. The program has five major focus areas:

- Providing accurate information about tobacco, alcohol, and drugs
- Teaching students techniques to resist peer pressure
- Teaching students respect for the law and law enforcers
- Giving students ideas for alternatives to drug use
- Building the self-esteem of students

DARE is based on the concept that young students need specific analytical and social skills to resist peer pressure and refuse drugs.[139] However, evaluations show that the program does little to reduce drug use or convince abusers that drugs are harmful.[140] Although there are indications that DARE may be effective with some subsets of the population, such as female and Hispanic students, overall success appears problematic at best.[141]

Drug-Testing Programs   Drug testing of private employees, government workers, and criminal offenders is believed to deter substance abuse. In the workplace, employees are tested to enhance on-the-job safety and productivity. In some industries, such as mining and transportation, drug testing is considered essential because abuse can pose a threat to the public.[142] Business leaders have been enlisted in the fight against drugs. Mandatory drug-testing programs in government and industry are common; more than 40 percent of the country's largest companies, including IBM and AT&T, have drug-testing programs. The federal government requires employee testing in regulated industries such as nuclear energy and defense contracting. About 4 million transportation workers are subject to testing.

Criminal defendants are now routinely tested at all stages of the justice system, from arrest to parole. The goal is to reduce criminal behavior by detecting current users and curbing their abuse. Can such programs reduce criminal activity? Two evaluations of pretrial drug-testing programs found little evidence that monitoring defendants' drug use influenced their behavior.[143]

Treatment Strategies   A number of approaches are taken to treat known users, getting them clean of drugs and alcohol and thereby reducing the at-risk population. One approach rests on the assumption that users have low self-esteem and treatment efforts must focus on building a sense of self. For example, users have been placed in worthwhile programs of outdoor activities and wilderness training to create self-reliance and a sense of accomplishment.[144] More intensive efforts use group therapy approaches, relying on group leaders who have been substance abusers; through such sessions, users get the skills and support to help them reject social pressure to use drugs. These programs are based on the Alcoholics Anonymous approach, which holds that users must find within themselves the strength to stay clean and that peer support from those who understand their experiences can help them achieve a drug-free life.

There are also residential programs for the more heavily involved, and a large network of drug treatment centers has been developed. Some detoxification units use medical procedures to wean patients from the more addicting drugs to others, such as methadone, that can be more easily regulated. Methadone is a drug similar to heroin, and addicts can be treated at clinics where they receive methadone under controlled conditions. However, methadone programs have been undermined because some users sell their methadone in the black market, and others supplement their dosages with illegally obtained heroin. Other programs utilized drugs such as Naxalone, which counters the effects of narcotics and eases the trauma of withdrawal, but results have not been conclusive.[145]

Other therapeutic programs attempt to deal with the psychological causes of drug use in "therapeutic communities." Hypnosis, aversion therapy (getting users to associate drugs with unpleasant sensations, such as nausea), counseling, biofeedback, and other techniques are often used. Some programs report significant success with clients who are able to complete the full course of the treatment.[146]

The long-term effects of treatment on drug abuse are still uncertain. Critics charge that a stay in a residential program can help stigmatize people as addicts even if they never used hard drugs; and in treatment they may be introduced to hard-core users with whom they will associate after release. Users do not often enter these programs voluntarily and have little motivation to change. Supporters of treatment argue that many addicts are helped by intensive inpatient and outpatient treatment, and the cost saving is considerable.[147] Moreover, it is estimated that less than half of the 5 million people who need drug treatment actually get it, so that treatment strategies have not been given a fair trial.

Employment Programs   Research indicates that drug abusers who obtain and keep employment will end or reduce the incidence of their substance abuse.[148] Not surprisingly, then, there have been a number of efforts to provide vocational rehabilitation for drug abusers. One approach is the supported work program, which typically involves jobsite training, ongoing assessment, and jobsite intervention. Rather than teach work skills in a classroom, support programs rely on helping drug abusers deal with real work settings. Other programs provide training to overcome barriers to employment, including help with motivation, education, experience, the job market, job-seeking skills, and personal issues. For example, female abusers may be unaware of child care resources that would enable them to seek employment opportunities. Another approach is to help addicts improve their interviewing skills so that once a job opportunity can be identified they are equipped to convince potential employers of their commitment and reliability.

Legalization

Considering these problems, some commentators have called for the legalization or decriminalization of restricted drugs. The so-called war on drugs is expensive, costing more than $500 billion over the past 20 years—money that could have been spent on education and economic development. Drug enforcement and treatment now costs federal, state, and local governments about $100 billion per year. For example, the National Center on Addiction and Substance Abuse at Columbia University claims states spent conservatively $81.3 billion on substance abuse and addiction—13.1 percent of the $620 billion in total state spending.[149] The federal government plans to spend close to $12 billion more on drug control, up from $7 billion in 1995; this figure does not reflect treatment costs.[150]

■ A protester is shown being arrested at a drug legalization rally in Seattle on August 16, 2003. Should recreational drugs be legalized or are they a "gateway" to more serious drug abuse?

And effectiveness is questionable. Two decades ago, a kilogram of cocaine sold for a wholesale price of $40,000; today it goes for $20,000 to $25,000. Translated into consumer prices, a gram of cocaine costs $50 today, compared to $100 in 1990. Declining prices suggest that the supply of cocaine is rising despite the billions spent to prevent its importation.[151]

Legalization is warranted, according to drug expert Ethan Nadelmann, because the use of mood-altering substances is customary in almost all human societies; people have always wanted, and will find ways of obtaining, psychoactive drugs.[152] Banning drugs creates networks of manufacturers and distributors, many of whom use violence as part of their standard operating procedures. Although some believe that drug use is immoral, Nadelmann questions whether it is any worse than the unrestricted use of alcohol and cigarettes, both of which are addicting and unhealthful. Far more people die each year because they abuse these legal substances than are killed in drug wars or from abusing illegal substances.

Nadelmann also states that just as Prohibition failed to stop the flow of alcohol in the 1920s while it increased the power of organized crime, the policy of prohibiting drugs is similarly doomed to failure. When drugs were legal and freely available early in the twentieth century, the proportion of Americans using drugs was not much greater than today. Most users led normal lives, most likely because of the legal status of their drug use.

If drugs were legalized, the argument goes, price and distribution could be controlled by the government. This would reduce addicts' cash requirements, so crime rates would drop because users would no longer need the same cash flow to support their habits. Drug-related deaths would decline because government control would reduce needle sharing and the spread of AIDS. Legalization would also destroy the drug-importing cartels and gangs. Because drugs would be bought and sold openly, the government would reap a tax windfall both from taxes on the sale of drugs and from income taxes paid by drug dealers on profits that have been part of the hidden economy. Of course, as with alcohol, drug distribution would be regulated, keeping drugs away from adolescents, public servants such as police and airline pilots, and known felons. Those who favor legalization point to the Netherlands as a country that has legalized drugs and remains relatively crime free.[153]

This approach might have the short-term effect of reducing the association between drug use and crime, but it might also have grave social consequences. Legalization might increase the nation's rate of drug usage, creating

CONCEPT SUMMARY   13.1 The Drug–Crime Relationship

RELATIONSHIP	DEFINITION	EXAMPLES
Drug-defined offenses	Violations of laws prohibiting or regulating the possession, use, distribution, or manufacture of illegal drugs	Drug possession or use; marijuana cultivation; cocaine, heroin, or marijuana sales
Drug-related offenses	Offenses in which a drug's pharmacologic effects contribute; offenses motivated by the user's need for money to support continued use; and offenses connected to drug distribution itself	Violent behavior resulting from drug effects; stealing to get money to buy drugs; violence against rival drug dealers
Drug-using lifestyle	Drug use and crime are common aspects of a deviant lifestyle. The likelihood and frequency of involvement in illegal activity is increased because drug users may not participate in the legitimate economy and are exposed to situations that encourage crime.	A life orientation with an emphasis on short-term goals supported by illegal activities; opportunities to offend resulting from contacts with offenders and illegal markets; criminal skills learned from other offenders

an even larger group of nonproductive, drug-dependent people who must be cared for by the rest of society.[154] In countries such as Iran and Thailand, where drugs are cheap and readily available, the rate of narcotics use is quite high. Historically, the availability of cheap narcotics has preceded drug use epidemics, as was the case when British and American merchants sold opium in nineteenth-century China.

If juveniles, criminals, and members of other at-risk groups were forbidden to buy drugs, who would be the customers? Noncriminal, nonabusing, middle-aged adults? And would not those prohibited from legally buying drugs create an underground market almost as vast as the current one? If the government tried to raise money by taxing legal drugs, as it now does with liquor and cigarettes, that might encourage drug smuggling to avoid tax payments; these "illegal" drugs might then fall into the hands of adolescents.

Decriminalization or legalization of controlled substances is unlikely in the near term, but further study is warranted. What effect would a policy of partial decriminalization (for example, legalizing small amounts of marijuana) have on drug use rates? Would a get-tough policy help to "widen the net" of the justice system and actually deepen some youths' involvement in substance abuse? Can society provide alternatives to drugs that will reduce teenage drug dependency?[155] The answers to these questions have proven elusive. The different types of drug control strategies are summarized in Concept Summary 13.1.

Summary

- Public order crimes are acts considered illegal because they conflict with social policy, accepted moral rules, and public opinion.

- There is usually great debate over public order crimes. Some charge that they are not really crimes at all and that it is foolish to legislate morality. Others view such morally tinged acts as prostitution, gambling, and drug abuse as harmful and therefore subject to public control.

- Many public order crimes are sex-related.

- Although homosexuality is not a crime, homosexual acts are subject to legal control.

- Gay people are still not allowed to marry and are barred from the military and other groups such as the Boy Scouts.

- In 2003 the Supreme Court ruled that sexual relations between gay people cannot be criminalized.

- Prostitution is another sex-related public order crime. Although prostitution has been practiced for thousands of years and is legal in some areas, most states outlaw commercial sex.

- There are a variety of prostitutes, including street-walkers, B-girls, and call girls. A new type of prostitution is cyber prostitution, which is Internet based.

- Studies indicate that prostitutes come from poor, troubled families and have abusive parents. However, there is little evidence that prostitutes are emotionally disturbed, addicted to drugs, or sexually abnormal.

- Although prostitution is illegal, some cities have set up adult entertainment areas where commercial sex is tolerated by law enforcement agents.

- Pornography involves the sale of sexually explicit material intended to sexually excite paying customers. The depiction of sex and nudity is not illegal, but it does violate the law when it is judged obscene.

- Obscenity is a legal term that today is defined as material offensive to community standards. Thus, each local jurisdiction must decide what pornographic material is obscene. A growing problem is the exploitation of children in obscene materials (kiddie porn), which has been has expanded through the Internet.

- The Supreme Court has ruled that local communities can pass statutes outlawing any sexually explicit material.

- There is no hard evidence that pornography is related to crime or aggression, but data suggest that sexual material with a violent theme is related to sexual violence by those who view it.

- Substance abuse is another type of public order crime. Most states and the federal government outlaw a wide variety of drugs they consider harmful, including narcotics, amphetamines, barbiturates, cocaine, hallucinogens, and marijuana.

- One of the main reasons for the continued ban on drugs is their relationship to crime. Numerous studies have found that drug addicts commit enormous amounts of property and violent crime.

- Alcohol is another commonly abused substance. Although alcohol is legal to possess, it too has been linked to crime. Drunk driving and deaths caused by drunk drivers are growing national problems.

- Strategies to control substance abuse range from source control to treatment. So far, no single method seems effective. Although legalization is debated, the fact that so many people already take drugs and the association of drug abuse with crime make legalization unlikely in the near term.

Thinking Like a Criminologist

You have been called upon by the director of the Department of Health and Human Services to give your opinion on a recent national survey that found that serious mental illness is highly correlated with illicit drug use. Among adults who used an illicit drug in the past year, 17.1 percent had serious mental illness in that year, whereas the rate of serious mental illness was 6.9 percent among adults who did not use an illicit drug. Among adults with serious mental illness, 28.9 percent used an illicit drug in the past year, whereas the rate of illicit drug use was 12.7 percent among those without serious mental illness. The relationship is illustrated in Figure A.

Among adults with serious mental illness, 23.2 percent (4 million) were dependent on or abused alcohol or illicit drugs, whereas the rate among adults without serious mental illness was only 8.2 percent. Adults with serious mental illness were more likely than those without serious mental illness to be dependent on or to abuse illicit drugs (9.6 percent versus 2.1 percent) and more likely to be dependent on or to abuse alcohol (18 percent

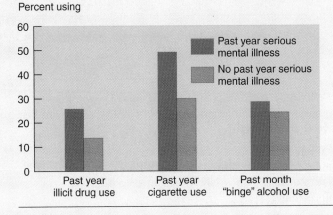

Percent using

Figure A

Rates of Serious Mental Illness Correlated with Illicit Drug, Alcohol, and Cigarette Use among Adults Aged 18 or Older, 2002

SOURCE: National Household Survey on Drug Abuse, 2002 (Washington, D.C.: U.S. Department of Health and Human Services, 2003).

versus 7 percent). Among adults with substance dependence or abuse, 20.4 percent had serious mental illness. The rate of serious mental illness was 7 percent among adults who did not have substance abuse or dependence.

The director realizes that one possible explanation of these data is that drugs cause people to become mentally

ill. He asks you to comment on other possible explanations. What will you tell her?

Go to the Criminology: The Core 2e Web site to review the content of this chapter.

Doing Research on the Web

For an up-to-date list of URLs, go to

http://www.cj.wadsworth.com/siegel_crimcore2e

To learn more about the association between mental illness and drug abuse, check out the Web site of the National Alliance for Mental Illness:

http://web.nami.org/helpline/dualdiagnosis.htm

You may also want to check out research at the Substance Abuse and Mental Health Service Administration Web site:

http://www.gainsctr.com/pdfs/fact_sheets/gainsjailprev.pdf

Pro/Con discussions and Viewpoint Essays on some of the topics in this chapter may be found at the Opposing Viewpoints Resource Center:

http://www.gale.com/OpposingViewpoints

Key Terms

public order crime 317
victimless crime 318
moral entrepreneur 319
gay bashing 320
homosexuality 320

sodomy 320
homophobia 320
paraphilia 322
prostitution 323
pornography 328

obscenity 328
temperance movement 333
Prohibition 333
narcotic 338

Critical Thinking Questions

1. Why do you think people take drugs? Do you know anyone with an addiction-prone personality, or do you believe that is a myth?

2. What policy might be the best strategy to reduce teenage drug use: source control, reliance on treatment, national education efforts, or community-level enforcement?

3. Under what circumstances, if any, might the legalization or decriminalization of sexually related material be beneficial to society?

4. Do you consider alcohol a drug? Should greater control be placed on the sale of alcohol?

5. Is prostitution really a crime? Should men or women have the right to sell sexual favors if they so choose?

part 4

The Criminal Justice System

The text's final section reviews the agencies and the process of justice designed to exert social control over criminal offenders. Chapter 14 provides an overview of the justice system and describes its major institutions and processes. This vast array of people and institutions is beset by conflicting goals and values. Some view the justice system as a mammoth agency of social control; others see it as a great social agency dispensing therapy to those who cannot fit within the boundaries of society.

Consequently, a major goal of justice system policymakers is to formulate and disseminate effective models of crime prevention and control. Efforts are now being undertaken at all levels of the justice system to improve information flow, experiment with new program concepts, and evaluate current operating procedures.

CHAPTER 14

The Criminal Justice System

Chapter Objectives

1. Be familiar with the history of the criminal justice system.
2. Know the component agencies of criminal justice.
3. Be familiar with the various stages in the process of justice.
4. Understand how criminal justice is shaped by the rule of law.
5. Know the elements of the crime control model.
6. Be able to discuss the problem of prisoner reentry.
7. Know what is meant by the justice model.
8. Discuss the elements of due process.
9. Be able to argue the merits of the rehabilitation model.
10. Understand the concept of nonintervention.
11. Know the elements of the restorative justice model.

N JANUARY 18, 2002, SARA JANE OLSON WAS SENTENCED TO 20 YEARS TO LIFE IN PRISON FOR HER ROLE IN A failed bomb plot to kill Los Angeles police officers in 1975. Then known as Kathy Soliah, a member of the radical Symbionese Liberation Army (SLA), Olson escaped capture and fled to Minnesota, where she led a quiet life. She married a doctor, raised a family, and became an upstanding member of the community en-

CNN View the CNN video clip of this story and answer related critical thinking questions on your *Criminology: The Core 2e* CD.

gaging in many charitable works. Then, in a segment of the TV show *America's Most Wanted,* pictures of Soliah and another SLA fugitive, James Kilgore, were broadcast, and the FBI offered a $20,000 reward for information leading to Soliah's capture. Identified by someone who watched the show, on June 16, 1999, she peacefully surrendered to the police after being pulled over a few blocks from her house in St. Paul, Minnesota.

During trial, Olson's defense suffered one setback after another. They argued she could not hope to get a fair hearing in light of the events of September 11; the motion was denied by the judge who sided with the prosecutor's argument that international acts of terrorism have no bearing on any case in the court system, even one that involves domestic terrorism. Her defense also suffered a blow when the judge ruled that prosecutors could present evidence of the Symbionese Liberation Army's criminal history during her trial even though Olson was not accused of committing these crimes; the judge ruled that all the acts were relevant because they showed the deadly intentions of the group.

he Olson case illustrates some of the dilemmas faced by the criminal justice system. Can such high-profile cases ever hope to get fair and unbiased juries? What is the effect on justice of pretrial publicity and televised trials? It also raises issues of the purpose of prosecuting and punishing criminal defendants. This middle-aged mother hardly presents a danger to society. Since Sarah Jane Olson had rehabilitated herself, was her prosecution and trial merely a cruel afterthought? On the other hand, should she be rewarded with lenient treatment because she was able to escape capture and elude the authorities for 25 years? Her sterling record as a wife and mother could only have been accomplished because she evaded the grasp of the law at the time her crimes were committed. Should we free a rapist merely because he escaped capture for 20 years? It is the role of the criminal justice system and its component agencies to deal with such thorny issues in an effective and efficient manner.

Although firmly entrenched in our culture, common criminal justice agencies have existed for only 150 years or so. At first these institutions operated independently, with little recognition that their functions could be coordinated or share common ground.

In 1931, President Herbert Hoover appointed the National Commission of Law Observance and Enforcement, commonly known as the Wickersham Commission. This national study group analyzed the American justice system in detail and helped usher in the era of treatment and rehabilitation. It showed the complex rules and regulations that govern the system and exposed how difficult it was for justice personnel to keep track of its legal and administrative complexity.

The modern era of criminal justice study began with a series of explorations of the criminal justice process conducted under the auspices of the American Bar Foundation.[1] As a group, the Bar Foundation studies brought to light some of the hidden or low-visibility processes at the heart of justice system operations. They showed how informal decision making and the use of personal discretion were essential ingredients of the justice process.

Another milestone occurred in 1967, when the President's Commission on Law Enforcement and the Administration of Justice (the Crime Commission), appointed by President Lyndon Johnson, published its final report, *The Challenge of Crime in a Free Society*.[2] This group of practitioners, educators, and attorneys had been charged with creating a comprehensive view of the criminal justice process and offering recommendations for its reform. Its efforts resulted in passage of the Safe Streets and Crime Control Act of 1968, which provided federal funds for state and local crime control efforts. This legislation helped launch a massive campaign to restructure the justice system by funding the Law Enforcement Assistance Administration (LEAA), an agency that provided hundreds of millions of dollars in aid to local and state justice agencies. Federal intervention through the LEAA ushered in a new era in research and development in criminal justice and established the concept that its component agencies actually make up a system.[3]

Though the LEAA is no longer in operation, its efforts helped identify the concept of a unified system of criminal justice. Rather than viewing police, courts, and correctional agencies as thousands of independent institutions, it has become common to see them as components of a large, integrated, people-processing system that manages law violators from the time of their arrest through trial, punishment, and release.

What Is the Criminal Justice System?

The **criminal justice system** refers to the agencies of government charged with enforcing law, adjudicating crime, and correcting criminal conduct. The criminal justice system is essentially an instrument of social control: Society considers some behaviors so dangerous and destructive that it either strictly controls their occurrence or outlaws them outright. It is the job of the agencies of justice to prevent social harm by apprehending and punishing those who violate the law and in so doing deter those who may be contemplating future wrongdoing. Although society maintains other forms of social control, such as the family, school, and church, these are designed to deal with moral, not legal, misbehavior. Only the criminal justice system has the power to control crime and punish criminals.

The contemporary criminal justice system in the United States is monumental in size. It consists of more than 55,000 public agencies and now costs federal, state, and local governments about $150 billion per year for civil and criminal justice, increasing more than 300 percent since 1982 (see Figure 14.1 and Figure 14.2).

One reason the justice system is so expensive to run is because it employs 2 million-plus people in more than 55,000 public agencies, including 17,000 police agencies, nearly 17,000 courts, more than 8,000 prosecutorial agencies,

criminal justice system
The agencies of government—police, courts, and corrections—responsible for apprehending, adjudicating, sanctioning, and treating criminal offenders.

Figure 14.1

Justice System Expenditures, 1982–1999

SOURCE: Bureau of Justice Statistics, "Justice Expenditure and Employment Extracts" [Online]. Available: http://www.ojp.usdoj.gov/bjs/glance/expgov.htm (2003)

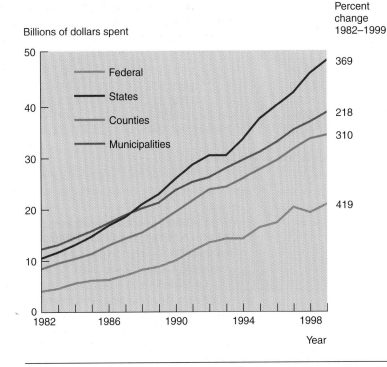

Figure 14.2

Direct Expenditure by Criminal Justice Functions, 1982–1999

SOURCE: Bureau of Justice Statistics, 2003.

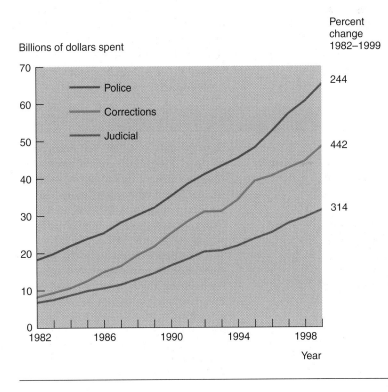

about 6,000 correctional institutions, and more than 3,500 probation and parole departments. There are also capital costs. State jurisdictions are now conducting a massive correctional building campaign, adding tens of thousands of prison cells. It costs about $70,000 to build a prison cell, and about $22,000 per year is needed to keep an inmate in prison; juvenile institutions cost about $30,000 per year per resident.

The system is so big because it must process, treat, and care for millions of people each year. Although the crime rate has declined substantially, close

TABLE	14.1 Number of People Under Correctional Supervision, 1990–2002				
TOTAL	POPULATION	PROBATION	PAROLE	JAIL	PRISON
1990	4,350,300	2,670,234	531,407	405,320	743,382
1995	5,342,900	3,077,861	679,421	507,044	1,078,542
2000	6,445,100	3,826,209	723,898	621,149	1,316,333
2001	6,592,800	3,932,751	731,147	631,240	1,330,980
2002	6,769,523	3,995,200	753,100	665,475	1,355,748

SOURCE: Bureau of Justice Statistics, 2002, updated 2003.

to 14 million people are still being arrested each year, including more than 2 million for serious felony offenses.[4] In addition, about 1.5 million juveniles are handled by the juvenile courts. Today state and federal courts convict a combined total of more than 1 million adults on felony charges.[5]

Considering the enormous number of people processed each year, it comes as no surprise that the correctional system population is at an all-time high. More than 6 million people are now under the control of the correctional system, with more than 2 million men and women in the nation's jails and prisons. About 4 million adult men and women are being supervised in the community while on probation or parole, a number that has been increasing by more than 3 percent each year since 1990 (see Table 14.1).

The major components of this immense system—the police, courts, and correctional agencies—are described in the sections that follow. What are their duties? What are the major stages in the formal criminal justice process, and how are decisions made at these critical junctures? What is the informal justice process, and how does it operate? These important questions are addressed next.

Police and Law Enforcement

Approximately 17,000 law enforcement agencies operate in the United States. State and local law enforcement agencies employ more than 1 million full-time personnel, including more than 700,000 sworn officers.[6] Most are municipal, general-purpose police forces, numbering about 12,000 in all. In addition, local jurisdictions maintain more than 1,000 special police units, including park rangers, harbor police, transit police, and campus security agencies at local universities. At the county level, there are approximately 3,000 sheriff's departments, which, depending on the jurisdiction, provide police protection in unincorporated areas of a county, perform judicial functions such as serving subpoenas, and maintain the county jail and detention facilities. Every state except Hawaii maintains a state police force. The federal government has its own law enforcement agencies, including the FBI and the Secret Service.

Law enforcement agencies have been charged with peacekeeping, deterring potential criminals, and apprehending law violators.[7] The traditional police role involved maintaining order through patrolling public streets and highways, responding to calls for assistance, investigating crimes, and identifying criminal suspects. The police role has gradually expanded to include a variety of human service functions, including preventing youth crime and diverting juvenile offenders from the criminal justice system, resolving family conflicts, facilitating the movement of people and vehicles, preserving civil order during emergencies, providing emergency medical care, and improving police–community relations.

Police are the most visible agents of the justice process. Their reactions to victims and offenders are carefully scrutinized in the news media. Police have

FIND IT ON INFOTRAC
College Edition

Despite its size and cost, some critics believe the criminal justice system does not work very well. To read one such critique, go to:

Barbara Dority, "The U.S. Criminal Injustice System," *The Humanist,* May 2000 v60 i3 p33

■ Law enforcement agencies are charged with peacekeeping, deterring potential criminals, and apprehending law violators. Here police officers attempt to keep a demonstration under control in Washington, D.C., on September 27, 2003.

© 2003 AP/Wide World Photos

been criticized for being too harsh or too lenient, too violent or too passive. Police response to minority groups, youths, political dissidents, protesters, and union workers has been publicly debated.

Compounding the problem is the tremendous **discretion** afforded police officers, who determine when a domestic dispute becomes disorderly conduct or criminal assault, whether it is appropriate to arrest juveniles or refer them to a social agency, and when to assume that probable cause exists to arrest a suspect for a crime. At the same time, police agencies have been criticized for such problems as internal corruption, inefficiency, lack of effectiveness, brutality, and discriminatory hiring.

Widely publicized cases of police brutality, such as the Rodney King beating in Los Angeles, have prompted calls for the investigation and prosecution of police officers. Although brutality may still exist, indications are that the number of violent incidents between the police and the public is actually quite rare. The most recent national survey on police contacts with civilians found that in a single year with an estimated 43 million police–citizen interactions, approximately 1 percent, or 422,000, involved the use or threatened use of force. Of these, an estimated 2 in 10 involved the threat of force only. When force was used, it typically involved the citizen being pushed or grabbed: Less than 20 percent of those experiencing force reported an injury.[8] Suspects who offer physical resistance are much more likely to receive some form of physical coercion in return, but those who offer verbal disrespect are not likely to be physically coerced.[9] However, this is not to say that a police officer's job is not dangerous or that violence is not a concern: At least 6,600 civilians have been killed by the police since 1976, and the true number is probably much higher.[10]

In recent years, police departments have experimented with new forms of law enforcement, including community policing and problem-oriented policing. Rather than respond to crime, police officers have taken on the role of community change agents, working with citizens to prevent crimes before they occur.

Community programs involve police in such activities as citizen crime patrols and councils that identify crime problems. Community policing often involves decentralized units that operate on the neighborhood level in order to be more sensitive to the particular concerns of the public; community policing creates a sense of security in a neighborhood and improves residents' opinions of the police.[11] Exhibit 14.1 shows what one expert considers the most notable changes in policing since 1960.

discretion
The use of personal decision making by those carrying out police, judicial, and sanctioning functions within the criminal justice system.

EXHIBIT 14.1 The Most Notable Achievements of American Police, 1960–Present

1. The intellectual caliber of the police has risen dramatically. American police today at all ranks are smarter, better informed, and more sophisticated than police in the 1960s.

2. Senior police managers are more ambitious for their organizations than they used to be. Chiefs and their deputies want to leave their own distinctive stamp on their organizations. Many recognize that management is an important specialized skill that must be developed.

3. An explicit scientific mindset has taken hold in American policing that involves an appreciation of the importance of evaluation and the timely availability of information.

4. The standards of police conduct have risen. Despite recent well-publicized incidents of brutality and corruption, American police today treat the public more fairly, more equitably, and less venally than police did 30 years ago.

5. Police are remarkably more diverse in terms of race and gender than a generation ago. This amounts to a revolution in American policing, changing both its appearance and, more slowly, its behavior.

6. Police work has become intellectually more demanding, requiring an array of new specialized knowledge about technology, forensic analysis, and crime. This has had profound effects on recruitment, notably adding civilian support, organizational structure, career patterns, and operational coordination.

7. Civilian review of police discipline has gradually become accepted by police. Although the struggle is not yet over, expansion is inevitable as more senior police executives see that civilian review reassures the public and validates their own favorable opinion of the overall quality of police performance.

SOURCE: David H. Bayley, "Policing in America," *Society* 36 (December 1998): 16–20.

The Criminal Court System

The criminal courts are considered by many to be the core element in the administration of criminal justice. The court is a complex social agency with many independent but interrelated subsystems—clerk, prosecutor, defense attorney, judge, and probation department—each having a role in the court's operation. It is also the scene of many important elements of criminal justice decision making—detention, jury selection, trial, and sentencing. Ideally, the judicatory process operates with absolute fairness and equality. The entire process—from filing the initial complaint to final sentencing of the defendant—is governed by precise rules of law designed to ensure fairness. No defendant tried before a U.S. court should suffer or benefit because of his or her personal characteristics, beliefs, or affiliations.

However, U.S. criminal justice can be selective. Discretion accompanies defendants through every step of the process, determining what will happen to them and how their cases will be resolved. Discretion means that two people committing similar crimes may receive highly dissimilar treatment. Table 14.2 shows that almost one-third of all people convicted of serious felonies receive a probation sentence; only 40 percent go to prison. Seventy percent of people convicted of rape go to prison whereas 30 percent receive a jail sentence that is generally a year or less or get probation only. Most people convicted of homicide receive a prison sentence, but about 5 percent receive probation as a sole sentence; murderers get probation more often than the death penalty.[12]

Court Structure   The typical state court structure is illustrated in Figure 14.3. Most states employ a multitiered court structure. Lower courts try misdemeanors and conduct the preliminary processing of felony offenses. Superior trial courts try felony cases. Appellate courts review the criminal procedures of trial courts to determine whether the offenders were treated fairly. Superior appellate courts or state supreme courts, used in about half the states, review lower appellate court decisions.

The independent federal court system has three tiers, as shown in Figure 14.4 on page 357. The U.S. district courts are the trial courts of the system;

FIND IT ON INFOTRAC
College Edition

Are the community police officers of today similar to the small-town doctors of yesteryear who knew every patient on a personal level and made house calls? To find out, read:

Joseph A. Harpold, "A Medical Model for Community Policing," *FBI Law Enforcement Bulletin*, June 2000 v69 i6 p23

TABLE 14.2 Types of Felony Sentences Imposed by State Courts, by Offense, 2000				
MOST SERIOUS CONVICTION OFFENSE	**PERCENTAGE OF FELONS SENTENCED TO INCARCERATION**			**PERCENTAGE OF FELONS SENTENCED TO PROBATION**
	TOTAL	**PRISON**	**JAIL**	
All Offenses	68	40	28	32
Violent Offenses	78	54	24	22
Murder[a]	95	93	2	5
Sexual assault[b]	84	64	20	16
Rape	90	70	20	10
Other sexual assault	80	60	20	20
Robbery	89	74	15	11
Aggravated assault	71	40	31	29
Other violent[c]	71	42	29	29
Property Offenses	64	37	27	36
Burglary	76	52	24	24
Larceny[d]	63	33	30	37
Motor vehicle theft	73	41	32	27
Fraud[e]	54	29	25	46
Drug Offenses	67	38	29	33
Possession	64	33	31	36
Trafficking	69	41	28	31
Weapon Offenses	70	41	29	30
Other Offenses[f]	66	32	34	34

Notes: For persons receiving a combination of sentences, the sentence designation came from the most severe penalty imposed—prison being the most severe, followed by jail, then probation. Prison includes death sentences. Felons receiving a sentence other than incarceration or probation are classified under "probation." This table is based on an estimated 919,387 cases.
[a]Includes nonnegligent manslaughter.
[b]Includes rape.
[c]Includes offenses such as negligent manslaughter and kidnapping.
[d]Includes motor vehicle theft.
[e]Includes forgery and embezzlement.
[f]Composed of nonviolent offenses such as receiving stolen property and vandalism.

they have jurisdiction over cases involving violations of federal law, such as interstate transportation of stolen vehicles and racketeering. Appeals from the district court are heard in one of the intermediate federal courts of appeal. The highest federal appeals court, the U.S. Supreme Court, is the court of last resort for all cases tried in the various federal and state courts.

The Supreme Court   The U.S. Supreme Court is composed of nine members, appointed for lifetime terms by the president with the approval of Congress. In general, the Court hears only cases it deems important and appropriate. When the Court decides to hear a case, it usually grants a writ of certiorari, requesting a transcript of the case proceedings for review.

The Supreme Court can word a decision so that it becomes a precedent that must be honored by all lower courts. For example, if the Court grants a particular litigant the right to counsel at a police lineup, then all people in similar situations must be given the same right. This type of ruling is usually referred to as a **landmark decision.** The use of precedent in the legal system gives the Supreme Court power to influence and mold the everyday operating procedures of police agencies, trial courts, and corrections institutions.

Prosecution and Defense   Within the structure of the court system, the prosecutor and the defense attorney are opponents in what is known as the **adversary system.** These two parties oppose each other in a hotly disputed

landmark decision
A ruling by the U.S. Supreme Court that serves as a precedent for similar legal issues; it often influences the everyday operating procedures of police agencies, trial courts, and corrections institutions.

adversary system
U.S. method of criminal adjudication in which prosecution (the state) and defense (the accused) each try to bring forward evidence and arguments, with guilt or innocence ultimately decided by an impartial judge or jury.

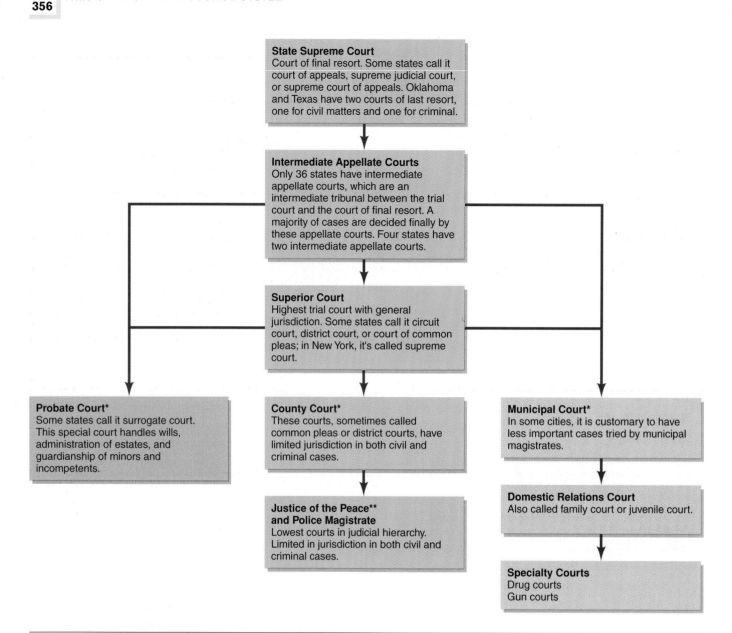

Figure 14.3
Structure of a State Judicial System

Notes: *Courts of special jurisdiction, such as probate, family, or juvenile courts, and the so-called inferior courts, such as common pleas or municipal courts, may be separate courts or part of the trial court of general jurisdiction.
**Justices of the peace do not exist in all states. Where they do exist, their jurisdictions vary greatly from state to state.
SOURCE: American Bar Association, *Law and the Courts* (Chicago: ABA, 1974), p. 20. Updated information provided by West Publishing, Eagen, Minnesota.

prosecutor
Public official who represents the government in criminal proceedings, presenting the case against the accused.

defendant
In criminal proceedings, the person accused of violating the law.

contest—the criminal trial—in accordance with rules of law and procedure. In every criminal case, the state acts against the defendant and the defense attorney acts for the defendant before an impartial judge or jury, with each side trying to bring forward evidence and arguments to advance its case. Theoretically, the ultimate objective of the adversary system is to seek the truth, determining the guilt or innocence of the defendant from the formal evidence presented at the trial. The adversary system is designed to ensure that the defendant is given a fair trial, that the relevant facts of a given case emerge, and that an impartial decision is reached.

Criminal Prosecution   The **prosecutor** is the public official who represents the government and presents its case against the **defendant,** who is charged with a violation of the criminal law. Traditionally, the prosecutor is a local attorney whose area of jurisdictional responsibility is limited to a particular county or city. The prosecutor is known variously as a district attorney or a prosecuting attorney and is either an elected or an appointed official. On the state level, the prosecutor may be referred to as the attorney general; in the federal jurisdiction the title is United States attorney.

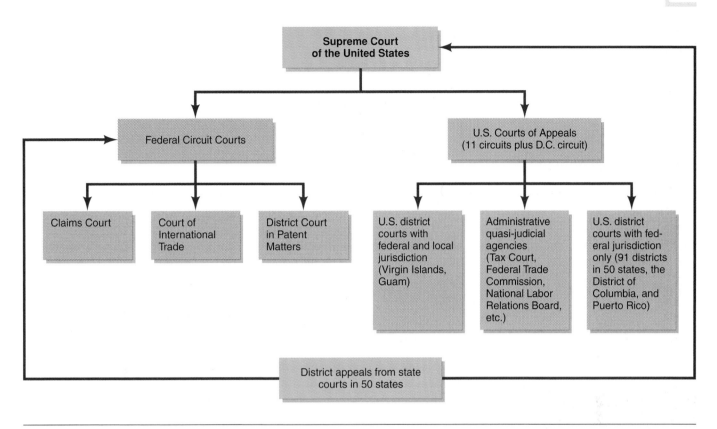

Figure 14.4
The Federal Judicial System

SOURCE: American Bar Association, *Law and the Courts* (Chicago: ABA, 1974), p. 21. Updated information provided by the Federal Courts Improvement Act of 1982 and West Publishing, Eagen, Minnesota.

The prosecutor is responsible not only for charging the defendant with the crime but also for bringing the case to trial and to a final conclusion. The prosecutor's authority ranges from determining the nature of the charge to reducing the charge by negotiation or recommending that the complaint be dismissed. The prosecutor also participates in bail hearings, presents cases before a grand jury, and appears for the state at arraignments. In sum, the prosecutor is responsible for presenting the state's case from the time of the defendant's arrest through conviction and sentencing in the criminal court.

The prosecutor, like the police officer, exercises a great deal of discretion; he or she can decide initially whether to file a criminal charge, determine what charge to bring, or explore the availability of noncriminal dispositions.[13] Prosecutorial discretion would not be as important as it is were it desirable to prosecute all violations of the law. However, full enforcement of every law is not practical because police officers and prosecutors ordinarily lack sufficient resources, staff, and support services to carry out that goal. Therefore, it makes sense to screen out cases where the accused is obviously innocent, where the evidence is negligible, or where criminal sanctions may seem inappropriate; the case must have **convictability**—that is, it must stand a good chance for a conviction. Instead of total or automatic law enforcement, a process of selective or discretionary enforcement exists; as a result, the prosecutor must make many decisions that significantly influence police operations and control the actual number of cases processed through the court and correctional systems.

Criminal Defense   The **defense attorney** is responsible for providing legal representation of the defendant. This role involves two major functions: (1) protecting the constitutional rights of the accused, and (2) presenting the best possible legal defense for the defendant.

The defense attorney represents a client from initial arrest through the trial stage, during the sentencing hearing, and, if needed, through the process

convictability
A case that has a good chance of a conviction.

defense attorney
The person responsible for protecting the constitutional rights of the accused and presenting the best possible legal defense; represents a defendant from initial arrest through trial, sentencing, and any appeal.

right to counsel
The right of a person accused of crime to
have the assistance of a defense attorney
in all criminal prosecutions.

public defender
An attorney employed by the state whose
job is to provide free legal counsel to indigent defendants.

pro bono
The provision of free legal counsel to indigent defendants by private attorneys as a
service to the profession and the
community.

probation
The conditional release of a convicted offender into the community under the supervision of a probation officer and
subject to certain conditions.

incarceration
Confinement in jail or prison.

jail
Institution, usually run by the county, for
short-term detention of those convicted of
misdemeanors and those awaiting trial or
other judicial proceedings.

prison or **penitentiary**
State or federally operated facility for the
incarceration of felony offenders sentenced by the criminal courts.

of appeal. The defense attorney is also expected to enter into plea negotiations and obtain for the defendant the most suitable bargain regarding type
and length of sentence.

Any person accused of a crime can obtain the services of a private attorney if he or she can afford to do so. One of the most critical questions in the
criminal justice system has been whether an indigent (poor) defendant has
a **right to counsel.** The federal court system has long provided counsel to
the indigent on the basis of the Sixth Amendment of the U.S. Constitution,
which gives the accused the right to have the assistance of defense counsel.
Through a series of landmark U.S. Supreme Court decisions, beginning with
Powell v. Alabama in 1932 and continuing with *Gideon v. Wainwright* in
1963 and *Argersinger v. Hamlin* in 1972, the right of a criminal defendant
to have counsel has become fundamental to the U.S. system of criminal justice.[14] Today, state courts must provide counsel to indigent defendants who
are charged with criminal offenses where the possibility of incarceration exists. Consequently, more than 1,000 **public defender** agencies have been
set up around the United States to provide free legal counsel to indigent defendants. In other jurisdictions, defense lawyers volunteer their services, referred to as working **pro bono,** and are assigned to criminal defendants. A
few rural counties have defense lawyers under contract who handle all criminal matters.

The Supreme Court has ruled that in addition to having an attorney,
every defendant is entitled to a legally competent defense. A conviction can be
overturned if it can be shown that an attorney did not meet this standard. To
prove legal assistance was legally ineffective, a defendant must show that her
lawyer's performance was deficient, and that the deficiency prejudiced the defense. Performance is deficient if it falls below an objective standard of reasonableness. For example, the performance of an attorney who did not
conduct a reasonable investigation of the facts of the case or hire expert witnesses when they were needed would be deficient.[15]

Corrections

After conviction and sentencing, the offender enters the correctional system.
Correctional agencies administer the postjudicatory care given to offenders,
which can range from informal monitoring in the community to solitary confinement in a maximum-security prison, depending on the seriousness of the
crime and the individual needs of the offender.

The most common correctional treatment, **probation,** is a legal disposition that allows the convicted offender to remain in the community, subject to
conditions imposed by court order, under the supervision of a probation officer. This lets the offender continue working and avoids the crippling effects of
incarceration.

A person given a sentence involving incarceration is ordinarily confined to
a correctional institution for a specified period. Different types of institutions
are used to hold offenders. **Jails,** or houses of correction, hold those convicted
of misdemeanors and those awaiting trial or involved in other proceedings,
such as grand jury deliberations, arraignments, or preliminary hearings.
Many of these institutions for short-term detention are administered by
county governments. Little is done to treat inmates because the personnel
and institutions lack the qualifications, services, and resources.

State and federally operated facilities that receive felony offenders sentenced by the criminal courts are called **prisons** or **penitentiaries.** They
may be minimum-, medium-, or maximum-security institutions. Prison
facilities vary throughout the country. Some have high walls, cells, and
large, heterogeneous inmate populations; others offer much freedom, good
correctional programs, and small, homogeneous populations. As Figure 14.5
shows, both the jail and prison populations have been steadily increasing de-

Figure 14.5

The Number of Adults in the Correctional Population, 1980–2002

SOURCE: Bureau of Justice Statistics Correctional Surveys, "National Prisoner Statistics, Survey of Jails, and the Annual Parole Survey," as presented in *Correctional Populations in the United States, Annual, Prisoners in 2002* and *Probation and Parole in the United States, 2002.*

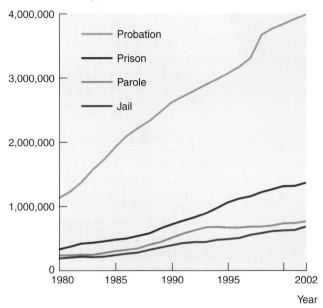

Adult correctional populations

parole
A conditional early release from prison, with the offender serving the remainder of the sentence in the community under the supervision of a parole officer.

spite a reduction in the crime rate. The increase is due to longer sentences for some crimes coupled with restrictions on early release mechanisms such as parole.

Most new inmates are first sent to a reception and classification center where they are given diagnostic evaluations and assigned to institutions that meet their individual needs as much as possible within the system's resources. The diagnostic process in the reception center may range from a physical examination and a single interview to an extensive series of psychiatric tests, orientation sessions, and numerous personal interviews. Classification is a way of evaluating inmates and assigning them to appropriate placements and activities within the state institutional system.

Because the gap between what correctional programs promise to deliver and their actual performance is often significant, many jurisdictions have instituted community-based correctional facilities. These programs emphasize the use of small neighborhood residential centers, halfway houses, prerelease centers, and work release and home furlough programs. Experts believe that only a small percentage of prison inmates require maximum security and that most can be more effectively rehabilitated in community-based facilities. Rather than totally confining offenders in an impersonal, harsh prison, such programs offer them the opportunity to maintain normal family and social relationships while providing rehabilitative services and resources at a lower cost to taxpayers.

The last segment of the corrections system, **parole,** is a process whereby an inmate is selected for early release and serves the remainder of the sentence in the community under the supervision of a parole officer. The main purpose of parole is to help the ex-inmate bridge the gap between institutional confinement and a positive adjustment within the community. All parolees must adhere to a set of rules of behavior while they are "on the outside." If these rules are violated, the parole privilege can be terminated (revoked), and the parolee will be sent back to the institution to serve the remainder of the sentence.

Other ways an offender may be released from an institution include mandatory release upon completion of the sentence and the pardon, a form of executive clemency. ✔ **Checkpoints**

The Process of Justice

In addition to viewing the criminal justice system as a collection of agencies, it is possible to see it as a series of decision points through which offenders flow. This process, illustrated in Figure 14.6, begins with initial contact with police and ends with the offender's reentry into society. At any point in the process, a decision may be made to drop further proceedings and allow the accused back into society without further penalty. In a classic statement, political scientist Herbert Packer described this process as follows:

> The image that comes to mind is an assembly line conveyor belt down which moves an endless stream of cases, never stopping, carrying them to workers who stand at fixed stations and who perform on each case as it comes by the same small but essential operation that brings it one step closer to being a finished product, or to exchange the metaphor for the reality, a closed file. The criminal process is seen as a screening process in which each successive stage—pre-arrest investigation, arrest, post-arrest investigation, preparation for trial, or entry of plea, conviction, disposition—involves a series of routinized operations whose success is gauged primarily by their tendency to pass the case along to a successful conclusion.[16]

Although each jurisdiction is somewhat different, a comprehensive view of the processing of a felony offender would probably contain the following decision points:

1. *Initial contact.* The initial contact an offender has with the justice system occurs when police officers observe a criminal act during their patrol of city streets, parks, or highways. They may also find out about a crime through a citizen or victim complaint. Similarly, an informer may alert them about criminal activity in return for financial or other consideration. Sometimes political officials, such as the mayor or city council, ask police to look into ongoing criminal activity, such as gambling, and during their subsequent investigations police officers encounter an illegal act.

2. *Investigation.* Regardless of whether the police observe, hear of, or receive a complaint about a crime, they may investigate to gather sufficient facts, or evidence, to identify the perpetrator, justify an arrest, and bring the offender to trial. An investigation may take a few minutes, as when patrol officers see a burglary in progress and apprehend the burglar at the scene of the crime. An investigation may also take years to complete and involve numerous investigators. For example, when federal agents tracked and captured Theodore Kaczinski (known as the Unabomber) in 1996, it completed an investigation that had lasted more than a decade.

3. *Arrest.* An **arrest** occurs when the police take a person into custody for allegedly committing a criminal act. An arrest is legal when all of the following conditions exist: (a) the officer believes there is sufficient evidence (**probable cause**) that a crime is being or has been committed and that the suspect committed the crime; (b) the officer deprives the individual of freedom; and (c) the suspect believes that he or she is in the custody of a police officer and cannot voluntarily leave. The police officer is not required to use the word "arrest" or any similar word to initiate an arrest; nor does the officer first have to bring the suspect to the police station. For all practical purposes, a person who has been deprived of liberty is under arrest. Arrests can be made at the scene of a crime or after a warrant is issued by a magistrate.

4. *Custody.* After arrest, the suspect remains in police custody. The person may be taken to the police station to be fingerprinted and photographed and to have personal information recorded—a procedure popularly referred to as **booking.** Witnesses may be brought in to view the suspect (in a lineup), and further evidence may be gathered on the case. Suspects may be interrogated by police officers to get their side of the story, they may be asked to sign a confession of guilt, or they may be asked to identify others involved in the

arrest
The taking into police custody of an individual suspected of a crime.

probable cause
Evidence of a crime, and of a suspect's involvement in it, sufficient to warrant an arrest.

booking
Fingerprinting, photographing, and recording personal information of a suspect in police custody.

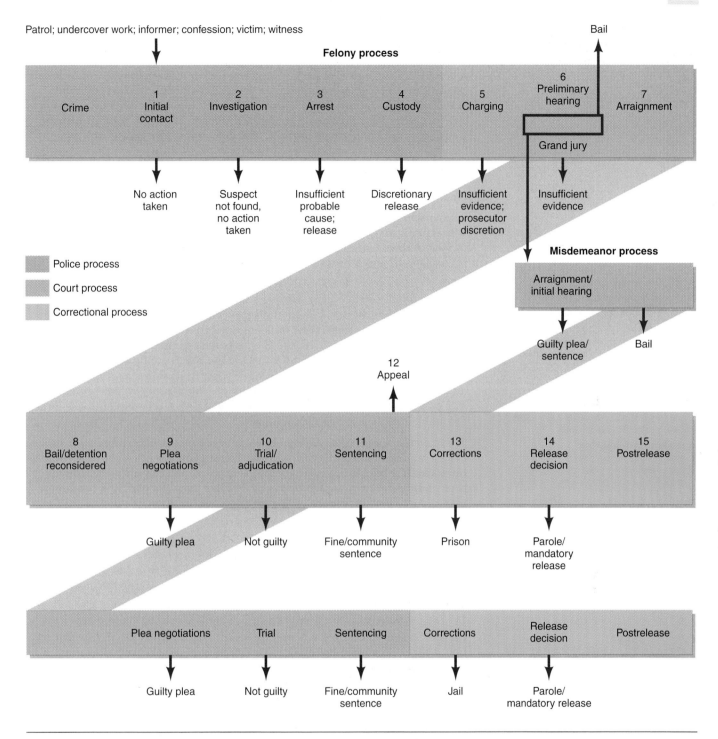

Felony process

Patrol; undercover work; informer; confession; victim; witness

Bail

| Crime | 1 Initial contact | 2 Investigation | 3 Arrest | 4 Custody | 5 Charging | 6 Preliminary hearing | 7 Arraignment |

Grand jury

No action taken

Suspect not found, no action taken

Insufficient probable cause; release

Discretionary release

Insufficient evidence; prosecutor discretion

Insufficient evidence

Misdemeanor process

Arraignment/ initial hearing

Guilty plea/ sentence

Bail

Police process
Court process
Correctional process

12 Appeal

| 8 Bail/detention reconsidered | 9 Plea negotiations | 10 Trial/ adjudication | 11 Sentencing | 13 Corrections | 14 Release decision | 15 Postrelease |

Guilty plea

Not guilty

Fine/community sentence

Prison

Parole/ mandatory release

| Plea negotiations | Trial | Sentencing | Corrections | Release decision | Postrelease |

Guilty plea

Not guilty

Fine/community sentence

Jail

Parole/ mandatory release

Figure 14.6
The Critical Stages of the Justice Process

interrogation
The questioning of a suspect in police custody.

crime. The law allows suspects to have their lawyer present when police conduct an in-custody **interrogation.**

5. *Complaint/charging.* After police turn the evidence in a case over to the prosecutor, who represents the state at any criminal proceedings, a decision will be made whether to file a complaint, information, or bill of indictment with the court having jurisdiction over the case. Complaints are used in misdemeanors; information and indictment are employed in felonies. Each is a charging document asking the court to bring a case forward to be tried.

6. *Preliminary hearing/grand jury.* Because it is a tremendous personal and financial burden to stand trial for a serious felony crime, the U.S. Constitution provides that the state must first prove to an impartial hearing board that there is probable cause that the accused committed the crime and,

therefore, that there is sufficient reason to try the person as charged. In about half the states and in the federal system, the decision of whether to bring a suspect to trial (**indictment**) is made by a group of citizens brought together to form a **grand jury.** The grand jury considers the case in a closed hearing in which only the prosecutor presents evidence. In the remaining states, an information is filed before an impartial lower-court judge who decides whether the case should go forward. This is known as a **preliminary hearing** or probable cause hearing. The defendant may appear at a preliminary hearing and dispute the prosecutor's charges. During either procedure, if the prosecution's evidence is accepted as factual and sufficient, the suspect is called to stand trial for the crime. These procedures are not used for misdemeanors because of their lesser importance and seriousness.

7. *Arraignment.* An **arraignment** brings the accused before the court that will actually try the case. The formal charges are read, and defendants are informed of their constitutional rights (such as the right to legal counsel). Bail is considered, and a trial date is set.

8. *Bail or detention.* If the bail decision has not been considered previously, it is evaluated at arraignment. **Bail** is a money bond, the amount of which is set by judicial authority; it is intended to ensure the presence of suspects at trial while allowing them their freedom until that time. Suspects who do not show up for trial forfeit their bail. Suspects who cannot afford bail or whose cases are so serious that a judge refuses them bail (usually restricted to capital cases) must remain in detention until trial. In most instances, this means an extended stay in the county jail. Many jurisdictions allow defendants awaiting trial to be released on their own **recognizance,** without bail, if they are stable members of the community.

9. *Plea bargaining.* After arraignment, it is common for the prosecutor to meet with the defendant and his or her attorney to discuss a possible **plea bargain.** If a bargain can be struck, the accused pleads guilty as charged, thus ending the criminal trial process. In return for the plea, the prosecutor may reduce charges, request a lenient sentence, or grant the defendant some other consideration.

10. *Adjudication.* If a plea bargain cannot be arranged, a criminal trial takes place. This involves a full-scale inquiry into the facts of the case before a judge, a jury, or both. The defendant can be found guilty or not guilty, or the jury can fail to reach a decision (**hung jury**), thereby leaving the case unresolved and open for a possible retrial.

11. *Disposition.* After a criminal trial, a defendant who is found guilty as charged is sentenced by the presiding judge. **Disposition** usually involves a fine, a term of community supervision (probation), a period of incarceration in a penal institution, or some combination of these penalties. In the most serious capital cases, it is possible to sentence the offender to death. Dispositions are usually made after a presentencing investigation is conducted by the court's probation staff. After disposition, the defendant may appeal the conviction to a higher court.

12. *Postconviction remedies.* After conviction, if the defendant believes he or she was not treated fairly by the justice system, the individual may **appeal** the conviction. An appellate court reviews trial procedures to determine whether an error was made. It considers such questions as whether evidence was used properly, whether the judge conducted the trial in an approved fashion, whether the jury was representative, and whether the attorneys in the case acted appropriately. If the court rules that the appeal has merit, it can hold that the defendant be given a new trial or, in some instances, order his or her outright release. Outright release can be ordered when the state prosecuted the case in violation of the double jeopardy clause of the U.S. Constitution or when it violated the defendant's right to a speedy trial.

indictment
A written accusation returned by a grand jury charging an individual with a specified crime, based on the prosecutor's presentation of probable cause.

grand jury
A group of citizens chosen to hear testimony in secret and to issue formal criminal accusations (indictments).

preliminary hearing
Alternative to a grand jury, in which an impartial lower-court judge decides whether there is probable cause sufficient for a trial.

arraignment
The step in the criminal justice process when the accused is brought before the trial judge, formal charges are read, defendants are informed of their rights, a plea is entered, bail is considered, and a trial date is set.

bail
A money bond intended to ensure that the accused will return for trial.

recognizance
Pledge by the accused to return for trial, which may be accepted in lieu of bail.

plea bargain
An agreement between prosecution and defense in which the accused pleads guilty in return for a reduction of charges, a more lenient sentence, or some other consideration.

hung jury
A jury that is unable to agree on a decision, thus leaving the case unresolved and open for a possible retrial.

disposition
Sentencing of a defendant who has been found guilty; usually involves a fine, probation, or incarceration.

appeal
Taking a criminal case to a higher court on the grounds that the defendant was found guilty because of legal error or violation of constitutional rights; a successful appeal may result in a new trial.

■ The initial contact an offender has with the justice system occurs when police officers observe a criminal act during their patrol of city streets, parks, or highways. Here, police attempt to capture Geraldo Sanchez on July 19, 2003, outside the Freedom Tower in Miami, Florida, where mourners were paying their respects to Celia Cruz. Sanchez allegedly threw rocks, small pipes, and a cup of urine on police, and threatened to kill himself by jumping off the 25-foot pole. Officers used a taser and bean bag guns to subdue Sanchez.

13. *Correctional treatment.* Offenders who are found guilty and are formally sentenced come under the jurisdiction of correctional authorities. They may serve a term of community supervision under control of the county probation department; they may have a term in a community correctional center; or they may be incarcerated in a large penal institution.

14. *Release.* At the end of the correctional sentence, the offender is released into the community. Most incarcerated offenders are granted parole before the expiration of the maximum term given them by the court and therefore finish their prison sentences in the community under supervision of the parole department. Offenders sentenced to community supervision, if successful, simply finish their terms and resume their lives unsupervised by court authorities.

15. *Postrelease/aftercare.* After termination of correctional treatment, the offender must successfully return to the community. This adjustment is usually aided by corrections department staff members, who attempt to counsel the offender through the period of reentry into society. The offender may be asked to spend some time in a community correctional center, which acts as a bridge between a secure treatment facility and absolute freedom. Offenders may find that their conviction has cost them some personal privileges, such as the right to hold certain kinds of jobs. These privileges may be returned by court order once the offenders have proven their trustworthiness and willingness to adjust to society's rules. Successful completion of the postrelease period marks the end of the criminal justice process.

At every stage of the criminal justice process, a decision is made by an agency of criminal justice whether to send the case farther down the line or "kick it" from the system. For example, an investigation is pursued for a few days, and if a suspect is not identified, the case is dropped. A prosecutor decides not to charge a person in police custody because he or she believes there is insufficient evidence to sustain a finding of guilt. A grand jury fails to hand down an indictment because it finds that the prosecutor presented insufficient evidence. A jury fails to convict the accused because it doubts his or her guilt. A parole board decides to release one inmate but denies another's request for early release. These decisions transform the identity of the individual passing through the system from an accused to a defendant, convicted criminal, inmate, and ex-con. Conversely, if decision makers take no action, people accused of crime can return to their daily lives with minimal interference in their lives or identities. Their friends and neighbors may not even know that they were once the subject of criminal investigation. Decision making and discretion mark each stage of the system. Thus, the criminal justice system acts like a funnel in which a great majority of cases are screened out before trial. As Figure 14.7 shows, cases are dismissed at each stage of the system, and relatively few actually reach trial. Those that do are more likely to be handled with a plea bargain than with a criminal trial. The funnel indicates that the justice system does not treat all felonies alike; only the relatively few serious cases make it through to the end of the formal process.[17]

Public perceptions about criminal justice are often formed on the basis of what happens in a few celebrated cases that receive widespread media attention. Some involve wealthy clients who can afford to be represented by high-powered attorneys who can hire the best experts to convince the jury that their client is innocent. The O. J. Simpson case is the best example of the

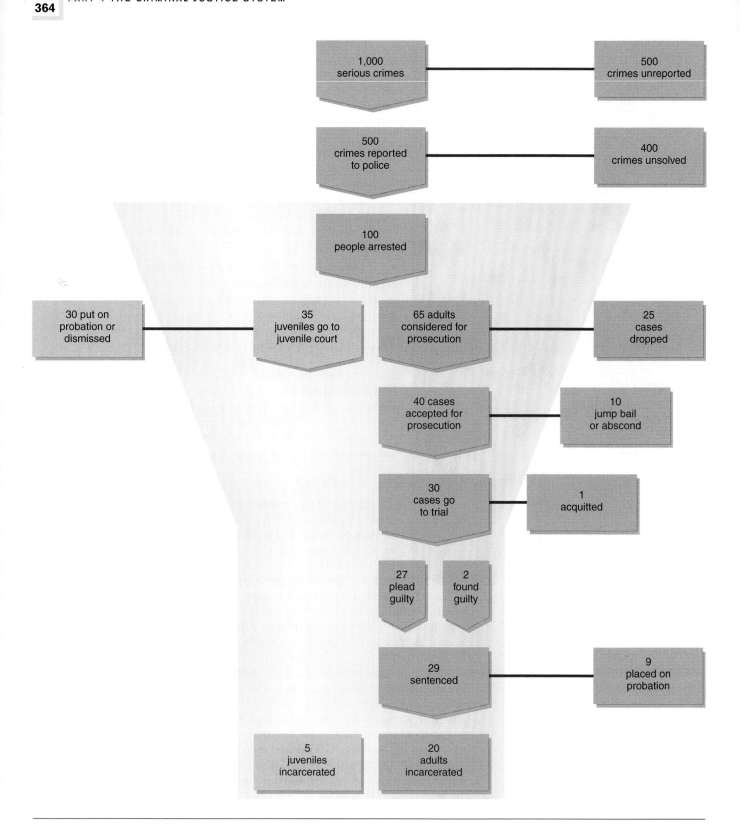

Figure 14.7
The Criminal Justice "Funnel"

SOURCES: Gerard Rainville and Brian Reaves, *Felony Defendants in Large Urban Counties, 2000* (Washington, D.C.: Bureau of Justice Statistics, 2003); Matthew Durose and Patrick Langan, *Felony Sentences in State Courts, 2000* (Washington, D.C.: Bureau of Justice Statistics, 2003).

celebrity defendant. Other defendants become celebrities when they are accused of particularly heinous or notorious crimes and draw the attention of both the press and accomplished defense attorneys.

In reality, these celebrity cases are few and far between. Most defendants are indigent people who cannot afford a comprehensive defense. The

FIND IT ON INFOTRAC
College Edition

For further information on the right to counsel, see:

Martin Gardner, "Sixth Amendment Right to Counsel and Its Underlying Values," *Journal of Criminal Law and Criminology*, 2000, v90 p397

system is actually dominated by judges, prosecutors, and public defenders who work in concert to get cases processed quickly and efficiently. Trials are rare; most cases are handled with a quick plea bargain and sentencing. This pattern of cooperation is referred to as the **courtroom work group.** By working together in a cooperative fashion, the prosecution and defense make sure that the cases flowing through the justice system proceed in an orderly and effective manner. Such "bargain justice" is estimated to occur in more than 90 percent of all criminal cases. If each defendant were afforded the full measure of constitutional rights, including a jury trial, the system would quickly become overloaded. Court dockets are too crowded and funds too scarce to grant each defendant a full share of justice.[18] Although the criminal court system is founded on the concept of equality before the law, poor and wealthy citizens receive unquestionably different treatment when they are accused of crimes.

Criminal Justice and the Rule of Law

✔ Checkpoints

✔ The criminal justice process can be best understood as a series of decision points.

✔ At each stage of the system, a decision is reached whether to process an offender to the next stage or terminate the case.

✔ Although a few celebrity cases receive the full range of justice procedures, most cases are handled in a cursory fashion and are settled with a plea bargain.

✔ The justice system is bound by the rule of law, which ensures that criminal defendants are protected from violations of their civil rights.

To quiz yourself on this material, go to questions 14.6–14.9 on the Criminology: The Core 2e Web site.

courtroom work group
Prosecution, defense, and judges working together to resolve criminal cases quickly and efficiently through plea bargaining.

law of criminal procedure
Judicial precedents that define and guarantee the rights of criminal defendants and control the various components of the criminal justice system.

Bill of Rights
The first 10 amendments to the U.S. Constitution, including guarantees against unreasonable search and seizure, self-incrimination, and cruel punishment.

For many years, U.S. courts exercised little control over the operations of criminal justice agencies, believing that their actions were not an area of judicial concern. This policy is referred to as the hands-off doctrine. However, in the 1960s, under the guidance of Chief Justice Earl Warren, the U.S. Supreme Court became more active in the affairs of the justice system. Today, each component of the justice system is closely supervised by state and federal courts through the **law of criminal procedure,** which sets out and guarantees citizens certain rights and privileges when they are accused of crime.

Procedural laws control the actions of the agencies of justice and define the rights of criminal defendants. They first come into play when people are suspected of committing crimes and the police wish to investigate them, search their property, or interrogate them. Here the law dictates, for example, whether police can search the homes of or interrogate unwilling suspects. If a formal charge is filed, procedural laws guide pretrial and trial activities; for example, they determine when and if people can obtain state-financed attorneys and when they can be released on bail. If a person is found guilty of committing a criminal offense, procedural laws guide the posttrial and correctional processes; for example, they determine when a conviction can be appealed.

Procedural laws have several different sources. Most important are the first 10 amendments to the U.S. Constitution, ratified in 1791 and generally called the **Bill of Rights.** Included within these amendments are the right of the people to be secure in their homes from unwarranted intrusion by government agents, to be free from self-incrimination, and to be protected against cruel punishments, such as torture.

The guarantees of freedom contained in the Bill of Rights initially applied only to the federal government and did not affect the individual states. In 1868, the Fourteenth Amendment made the first 10 amendments to the Constitution binding on the state governments. However, it has remained the duty of state and federal court systems to interpret constitutional law and develop a body of case law that spells out the exact procedural rights to which a person is entitled. Thus, it is the U.S. Supreme Court that interprets the Constitution and sets out the procedural laws that must be followed by the lower federal and state courts. If the Supreme Court has not ruled on a procedural issue, then the lower courts are free to interpret the Constitution as they see fit.

Today, procedural rights protect defendants from illegal searches and seizures and overly aggressive police interrogations. According to the *exclusionary rule,* such illegally seized evidence cannot be used during a trial.

✔ Checkpoints

Concepts of Justice

Many justice system operations are controlled by the rule of law, but they are also influenced by the various philosophies or viewpoints held by its practitioners and policymakers. These, in turn, have been influenced by criminological theory and research. Knowledge about crime, its causes, and its control has significantly affected perceptions of how criminal justice should be managed.

Not surprisingly, many competing views of justice exist simultaneously in U.S. culture. Those in favor of one position or another try to win public opinion to their side, hoping to influence legislative, judicial, or administrative decision making. Over the years, different philosophical viewpoints tend to predominate, only to fall into disfavor as programs based on their principles fail to prove effective.

The remainder of this chapter briefly discusses the most important concepts of criminal justice.

Crime Control Model

Those espousing the **crime control model** believe that the overriding purpose of the justice system is to protect the public, deter criminal behavior, and incapacitate known criminals. Those who embrace its principles view the justice system as a barrier between destructive criminal elements and conventional society. Speedy, efficient justice, unencumbered by legal red tape and followed by punishment designed to fit the crime, is the goal of advocates of the crime control model. Its disciples promote such policies as increasing the size of police forces, maximizing the use of discretion, building more prisons, using the death penalty, and reducing legal controls on the justice system. They point to evidence showing that as many as 30,000 violent criminals, 62,000 drunk drivers, 46,000 drug dealers, and several hundred thousand other criminals go free every year in cases dropped because police believe they have violated the suspects' **Miranda rights**.[19] They lobby for abolition of the **exclusionary rule** and applaud when the Supreme Court hands down rulings that increase police power.

The crime control philosophy emphasizes protecting society and compensating victims. The criminal is responsible for his or her actions, has broken faith with society, and has chosen to violate the law for reasons such as anger, greed, or revenge. Therefore, money spent should be directed not at making criminals more comfortable but at increasing the efficiency of police in apprehending them and the courts in trying them effectively and the corrections system in meting out criminal punishment. This element of justice is quite critical because punishment symbolizes the legitimate social order and the power societies have to regulate behavior and punish those who break social rules.[20]

The crime control philosophy has become a dominant force in American justice. Fear of crime in the 1960s and 1970s was coupled with a growing skepticism about the effectiveness of rehabilitation efforts. A number of important reviews claimed that treatment and rehabilitation efforts directed at known criminals just did not work.[21] There is more evidence that most criminals recidivate after their release from prison and that their reentry into society can destabilize the neighborhoods to which they return. The Current Issues in Crime feature discusses this problem.

The lack of clear evidence that criminals can be successfully treated has produced a climate in which conservative, hard-line solutions to the crime problem are being sought. The results of this swing can be seen in such phenomena as the increasing use of the death penalty, erosion of the exclusionary rule, prison overcrowding, and attacks on the insanity defense. In the past few years, a number of states, including Tennessee, Utah, Iowa, Ohio, and West Virginia, have changed their juvenile codes, making it easier to try juveniles as adults. Other states have expanded their control over ex-offenders by

Connections

The crime control model is rooted in choice theory, discussed in Chapter 4. Fear of criminal sanctions is viewed as the primary deterrent to crime. Because criminals are rational and choose to commit crime, it stands to reason that their activities can be controlled if the costs of crime become too high. Swift, sure, and efficient justice is considered an essential element of an orderly society.

crime control model
View that the overriding purpose of the justice system is to protect the public, deter criminal behavior, and incapacitate known criminals; favors speedy, efficient justice and punishment.

Miranda rights
Rights of criminal defendants, including the right against self-incrimination and right to counsel, spelled out in the case of *Miranda v. Arizona*.

exclusionary rule
The rule that evidence against a defendant may not be presented in court if it was obtained in violation of the defendant's rights.

■ The crime control philosophy emphasizes that criminals are responsible for their actions, and therefore the justice system should be willing to punish them for their misdeeds. The harsher the punishment the less likely they will repeat their criminal acts, and others, observing the punishment, will be less willing to risk crime themselves.

requiring registration of sex offenders. New York has passed a death penalty statute, and other states, including Delaware and South Dakota, have expanded the circumstances under which a person may be eligible for the death penalty.[22]

Can such measures deter crime? There is some evidence that strict crime control measures can have a deterrent effect.[23] A study by the National Center for Policy Analysis uncovered a direct correlation between the probability of imprisonment for a particular crime and a subsequent decline in the rate of that crime.[24] The probability of going to prison for murder increased 17 percent between 1993 and 1997, and the murder rate dropped 23 percent during that period; robbery declined 21 percent as the probability of prison increased 14 percent. These data support the crime control model.

Justice Model

According to the **justice model,** it is futile to rehabilitate criminals, both because treatment programs are ineffective and because they deny people equal protection under the law.[25] It is unfair if two people commit the same crime but receive different sentences because only one is receptive to treatment. The consequence is a sense of injustice in the criminal justice system.

Beyond these problems, justice model advocates question the crime control perspective's reliance on deterrence. Is it fair to punish or incarcerate based on predictions of what offenders will do in the future or on whether others will be deterred by their punishment? Justice model advocates are also concerned with unfairness in the system, such as racism and discrimination, that causes sentencing disparity and unequal treatment before the law.[26]

As an alternative, the justice model calls for fairness in criminal procedure. This would require **determinate sentencing,** in which all offenders in a particular crime category would receive the same sentence. Prisons would be viewed as places of just, evenhanded punishment, not rehabilitation. Parole would be abolished to avoid the discretionary unfairness associated with that mechanism of early release.

The justice model has had an important influence on criminal justice policy. Some states have adopted flat sentencing statutes and have limited the use of parole. There is a trend toward giving prison sentences because people deserve punishment rather than because the sentences will deter or

justice model
View that emphasizes fairness and equal treatment in criminal procedures and sentencing.

determinate sentencing
Principle that all offenders who commit the same crime should receive the same sentence.

CURRENT ISSUES IN CRIME

The Problems of Reentry

Because of America's two-decade-long imprisonment boom, more than 500,000 inmates are now being released back into the community each year. As Figure A shows, the number of people being paroled into the community has almost tripled since 1980. And as Figure B shows, more than 60 percent are re-arrested within three years of their release.

Criminologist Joan Petersilia warns that as the number of inmates released from prison increases—many of whom have not received adequate treatment and are unprepared for life in conventional society—a number of unfortunate collateral consequences will follow. Among them are increases in child abuse, family violence, the spread of infectious diseases, homelessness, and community disorganization.

Reentry risks have increased and can be tied to legal changes in the way people are released from prison. In the past, offenders were granted early release only if a parole board believed they were rehabilitated and had ties to the community—such as a family or a job. Inmates were encouraged to enter treatment programs to earn parole. Changes in sentencing law have resulted in the growth of mandatory release and the limits on discretionary parole. People now serve a fixed sentence, and the discretion of parole boards has been blunted. Inmates may be discouraged from seeking involvement in rehabilitation programs (they do not influence the chance of parole), and the lack of incentive means that fewer inmates leaving prison have participated in programs to address work, education, and substance use deficiencies. For example, only 13 percent of inmates who suffer addiction receive any kind of drug abuse treatment in prison. Nor does the situation improve upon release. Many inmates are not assigned to supervision caseloads once released into the community; about 100,000 re-leased inmates go unsupervised each year.

Petersilia argues that once back in the community offenders may increase their criminal activity because they want to "make up for lost time" and resume their criminal careers. The majority leave prison with no savings, no immediate entitlement to unemployment benefits, and few employment prospects. One year after release, as many as 60 percent of former inmates are not employed in the regular labor market, and there is increasing reluctance among employers to hire ex-offenders. Unemployment is closely related to drug and alcohol abuse. Losing a job can lead to substance abuse, which in turn is related to child and family violence. Mothers released from prison have difficulty finding services such as housing, employment, and child care, and this causes stress for them and their children. Children of incarcerated and released parents often suffer confusion, sadness, and social stigma, and these feelings may result in school-related difficulties, low self-esteem, aggressive behavior, and general emotional dysfunction. If the parents are negative role models, children fail to develop positive attitudes about work and responsibility. Children of incarcerated parents are five times more likely to serve time in prison than are children whose parents are not incarcerated.

Prisoners have significantly more medical and mental health problems than the general population due to lifestyles that often include crowded or itinerant living conditions, intravenous drug use, poverty, and high rates of substance abuse. Inmates with mental illness (about 16 percent of all inmates) also are increasingly being imprisoned—and being released. Even when public mental health services are available, many mentally ill individuals fail to use them because they fear institutionalization, deny they are mentally ill, or distrust the mental health system. The situation will become more serious as more and more parolees are released back into the disorganized communities whose deteriorated conditions may have motivated their original crimes.

Fear of a prison stay has less of an impact on behavior than ever before. As the prison population grows, the negative impact of incarceration may be lessening. In neighborhoods where "doing time" is more a rule than the exception, it becomes less of a stigma and more a badge of acceptance. It also becomes a way of life from which some ex-convicts do rebound. Teens may encounter older men who have gone to prison and have returned to begin their lives again. With the proper skills and survival techniques, prison is considered "manageable." A prison stay is still unpleasant, but it has lost its aura of shame and fear. By becoming commonplace and mundane, the "myth" and fear of the prison experience has been exposed and its deterrent power reduced.

The Effect on Communities

Parole expert Richard Seiter has written on the effect returnees have on communities. When there were only a few hundred thousand prisoners, and a few thousand releasees per year, the issues surrounding the release of offenders did not overly challenge communities. Families could house ex-inmates, job-search organizations could find them jobs, and community social service agencies could respond to their individual needs for mental health or substance abuse treatment. Today, the sheer number of reentering inmates has taxed the communities to which they are returning. The challenges of prisoner reentry can be observed by conditions in the state of Illinois. In 2001, 30,068 men and women were released from Illinois prisons, compared to just 11,715 in 1983. Just over half of those prisoners (15,488) returned to the

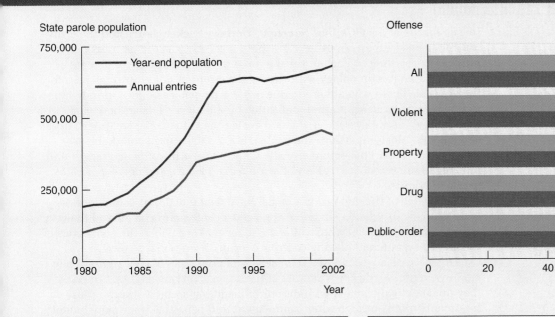

Figure A

Annual State Parole Population and Entries to State Parole, 1980–2002

SOURCE: Timothy Hughes and Doris James Wilson, *Reentry Trends in the United States, Inmates Returning to the Community After Serving Time in Prison* (Washington, D.C.: Bureau of Justice Statistics, 2003).

Figure B

Percentage of Released Prisoners Rearrested within Three Years, by Offense, 1983 and 1994

city of Chicago where they were concentrated in relatively few neighborhoods; 6 of Chicago's 77 communities accounted for 34 percent of the prisoners returning to Chicago. These communities already face great social and economic disadvantages, and the influx of returning inmates can magnify their problems.

The results of this system overload were recently encountered in Tallahassee, Florida, by Todd Clear and his associates. Data collected indicate that crime rates increase markedly one year after large numbers of inmates are released into the community. Disturbingly, the Clear research found that high rates of prison admissions produce high crime rates. Clearly the national policy of relying on prison as a deterrent to crime may produce results that policymakers had not expected or wanted.

Critical Thinking

1. All too often, government leaders jump on the incarceration bandwagon as a panacea for the nation's crime problem. Is it a "quick fix" whose long-term consequences may be devastating for the nation's cities, or are these problems counterbalanced by the crime-reducing effect of putting large numbers of high-rate offenders behind bars?

2. If you agree that incarceration undermines neighborhoods, can you think of some other indirect ways that high incarceration rates help increase crime rates?

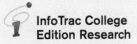

InfoTrac College Edition Research

Alternatives to prison are now being sought because high incarceration may undermine a community's viability.

What do you think? For some interesting developments, check out these articles:

Joe Loconte, "Making Criminals Pay: A New York County's Bold Experiment in Biblical Justice," *Policy Review,* Jan-Feb 1998 n87 p26

Katarina Ivanko, "Shifting Gears to Rehabilitation," *Corrections Today,* April 1997 v59 n2 p20.

SOURCES: Joan Petersilia, *When Prisoners Come Home: Parole and Prisoner Reentry* (New York: Oxford University Press, 2003); Nancy La Vigne, Cynthia Mamalian, Jeremy Travis, and Christy Visher, *A Portrait of Prisoner Reentry in Illinois* (Washington, D.C.: Urban Institute, 2003); Joan Petersilia, When prisoners return to communities: political, economic, and social consequences," *Federal Probation* 65 (2001): 3–9; Todd Clear, Dina Rose, Elin Waring, and Kristen Scully, "Coercive mobility and crime: a preliminary examination of concentrated incarceration and social disorganization," *Justice Quarterly* 20 (2003): 33–65; Richard Seiter, "Prisoner reentry and the role of parole officers," *Federal Probation* 66 (2002).

rehabilitate them. Such measures as sentencing guidelines, which are aimed at reducing sentencing disparity, are a direct offshoot of the justice model.

Due Process Model

In *The Limits of the Criminal Sanction,* Herbert Packer contrasted the crime control model with an opposing view that he refers to as the **due process model**.[27] According to Packer, the due process model combines elements of liberal/positivist criminology with the legal concept of procedural fairness for the accused. Those who adhere to due process principles believe in individualized justice, treatment, and rehabilitation of offenders. If discretion exists in the criminal justice system, it should be used to evaluate the treatment needs of offenders. Most important, the civil rights of the accused should be protected at all costs. This emphasis calls for strict scrutiny of police search and interrogation procedures, review of sentencing policies, and development of prisoners' rights.

Advocates of the due process model have demanded that competent defense counsel, jury trials, and other procedural safeguards be offered to every criminal defendant. They have also called for making public the operations of the justice system and placing controls over its discretionary power.

Due process advocates see themselves as protectors of civil rights. They view overzealous police as violators of basic constitutional rights. Similarly, they are skeptical about the intentions of meddling social workers, whose treatments often entail greater confinement and penalties than punishment does. Their concern is magnified by data showing that the poor and minority group members are often maltreated in the criminal justice system. In some jurisdictions, such as Washington, D.C., almost half of all African American young men are under the control of the justice system. Is it possible that this reflects racism, discrimination, and a violation of their civil rights?[28] Research shows that in at least some states African Americans are more likely to be sent to prison than European Americans; these racial differences in the incarceration rate cannot be explained by the fact that blacks are arrested more often than whites.[29] The Race, Culture, Gender, and Criminology feature explores the issue of racial discrimination in the sentencing process.

Due process exists to protect citizens—both from those who wish to punish them and from those who wish to treat them without regard for legal and civil rights. Due process model advocates worry about the government's expanding ability to use computers to intrude into people's private lives. In 1996, for example, the federal government announced plans for a computerized registry of sex offenders; there are plans for nationwide computer-based mug shot and fingerprint systems. These measures can harm privacy and civil liberties, although research shows that they may have relatively little impact on controlling crime.[30]

Advocates of the due process orientation are quick to point out that the justice system remains an adversary process that pits the forces of an all-powerful state against those of a solitary individual accused of crime. If an overriding concern for justice and fairness did not exist, the defendant who lacked resources could easily be overwhelmed. They point to miscarriages of justice such as the case of Jeffrey Blake, who went to prison for a double murder in 1991 and spent seven years behind bars before his conviction was overturned in 1998. The prosecution's star witness conceded that he had lied on the stand, forcing Blake to spend a quarter of his life in prison for a crime he did not commit.[31] His wrongful conviction would have been even more tragic if he had been executed for his alleged crime. The Institute for Law and Justice, a Virginia-based research firm, found that at least 28 cases of sexual assault have been overturned because DNA evidence proved that the convicted men could not have committed the crimes; the inmates averaged seven years in prison before their release.[32] Because such mistakes can happen, even the most apparently guilty offender deserves all the protection the justice system can offer.

due process model
View that focuses on protecting the civil rights of those accused of crime.

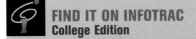

FIND IT ON INFOTRAC
College Edition

The concept of due process guaranteed by the Fifth and Fourteenth Amendments to the U.S. Constitution is one of the most complex issues in the criminal justice system. To read more on this topic, use "due process" as a key word.

The due process orientation has not fared well in recent years. The movement to grant greater civil rights protections to criminal defendants has been undermined by Supreme Court decisions expanding police ability to search and seize evidence and to question suspects. Similarly, the movement between 1960 and 1980 to grant prison inmates an ever-increasing share of constitutional protections has been curtailed. There is growing evidence that the desire to protect the public has overshadowed concerns for the rights of criminal defendants. Although the most important legal rights won by criminal defendants in the 1960s and 1970s remain untouched (for example, the right to a fair and impartial jury of one's peers), there was little urgency to increase the scope of civil rights in the more conservative 1990s.

Rehabilitation Model

The **rehabilitation model** embraces the notion that given the proper care and treatment, criminals can be changed into productive, law-abiding citizens. Influenced by positivist criminology, the rehabilitation school suggests that people commit crimes through no fault of their own. Instead, criminals themselves are the victims of social injustice, poverty, and racism; their acts are a response to a society that has betrayed them. And because of their disturbed and impoverished upbringing, they may be suffering psychological problems and personality disturbances that further enhance their crime-committing capabilities. Although the general public wants protection from crime, the argument goes, it also favors programs designed to help unfortunate people who commit crime because of emotional or social problems.[33]

Dealing effectively with crime requires attacking its root causes. Funds must be devoted to equalizing access to conventional means of success. This requires supporting such programs as public assistance, educational opportunity, and job training. If individuals run afoul of the law, efforts should be made to treat them, not punish them, by emphasizing counseling and psychological care in community-based treatment programs. Whenever possible, offenders should be placed on probation in halfway houses or in other rehabilitation-oriented programs.

This view of the justice system portrays it as a method for dispensing "treatment" to needy "patients." Also known as the medical model, it portrays offenders as people who, because they have failed to exercise self-control, need the help of the state. The medical model rejects the crime control philosophy on the ground that it ignores the needs of offenders, who are people whom society has failed to help.

Connections

The rehabilitation model is linked to social structure and social process theories because it assumes that if lifestyle and socialization could be improved, crime rates would decline. See Chapters 6 and 7 for more on these theories.

■ Sometimes rehabilitation can involve "tough love." Here Sister Mary Gregory George talks with Ron Poessy, the coordinator of the Benchmark Program at the Erie County Probation Office in Sandusky, Ohio. After nearly 20 years counseling drug addicts and alcoholics, everyone has come to know what Sister Gregory's tough love means: Her nickname, in fact, is Attila the Nun.

© 2003 AP/Wide World Photos

rehabilitation model
View that sees criminals as victims of social injustice, poverty, and racism and suggests that appropriate treatment can change them into productive, law-abiding citizens.

Race and Sentencing

Although critics of American race relations may think otherwise, research on sentencing has failed to show a definitive pattern of racial discrimination. Some research does indicate that a defendant's race has a direct impact on sentencing outcomes, but other efforts show that the influence of race on sentencing is less clear-cut than anticipated. It is possible that the disproportionate number of minority group members in prison are a result of crime and arrest patterns and not racial bias by judges when they hand out criminal sentences; racial and ethnic minorities commit more crime, the argument goes, and therefore they are more likely to wind up in prison.

Some studies have found that minorities receive significantly longer sentences than whites merely because of their race. For example, Shawn Bushway and Anne Morrison Piehl studied sentencing outcomes in Maryland and found that, on average, African Americans have 20 percent longer sentences than whites, even when holding constant age, gender, and recommended sentence length. Tracy Nobiling, Cassia Spohn, and Miriam DeLone also found that racial status influences sentencing partially because minority group members have a lower income than whites and are more likely to be unemployed. Judges may possibly view their status as "social dynamite," considering them more dangerous and more likely to recidivate than white offenders.

Patterns of Racial Disparity

Why does the critical issue of racial disparity remain so murky? One reason may be that if disparity is a factor in sentencing its cause may lay outside of judicial sentencing practices. For example, research efforts show that minority defendants suffer discrimination in a variety of court actions: they are more likely to be detained before trial than whites and, upon conviction, are more likely to receive jail sentences rather than fines. Prosecutors are less likely to divert minorities from the legal system than whites who commit the same crimes; minorities are less likely to win appeals than are white appellants.

The relationship between race and sentencing may be difficult to establish because their association may not be linear: minority defendants may be punished more severely for some crimes, and under some circumstances, but they are treated more leniently for others. Sociologist Darnell Hawkins explains this phenomenon as a matter of "appropriateness":

> Certain crime types are considered less "appropriate" for blacks than for whites. Blacks who are charged with committing these offenses will be treated more severely than blacks who commit crimes that are considered more "appropriate." Included in the former category are various white collar offenses and crimes against political and social structures of authority. The latter groups of offenses would include various forms of victimless crimes associated with lower social status (e.g., prostitution, minor drug use, or drunkenness). This may also include various crimes against the person, especially those involving black victims.

Race may have an impact on sentencing because some race-specific crimes are punished more harshly than others. African Americans receive longer sentences for drug crimes than Anglos because (a) they are more likely to be arrested for crack possession and sales and (b) crack dealing is more severely punished by state and federal laws than other drug crimes. Because whites are more likely to use marijuana and methamphetamines, prosecutors are more willing to plea-bargain and offer shorter jail terms.

Racial bias has also been linked to victim–offender status. Minority defendants are sanctioned more severely if their victim is white than if their target is a fellow minority group member; minorities who kill whites are more likely to get the death penalty than those who kill other minorities. Judges may base sentencing decisions on the race of the victim and not the race of the defendant. For example, Charles Crawford, Ted Chiricos, and Gary Kleck found that African American defendants are more likely to be prosecuted under habitual offender statutes if they commit crimes where there is a greater likelihood of a white victim (larceny and burglary) than if they commit violent crimes that are largely intraracial. Where there is a perceived "racial threat," punishments are enhanced.

System Effects

Sentencing disparity may also reflect race-based differences in criminal justice practices and policies associated with sentencing outcome. Probation presentence reports may favor white over minority defendants, causing judges to award whites probation more often than minorities. Whites are more likely to receive probation in jurisdictions where African Americans and whites receive prison sentences of similar duration; this is referred to as the "in-out" decision.

Research evidence suggests that correctional treatment can have an important influence on offenders.[34] Programs that teach interpersonal skills and use individual counseling and behavioral modification techniques have produced positive results both in the community and within correctional institutions.[35] And while some politicians call for a strict law-and-order approach, the general public is quite supportive of treatment programs such as early childhood intervention and services for at-risk children.[36]

Defendants who can afford bail receive more lenient sentences than those who remain in pretrial detention; minority defendants are less likely to make bail because they suffer a higher degree of income inequality. That is, minorities earn less on average and therefore are less likely to be able to make bail. Sentencing outcome is also affected by the defendant's ability to afford a private attorney and put on a vigorous legal defense that makes use of high-paid expert witnesses. These factors place the poor and minority group members at a disadvantage in the sentencing process and result in sentencing disparity. Considerations of prior record may be legitimate in forming sentencing decisions, and there is evidence that minorities are more likely to have prior records because of organizational and individual bias on the part of police.

Are Sentencing Practices Changing?

If in fact racial discrepancies exist, new sentencing laws featuring determinate and mandatory sentences may be helping to reduce disparity. For example, Jon'a Meyer and Tara Gray found that jurisdictions in California that use mandatory sentences for crimes such as drunk driving also show little racial disparity in sentences between whites and minority group members. Similarly, a national survey of sentencing practices conducted by the Bureau of Justice Statistics found that white defendants were somewhat more likely to receive probation and other nonincarceration sentences than black defendants (34 percent versus 31 percent), but there was little racial disparity in the length of prison sentences.

These results are encouraging, but it is also possible that some studies miss a racial effect because they combine Anglo and Hispanic cases into a single category of "white" defendants and then compare them with the sentencing of black defendants. Darrell Steffensmeier and Stephen Demuth's analysis of sentencing in Pennsylvania found that Hispanics are punished considerably more severely than non-Hispanic Anglos and that combining the two groups masks the ethnic differences in sentencing. Steffensmeier and Demuth also found that federal court judges in Pennsylvania were less likely to consider race and ethnic origin in their sentencing decisions than state court judges. This outcome suggests that federal judges, who are insulated from community pressures and values and hold a lifetime appointment, are better able to render objective decisions. By implication, justice may become more objective if judges hold life tenure and are selected from a pool of qualified applicants who reside outside the county in which they serve.

Critical Thinking

Do you feel that sentences should be influenced by the fact that one ethnic or racial group is more likely to commit that crime? For example, critics have called for change in the way federal sentencing guidelines are designed, asking that the provisions that punish crack possession more heavily than powdered cocaine possession be repealed because African Americans are more likely to use crack and whites powdered cocaine. Do you approve of such a change? Because of the lingering problem of racial and class bias in the sentencing process, one primary goal of the criminal justice system in the 1990s was to reduce disparity by creating new forms of criminal sentences that limit judicial discretion and are aimed at uniformity and fairness.

InfoTrac College Edition Research

Use the terms *race* and *sentencing* as key words to find out more about the relationship between these two factors.

SOURCES: Shawn Bushway and Anne Morrison Piehl, "Judging judicial discretion: legal factors and racial discrimination in sentencing," *Law and Society Review* 35 (2001): 733–765; Barbara Koons-Witt, "The effect of gender on the decision to incarcerate before and after the introduction of sentencing guidelines," *Criminology* 40 (2002): 97–129; Marian R. Williams and Jefferson E. Holcomb, "Racial disparity and death sentences in Ohio," *Journal of Criminal Justice* 29 (2001): 207–218; Rodney Engen and Randy Gainey, "Modeling the effects of legally relevant and extra-legal factors under sentencing guidelines: the rules have changed," *Criminology* 38 (2000) 1207–1230; Darrell Steffensmeier and Stephen Demuth, "Ethnicity and judges' sentencing decisions: Hispanic-black-white comparisons," *Criminology* 39 (2001): 145–178; Tracy Nobiling, Cassia Spohn, and Miriam DeLone, "A Tale of two counties: unemployment and sentence severity," *Justice Quarterly* 15 (1998): 459–486; Travis Pratt, "Race and sentencing: a meta-analysis of conflicting empirical research results," *Journal of Criminal Justice* 26 (1998): 513–525; Charles Crawford, Ted Chiricos, and Gary Kleck, "Race, racial threat, and sentencing of habitual offenders," *Criminology* 36 (1998): 481–511; Jon'a Meyer and Tara Gray, "Drunk drivers in the courts: legal and extra-legal factors affecting pleas and sentences," *Journal of Criminal Justice* 25 (1997): 155–163; Alexander Alvarez and Ronet Bachman, "American Indians and sentencing disparity: an Arizona test," *Journal of Criminal Justice* 24 (1996): 549–561; Carole Wolff Barnes and Rodney Kingsnorth, "Race, drug, and criminal sentencing: hidden effects of the criminal law," *Journal of Criminal Justice* 24 (1996): 39–55; Samuel Walker, Cassia Spohn and Miriam DeLone, *The Color of Justice, Race, Ethnicity and Crime in America* (Belmont, Calif.: Wadsworth, 1996), pp. 145–146; Jo Dixon, "The organizational context of sentencing," *American Journal of Sociology* 100 (1995): 1157–1198; Celesta Albonetti and John Hepburn, "Prosecutorial discretion to defer criminalization: the effects of defendant's ascribed and achieved status characteristics," *Journal of Quantitative Criminology* 12 (1996): 63–81; Darnell Hawkins, "Race, crime type and imprisonment," *Justice Quarterly* 3 (1986): 251–269.

Nonintervention Model

In the late 1960s and 1970s, both the rehabilitation ideal and the due process movement were viewed suspiciously by experts concerned by the stigmatization of offenders. Regardless of the purpose, the more the government intervenes in the lives of people, the greater the harm done to their future behavior patterns. Once arrested and labeled, the offender is placed at a disadvantage at home, at school, and in the job market.[37] Rather than deter crime, the stigma of a criminal label erodes social capital and jeopardizes future success and achievement.

The **noninterventionist model** calls for limiting government intrusion into the lives of people, especially minors, who run afoul of the law.[38] Noninterventionists advocate deinstitutionalization of nonserious offenders, diversion from formal court processes into informal treatment programs, and decriminalization of nonserious offenses, such as possessing small amounts of marijuana. Under this concept, the justice system should interact as little as possible with offenders. Police, courts, and correctional agencies would concentrate their efforts on diverting law violators out of the formal justice system, thereby helping them avoid the stigma of formal labels such as "delinquent" or "ex-con." Programs instituted under this model include mediation (instead of trial), diversion (instead of formal processing), and community-based corrections (instead of secure corrections).

Nonintervention advocates are also skeptical about the creation of laws that criminalize acts that were previously legal, thus expanding the reach of justice and creating new classes of offenders. For example, it has become popular to expand control over youthful offenders by passing local curfew laws that make it a crime for young people to be out at night after a certain hour, such as 11 P.M. An adolescent who was formerly a night owl is now a criminal![39]

There are many examples of nonintervention ideas in practice. The juvenile justice system has made a major effort to remove youths from adult jails and to reduce the use of pretrial detention. Mediation programs have proven successful alternatives to the formal trial process. In the adult system, pretrial release programs (alternatives to bail) are now the norm instead of an experimental innovation. And, although the prison population is rising, probation and community treatment have become the most common forms of criminal sanction.

There has also been criticism of the noninterventionist philosophy. There is little evidence that alternative programs actually reduce recidivism rates. Some critics charge that alternative programs actually result in "widening the net."[40] That is, efforts to remove people from the justice system actually enmesh them further within it by ordering them to spend more time in treatment than they would have had to spend in the formal legal process.

In the future, the nonintervention philosophy will be aided by the rising cost of justice. Although low-impact, nonintrusive programs may work no better than prison, they are certainly cheaper; program costs may receive greater consideration than program effectiveness.

Restorative Justice Model

A number of liberal and left-oriented scholars have devised the concept of restorative justice. They believe that the true purpose of the criminal justice system is to promote a peaceful, just society; they advocate peacemaking, not punishment.[41]

The **restorative justice model** draws its inspiration from religious and philosophical teachings ranging from Quakerism to Zen. Advocates of restorative justice say that state efforts to punish and control encourage crime. The violent punishing acts of the state, they claim, are not dissimilar from the violent acts of individuals.[42] Whereas crime control advocates associate lower crime rates with increased punishment, restorative justice advocates counter that studies show that punitive methods of correction (such as jail) are no more effective than more humanitarian efforts (such as probation with treatment).[43] Therefore, mutual aid rather than coercive punishment is the key to a harmonious society. Without the capacity to restore damaged social relations, society's response to crime has been almost exclusively punitive.

Restorative justice is guided by three essential principles: community "ownership" of conflict (including crime), material and symbolic reparation for

noninterventionist model
The view that arresting and labeling offenders does more harm than good, that youthful offenders in particular should be diverted into informal treatment programs, and that minor offenses should be decriminalized.

restorative justice model
View that emphasizes the promotion of a peaceful, just society through reconciliation and reintegration of the offender into society.

crime victims, and social reintegration of the offender.[44] Maintaining ownership, or jurisdiction, over the conflict means that the conflict between criminal and victim should be resolved in the community in which it originated, not in some faraway prison. The victim should be given a chance to voice his or her story, and the offender should help compensate the victim financially or by providing some service. The goal is to enable the offender to appreciate the damage caused, to make amends, and to be reintegrated into society.

Restorative justice programs are geared to these principles. The ability of police officers to mediate disputes rather than resort to formal arrest has long been recognized; it is an essential element of community policing.[45] Mediation and conflict resolution programs are now common. Financial and community-service restitution programs as an alternative to imprisonment have been in operation for more than two decades.

Although restorative justice has become an important perspective in recent years, there are so many diverse programs calling themselves "restorative" that there is still no single definition of what constitutes restorative justice.[46] Restorative justice programs must also be wary of the cultural and social differences that can be found throughout our heterogeneous society; what may be considered "restorative" in one subculture may be considered insulting and damaging in another.[47]

Concepts of Justice Today

The various philosophies of justice compete today for dominance in the criminal justice system (see Figure 14.8). Each has supporters who lobby diligently for their positions. At the time of this writing, it seems that the crime control and justice models have captured the support of legislators and the general public. There is a growing emphasis on protecting the public by increasing criminal sentences and swelling prison populations. Yet advocates of the rehabilitation model claim that the recent imprisonment binge may be a false panacea. For example, in his 1998 book *Crime and Punishment in America*, liberal scholar Elliott Currie concedes that the crime rate has declined as the

Figure 14.8
Perspectives on Justice: Key Concerns and Concepts

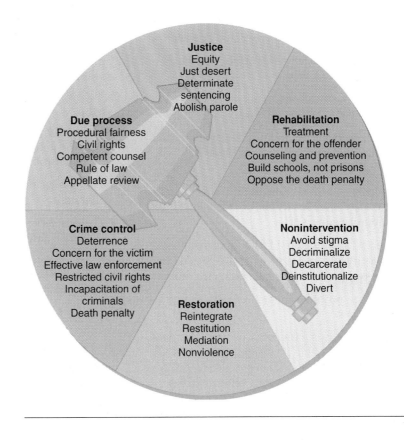

✔ Checkpoints

✔ The most conservative view is the crime control model, which holds that the justice system is designed to protect the public and deter criminal behavior.

✔ In contrast, the rehabilitation model holds that the justice system can help treat needy people and help them turn their lives around.

✔ Some justice experts believe that the system must be on the lookout for violations of due process.

✔ The restorative justice model holds that the system is an ideal venue for reconciliation and healing.

To quiz yourself on this material, go to questions 14.10–14.15 on the Criminology: The Core 2e Web site.

incarceration rate has increased.[48] Nonetheless, he claims that the association may be misleading because the crime rate is undergoing a natural revision from the abnormally high, unprecedented increases brought about by the crack cocaine epidemic in the 1980s. He claims that punitive, incarceration-based models of justice are doomed to fail in the long run. Most offenders eventually return to society, and if the justice system does not help inmates achieve a productive lifestyle, a steadily increasing cohort of ex-offenders with limited life chances will be on the street. Their chances of success in the legitimate world have, if anything, been severely diminished by their prison experiences. Punishment may produce short-term reductions in the crime rate, but only rehabilitation and treatment can produce long-term gains.

So, despite the demand for punishing serious, chronic offenders, the door to treatment for nonviolent, nonchronic offenders has not been closed. The number of noninterventionist and restorative justice programs featuring restitution and nonpunitive sanctions is growing. As the cost of justice skyrockets and the correctional system becomes increasingly overcrowded, alternatives such as house arrest, electronic monitoring, intensive probation supervision, and other cost-effective programs have come to the forefront.

✔ Checkpoints

Summary

- Criminal justice refers to the formal processes and institutions that have been established to apprehend, try, punish, and treat law violators.

- The major components of the criminal justice system are the police, the courts, and correctional agencies.

- Police maintain public order, deter crime, and apprehend law violators.

- Police departments are now experimenting with community and problem-oriented policing.

- The courts determine the criminal liability of accused offenders brought before them and dispense sanctions to those found guilty of crime.

- Corrections agencies provide postadjudicatory care to offenders who are sentenced by the courts to confinement or community supervision.

- Dissatisfaction with traditional forms of corrections has spurred the development of community-based facilities and work release and work furlough programs.

- Justice can also be conceived of as a process through which offenders flow.

- The justice process begins with initial contact by a police agency and proceeds through investigation and custody, trial stages, and correctional system processing. At any stage of the process, the offender may be excused because evidence is lacking, the case is trivial, or a decision maker simply decides to discontinue interest in the case.

- Procedures, policies, and practices employed within the criminal justice system are scrutinized by the courts to make sure they do not violate the guidelines in the first 10 amendments to the U.S. Constitution. If a violation occurs, the defendant can appeal the case and seek to overturn the conviction. Among the rights that must be honored are freedom from illegal searches and seizures and treatment with overall fairness and due process.

- Several different philosophies or perspectives dominate the justice process. The crime control model asserts that the goals of justice are protection of the public and incapacitation of known offenders.

- The justice model calls for fair, equal treatment for all offenders.

- The due process model emphasizes liberal principles, such as legal rights and procedural fairness for the offender.

- The rehabilitation model views the justice system as a wise and caring parent.

- The noninterventionist perspective calls for minimal interference in offenders' lives.

- The restorative justice model seeks nonpunitive, humane solutions to the conflict inherent in crime and victimization.

Thinking Like a Criminologist

You have been appointed assistant to the president's drug czar, who is in charge of coordinating the nation's drug control policy. She has asked you to develop a plan to reduce drug abuse by 25 percent within three years.

You realize that multiple perspectives of justice exist and that the agencies of the criminal justice system can use a number of strategies to reduce drug trafficking and the use of drugs. It might be possible to control the drug trade through a strict crime control effort, for example, using law enforcement officers to cut off supplies of drugs by destroying crops and arresting members of drug cartels in drug-producing countries. Border patrols and military personnel using sophisticated hardware could also help prevent drugs from entering the country. According to the justice model, if drug violations were punished with criminal sentences commensurate with their harm, then the rational drug trafficker might look for a new line of employment. The adoption of mandatory sentences for drug crimes to ensure that all offenders receive similar punishment for their acts might reduce crime. The rehabilitation model suggests that strategies should be aimed at reducing the desire to use drugs and increasing incentives for users to eliminate substance abuse. A noninterventionist strategy calls for the legalization of drugs so distribution could be controlled by the government. Crime rates would be cut because drug users would no longer need the same cash flow to support their habit.

Considering these different approaches, how would you shape drug control strategies?

Go to the Criminology: The Core 2e Web site to review the content of this chapter.

Doing Research on the Web

For an up-to-date list of URLs, go to

http://www.cj.wadsworth.com/siegel_crimcore2e

The Drug Policy Alliance is a leading organization working to end the war on drugs and to reform drug policy. To help research the Thinking Like a Criminologist question, go to their Web site at:

http://www.dpf.org/homepage.cfm

To read about the drug problem in Europe and what is being done about it, go to the Web site of the European Monitoring Centre for Drugs and Drug Addiction (EMCDDA):

http://www.emcdda.eu.int/

Pro/Con discussions and Viewpoint Essays on some of the topics in this chapter may be found at the Opposing Viewpoints Resource Center:

http://www.gale.com/OpposingViewpoints

Key Terms

criminal justice system 350
discretion 353
landmark decision 355
adversary system 355
prosecutor 356
defendant 356
convictability 357
defense attorney 357
right to counsel 358
public defender 358

pro bono 358
probation 358
incarceration 358
jail 358
prison or penitentiary 358
parole 359
arrest 360
probable cause 360
booking 360
interrogation 361

indictment 362
grand jury 362
preliminary hearing 362
arraignment 362
bail 362
recognizance 362
plea bargain 362
hung jury 362
disposition 362
appeal 362

courtroom work group 365
law of criminal procedure 365
Bill of Rights 365
crime control model 366

Miranda rights 366
exclusionary rule 366
justice model 367
determinate sentencing 367

due process model 370
rehabilitation model 371
noninterventionist model 374
restorative justice model 374

Critical Thinking Questions

1. Describe the differences between the formal and informal justice systems. Is it fair to treat some offenders informally?

2. What are the basic elements of each model or perspective on justice? Which best represents your own point of view?

3. How would each perspective on criminal justice consider the use of the death penalty as a sanction for first-degree murder? In your opinion, does the death penalty serve as a deterrent to murder? If not, why not?

4. Discuss the trends that will influence policing during the coming decade.

5. Why does the problem of sentencing disparity exist? Do programs exist that can reduce disparate sentences? If so, what are they?

6. Should all people who commit the same crime receive the same sentence?

NOTES

Chapter 1

1. John Hagan and Alberto Palloni, "Sociological Criminology and the Mythology of Hispanic Immigration and Crime," *Social Problems* 46 (1999): 617–632.
2. Eugene Weber, *A Modern History of Europe* (New York: W. W. Norton, 1971), p. 398.
3. Marvin Wolfgang, *Patterns in Criminal Homicide* (Philadelphia: University of Pennsylvania Press, 1958).
4. Described in David Lykken, "Psychopathy, Sociopathy, and Crime," *Society* 34 (1996): 29–38.
5. See Peter Scott, "Henry Maudsley," in *Pioneers in Criminology,* ed. Hermann Mannheim (Montclair, N.J.: Prentice-Hall, 1981).
6. Nicole Hahn Rafter, "Criminal Anthropology in the United States," *Criminology* 30 (1992): 525–547.
7. Ibid., p. 535.
8. See, generally, Robert Nisbet, *The Sociology of Emile Durkheim* (New York: Oxford University Press, 1974).
9. L. A. J. Quetelet, *A Treatise on Man and the Development of His Faculties* (Gainesville, Fla.: Scholars' Facsimiles and Reprints, 1969), pp. 82–96.
10. Ibid., p. 85.
11. Emile Durkheim, *Rules of the Sociological Method,* reprint ed., trans. W. D. Halls (New York: Free Press, 1982).
12. Emile Durkheim, *The Division of Labor in Society,* reprint ed. (New York: Free Press, 1997).
13. Robert Park and Ernest Burgess, *The City* (Chicago: University of Chicago Press, 1925).
14. Karl Marx and Friedrich Engels, *Capital: A Critique of Political Economy,* trans. E. Aveling (Chicago: Charles Kern, 1906); Karl Marx, *Selected Writings in Sociology and Social Philosophy,* trans. P. B. Bottomore (New York: McGraw-Hill, 1956). For a general discussion of Marxist thought, see Michael Lynch and W. Byron Groves, *A Primer in Radical Criminology* (New York: Harrow and Heston, 1986), pp. 6–26.
15. Irvin Wolfgang and Franco Ferracuti, *The Subculture of Violence* (London: Social Science Paperbacks, 1967), p. 20.
16. *Smith et al. v. Doe et al.,* No. 01-729, March 5, 2003.
17. Ronald Simons, Eric Stewart, Leslie Gordon, Rand Conger, and Glen Elder Jr., "Test of Life-Course Explanations for Stability and Change in Antisocial Bebopper from Adolescence to Young Adulthood" *Criminology* 40 (2002): 401–434.
18. Marvin Wolfgang, *Patterns in Criminal Homicide* (Philadelphia: University of Pennsylvania Press, 1958).
19. Hans von Hentig, *The Criminal and His Victim* (New Haven: Yale University Press, 1948); Stephen Schafer, *The Victim and His Criminal* (New York: Random House, 1968).
20. Charles McCaghy, *Deviant Behavior* (New York: Macmillan, 1976), pp. 2–3.
21. Edwin Sutherland and Donald Cressey, *Criminology,* 8th ed. (Philadelphia: J. B. Lippincott, 1960), p. 8.
22. Howard Becker, *Outsiders: Studies in the Sociology of Deviance* (New York: Free Press, 1963), p. 9.
23. Ibid.
24. Oliver Wendell Holmes, *The Common Law,* ed. Mark De Wolf (Boston: Little, Brown, 1881), p. 36.
25. National Institute of Justice, *Project to Develop a Model Anti-Stalking Statute* (Washington, D.C.: National Institute of Justice, 1994).
26. "Clinton Signs Tougher 'Megan's Law,'" *CNN News Service,* May 17, 1996.
27. Associated Press, "Judge Upholds State's Sexual Predator Law," *Bakersfield Californian,* October 2, 1996.
28. *Lawrence et al. v. Texas,* No. 02-102, June 26, 2003.
29. Michael Gottfredson and Travis Hirschi, "The Methodological Adequacy of Longitudinal Research on Crime," *Criminology* 25 (1987): 581–614.
30. The most recent version available at the time of this writing is Federal Bureau of Investigation, *Crime in the United States, 2002* (Washington, D.C.: U.S. Government Printing Office, 2003).
31. Claire Sterk, "Just for Fun? Cocaine Use Among Middle-Class Women," *Journal of Drug Issues* 26 (1996): 63–76.
32. Ibid., p. 63.
33. William F. Whyte, *Street Corner Society* (Chicago: University of Chicago Press, 1955).
34. Herman Schwendinger and Julia Schwendinger, *Adolescent Subcultures and Delinquency* (New York: Praeger, 1985).
35. Joachim Savelsberg, Ryan King, and Lara Cleveland, "Politicized Scholarship? Science on Crime and the State," *Social Problems* 49 (2002): 327–349.
36. See, for example, Michael Hindelang and Travis Hirschi, "Intelligence and Delinquency: A Revisionist Review," *American Sociological Review* 42 (1977): 471–486.
37. Richard Herrnstein and Charles Murray, *The Bell Curve* (New York: Free Press, 1994).
38. Dermot Feenan, "Legal Issues in Acquiring Information about Illegal Behaviour through Criminological Research," *British Journal of Criminology* 42 (2002): 762–781.
39. Anthony Petrosino, Carolyn Turpin-Petrosino, and James Finckenauer, "Well-Meaning Programs Can Have Harmful Effects! Lessons from Experiments of Programs Such as Scared Straight," *Crime and Delinquency* 46 (2000): 354–379.
40. Victor Boruch, Timothy Victor, and Joe Cecil, "Resolving Ethical and Legal Problems in Randomized Experiments," *Crime and Delinquency* 46 (2000): 330–353.

Chapter 2

1. Information on the Rudolph case can be obtained at http://www.cnn.com/2003/US/05/31/rudolph.arrest/ http://www.belleville.com/mld/newsdemocrat/6027216.htm
2. Federal Bureau of Investigation, *Crime in the United States, 2002* (Washington, D.C.: U.S. Government Printing Office, 2003). Herein cited in notes as FBI, Uniform Crime Report, and referred to in text as Uniform Crime Report or UCR.
3. Callie Marie Rennison, *Criminal Victimization 1999: Changes 1998–99 with Trends 1993–98* (Washington, D.C.: Bureau of Justice Statistics, 2000).
4. Richard Felson, Steven Messner, Anthony Hoskin, and Glenn Deane, "Reasons for Reporting and Not Reporting Domestic Violence to the Police." *Criminology* 40 (2002): 617–648.
5. Bonnie Fisher, Leah Daigle, Francis Cullen, and Michael Turner, "Reporting Sexual Victimization to the Police and Others: Results from a National-Level Study of College Women," *Criminal Justice and Behavior* 30 (2003): 6–39.
6. Duncan Chappell, Gilbert Geis, Stephen Schafer, and Larry Siegel, "Forcible Rape: A Comparative Study of Offenses Known to the Police in Boston and Los Angeles," in *Studies in the Sociology of Sex,* ed. James Henslin (New York: Appleton Century Crofts, 1971), pp. 169–193.
7. Robert O'Brien, "Police Productivity and Crime Rates: 1973–1992," *Criminology* 34 (1996): 183–207.
8. FBI, *UCR Handbook* (Washington, D.C.: U.S. Government Printing Office, 1998), p. 33.
9. Callie Marie Rennison and Michael Rand, *Criminal Victimization 2002* (Washington, D.C.: Bureau of Justice

Statistics, 2003). Data in this section come from this report.

10. L. Edward Wells and Joseph Rankin, "Juvenile Victimization: Convergent Validation of Alternative Measurements," *Journal of Research in Crime and Delinquency* 32 (1995): 287–307.

11. A pioneering effort in self-report research is A. L. Porterfield, *Youth in Trouble* (Fort Worth, Tex.: Leo Potishman Foundation, 1946); for a review, see Robert Hardt and George Bodine, *Development of Self-Report Instruments in Delinquency Research: A Conference Report* (Syracuse, N.Y.: Syracuse University Youth Development Center, 1965). See also Fred Murphy, Mary Shirley, and Helen Witner, "The Incidence of Hidden Delinquency," *American Journal of Orthopsychology* 16 (1946): 686–696.

12. See, for example, John Paul Wright and Francis Cullen, "Juvenile Involvement in Occupational Delinquency," *Criminology* 38 (2000): 863–896.

13. For example, the following studies have noted the great discrepancy between official statistics and self-report studies: Martin Gold, "Undetected Delinquent Behavior," *Journal of Research in Crime and Delinquency* 3 (1966): 27–46; James Short and F. Ivan Nye, "Extent of Undetected Delinquency: Tentative Conclusions," *Journal of Criminal Law, Criminology and Police Science* 49 (1958): 296–302; Michael Hindelang, "Causes of Delinquency: A Partial Replication and Extension," *Social Problems* 20 (1973): 471–487.

14. D. Wayne Osgood, Lloyd Johnston, Patrick O'Malley, and Jerald Bachman, "The Generality of Deviance in Late Adolescence and Early Adulthood," *American Sociological Review* 53 (1988): 81–93.

15. See, for example, Spencer Rathus and Larry Siegel, "Crime and Personality Revisited: Effects of MMPI Sets on Self-Report Studies," *Criminology* 18 (1980): 245–251; John Clark and Larry Tifft, "Polygraph and Interview Validation of Self-Reported Deviant Behavior," *American Sociological Review* 31 (1966): 516–523.

16. Mallie Paschall, Miriam Ornstein, and Robert Flewelling, "African-American Male Adolescents' Involvement in the Criminal Justice System: The Criterion Validity of Self-Report Measures in Prospective Study," *Journal of Research in Crime and Delinquency* 38 (2001): 174–187.

17. Leonore Simon, "Validity and Reliability of Violent Juveniles: A Comparison of Juvenile Self-Reports with Adult Self-Reports Incarcerated in Adult Prisons," paper presented at the annual meeting of the American Society of Criminology, Boston, November 1995, p. 26.

18. Terence Thornberry, Beth Bjerregaard, and William Miles, "The Consequences of Respondent Attrition in Panel Studies: A Simulation Based on the Rochester Youth Development Study," *Journal of Quantitative Criminology* 9 (1993): 127–158.

19. Julia Yun Soo Kim, Michael Fendrich, and Joseph S. Wislar, "The Validity of Juvenile Arrestees' Drug Use Reporting: A Gender Comparison," *Journal of Research in Crime and Delinquency* 37 (2000): 419–432.

20. Barbara Warner and Brandi Wilson Coomer, "Neighborhood Drug Arrest Rates: Are They a Meaningful Indicator of Drug Activity? A Research Note," *Journal of Research in Crime and Delinquency* 40 (2003): 123–139.

21. Alfred Blumstein, Jacqueline Cohen, and Richard Rosenfeld, "Trend and Deviation in Crime Rates: A Comparison of UCR and NCVS Data for Burglary and Robbery," *Criminology* 29 (1991): 237–248. See also Michael Hindelang, Travis Hirschi, and Joseph Weis, *Measuring Delinquency* (Beverly Hills, Calif.: Sage, 1981).

22. Clarence Schrag, *Crime and Justice: American Style* (Washington, D.C.: U.S. Government Printing Office, 1971), p. 17.

23. Thomas Bernard, "Juvenile Crime and the Transformation of Juvenile Justice: Is There a Juvenile Crime Wave?" *Justice Quarterly* 16 (1999): 336–356.

24. Lloyd Johnston, Patrick O'Malley, and Jerald Bachman, *Monitoring the Future, 1990* (Ann Arbor, Mich.: Institute for Social Research, 1991); Timothy Flanagan and Kathleen Maguire, *Sourcebook of Criminal Justice Statistics, 1989* (Washington, D.C.: U.S. Government Printing Office, 1990), pp. 290–291.

25. James A. Fox, *Trends in Juvenile Violence: A Report to the United States Attorney General on Current and Future Rates of Juvenile Offending* (Boston: Northeastern University, 1996).

26. Steven Levitt, "The Limited Role of Changing Age Structure in Explaining Aggregate Crime Rates," *Criminology* 37 (1999): 581–599.

27. Steven Levitt, "Understanding Why Crime Fell in the 1990s: Four Factors that Explain the Decline and Six That Do Not," *Journal of Economic Perspectives* (in press, 2004).

28. Peter Van Koppen and Robert Jansen, "The Time to Rob: Variations in Time of Number of Commercial Robberies," *Journal of Research in Crime and Delinquency* 36 (1999): 7–29.

29. Ellen Cohn, "The Effect of Weather and Temporal Variations on Calls for Police Service," *American Journal of Police* 15 (1996): 23–43.

30. R. A. Baron, "Aggression as a Function of Ambient Temperature and Prior Anger Arousal," *Journal of Personality and Social Psychology* 21 (1972): 183–189.

31. Ellen Cohn, "The Prediction of Police Calls for Service: The Influence of Weather and Temporal Variables on Rape and Domestic Violence," *Journal of Environmental Psychology* 13 (1993): 71–83.

32. See, generally, Franklin Zimring and Gordon Hawkins, *Crime Is Not the Problem: Lethal Violence in America* (New York: Oxford University Press, 1997).

33. Ibid., p. 36.

34. Robert Nash Parker, "Bringing 'Booze' Back In: The Relationship between Alcohol and Homicide," *Journal of Research in Crime and Delinquency* 32 (1995): 3–38.

35. Victoria Brewer and M. Dwayne Smith, "Gender Inequality and Rates of Female Homicide Victimization across U.S. Cities," *Journal of Research in Crime and Delinquency* 32 (1995): 175–190.

36. R. Gregory Dunaway, Francis Cullen, Velmer Burton, and T. David Evans, "The Myth of Social Class and Crime Revisited: An Examination of Class and Adult Criminality," *Criminology* 38 (2000): 589–632.

37. Ivan Nye, James Short, and Virgil Olsen, "Socioeconomic Status and Delinquent Behavior," *American Journal of Sociology* 63 (1958): 381–389; Robert Dentler and Lawrence Monroe, "Social Correlates of Early Adolescent Theft," *American Sociological Review* 63 (1961): 733–743. See also Terence Thornberry and Margaret Farnworth, "Social Correlates of Criminal Involvement: Further Evidence of the Relationship between Social Status and Criminal Behavior," *American Sociological Review* 47 (1982): 505–518.

38. Charles Tittle, Wayne Villemez, and Douglas Smith, "The Myth of Social Class and Criminality: An Empirical Assessment of the Empirical Evidence," *American Sociological Review* 43 (1978): 643–656. See also Charles Tittle and Robert Meier, "Specifying the SES/Delinquency Relationship," *Criminology* 28 (1990): 271–301.

39. Delbert Elliott and Suzanne Ageton, "Reconciling Race and Class Differences in Self-Reported and Official Estimates of Delinquency," *American Sociological Review* 45 (1980): 95–110.

40. See also Delbert Elliott and David Huizinga, "Social Class and Delinquent Behavior in a National Youth Panel: 1976–1980," *Criminology* 21 (1983): 149–177. For a similar view, see John Braithwaite, "The Myth of Social Class and Criminality Reconsidered," *American Sociological Review* 46 (1981): 35–58; Hindelang, Hirschi, and Weis, *Measuring Delinquency,* p. 196.

41. Dunaway, Cullen, Burton, and Evans, "The Myth of Social Class and Crime Revisited."

42. Judith Blau and Peter Blau, "The Cost of Inequality: Metropolitan Structure and Violent Crime," *American Sociological Review* 147 (1982): 114–129; Richard Block, "Community Environment and Violent Crime," *Criminology* 17 (1979): 46–57; Robert Sampson, "Structural Sources of Variation in Race-Age-Specific Rates of Offending across Major U.S. Cities," *Criminology* 23 (1985): 647–673.

43. Chin-Chi Hsieh and M. D. Pugh, "Poverty, Income Inequality, and Violent Crime: A Meta-Analysis of Recent

Aggregate Data Studies," *Criminal Justice Review* 18 (1993): 182–199.

44. Robert Agnew, "A General Strain Theory of Community Differences in Crime Rates," *Journal of Research in Crime and Delinquency* 36 (1999): 123–155.

45. Bonita Veysey and Steven Messner, "Further Testing of Social Disorganization Theory: An Elaboration of Sampson and Groves's 'Community Structure and Crime,'" *Journal of Research in Crime and Delinquency* 36 (1999): 156–174.

46. Lance Hannon and James Defronzo, "Welfare and Property Crime," *Justice Quarterly* 15 (1998): 273–288.

47. Travis Hirschi and Michael Gottfredson, "Age and the Explanation of Crime," *American Journal of Sociology* 89 (1983): 552–584, at p. 581.

48. Darrell Steffensmeier and Cathy Streifel, "Age, Gender, and Crime across Three Historical Periods: 1935, 1960 and 1985," *Social Forces* 69 (1991): 869–894.

49. For a comprehensive review of crime and the elderly, see Kyle Kercher, "Causes and Correlates of Crime Committed by the Elderly," in *Critical Issues in Aging Policy,* eds. E. Borgatta and R. Montgomery (Beverly Hills, Calif.: Sage, 1987), pp. 254–306; Darrell Steffensmeier, "The Invention of the 'New' Senior Citizen Criminal," *Research on Aging* 9 (1987): 281–311.

50. Margo Wilson and Martin Daly, "Life Expectancy, Economic Inequality, Homicide, and Reproductive Timing in Chicago Neighbourhoods," *British Journal of Medicine* 314 (1997): 1271–1274.

51. Edward Mulvey and John LaRosa, "Delinquency Cessation and Adolescent Development: Preliminary Data," *American Journal of Orthopsychiatry* 56 (1986): 212–224.

52. Gordon Trasler, "Cautions for a Biological Approach to Crime," in *The Causes of Crime: New Biological Approaches,* eds. Sarnoff Mednick, Terrie Moffitt, and Susan Stack (Cambridge: Cambridge University Press, 1987), pp. 7–25.

53. Walter Gove, "The Effect of Age and Gender on Deviant Behavior: A Biopsychosocial Perspective," in *Gender and the Life Course,* ed. A. Ross (Chicago: Aldine, 1985), p. 131.

54. Cesare Lombroso, *The Female Offender* (New York: Appleton, 1920), p. 122.

55. Ibid.

56. Alan Booth and D. Wayne Osgood, "The Influence of Testosterone on Deviance in Adulthood: Assessing and Explaining the Relationship," *Criminology* 31 (1993): 93–118.

57. Gisela Konopka, *The Adolescent Girl in Conflict* (Englewood Cliffs, N.J.: Prentice-Hall, 1966); Clyde Vedder and Dora Somerville, *The Delinquent Girl* (Springfield, Ill.: Charles C. Thomas, 1970).

58. Robert Hoge, D. A. Andrews, and Alan Leschied, "Tests of Three Hypotheses Regarding the Predictors of Delinquency," *Journal of Abnormal Child Psychology* 22 (1994): 547–559.

59. Emily Gaarder and Joanne Belknap, "Tenuous Borders: Girls Transferred to Adult Court," *Criminology* 40 (2002): 481–517.

60. Rita James Simon, *The Contemporary Woman and Crime* (Washington, D.C.: U.S. Government Printing Office, 1975).

61. See generally, Mari DeWees and Karen Parker, "The Political Economy of Urban Homicide: Assessing the Relative Impact of Gender Inequality on Sex-Specific Victimization," *Violence and Victims* 18 (2003): 35–54.

62. David Rowe, Alexander Vazsonyi, and Daniel Flannery, "Sex Differences in Crime: Do Mean and Within-Sex Variation Have Similar Causes?" *Journal of Research in Crime and Delinquency* 32 (1995): 84–100; Michael Hindelang, "Age, Sex, and the Versatility of Delinquency Involvements," *Social Forces* 14 (1971): 525–534; Martin Gold, *Delinquent Behavior in an American City* (Belmont, Calif.: Brooks/Cole, 1970); Gary Jensen and Raymond Eve, "Sex Differences in Delinquency: An Examination of Popular Sociological Explanations," *Criminology* 13 (1976): 427–448.

63. David Huizinga and Delbert Elliott, "Juvenile Offenders: Prevalence, Offender Incidence, and Arrest Rates by Race," *Crime and Delinquency* 33 (1987): 206–223. See also Dale Dannefer and Russell Schutt, "Race and Juvenile Justice Processing in Court and Police Agencies," *American Journal of Sociology* 87 (1982): 1113–1132.

64. Paul Tracy, "Race and Class Differences in Official and Self-Reported Delinquency," in *From Boy to Man, from Delinquency to Crime,* eds. Marvin Wolfgang, Terence Thornberry, and Robert Figlio (Chicago: University of Chicago Press, 1987), p. 120.

65. Phillipe Rushton, "Race and Crime: An International Dilemma," *Society* 32 (1995): 37–42; for a rebuttal, see Jerome Neapolitan, "Cross-National Variation in Homicides: Is Race a Factor?" *Criminology* 36 (1998): 139–156.

66. Miriam Sealock and Sally Simpson, "Unraveling Bias in Arrest Decisions: The Role of Juvenile Offender Type-Scripts," *Justice Quarterly* 15 (1998): 427–457.

67. "Law Enforcement Seeks Answers to 'Racial Profiling' Complaints," *Criminal Justice Newsletter* 29 (1998): 5.

68. David Eitle, Stewart D'Alessio, and Lisa Stolzenberg, "Racial Threat and Social Control: A Test of the Political, Economic, and Threat of Black Crime Hypotheses," *Social Forces* 81 (2002): 557–576.

69. Michael Leiber and Jayne Stairs, "Race, Contexts and the Use of Intake Diversion," *Journal of Research in Crime and Delinquency* 36 (1999): 56–86; Darrell Steffensmeier, Jeffery Ulmer, and John Kramer, "The Interaction of Race, Gender, and Age in Criminal Sentencing: The Punishment Cost of Being Young, Black, and Male," *Criminology* 36 (1998): 763–798.

70. Rodney Engen, Sara Steen, and George Bridges, "Racial Disparities in the Punishment of Youth: A Theoretical and Empirical Assessment of the Literature," *Social Problems* 49 (2002): 194–221.

71. Tracy Nobiling, Cassia Spohn, and Miriam DeLone, "A Tale of Two Counties: Unemployment and Sentence Severity," *Justice Quarterly* 15 (1998): 459–486.

72. Alexander Weiss and Steven Chermak, "The News Value of African-American Victims: An Examination of the Media's Presentation of Homicide," *Journal of Crime and Justice* 21 (1998): 71–84.

73. Daniel Georges-Abeyie, "Definitional Issues: Race, Ethnicity and Official Crime/Victimization Rates," in *The Criminal Justice System and Blacks,* ed. D. Georges-Abeyie (New York: Clark Boardman, 1984), p. 12; Robert Sampson, "Race and Criminal Violence: A Demographically Disaggregated Analysis of Urban Homicide," *Crime and Delinquency* 31 (1985): 47–82.

74. Fox Butterfield, *All God's Children: The Bosket Family and the American Tradition of Violence* (New York: Avon, 1996).

75. Barry Sample and Michael Philip, "Perspectives on Race and Crime in Research and Planning," in *The Criminal Justice System and Blacks,* ed. D. Georges-Abeyie (New York: Clark Boardman, 1984), pp. 21–36.

76. Leiber and Stairs, "Race, Contexts and the Use of Intake Diversion"; Steffensmeier, Ulmer, and Kramer, "The Interaction of Race, Gender, and Age in Criminal Sentencing."

77. Mallie Paschall, Robert Flewelling, and Susan Ennett, "Racial Differences in Violent Behavior among Young Adults: Moderating and Confounding Effects," *Journal of Research in Crime and Delinquency* 35 (1998): 148–165.

78. Julie Phillips, "White, Black, and Latino Homicide Rates: Why the Difference?" *Social Problems* 49 (2002): 349–374.

79. Marvin Wolfgang, Robert Figlio, and Thorsten Sellin, *Delinquency in a Birth Cohort* (Chicago: University of Chicago Press, 1972).

80. Lyle Shannon, *Criminal Career Opportunity* (New York: Human Sciences Press, 1988); D. J. West and David P. Farrington, *The Delinquent Way of Life* (London: Heinemann, 1977).

Chapter 3

1. Mark Pazniokas, "Mayor Again Denied Bail, Giordano Remains Flight Risk, Judge Says," *Hartford Courant,* November 9, 2001, p. A1; Associated Press, "Waterbury Mayor Paid Teenager for Sex, Reports Say," *New York Times,* August 16, 2001, p. 1.

2. Associated Press, "Giordano Guilty in Federal Trial Involving Child Sex Abuse," *Hartford Courant,* March 25, 2003, p. 1.

3. Richard Estes and Neil Alan Weiner, *The Commercial Sexual Exploitation of Children in the U.S., Canada and Mexico* (Philadelphia, Pa.: University of Pennsylvania, 2001).

4. Children's Safety Network Economics and Insurance Resource Center, "State Costs of Violence Perpetrated by Youth." Available: http://www.csneirc.org/pubs/tables/youth-viol.htm (accessed July 12, 2000).

5. Ted Miller, Mark Cohen, and Brian Wiersema, *The Extent and Costs of Crime Victimization: A New Look* (Washington, D.C.: National Institute of Justice, 1996).

6. Ted R. Miller, Mark A. Cohen, and Brian Wiersema, *Victim Costs and Consequences: A New Look* (Washington, D.C.: National Institute of Justice, 1996), p. 9, table 2.

7. Ross Macmillan, "Adolescent Victimization and Income Deficits in Adulthood: Rethinking the Costs of Criminal Violence from a Life-Course Perspective," *Criminology* 38 (2000): 553–588.

8. Rebecca Campbell and Sheela Raja, "Secondary Victimization of Rape Victims: Insights from Mental Health Professionals Who Treat Survivors of Violence," *Violence and Victims* 14 (1999): 261–274.

9. Peter Finn, *Victims* (Washington, D.C.: Bureau of Justice Statistics, 1988), p. 1.

10. Catherine Grus, "Child Abuse: Correlations with Hostile Attributions," *Journal of Developmental & Behavioral Pediatrics* 24 (2003): 296–298.

11. Michael Wiederman, Randy Sansone, and Lori Sansone, "History of Trauma and Attempted Suicide among Women in a Primary Care Setting," *Violence and Victims* 13 (1998): 3–11; Susan Leslie Bryant and Lillian Range, "Suicidality in College Women Who Were Sexually and Physically Abused and Physically Punished by Parents," *Violence and Victims* 10 (1995): 195–215; William Downs and Brenda Miller, "Relationships between Experiences of Parental Violence During Childhood and Women's Self-Esteem," *Violence and Victims* 13 (1998): 63–78; Sally Davies-Netley, Michael Hurlburt, and Richard Hough, "Childhood Abuse as a Precursor to Homelessness for Homeless Women with Severe Mental Illness," *Violence and Victims* 11 (1996): 129–142.

12. Jane Siegel and Linda Williams, "Risk Factors for Sexual Victimization of Women," *Violence Against Women* 9 (2003): 902–930.

13. Jeanne Kaufman and Cathy Spatz Widom, "Childhood Victimization, Running Away, and Delinquency," *Journal of Research in Crime and Delinquency* 36 (1999): 347–370.

14. Kim Logio, "Gender, Race, Childhood Abuse, and Body Image among Adolescents," *Violence Against Women* 9 (2003): 931–955.

15. Lana Stermac and Emily Paradis, "Homeless Women and Victimization: Abuse and Mental Health History among Homeless Rape Survivors," *Resources for Feminist Research* 28 (2001): 65–81.

16. Dina Vivian and Jean Malone, "Relationship Factors and Depressive Symptomology Associated with Mild and Severe Husband-to-Wife Physical Aggression," *Violence and Victims* 12 (1997): 19–37; Walter Gleason, "Mental Disorders in Battered Women," *Violence and Victims* 8 (1993): 53–66; Daniel Saunders, "Posttraumatic Stress Symptom Profiles of Battered Women: A Comparison of Survivors in Two Settings," *Violence and Victims* 9 (1994): 31–43.

17. K. Daniel O'Leary, "Psycholgocial Abuse: A Variable Deserving Critical Attention in Domestic Violence," *Violence and Victims* 14 (1999): 1–21.

18. James Anderson, Terry Grandison, and Laronistine Dyson, "Victims of Random Violence and the Public Health Implication: A Health Care of Criminal Justice Issue," *Journal of Criminal Justice* 24 (1996): 379–393.

19. Susan Popkin, Victoria Gwlasda, Dennis Rosenbaum, Jean Amendolla, Wendell Johnson, and Lynn Olson, "Combating Crime in Public Housing: A Qualitative and Quantitative Longitudinal Analysis of the Chicago Housing Authority's Anti-drug Initiative," *Justice Quarterly* 16 (1999): 519–557.

20. Pamela Wilcox Rountree, "A Reexamination of the Crime–Fear Linkage," *Journal of Research in Crime and Delinquency* 35 (1998): 341–372.

21. Susan Brison, *Aftermath: Violence and the Remaking of a Self* (Princeton, N.J.: Princeton University Press, 2001).

22. Timothy Ireland and Cathy Spatz Widom, *Childhood Victimization and Risk for Alcohol and Drug Arrests* (Washington, D.C.: National Institute of Justice, 1995).

23. Brigette Erwin, Elana Newman, Robert McMackin, Carlo Morrissey, and Danny Kaloupek, "PTSD, Malevolent Environment, and Criminality among Criminally Involved Male Adolescents," *Criminal Justice and Behavior* 27 (2000): 196–215.

24. Cathy Spatz Widom, *The Cycle of Violence* (Washington, D.C.: National Institute of Justice, 1992), p. 1.

25. Steve Spaccarelli, J. Douglas Coatsworth, and Blake Sperry Bowden, "Exposure to Serious Family Violence among Incarcerated Boys: Its Association with Violent Offending and Potential Mediating Variables," *Violence and Victims* 10 (1995): 163–180; Jerome Kolbo, "Risk and Resilience among Children Exposed to Family Violence," *Violence and Victims* 11 (1996): 113–127.

26. Victim data used in these sections is from Callie Marie Rennison and Michael Rand, *Criminal Victimization 2002* (Washington, D.C.: Bureau of Justice Statistics, 2003). The data in this section comes from this report.

27. Lamar Jordan, "Law Enforcement and the Elderly: A Concern for the 21st Century," *FBI Law Enforcement Bulletin* 71 (2002): 20–24.

28. Karin Wittebrood and Paul Nieuwbeerta, "Criminal Victimization During One's Life Course: The Effects of Previous Victimization and Patterns of Routine Activities," *Journal of Research in Crime and Delinquency* 37 (2000): 91–122; Janet Lauritsen and Kenna Davis Quinet, "Repeat Victimizations among Adolescents and Young Adults," *Journal of Quantitative Criminology* 11 (1995): 143–163.

29. Denise Osborn, Dan Ellingworth, Tim Hope, and Alan Trickett, "Are Repeatedly Victimized Households Different?" *Journal of Quantitative Criminology* 12 (1996): 223–245.

30. Graham Farrell, "Predicting and Preventing Revictimization," in *Crime and Justice: An Annual Review of Research,* eds. Michael Tonry and David Farrington, vol. 20 (Chicago: University of Chicago Press, 1995), pp. 61–126.

31. Ibid., p. 61.

32. David Finkelhor and Nancy Asigian, "Risk Factors for Youth Victimization: Beyond a Lifestyles/Routine Activities Theory Approach," *Violence and Victimization* 11 (1996): 3–19.

33. Graham Farrell, Coretta Phillips, and Ken Pease, "Like Taking Candy: Why Does Repeat Victimization Occur?" *British Journal of Criminology* 35 (1995): 384–399.

34. Christopher Innes and Lawrence Greenfeld, *Violent State Prisoners and Their Victims* (Washington, D.C.: Bureau of Justice Statistics, 1990).

35. Hans Von Hentig, *The Criminal and His Victim: Studies in the Sociobiology of Crime* (New Haven, Conn.: Yale University Press, 1948), p. 384.

36. Marvin Wolfgang, *Patterns of Criminal Homicide* (Philadelphia: University of Pennsylvania Press, 1958).

37. Menachem Amir, *Patterns in Forcible Rape* (Chicago: University of Chicago Press, 1971).

38. Susan Estrich, *Real Rape* (Cambridge, Mass.: Harvard University Press, 1987).

39. Edem Avakame, "Female's Labor Force Participation and Intimate Femicide: An Empirical Assessment of the Backlash Hypothesis," *Violence and Victims* 14 (1999): 277–283.

40. Martin Daly and Margo Wilson, *Homicide* (New York: Aldine de Gruyter, 1988).

41. Lening Zhang, John W. Welte, and William F. Wieczorek, "Deviant Lifestyle and Crime Victimization," *Journal of Criminal Justice* 29 (2001): 133–143.

42. Dan Hoyt, Kimberly Ryan, and Mari Cauce, "Personal Victimization in a High-Risk Environment: Homeless and Runaway Adolescents," *Journal of Research in Crime and Delinquency* 36 (1999): 371–392.

43. See, generally, Gary Gottfredson and Denise Gottfredson, *Victimization in Schools* (New York: Plenum Press, 1985).

44. Gary Jensen and David Brownfield, "Gender, Lifestyles, and Victimization: Beyond Routine Activity Theory," *Violence and Victims* 1 (1986): 85–99.

45. Rolf Loeber, Mary DeLamatre, George Tita, Jacqueline Cohen, Magda Stouthamer-Loeber, and David Farrington, "Gun Injury and Mortality: The Delinquent Backgrounds of Juvenile Offenders," *Violence and Victims* 14 (1999): 339–351.

46. Bonnie Fisher, John Sloan, Francis Cullen, and Chunmeng Lu, "Crime in the Ivory Tower: The Level and Sources of Student Victimization," *Criminology* 36 (1998): 671–710.

47. Adam Dobrin, "The Risk of Offending on Homicide Victimization: A Case Control Study," *Journal of Research in Crime and Delinquency* 38 (2001): 154–173.

48. S. Farrall and S. Maltby, "The Victimisation of Probationers," *Howard Journal of Criminal Justice* 42 (2003): 32–55.

49. Rolf Loeber, Larry Kalb, and David Huizinga, *Juvenile Delinquency and Serious Injury Victimization* (Washington, D.C.: Office of Juvenile Justice and Delinquency Prevention, 2001).

50. James Garofalo, "Reassessing the Lifestyle Model of Criminal Victimization," in *Positive Criminology,* eds. Michael Gottfredson and Travis Hirschi (Newbury Park, Calif.: Sage, 1987), pp. 23–42.

51. Terance Miethe and David McDowall, "Contextual Effects in Models of Criminal Victimization," *Social Forces* 71 (1993): 741–759.

52. Rodney Stark, "Deviant Places: A Theory of the Ecology of Crime," *Criminology* 25 (1987): 893–911.

53. Ibid., p. 902.

54. Pamela Wilcox Rountree, Kenneth Land, and Terance Miethe, "Macro–Micro Integration in the Study of Victimization: A Hierarchical Logistic Model Analysis across Seattle Neighborhoods," paper presented at the annual meeting of the American Society of Criminology, Phoenix, Arizona, November 1993.

55. Lawrence Cohen and Marcus Felson, "Social Change and Crime Rate Trends: A Routine Activities Approach," *American Sociological Review* 44 (1979): 588–608.

56. For a review, see James LeBeau and Thomas Castellano, "The Routine Activities Approach: An Inventory and Critique," unpublished paper, Center for the Studies of Crime, Delinquency, and Corrections, Southern Illinois University, Carbondale, 1987.

57. Teresa LaGrange, "The Impact of Neighborhoods, Schools, and Malls on the Spatial Distribution of Property Damage," *Journal of Research in Crime and Delinquency* 36 (1999): 393–422.

58. Lawrence Cohen, Marcus Felson, and Kenneth Land, "Property Crime Rates in the United States: A Macrodynamic Analysis, 1947–1977, with Ex-ante Forecasts for the Mid-1980s," *American Journal of Sociology* 86 (1980): 90–118.

59. Steven Messner, Lawrence Raffalovich, and Richard McMillan, "Economic Deprivation and Changes in Homicide Arrest Rates for White and Black Youths, 1967–1998: A National Time Series Analysis," *Criminology* 39 (2001): 591–614.

60. Terence Miethe and Robert Meier, *Crime and Its Social Context: Toward an Integrated Theory of Offenders, Victims, and Situations* (Albany: State University of New York Press, 1994).

61. Richard Felson, "Routine Activities and Involvement in Violence as Actor, Witness, or Target," *Violence and Victimization* 12 (1997): 209–223.

62. Georgina Hammock and Deborah Richardson, "Perceptions of Rape: The Influence of Closeness of Relationship, Intoxication, and Sex of Participant," *Violence and Victimization* 12 (1997): 237–247.

63. Wittebrood and Nieuwbeerta, "Criminal Victimization During One's Life Course," pp. 112–113.

64. Patricia Resnick, "Psychological Effects of Victimization: Implications for the Criminal Justice System," *Crime and Delinquency* 33 (1987): 468–478.

65. Dean Kilpatrick, Benjamin Saunders, Lois Veronen, Connie Best, and Judith Von, "Criminal Victimization: Lifetime Prevalence, Reporting to Police, and Psychological Impact," *Crime and Delinquency* 33 (1987): 479–489.

66. U.S. Department of Justice, *Report of the President's Task Force on Victims of Crime* (Washington, D.C.: U.S. Government Printing Office, 1983).

67. Ibid., pp. 2–10; "Review on Victims: Witnesses of Crime," *Massachusetts Lawyers Weekly,* April 25, 1983, p. 26.

68. Robert Davis, *Crime Victims: Learning How to Help Them* (Washington, D.C.: National Institute of Justice, 1987).

69. This section leans heavily on Albert Roberts, "Delivery of Services to Crime Victims: A National Survey," *American Journal of Orthopsychiatry* 6 (1991): 128–137; see also Albert Roberts, *Helping Crime Victims: Research, Policy, and Practice* (Newbury Park, Calif.: Sage, 1990).

70. Randall Schmidt, "Crime Victim Compensation Legislation: A Comparative Study," *Victimology* 5 (1980): 428–437.

71. Ibid.

72. National Association of Crime Victim Compensation Boards. Available: http://nacvcb.org/ (accessed September 24, 2003).

73. *Payne v. Tennessee,* 111 S.Ct. 2597, 115 L.Ed.2d 720 (1991).

74. Robert Davis and Barbara Smith, "The Effects of Victim Impact Statements on Sentencing Decisions: A Test in an Urban Setting," *Justice Quarterly* 11 (1994): 453–69; Edna Erez and Pamela Tontodonato, "The Effect of Victim Participation in Sentencing on Sentence Outcome," *Criminology* 28 (1990): 451–474.

75. Douglas E. Beloof, "Constitutional Implications of Crime Victims as Participants," *Cornell Law Review* 88(2003): 282–305.

76. Pater Jaffe, Marlies Sudermann, Deborah Reitzel, and Steve Killip, "An Evaluation of a Secondary School Primary Prevention Program on Violence in Intimate Relationships," *Violence and Victims* 7 (1992): 129–145.

77. Andrew Karmen, "Victim–Offender Reconciliation Programs: Pro and Con," *Perspectives of the American Probation and Parole Association* 20 (1996): 11–14.

78. National Center for Victims of Crime. Available: http://www.ncvc.org/policy/issues/rights/ (accessed September 24, 2003).

79. Ibid., pp. 9–10.

Chapter 4

1. *Lockyer v. Andrade* No. 01-1127 March 5, 2003

2. Bob Roshier, *Controlling Crime* (Chicago: Lyceum Books, 1989), p. 10.

3. Gary Becker, "Crime and Punishment: An Economic Approach," *The Journal of Political Economy* 76 (1968) 169–217.

4. James Q. Wilson, *Thinking About Crime,* rev. ed. (New York: Vintage Books, 1983), p. 260.

5. See, generally, Derek Cornish and Ronald Clarke, eds., *The Reasoning Criminal: Rational Choice Perspectives on Offending* (New York: Springer Verlag, 1986); Philip Cook, "The Demand and Supply of Criminal Opportunities," in *Crime and Justice,* vol. 7, eds. Michael Tonry and Norval Morris (Chicago: University of Chicago Press, 1986), pp. 1–28; Ronald Clarke and Derek Cornish, "Modeling Offenders' Decisions: A Framework for Research and Policy," in *Crime and Justice,* vol. 6, eds. Michael Tonry and Norval Morris (Chicago: University of Chicago Press, 1985), pp. 147–187; Morgan Reynolds, *Crime by Choice: An Economic Analysis* (Dallas: Fisher Institute, 1985).

6. George Rengert and John Wasilchick, *Suburban Burglary: A Time and Place for Everything* (Springfield, Ill.: Charles Thomas, 1985).

7. John McIver, "Criminal Mobility: A Review of Empirical Studies," in *Crime Spillover,* eds. Simon Hakim and George Rengert (Beverly Hills, Calif.: Sage, 1981), pp. 110–121; Carol Kohfeld and John Sprague, "Demography, Police Behavior, and Deterrence," *Criminology* 28 (1990): 111–136.

8. Derek Cornish and Ronald Clarke, "Understanding Crime Displacement: An Application of Rational Choice Theory," *Criminology* 25 (1987): 933–947.

9. Lloyd Phillips and Harold Votey, "The Influence of Police Interventions and Alternative Income Sources on the Dynamic Process of Choosing Crime as a Career," *Journal of Quantitative Criminology* 3 (1987): 251–274.

10. Michael Gottfredson and Travis Hirschi, *A General Theory of Crime* (Stanford, Calif.: Stanford University Press, 1990).

11. Liliana Pezzin, "Earnings Prospects, Matching Effects, and the Decision to Terminate a Criminal Career," *Journal of Quantitative Criminology* 11 (1995): 29–50.

12. Pierre Tremblay and Carlo Morselli, "Patterns in Criminal Achievement: Wilson and Abrahmse Revisited," *Criminology* 38 (2000): 633–660.

13. Steven Levitt and Sudhir Alladi Venkatesh, "An Economic Analysis of a Drug-Selling Gang's Finances," NBER Working Papers 6592 (Cambridge, Mass.: National Bureau of Economic Research, Inc., 1998).

14. Bill McCarthy, " New Economics of Sociological Criminology," *Annual Review of Sociology* (2002): 417–442.

15. Ronald Akers, "Rational Choice, Deterrence and Social Learning Theory in Criminology: The Path Not Taken," *Journal of Criminal Law and Criminology* 81 (1990): 653–676.

16. Neal Shover, *Aging Criminals* (Beverly Hills, Calif.: Sage, 1985).

17. Robert Agnew, "Determinism, Indeterminism, and Crime: An Empirical Exploration," *Criminology* 33 (1995): 83–109.

18. Ibid., pp. 103–104.

19. Bruce Jacobs, "Crack Dealers' Apprehension Avoidance Techniques: A Case of Restrictive Deterrence," *Justice Quarterly* 13 (1996): 359–381.

20. Ibid., p. 367.

21. Ibid., p. 372.

22. Michael Rand, *Crime and the Nation's Households, 1989* (Washington, D.C.: Bureau of Justice Statistics, 1990), p. 4.

23. Paul Cromwell, James Olson, and D'Aunn Wester Avary, *Breaking and Entering: An Ethnographic Analysis of Burglary* (Newbury Park, Calif.: Sage, 1989), p. 24.

24. Ibid., pp. 30–32.

25. George Rengert and John Wasilchick, *Space, Time, and Crime: Ethnographic Insights into Residential Burglary* (Washington, D.C.: National Institute of Justice, 1989); see also Rengert and Wasilchick, *Suburban Burglary*.

26. Matthew Robinson, "Lifestyles, Routine Activities, and Residential Burglary Victimization," *Journal of Criminal Justice* 22 (1999): 27–52.

27. Patrick Donnelly and Charles Kimble, "Community Organizing, Environmental Change, and Neighborhood Crime," *Crime and Delinquency* 43 (1997): 493–511.

28. Leanne Fiftal Alarid, James Marquart, Velmer Burton, Francis Cullen, and Steven Cuvelier, "Women's Roles in Serious Offenses: A Study of Adult Felons," *Justice Quarterly* 13 (1996): 431–454, at p. 448.

29. Ronald Clarke and Marcus Felson, "Introduction: Criminology, Routine Activity and Rational Choice," in *Routine Activity and Rational Choice* (New Brunswick, N.J.: Transaction, 1993), pp. 1–14.

30. Associated Press, "Thrift Hearings Resume Today in Senate," *Boston Globe,* January 2, 1991, p. 10.

31. Ronald Clarke and Patricia Harris, "Auto Theft and Its Prevention," in *Crime and Justice: An Annual Edition,* eds. Michael Tonry and Norval Morris (Chicago: University of Chicago Press, 1992), pp. 1–54, at pp. 20–21.

32. William Smith, Sharon Glave Frazee, and Elizabeth Davison, "Furthering the Integration of Routine Activity and Social Disorganization Theories: Small Units of Analysis and the Study of Street Robbery as a Diffusion Process," *Criminology* 38 (2000): 489–521.

33. Paul Bellair, "Informal Surveillance and Street Crime: A Complex Relationship," *Criminology* 38 (2000): 137–167.

34. John Gibbs and Peggy Shelly, "Life in the Fast Lane: A Retrospective View by Commercial Thieves," *Journal of Research in Crime and Delinquency* 19 (1982): 229–230.

35. Gary Kleck and Don Kates, *Armed: New Perspectives on Guns* (Amherst, N.Y.: Prometheus Books, 2001).

36. Elizabeth Ehrhardt Mustaine and Richard Tewksbury, "Predicting Risks of Larceny Theft Victimization: A Routine Activity Analysis Using Refined Lifestyle Measures," *Criminology* 36 (1998): 829–858.

37. Gordon Knowles, "Deception, Detection, and Evasion: A Trade Craft Analysis of Honolulu, Hawaii's Street Crack Cocaine Traffickers," *Journal of Criminal Justice* 27 (1999): 443–455.

38. John Petraitis, Brian Flay, and Todd Miller, "Reviewing Theories of Adolescent Substance Use: Organizing Pieces in the Puzzle," *Psychological Bulletin* 117 (1995): 67–86.

39. George Rengert, *The Geography of Illegal Drugs* (Boulder, Colo.: Westview Press, 1996).

40. Levitt and Venkatesh, "An Economic Analysis of a Drug-Selling Gang's Finances."

41. Richard Felson and Steven Messner, "To Kill or Not to Kill? Lethal Outcomes in Injurious Attacks," *Criminology* 34 (1996): 519–545, at p. 541.

42. Richard Wright and Scott Decker, *Armed Robbers in Action: Stickups and Street Culture* (Boston, Mass.: Northeastern University Press, 1997).

43. Ibid., p. 52.

44. James Wright and Peter Rossi, *Armed and Considered Dangerous: A Survey of Felons and Their Firearms* (Hawthorne, N.Y.: Aldine De Gruyter, 1983), pp. 141–159.

45. Bruce A. Jacobs, *Robbing Drug Dealers: Violence Beyond the Law* (Hawthorne, N.Y.: Aldine de Gruyter, 2000).

46. Andy Hochstetler, "Opportunities and Decisions: Interactional Dynamics in Robbery and Burglary Groups, *Criminology* 39 (2001): 737–763.

47. Peter Wood, Walter Gove, James Wilson, and John Cochran, "Nonsocial Reinforcement and Habitual Criminal Conduct: An Extension of Learning," *Criminology* 35 (1997): 335–366.

48. Jeff Ferrell, "Criminological Verstehen: Inside the Immediacy of Crime," *Justice Quarterly* 14 (1997): 3–23, at p. 12.

49. Jack Katz, *Seductions of Crime* (New York: Basic Books, 1988).

50. Bill McCarthy, "Not Just 'For the Thrill of It': An Instrumentalist Elaboration of Katz's Explanation of Sneaky Thrill Property Crime," *Criminology* 33 (1995): 519–539.

51. George Rengert, "Spatial Justice and Criminal Victimization," *Justice Quarterly* 6 (1989): 543–564.

52. Ronald Clarke, *Situational Crime Prevention: Successful Case Studies* (Albany, N.Y.: Harrow and Heston, 1992).

53. Nancy LaVigne, "Gasoline Drive-Offs: Designing a Less Convenient Environment," in *Crime Prevention Studies,* vol. 2, ed. Ronald Clarke (Monsey, N.Y.: Criminal Justice Press, 1994), pp. 91–114.

54. Barry Webb, "Steering Column Locks and Motor Vehicle Theft: Evaluations for Three Countries," in *Crime Prevention Studies,* vol. 2, ed. Ronald Clarke (Monsey, N.Y.: Criminal Justice Press, 1994), pp. 71–89.

55. Andrew Fulkerson, "Blow and Go: The Breath-Analyzed Ignition Interlock Device as a Technological Response to DWI," *American Journal of Drug and Alcohol Abuse* 29 (2003): 219–235.

56. Brandon Welsh and David Farrington, "Effects of Closed-Circuit Television on Crime," *Annals of the American Academy of Political and Social Science* 587 (2003): 110–136.

57. Ronald Clarke, "Deterring Obscene Phone Callers: The New Jersey Experience," in *Situational Crime Prevention,* ed. Ronald Clarke (Albany, N.Y.: Harrow & Heston, 1992), pp. 124–132.

58. Robert Barr and Ken Pease, "Crime Placement, Displacement, and Deflection," in *Crime and Justice, A Review of Research,* vol. 12, eds. Michael Tonry and Norval Morris (Chicago: University of Chicago Press, 1990), pp. 277–319.

59. Clarke, *Situational Crime Prevention,* p. 27.

60. Ibid., p. 35.

61. Ronald Clarke and David Weisburd, "Diffusion of Crime Control Benefits: Observations of the Reverse of Displacement," in *Crime Prevention Studies,* vol. 2, ed. Ronald Clarke (New York: Criminal Justice Press, 1994).

62. David Weisburd and Lorraine Green, "Policing Drug Hot Spots: The Jersey City Drug Market Analysis Experiment," *Justice Quarterly* 12 (1995): 711–734.

63. Ian Ayres and Steven D. Levitt, "Measuring Positive Externalities from Unobservable Victim Precaution: An Empirical Analysis of Lojack," *Quarterly Journal of Economics* 113 (1998): 43–78.

64. R. Steven Daniels, Lorin Baumhover, William Formby, and Carolyn Clark-Daniels, "Police Discretion and Elder Mistreatment: A Nested Model of Observation, Reporting, and Satisfaction," *Journal of Criminal Justice* 27 (1999): 209–225.

65. Daniel Nagin and Greg Pogarsky, "Integrating Celerity, Impulsivity, and Ex-

tralegal Sanction Threats into a Model of General Deterrence: Theory and Evidence," *Criminology* 39 (2001): 865–892.

66. Daniel Nagin, "Criminal Deterrence Theory at the Outset of the Twenty-First Century," in *Crime and Justice: An Annual Review of Research,* vol. 23, ed. Michael Tonry (Chicago, Ill.: University of Chicago Press, 1998), pp. 51–92; for an opposing view, see Robert Bursik, Harold Grasmick, and Mitchell Chamlin, "The Effect of Longitudinal Arrest Patterns on the Development of Robbery Trends at the Neighborhood Level," *Criminology* 28 (1990): 431–450.

67. Daniel Nagin and Greg Pogarsky, "An Experimental Investigation of Deterrence: Cheating, Self-Serving Bias and Impulsivity," *Criminology* 41 (2003): 167–195.

68. David Bayley, *Policing for the Future* (New York: Oxford, 1994).

69. Tomislav V. Kovandzic and John J. Sloan, "Police Levels and Crime Rates Revisited: A County-Level Analysis from Florida (1980–1998)," *Journal of Criminal Justice* 30 (2002): 65–76. For a review, see Thomas Marvell and Carlisle Moody, "Specification Problems, Police Levels, and Crime Rates," *Criminology* 34 (1996): 609–646; Steven Levitt, "Using Electoral Cycles in Police Hiring to Estimate the Effect of Police on Crime," *American Economic Review* 87 (1997): 270–291.

70. Charles Tittle and Alan Rowe, "Certainty of Arrest and Crime Rates: A Further Test of the Deterrence Hypothesis," *Social Forces* 52 (1974): 455–462.

71. Michael White, James Fyfe, Suzanne Campbell, and John Goldkamp, "The Police Role in Preventing Homicide: Considering the Impact of Problem-Oriented Policing on the Prevalence of Murder," *Journal of Research in Crime and Delinquency* 40 (2003): 194–226.

72. Janice Puckett and Richard Lundman," Factors Affecting Homicide Clearances: Multivariate Analysis of a More Complete Conceptual Framework," *Journal of Research in Crime and Delinquency* 40 (2003): 171–194.

73. Kenneth Novak, Jennifer Hartman, Alexander Holsinger, and Michael Turner, "The Effects of Aggressive Policing of Disorder on Serious Crime," *Policing* 22 (1999): 171–190.

74. Lawrence Sherman, "Police Crackdowns," *NIJ Reports* (March/April 1990): 2–6, at p. 2.

75. Anthony Braga, David Weisburd, Elin Waring, Lorraine Green Mazerolle, William Spelman, and Francis Gajewski, "Problem-Oriented Policing in Violent Crime Places: A Randomized Controlled Experiment," *Criminology* 37 (1999): 541–580.

76. Greg Pogarsky, "Identifying 'Deterrable' Offenders: Implications for Research on Deterrence," *Justice Quarterly* 19 (2002): 431–453.

77. Ed Stevens and Brian Payne, "Applying Deterrence Theory in the Context of Corporate Wrongdoing: Limitations on Punitive Damages," *Journal of Criminal Justice* 27 (1999): 195–209; Jeffrey Roth, *Firearms and Violence* (Washington, D.C.: National Institute of Justice, 1994); Thomas Marvell and Carlisle Moody, "The Impact of Enhanced Prison Terms for Felonies Committed with Guns," *Criminology* 33 (1995): 247–281; and Gary Green, "General Deterrence and Television Cable Crime: A Field Experiment in Social Crime," *Criminology* 23 (1986): 629–645.

78. William Bowers and Glenn Pierce, "Deterrence or Brutalization: What Is the Effect of Executions?" *Crime and Delinquency* 26 (1980): 453–484.

79. John Cochran, Mitchell Chamlin, and Mark Seth, "Deterrence or Brutalization? An Impact Assessment of Oklahoma's Return to Capital Punishment," *Criminology* 32 (1994): 107–134.

80. David Phillips, "The Deterrent Effect of Capital Punishment," *American Journal of Sociology* 86 (1980): 139–148; Hans Zeisel, "A Comment on 'The Deterrent Effect of Capital Punishment' by Phillips," *American Journal of Sociology* 88 (1982): 167–169; see also Sam McFarland, "Is Capital Punishment a Short-Term Deterrent to Homicide? A Study of the Effects of Four Recent American Executions," *Journal of Criminal Law and Criminology* 74 (1984): 1014–1032.

81. Karl Schuessler, "The Deterrent Influence of the Death Penalty," *Annals of the Academy of Political and Social Sciences* 284 (1952): 54–62.

82. Thorsten Sellin, *The Death Penalty* (Philadelphia: American Law Institute, 1959); Walter Reckless, "Use of the Death Penalty," *Crime and Delinquency* 15 (1969): 43–51.

83. Richard Lempert, "The Effect of Executions on Homicides: A New Look in an Old Light," *Crime and Delinquency* 29 (1983): 88–115.

84. Derral Cheatwood, "Capital Punishment and the Deterrence of Violent Crime in Comparable Counties," *Criminal Justice Review* 18 (1993): 165–181.

85. Dane Archer, Rosemary Gartner, and Marc Beittel, "Homicide and the Death Penalty: A Cross-National Test of a Deterrence Hypothesis," *Journal of Criminal Law and Criminology* 74 (1983): 991–1014.

86. Isaac Ehrlich, "The Deterrent Effect of Capital Punishment: A Question of Life and Death," *American Economic Review* 65 (1975): 397–417.

87. James Fox and Michael Radelet, "Persistent Flaws in Econometric Studies of the Deterrent Effect of the Death Penalty," *Loyola of Los Angeles Law Review* 23 (1987): 29–44; William B. Bowers and Glenn Pierce, "The Illusion of Deterrence in Isaac Ehrlich's Research on Capital Punishment," *Yale Law Journal* 85 (1975): 187–208.

88. Jon Sorenson, Robert Wrinkle, Victoria Brewer, and James Marquart, "Capital Punishment and Deterrence: Examining the Effect of Executions on Murder in Texas," *Crime and Delinquency* 45 (1999): 481–493.

89. William Bailey, "Disaggregation in Deterrence and Death Penalty Research: The Case of Murder in Chicago," *Journal of Criminal Law and Criminology* 74 (1983): 827–859.

90. Steven Messner and Kenneth Tardiff, "Economic Inequality and Level of Homicide: An Analysis of Urban Neighborhoods," *Criminology* 24 (1986): 297–317.

91. Stuart Banner, *The Death Penalty: An American History* (Cambridge, Mass.: Harvard University Press, 2002).

92. Steven Levitt, "Understanding Why Crime Fell in the 1990s: Four Factors That Explain the Decline and Six That Do Not," *Journal of Economic Perspectives* (in press, 2004).

93. Donald Green, "Past Behavior as a Measure of Actual Future Behavior: An Unresolved Issue in Perceptual Deterrence Research," *Journal of Criminal Law and Criminology* 80 (1989): 781–804.

94. Donna Bishop, "Deterrence: A Panel Analysis," *Justice Quarterly* 1 (1984): 311–328; Julie Horney and Ineke Haen Marshall, "Risk Perceptions among Serious Offenders: The Role of Crime and Punishment," *Criminology* 30 (1992): 575–594.

95. Wanda Foglia, "Perceptual Deterrence and the Mediating Effect of Internalized Norms among Inner-City Teenagers," *Journal of Research in Crime and Delinquency* 34 (1997): 414–442; Raymond Paternoster, "Decisions to Participate in and Desist from Four Types of Common Delinquency: Deterrence and the Rational Choice Perspective," *Law and Society Review* 23 (1989): 7–29; Raymond Paternoster, "Examining Three-Wave Deterrence Models: A Question of Temporal Order and Specification," *Journal of Criminal Law and Criminology* 79 (1988): 135–163; Raymond Paternoster, Linda Saltzman, Gordon Waldo, and Theodore Chiricos, "Estimating Perceptual Stability and Deterrent Effects: The Role of Perceived Legal Punishment in the Inhibition of Criminal Involvement," *Journal of Criminal Law and Criminology* 74 (1983): 270–297; M. William Minor and Joseph Harry, "Deterrent and Experiential Effects in Perceptual Deterrence Research: A Replication and Extension," *Journal of Research in Crime and Delinquency* 19 (1982): 190–203; Lonn Lanza-Kaduce, "Perceptual Deterrence and Drinking and Driving among College Students," *Criminology* 26 (1988): 321–341.

96. Steven Klepper and Daniel Nagin, "The Deterrent Effect of Perceived Certainty and Severity of Punishment Revisited," *Criminology* 27 (1989): 721–746; Scott Decker, Richard Wright, and Robert Logie, "Perceptual Deterrence among Active Residential Burglars: A Research Note," *Criminology* 31 (1993): 135–147.

97. Alex Piquero and George Rengert, "Studying Deterrence with Active Residential Burglars," *Justice Quarterly* 16 (1999): 451–462.

98. Ernest Van Den Haag, "The Criminal Law as a Threat System," *Journal of Criminal Law and Criminology* 73 (1982): 709–785.

99. David Lykken, "Psychopathy, Sociopathy, and Crime," *Society* 34 (1996): 30–38.

100. George Lowenstein, Daniel Nagin, and Raymond Paternoster, "The Effect of Sexual Arousal on Expectations of Sexual Forcefulness," *Journal of Research in Crime and Delinquency* 34 (1997): 443–473.

101. Lyn Exum, "The Application and Robustness of the Rational Choice Perspective in the Study of Intoxicated and Angry Intentions to Aggress," *Criminology* 40 (2002): 933–967.

102. David Klinger, "Policing Spousal Assault," *Journal of Research in Crime and Delinquency* 32 (1995): 308–324.

103. James Williams and Daniel Rodeheaver, "Processing of Criminal Homicide Cases in a Large Southern City," *Sociology and Social Research* 75 (1991): 80–88.

104. Greg Pogarsky, "Identifying *Deterrable* Offenders: Implications for Deterrence Research," *Justice Quarterly* 19 (2002): 431–453.

105. Nagin and Pogarsky, "Integrating Celerity, Impulsivity, and Extralegal Sanction Threats into a Model of General Deterrence: Theory and Evidence."

106. James Q. Wilson, *Thinking About Crime* (New York: Basic Books, 1975).

107. James Q. Wilson and Richard Herrnstein, *Crime and Human Nature* (New York: Simon & Schuster, 1985), p. 494.

108. Christina Dejong, "Survival Analysis and Specific Deterrence: Integrating Theoretical and Empirical Models of Recidivism," *Criminology* 35 (1997): 561–576; Paul Tracy and Kimberly Kempf-Leonard, *Continuity and Discontinuity in Criminal Careers* (New York: Plenum Press, 1996).

109. Allen Beck and Bernard Shipley, *Recidivism of Prisoners Released in 1983* (Washington, D.C.: Bureau of Justice Statistics, 1989).

110. Dejong, "Survival Analysis and Specific Deterrence," p. 573.

111. Ibid.; Raymond Paternoster and Alex Piquero, "Reconceptualizing Deterrence: An Empirical Test of Personal and Vicarious Experiences," *Journal of Research in Crime and Delinquency* 32 (1995): 251–258.

112. Cassia Spohn and David Holleran, "The Effect of Imprisonment on Recidivism Rates of Felony Offenders: A Focus on Drug Offenders," *Criminology* 40 (2002): 329–359.

113. Greg Pogarsky and Alex R. Piquero "Can Punishment Encourage Offending? Investigating the 'Resetting' Effect," *Journal of Research in Crime and Delinquency* 40 (2003): 92–117.

114. Doris Layton MacKenzie and Spencer De Li, "The Impact of Formal and Informal Social Controls on the Criminal Activities of Probationers," *Journal of Research in Crime and Delinquency* 39 (2002): 243–276.

115. See, generally, Raymond Paternoster, "Absolute and Restrictive Deterrence in a Panel of Youth: Explaining the Onset, Persistence/Desistance, and Frequency of Delinquent Offending," *Social Problems* 36 (1989): 289–307; Raymond Paternoster, "The Deterrent Effect of Perceived Severity of Punishment: A Review of the Evidence and Issues," *Justice Quarterly* 42 (1987): 173–217.

116. Isaac Ehrlich, "Participation in Illegitimate Activities: An Economic Analysis," *Journal of Political Economy* 81 (1973): 521–567; Lee Bowker, "Crime and the Use of Prisons in the United States: A Time Series Analysis," *Crime and Delinquency* 27 (1981): 206–212.

117. David Greenberg, "The Incapacitative Effects of Imprisonment: Some Estimates," *Law and Society Review* 9 (1975): 541–580.

118. Reuel Shinnar and Shlomo Shinnar, "The Effects of the Criminal Justice System on the Control of Crime: A Quantitative Approach," *Law and Society Review* 9 (1975): 581–611.

119. David Greenberg and Nancy Larkin, "The Incapacitation of Criminal Opiate Users," *Crime and Delinquency* 44 (1998): 205–228.

120. John Wallerstedt, *Returning to Prison: Bureau of Justice Statistics Special Report* (Washington, D.C.: U.S. Department of Justice, 1984).

121. James Marquart, Victoria Brewer, Janet Mullings, and Ben Crouch, "The Implications of Crime Control Policy on HIV/AIDS-Related Risk among Women Prisoners, *Crime and Delinquency* 45 (1999): 82–98.

122. Jose Canela-Cacho, Alfred Blumstein, and Jacqueline Cohen, "Relationship between the Offending Frequency of Imprisoned and Free Offenders," *Criminology* 35 (1997): 133–171.

123. Kate King and Patricia Bass, "Southern Prisons and Elderly Inmates: Taking a Look Inside," paper presented at the annual meeting of the American Society of Criminology, San Diego, November 1997.

124. Marc Mauer, testimony before the U.S. Congress, House Judiciary Committee, on "Three Strikes and You're Out," March 1, 1994.

125. Canela-Cacho, Blumstein, and Cohen, "Relationship Between the Offending Frequency of Imprisoned and Free Offenders."

126. Thomas Marvell and Carlisle Moody, "The Impact of Out-of-State Prison Population on State Homicide Rates: Displacement and Free-Rider Effects," *Criminology* 36 (1998): 513–538; Thomas Marvell and Carlisle Moody, "The Impact of Prison Growth on Homicide," *Homicide Studies* 1 (1997): 205–233.

127. Ilyana Kuziemko and Steven D. Levitt, "An Empirical Analysis of Imprisoning Drug Offenders," NBER Working Papers 8489 (Cambridge, Mass.: National Bureau of Economic Research, Inc., 2001).

128. Stephen Markman and Paul Cassell, "Protecting the Innocent: A Response to the Bedeau-Radelet Study," *Stanford Law Review* 41 (1988): 121–170, at p. 153.

129. James Stephan and Tracy Snell, *Capital Punishment, 1994* (Washington, D.C: Bureau of Justice Statistics, 1996), p. 8.

130. Andrew Von Hirsch, *Doing Justice* (New York: Hill & Wang, 1976).

131. Ibid., pp. 15–16.

132. Ibid.

Chapter 5

1. Lee Ellis, "A Discipline in Peril: Sociology's Future Hinges on Curing Biophobia," *American Sociologist* 27 (1996): 21–41.

2. Edmund O. Wilson, *Sociobiology* (Cambridge, Mass.: Harvard University Press, 1975).

3. Per-Olof Wikstrom and Rolf Loeber, "Do Disadvantaged Neighborhoods Cause Well-Adjusted Children to Become Adolescent Delinquents?" *Criminology* 38 (2000): 1109–1142.

4. See, generally, Lee Ellis, *Theories of Rape* (New York: Hemisphere, 1989).

5. Anthony Walsh, "Behavior Genetics and Anomie/Strain Theory," *Criminology* 38 (2000): 1075–1108.

6. Dalton Conley and Neil Bennett, "Is Biology Destiny? Birth Weight and Life Chances," *American Sociological Review* 654 (2000): 458–467.

7. Anthony Walsh and Lee Ellis, "Shoring Up the Big Three: Improving Criminological Theories with Biosocial Concepts," paper presented at the annual meeting of the Society of Criminology, San Diego, November 1997, p. 16.

8. Israel Nachshon, "Neurological Bases of Crime, Psychopathy and Aggression," in *Crime in Biological, Social and Moral Contexts,* eds. Lee Ellis and Harry Hoffman (New York: Praeger, 1990), p. 199.

9. *Time*, May 28, 1979, p. 57.

10. G. B. Ramirez, O. Pagulayan, H. Akagi, A. Francisco Rivera, L. V. Lee, A. Berroya, M. C. Vince Cruz, and D. Casintahan, "Tagum Study II: Follow-Up Study at Two Years of Age after Prenatal Exposure to Mercury," *Pediatrics* 111 (2003): 289–295.

11. Harold Milman and Suzanne Arnold, "Neurologic, Psychological, and Aggressive Disturbances with Sildenafil," *Annals of Pharmacotherapy* 3 (2002): 1129–1134.

12. Sue Dengate and Alan. Ruben, "Controlled Trial of Cumulative Behavioural Effects of a Common Bread Preservative," *Journal of Pediatrics and Child Health* 38 (2002): 373–376.

13. J. Kershner and W. Hawke, "Megavitamins and Learning Disorders: A Controlled Double-Blind Experiment," *Journal of Nutrition* 109 (1979): 819–826.

14. Stephen Schoenthaler and Walter Doraz, "Types of Offenses Which Can Be Reduced in an Institutional Setting

Using Nutritional Intervention," *International Journal of Biosocial Research* 4 (1983): 74–84; Stephen Schoenthaler and Walter Doraz, "Diet and Crime," *International Journal of Biosocial Research* 4 (1983): 74–84.

15. Mark Wolraich, Scott Lindgren, Phyllis Stumbo, Lewis Steglink, Mark Appelbaum, and Mary Kiritsy, "Effects of Diets High in Sucrose or Aspartame on the Behavior and Cognitive Performance of Children," *New England Journal of Medicine* 330 (1994): 303–306; Dian Gans, "Sucrose and Unusual Childhood Behavior," *Nutrition Today* 26 (1991): 8–14.

16. Diana Fishbein, "Neuropsychological Function, Drug Abuse, and Violence: A Conceptual Framework," *Criminal Justice and Behavior* 27 (2000): 139–159.

17. E. Podolsky, "The Chemistry of Murder," *Pakistan Medical Journal* 15 (1964): 9–14.

18. J. A. Yaryura-Tobias and F. Neziroglu, "Violent Behavior, Brain Dysrhythmia and Glucose Dysfunction: A New Syndrome," *Journal of Orthopsychiatry* 4 (1975): 182–188.

19. Matti Virkkunen, "Reactive Hypoglycemic Tendency among Habitually Violent Offenders," *Nutrition Reviews Supplement* 44 (1986): 94–103.

20. James Q. Wilson, *The Moral Sense* (New York: Free Press, 1993).

21. Lee Ellis, "Evolutionary and Neurochemical Causes of Sex Differences in Victimizing Behavior: Toward a Unified Theory of Criminal Behavior and Social Stratification," *Social Science Information* 28 (1989): 605–636.

22. Lee Ellis and Phyllis Coontz, "Androgens, Brain Functioning, and Criminality: The Neurohormonal Foundations of Antisociality," in *Crime in Biological, Social and Moral Contexts,* eds. Lee Ellis and Harry Hoffman (New York: Praeger, 1990), pp. 162–193, at p. 181.

23. Stephanie H.M. van Goozen, Walter Matthys, Peggy Cohen-Kettenis, Jos Thijssen, and Herman van Engeland, "Adrenal Androgens and Aggression in Conduct Disorder Prepubertal Boys and Normal Controls," *Biological Psychiatry* 43 (1998): 156–158.

24. Paul Bernhardt, "Influences of Serotonin and Testosterone in Aggression and Dominance: Convergence with Social Psychology," *Current Directions in Psychological Science* 6 (1997): 44–48.

25. Christy Miller Buchanan, Jacquelynne Eccles, and Jill Becker, "Are Adolescents the Victims of Raging Hormones? Evidence for Activational Effects of Hormones on Moods and Behavior at Adolescence," *Psychological Bulletin* 111 (1992): 62–107.

26. Alan Booth and D. Wayne Osgood, "The Influence of Testosterone on Deviance in Adulthood: Assessing and Explaining the Relationship," *Criminology* 31 (1993): 93–117.

27. Albert Reiss and Jeffrey Roth, eds., *Understanding and Preventing Violence* (Washington, D.C.: National Academy Press, 1993), p. 118.

28. Anthony Walsh, "Genetic and Cytogenetic Intersex Anomalies: Can They Help Us to Understand Gender Differences in Deviant Behavior?" *International Journal of Offender Therapy and Comparative Criminology* 39 (1995): 151–166.

29. Walter Gove, "The Effect of Age and Gender on Deviant Behavior: A Biopsychosocial Perspective," in *Gender and the Life Course,* ed. A. S. Rossi (New York: Aldine, 1985), pp. 115–144.

30. For a review of this concept, see Anne E. Figert, "The Three Faces of PMS: The Professional, Gendered, and Scientific Structuring of a Psychiatric Disorder," *Social Problems* 42 (1995): 56–72.

31. Katharina Dalton, *The Premenstrual Syndrome* (Springfield, Ill.: Charles C. Thomas, 1971).

32. Julie Horney, "Menstrual Cycles and Criminal Responsibility," *Law and Human Nature* 2 (1978): 25–36.

33. Diana Fishbein, "Selected Studies on the Biology of Antisocial Behavior," in *New Perspectives in Criminology,* ed. John Conklin (Needham Heights, Mass.: Allyn & Bacon, 1996), pp. 26–38.

34. Ibid.; Karen Paige, "Effects of Oral Contraceptives on Affective Fluctuations Associated with the Menstrual Cycle," *Psychosomatic Medicine* 33 (1971): 515–537.

35. Press Release, "CDC Releases Most Extensive Assessment Ever of Americans' Exposure to Environmental Chemicals," Center for Disease Control. Atlanta, Ga., January 31, 2003.

36. Alexander Schauss, *Diet, Crime and Delinquency* (Berkeley, Calif.: Parker House, 1980).

37. Herbert Needleman, Christine McFarland, Roberta Ness, Stephen Fienberg, and Michael Tobin, "Bone Lead Levels in Adjudicated Delinquents: A Case Control Study," *Neurotoxicology and Teratology* 24 (2002): 711–717.

38. Deborah Denno, "Considering Lead Poisoning as a Criminal Defense," *Fordham Urban Law Journal* 20 (1993): 377–400.

39. Jeff Evans, "Asymptomatic, High Lead Levels Tied to Delinquency," *Pediatric News* 37 (2003): 13.

40. Jens Walkowiak, Jörg Wiener, Annemarie Fastabend, Birger Heinzow, Ursula Krämer, Eberhard Schmidt, Hans Steingürber, Sabine Wundram, and Gerhard Winneke, "Environmental Exposure to Polychlorinated Biphenyls and Quality of the Home Environment: Effects on Psychodevelopment in Early Childhood," *The Lancet* 358 (2001): 92–93.

41. Terrie Moffitt, "The Neuropsychology of Juvenile Delinquency: A Critical Review," in *Crime and Justice: An Annual Review,* vol. 12, eds. Norval Morris and Michael Tonry (Chicago: University of Chicago Press, 1990), pp. 99–169.

42. Terrie Moffitt, Donald Lynam, and Phil Silva, "Neuropsychological Tests Predicting Persistent Male Delinquency," *Criminology* 32 (1994): 277–300; Eliza-beth Kandel and Sarnoff Mednick, "Perinatal Complications Predict Violent Offending," *Criminology* 29 (1991): 519–529; Sarnoff Mednick, Ricardo Machon, Matti Virkkunen, and Douglas Bonett, "Adult Schizophrenia Following Prenatal Exposure to an Influenza Epidemic," *Archives of General Psychiatry* 44 (1987): 35–46; C. A. Fogel, S. A. Mednick, and N. Michelson, "Hyperactive Behavior and Minor Physical Anomalies," *Acta Psychiatrica Scandinavia* 72 (1985): 551–556.

43. Jean Seguin, Robert Pihl, Philip Harden, Richard Tremblay, and Bernard Boulerice, "Cognitive and Neuropsychological Characteristics of Physically Aggressive Boys," *Journal of Abnormal Psychology* 104 (1995): 614–624; Deborah Denno, "Gender, Crime and the Criminal Law Defenses," *Journal of Criminal Law and Criminology* 85 (1994): 80–180.

44. Adrian Raine, Patricia Brennan, Brigitte Mednick, and Sarnoff Mednick, "High Rates of Violence, Crime, Academic Problems, and Behavioral Problems in Males with Both Early Neuromotor Deficits and Unstable Family Environments," *Archives of General Psychiatry* 53 (1996): 544–549; Deborah Denno, *Biology, Crime and Violence: New Evidence* (Cambridge: Cambridge University Press, 1989).

45. Diana Fishbein and Robert Thatcher, "New Diagnostic Methods in Criminology: Assessing Organic Sources of Behavioral Disorders," *Journal of Research in Crime and Delinquency* 23 (1986): 240–267.

46. Lorne Yeudall, "A Neuropsychosocial Perspective on Persistent Juvenile Delinquency and Criminal Behavior," paper presented at the New York Academy of Sciences, September 26, 1979.

47. See, generally, Jan Volavka, "Electroencephalogram among Criminals," in *The Causes of Crime: New Biological Approaches,* eds. Sarnoff Mednick, Terrie Moffitt, and Susan Stack (Cambridge: Cambridge University Press, 1987), pp. 137–145; Z. A. Zayed, S. A. Lewis, and R. P. Britain, "An Encephalographic and Psychiatric Study of 32 Insane Murderers," *British Journal of Psychiatry* 115 (1969): 1115–1124.

48. Nathaniel Pallone and James Hennessy, "Brain Dysfunction and Criminal Violence," *Society* 35 (1998): 21–27; P. F. Goyer, P. J. Andreason, and W. E. Semple, "Positronic Emission Tomography and Personality Disorders," *Neuropsychopharmacology* 10 (1994): 21–28.

49. Fishbein, "Neuropsychological Function, Drug Abuse, and Violence"; Adrian Raine, Monte Buchsbaum, and Lori LaCasse, "Brain Abnormalities in Murderers Indicated by Positron Emission Tomography," *Biological Psychiatry* 42 (1997): 495–508.

50. Pallone and Hennessy, "Brain Dysfunction and Criminal Violence," p. 25.

51. D. R. Robin, R. M. Starles, T. J. Kenney, B. J. Reynolds, and F. P. Heald,

"Adolescents Who Attempt Suicide," *Journal of Pediatrics* 90 (1977): 636–638.

52. Raine, Buchsbaum, and LaCasse, "Brain Abnormalities in Murderers Indicated by Positron Emission Tomography."

53. Leonore Simon, "Does Criminal Offender Treatment Work?" *Applied and Preventive Psychology* (Summer 1998); Stephen Faraone et al., "Intellectual Performance and School Failure in Children with Attention Deficit Hyperactivity Disorder and in Their Siblings," *Journal of Abnormal Psychology* 102 (1993): 616–623.

54. Simon, "Does Criminal Offender Treatment Work?"

55. Ibid.

56. Terrie Moffitt and Phil Silva, "Self-Reported Delinquency, Neuropsychological Deficit, and History of Attention Deficit Disorder," *Journal of Abnormal Child Psychology* 16 (1988): 553–569.

57. D. R. Blachman and S. P. Hinshaw, "Patterns of Friendship among Girls with and without Attention-Deficit/Hyperactivity Disorder," *Journal of Abnormal Child Psychology* 30 (2002): 625–640.

58. Elizabeth Hart et al., "Developmental Change in Attention-Deficit Hyperactivity Disorder in Boys: A Four-Year Longitudinal Study," *Journal of Consulting and Clinical Psychology* 62 (1994): 472–491.

59. Eugene Maguin, Rolf Loeber, and Paul LeMahieu, "Does the Relationship between Poor Reading and Delinquency Hold for Males of Different Ages and Ethnic Groups?" *Journal of Emotional and Behavioral Disorders* 1 (1993): 88–100.

60. Susan Young, Andrew Smolen, Robin Corley, Kenneth Krauter, John DeFries, Thomas Crowley, and John Hewitt, "Dopamine Transporter Polymorphism Associated with Externalizing Behavior Problems in Children," *American Journal of Medical Genetics* 114 (2002): 144–149.

61. Avshalom Caspi, Joseph McClay, Terrie E. Moffitt, Jonathan Mill, Judy Martin, Ian W. Craig, Alan Taylor, and Richie Poulton, " Role of Genotype in the Cycle of Violence in Maltreated Children," *Science* 297 (2002): 851–854.

62. Matti Virkkunen, David Goldman, and Markku Linnoila, "Serotonin in Alcoholic Violent Offenders," *The Ciba Foundation Symposium: Genetics of Criminal and Antisocial Behavior* (Chichester, England: Wiley, 1995).

63. Lee Ellis, "Left- and Mixed-Handedness and Criminality: Explanations for a Probable Relationship," in *Left-Handedness: Behavioral Implications and Anomalies,* ed. S. Coren (Amsterdam: Elsevier, 1990), pp. 485–507.

64. Lee Ellis, "Monoamine Oxidase and Criminality: Identifying an Apparent Biological Marker for Antisocial Behavior," *Journal of Research in Crime and Delinquency* 28 (1991): 227–251.

65. Lee Ellis, "Arousal Theory and the Religiosity–Criminality Relationship," in *Contemporary Criminological Theory,* eds. Peter Cordella and Larry Siegel (Boston, Mass.: Northeastern University, 1996), pp. 65–84.

66. Adrian Raine, Peter Venables, and Sarnoff Mednick, "Low Resting Heart Rate at Age 3 Years Predisposes to Aggression at Age 11 Years: Evidence from the Mauritius Child Health Project," *Journal of the American Academy of Adolescent Psychiatry* 36 (1997): 1457–1464.

67. David Rowe, "As the Twig Is Bent: The Myth of Child-Rearing Influences on Personality Development," *Journal of Counseling and Development* 68 (1990): 606–611; David Rowe, Joseph Rogers, and Sylvia Meseck-Bushey, "Sibling Delinquency and the Family Environment: Shared and Unshared Influences," *Child Development* 63 (1992): 59–67; Gregory Carey and David DiLalla, "Personality and Psychopathology: Genetic Perspectives," *Journal of Abnormal Psychology* 103 (1994): 32–43.

68. T. R. Sarbin and L. E. Miller, "Demonism Revisited: The XYY Chromosome Anomaly," *Issues in Criminology* 5 (1970): 195–207.

69. Sarnoff Mednick and Jan Volavka, "Biology and Crime," in *Crime and Justice,* eds. Norval Morris and Michael Tonry (Chicago: University of Chicago Press, 1980), pp. 85–159, at p. 93.

70. For an early review, see Barbara Wooton, *Social Science and Social Pathology* (London: Allen & Unwin, 1959); John Laub and Robert Sampson, "Unraveling Families and Delinquency: A Reanalysis of the Gluecks' Data," *Criminology* 26 (1988): 355–380.

71. D. J. West and D. P. Farrington, "Who Becomes Delinquent?" in *The Delinquent Way of Life,* eds. D. J. West and D. P. Farrington (London: Heinemann, 1977), pp. 1–28; D. J. West, *Delinquency: Its Roots, Careers, and Prospects* (Cambridge, Mass.: Harvard University Press, 1982).

72. West, *Delinquency,* p. 114.

73. David Farrington, "Understanding and Preventing Bullying," in *Crime and Justice,* vol. 17, ed. Michael Tonry (Chicago: University of Chicago Press, 1993), pp. 381–457.

74. Terence Thornberry, Adrienne Freeman-Gallant, Alan Lizotte, Marvin Krohn, and Carolyn Smith, "Linked Lives: The Intergenerational Transmission of Antisocial Behavior," *Journal of Abnormal Child Psychology* 31 (2003): 171–185.

75. David Rowe and David Farrington, "The Familial Transmission of Criminal Convictions," *Criminology* 35 (1997): 177–201.

76. Mednick and Volavka, "Biology and Crime," p. 94.

77. Edwin J. C. G. van den Oord, Frank Verhulst, and Dorret Boomsma, "A Genetic Study of Maternal and Paternal Ratings of Problem Behaviors in 3-Year-Old Twins," *Journal of Abnormal Psychology* 105 (1996): 349–357.

78. Ibid., p. 95.

79. David Rowe, "Genetic and Environmental Components of Antisocial Behavior: A Study of 265 Twin Pairs," *Criminology* 24 (1986): 513–532; David Rowe and D. Wayne Osgood, "Heredity and Sociological Theories of Delinquency: A Reconsideration," *American Sociological Review* 49 (1984): 526–540.

80. Michael Lyons, "A Twin Study of Self-Reported Criminal Behavior," and Judy Silberg, Joanne Meyer, Andrew Pickles, Emily Simonoff, Lindon Eaves, John Hewitt, Hermine Maes, and Michael Rutter, "Heterogeneity among Juvenile Antisocial Behaviors: Findings from the Virginia Twin Study of Adolescent Behavioral Development," in *The Ciba Foundation Symposium, Genetics of Criminal and Antisocial Behavior* (Chichester, England: Wiley), 1995.

81. Thomas Bouchard, "Genetic and Environmental Influences on Intelligence and Special Mental Abilities," *American Journal of Human Biology* 70 (1998): 253–275; some findings from the Minnesota study can be accessed from their Web site: http://www.cla.umn.edu/psych/psylabs/mtfs/mtfsspec.htm

82. Gregory Carey, "Twin Imitation for Antisocial Behavior: Implications for Genetic and Family Environment Research," *Journal of Abnormal Psychology* 101 (1992): 18–25.

83. David Rowe, *The Limits of Family Influence: Genes, Experiences and Behavior* (New York: Guilford Press, 1995), p. 64.

84. R. J. Cadoret, C. Cain, and R. R. Crowe, "Evidence for a Gene–Environment Interaction in the Development of Adolescent Antisocial Behavior," *Behavior Genetics* 13 (1983): 301–310.

85. Barry Hutchings and Sarnoff A. Mednick, "Criminality in Adoptees and Their Adoptive and Biological Parents: A Pilot Study," in *Biological Bases in Criminal Behavior,* eds. S. A. Mednick and K. O. Christiansen (New York: Gardner Press, 1977).

86. For similar results, see Sarnoff Mednick, Terrie Moffitt, William Gabrielli, and Barry Hutchings, "Genetic Factors in Criminal Behavior: A Review," *Development of Antisocial and Prosocial Behavior* (New York: Academic Press, 1986), pp. 3–50; Sarnoff Mednick, William Gabrielli, and Barry Hutchings, "Genetic Influences in Criminal Behavior: Evidence from an Adoption Cohort," in *Perspective Studies of Crime and Delinquency,* eds. Katherine Teilmann Van Dusen and Sarnoff Mednick (Boston: Kluwer-Nijhoff, 1983), pp. 39–57.

87. Glenn Walters, "A Meta-Analysis of the Gene–Crime Relationship," *Criminology* 30 (1992): 595–613.

88. Lawrence Cohen and Richard Machalek, "A General Theory of Expropriative Crime: An Evolutionary Ecological Approach," *American Journal of Sociology* 94 (1988): 465–501.

89. For a general review, see Martin Daly and Margo Wilson, "Crime and Conflict: Homicide in Evolutionary Psychological Theory," in *Crime and Justice: An Annual Edition,* ed. Michael Tonry (Chicago: University of Chicago Press, 1997), pp. 51–100.

90. Lee Ellis, "The Evolution of Violent Criminal Behavior and Its Nonlegal Equivalent," in *Crime in Biological, Social and Moral Contexts,* eds. Lee Ellis and Harry Hoffman (New York: Praeger, 1990), pp. 63–65.

91. David Rowe, Alexander Vazsonyi, and Aurelio Jose Figuerdo, "Mating-Effort in Adolescence: A Conditional Alternative Strategy," *Personal Individual Differences* 23 (1997): 105–115.

92. Ibid., p. 101.

93. Todd Shackelford," Risk of Multiple-Offender Rape–Murder Varies with Female Age," *Journal of Criminal Justice* 30 (2002): 135–142.

94. Margo Wilson, Holly Johnson, and Martin Daly, "Lethal and Nonlethal Violence against Wives," *Canadian Journal of Criminology* 37 (1995): 331–361.

95. Lee Ellis and Anthony Walsh, "Gene-Based Evolutionary Theories of Criminology," *Criminology* 35 (1997): 229–276.

96. Byron Roth, "Crime and Child Rearing," *Society* 34 (1996): 39–45.

97. Deborah Denno, "Sociological and Human Developmental Explanations of Crime: Conflict or Consensus," *Criminology* 23 (1985): 711–741.

98. Glenn Walters and Thomas White, "Heredity and Crime: Bad Genes or Bad Research?" *Criminology* 27 (1989): 455–486, at p. 478.

99. Edwin Driver, "Charles Buckman Goring," in *Pioneers in Criminology,* ed. Hermann Mannheim (Montclair, N.J.: Patterson Smith, 1970), p. 440.

100. Gabriel Tarde, *Penal Philosophy,* trans. R. Howell (Boston: Little, Brown, 1912).

101. See, generally, Donn Byrne and Kathryn Kelly, *An Introduction to Personality* (Englewood Cliffs, N.J.: Prentice-Hall, 1981).

102. David Abrahamsen, *Crime and the Human Mind* (New York: Columbia University Press, 1944), p. 137; also see, generally, Fritz Redl and Hans Toch, "The Psychoanalytic Perspective," in *Psychology of Crime and Criminal Justice,* ed. Hans Toch (New York: Holt, Rinehart & Winston, 1979), pp. 193–195.

103. See, generally, D. A. Andrews and James Bonta, *The Psychology of Criminal Conduct* (Cincinnati: Anderson, 1994), pp. 72–75.

104. Paige Crosby Ouimette, "Psychopathology and Sexual Aggression in Nonincarcerated Men," *Violence and Victimization* 12 (1997): 389–397.

105. Robert Krueger, Avshalom Caspi, Phil Silva, and Rob McGee, "Personality Traits Are Differentially Linked to Mental Disorders: A Multitrait–Multidiagnosis Study of an Adolescent Birth Cohort," *Journal of Abnormal Psychology* 105 (1996): 299–312.

106. Seymour Halleck, *Psychiatry and the Dilemmas of Crime* (Berkeley: University of California Press, 1971).

107. Jennifer Beyers and Rolf Loeber, "Untangling Developmental Relations between Depressed Mood and Delinquency in Male Adolescents," *Journal of Abnormal Child Psychology* 31 (2003): 247–267.

108. Bruce Link, Howard Andrews, and Francis Cullen, "The Violent and Illegal Behavior of Mental Patients Reconsidered," *American Sociological Review* 57 (1992): 275–292; Ellen Hochstedler Steury, "Criminal Defendants with Psychiatric Impairment: Prevalence, Probabilities and Rates," *Journal of Criminal Law and Criminology* 84 (1993): 354–374.

109. John Monahan, *Mental Illness and Violent Crime* (Washington, D.C.: National Institute of Justice, 1996).

110. Richard Rosner, "Adolescents Accused of Murder and Manslaughter: A Five-Year Descriptive Study," *Bulletin of the American Academy of Psychiatry and the Law* 7 (1979): 342–351.

111. Richard Famularo, Robert Kinscherff, and Terence Fenton, "Psychiatric Diagnoses of Abusive Mothers: A Preliminary Report," *Journal of Nervous and Mental Disease* 180 (1992): 658–660.

112. Henrik Belfrage "A Ten-Year Follow-Up of Criminality in Stockholm Mental Patients: New Evidence for a Relation between Mental Disorder and Crime," *British Journal of Criminology* 38 (1998): 145–155.

113. C. Wallace, P. Mullen, P. Burgess, S. Palmer, D. Ruschena, and C. Browne, "Serious Criminal Offending and Mental Disorder. Case Linkage Study," *British Journal of Psychiatry* 174 (1998): 477–484.

114. Patricia Brennan, Sarnoff Mednick, and Sheilagh Hodgins, "Major Mental Disorders and Criminal Violence in a Danish Birth Cohort," *Archives of General Psychiatry* 57 (2000): 494–500.

115. Marc Hillbrand, John Krystal, Kimberly Sharpe, and Hilliard Foster, "Clinical Predictors of Self-Mutilation in Hospitalized Patients," *Journal of Nervous and Mental Disease* 182 (1994): 9–13.

116. Carmen Cirincione, Henry Steadman, Pamela Clark Robbins, and John Monahan, *Mental Illness as a Factor in Criminality: A Study of Prisoners and Mental Patients* (Delmar, N.Y.: Policy Research Associates, 1991); see also Carmen Cirincione, Henry Steadman, Pamela Clark Robbins, and John Monahan, *Schizophrenia as a Contingent Risk Factor for Criminal Violence* (Delmar, N.Y.: Policy Research Associates, 1991).

117. Eric Silver, "Mental Disorder and Violent Victimization: The Mediating Role of Involvement in Conflicted Social Relationships," *Criminology* 40 (2002): 191–212.

118. Stacy De Coster and Karen Heimer, "The Relationship between Law Violation and Depression: An Interactionist Analysis," *Criminology* 39 (2001): 799–836.

119. This discussion is based on three works by Albert Bandura: *Aggression: A Social Learning Analysis* (Englewood Cliffs, N.J.: Prentice-Hall, 1973); *Social Learning Theory* (Englewood Cliffs, N.J.: Prentice-Hall, 1977); and "The Social Learning Perspective: Mechanisms of Aggression," in *Psychology of Crime and Criminal Justice,* ed. Hans Toch (New York: Holt, Rinehart & Winston, 1979), pp. 198–236.

120. Amy Street, Lynda King, Daniel King, and David Riges, "The Associations among Male-Perpetrated Partner Violence, Wives' Psychological Distress and Children's Behavior Problems: A Structural Equation Modeling Analysis," *Journal of Comparative Family Studies* 34 (2003): 23–46.

121. David Phillips, "The Impact of Mass Media Violence on U.S. Homicides," *American Sociological Review* 48 (1983): 560–568.

122. K. A. Dodge, "A Social Information Processing Model of Social Competence in Children," in *Minnesota Symposium in Child Psychology,* vol. 18, ed. M. Perlmutter (Hillsdale, N.J.: Erlbaum, 1986), pp. 77–125.

123. Adrian Raine, Peter Venables, and Mark Williams, "Better Autonomic Conditioning and Faster Electrodermal Half-Recovery Time at Age 15 Years as Possible Protective Factors against Crime at Age 29 Years," *Developmental Psychology* 32 (1996): 624–630.

124. Jean Marie McGloin and Travis Pratt, "Cognitive Ability and Delinquent Behavior among Inner-City Youth: A Life-Course Analysis of Main, Mediating, and Interaction Effects," *International Journal of Offender Therapy & Comparative Criminology* 47 (2003): 253–271.

125. Tony Ward and Claire Stewart, "The Relationship between Human Needs and Criminogenic Needs," *Psychology, Crime & Law* 9 (2003): 219–225.

126. L. Huesman and L. Eron, "Individual Differences and the Trait of Aggression," *European Journal of Personality* 3 (1989): 95–106.

127. Rolf Loeber and Dale Hay, "Key Issues in the Development of Aggression and Violence from Childhood to Early Adulthood," *Annual Review of Psychology* 48 (1997): 371–410.

128. D. Lipton, E. C. McDonel, and R. McFall, "Heterosocial Perception in Rapists," *Journal of Consulting and Clinical Psychology* 55 (1987): 17–21.

129. See, generally, Walter Mischel, *Introduction to Personality,* 4th ed. (New York: Holt, Rinehart & Winston, 1986).

130. See, generally, Hans Eysenck, *Personality and Crime* (London: Routledge & Kegan Paul, 1977).

131. Edelyn Verona and Joyce Carbonell, "Female Violence and Personality," *Criminal Justice and Behavior* 27 (2000): 176–195.

132. Hans Eysenck and M. W. Eysenck, *Personality and Individual Differences* (New York: Plenum, 1985).

133. Catrien Bijleveld and Jan Hendriks, "Juvenile Sex Offenders: Differences

between Group and Solo Offenders," *Psychology, Crime & Law* 9 (2003): 237–246.

134. Laurie Frost, Terrie Moffitt, and Rob McGee, "Neuropsychological Correlates of Psychopathology in an Unselected Cohort of Young Adolescents," *Journal of Abnormal Psychology* 98 (1989): 307–313.

135. David Lykken, "Psychopathy, Sociopathy, and Crime," *Society* 34 (1996): 30–38.

136. Avshalom Caspi, Terrie Moffitt, Phil Silva, Magda Stouthamer-Loeber, Robert Krueger, and Pamela Schmutte, "Are Some People Crime-Prone? Replications of the Personality–Crime Relationship across Countries, Genders, Races and Methods," *Criminology* 32 (1994): 163–195.

137. Lykken, "Psychopathy, Sociopathy, and Crime."

138. Kent Kiehl, Andra Smith, Robert Hare, Adrianna Mendrek, Bruce Forster, Johann Brink, and Peter F. Liddle, "Limbic Abnormalities in Affective Processing by Criminal Psychopaths as Revealed by Functional Magnetic Resonance Imaging," *Biological Psychiatry* 5 (2001): 677–684.

139. Henry Goddard, *Efficiency and Levels of Intelligence* (Princeton, N.J.: Princeton University Press, 1920); Edwin Sutherland, "Mental Deficiency and Crime," in *Social Attitudes,* ed. Kimball Young (New York: Henry Holt, 1931), chap. 15.

140. William Healy and Augusta Bronner, *Delinquency and Criminals: Their Making and Unmaking* (New York: McMillan, 1926).

141. Joseph Lee Rogers, H. Harrington Cleveland, Edwin van den Oord, and David Rowe, "Resolving the Debate over Birth Order, Family Size and Intelligence," *American Psychologist* 55 (2000): 599–612.

142. Sutherland, "Mental Deficiency and Crime."

143. Travis Hirschi and Michael Hindelang, "Intelligence and Delinquency: A Revisionist Review," *American Sociological Review* 42 (1977): 471–586.

144. Deborah Denno, "Sociological and Human Developmental Explanations of Crime: Conflict or Consensus," *Criminology* 23 (1985): 711–741; Christine Ward and Richard McFall, "Further Validation of the Problem Inventory for Adolescent Girls: Comparing Caucasian and Black Delinquents and Nondelinquents," *Journal of Consulting and Clinical Psychology* 54 (1986): 732–733; L. Hubble and M. Groff, "Magnitude and Direction of WISC-R Verbal Performance IQ Discrepancies among Adjudicated Male Delinquents," *Journal of Youth and Adolescence* 10 (1981): 179–183; Robert Gordon, "IQ Commensurability of Black–White Differences in Crime and Delinquency," paper presented at the annual meeting of the American Psychological Association, Washington, D.C., August 1986; Robert Gordon, "Two Illustrations of the IQ-Surrogate Hypothesis: IQ versus Parental Education and Occupational Status in the Race–IQ–Delinquency Model," paper presented at the annual meeting of the American Society of Criminology, Montreal, November 1987.

145. James Q. Wilson and Richard Herrnstein, *Crime and Human Nature* (New York: Simon & Schuster, 1985), p. 148.

146. Ibid., p. 171.

147. Richard Herrnstein and Charles Murray, *The Bell Curve: Intelligence and Class Structure in American Life* (New York: Free Press, 1994).

148. H. D. Day, J. M. Franklin, and D. D. Marshall, "Predictors of Aggression in Hospitalized Adolescents," *Journal of Psychology* 132 (1998): 427–435; Scott Menard and Barbara Morse, "A Structuralist Critique of the IQ–Delinquency Hypothesis: Theory and Evidence," *American Journal of Sociology* 89 (1984): 1347–1378; Denno, "Sociological and Human Developmental Explanations of Crime."

149. Ulric Neisser et al., "Intelligence: Knowns and Unknowns," *American Psychologist* 51 (1996): 77–101, at p. 83.

150. Susan Pease and Craig T. Love, "Optimal Methods and Issues in Nutrition Research in the Correctional Setting," *Nutrition Reviews Supplement* 44 (1986): 122–131.

151. Mark O'Callaghan and Douglas Carroll, "The Role of Psychosurgical Studies in the Control of Antisocial Behavior," in *The Causes of Crime: New Biological Approaches,* eds. Sarnoff Mednick, Terrie Moffitt, and Susan Stack (Cambridge: Cambridge University Press, 1987), pp. 312–328.

152. Reiss and Roth, *Understanding and Preventing Violence,* p. 389.

153. Kathleen Cirillo, B. E. Pruitt, Brian Colwell, Paul M. Kingery, Robert S. Hurley, and Danny Ballard, "School Violence: Prevalence and Intervention Strategies for At-Risk Adolescents," *Adolescence* 33 (1998): 319–331.

Chapter 6

1. Arlen Egley and Aline Major, *2001 Youth Gang Survey* (Washington, DC: Office of Juvenile Justice and Delinquency Prevention, 2003). Herein cited as 2001 National Youth Gang Survey; Arlen Egley, Aline Major and James Howell, J *National Youth Gang Survey: 1999-2001.* Tallahassee, FL: National Youth Gang Center, 2004 (forthcoming).

2. Arlen Egley National Youth Gang Survey Trends From 1996 to 2000 Series: Fact Sheet (Washington, D.C.: Bureau of Justice Statistics, 2002)

3. Steven Messner and Richard Rosenfeld, *Crime and the American Dream* (Belmont, CA: Wadsworth, 1994), p. 11.

4. Steven Messner and Richard Rosenfeld, *Crime and the American Dream* (Belmont, Calif.: Wadsworth, 1994), p. 11.

5. Edwin Lemert, *Human Deviance, Social Problems and Social Control* (Englewood Cliffs, N.J.: Prentice-Hall, 1967).

6. Carmen DeNavas Walt, Robert Cleveland, and Bruce Webster, *Income in the United States, 2003* (Washington, D.C.: U.S. Census Bureau, 2003) Available: http://www.census.gov/prod/2003pubs/p60-221.pdf (accessed November 6, 2003).

7. U.S. Department of Census Data, *Race and Income* (Washington, D.C.: U.S. Census Bureau, 2003).

8. UCLA Center for Health Policy Research, *The Health of Young Children in California: Findings from the 2001 California Health Interview Survey* (Los Angeles: California UCLA Center for Health Policy Research, 2003).

9. James Ainsworth-Darnell and Douglas Downey, "Assessing the Oppositional Culture Explanation for Racial/Ethnic Differences in School Performances," *American Sociological Review* 63 (1998): 536–553.

10. Julie A. Phillips, "White, Black, and Latino Homicide Rates: Why the Difference?" *Social Problems* 49 (2002): 349–374.

11. Jeanne Brooks-Gunn and Greg J. Duncan, "The Effects of Poverty on Children," *Future of Children* 7 (1997): 34–39.

12. Ibid.

13. Greg Duncan, W. Jean Yeung, Jeanne Brooks-Gunn, and Judith Smith, "How Much Does Childhood Poverty Affect the Life Chances of Children?" *American Sociological Review* 63 (1998): 406–423.

14. Ibid., p. 409.

15. Gary Evans, Nancy Wells, and Annie Moch, "Housing and Mental Health: A Review of the Evidence and a Methodological and Conceptual Critique," *Journal of Social Issues* 59 (2003): 475–501.

16. Jonathan Crane, "The Epidemic Theory of Ghettos and Neighborhood Effects on Dropping Out and Teenage Childbearing," *American Journal of Sociology* 96 (1991): 1226–1259; see also Rodrick Wallace, "Expanding Coupled Shock Fronts of Urban Decay and Criminal Behavior: How U.S. Cities Are Becoming 'Hollowed Out,'" *Journal of Quantitative Criminology* 7 (1991): 333–355.

17. Oscar Lewis, "The Culture of Poverty," *Scientific American* 215 (1966): 19–25.

18. Gunnar Myrdal, *The Challenge of World Poverty* (New York: Vintage Books, 1970).

19. Barbara Warner, "The Role of Attenuated Culture in Social Disorganization Theory," *Criminology* 41 (2003): 73–97.

20. See Charles Tittle and Robert Meier, "Specifying the SES/Delinquency Relationship," *Criminology* 28 (1990): 271–295, at p. 293.

21. See Ruth Kornhauser, *Social Sources of Delinquency* (Chicago: University of Chicago Press, 1978), p. 75.

22. Clifford R. Shaw and Henry D. McKay, *Juvenile Delinquency and Urban Areas,* rev. ed. (Chicago: University of Chicago Press, 1972).

23. Ibid., p. 52.

24. Ibid., p. 171.

25. Claire Valier, "Foreigners, Crime and Changing Mobilities," *British Journal of Criminology* 43 (2003): 1–21.

26. The best-known of these critiques is Kornhauser, *Social Sources of Delinquency.*

27. For a general review, see James Byrne and Robert Sampson, eds., *The Social Ecology of Crime* (New York: Springer Verlag, 1985).

28. See, generally, Robert Bursik, "Social Disorganization and Theories of Crime and Delinquency: Problems and Prospects," *Criminology* 26 (1988): 521–539.

29. D. Wayne Osgood and Jeff Chambers, "Social Disorganization Outside the Metropolis: An Analysis of Rural Youth Violence," *Criminology* 38 (2000): 81–117.

30. William Spelman, "Abandoned Buildings: Magnets for Crime?" *Journal of Criminal Justice* 21 (1993): 481–493.

31. Keith Harries and Andrea Powell, "Juvenile Gun Crime and Social Stress: Baltimore, 1980–1990," *Urban Geography* 15 (1994): 45–63.

32. Ellen Kurtz, Barbara Koons, and Ralph Taylor, "Land Use, Physical Deterioration, Resident-Based Control, and Calls for Service on Urban Streetblocks," *Justice Quarterly* 15 (1998): 121–149.

33. Charis E. Kubrin, "Structural Covariates of Homicide Rates: Does Type of Homicide Matter?" *Journal of Research in Crime and Delinquency* 40 (2003): 139–170.

34. Steven Messner and Kenneth Tardiff, "Economic Inequality and Levels of Homicide: An Analysis of Urban Neighborhoods," *Criminology* 24 (1986): 297–317.

35. G. David Curry and Irving Spergel, "Gang Homicide, Delinquency, and Community," *Criminology* 26 (1988): 381–407.

36. Darrell Steffensmeier and Dana Haynie, "Gender, Structural Disadvantage, and Urban Crime: Do Macrosocial Variables Also Explain Female Offending Rates?" *Criminology* 38 (2000): 403–438.

37. Bursik, "Social Disorganization and Theories of Crime and Delinquency," p. 520.

38. Richard McGahey, "Economic Conditions, Organization, and Urban Crime," in *Communities and Crime,* eds. Albert Reiss and Michael Tonry (Chicago: University of Chicago Press, 1986), pp. 231–270.

39. Scott Menard and Delbert Elliott, "Self-Reported Offending, Maturational Reform, and the Easterlin Hypothesis," *Journal of Quantitative Criminology* 6 (1990): 237–268.

40. Elijah Anderson, *Streetwise: Race, Class and Change in an Urban Community* (Chicago: University of Chicago Press, 1990), pp. 243–244.

41. Matthew Lee and Terri Earnest, "Perceived Community Cohesion and Perceived Risk of Victimization: A Cross-National Analysis," *Justice Quarterly* 20 (2003): 131–158.

42. Pamela Wilcox, Neil Quisenberry, and Shayne Jones, "The Built Environment and Community Crime Risk Interpretation," *Journal of Research in Crime and Delinquency* 40 (2003): 322–345.

43. Pamela Wilcox Rountree and Kenneth Land, "Burglary Victimization, Perceptions of Crime Risk, and Routine Activities: A Multilevel Analysis across Seattle Neighborhoods and Census Tracts," *Journal of Research in Crime and Delinquency* 33 (1996): 147–180.

44. Randy LaGrange, Kenneth Ferraro, and Michael Supancic, "Perceived Risk and Fear of Crime: Role of Social and Physical Incivilities," *Journal of Research in Crime and Delinquency* 29 (1992): 311–334.

45. Ted Chiricos, Ranee McEntire, and Marc Gertz, "Social Problems, Perceived Racial and Ethnic Composition of Neighborhood and Perceived Risk of Crime," *Social Problems* 48 (2001): 322–341; Wesley Skogan, "Fear of Crime and Neighborhood Change," in *Communities and Crime,* eds. Albert Reiss and Michael Tonry (Chicago: University of Chicago Press, 1986), pp. 191–232.

46. Stephanie Greenberg, "Fear and Its Relationship to Crime, Neighborhood Deterioration, and Informal Social Control," in *The Social Ecology of Crime,* eds. James Byrne and Robert Sampson (New York: Springer Verlag, 1985), pp. 47–62.

47. Catherine E. Ross, John Mirowsky, and Shana Pribesh, "Powerlessness and the Amplification of Threat: Neighborhood Disadvantage, Disorder, and Mistrust," *American Sociological Review* 66 (2001): 568–580.

48. William Terrill and Michael Reisig, "Neighborhood Context and Police Use of Force," *Journal of Research in Crime and Delinquency* 40 (2003): 291–321.

49. Finn Aage-Esbensen and David Huizinga, "Community Structure and Drug Use: From a Social Disorganization Perspective," *Justice Quarterly* 7 (1990): 691–709.

50. Allen Liska and Paul Bellair, "Violent-Crime Rates and Racial Composition: Convergence over Time," *American Journal of Sociology* 101 (1995): 578–610.

51. Wesley Skogan, *Disorder and Decline: Crime and the Spiral of Decay in American Neighborhoods* (New York: Free Press, 1990), pp. 15–35.

52. Ralph Taylor and Jeanette Covington, "Neighborhood Changes in Ecology and Violence," *Criminology* 26 (1988): 553–589.

53. Barbara Warner, " The Role of Attenuated Culture in Social Disorganization Theory," *Criminology* 41 (2003): 73–99.

54. Leo Scheurman and Solomon Kobrin, "Community Careers in Crime," in *Communities and Crime,* eds. Albert Reiss and Michael Tonry (Chicago: University of Chicago Press, 1986), pp. 67–100.

55. Ibid.

56. Jeffrey Morenoff, Robert Sampson, and Stephen Raudenbush, "Neighborhood Inequality, Collective Efficacy, and the Spatial Dynamics of Urban Violence," *Criminology* 39 (2001): 517–560.

57. Karen Parker and Matthew Pruitt, "Poverty, Poverty Concentration, and Homicide," *Social Science Quarterly* 81 (2000): 555–582.

58. Matthew Lee, Michael Maume, and Graham Ousey, "Social Isolation and Lethal Violence across the Metro/Nonmetro Divide: The Effects of Socioeconomic Disadvantage and Poverty Concentration on Homicide," *Rural Sociology* 68 (2003): 107–131.

59. Carolyn Rebecca Block and Richard Block, *Street Gang Crime in Chicago* (Washington, D.C.: National Institute of Justice, 1993), p. 7.

60. Chris Gibson, Jihong Zhao, Nicholas Lovrich, and Michael Gaffney, "Social Integration, Individual Perceptions of Collective Efficacy, and Fear of Crime in Three Cities," *Justice Quarterly* 19 (2002): 537–564; Felton Earls, *Linking Community Factors and Individual Development* (Washington, D.C.: National Institute of Justice, 1998).

61. Robert J. Sampson and Stephen W. Raudenbush, *Disorder in Urban Neighborhoods: Does It Lead to Crime?* (Washington, D.C.: National Institute of Justice, 2001).

62. Robert Sampson, Jeffrey Morenoff, and Felton Earls, "Beyond Social Capital: Spatial Dynamics of Collective Efficacy for Children," *American Sociological Review* 64 (1999): 633–660.

63. Donald Black, "Social Control as a Dependent Variable," in *Toward a General Theory of Social Control,* ed. D. Black (Orlando: Academic Press, 1990).

64. Jennifer Beyers, John Bates, Gregory Pettit, and Kenneth Dodge, "Neighborhood Structure, Parenting Processes, and the Development of Youths' Externalizing Behaviors: A Multilevel Analysis," *American Journal of Community Psychology* 31 (2003): 35–53.

65. Paul Bellair, "Informal Surveillance and Street Crime: A Complex Relationship," *Criminology* 38 (2000): 137–170.

66. Skogan, *Disorder and Decline.*

67. Robert Sampson and W. Byron Groves, "Community Structure and Crime: Testing Social Disorganization Theory," *American Journal of Sociology* 94 (1989): 774–802; Denise Gottfredson, Richard McNeill, and Gary Gottfredson, "Social Area Influences on Delinquency: A Multilevel Analysis," *Journal of Research in Crime and Delinquency* 28 (1991): 197–206.

68. Fred Markowitz, Paul Bellair, Allen Liska, and Jianhong Liu, "Extending Social Disorganization Theory: Modeling the Relationships between Cohesion, Disorder, and Fear," *Criminology* 39 (2001): 293–320.

69. Robert Bursik and Harold Grasmick, "The Multiple Layers of Social Disorganization," paper presented at the annual meeting of the American Society of Criminology, New Orleans, November 1992.

70. George Capowich, "The Conditioning Effects of Neighborhood Ecology on Burglary Victimization," *Criminal Justice and Behavior* 30 (2003): 39–62.

71. Ruth Perterson, Lauren Krivo, and Mark Harris, "Disadvantage and Neighborhood Violent Crime: Do Local Institutions Matter?" *Journal of Research in Crime and Delinquency* 37 (2000): 31–63.

72. Maria Velez, "The Role of Public Social Control in Urban Neighborhoods: A Multi-Level Analysis of Victimization Risk," *Criminology* 39 (2001): 837–864.

73. David Klinger, "Negotiating Order in Patrol Work: An Ecological Theory of Police Response to Deviance," *Criminology* 35 (1997): 277–306.

74. Rodney Stark, "Deviant Places: A Theory of the Ecology of Crime," *Criminology* 25 (1987): 893–911.

75. Robert Bursik and Harold Grasmick, "Economic Deprivation and Neighborhood Crime Rates, 1960–1980," *Law and Society Review* 27 (1993): 263–278.

76. Delbert Elliott, William Julius Wilson, David Huizinga, Robert Sampson, Amanda Elliott, and Bruce Rankin, "The Effects of Neighborhood Disadvantage on Adolescent Development," *Journal of Research in Crime and Delinquency* 33 (1996): 389–426.

77. Ibid., p. 414.

78. Ruth Peterson, Lauren Krivo, and Mark Harris, "Disadvantage and Neighborhood Violent Crime: Do Local Institutions Matter?" *Journal of Research in Crime and Delinquency* 37 (2000): 31–63.

79. Ralph Taylor, "Social Order and Disorder of Street Blocks and Neighborhoods: Ecology, Microecology, and the Systemic Model of Social Disorganization," *Journal of Research in Crime and Delinquency* 34 (1997): 113–155.

80. Mitchell Chamlin and John Cochran, "Social Altruism and Crime," *Criminology* 35 (1997): 203–227.

81. James DeFronzo, "Welfare and Homicide," *Journal of Research in Crime and Delinquency* 34 (1997): 395–406.

82. Sampson, Morenoff, and Earls, "Beyond Social Capital: Spatial Dynamics of Collective Efficacy for Children."

83. Thomas McNulty, "Assessing the Race–Violence Relationship at the Macro Level: The Assumption of Racial Invariance and the Problem of Restricted Distribution," *Criminology* 39 (2001): 467–490.

84. Robert Merton, *Social Theory and Social Structure,* enlarged ed. (New York: Free Press, 1968).

85. Albert Cohen, "The Sociology of the Deviant Act: Anomie Theory and Beyond," *American Sociological Review* 30 (1965): 5–14.

86. Steven Messner and Richard Rosenfeld, *Crime and the American Dream* (Belmont, Calif.: Wadsworth, 1994).

87. Jon Gunnar Bernburg, "Anomie, Social Change and Crime: A Theoretical Examination of Institutional-Anomie Theory," *British Journal of Criminology* 42 (2002): 729–743.

88. John Hagan, Gerd Hefler, Gabriele Classen, Klaus Boehnke, and Hans Merkens, "Subterranean Sources of Subcultural Delinquency Beyond the American Dream," *Criminology* 36 (1998): 309–340.

89. Morenoff, Sampson, and Raudenbush, "Neighborhood Inequality, Collective Efficacy, and the Spatial Dynamics of Urban Violence."

90. John Braithwaite, "Poverty, Power, White-Collar Crime and the Paradoxes of Criminological Theory," *Australian and New Zealand Journal of Criminology* 24 (1991): 40–58.

91. Margo Wilson and Martin Daly, "Life Expectancy, Economic Inequality, Homicide, and Reproductive Timing in Chicago Neighbourhoods," *British Journal of Medicine* 314 (1997): 1271–1274.

92. Judith Blau and Peter Blau, "The Cost of Inequality: Metropolitan Structure and Violent Crime," *American Sociological Review* 147 (1982): 114–129.

93. Ibid.

94. Tomislav Kovandzic, Lynne Vieraitis, and Mark Yeisley, "The Structural Covariates of Urban Homicide: Reassessing the Impact of Income Inequality and Poverty in the Post-Reagan Era," *Criminology* 36 (1998): 569–600.

95. Scott South and Steven Messner, "Structural Determinants of Intergroup Association," *American Journal of Sociology* 91 (1986): 1409–1430; Steven Messner and Scott South, "Economic Deprivation, Opportunity Structure, and Robbery Victimization," *Social Forces* 64 (1986): 975–991.

96. Richard Fowles and Mary Merva, "Wage Inequality and Criminal Activity: An Extreme Bounds Analysis for the United States 1975–1990," *Criminology* 34 (1996): 163–182.

97. Beverly Stiles, Xiaoru Liu, and Howard Kaplan, "Relative Deprivation and Deviant Adaptations: The Mediating Effects of Negative Self Feelings," *Journal of Research in Crime and Delinquency* 37 (2000): 64–90.

98. Robert Agnew, "Foundation for a General Strain Theory of Crime and Delinquency," *Criminology* 30 (1992): 47–87.

99. Ibid., p. 57.

100. Timothy Brezina, "Adolescent Maltreatment and Delinquency: The Question of Intervening Processes," *Journal of Research in Crime and Delinquency* 35 (1998): 71–99.

101. Paul Mazerolle, Velmer Burton, Francis Cullen, T. David Evans, and Gary Payne, "Strain, Anger, and Delinquent Adaptations Specifying General Strain Theory," *Journal of Criminal Justice* 28 (2000): 89–101; Paul Mazerolle and Alex Piquero, "Violent Responses to Strain: An Examination of Conditioning Influences," *Violence and Victimization* 12 (1997): 323–345.

102. George E. Capowich, Paul Mazerolle, and Alex Piquero, "General Strain Theory, Situational Anger, and Social Networks: An Assessment of Conditioning Influences," *Journal of Criminal Justice* 29 (2001): 445–461.

103. Robert Agnew, Timothy Brezina, John Paul Wright, and Francis T. Cullen, "Strain, Personality Traits, and Delinquency: Extending General Strain Theory," *Criminology* 40 (2002): 43–71.

104. Robert Agnew, "Stability and Change in Crime over the Life Course: A Strain Theory Explanation," in *Advances in Criminological Theory: Vol. 7. Developmental Theories of Crime and Delinquency,* ed. Terence Thornberry (New Brunswick, N.J.: Transaction Books, 1995), pp. 113–137.

105. Lawrence Wu, "Effects of Family Instability, Income, and Income Instability on the Risk of Premarital Birth," *American Sociological Review* 61 (1996): 386–406.

106. Robert Agnew and Helene Raskin White, "An Empirical Test of General Strain Theory," *Criminology* 30 (1992): 475–499.

107. John Hoffman and Alan Miller, "A Latent Variable Analysis of General Strain Theory," *Journal of Quantitative Criminology* 13 (1997): 111–113; Raymond Paternoster and Paul Mazerolle, "General Strain Theory and Delinquency: A Replication and Extension," *Journal of Research in Crime and Delinquency* 31 (1994): 235–263; G. Roger Jarjoura, "The Conditional Effect of Social Class on the Dropout–Delinquency Relationship," *Journal of Research in Crime and Delinquency* 33 (1996): 232–255.

108. Paul Mazerolle, Velmer Burton, Francis Cullen, T. David Evans, and Gary Payne, "Strain, Anger, and Delinquent Adaptations: Specifying General Strain Theory," *Journal of Criminal Justice* 28 (2000): 89–101.

109. Timothy Brezina, "Adapting to Strain: An Examination of Delinquent Coping Responses," *Criminology* 34 (1996): 39–61.

110. Stephen Cernkovich, Peggy Giordano, and Jennifer Rudolph, "Race, Crime and the American Dream," *Journal of Research in Crime and Delinquency* 37 (2000): 131–170.

111. Robert Agnew, "Experienced, Vicarious, and Anticipated Strain: An Exploratory Study on Physical Victimization and Delinquency," *Justice Quarterly* 19 (2002): 603–633.

112. Walter Miller, "Lower-Class Culture as a Generating Milieu of Gang Delinquency," *Journal of Social Issues* 14 (1958): 5–19.

113. Ibid., pp. 14–17.

114. Fred Markowitz and Richard Felson, "Social-Demographic Attitudes and Violence," *Criminology* 36 (1998): 117–138.

115. Jeffrey Fagan, *Adolescent Violence: A View from the Street,* NIJ Research Preview (Washington, D.C.: National Institute of Justice, 1998).

116. Albert Cohen, *Delinquent Boys* (New York: Free Press, 1955).

117. Ibid., p. 25.

118. Ibid., p. 28.

119. Ibid.

120. Ibid., p. 30.

121. Ibid., p. 133.

122. Richard Cloward and Lloyd Ohlin, *Delinquency and Opportunity* (New York: Free Press, 1960).

123. Ibid., p. 171.

124. Ibid., p. 73.

125. James DeFronzo, "Welfare and Burglary," *Crime and Delinquency* 42 (1996): 223–230.

Chapter 7

1. *Smith et al. v. Doe et al.* No. 01-729. Decided March 5, 2003;

2. Charles Tittle and Robert Meier, "Specifying the SES/Delinquency Relationship," *Criminology* 28 (1990): 271–299, at p. 274.

3. Eric Stewart, Ronald Simons, and Rand Conger, "Assessing Neighborhood and Social Psychological Influences on Childhood Violence in an African-American Sample," *Criminology* 40 (2002): 801–830.

4. Sheldon Glueck and Eleanor Glueck, *Unraveling Juvenile Delinquency* (Cambridge, Mass.: Harvard University Press, 1950); Ashley Weeks, "Predicting Juvenile Delinquency," *American Sociological Review* 8 (1943): 40–46.

5. Alexander Vazsonyi and Lloyd Pickering, "The Importance of Family and School Domains in Adolescent Deviance: African American and Caucasian Youth," *Journal of Youth and Adolescence* 32 (2003): 115–129; Denise Kandel, "The Parental and Peer Contexts of Adolescent Deviance: An Algebra of Interpersonal Influences," *Journal of Drug Issues* 26 (1996): 289–315; Ann Goetting, "The Parenting–Crime Connection," *Journal of Primary Prevention* 14 (1994): 167–184.

6. John Paul Wright and Francis Cullen, "Parental Efficacy and Delinquent Behavior: Do Control and Support Matter?" *Criminology* 39 (2001): 677–706.

7. Carter Hay, "Parenting, Self-Control, and Delinquency: A Test of Self-Control Theory," *Criminology* 39 (2001): 707–736.

8. Robert Roberts and Vern Bengston, "Affective Ties to Parents in Early Adulthood and Self-Esteem across 20 Years," *Social Psychology Quarterly* 59 (1996): 96–106.

9. Joseph Rankin and L. Edward Wells, "The Effect of Parental Attachments and Direct Controls on Delinquency," *Journal of Research in Crime and Delinquency* 27 (1990): 140–165.

10. Tiffany Field, "Violence and Touch Deprivation in Adolescents," *Adolescence* 37 (2002): 735–749.

11. Robert Johnson, S. Susan Su, Dean Gerstein, Hee-Choon Shin, and John Hoffman, "Parental Influences on Deviant Behavior in Early Adolescence: A Logistic Response Analysis of Age- and Gender-Differentiated Effects," *Journal of Quantitative Criminology* 11 (1995): 167–192.

12. Thomas Ashby Wills, Donato Vaccaro, Grace McNamara, and A. Elizabeth Hirky, "Escalated Substance Use: A Longitudinal Grouping Analysis from Early to Middle Adolescence," *Journal of Abnormal Psychology* 105 (1996): 166–180.

13. Carolyn Smith and Terence Thornberry, "The Relationship between Childhood Maltreatment and Adolescent Involvement in Delinquency," *Criminology* 33 (1995): 451–479.

14. Ronald Simons, Chyi-In Wu, Kuei-Hsiu Lin, Leslie Gordon, and Rand Conger, "A Cross-Cultural Examination of the Link between Corporal Punishment and Adolescent Antisocial Behavior," *Criminology* 38 (2000): 47–79.

15. Murray A. Straus, "Spanking and the Making of a Violent Society: The Short- and Long-Term Consequences of Corporal Punishment," *Pediatrics* 98 (1996): 837–843.

16. *The Forgotten Half: Pathways to Success for America's Youth and Young Families* (Washington, D.C.: William T. Grant Foundation, 1988); Lee Jussim, "Teacher Expectations: Self-Fulfilling Prophecies, Perceptual Biases, and Accuracy," *Journal of Personality and Social Psychology* 57 (1989): 469–480.

17. Eugene Maguin and Rolf Loeber, "Academic Performance and Delinquency," in *Crime and Justice: A Review of Research,* vol. 20, ed. Michael Tonry (Chicago: University of Chicago Press, 1995), pp. 145–264.

18. Jeannie Oakes, *Keeping Track: How Schools Structure Inequality* (New Haven, Conn.: Yale University Press, 1985); Marc LeBlanc, Evelyne Valliere, and Pierre McDuff, "Adolescents' School Experience and Self-Reported Offending: A Longitudinal Test of Social Control Theory," paper presented at the annual meeting of the American Society of Criminology, Baltimore, November 1990.

19. G. Roger Jarjoura, "Does Dropping Out of School Enhance Delinquent Involvement? Results from a Large-Scale National Probability Sample," *Criminology* 31 (1993): 149–172; Terence Thornberry, Melanie Moore, and R. L. Christenson, "The Effect of Dropping Out of High School on Subsequent Criminal Behavior," *Criminology* 23 (1985): 3–18.

20. Irving Janis, *Groupthink: Psychological Studies of Policy Decisions and Fiascoes* (Boston: Houghton Mifflin, 1982).

21. Delbert Elliott, David Huizinga, and Suzanne Ageton, *Explaining Delinquency and Drug Use* (Beverly Hills, Calif.: Sage, 1985); Helene Raskin White, Robert Padina, and Randy LaGrange, "Longitudinal Predictors of Serious Substance Use and Delinquency," *Criminology* 6 (1987): 715–740.

22. Robert Agnew and Timothy Brezina, "Relational Problems with Peers, Gender and Delinquency," *Youth and Society* 29 (1997): 84–111.

23. Mark Warr, "Age, Peers, and Delinquency," *Criminology* 31 (1993): 17–40.

24. Sara Battin, Karl Hill, Robert Abbott, Richard Catalano, and J. David Hawkins, "The Contribution of Gang Membership to Delinquency Beyond Delinquent Friends," *Criminology* 36 (1998): 93–116.

25. David Fergusson, L. John Horwood, and Daniel Nagin, "Offending Trajectories in a New Zealand Birth Cohort," *Criminology* 38 (2000): 525–551.

26. Colin Baier and Bradley Wright, "If You Love Me, Keep My Commandments": A Meta-Analysis of the Effect of Religion on Crime," *Journal of Research in Crime and Delinquency* 38 (2001): 3–21; Byron Johnson, Sung Joon Jang, David Larson and Spencer De Li, "Does Adolescent Religious Commitment Matter? A Reexamination of the Effects of Religiosity on Delinquency," *Journal of Research in Crime and Delinquency* 38 (2001): 22–44.

27. Sung Joon Jang and Byron Johnson, "Neighborhood Disorder, Individual Religiosity, and Adolescent Use of Illicit Drugs: A Test of Multilevel Hypothesis," *Criminology* 39 (2001): 109–144.

28. T. David Evans, Francis Cullen, R. Gregory Dunaway, and Velmer Burton Jr., "Religion and Crime Reexamined: The Impact of Religion, Secular Controls, and Social Ecology on Adult Criminality," *Criminology* 33 (1995): 195–224.

29. Edwin H. Sutherland, *Principles of Criminology* (Philadelphia: Lippincott, 1939).

30. See, for example, Edwin Sutherland, "White-Collar Criminality," *American Sociological Review* 5 (1940): 2–10.

31. See Edwin Sutherland and Donald Cressey, *Criminology,* 8th ed. (Philadelphia: Lippincott, 1970), pp. 77–79.

32. Sandra Brown, Vicki Creamer, and Barbara Stetson, "Adolescent Alcohol Expectancies in Relation to Personal and Parental Drinking Patterns," *Journal of Abnormal Psychology* 96 (1987): 117–121.

33. Leanne Fiftal Alarid, Velmer Burton, and Francis Cullen, "Gender and Crime among Felony Offenders: Assessing the Generality of Social Control and Differential Association Theory," *Journal of Research in Crime and Delinquency* 37 (2000): 171–199.

34. Terence Thornberry, Adrienne Freeman-Gallant, Alan Lizotte, Marvin Krohn, and Carolyn Smith, "Linked Lives: The Intergenerational Transmission of Antisocial Behavior," *Journal of Abnormal Child Psychology* 31 (2003): 171–184.

35. Joel Hektner, Gerald August, and George Realmuto, "Effects of Pairing Aggressive and Nonaggressive Children in Strategic Peer Affiliation," *Journal of Abnormal Child Psychology* 31 (2003): 399–412.

36. Matthew Ploeger, "Youth Employment and Delinquency: Reconsidering a Problematic Relationship," *Criminology* 35 (1997): 659–675.

37. William Skinner and Anne Fream, "A Social Learning Theory Analysis of Computer Crime among College Students," *Journal of Research in Crime and Delinquency* 34 (1997): 495–518; Denise Kandel and Mark Davies,

"Friendship Networks, Intimacy, and Illicit Drug Use in Young Adulthood: A Comparison of Two Competing Theories," *Criminology* 29 (1991): 441–467.

38. Mallie Paschall, Christopher Ringwalt, and Robert Flewelling, "Explaining Higher Levels of Alcohol Use among Working Adolescents: An Analysis of Potential Explanatory Variables," *Journal of Studies on Alcohol* 63 (2002): 169–178.

39. Warr, "Age, Peers, and Delinquency."

40. Craig Reinerman and Jeffrey Fagan, "Social Organization and Differential Association: A Research Note from a Longitudinal Study of Violent Juvenile Offenders," *Crime and Delinquency* 34 (1988): 307–327.

41. Sue Titus Reed, *Crime and Criminology,* 2nd ed. (New York: Holt, Rinehart & Winston, 1979), p. 234.

42. Gresham Sykes and David Matza, "Techniques of Neutralization: A Theory of Delinquency," *American Sociological Review* 22 (1957): 664–670; David Matza, *Delinquency and Drift* (New York: John Wiley, 1964).

43. Matza, *Delinquency and Drift,* p. 51.

44. Sykes and Matza, "Techniques of Neutralization"; see also David Matza, "Subterranean Traditions of Youths," *Annals of the American Academy of Political and Social Science* 378 (1961): 116.

45. Sykes and Matza, "Techniques of Neutralization."

46. Ibid.

47. Ian Shields and George Whitehall, "Neutralization and Delinquency among Teenagers," *Criminal Justice and Behavior* 21 (1994): 223–235; Robert A. Ball, "An Empirical Exploration of Neutralization Theory," *Criminologica* 4 (1966): 22–32. See also M. William Minor, "The Neutralization of Criminal Offense," *Criminology* 18 (1980): 103–120; Robert Gordon, James Short, Desmond Cartwright, and Fred Strodtbeck, "Values and Gang Delinquency: A Study of Street Corner Groups," *American Journal of Sociology* 69 (1963): 109–128.

48. Michael Hindelang, "The Commitment of Delinquents to Their Misdeeds: Do Delinquents Drift?" *Social Problems* 17 (1970): 500–509; Robert Regoli and Eric Poole, "The Commitment of Delinquents to Their Misdeeds: A Reexamination," *Journal of Criminal Justice* 6 (1978): 261–269.

49. Larry Siegel, Spencer Rathus, and Carol Ruppert, "Values and Delinquent Youth: An Empirical Reexamination of Theories of Delinquency," *British Journal of Criminology* 13 (1973): 237–244.

50. Robert Agnew, "The Techniques of Neutralization and Violence," *Criminology* 32 (1994): 555–580.

51. Jeffrey Fagan, *Adolescent Violence: A View from the Street,* NIJ Research Preview (Washington, D.C.: National Institute of Justice, 1998).

52. Eric Wish, *Drug Use Forecasting 1990* (Washington, D.C.: National Institute of Justice, 1991).

53. Scott Briar and Irving Piliavin, "Delinquency: Situational Inducements and Commitment to Conformity," *Social Problems* 13 (1965–1966): 35–45.

54. Lawrence Sherman and Douglas Smith, with Janell Schmidt and Dennis Rogan, "Crime, Punishment, and Stake in Conformity: Legal and Informal Control of Domestic Violence," *American Sociological Review* 57 (1992): 680–690.

55. Albert Reiss, "Delinquency as the Failure of Personal and Social Controls," *American Sociological Review* 16 (1951): 196–207.

56. Briar and Piliavin, "Delinquency."

57. Walter Reckless, *The Crime Problem* (New York: Appleton-Century Crofts, 1967), pp. 469–483.

58. Among the many research reports by Reckless and his colleagues are Walter Reckless, Simon Dinitz, and Ellen Murray, "Self-Concept as an Insulator Against Delinquency," *American Sociological Review* 21 (1956): 744–746; Walter Reckless, Simon Dinitz, and Barbara Kay, "The Self-Component in Potential Delinquency and Potential Non-Delinquency," *American Sociological Review* 22 (1957): 566–570; Walter Reckless, Simon Dinitz, and Ellen Murray, "The Good Boy in a High Delinquency Area," *Journal of Criminal Law, Criminology, and Police Science* 48 (1957): 12–26; Frank Scarpitti, Ellen Murray, Simon Dinitz, and Walter Reckless, "The Good Boy in a High Delinquency Area: Four Years Later," *American Sociological Review* 23 (1960): 555–558; Walter Reckless and Simon Dinitz, "Pioneering with Self-Concept as a Vulnerability Factor in Delinquency," *Journal of Criminal Law, Criminology, and Police Science* 58 (1967): 515–523.

59. Travis Hirschi, *Causes of Delinquency* (Berkeley: University of California Press, 1969).

60. Ibid., p. 231.

61. Ibid., pp. 66–74.

62. Michael Wiatroski, David Griswold, and Mary K. Roberts, "Social Control Theory and Delinquency," *American Sociological Review* 46 (1981): 525–541.

63. Bobbi Jo Anderson, Malcolm Holmes, and Erik Ostresh, "Male and Female Delinquents' Attachments and Effects of Attachments on Severity of Self-Reported Delinquency," *Criminal Justice and Behavior* 26 (1999): 435–452.

64. Robert Laird, Gregory Pettit, John Bates, and Kenneth. Dodge, "Parents' Monitoring-Relevant Knowledge and Adolescents' Delinquent Behavior: Evidence of Correlated Developmental Changes and Reciprocal Influences," *Child Development* 74 (2003): 752–768.

65. Mallie Paschall, Christopher Ringwalt, and Robert Flewelling, "Effects of Parenting, Father Absence, and Affiliation with Delinquent Peers on Delinquent Behavior among African-American Male Adolescents," *Adolescence* 38 (2003): 15–34.

66. Patricia Jenkins, "School Delinquency and the School Social Bond," *Journal of Research in Crime and Delinquency* 34 (1997): 337–367.

67. Thomas Vander Ven, Francis Cullen, Mark Carrozza, and John Paul Wright, "Home Alone: The Impact of Maternal Employment on Delinquency," *Social Problems* 48 (2001): 236–257; Patricia Jenkins, "School Delinquency and the School Social Bond," *Journal of Research in Crime and Delinquency* 34 (1997): 337–367.

68. Alexander Vazsonyi and Lloyd Pickering, "The Importance of Family and School Domains in Adolescent Deviance: African American and Caucasian Youth," *Journal of Youth and Adolescence* 32 (2003): 115–128.

69. Helen Garnier and Judith Stein, "An 18-Year Model of Family and Peer Effects on Adolescent Drug Use and Delinquency," *Journal of Youth and Adolescence* 31 (2002): 45–56.

70. Peggy Giordano, Stephen Cernkovich, and M. D. Pugh, "Friendships and Delinquency," *American Journal of Sociology* 91 (1986): 1170–1202.

71. Denise Kandel and Mark Davies, "Friendship Networks, Intimacy, and Illicit Drug Use in Young Adulthood: A Comparison of Two Competing Theories," *Criminology* 29 (1991): 441–467.

72. Stephen Cernkovich, Peggy Giordano, and Jennifer Rudolph, "Race, Crime and the American Dream," *Journal of Research in Crime and Delinquency* 37 (2000): 131–170.

73. Velmer Burton, Francis Cullen, T. David Evans, R. Gregory Dunaway, Sesha Kethineni, and Gary Payne, "The Impact of Parental Controls on Delinquency," *Journal of Criminal Justice* 23 (1995): 111–126.

74. Michael Hindelang, "Causes of Delinquency: A Partial Replication and Extension," *Social Problems* 21 (1973): 471–487.

75. Gary Jensen and David Brownfield, "Parents and Drugs," *Criminology* 21 (1983): 543–554. See also M. Wiatrowski, D. Griswold, and M. Roberts, "Social Control Theory and Delinquency," *American Sociological Review* 46 (1981): 525–541.

76. Leslie Samuelson, Timothy Hartnagel, and Harvey Krahn, "Crime and Social Control among High School Dropouts," *Journal of Crime and Justice* 18 (1990): 129–161.

77. Alan E. Liska and M. D. Reed, "Ties to Conventional Institutions and Delinquency: Estimating Reciprocal Effects," *American Sociological Review* 50 (1985): 547–560.

78. Wiatrowski, Griswold, and Roberts, "Social Control Theory and Delinquency."

79. Linda Jackson, John Hunter, and Carole Hodge, "Physical Attractiveness and Intellectual Competence: A Meta-Analytic Review," *Social Psychology Quarterly* 58 (1995): 108–122.

80. Howard Becker, *Outsiders: Studies in the Sociology of Deviance* (New York: Macmillan, 1963), p. 9.

81. Laurie Goodstein, "The Architect of the 'Gay Conversion' Campaign," *New York Times,* August 13, 1998, p. A10.

82. Harold Garfinkle, "Conditions of Successful Degradation Ceremonies," *American Journal of Sociology* 61 (1956): 420–424.

83. Stacy DeCoster and Karen Heimer, "The Relationship between Law Violation and Depression: An Interactionist Analysis," *Criminology* 39 (2001): 799–837.

84. Karen Heimer and Ross Matsueda, "Role-Taking, Role-Commitment and Delinquency: A Theory of Differential Social Control," *American Sociological Review* 59 (1994): 365–390.

85. See, for example, Howard Kaplan and Hiroshi Fukurai, "Negative Social Sanctions, Self-Rejection, and Drug Use," *Youth and Society* 23 (1992): 275–298; Howard Kaplan and Robert Johnson, "Negative Social Sanctions and Juvenile Delinquency: Effects of Labeling in a Model of Deviant Behavior," *Social Science Quarterly* 72 (1991): 98–122; Howard Kaplan, Robert Johnson, and Carol Bailey, "Deviant Peers and Deviant Behavior: Further Elaboration of a Model," *Social Psychology Quarterly* 30 (1987): 277–284.

86. John Lofland, *Deviance and Identity* (Englewood Cliffs, N.J.: Prentice-Hall, 1969).

87. Frank Tannenbaum, *Crime and the Community* (New York: Columbia University Press, 1938), pp. 19–20.

88. Edwin Lemert, *Social Pathology* (New York: McGraw-Hill, 1951).

89. Ibid., p. 75.

90. Christy Visher, "Gender, Police Arrest Decision, and Notions of Chivalry," *Criminology* 21 (1983): 5–28.

91. Marjorie Zatz, "Race, Ethnicity and Determinate Sentencing," *Criminology* 22 (1984): 147–171.

92. Christina DeJong and Kenneth Jackson, "Putting Race into Context: Race, Juvenile Justice Processing, and Urbanization," *Justice Quarterly* 15 (1998): 487–504.

93. Joan Petersilia, "Racial Disparities in the Criminal Justice System: A Summary," *Crime and Delinquency* 31 (1985): 15–34.

94. Carl Pope and William Feyerherm, "Minority Status and Juvenile Justice Processing," *Criminal Justice Abstracts* 22 (1990): 327–336. See also Carl Pope, "Race and Crime Revisited," *Crime and Delinquency* 25 (1979): 347–357; National Minority Council on Criminal Justice, *The Inequality of Justice* (Washington, D.C.: National Minority Advisory Council on Criminal Justice, 1981), p. 200.

95. Howard Kaplan and Robert Johnson, "Negative Social Sanctions and Juvenile Delinquency: Effects of Labeling in a Model of Deviant Behavior," *Social Science Quarterly* 72 (1991): 98–122.

96. Ruth Triplett, "The Conflict Perspective, Symbolic Interactionism, and the Status Characteristics Hypothesis," *Justice Quarterly* 10 (1993): 540–558.

97. Lening Zhang, "Official Offense Status and Self-Esteem among Chinese Youths," *Journal of Criminal Justice* 31(2003): 99–105.

98. Ross Matsueda, "Reflected Appraisals: Parental Labeling, and Delinquency: Specifying a Symbolic Interactionist Theory," *American Journal of Sociology* 97 (1992): 1577–1611.

99. Xiaoru Liu, "The Conditional Effect of Peer Groups on the Relationship between Parental Labeling and Youth Delinquency," *Sociological Perspectives* 43 (2000): 499–515.

100. Suzanne Ageton and Delbert Elliott, *The Effect of Legal Processing on Self-Concept* (Boulder, Colo.: Institute of Behavioral Science, 1973).

101. Mike Adams, Craig Robertson, Phyllis Gray-Ray, and Melvin Ray, "Labeling and Delinquency," *Adolescence* 38 (2003): 171–186.

102. Christine Bowditch, "Getting Rid of Troublemakers: High School Disciplinary Procedures and the Production of Dropouts," *Social Problems* 40 (1993): 493–507.

103. Melvin Ray and William Downs, "An Empirical Test of Labeling Theory Using Longitudinal Data," *Journal of Research in Crime and Delinquency* 23 (1986): 169–194.

104. Sherman and Smith, with Schmidt and Rogan, "Crime, Punishment, and Stake in Conformity."

105. Charles Tittle, "Two Empirical Regularities (Maybe) in Search of an Explanation: Commentary on the Age/Crime Debate," *Criminology* 26 (1988): 75–85.

106. Robert Sampson and John Laub, "A Life-Course Theory of Cumulative Disadvantage and the Stability of Delinquency," in *Developmental Theories of Crime and Delinquency,* ed. Terence Thornberry (New Brunswick, N.J.: Transaction Press, 1997): 133–161; Douglas Smith and Robert Brame, "On the Initiation and Continuation of Delinquency," *Criminology* 4 (1994): 607–630.

107. Raymond Paternoster and Leeann Iovanni, "The Labeling Perspective and Delinquency: An Elaboration of the Theory and an Assessment of the Evidence," *Justice Quarterly* 6 (1989): 358–394.

Chapter 8

1. Ibid., p. 4.

2. Michael Lynch, "Rediscovering Criminology: Lessons from the Marxist Tradition," in *Marxist Sociology: Surveys of Contemporary Theory and Research,* eds. Donald McQuarie and Patrick McGuire (New York: General Hall Press, 1994).

3. James Short and F. Ivan Nye, "Extent of Undetected Delinquency: Tentative Conclusions," *Journal of Criminal Law, Criminology, and Police Science* 49 (1958): 296–302.

4. See, generally, Robert Meier, "The New Criminology: Continuity in Criminological Theory," *Journal of Criminal Law and Criminology* 67 (1977): 461–469.

5. David Greenberg, ed., *Crime and Capitalism* (Palo Alto, Calif.: Mayfield, 1981), p. 3.

6. William Chambliss and Robert Seidman, *Law, Order, and Power* (Reading, Mass.: Addison-Wesley, 1971), p. 503.

7. Richard Quinney, *The Social Reality of Crime* (Boston: Little, Brown, 1970).

8. John Braithwaite, "Retributivism, Punishment, and Privilege," in *Punishment and Privilege,* eds. W. Byron Groves and Graeme Newman (Albany, N.Y.: Harrow & Heston, 1986), pp. 55–66.

9. David Jacobs and David Britt, "Inequality and Police Use of Deadly Force: An Empirical Assessment of a Conflict Hypothesis," *Social Problems* 26 (1979): 403–412.

10. Ronald Weitzer and Steven Tuch, "Perceptions of Racial Profiling: Race, Class and Personal Experience," *Criminology* 40 (2002): 435–456.

11. Albert Meehan and Michael Ponder, "Race and Place: The Ecology of Racial Profiling African American Motorists," *Justice Quarterly* 29 (2002): 399–431.

12. Malcolm Homes, "Minority Threat and Police Brutality: Determinants of Civil Rights Criminal Complaints in U.S. Municipalities," *Criminology* 38 (2000): 343–368.

13. Darrell Steffensmeier and Stephen Demuth, "Ethnicity and Judges' Sentencing Decisions: Hispanic-Black-White Comparisons," *Criminology* 39 (2001): 145–178; Alan Lizotte, "Extra-Legal Factors in Chicago's Criminal Courts: Testing the Conflict Model of Criminal Justice," *Social Problems* 25 (1978): 564–580.

14. Terance Miethe and Charles Moore, "Racial Differences in Criminal Processing: The Consequences of Model Selection on Conclusions about Differential Treatment," *Sociological Quarterly* 27 (1987): 217–237.

15. Tracy Nobiling, Cassia Spohn, and Miriam DeLone, "A Tale of Two Counties: Unemployment and Sentence Severity," *Justice Quarterly* 15 (1998): 459–485.

16. Charles Crawford, Ted Chiricos, and Gary Kleck, "Race, Racial Threat, and Sentencing of Habitual Offenders," *Criminology* 36 (1998): 481–511.

17. Thomas Arvanites, "Increasing Imprisonment: A Function of Crime or Socioeconomic Factors?" *American Journal of Criminal Justice* 17 (1992): 19–38.

18. David Greenberg and Valerie West, "State Prison Populations and Their Growth, 1971–1991," *Criminology* 39 (2001): 615–654.

19. Michael Lynch and W. Byron Groves, *A Primer in Radical Criminology,* 2nd ed. (Albany, N.Y.: Harrow & Heston, 1989), pp. 32–33.

20. Ian Taylor, Paul Walton, and Jock Young, *The New Criminology: For a Social Theory of Deviance* (London: Routledge & Kegan Paul, 1973).

21. See, for example, Larry Tifft and Dennis Sullivan, *The Struggle to Be Human: Crime, Criminology, and Anarchism* (Over-the-Water-Sanday, Scotland: Cienfuegos Press, 1979); Dennis Sullivan, *The Mask of Love* (Port Washington, N.Y.: Kennikat Press, 1980).

22. Tony Platt and Cecilia O'Leary, "Patriot Acts," *Social Justice* 30 (2003): 5–21.

23. Garrett Brown, "The Global Threats to Workers' Health and Safety on the Job," *Social Justice* 29 (2002): 12–25.

24. Robert Bohm, "Radical Criminology: Back to the Basics," paper presented at the annual meeting of the American Society of Criminology, Phoenix, Arizona, November 1993, p. 2.

25. Ibid., p. 4.

26. Lynch and Groves, *A Primer in Radical Criminology,* p. 7.

27. This section borrows heavily from Richard Sparks, "A Critique of Marxist Criminology," in *Crime and Justice,* vol. 2, eds. Norval Morris and Michael Tonry (Chicago: University of Chicago Press, 1980), pp. 159–208.

28. Barbara Sims, "Crime, Punishment, and the American Dream: Toward a Marxist Integration," *Journal of Research in Crime and Delinquency* 34 (1997): 5–24.

29. Jeffery Reiman, *The Rich Get Richer and the Poor Get Prison* (New York: Wiley, 1984), pp. 43–44.

30. Rob White, "Environmental Harm and the Political Economy of Consumption," *Social Justice* 29 (2002): 82–102.

31. Sims, "Crime, Punishment, and the American Dream."

32. Gresham Sykes, "The Rise of Critical Criminology," *Journal of Criminal Law and Criminology* 65 (1974): 211–229.

33. David Jacobs, "Corporate Economic Power and the State: A Longitudinal Assessment of Two Explanations," *American Journal of Sociology* 93 (1988): 852–881.

34. Deanna Alexander, "Victims of the L.A. Riots: A Theoretical Consideration," paper presented at the annual meeting of the American Society of Criminology, Phoenix, Arizona, November 1993.

35. Richard Quinney, "Crime Control in Capitalist Society," in *Critical Criminology,* eds. Ian Taylor, Paul Walton, and Jock Young (London: Routledge & Kegan Paul, 1975), p. 199.

36. Ibid.

37. John Hagan, *Structural Criminology* (New Brunswick, N.J.: Rutgers University Press, 1989), pp. 110–119.

38. Michael Lynch, "Assessing the State of Radical Criminology: Toward the Year 2000," paper presented at the annual meeting of the American Society of Criminology, Phoenix, Arizona, November 1993.

39. Steven Box, *Recession, Crime, and Unemployment* (London: MacMillan, 1987).

40. David Barlow, Melissa Hickman-Barlow, and W. Wesley Johnson, "The Political Economy of Criminal Justice Policy: A Time-Series Analysis of Economic Conditions, Crime, and Federal Criminal Justice Legislation, 1948–1987," *Justice Quarterly* 13 (1996): 223–241.

41. Mahesh Nalla, Michael Lynch, and Michael Leiber, "Determinants of Police Growth in Phoenix, 1950–1988," *Justice Quarterly* 14 (1997): 144–163.

42. David Friedrichs and Jessica Friedrichs, "The World Bank and Crimes of Globalization: A Case Study," *Social Justice* 29 (2002): 13–36.

43. Roy Bhaskar, "Empiricism," in *A Dictionary of Marxist Thought,* ed. T. Bottomore (Cambridge, Mass.: Harvard University Press, 1983), pp. 149–150.

44. Byron Groves, "Marxism and Positivism," *Crime and Social Justice* 23 (1985): 129–150; Michael Lynch, "Quantitative Analysis and Marxist Criminology: Some Old Answers to a Dilemma in Marxist Criminology," *Crime and Social Justice* 29 (1987): 110–117.

45. Alan Lizotte, James Mercy, and Eric Monkkonen, "Crime and Police Strength in an Urban Setting: Chicago, 1947–1970," in *Quantitative Criminology,* ed. John Hagan (Beverly Hills, Calif.: Sage, 1982), pp. 129–148.

46. William Chambliss, "The State, the Law, and the Definition of Behavior as Criminal or Delinquent," in *Handbook of Criminology,* ed. D. Glazer (Chicago: Rand McNally, 1974), pp. 7–44.

47. Timothy Carter and Donald Clelland, "A Neo-Marxian Critique, Formulation, and Test of Juvenile Dispositions as a Function of Social Class," *Social Problems* 27 (1979): 96–108.

48. David Greenberg, "Socio-Economic Status and Criminal Sentences: Is There an Association?" *American Sociological Review* 42 (1977): 174–175; David Greenberg and Drew Humphries, "The Co-optation of Fixed Sentencing Reform," *Crime and Delinquency* 26 (1980): 206–225.

49. Steven Box, *Power, Crime and Mystification* (London: Tavistock, 1984); Gregg Barak, *In Defense of Whom? A Critique of Criminal Justice Reform* (Cincinnati: Anderson, 1980). For an opposing view, see Franklin Williams, "Conflict Theory and Differential Processing: An Analysis of the Research Literature," in *Radical Criminology: The Coming Crisis,* ed. J. Inciardi (Beverly Hills, Calif.: Sage, 1980), pp. 213–231.

50. Robert Weiss, "Repatriating Low-Wage Work: The Political Economy of Prison Labor Reprivatization in the Postindustrial United States," *Criminology* 39 (2001): 253–292.

51. Dragan Milovanovic, "Postmodern Criminology: Mapping the Terrain," *Justice Quarterly* 13 (1996): 567–610.

52. Michael Rustigan, "A Reinterpretation of Criminal Law Reform in Nineteenth-Century England," in *Crime and Capitalism,* ed. D. Greenberg (Palo Alto, Calif.: Mayfield, 1981), pp. 255–278.

53. Rosalind Petchesky, "At Hard Labor: Penal Confinement and Production in Nineteenth-Century America," in *Crime and Capitalism,* ed. D. Greenberg (Palo Alto, Calif.: Mayfield, 1981), pp. 341–357; Paul Takagi, "The Walnut Street Jail: A Penal Reform to Centralize the Powers of the State," *Federal Probation* 49 (1975): 18–26.

54. Jack Gibbs, "An Incorrigible Positivist," *Criminologist* 12 (1987): 2–3.

55. Jackson Toby, "The New Criminology Is the Old Sentimentality," *Criminology* 16 (1979): 513–526.

56. Richard Sparks, "A Critique of Marxist Criminology," in *Crime and Justice,* vol. 2, eds. Norval Morris and Michael Tonry (Chicago: University of Chicago Press, 1980), pp. 159–208.

57. Carl Klockars, "The Contemporary Crises of Marxist Criminology," in *Radical Criminology: The Coming Crisis,* ed. J. Inciardi (Beverly Hills, Calif.: Sage, 1980), pp. 92–123.

58. Matthew Petrocelli, Alex Piquero, and Michael Smith, "Conflict Theory and Racial Profiling: An Empirical Analysis of Police Traffic Stop Data," *Journal of Criminal Justice* 31 (2003): 1–10.

59. Ibid.

60. Anthony Platt, "Criminology in the 1980s: Progressive Alternatives to 'Law and Order,'" *Crime and Social Justice* 21–22 (1985): 191–199.

61. See, generally, Roger Matthews and Jock Young, eds., *Confronting Crime* (London: Sage, 1986); for a thorough review of left realism, see Martin Schwartz and Walter DeKeseredy, "Left Realist Criminology: Strengths, Weaknesses, and the Feminist Critique," *Crime, Law, and Social Change* 15 (1991): 51–72.

62. John Lea and Jock Young, *What Is to Be Done About Law and Order?* (Harmondsworth, England: Penguin, 1984).

63. Ibid., p. 88.

64. Ian Taylor, *Crime in Context: A Critical Criminology of Market Societies* (Boulder, Colo.: Westview Press, 1999).

65. Ibid., pp. 30–31.

66. Richard Kinsey, John Lea, and Jock Young, *Losing the Fight Against Crime* (London: Blackwell, 1986).

67. Martin Schwartz and Walter DeKeseredy, *Contemporary Criminology* (Belmont, Calif.: Wadsworth, 1993), p. 249.

68. Schwartz and DeKeseredy, "Left Realist Criminology."

69. For a general review of this issue, see Kathleen Daly and Meda Chesney-Lind, "Feminism and Criminology," *Justice Quarterly* 5 (1988): 497–538; Douglas Smith and Raymond Paternoster, "The Gender Gap in Theories of Deviance: Issues and Evidence," *Journal of Research in Crime and Delinquency* 24 (1987): 140–172; and Pat Carlen, "Women, Crime, Feminism, and Realism," *Social Justice* 17 (1990): 106–123.

70. Herman Schwendinger and Julia Schwendinger, *Rape and Inequality* (Newbury Park, Calif.: Sage, 1983).

71. Daly and Chesney-Lind, "Feminism and Criminology."

72. Janet Saltzman Chafetz, "Feminist Theory and Sociology: Underutilized Contributions for Mainstream Theory," *Annual Review of Sociology* 23 (1997): 97–121.

73. Ibid.

74. James Messerschmidt, *Capitalism, Patriarchy, and Crime* (Totowa, N.J.: Rowman & Littlefield, 1986); for a critique of this work, see Herman

Schwendinger and Julia Schwendinger, "The World According to James Messerschmidt," *Social Justice* 15 (1988): 123–145.

75. Kathleen Daly, "Gender and Varieties of White-Collar Crime," *Criminology* 27 (1989): 769–793.

76. Jane Roberts Chapman, "Violence against Women as a Violation of Human Rights," *Social Justice* 17 (1990): 54–71.

77. James Messerschmidt, *Masculinities and Crime: Critique and Reconceptualization of Theory* (Lanham, Md.: Rowman & Littlefield, 1993).

78. Angela P. Harris, "Gender, Violence, Race, and Criminal Justice," *Stanford Law Review* 52 (2000): 777–810.

79. Suzie Dod Thomas and Nancy Stein, "Criminality, Imprisonment, and Women's Rights in the 1990s," *Social Justice* 17 (1990): 1–5.

80. Walter DeKeseredy and Martin Schwartz, "Male Peer Support and Woman Abuse: An Expansion of DeKeseredy's Model," *Sociological Spectrum* 13 (1993): 393–413.

81. Daly and Chesney-Lind, "Feminism and Criminology." See also, Drew Humphries and Susan Caringella-MacDonald, "Murdered Mothers, Missing Wives: Reconsidering Female Victimization," *Social Justice* 17 (1990): 71–78.

82. Hagan, *Structural Criminology.*

83. John Hagan, A. R. Gillis, and John Simpson, "The Class Structure and Delinquency: Toward a Power–Control Theory of Common Delinquent Behavior," *American Journal of Sociology* 90 (1985): 1151–1178; John Hagan, John Simpson, and A. R. Gillis, "Class in the Household: A Power–Control Theory of Gender and Delinquency," *American Journal of Sociology* 92 (1987): 788–816.

84. John Hagan, Bill McCarthy, and Holly Foster, "A Gendered Theory of Delinquency and Despair in the Life Course," *Acta Sociologica* 45 (2002): 37–47.

85. Brenda Sims Blackwell, Christine Sellers, Sheila Schlaupitz, "A Power–Control Theory of Vulnerability to Crime and Adolescent Role Exits—Revisited," *Canadian Review of Sociology and Anthropology* 39 (2002): 199–219.

86. Brenda Sims Blackwell, "Perceived Sanction Threats, Gender, and Crime: A Test and Elaboration of Power–Control Theory," *Criminology* 38 (2000): 439–488.

87. Christopher Uggen, "Class, Gender, and Arrest: An Intergenerational Analysis of Workplace Power and Control," *Criminology* 38 (2001): 835–862.

88. Gary Jensen, "Power–Control versus Social-Control Theory: Identifying Crucial Differences for Future Research," paper presented at the annual meeting of the American Society of Criminology, Baltimore, November 1990.

89. Gary Jensen and Kevin Thompson, "What's Class Got to Do with It? A Further Examination of Power–Control Theory," *American Journal of Sociology* 95 (1990): 1009–1023. For some critical research, see Simon Singer and Murray Levine, "Power–Control Theory, Gender and Delinquency: A Partial Replication with Additional Evidence on the Effects of Peers," *Criminology* 26 (1988): 627–648.

90. Kevin Thompson, "Gender and Adolescent Drinking Problems: The Effects of Occupational Structure," *Social Problems* 36 (1989): 30–38.

91. See, generally, Uggen, "Class, Gender, and Arrest."

92. See, generally, Lynch, "Rediscovering Criminology," pp. 27–28.

93. See, generally, Stuart Henry and Dragan Milovanovic, *Constitutive Criminology: Beyond Postmodernism* (London: Sage, 1996).

94. Dragan Milovanovic, *A Primer in the Sociology of Law* (Albany, N.Y.: Harrow & Heston, 1988), pp. 127–128.

95. See, generally, Henry and Milovanovic, *Constitutive Criminology.*

96. Bruce Arrigo and Thomas Bernard, "Postmodern Criminology in Relation to Radical and Conflict Criminology," *Critical Criminology* 8 (1997): 39–60.

97. Liz Walz, "One Blood," *Contemporary Justice Review* 6 (2003): 25–36.

98. See, for example, Tifft and Sullivan, *The Struggle to Be Human;* Sullivan, *The Mask of Love.*

99. Larry Tifft, "Foreword," in Sullivan, *The Mask of Love,* p. 6.

100. Sullivan, *The Mask of Love,* p. 141.

101. Dennis Sullivan and Larry Tifft, *Restorative Justice* (Monsey, N.Y.: Willow Tree Press, 2001).

102. Richard Quinney, "The Way of Peace: On Crime, Suffering, and Service," in *Criminology as Peacemaking,* eds. Harold Pepinsky and Richard Quinney (Bloomington: Indiana University Press, 1991), pp. 8–9.

103. For a review of Quinney's ideas, see Kevin B. Anderson, " Richard Quinney's Journey: The Marxist Dimension," *Crime and Delinquency* 48 (2002): 232–242.

104. Robert DeFina and Thomas Arvanites, "The Weak Effect of Imprisonment on Crime: 1971–1998," *Social Science Quarterly* 83 (2002): 635–654.

105. Kathleen Daly and Russ Immarigeon, "The Past, Present and Future of Restorative Justice: Some Critical Reflections," *Contemporary Justice Review* 1 (1998): 21–45.

106. Howard Zehr, *The Little Book of Restorative Justice* (Intercourse, Pa.: Good Books, 2002): 1–10.

107. Mark Lewis Taylor, *The Executed God: The Way of the Cross in Lockdown America* (Minneapolis, Minn.: Fortress Press, 2001).

108. Gene Stephens, "The Future of Policing: From a War Model to a Peace Model," in *The Past, Present and Future of American Criminal Justice,* eds. Brendan Maguire and Polly Radosh (Dix Hills, N.Y.: General Hall, 1996), pp. 77–93.

109. Rick Shifley, "The Organization of Work as a Factor in Social Well-Being," *Contemporary Justice Review* 6 (2003): 105–126.

110. Kay Pranis, "Peacemaking Circles: Restorative Justice in Practice Allows Victims and Offenders to Begin Repairing the Harm," *Corrections Today* 59 (1997): 74–78.

111. Carol LaPrairie, "The 'New' Justice: Some Implications for Aboriginal Communities," *Canadian Journal of Criminology* 40 (1998): 61–79.

112. Diane Schaefer, "A Disembodied Community Collaborates in a Homicide: Can Empathy Transform a Failing Justice System?" *Contemporary Justice Review* 6 (2003): 133–143.

113. David R. Karp and Beau Breslin, "Restorative Justice in School Communities," *Youth & Society* 33 (2001): 249–272.

114. Paul Jesilow and Deborah Parsons, "Community Policing as Peacemaking," *Policing & Society* 10 (2000): 163–183.

115. Gordon Bazemore and Curt Taylor Griffiths, "Conferences, Circles, Boards, and Mediations: The 'New Wave' of Community Justice Decision Making," *Federal Probation* 61 (1997): 25–37.

116. John Braithwaite, "Setting Standards for Restorative Justice," *British Journal of Criminology* 42 (2002): 563–577.

117. David Altschuler, "Community Justice Initiatives: Issues and Challenges in the U.S. Context," *Federal Probation* 65 (2001): 28–33.

118. Lois Presser and Patricia Van Voorhis, "Values and Evaluation: Assessing Processes and Outcomes of Restorative Justice Programs," *Crime & Delinquency* 48 (2002): 162–189.

119. Sharon Levrant, Francis Cullen, Betsy Fulton, and John Wozniak, "Reconsidering Restorative Justice: The Corruption of Benevolence Revisited?" *Crime & Delinquency* 45 (1999): 3–28.

Chapter 9

1. Gerald Patterson and Karen Yoerger, "Developmental Models for Delinquent Behavior," in *Mental Disorder and Crime,* ed. Sheilagh Hodgins (Newbury Park, Calif.: Sage, 1993), pp. 150–159.

2. James Q. Wilson and Richard Herrnstein, *Crime and Human Nature* (New York: Simon & Schuster, 1985).

3. David Rowe, D. Wayne Osgood, and W. Alan Nicewander, "A Latent Trait Approach to Unifying Criminal Careers," *Criminology* 28 (1990): 237–270.

4. Lee Ellis, "Neurohormonal Bases of Varying Tendencies to Learn Delinquent and Criminal Behavior," in *Behavioral Approaches to Crime and Delinquency,* eds. E. Morris and C. Braukmann (New York: Plenum, 1988), pp. 499–518.

5. David Rowe, Alexander Vazsonyi, and Daniel Flannery, "Sex Differences in Crime: Do Means and Within-Sex Variation Have Similar Causes?" *Journal of Research in Crime and Delinquency* 32 (1995): 84–100.

6. Michael Gottfredson and Travis Hirschi, *A General Theory of Crime* (Stanford, Calif.: Stanford University Press, 1990).

7. Ibid., p. 27.

8. Ibid., p. 90.

9. Ibid., p. 89.

10. Alex Piquero and Stephen Tibbetts, "Specifying the Direct and Indirect Effects of Low Self-Control and Situational Factors in Offenders' Decision Making: Toward a More Complete Model of Rational Offending," *Justice Quarterly* 13 (1996): 481–508.

11. David Forde and Leslie Kennedy, "Risky Lifestyles, Routine Activities, and the General Theory of Crime," *Justice Quarterly* 14 (1997): 265–294.

12. Marianne Junger and Richard Tremblay, "Self-Control, Accidents, and Crime," *Criminal Justice and Behavior* 26 (1999): 485–501.

13. Gottfredson and Hirschi, *A General Theory of Crime*, p. 112.

14. Ibid.

15. Dennis Giever, "An Empirical Assessment of the Core Elements of Gottfredson and Hirschi's General Theory of Crime," paper presented at the annual meeting of the American Society of Criminology, Boston, November 1995.

16. David Farrington, Darrick Jolliffe, Rolf Loeber, Madga Southamer-Loeber, and Larry Kalb, "The Concentration of Offenders in Families, and Family Criminality in the Prediction of Boy's Delinquency," *Journal of Adolescence* 24 (2001): 579–596.

17. Robert Agnew, "The Contribution of Social-Psychological Strain Theory to the Explanation of Crime and Delinquency," *Advances in Criminological Theory* 6 (1994): 211–213.

18. John Gibbs, Dennis Giever, and George Higgins, "A Test of Gottfredson and Hirschi's General Theory Using Structural Equation Modeling," *Criminal Justice and Behavior* 30 (2003): 441–458; David Brownfield and Ann Marie Sorenson, "Self-Control and Juvenile Delinquency: Theoretical Issues and an Empirical Assessment of Selected Elements of a General Theory of Crime," *Deviant Behavior* 14 (1993): 243–264; Harold Grasmick, Charles Tittle, Robert Bursik, and Bruce Arneklev, "Testing the Core Empirical Implications of Gottfredson and Hirschi's General Theory of Crime," *Journal of Research in Crime and Delinquency* 30 (1993): 5–29; John Cochran, Peter Wood, and Bruce Arneklev, "Is the Religiosity–Delinquency Relationship Spurious? A Test of Arousal and Social Control Theories," *Journal of Research in Crime and Delinquency* 31 (1994): 92–123; Marc LeBlanc, Marc Ouimet, and Richard Tremblay, "An Integrative Control Theory of Delinquent Behavior: A Validation 1976–1985," *Psychiatry* 51 (1988): 164–176.

19. Ronald Akers, "Self-Control as a General Theory of Crime," *Journal of Quantitative Criminology* 7 (1991): 201–211.

20. Estrella Romero, J. Antonio Gomez-Fraguela, Angeles Luengo, Jorge Sobral, "The Self-Control Construct in the General Theory of Crime: An Investigation in Terms of Personality Psychology," *Psychology, Crime and Law* 9 (2003): 61–86.

21. Richard Wiebe, "Reconciling Psychopathy and Low Self-Control," *Justice Quarterly* 20 (2003): 297–336.

22. Alan Feingold, "Gender Differences in Personality: A Meta Analysis," *Psychological Bulletin* 116 (1994): 429–456.

23. Gottfredson and Hirschi, *A General Theory of Crime*, p. 153.

24. Scott Menard, Delbert Elliott, and Sharon Wofford, "Social Control Theories in Developmental Perspective," *Studies on Crime and Crime Prevention* 2 (1993): 69–87.

25. Charles Tittle, David Ward, and Harold Grasmick, "Gender, Age, and Crime/Deviance: A Challenge to Self-Control Theory," *Journal of Research in Crime and Delinquency* 40 (2003): 426–453; Charles Tittle and Harold Grasmick, "Criminal Behavior and Age: A Test of Three Provocative Hypotheses," *Journal of Criminal Law and Criminology* 88 (1997): 309–342.

26. Tittle, Ward, and Grasmick, "Gender, Age, and Crime/Deviance: A Challenge to Self-Control Theory"; Travis Pratt and Frank Cullen, "The Empirical Status of Gottfredson and Hirschi's General Theory of Crime: A Meta-Analysis," *Criminology* 38 (2000): 938–964; Douglas Longshore, "Self-Control and Criminal Opportunity: A Prospective Test of the General Theory of Crime," *Social Problems* 45 (1998): 102–114.

27. Otwin Marenin and Michael Resig, "A General Theory of Crime and Patterns of Crime in Nigeria: An Exploration of Methodological Assumptions," *Journal of Criminal Justice* 23 (1995): 501–518.

28. Bruce Arneklev, Harold Grasmick, Charles Tittle, and Robert Bursik, "Low Self-Control and Imprudent Behavior," *Journal of Quantitative Criminology* 9 (1993): 225–246.

29. Alexander Vazsonyi, Lloyd Pickering, Marianne Junger, and Dick Hessing, "An Empirical Test of a General Theory of Crime: A Four-Nation Comparative Study of Self-Control and the Prediction of Deviance," *Journal of Research in Crime and Delinquency* 38 (2001): 91–131.

30. Kevin Thompson, "Sexual Harassment and Low Self-Control: An Application of Gottfredson and Hirschi's General Theory of Crime," paper presented at the annual meeting of the American Society of Criminology, Phoenix, Arizona, November 1993.

31. Marvin Krohn, Alan Lizotte, and Cynthia Perez, "The Interrelationship between Substance Use and Precocious Transitions to Adult Sexuality," *Journal of Health and Social Behavior* 38 (1997): 87–103, at p. 88.

32. G. R. Patterson, Barbara DeBaryshe, and Elizabeth Ramsey, "A Developmental Perspective on Antisocial Behavior," *American Psychologist* 44 (1989): 329–335.

33. Joan McCord, "Family Relationships, Juvenile Delinquency, and Adult Criminality," *Criminology* 29 (1991): 397–417.

34. Paul Mazerolle, "Delinquent Definitions and Participation Age: Assessing the Invariance Hypothesis," *Studies on Crime and Crime Prevention* 6 (1997): 151–168.

35. See, generally, Sheldon Glueck and Eleanor Glueck, *500 Criminal Careers* (New York: Knopf, 1930); Sheldon Glueck and Eleanor Glueck, *One Thousand Juvenile Delinquents* (Cambridge, Mass.: Harvard University Press, 1934); Sheldon Glueck and Eleanor Glueck, *Predicting Delinquency and Crime* (Cambridge, Mass.: Harvard University Press, 1967), pp. 82–83.

36. Sheldon Glueck and Eleanor Glueck, *Unraveling Juvenile Delinquency* (Cambridge, Mass.: Harvard University Press, 1950).

37. Ibid., p. 48.

38. Rolf Loeber and Marc LeBlanc, "Toward a Developmental Criminology," in *Crime and Justice,* vol. 12, eds. Norval Morris and Michael Tonry (Chicago: University of Chicago Press, 1990), pp. 375–473; Rolf Loeber and Marc LeBlanc, "Developmental Criminology Updated," in *Crime and Justice,* vol. 23, ed. Michael Tonry (Chicago: University of Chicago Press, 1998), pp. 115–198.

39. Alex R. Piquero and He Len Chung, "On the Relationships between Gender, Early Onset, and the Seriousness of Offending," *Journal of Criminal Justice* 29 (2001): 189–206.

40. David Nurco, Timothy Kinlock, and Mitchell Balter, "The Severity of Preaddiction Criminal Behavior among Urban, Male Narcotic Addicts and Two Nonaddicted Control Groups," *Journal of Research in Crime and Delinquency* 30 (1993): 293–316.

41. Rolf Loeber and David Farrington, "Young Children Who Commit Crime: Epidemiology, Developmental Origins, Risk Factors, Early Interventions, and Policy Implications," *Development and Psychopathology* 12 (2000): 737–762.

42. Ick-Joong Chung, Karl G Hill, J. David Hawkins, Lewayne Gilchrist, and Daniel Nagin, "Childhood Predictors of Offense Trajectories," *Journal of Research in Crime and Delinquency* 39 (2002): 60–91.

43. Elaine Eggleston and John Laub, "The Onset of Adult Offending: A Neglected Dimension of the Criminal Career," *Journal of Criminal Justice* 30 (2002): 603–622.

44. Alex R. Piquero, Robert Brame, Paul Mazerolle, and Rudy Haapanen, "Crime in Emerging Adulthood," *Criminology* 40 (2002): 137–169.

45. Amy D'Unger, Kenneth Land, Patricia McCall, and Daniel Nagin, "How Many Latent Classes of Delinquent/Criminal Careers? Results from Mixed Poisson Regression Analyses," *American Journal of Sociology* 103 (1998): 1593–1630.

46. Terrie Moffitt, "Natural Histories of Delinquency," in *Cross-National Longitudinal Research on Human Development and Criminal Behavior*, eds.

Elmar Weitekamp and Hans-Jurgen Kerner (Dordrecht, Netherlands: Kluwer, 1994), pp. 3–65.

47. Michael Newcomb, "Pseudomaturity among Adolescents: Construct Validation, Sex Differences, and Associations in Adulthood," *Journal of Drug Issues* 26 (1996): 477–504.

48. Rolf Loeber and Magda Stouthamer-Loeber, "Development of Juvenile Aggression and Violence," *American Psychologist* 53 (1998): 242–259.

49. Terrie Moffitt, "Adolescence-Limited and Life-Course-Persistent Antisocial Behavior: A Developmental Taxonomy," *Psychological Review* 100 (1993): 674–701.

50. David Fergusson, L. John Horwood, and Daniel Nagin, "Offending Trajectories in a New Zealand Birth Cohort," *Criminology* 38 (2000): 525–551.

51. Alex Piquero and Timothy Brezina, "Testing Moffitt's Account of Adolescent-Limited Delinquency," *Criminology* 39 (2001): 353–370.

52. Ronald Simons, Chyi-In Wu, Rand Conger, and Frederick Lorenz, "Two Routes to Delinquency: Differences between Early and Later Starters in the Impact of Parenting and Deviant Careers," *Criminology* 32 (1994): 247–275.

53. Magda Stouthamer-Loeber and Evelyn Wei, "The Precursors of Young Fatherhood and Its Effect on Delinquency of Teenage Males," *Journal of Adolescent Health* 22 (1998): 56–65; Richard Jessor, John Donovan, and Francis Costa, *Beyond Adolescence: Problem Behavior and Young Adult Development* (New York: Cambridge University Press, 1991).

54. Marvin Krohn, Alan Lizotte, and Cynthia Perez, "The Interrelationship between Substance Use and Precocious Transitions to Adult Sexuality," *Journal of Health and Social Behavior* 38 (1997): 87–103, at p. 88; Richard Jessor, "Risk Behavior in Adolescence: A Psychosocial Framework for Understanding and Action," in *Adolescents at Risk: Medical and Social Perspectives,* eds. D. E. Rogers and E. Ginzburg (Boulder, Colo.: Westview, 1992).

55. Ick-Joong Chung, J. David Hawkins, Lewayne Gilchrist; Karl Hill, and Daniel Nagin, "Identifying and Predicting Offending Trajectories among Poor Children," *Social Service Review* 76 (2002): 663–687.

56. Deborah Capaldi and Gerald Patterson, "Can Violent Offenders Be Distinguished from Frequent Offenders: Prediction from Childhood to Adolescence," *Journal of Research in Crime and Delinquency* 33 (1996): 206–231; D. Wayne Osgood, "The Covariation among Adolescent Problem Behaviors," paper presented at the annual meeting of the American Society of Criminology, Baltimore, November 1990.

57. Terence Thornberry, Carolyn Smith, and Gregory Howard, "Risk Factors for Teenage Fatherhood," *Journal of Marriage and the Family* 59 (1997): 505–522; Todd Miller, Timothy Smith,

Charles Turner, Margarita Guijarro, and Amanda Hallet, "A Meta-Analytic Review of Research on Hostility and Physical Health," *Psychological Bulletin* 119 (1996): 322–348; Marianne Junger, "Accidents and Crime," in *The Generality of Deviance,* eds. T. Hirschi and M. Gottfredson (New Brunswick, N.J.: Transaction Press, 1993).

58. Robert Johnson, S. Susan Su, Dean Gerstein, Hee-Choon Shin, and John Hoffman, "Parental Influences on Deviant Behavior in Early Adolescence: A Logistic Response Analysis of Age- and Gender-Differentiated Effects," *Journal of Quantitative Criminology* 11 (1995): 167–192; Judith Brooks, Martin Whiteman, and Patricia Cohen, "Stage of Drug Use, Aggression, and Theft/Vandalism," in *Drugs, Crime and Other Deviant Adaptations: Longitudinal Studies,* ed. Howard Kaplan (New York: Plenum, 1995), pp. 83–96; Robert Hoge, D. A. Andrews, and Alan Leschied, "Tests of Three Hypotheses Regarding the Predictors of Delinquency," *Journal of Abnormal Child Psychology* 22 (1994): 547–559.

59. David Huizinga, Rolf Loeber, and Terence Thornberry, "Longitudinal Study of Delinquency, Drug Use, Sexual Activity, and Pregnancy among Children and Youth in Three Cities," *Public Health Reports* 108 (1993): 90–96.

60. Margit Wiesner and Deborah Capaldi, "Relations of Childhood and Adolescent Factors to Offending Trajectories of Young Men," *Journal of Research in Crime and Delinquency* 40 (2003): 231–262.

61. Rolf Loeber, Phen Wung, Kate Keenan, Bruce Giroux, Magda Stouthamer-Loeber, Wemoet Van Kammen, and Barbara Maughan, "Developmental Pathways in Disruptive Behavior," *Development and Psychopathology* (1993): 12–48.

62. Mark Lipsey and James Derzon, "Predictors of Violent or Serious Delinquency in Adolescence and Early Adulthood: A Synthesis of Longitudinal Research," in *Serious and Violent Juvenile Offenders: Risk Factors and Successful Interventions,* eds. Rolf Loeber and David Farrington (Thousand Oaks, Calif.: Sage, 1998).

63. G. R. Patterson and Karen Yoerger, "Differentiating Outcomes and Histories for Early and Late Onset Arrests," paper presented at the annual meeting of the American Society of Criminology, Phoenix, Arizona, November 1993.

64. Marshall Jones and Donald Jones, "The Contagious Nature of Antisocial Behavior," *Criminology* 38 (2000): 25–46.

65. See, for example, the Rochester Youth Development Study, Hindelang Criminal Justice Research Center, 135 Western Avenue, Albany, New York 12222.

66. David Farrington, "The Development of Offending and Antisocial Behavior from Childhood to Adulthood," paper presented at the Congress on Rethinking Delinquency, University of Minho, Braga, Portugal, July 1992.

67. Joseph Weis and J. David Hawkins, *Reports of the National Juvenile Assessment Centers: Preventing Delinquency* (Washington, D.C.: U.S. Department of Justice, 1981); Joseph Weis and John Sederstrom, *Reports of the National Juvenile Justice Assessment Centers: The Prevention of Serious Delinquency: What to Do* (Washington, D.C.: U.S. Department of Justice, 1981).

68. Bu Huang, Rick Kosterman, Richard Catalano, J. David Hawkins, and Robert Abbott, "Modeling Mediation in the Etiology of Violent Behavior in Adolescence: A Test of the Social Development Model," *Criminology* 39 (2001): 75–107.

69. Julie O'Donnell, J. David Hawkins, and Robert Abbott, "Predicting Serious Delinquency and Substance Use among Aggressive Boys," *Journal of Consulting and Clinical Psychology* 63 (1995): 529–537.

70. Todd Herrenkohl, Bu Huang, Rick Kosterman, J. David Hawkins, Richard Catalano, and Brian Smith, "A Comparison of Social Development Processes Leading to Violent Behavior in Late Adolescence for Childhood Initiators and Adolescent Initiators of Violence," *Journal of Research in Crime and Delinquency* 38 (2001): 45–63.

71. Terence Thornberry, "Toward an Interactional Theory of Delinquency," *Criminology* 25 (1987): 863–891.

72. Ross Matsueda and Kathleen Anderson, "The Dynamics of Delinquent Peers and Delinquent Behavior," *Criminology* 36 (1998): 269–308.

73. Thornberry, "Toward an Interactional Theory of Delinquency."

74. Ibid., p. 863.

75. Terence Thornberry and Marvin Krohn, " The Development of Delinquency: An Interactional Perspective," in *Handbook of Youth and Justice,* ed. Susan White (New York: Plenum, 2001), pp. 289–305.

76. Kee Jeong Kim, Rand Conger, Glen Elder Jr., and Frederick Lorenz, "Reciprocal Influences between Stressful Life Events and Adolescent Internalizing and Externalizing Problems," *Child Development* 74 (2003): 127–143.

77. Terence Thornberry, Adrienne Freeman-Gallant, Alan Lizotte; Marvin Krohn, and Carolyn Smith, "Linked Lives: The Intergenerational Transmission of Antisocial Behavior," *Journal of Abnormal Child Psychology* 31 (2003): 171–185.

78. Terrence Thornberry, Alan Lizotte, Marvin Krohn, Margaret Farnworth, and Sung Joon Jang, *Delinquent Peers, Beliefs, and Delinquent Behavior: A Longitudinal Test of Interactional Theory,* working paper no. 6, rev., Rochester Youth Development Study (Albany, N.Y.: Hindelang Criminal Justice Research Center, 1992), pp. 628–629.

79. Robert Sampson and John Laub, *Crime in the Making: Pathways and Turning Points Through Life* (Cambridge, Mass.: Harvard University Press, 1993); John Laub and Robert Sampson, "Turning Points in the Life

Course: Why Change Matters to the Study of Crime," paper presented at the annual meeting of the American Society of Criminology, New Orleans, November 1992.

80. Terri Orbuch, James House, Richard Mero, and Pamela Webster, "Marital Quality Over the Life Course," *Social Psychology Quarterly* 59 (1996): 162–171; Lee Lillard and Linda Waite, "'Til Death Do Us Part: Marital Disruption and Mortality," *American Journal of Sociology* 100 (1995): 1131–1156.

81. Mark Warr, "Life-Course Transitions and Desistance from Crime," *Criminology* 36 (1998): 183–216.

82. Pamela Webster, Terri Orbuch, and James House, "Effects of Childhood Family Background on Adult Marital Quality and Perceived Stability," *American Journal of Sociology* 101 (1995): 404–432.

83. Nan Lin, *Social Capital: A Theory of Social Structure and Action* (Cambridge, UK: Cambridge University Press, 2002).

84. John Hagan, Ross MacMillan, and Blair Wheaton, "New Kid in Town: Social Capital and the Life Course Effects of Family Migration on Children," *American Sociological Review* 61 (1996): 368–385.

85. Sampson and Laub, *Crime in the Making*, p. 249.

86. Erich Labouvie, "Maturing Out of Substance Use: Selection and Self-Correction," *Journal of Drug Issues* 26 (1996): 457–474.

87. Mark Warr, "Life-Course Transitions and Desistance from Crime," *Criminology* 36 (1998): 502–535.

88. Doris Layton MacKenzie and Spencer De Li, "The Impact of Formal and Informal Social Controls on the Criminal Activities of Probationers," *Journal of Research in Crime and Delinquency* 39 (2002): 243–278.

89. Pamela Webster, Terri Orbuch, and James House, "Effects of Childhood Family Background on Adult Marital Quality and Perceived Stability," *American Journal of Sociology* 101 (1995): 404–432.

90. Alex Piquero, John MacDonald, and Karen Parker, "Race, Local Life Circumstances, and Criminal Activity over the Life-Course," *Social Science Quarterly* 83 (2002): 654–671.

91. Personal communication with Alex Piquero, September 24, 2002.

92. Ronald Simons, Eric Stewart, Leslie Gordon, Rand Conger, and Glen Elder Jr., "Test of Life-Course Explanations for Stability and Change in Antisocial Behavior from Adolescence to Young Adulthood," *Criminology* 40 (2002): 401–435.

93. Raymond Paternoster and Robert Brame, "Multiple Routes to Delinquency? A Test of Developmental and General Theories of Crime," *Criminology* 35 (1997): 49–84.

94. Robert Hoge, D. A. Andrews, and Alan Leschied, "An Investigation of Risk and Protective Factors in a Sample of Youthful Offenders," *Journal of Child Psychology and Psychiatry* 37 (1996): 419–424.

95. Candace Kruttschnitt, Christopher Uggen, and Kelly Shelton, "Individual Variability in Sex Offending and Its Relationship to Informal and Formal Social Controls," paper presented at the annual meeting of the American Society of Criminology, San Diego, 1997; Mark Collins and Don Weatherburn, "Unemployment and the Dynamics of Offender Populations," *Journal of Quantitative Criminology* 11 (1995): 231–245.

96. Shadd Maruna, *Making Good: How Ex-Convicts Reform and Rebuild Their Lives* (Washington, D.C.: American Psychological Association, 2000).

97. Avshalom Caspi, Terrie Moffitt, Bradley Entner Wright, and Phil Silva, "Early Failure in the Labor Market: Childhood and Adolescent Predictors of Unemployment in the Transition to Adulthood," *American Sociological Review* 63 (1998): 424–451.

98. Robert Sampson and John Laub, "Socioeconomic Achievement in the Life Course of Disadvantaged Men: Military Service as a Turning Point, circa 1940–1965," *American Sociological Review* 61 (1996): 347–367.

99. Daniel Nagin and Raymond Paternoster, "Personal Capital and Social Control: The Deterrence Implications of a Theory of Criminal Offending," *Criminology* 32 (1994): 581–606.

100. David P. Farrington, "Developmental and Life-Course Criminology: Key Theoretical and Empirical Issues," Sutherland Award address at the American Society of Criminology meeting in Chicago, November 2002 (revised March 2003).

101. Bradley Entner Wright, Avashalom Caspi, Terrie Moffitt, and Phil Silva, "Low Self-Control, Social Bonds, and Crime: Social Causation, Social Selection, or Both?" *Criminology* 37 (1999): 479–514.

102. Ibid., p. 504.

103. Stephen Cernkovich and Peggy Giordano, "Stability and Change in Antisocial Behavior: The Transition from Adolescence to Early Adulthood," *Criminology* 39 (2001): 371–410.

Chapter 10

1. Elissa Gootman, "The Hunt for a Sniper: The Victim; 10th Victim Is Recalled as Motivator on Mission," *New York Times,* October 14, 2002, p. A15; Sarah Kershaw, "The Hunt for a Sniper: The Investigation; Endless Frustration But Little Evidence in Search for Sniper," *New York Times,* October 14, 2002, p. A 1.

2. Francis X. Clines, with Christopher Drew, "Prosecutors to Discuss Charges as Rifle Is Tied to Sniper Killings," *New York Times,* October 25, 2002, p. A1.

3. Kathleen Maguire and Ann Pastore, eds., *Sourcebook of Criminal Justice Statistics* [Online], p. 129. Available: http://www.albany.edu/sourcebook/ [Accessed September 22, 2001].

4. Robert Nash Parker and Catherine Colony, "Relationships, Homicides, and Weapons: A Detailed Analysis." Paper presented at the annual meeting of the American Society of Criminology, Montreal, November 1987.

5. Stryker McGuire, "The Dunblane Effect," *Newsweek,* October 28, 1996, p. 46.

6. Dorothy Otnow Lewis, Ernest Moy, Lori Jackson, Robert Aaronson, Nicholas Restifo, Susan Serra, and Alexander Simos, "Biopsychosocial Characteristics of Children Who Later Murder," *American Journal of Psychiatry* 142 (1985): 1161–1167.

7. Dorothy Otnow Lewis, *Guilty by Reason of Insanity* (New York: Fawcett Columbine, 1998).

8. Richard Rogers, Randall Salekin, Kenneth Sewell, and Keith Cruise, "Prototypical Analysis of Antisocial Personality Disorder," *Criminal Justice and Behavior* 27 (2000): 234–255; Amy Holtzworth-Munroe and Gregory Stuart, "Typologies of Male Batterers: Three Subtypes and the Differences among Them," *Psychological Bulletin* 116 (1994): 476–497.

9. Katherine Van Wormer and Chuk Odiah, "The Psychology of Suicide-Murder and the Death Penalty," *Journal of Criminal Justice* 27 (1999): 361–370.

10. Albert Reiss and Jeffrey Roth, *Understanding and Preventing Violence* (Washington, D.C.: National Academy Press, 1993) pp. 112–113.

11. Todd Herrenkhol, Bu Huan, Emiko Tajima, and Stephen Whitney, "Examining the Link between Child Abuse and Youth Violence," *Journal of Interpersonal Violence* 18 (2003): 1189–1208; Pamela Lattimore, Christy Visher, and Richard Linster, "Predicting Rearrest for Violence among Serious Youthful Offenders," *Journal of Research in Crime and Delinquency* 32 (1995): 54–83.

12. Rolf Loeber and Dale Hay, "Key Issues in the Development of Aggression and Violence from Childhood to Early Adulthood," *Annual Review of Psychology* 48 (1997): 371–410.

13. Deborah Capaldi and Gerald Patterson, "Can Violent Offenders Be Distinguished from Frequent Offenders: Prediction from Childhood to Adolescence," *Journal of Research in Crime and Delinquency* 33 (1996): 206–231.

14. Adrian Raine, Patricia Brennan, and Sarnoff Mednick, "Interaction between Birth Complications and Early Maternal Rejection in Predisposing Individuals to Adult Violence: Specificity to Serious, Early-Onset Violence," *American Journal of Psychiatry* 154 (1997): 1265–1271.

15. Timothy Ireland, Carolyn Smith, and Terence Thornberry, "Developmental Issues in the Impact of Child Maltreatment on Later Delinquency and Drug Use," *Criminology* 40 (2002): 359–401.

16. Murray Straus, "Discipline and Deviance: Physical Punishment of Children and Violence and Other Crime in

Adulthood," *Social Problems* 38 (1991): 133–154.

17. Alan Rosenbaum and Penny Leisring, "Beyond Power and Control: Towards an Understanding of Partner Abusive Men," *Journal of Comparative Family Studies* 34 (2003): 7–26.

18. Sigmund Freud, *Beyond the Pleasure Principle* (London: Inter-Psychoanalytic Press, 1922).

19. Konrad Lorenz, *On Aggression* (New York: Harcourt Brace Jovanovich, 1966).

20. Wade Myers, *Sexual Homicide by Juveniles* (London, Academic Press, 2002).

21. Eric Stewart, Ronald Simons, and Rand Conger, "Assessing Neighborhood and Social Psychological Influences on Childhood Violence in an African-American Sample," *Criminology* 40 (2002): 801–830.

22. David Farrington, Rolf Loeber, and Magda Stouthamer-Loeber, "How Can the Relationship between Race and Violence Be Explained?" in *Violent Crimes: Assessing Race and Ethnic Differences,* ed. D. F. Hawkins (New York: Cambridge University Press, 2003), pp. 213–237.

23. Paul Goldstein, Henry Brownstein, and Patrick Ryan, "Drug-Related Homicide in New York: 1984–1988," *Crime and Delinquency* 38 (1992): 459–476.

24. James Collins and Pamela Messerschmidt, "Epidemiology of Alcohol-Related Violence," *Alcohol Health and Research World* 17 (1993): 93–100.

25. Paul Goldstein, Patricia Bellucci, Barry Spunt, and Thomas Miller, "Volume of Cocaine Use and Violence: A Comparison between Men and Women," *Journal of Drug Issues* 21 (1991): 345–367.

26. Kenneth Tardiff, Peter Marzuk, Kira Lowell, Laura Portera, and Andrew Leon, "A Study of Drug Abuse and Other Causes of Homicide in New York," *Journal of Criminal Justice* 30 (2002): 317–325.

27. Pamela Wilcox and Richard Clayton, "A Multilevel Analysis of School-Based Weapon Possession," *Justice Quarterly* 18 (2001): 509–542.

28. Federal Bureau of Investigation, *Crime in the United States, 2002* (Washington, D.C: U.S. Government Printing Office, 2003).

29. David Brent, Joshua Perper, Christopher Allman, Grace Moritz, Mary Wartella, and Janice Zelenak, "The Presence and Accessibility of Firearms in the Home and Adolescent Suicides," *Journal of the American Medical Association* 266 (1991): 2989–2995.

30. Robert Baller, Luc Anselin, Steven Messner, Glenn Deane, and Darnell Hawkins, "Structural Covariates of U.S. County Homicide Rates Incorporating Spatial Effects," *Criminology* 39 (2001): 561–590.

31. Marvin Wolfgang and Franco Ferracuti, *The Subculture of Violence* (London: Tavistock, 1967).

32. David Luckenbill and Daniel Doyle, "Structural Position and Violence: De-veloping a Cultural Explanation," *Criminology* 27 (1989): 419–436.

33. Charis Kubrin and Ronald Weitzer, "Retaliatory Homicide: Concentrated Disadvantage and Neighborhood Culture," *Social Problems* 50 (2003): 157–180.

34. Beth Bjerregaard and Alan Lizotte, "Gun Ownership and Gang Membership," *Journal of Criminal Law and Criminology* 86 (1995): 37–58.

35. James Howell, "Youth Gang Homicides: A Literature Review," *Crime and Delinquency* 45 (1999): 208–241.

36. Scott Decker, "Gangs and Violence: The Expressive Character of Collective Involvement." Unpublished manuscript, University of Missouri–St. Louis, 1994, p. 11.

37. William Green, *Rape* (Lexington, Mass.: Lexington Books, 1988), p. 5.

38. Barbara Krah, Renate Scheinberger-Olwig, and Steffen Bieneck, "Men's Reports of Nonconsensual Sexual Interactions with Women: Prevalence and Impact," *Archives of Sexual Behavior* 32 (2003): 165–176.

39. Susan Brownmiller, *Against Our Will: Men, Women and Rape* (New York: Simon & Schuster, 1975).

40. Green, *Rape,* p. 6.

41. FBI, Uniform Crime Report, 2001, pp. 29. Updated with Preliminary Uniform Crime Reports Data 2002, released June 16, 2003.

42. Callie Marie Rennison and Michael Rand, *Criminal Victimization 2002: Changes 2001–2002* (Washington, D.C.: Bureau of Justice Statistics, 2003), p. 2.

43. Arnold Kahn, Jennifer Jackson, Christine Kully, Kelly Badger, and Jessica Halvorsen, "Calling It Rape: Differences in Experiences of Women Who Do or Do Not Label Their Sexual Assault as Rape," *Psychology of Women Quarterly* 27 (2003): 233–242.

44. Angela Browne, "Violence against Women: Relevance for Medical Practitioners," *Journal of the American Medical Association* 267 (1992): 3184–3189.

45. Mark Warr, "Rape, Burglary and Opportunity," *Journal of Quantitative Criminology* 4 (1988): 275–288.

46. A. Nicholas Groth and Jean Birnbaum, *Men Who Rape* (New York: Plenum Press, 1979).

47. For another typology, see Raymond Knight, "Validation of a Typology of Rapists," in *Sex Offender Research and Treatment: State-of-the-Art in North America and Europe,* eds. W. L. Marshall and J. Frenken (Beverly Hills, Calif.: Sage, 1997), pp. 58–75.

48. R. Lance Shotland, "A Model of the Causes of Date Rape in Developing and Close Relationships," in *Close Relationships,* ed. C. Hendrick (Newbury Park, Calif.: Sage, 1989), pp. 247–270.

49. Kimberly Tyler, Danny Hoyt, and Les Whitbeck, "Coercive Sexual Strategies," *Violence and Victims* 13 (1998): 47–63.

50. Bonnie Fisher, Leah Daigle, Francis Cullen, and Michael Turner, "Report-ing Sexual Victimization to the Police and Others: Results from a National-Level Study of College Women," *Criminal Justice and Behavior* 30 (2003): 6–39.

51. David Finkelhor and K. Yllo, *License to Rape: Sexual Abuse of Wives* (New York: Holt, Rinehart and Winston, 1985).

52. Jill Elaine Hasday, "Contest and Consent: A Legal History of Marital Rape," *California Law Review* 88 (2000): 1373–1433.

53. Sharon Elstein and Roy Davis, *Sexual Relationships between Adult Males and Young Teen Girls: Exploring the Legal and Social Responses* (Chicago, Ill.: American Bar Association, 1997).

54. Donald Symons, *The Evolution of Human Sexuality* (Oxford: Oxford University Press, 1979).

55. Lee Ellis and Anthony Walsh, "Gene-Based Evolutionary Theories in Criminology," *Criminology* 35 (1997): 229–276.

56. Suzanne Osman, "Predicting Men's Rape Perceptions Based on the Belief That 'No' Really Means 'Yes,'" *Journal of Applied Social Psychology* 33 (2003): 683–692.

57. Martin Schwartz, Walter DeKeseredy, David Tait, and Shahid Alvi, "Male Peer Support and a Feminist Routine Activities Theory: Understanding Sexual Assault on the College Campus," *Justice Quarterly* 18 (2001): 623–650.

58. Diana Russell and Rebecca M. Bolen, *The Epidemic of Rape and Child Sexual Abuse in the United States* (Thousand Oaks, Calif.: Sage, 2000).

59. Paul Gebhard, John Gagnon, Wardell Pomeroy, and Cornelia Christenson, *Sex Offenders: An Analysis of Types* (New York: Harper & Row, 1965), pp. 198–205; Richard Rada, ed., *Clinical Aspects of the Rapist* (New York: Grune & Stratton, 1978), pp. 122–130.

60. Stephen Porter, David Fairweather, Jeff Drugge, Huues Herve, Angela Birt, and Douglas Boer, "Profiles of Psychopathy in Incarcerated Sexual Offenders," *Criminal Justice and Behavior* 27 (2000): 216–233.

61. Brad Bushman, Angelica Bonacci, Mirjam van Dijk, and Roy Baumeister, "Narcissism, Sexual Refusal, and Aggression: Testing a Narcissistic Reactance Model of Sexual Coercion," *Journal of Personality and Social Psychology* 84 (2003): 1027–1040.

62. Schwartz, DeKeseredy, Tait, and Alvi, "Male Peer Support and a Feminist Routine Activities Theory."

63. Groth and Birnbaum, *Men Who Rape,* p. 101.

64. See, generally, Edward Donnerstein, Daniel Linz, and Steven Penrod, *The Question of Pornography* (New York: Free Press, 1987); Diana Russell, *Sexual Exploitation* (Beverly Hills: Sage, 1985), pp. 115–116.

65. Neil Malamuth and John Briere, "Sexual Violence in the Media: Indirect Effects on Aggression against Women," *Journal of Social Issues* 42 (1986): 75–92.

66. Richard Felson and Marvin Krohn, "Motives for Rape," *Journal of Research in Crime and Delinquency* 27 (1990): 222–242.

67. Julie Horney and Cassia Spohn, "The Influence of Blame and Believability Factors on the Processing of Simple versus Aggravated Rape Cases," *Criminology* 34 (1996): 135–163.

68. Patricia Landwehr, Robert Bothwell, Matthew Jeanmard, Luis Luque, Roy Brown III, and Marie-Anne Breaux, "Racism in Rape Trials," *Journal of Social Psychology* 142 (2002): 667–670.

69. Cassia Spohn, Dawn Beichner, and Erika Davis-Frenzel, "Prosecutorial Justifications for Sexual Assault Case Rejection," *Social Problems* 48 (2001): 206–235.

70. "Man Wrongly Convicted of Rape Released 19 Years Later," *The Forensic Examiner* (May-June 2003): 44.

71. Gerald Robin, "Forcible Rape: Institutionalized Sexism in the Criminal Justice System," *Crime and Delinquency* 23 (1977): 136–153.

72. Rodney Kingsworth, Randall MacIntosh, and Jennifer Wentworth, "Sexual Assault: The Role of Prior Relationship and Victim Characteristics in Case Processing," *Justice Quarterly* 16 (1999): 276–302.

73. Susan Estrich, *Real Rape* (Cambridge: Harvard University Press, 1987), pp. 58–59.

74. *Michigan v. Lucas* 90-149 (1991); Comment, "The Rape Shield Paradox: Complainant Protection Amidst Oscillating Trends of State Judicial Interpretation," *Journal of Criminal Law and Criminology* 78 (1987): 644–698.

75. Andrew Karmen, *Crime Victims* (Pacific Grove, Calif.: Brooks/Cole, 1990), p. 252.

76. "Court Upholds Civil Rights Portion of Violence against Women Act," *Criminal Justice Newsletter* 28 (December 1, 1997), p. 3.

77. Cassia Spohn and David Holleran, "Prosecuting Sexual Assault: A Comparison of Charging Decisions in Sexual Assault Cases Involving Strangers, Acquaintances, and Intimate Partners," *Justice Quarterly* 18 (2001): 651–688; Colleen Fitzpatrick and Philip Reichel, "Conceptions of Rape and Perceptions of Prosecution." Paper presented at the American Society of Criminology meeting, San Diego, 1997.

78. Donald Lunde, *Murder and Madness* (San Francisco: San Francisco Book, 1977), p. 3.

79. Lisa Baertlein, "HIV Ruled Deadly Weapon in Rape Case," *Boston Globe,* March 2, 1994, p. 3.

80. The legal principles here come from Wayne LaFave and Austin Scott, *Criminal Law* (St. Paul: West, 1986; updated 1993). The definitions and discussion of legal principles used in this chapter lean heavily on this work.

81. LaFave and Scott, *Criminal Law.*

82. Evelyn Nieves, "Woman Gets 4-Year Term in Fatal Dog Attack," *New York Times,* July 16, 2002, p.1.

83. James Alan Fox and Marianne Zawitz, *Homicide Trends in the United States* (Washington, D.C.: Bureau of Justice Statistics, 2001).

84. Ibid.

85. Ibid.

86. See, generally, Marc Reidel and Margaret Zahn, *The Nature and Pattern of American Homicide* (Washington, D.C.: U.S. Government Printing Office, 1985).

87. Tomislav Kovandzic, John Sloan, and Lynne Vieraitis, "Unintended Consequences of Politically Popular Sentencing Policy: The Homicide Promoting Effects of 'Three Strikes' in U.S. Cities (1980-1999)," *Criminology and Public Policy* 3 (2002): 399–424.

88. James L. Williams, "A Discriminant Analysis of Urban Homicide Patterns." Paper presented at the annual meeting of the American Society of Criminology, Baltimore, November 1990.

89. Scott Decker, "Deviant Homicide: A New Look at the Role of Motives and Victim–Offender Relationships," *Journal of Research in Crime and Delinquency* 33 (1996): 427–449.

90. David Luckenbill, "Criminal Homicide as a Situational Transaction," *Social Problems* 25 (1977): 176–186.

91. Mark Anderson, Joanne Kaufman, Thomas Simon, Lisa Barrios, Len Paulozzi, George Ryan, Rodney Hammond, William Modzeleski, Thomas Feucht, Lloyd Potter, and the School-Associated Violent Deaths Study Group, "School-Associated Violent Deaths in the United States, 1994–1999," *Journal of the American Medical Association* 286 (2001): 2695–2702.

92. Pamela Wilcox and Richard Clayton, "A Multilevel Analysis of School-based Weapon Possession," *Justice Quarterly* 18 (2001): 509–542.

93. Larry Rohter, "In the Chaos of Colombia, the Makings of a Mass Killer," *New York Times,* November 1, 1999, p. 3.

94. "Police Suspect 'Something Snapped' to Ignite Wilder's Crime Spree," *Omaha World Herald,* April 15, 1984, p. 21A.

95. Mark Starr, "The Random Killers," *Newsweek,* November 26, 1984, pp. 100–106.

96. Thomas Palmer, "Ex-Hospital Aide Admits Killing 24 in Cincinnati," *Boston Globe,* August 19, 1987, p. 3.

97. Christopher Ferguson, Diana White, Stacey Cherry, Marta Lorenz, and Zhara Bhimani, "Defining and Classifying Serial Murder in the Context of Perpetrator Motivation," *Journal of Criminal Justice* 31 (2003): 287–293.

98. James Alan Fox and Jack Levin, "Multiple Homicide: Patterns of Serial and Mass Murder," in *Crime and Justice, An Annual Edition,* vol. 23, ed. Michael Tonry (Chicago, Ill.: University of Chicago Press, 1998): 407–455; see also, James Alan Fox and Jack Levin, *Overkill: Mass Murder and Serial Killing Exposed* (New York: Plenum, 1994); James Allan Fox and Jack Levin, "A Psycho-Social Analysis of Mass Murder," in *Serial and Mass Murder: Theory, Policy, and Research,* eds. Thomas O'Reilly-Fleming and Steven Egger (Toronto: University of Toronto Press, 1993); James Alan Fox and Jack Levin, "Serial Murder: A Survey," in *Serial and Mass Murder: Theory, Policy, and Research,* eds. Thomas O'Reilly-Fleming and Steven Egger (Toronto: University of Toronto Press, 1993); Jack Levin and James Alan Fox, *Mass Murder* (New York: Plenum Press, 1985).

99. Ibid.

100. Belea Keeney and Kathleen Heide, "Gender Differences in Serial Murderers: A Preliminary Analysis," *Journal of Interpersonal Violence* 9 (1994): 37–56.

101. Federal Bureau of Investigation, *Crime in the United States, 2000* (Washington, D.C.: U.S. Government Printing Office, 2001), p. 34.

102. Keith Harries, "Homicide and Assault: A Comparative Analysis of Attributes in Dallas Neighborhoods, 1981–1985," *Professional Geographer* 41 (1989): 29–38.

103. Laurence Zuckerman, "The Air-Rage Rage: Taking a Cold Look at a Hot Topic," *New York Times,* October 4, 1998, p. A3.

104. See, generally, Ruth S. Kempe and C. Henry Kempe, *Child Abuse* (Cambridge: Harvard University Press, 1978).

105. National Clearinghouse on Child Abuse and Neglect Information, "Child Maltreatment 2001: Summary of Key Findings" [Online]. Available: http://nccanch.acf.hhs.gov/pubs/factsheets/canstats.cfm (accessed December 15, 2003).

106. Diana Russell, "The Incidence and Prevalence of Intrafamilial and Extrafamilial Sexual Abuse of Female Children," *Child Abuse and Neglect* 7 (1983): 133–146; see also David Finkelhor, *Sexually Victimized Children* (New York: Free Press, 1979), p. 88.

107. Jeanne Hernandez, "Eating Disorders and Sexual Abuse in Adolescents." Paper presented at the annual meeting of the American Psychosomatic Society, Charleston, S.C., March 1993; Glenn Wolfner and Richard Gelles, "A Profile of Violence toward Children: A National Study," *Child Abuse and Neglect* 17 (1993): 197–212.

108. Lisa Jones and David Finkelhor, *The Decline in Child Sexual Abuse Cases* (Washington, D.C.: Office of Juvenile Justice and Delinquency Prevention, 2001).

109. Lisa Jones, David Finkelhor, and Kathy Kopie, "Why Is Sexual Abuse Declining? A Survey of State Child Protection Administrators," *Child Abuse and Neglect* 25 (2001): 1139–1141.

110. Jane Siegel and Linda Williams, "Risk Factors for Sexual Victimization of Women," *Violence Against Women* 9 (2003): 902-930.

111. Wolfner and Gelles, "A Profile of Violence toward Children."

112. Martin Daly and Margo Wilson, "Violence against Step Children," *Current*

Directions in Psychological Science 5 (1996): 77–81.

113. Ruth Inglis, *Sins of the Fathers: A Study of the Physical and Emotional Abuse of Children* (New York: St. Martins Press, 1978), p. 53.

114. Arina Ulman and Murray Straus, "Violence by Children against Mothers in Relation to Violence between Parents and Corporal Punishment by Parents," *Journal of Comparative Family Studies* 34 (2003): 41–63.

115. Richard Gelles and Murray Straus, "Violence in the American Family," *Journal of Social Issues* 35 (1979): 15–39.

116. Miguel Schwartz, Susan O'Leary, and Kimberly Kendziora, "Dating Aggression among High School Students," *Violence and Victimization* 12 (1997): 295–307.

117. Jay Silverman, Anita Raj, Lorelei Mucci, and Jeanne Hathaway, "Dating Violence against Adolescent Girls and Associated Substance Abuse, Unhealthy Weight Control, Sexual Risk Behavior, Pregnancy and Suicidality," *Journal of the American Medical Association* 286 (2001): 572–579.

118. Jacquelyn Campbell, Daniel Webster, Jane Koziol-McLain, Carolyn Block, Doris Campbell, Mary Ann Curry, Faye Gary, Nancy Glass, Judith McFarlane, Carolyn Sachs, Phyllis Sharps, Yvonne Ulrich, Susan Wilt, Jennifer Manganello, Xiao Xu, Janet Schollenberger, Victoria Frye, and Kathryn Laughon, "Risk Factors for Femicide in Abusive Relationships: Results from a Multisite Case Control Study," *American Journal of Public Health* 93 (2003): 1089–1097.

119. FBI, *Crime in the United States, 2000*, p. 29.

120. James Calder and John Bauer, "Convenience Store Robberies: Security Measures and Store Robbery Incidents," *Journal of Criminal Justice* 20 (1992): 553–566.

121. Peter Van Koppen and Robert Jansen, "The Time to Rob: Variations in Time of Number of Commercial Robberies," *Journal of Research in Crime and Delinquency* 36 (1999): 7–29.

122. Jody Miller, "Up It Up: Gender and the Accomplishment of Street Robbery," *Criminology* 36 (1998): 37–67.

123. Ibid., pp. 54–55.

124. Volkan Topalli, Richard Wright, and Robert Fornango, "Drug Dealers, Robbery and Retaliation: Vulnerability, Deterrence and the Contagion of Violence," *British Journal of Criminology* 42 (2002): 337–351.

125. Richard Felson, Eric Baumer, and Steven Messner, "Acquaintance Robbery," *Journal of Research in Crime and Delinquency* 37 (2000): 284–305.

126. Ibid., p. 287.

127. Ibid.

128. Richard Wright and Scott Decker, *Armed Robbers in Action, Stickups and Street Culture* (Boston, Mass.: Northeastern University Press, 1997).

129. James Brooke, "Gay Student Who Was Kidnapped and Beaten Dies," *New York Times*, October 13, 1998, p. A1.

130. James Garofalo, "Bias and Non-Bias Crimes in New York City: Preliminary Findings." Paper presented at the annual meeting of the American Society of Criminology, Baltimore, November 1990.

131. "Boy Gets 18 Years in Fatal Park Beating of Transient," *Los Angeles Times*, December 24, 1987, p. 9B.

132. Jack McDevitt, Jack Levin, and Susan Bennett, "Hate Crime Offenders: An Expanded Typology," *Journal of Social Issues* 58 (2002): 303–318; Jack Levin and Jack McDevitt, *Hate Crimes: The Rising Tide of Bigotry and Bloodshed* (New York: Plenum, 1993).

133. FBI, Fact Sheet for Hate Crime Statistics, 2002 [News Release], Washington, D.C.: November 12, 2003.

134. Kevin J. Strom, *Hate Crimes Reported in NIBRS, 1997–99* (Washington, D.C: Bureau of Justice Statistics, 2001).

135. Gregory Herek, Jeanine Cogan, and Roy Gillis, "Victim Experiences in Hate Crimes Based on Sexual Orientation," *Journal of Social Issues* 58 (2002): 319–340.

136. Garofalo, "Bias and Non-Bias Crimes in New York City," p. 3.

137. Brian Levin, "From Slavery to Hate Crime Laws: The Emergence of Race and Status-based Protection in American Criminal Law," *Journal of Social Issues* 58 (2002): 227–246.

138. *Virginia v. Black et al.*, No. 01-1107, 2003.

139. James Alan Fox and Jack Levin, "Firing Back: The Growing Threat of Workplace Homicide," *Annals* 536 (1994): 16–30.

140. John King, "Workplace Violence: A Conceptual Framework." Paper presented at the annual meeting of the American Society of Criminology, Phoenix, Arizona, November 1993.

141. Robert Simon, *Bad Men Do What Good Men Dream* (Washington, D.C.: American Psychiatric Press, 1999).

142. Greg Warchol, *Workplace Violence, 1992–96* (Washington, D.C.: Bureau of Justice Statistics, 1998).

143. The following sections rely heavily on Patricia Tjaden, *The Crime of Stalking: How Big Is the Problem?* (Washington, D.C: National Institute of Justice, 1997); see also, Robert M. Emerson, Kerry O. Ferris, and Carol Brooks Gardner, "On Being Stalked," *Social Problems* 45 (1998): 289–298.

144. Tjaden, *The Crime of Stalking: How Big Is the Problem?*

145. Bonnie Fisher, Francis Cullen, and Michael Turner, "Being Pursued: Stalking Victimization in a National Study of College Women," *Criminology and Public Policy* 1 (2002): 257–309.

146. Carol Jordan, T. K. Logan, and Robert Walker, "Stalking: An Examination of the Criminal Justice Response," *Journal of Interpersonal Violence* 18 (2003): 148–165.

147. Title 22 of the United States Code section 2656f(d) (1999).

148. Paul Wilkinson, *Terrorism and the Liberal State* (New York: John Wiley, 1977), p. 49.

149. Jack Gibbs, "Conceptualization of Terrorism," *American Sociological Review* 54 (1989): 329–40, at 330.

150. Associated Press, "Malaysia Arrests Five Militants," *New York Times*, October 15, 2002, p. A2.

151. Jocelyn Parker, "Vehicles Burn at Dealership: SUV Attacks Turn Violent," *Detroit Free Press*, August 23, 2003, p 1.

152. "Brutal Elves in the Woods," *The Economist* 359 (April 14, 2001): 28–30.

153. Mark Jurgensmeyer, *Terror in the Mind of God* (Berkeley and Los Angeles: University of California Press, 2000).

154. "Hunting Terrorists Using Confidential Informant Reward Programs," *FBI Law Enforcement Bulletin* 71 (2002): 26–28; Sara Sun Beale and James Felman, "The Consequences of Enlisting Federal Grand Juries in the War on Terrorism: Assessing the USA Patriot Act's Changes to Grand Jury Secrecy," *Harvard Journal of Law and Public Policy* 25 (2002): 699–721.

Chapter 11

1. Rick Lyman, "Winona Ryder Found Guilty of 2 Counts in Shoplifting Case," *New York Times*, November 6, 2002, p. A1.

2. Andrew McCall, *The Medieval Underworld* (London: Hamish Hamilton, 1979), p. 86.

3. Ibid., p. 104.

4. J. J. Tobias, *Crime and Police in England, 1700–1900* (London: Gill and Macmillan, 1979).

5. Ibid., p. 9.

6. Marilyn Walsh, *The Fence* (Westport, Conn.: Greenwood Press, 1977), pp. 18–25.

7. John Hepburn, "Occasional Criminals," in *Major Forms of Crime*, ed. Robert Meier (Beverly Hills, Calif.: Sage, 1984), pp. 73–94.

8. James Inciardi, "Professional Crime," in *Major Forms of Crime*, ed. Robert Meier (Beverly Hills, Calif.: Sage, 1984), p. 223.

9. This section depends heavily on a classic book: Wayne La Fave and Austin Scott, *Handbook on Criminal Law* (St. Paul, Minn.: West, 1972).

10. La Fave and Scott, *Handbook on Criminal Law*, p. 622.

11. FBI, *Crime in the United States, 2001* (Washington, D.C.: U.S. Government Printing Office, 2002). Updated with preliminary 2002 data issued June 16, 2003.

12. Margaret Loftus, "Gone: One TV," *U.S. News & World Report*, July 14, 1997, p. 61.

13. "Hot Cars: Parts Crooks Love Best," *Business Week*, September 15, 2003, p. 104.

14. Jill Jordan Siedfer, "To Catch a Thief, Try This: Peddling High-Tech Solutions to Shoplifting," *U.S. News & World Report*, September 23, 1996, p. 71.

15. Mary Owen Cameron, *The Booster and the Snitch* (New York: Free Press, 1964).

16. Ibid., p. 57.

17. Lawrence Cohen and Rodney Stark, "Discriminatory Labeling and the Five-Finger Discount: An Empirical Analysis of Differential Shoplifting Dispositions," *Journal of Research on Crime and Delinquency* 11 (1974): 25–35.

18. Lloyd Klemke, "Does Apprehension for Shoplifting Amplify or Terminate Shoplifting Activity?" *Law and Society Review* 12 (1978): 390–403.

19. Erhard Blankenburg, "The Selectivity of Legal Sanctions: An Empirical Investigation of Shoplifting," *Law and Society Review* 11 (1976): 109–129.

20. George Keckeisen, *Retail Security versus the Shoplifter* (Springfield, Ill.: Charles Thomas, 1993), pp. 31–32.

21. "Tesco Trials Electronic Product Tagging," *Computing and Control Engineering* 14 (2003): 3.

22. Siedfer, "To Catch a Thief, Try This."

23. *Ruditys v. J.C. Penney Co.,* No. 02-4114 (Delaware Co., Pa., Ct. C.P. 2003).

24. Edwin Lemert, "An Isolation and Closure Theory of Naive Check Forgery," *Journal of Criminal Law, Criminology and Police Science* 44 (1953): 297–298.

25. Paul Beckett and Jathon Sapsford, "As Credit-Card Theft Grows, a Tussle Over Paying to Stop It," *Wall Street Journal* [Eastern Edition], May 1, 2003, p. A1.

26. Matt Richtell, "Credit Card Theft Is Thriving Online as Global Market," *New York Times,* May 13, 2002, p. A1.

27. La Fave and Scott, *Handbook on Criminal Law,* p. 672.

28. Beckett and Sapsford, "As Credit-Card Theft Grows, a Tussle Over Paying to Stop It."

29. Peter Wayner, "Bogus Web Sites Troll for Credit Card Numbers," *New York Times,* February 12, 1997, p. A18.

30. National Insurance Crime Bureau, *SUV's, Pickups, Mini-Vans Favorites on Thieves Shopping List; Popular Vehicles Stolen for Parts or Illegal Export* (Palos Hills, Ill.: Author, December 10, 2002).

31. Kim Hazelbaker, "Insurance Industry Analyses and the Prevention of Motor Vehicle Theft," in *Business and Crime Prevention,* eds. Marcus Felson and Ronald Clarke (Monsey, N.Y.: Criminal Justice Press, 1997), pp. 283–293, at p. 287.

32. Charles McCaghy, Peggy Giordano, and Trudy Knicely Henson, "Auto Theft," *Criminology* 15 (1977): 367–381.

33. Donald Gibbons, *Society, Crime and Criminal Careers* (Englewood Cliffs, N.J.: Prentice-Hall, 1977), p. 310.

34. Hazelbaker, "Insurance Industry Analyses and the Prevention of Motor Vehicle Theft."

35. Ian Ayres and Steven D. Levitt, "Measuring Positive Externalities from Unobservable Victim Precaution: An Empirical Analysis of Lojack," *Quarterly Journal of Economics* 113 (1998): 43–78.

36. Hazelbaker, "Insurance Industry Analyses and the Prevention of Motor Vehicle Theft," p. 289.

37. La Fave and Scott, *Handbook on Criminal Law,* p. 655.

38. 30 Geo. III, C.24 (1975).

39. Susan Gembrowski and Tim Dahlberg, "Over 100 Here Indicted After Telemarketing Fraud Probe Around the U.S," *San Diego Daily Transcript Online,* December 8, 1995. Available: http://www.sddt.com/files/library/95headlines/DN951208/DN95120802.html

40. Jerome Hall, *Theft, Law and Society* (Indianapolis: Bobbs-Merrill, 1952), p. 36.

41. La Fave and Scott, *Handbook on Criminal Law,* p. 644.

42. Ibid., p. 649.

43. Ibid., p. 708.

44. E. Blackstone, *Commentaries on the Laws of England* (London: 1769), p. 224.

45. Frank Hoheimer, *The Home Invaders: Confessions of a Cat Burglar* (Chicago: Chicago Review, 1975).

46. Richard Wright, Robert Logie, and Scott Decker, "Criminal Expertise and Offender Decision Making: An Experimental Study of the Target Selection Process in Residential Burglary," *Journal of Research in Crime and Delinquency* 32 (1995): 39–53.

47. Richard Wright and Scott Decker, *Burglars on the Job: Streetlife and Residential Break-ins* (Boston, Mass.: Northeastern University Press, 1994).

48. Elizabeth Groff and Nancy La Vigne, "Mapping an Opportunity Surface of Residential Burglary," *Journal of Research in Crime and Delinquency* 38 (2001): 257–278.

49. Frank Hoheimer, *The Home Invaders: Confessions of a Cat Burglar* (Chicago: Chicago Review, 1975).

50. Wright, Logie, and Decker, "Criminal Expertise and Offender Decision Making: An Experimental Study of the Target Selection Process in Residential Burglary."

51. Matthew Robinson, "Accessible Targets, but Not Advisable Ones: The Role of 'Accessibility' in Student Apartment Burglary," *Journal of Security Administration* 21 (1998): 28–44.

52. Matt Hopkins, "Crimes against Businesses: The Way Forward for Future Research," *British Journal of Criminology* 42 (2002): 782–797.

53. Simon Hakim and Yochanan Shachmurove, "Spatial and Temporal Patterns of Commercial Burglaries," *American Journal of Economics and Sociology* 55 (1996): 443–457.

54. Roger Litton, "Crime Prevention and the Insurance Industry," in *Business and Crime Prevention,* eds. Marcus Felson and Ronald Clarke (Monsey, N.Y.: Criminal Justice Press, 1997), p. 162.

55. Graham Farrell, Coretta Phillips, and Ken Pease, "Like Taking Candy: Why Does Repeat Victimization Occur?" *British Journal of Criminology* 35 (1995): 384–399, at p. 391.

56. Ronald Clarke, Elizabeth Perkins, and Donald Smith, "Explaining Repeat Residential Burglaries: An Analysis of Property Stolen," in *Repeat Victimization (Crime Prevention Studies, vol. 12),* eds. Graham Farrell and Ken Pease (Monsey, N.Y.: Criminal Justice Press, 2001): 119–132.

57. Michael Townsley, Ross Homel, and Janet Chaseling, "Infectious Burglaries," *British Journal of Criminology* 43 (2003): 615–634.

58. See, generally, Neal Shover, "Structures and Careers in Burglary," *Journal of Criminal Law, Criminology and Police Science* 63 (1972): 540–549.

59. Richard Stevenson, Lubica Forsythe, and M. V. Weatherburn, "The Stolen Goods Market in New South Wales, Australia: An Analysis of Disposal Avenues and Tactics," *British Journal of Criminology* 41 (Winter 2001): 101–118.

60. Paul Cromwell, James Olson, and D'Aunn Wester Avary, *Breaking and Entering: An Ethnographic Analysis of Burglary* (Newbury Park, Calif.: Sage, 1991), pp. 48–51.

61. Jeffrey Zaslow, "Dangerous Games—Medical Mystery: Why Some Children Keep Setting Fires—Without Consensus on Cure, Groups Try Safety Lessons, Therapy and Scare Tactics—Sleeping Mom's Singed Hair," *Wall Street Journal,* June 27, 2003, p. A.1.

62. Arson Prevention Bureau of Justice, "Key Facts" [Online]. Available: http://www.arsonpreventionbureau.org.uk/News/ (accessed October 15, 2003).

63. Nancy Webb, George Sakheim, Luz Towns-Miranda, and Charles Wagner, "Collaborative Treatment of Juvenile Firestarters: Assessment and Outreach," *American Journal of Orthopsychiatry* 60 (1990): 305–310.

64. Pekka Santtila, Helina Haikkanen, Laurence Alison, and Carrie Whyte, "Juvenile Firesetters: Crime Scene Actions and Offender Characteristics," *Legal and Criminological Psychology* 8 (2003): 1–20.

65. John Taylor, Ian Thorne, Alison Robertson, and Ginny Avery, "Evaluation of a Group Intervention for Convicted Arsonists with Mild and Borderline Intellectual Disabilities," *Criminal Behaviour and Mental Health* 12 (2002): 282–294.

66. Scott Turner, "Funding Sparks Effort to Cut Juvenile Arson Rate" [Online], *George Street Journal* 27 (January 31, 2003): 1. Available: http://www.brown.edu/Administration/George_Street_Journal/vol27/27GSJ16f.html

Chapter 12

1. Constance Hays, "ImClone Founder Pleads Guilty to 6 Charges," *New York Times,* October 16, 2002, p. A1.

2. Nikos Passas and David Nelken, "The Thin Line between Legitimate and Criminal Enterprises: Subsidy Frauds in the European Community," *Crime, Law and Social Change* 19 (1993): 223–243.

3. For a thorough review, see David Friedrichs, *Trusted Criminals* (Belmont, Calif.: Wadsworth, 1996).

4. Kitty Calavita and Henry Pontell, "Savings and Loan Fraud as Orga-

nized Crime: Toward a Conceptual Typology of Corporate Illegality," *Criminology* 31 (1993): 519–548.

5. Mark Haller, "Illegal Enterprise: A Theoretical and Historical Interpretation," *Criminology* 28 (1990): 207–235.

6. Edwin Sutherland, *White-Collar Crime: The Uncut Version* (New Haven: Yale University Press, 1983).

7. Edwin Sutherland, "White-Collar Criminality," *American Sociological Review* 5 (1940): 2–10.

8. David Weisburd and Kip Schlegel, "Returning to the Mainstream," in *White-Collar Crime Reconsidered*, eds. Kip Schlegel and David Weisburd (Boston: Northeastern University Press, 1992), pp. 352–365.

9. Elizabeth Moore and Michael Mills, "The Neglected Victims and Unexamined Costs of White-Collar Crime," *Crime and Delinquency* 36 (1990): 408–418.

10. Natalie Taylor, "Under-Reporting of Crime against Small Businesses: Attitudes Towards Police and Reporting Practices," *Policing and Society* 13 (2003): 79–90.

11. This text employs categories of white-collar crime first identified in Mark Moore, "Notes Toward a National Strategy to Deal with White-Collar Crime," in *A National Strategy for Containing White-Collar Crime,* eds. Herbert Edelhertz and Charles Rogovin (Lexington, Mass.: Lexington Books, 1980), pp. 32–44.

12. David Firestone, "In Racketeering Trial, Well-Dressed Strip Club Takes the Stage," *New York Times,* May 5, 2001, p. 3.

13. Earl Gottschalk, "Churchgoers Are the Prey as Scams Rise," *Wall Street Journal,* August 7, 1989, p. C1.

14. Richard Quinney, "Occupational Structure and Criminal Behavior: Prescription Violation of Retail Pharmacists," *Social Problems* 11 (1963): 179–185; see also John Braithwaite, *Corporate Crime in the Pharmaceutical Industry* (London: Routledge and Kegan Paul, 1984).

15. Pam Belluck, "Prosecutors Say Greed Drove Pharmacist to Dilute Drugs," *New York Times,* August 18, 2001, p. 3.

16. Press Release, April 22, 2002, Kansas City Division, Federal Bureau of Investigation.

17. James Armstrong et al., "Securities Fraud," *American Criminal Law Review* 33 (1995): 973–1016.

18. Scott McMurray, "Futures Pit Trader Goes to Trial," *Wall Street Journal,* May 8, 1990, p. C1; Scott McMurray, "Chicago Pits' Dazzling Growth Permitted a Free-for-All Mecca," *Wall Street Journal,* August 3, 1989, p. A4.

19. Security and Exchange Commission Press Release, "Ten of Nation's Top Investment Firms Settle Enforcement Actions Involving Conflicts of Interest between Research and Investment Banking: Historic Settlement Requires Payments of Penalties of $487.5 Million, Disgorgement of $387.5 Million, Payments of $432.5 Million to Fund Independent Research, and Payments of $80 Million to Fund Investor Education and Mandates Sweeping Structural Reforms," April 28, 2003.

20. United Press International, "Minority Leader in N.Y. Senate Is Charged," *Boston Globe,* September 17, 1987, p. 20.

21. Al Baker, "Wide Inquiry Into Lobbyists' Gifts and Payments to Legislators," *New York Times,* January 17, 2003, p. B1.

22. James C. McKinley Jr., "Company Gets Record Fine for Its Giving to Lawmakers," *New York Times,* February 27, 2003, p. B1.

23. Cited in Hugh Barlow, *Introduction to Criminology,* 2nd ed. (Boston: Little, Brown, 1984).

24. PL No. 95-213, 101-104, 91 Stat. 1494.

25. Associated Press, "F.B.I. Arrests 8 in McDonald's Prize Scheme," *New York Times,* August 21, 2001, p. B1.

26. Adrian Cho, "Hey Buddy…Wanna Buy a Moon Rock?" *Science Now,* July 23, 2002, p. 1.

27. Charles McCaghy, *Deviant Behavior* (New York: Macmillan, 1976), p. 178.

28. "While Stocks Last," *Economist* (2002, September 21): 64–67.

29. The National Food Service Council, 2002. Available: http://www.nfssc.com/

30. Joshua Kurlantzick, "Those Sticky Fingers," *U.S. News & World Report* 130 (2001, June 4): 44.

31. J. Sorenson, H. Grove, and T. Sorenson, "Detecting Management Fraud: The Role of the Independent Auditor," in *White-Collar Crime, Theory and Research,* eds. G. Geis and E. Stotland (Beverly Hills: Sage, 1980), pp. 221–251.

32. Kurt Eichenwald, "Ex-Andersen Partner Pleads Guilty in Record-Shredding," *New York Times,* April 12, 2002, p. C1; John A. Byrne, "At Enron, the Environment Was Ripe for Abuse," *Business Week,* February 25, 2002, p. 12.

33. Peter Behr and Carrie Johnson, "Govt. Expands Charges against Enron Execs," *Washington Post,* May 1, 2003, p. 1.

34. John Rendleman, "Former WorldCom Execs Invoke the Fifth; Bernie Ebbers and Scott Sullivan Refuse to Testify at a Congressional Hearing about Their Roles in the Company's Accounting Scandal," *InformationWeek,* July 9, 2002.

35. Associated Press, "Ex-Chairman of Tyco Asked about Bonuses," *New York Times,* October 16, 2003, p. B1.

36. Joe Sexton, "In Brooklyn Neighborhood, Welfare Fraud Is Nothing New," *New York Times,* March 19, 1997, p. A1.

37. Metropolitan Desk, "False Claims from Fake Crashes Lead to Charges against 172," *New York Times,* July 20, 2001, p. C1.

38. 42 USC 1320a-7b(b); 42 USC 1320a-7b(b)(3); 42 CFR 1001.952 (regulatory safe harbors); 42 USC 1395nn (codifying "Stark I" and "Stark II" statutes).

39. 18 U.S.C. section 1344 (1994).

40. *United States v. Bishop,* 412 U.S. 346 (1973).

41. David Cay Johnston, "Departing Chief Says I.R.S. Is Losing War on Tax Cheats," *New York Times,* November 5, 2002, p.1.

42. Ibid.

43. Cited in Nancy Frank and Michael Lynch, *Corporate Crime, Corporate Violence* (Albany, N.Y.: Harrow and Heston, 1992), , pp. 12–13.

44. Sutherland, "White-Collar Criminality," pp. 2–10.

45. Joseph S. Hall, "Corporate Criminal Liability," *American Criminal Law Review* 35 (1998): 549–560.

46. 15 U.S.C. section 1 (1994).

47. 15 U.S.C. 1–7 (1976).

48. *Northern Pacific Railways v. United States,* 356 U.S. 1 (1958).

49. Tim Carrington, "Federal Probes of Contractors Rise for Year," *Wall Street Journal,* February 23, 1987, p. 50.

50. *Illinois Ex Rel. Madigan, Attorney General of Illinois v. Telemarketing Associates, Inc., et al.,* Number 01-1806 (2003).

51. Environmental Protection Agency, Criminal Enforcement Division [Online]. Available: http://www.epa.gov/compliance/criminal/index.html

52. Herbert Edelhertz and Charles Rogovin, eds., *A National Strategy for Containing White-Collar Crime* (Lexington, Mass.: Lexington Books, 1980), Appendix A, pp. 122–123.

53. Belluck, "Prosecutors Say Greed Drove Pharmacist to Dilute Drugs," p. 3.

54. Kathleen Daly, "Gender and Varieties of White-Collar Crime," *Criminology* 27 (1989): 769–793.

55. Donald Cressey, *Other People's Money: A Study of the Social Psychology of Embezzlement* (Glencoe, Ill.: Free Press, 1973), p. 96.

56. Byrne, "At Enron, the Environment Was Ripe for Abuse," p. 14.

57. Travis Hirschi and Michael Gottfredson, "Causes of White-Collar Crime," *Criminology* 25 (1987): 949–974.

58. Michael Gottfredson and Travis Hirschi, *A General Theory of Crime* (Stanford, Calif.: Stanford University Press, 1990), p. 191.

59. This section relies heavily on Daniel Skoler, "White-Collar Crime and the Criminal Justice System: Problems and Challenges," in *A National Strategy for Containing White-Collar Crime,* eds. Herbert Edelhertz and Charles Rogovin (Lexington, Mass.: Lexington Books, 1980), pp. 57–76.

60. Theodore Hammett and Joel Epstein, *Prosecuting Environmental Crime: Los Angeles County* (Washington, D.C.: National Institute of Justice, 1993).

61. Information provided by Los Angeles County District Attorney's Office, April 2003.

62. David Simon and D. Stanley Eitzen, *Elite Deviance* (Boston: Allyn and Bacon, 1982), p. 28.

63. This section relies heavily on Albert Reiss Jr., "Selecting Strategies of Social Control over Organizational Life," in *Enforcing Regulation,* eds. Keith

Hawkins and John M. Thomas (Boston: Klowver, 1984), pp. 25–37.

64. John Braithwaite, "The Limits of Economism in Controlling Harmful Corporate Conduct," *Law and Society Review* 16 (1981–1982): 481–504.

65. "Status Report: Criminal Fines," Criminal Enforcement Division, Anti-Trust Division, United States Department of Justice, June 1, 2002.

66. Michael Benson, "Emotions and Adjudication: Status Degradation among White-Collar Criminals," *Justice Quarterly* 7 (1990): 515–528; John Braithwaite, *Crime, Shame and Reintegration* (Sydney: Cambridge University Press, 1989).

67. Christopher M. Brown and Nikhil S. Singhvi, "Antitrust Violations," *American Criminal Law Review* 35 (1998): 467–501.

68. Howard Adler, "Current Trends in Criminal Antitrust Enforcement," *Business Crimes Bulletin* (1996, April): 1.

69. Robert Bennett, "Eighth Survey of White Collar Crime" (Foreword), *American Criminal Law Review* 30 (1993).

70. David Weisburd, Elin Waring, and Stanton Wheeler, "Class, Status, and the Punishment of White-Collar Criminals," *Law and Social Inquiry* 15 (1990): 223–243.

71. Sean Rosenmerkel, "Wrongfulness and Harmfulness as Components of Seriousness of White-Collar Offenses," *Journal of Contemporary Criminal Justice* 17 (2001): 308–328.

72. Mark Cohen, "Environmental Crime and Punishment: Legal/Economic Theory and Empirical Evidence on Enforcement of Federal Environmental Statutes," *Journal of Criminal Law and Criminology* 82 (1992): 1054–1109.

73. Russell Mokhiber, "White Collar Crime Penalties," *Multinational Monitor* 22 (2001): 30.

74. Jonathan Lechter, Daniel Posner, and George Morris, "Antitrust Violations," *American Criminal Law Review* 39 (2002): 225–273.

75. "Gartner G2 Says 2001 Online Fraud Losses Were 19 Times as High as Offline Fraud Losses, Consumers Are Beginning to Embrace Online Credit Card Security Systems." Unpublished Report, Gartner Inc., Stamford, Conn., 2002.

76. "Internet Fraud Complaint Center Referred More Than 48,000 Fraud Complaints to Law Enforcement in 2002: Referrals Triple Since 2001, Fraud Losses Total $54 Million" [Online]. Available: http://www1.ifccfbi.gov/strategy/wn030409.asp

77. Richard Powers, "2002 Computer Crime and Security Survey." Computer Security Institute, San Francisco, Calif., 2002.

78. Jeanne Capachin and Dave Potterton, "Online Card Payments, Fraud Solutions Bid to Win," Meridien Research Report, Newton, Mass., January 18, 2001.

79. Bruce Swartz, Deputy Assistant General, Criminal Division, Justice Department, Internet Fraud Testimony Before the House Energy and Commerce Committee, May 23, 2001.

80. Ibid.

81. This section is based on Richard Walker and David M. Levine, "'You've Got Jail': Current Trends in Civil and Criminal Enforcement of Internet Securities Fraud," *American Criminal Law Review* 38 (2001): 405–430.

82. Jim Wolf, "Internet Scams Targeted in Sweep: A 10-Day Crackdown Leads to 62 Arrests and 88 Indictments," *Boston Globe,* May 22, 2001, p. A2.

83. M. Swanson and J. Terriot, "Computer Crime: Dimensions, Types, Causes and Investigations," *Journal of Political Science and Administration* 8 (1980): 305–306; see Donn Parker, "Computer-Related White-Collar Crime," in *White Collar Crime, Theory and Research,* eds. G. Geis and E. Stotland (Beverly Hills: Sage, 1980), pp. 199–220.

84. Business Software Alliance, "BSA Seventh Annual Global Software Piracy Study (2002)" [Online]. Available: http://www.bsa.org/resources/ 2001-05-21.55.pdf (accessed October 21, 2002).

85. Anne Branscomb, "Rogue Computer Programs and Computer Rogues: Tailoring Punishment to Fit the Crime," *Rutgers Computer and Technology Law Journal* 16 (1990): 24–26.

86. Heather Jacobson and Rebecca Green, "Computer Crimes," *American Criminal Law Review* 39 (2002): 272–326.

87. Pub. L. No. 98-473, Title H, Chapter XXI, [sections] 2102(a), 98 Stat. 1837, 2190 (1984)

88. Pub. L. No. 104-294, Title II, [sections] 201, 110 Stat. 3488, 3491-94 (1996).

89. William Jackson. "Survey Shows Drop in Cybercrime," *Government Computer News* 22 (2003, September 29): 32.

90. See, generally, President's Commission on Organized Crime, *Report to the President and the Attorney General, The Impact: Organized Crime Today* (Washington, D.C.: U.S. Government Printing Office, 1986). Herein cited as *Organized Crime Today.*

91. Frederick Martens and Michele Cunningham-Niederer, "Media Magic, Mafia Mania," *Federal Probation* 49 (1985): 60–68.

92. *Organized Crime Today,* pp. 7–8.

93. Alan Block and William Chambliss, *Organizing Crime* (New York: Elsevier, 1981).

94. Alan Block, *East Side / West Side* (New Brunswick, N.J.: Transaction Books, 1983), pp. 10–11.

95. Statement for the Record of Thomas V. Fuentes, Chief Organized Crime Section Criminal Investigative Division Federal Bureau of Investigation on Organized Crime Before the House Subcommittee on Finance and Hazardous Materials, Washington, D.C., September 13, 2000.

96. Donald Cressey, *Theft of the Nation* (New York: Harper and Row, 1969).

97. Dwight Smith, *The Mafia Mystique* (New York: Basic Books, 1975).

98. Stanley Einstein and Menachem Amir, *Organized Crime: Uncertainties and Dilemmas* (Chicago: University of Illinois at Chicago, Office of International Criminal Justice, 1999); William Kleinknecht, *The New Ethnic Mobs: The Changing Face of Organized Crime in America* (New York: Free Press, 1996); Don Liddick, *An Empirical, Theoretical, and Historical Overview of Organized Crime* (Lewiston, N.Y.: Edwin Mellen Press, 1999); Maria Minniti, "Membership Has Its Privileges: Old and New Mafia Organizations," *Comparative Economic Studies* 37 (1995): 31–47.

99. *Organized Crime Today,* p. 11.

100. David Binder, "In Europe, Sex Slavery Is Thriving Despite Raids," *New York Times,* October 19, 2002, p. A3.

101. Richard A. Ballezza, "YACS Crime Groups: An FBI Major Crime Initiative," *FBI Law Enforcement Bulletin* 67 (1998): 7–13.

102. Omar Bartos, "Growth of Russian Organized Crime Poses Serious Threat," *CJ International* 11 (1995): 8–9.

103. George Vold, *Theoretical Criminology,* 2nd ed., rev. Thomas Bernard (New York: Oxford University Press, 1979).

104. 18 U.S.C. 1952 (1976).

105. PL No. 91-452, Title IX, 84 Stat. 922 (1970) (codified at 18 U.S.C. 1961–68, 1976).

106. *Richard McFeely,* "Enterprise Theory of Investigation," *FBI Law Enforcement Bulletin* 70 (2001): 19–26.

Chapter 13

1. *Hillary Goodridge and Others v. Department of Public Health,* SJC-08860, November 18, 2003.

2. Edwin Schur, *Crimes without Victims* (Englewood Cliffs, N.J.: Prentice-Hall, 1965).

3. Andrea Dworkin, quoted in "Where Do We Stand on Pornography?" *Ms* (1994, January–February), p. 34.

4. Russel Falck, Jichuan Wang, and Robert Carlson, "The Epidemiology of Physical Attack and Rape among Crack-Using Women," *Violence and Victims* 16 (2001): 79–89.

5. Morris Cohen, "Moral Aspects of the Criminal Law," *Yale Law Journal* 49 (1940): 1017.

6. See Joel Feinberg, *Social Philosophy* (Englewood Cliffs, N.J.: Prentice-Hall, 1973), chaps. 2, 3.

7. *United States v. 12 200-ft Reels of Super 8mm Film,* 413 U.S. 123 (1973), at p. 137.

8. Irving Kristol, "Liberal Censorship and the Common Culture," *Society* 36 (1999, September): 5.

9. Wayne La Fave and Austin Scott Jr., *Criminal Law* (St. Paul, Minn.: West, 1986), p. 12.

10. Ibid.

11. Judith Levine, *Harmful to Minors: The Perils of Protecting Children from Sex* (Minneapolis: University of Minnesota Press, 2002).

12. Howard Becker, *Outsiders* (New York: Macmillan, 1963), pp. 13–14.

13. Andrea Friedman, "Sadists and Sissies: Anti-Pornography Campaigns

in Cold War America," *Gender and History* 15 (2003): 201–228.

14. Judd Marmor, "The Multiple Roots of Homosexual Behavior," in *Homosexual Behavior,* ed. J. Marmor (New York: Basic Books, 1980), p. 5.

15. J. Money, "Sin, Sickness, or Status? Homosexual Gender Identity and Psychoneuroendocrinology," *American Psychologist* 42 (1987): 384–399.

16. J. McNeil, *The Church and the Homosexual* (Kansas City, Mo.: Sheed, Andrews, and McNeel, 1976).

17. Laurie Goodstein, "The Architect of the 'Gay Conversion' Campaign," *New York Times,* August 13, 1998, p. A10.

18. "Executing Injustice," *The Advocate* (2002, February 5): 16.

19. Sue Headley, "Anti-Homosexual Homicides Most Often Perpetrated by Young Males," *Youth Studies Australia* 22 (2003): 55.

20. Marmor, "The Multiple Roots of Homosexual Behavior," pp. 18–19.

21. Ibid., p. 19.

22. Henry Adams, Lester Wright, and Bethany Lohr, "Is Homophobia Associated with Homosexual Arousal?" *Journal of Abnormal Psychology* 105 (1996): 440–445.

23. 376 U.S. 660; 82 S.Ct. 1417; 8 L.Ed.2d 758 (1962).

24. Associated Press, "Governor Signs Defense of Marriage Act into Law," *Houston Chronicle,* May 27, 2003, p.1.

25. John Biskupic, "Justice Let Stand 'Don't Ask, Don't Tell' Policy," *Boston Globe,* October 22, 1996, p. A6.

26. Michael Joseph Gross, "A Problem with Privacy, and with Openness," *Boston Globe,* February 15, 1998, p. C3.

27. Associated Press, "Court Gives Sons Back to Gay Father," *Boston Globe,* October 16, 1996, p. A5.

28. *Boy Scouts of America v. Dale* 530 U.S. 640 (2000).

29. National Gay and Lesbian Task Force, "Eye on Equality: Pride and Public Opinion," Press Release, July 5, 1998.

30. Mireya Navarro, "Miami Restores Gay Rights Law," *New York Times,* December 2, 1998, p. B1.

31. *Romer v. Evans,* 517 U.S. 620 (1996).

32. *Lawrence et al. v. Texas,* No. 02-102, June 26, 2003.

33. *Bowers v. Hardwick,* 106 S.Ct. 2841 (1986); reh. den. 107 S.Ct. 29 (1986).

34. See, generally, Spencer Rathus and Jeffery Nevid, *Abnormal Psychology* (Englewood Cliffs, N.J.: Prentice-Hall, 1991), pp. 373–411.

35. W. P. de Silva, "Sexual Variations," *British Medical Journal* 318 (1999): 654–655.

36. Kathy Smiljanich and John Briere, "Self-Reported Sexual Interest in Children: Sex Differences and Psychosocial Correlates in a University Sample," *Violence and Victims* 11 (1996): 39–50.

37. See, generally, V. Bullogh, *Sexual Variance in Society and History* (Chicago: University of Chicago Press, 1958), pp. 143–144.

38. Spencer Rathus, *Human Sexuality* (New York: Holt, Rinehart and Winston, 1983), p. 463.

39. Charles McCaghy, *Deviant Behavior* (New York: Macmillan, 1976), pp. 348–349.

40. Ibid.

41. Michael Waldholz, "HTLV–I Virus Found in Blood of Prostitutes," *Wall Street Journal,* January 5, 1990, p. B2.

42. Monica Prasad, "The Morality of Market Exchange: Love, Money, and Contractual Justice," *Sociological Perspectives* 42 (1999): 181–187.

43. Elizabeth Bernstein, "The Meaning of the Purchase: Desire, Demand and the Commerce of Sex," *Ethnography* 2 (2001): 389–420.

44. David Enrich, "Trafficking in People," *U.S. News & World Report* 131 (2001, July 23): 34.

45. Charles Winick and Paul Kinsie, *The Lively Commerce* (Chicago: Quadrangle, 1971), p. 58.

46. Mark-David Janus, Barbara Scanlon, and Virginia Price, "Youth Prostitution," in *Child Pornography and Sex Rings,* ed. Ann Wolbert Burgess (Lexington, Mass.: Lexington Books, 1989), pp. 127–146.

47. Jennifer James, "Prostitutes and Prostitution," in *Deviants: Voluntary Action in a Hostile World,* eds. E. Sagarin and F. Montanino (New York: Scott, Foresman, 1977), p. 384.

48. Winick and Kinsie, *The Lively Commerce,* pp. 172–173.

49. Paul Goldstein, "Occupational Mobility in the World of Prostitution: Becoming a Madam," *Deviant Behavior* 4 (1983): 267–279.

50. Ibid.

51. Mireya Navarro, "Group Forced Illegal Aliens into Prostitution, U.S. Says," *New York Times,* April 24, 1998, p. A10.

52. D. Kelly Weisberg, *Children of the Night: A Study of Adolescent Prostitution* (Lexington, Mass.: Lexington Books, 1985), pp. 44–55.

53. Gerald Hotaling and David Finkelhor, *The Sexual Exploitation of Missing Children* (Washington, D.C.: U.S. Department of Justice, 1988).

54. Richard Estes and Neil Alan Weiner, "The Commercial Sexual Exploitation of Children in the U.S., Canada and Mexico," (Philadelphia: University of Pennsylvania, 2001).

55. N. Jackman, Richard O'Toole, and Gilbert Geis, "The Self-Image of the Prostitute," in *Sexual Deviance,* eds. J. Gagnon and W. Simon (New York: Harper and Row, 1967), pp. 152–153.

56. Weisberg, *Children of the Night,* p. 98.

57. Barbara G. Brents and Kathryn Hausbeck, "State-Sanctioned Sex: Negotiating Formal and Informal Regulatory Practices in Nevada Brothels," *Sociological Perspectives* 44 (2001): 307–335.

58. Ibid.

59. Mara Keire, "The Vice Trust: A Reinterpretation of the White Slavery Scare in the United States, 1907–1917," *Journal of Social History* 35 (2001): 5–42.

60. Ronald Weitzer, "The Politics of Prostitution in America," in *Sex for Sale,* ed.

R. Weitzer (New York: Routledge, 2000), pp. 159–180.

61. Andrea Dworkin, *Pornography* (New York: Dutton, 1989).

62. Annette Jolin, "On the Backs of Working Prostitutes: Feminist Theory and Prostitution Policy," *Crime and Delinquency* 40 (1994): 60–83, at pp. 76–77.

63. Alexa Albert, *Brothel: Mustang Ranch and Its Women* (New York: Random House, 2001).

64. *Merriam-Webster Dictionary* (New York: Pocket Books, 1974), p. 484.

65. Attorney General's Commission, Report on Pornography, *Final Report* (Washington, D.C.: U.S. Government Printing Office, 1986), pp. 837–901. Hereafter cited as Pornography Commission.

66. Philip Jenkins, *Beyond Tolerance: Child Pornography Online* (New York: New York University Press, 2001).

67. Christopher Bagley, "Diminishing Incidence of Internet Child Pornographic Images," *Psychological Reports* 93 (2003): 305–306.

68. *Report of the Commission on Obscenity and Pornography* (Washington, D.C.: U.S. Government Printing Office, 1970).

69. Berl Kutchinsky, "The Effect of Easy Availability of Pornography on the Incidence of Sex Crimes," *Journal of Social Issues* 29 (1973): 95–112.

70. Michael Goldstein, "Exposure to Erotic Stimuli and Sexual Deviance," *Journal of Social Issues* 29 (1973): 197–219.

71. See Edward Donnerstein, Daniel Linz, and Steven Penrod, *The Question of Pornography* (New York: Free Press, 1987).

72. Edward Donnerstein, "Pornography and Violence against Women," *Annals of the New York Academy of Science* 347 (1980): 277–288; E. Donnerstein and J. Hallam, "Facilitating Effects of Erotica on Aggression against Women," *Journal of Personality and Social Psychology* 36 (1977): 1270–1277; Seymour Fishbach and Neil Malamuth, "Sex and Aggression: Proving the Link," *Psychology Today* 12 (1978): 111–122.

73. Don Smith, "Sexual Aggression in American Pornography: The Stereotype of Rape," paper presented at the annual meeting of the American Sociological Association, Salt Lake City, August 1976.

74. Diana Russel, *Dangerous Relationships: Pornography, Misogyny, and Rape* (Thousand Oaks, Calif.: Sage, 1998).

75. 354 U.S. 476; 77 S.Ct. 1304 (1957).

76. 413 U.S. 15 (1973).

77. R. George Wright, "Defining Obscenity: The Criterion of Value," *New England Law Review* 22 (1987): 315–341.

78. *Pope v. Illinois,* 107 S.Ct. 1918 (1987).

79. ACLU, "*ACLU v. Reno,* Round 2: Broad Coalition Files Challenge to New Federal Net Censorship Law," News Release, October 22, 1998.

80. *Ashcroft, Attorney General, et al. v. Free Speech Coalition et al.,* No. 00-795, April 16, 2002.

81. Anthony Flint, "Skin Trade Spreading Across U.S.," *Boston Globe,* December 1, 1996, pp. 1, 36–37.

82. Thomas J. Lueck, "At Sex Shops, Fear That Ruling Means the End Is Near," *New York Times,* February 25, 1998, p. 1.

83. David Rohde, "In Giuliani's Crackdown on Porn Shops, Court Ruling Is a Setback," *New York Times,* August 29, 1998, p. A11.

84. ACLU, *Reno v. ACLU,* No. 96-511.

85. Ralph Weisheit, "Studying Drugs in Rural Areas: Notes from the Field," *Journal of Research in Crime and Delinquency* 30 (1993): 213–232.

86. Substance Abuse and Mental Health Services Administration (SAMHSA), *Emergency Data from the Drug Abuse Warning Network* (Rockville, Md.: SAMHSA, March 2003).

87. Arnold Trebach, *The Heroin Solution* (New Haven, Conn.: Yale University Press, 1982).

88. James Inciardi, *The War on Drugs* (Palo Alto, Calif.: Mayfield, 1986), p. 2.

89. See, generally, David Pittman, "Drug Addiction and Crime," in *Handbook of Criminology,* ed. D. Glazer (Chicago: Rand McNally, 1974), pp. 209–232; Board of Directors, National Council on Crime and Delinquency, "Drug Addiction: A Medical, Not a Law Enforcement Problem," *Crime and Delinquency* 20 (1974): 4–9.

90. Associated Press, "Records Detail Royals' Turn-of-Century Drug Use," *Boston Globe,* August 29, 1993, p. 13.

91. See Edwin Brecher, *Licit and Illicit Drugs* (Boston: Little, Brown, 1972).

92. James Inciardi, *Reflections on Crime* (New York: Holt, Rinehart and Winston, 1978), pp. 8–10; see also A. Greeley, William McCready, and Gary Theisen, *Ethnic Drinking Subcultures* (New York: Praeger, 1980).

93. Joseph Gusfield, *Symbolic Crusade* (Urbana: University of Illinois Press, 1963), chap. 3.

94. McCaghy, *Deviant Behavior,* p. 280.

95. Ibid.

96. The annual survey is conducted by Lloyd Johnston, Jerald Bachman, and Patrick O'Malley of the Institute of Social Research, University of Michigan, Ann Arbor.

97. National Household Survey on Drug Abuse and Health, 2002

98. National Center on Addiction and Substance Abuse, *Teen Tipplers: America's Underage Drinking Epidemic,* rev. ed. (New York City: Author, February 2003).

99. C. Bowden, "Determinants of Initial Use of Opioids," *Comprehensive Psychiatry* 12 (1971): 136–140.

100. Marvin Krohn, Alan Lizotte, Terence Thornberry, Carolyn Smith, and David McDowall, "Reciprocal Causal Relationships among Drug Use, Peers, and Beliefs: A Five-Wave Panel Model," *Journal of Drug Issues* 26 (1996): 205–228.

101. R. Cloward and L. Ohlin, *Delinquency and Opportunity: A Theory of Delinquent Gangs* (Glencoe, Ill.: Free Press, 1960).

102. Lening Zhang, John Welte, and William Wieczorek, "Youth Gangs, Drug Use and Delinquency," *Journal of Criminal Justice* 27 (1999): 101–109.

103. Peter Giancola, "Constructive Thinking, Antisocial Behavior, and Drug Use in Adolescent Boys with and without a Family History of a Substance Use Disorder," *Personality and Individual Differences* 35 (2003): 1315–1331.

104. Amy Young, Carol Boyd, and Amy Hubbell, "Social Isolation and Sexual Abuse among Women Who Smoke Crack," *Journal of Psychosocial Nursing* 39 (2001): 16–19.

105. Substance Abuse and Mental Health Services Administration, Office of Applied Studies, "The Relationship between Mental Health and Substance Abuse among Adolescents," Analytic Series: A-9, 1999.

106. D. W. Goodwin, "Alcoholism and Genetics," *Archives of General Psychiatry* 42 (1985): 171–174.

107. For a thorough review of this issue, see John Petraitis, Brian Flay, and Todd Miller, "Reviewing Theories of Adolescent Substance Use: Organizing Pieces in the Puzzle," *Psychological Bulletin* 117 (1995): 67–86.

108. Judith Brooks and Li-Jung Tseng, "Influences of Parental Drug Use, Personality, and Child Rearing on the Toddler's Anger and Negativity," *Genetic, Social and General Psychology Monographs* 122 (1996): 107–128.

109. Thomas Ashby Wills, Donato Vaccaro, Grace McNamara, and A. Elizabeth Hirky, "Escalated Substance Use: A Longitudinal Grouping Analysis from Early to Middle Adolescence," *Journal of Abnormal Psychology* 105 (1996): 166–180.

110. Denise Kandel and Mark Davies, "Friendship Networks, Intimacy, and Illicit Drug Use in Young Adulthood: A Comparison of Two Competing Theories," *Criminology* 29 (1991): 441–471.

111. J. S. Mio, G. Nanjundappa, D. E. Verlur, and M. D. DeRios, "Drug Abuse and the Adolescent Sex Offender: A Preliminary Analysis," *Journal of Psychoactive Drugs* 18 (1986): 65–72.

112. D. Baer and J. Corrado, "Heroin Addict Relationships with Parents During Childhood and Early Adolescent Years," *Journal of Genetic Psychology* 124 (1974): 99–103.

113. The National Center on Addiction and Substance Abuse, "Reducing Teen Smoking Can Cut Marijuana Use Significantly," Press Release, September 16, 2003.

114. John Wallace and Jerald Bachman, "Explaining Racial/Ethnic Differences in Adolescent Drug Use: The Impact of Background and Lifestyle," *Social Problems* 38 (1991): 333–357.

115. John Donovan, "Problem-Behavior Theory and the Explanation of Adolescent Marijuana Use," *Journal of Drug Issues* 26 (1996): 379–404.

116. A. Christiansen, G. T. Smith, P. V. Roehling, and M. S. Goldman, "Using Alcohol Expectancies to Predict Adolescent Drinking Behavior After One Year," *Journal of Counseling and Clinical Psychology* 57 (1989): 93–99.

117. Icek Ajzen, *Attitudes, Personality and Behavior* (Homewood, Ill.: Dorsey Press, 1988).

118. Judith Brook, Martin Whiteman, Elinor Balka, and Beatrix Hamburg, "African-American and Puerto Rican Drug Use: Personality, Familial, and Other Environmental Risk Factors," *Genetic, Social, and General Psychology Monographs* 118 (1992): 419–438.

119. Bu Huang, Helene White, Rick Kosterman, Richard Catalano, and J. David Hawkins, "Developmental Associations between Alcohol and Interpersonal Aggression During Adolescence," *Journal of Research in Crime and Delinquency* 38 (2001): 64–83.

120. Andrew Golub and Bruce D. Johnson, *The Rise of Marijuana as the Drug of Choice among Youthful Adult Arrestees* (Washington, D.C.: National Institute of Justice, 2001).

121. Marvin Dawkins, "Drug Use and Violent Crime among Adolescents," *Adolescence* 32 (1997): 395–406.

122. Jeffrey Fagan, *Adolescent Violence: A View from the Street,* NIJ Research Preview (Washington, D.C.: National Institute of Justice, 1998); Eric Baumer, Janet Lauritsen, Richard Rosenfeld, and Richard Wright, "The Influence of Crack Cocaine on Robbery, Burglary, and Homicide Rates: A Cross-City, Longitudinal Analysis," *Journal of Research in Crime and Delinquency* 35 (1998): 316–340; Carolyn Rebecca Block and Antigone Christakos, "Intimate Partner Homicide in Chicago over 29 Years," *Crime and Delinquency* 41 (1995): 496–526.

123. George Speckart and M. Douglas Anglin, "Narcotics Use and Crime: An Overview of Recent Research Advances," *Contemporary Drug Problems* 13 (1986): 741–769; Charles Faupel and Carl Klockars, "Drugs–Crime Connections: Elaborations from the Life Histories of Hard-Core Heroin Addicts," *Social Problems* 34 (1987): 54–68.

124. M. Douglas Anglin, Elizabeth Piper Deschenes, and George Speckart, "The Effect of Legal Supervision on Narcotic Addiction and Criminal Behavior," paper presented at the annual meeting of the American Society of Criminology, Montreal, November 1987, p. 2.

125. Speckart and Anglin, "Narcotics Use and Crime," p. 752.

126. Arrestee Drug Abuse Monitoring Program (ADAM), *Annual Report on Drug Use among Adult and Juvenile Arrestees* (Washington, D.C.: National Institute of Justice, 2003).

127. Marvin Krohn, Alan Lizotte, and Cynthia Perez, "The Interrelationship between Substance Use and Precocious Transitions to Adult Sexuality," *Journal of Health and Social Behavior* 38 (1997): 87–103, at p. 88; Richard Jessor, "Risk Behavior in Adolescence: A Psychosocial Framework for Understanding and Action," in *Adolescents at Risk: Medical and Social Perspectives,*

128. See Kenneth Jones, Louis Shainberg, and Carter Byer, *Drugs and Alcohol* (New York: Harper and Row, 1979) pp. 137–146.

129. Controlled Substance Act, 21 U.S.C. 848 (1984).

130. Anti–Drug Abuse Act of 1986, Pub. L. No. 99-570, U.S.C. 841 (1986).

131. Anti–Drug Abuse Act of 1988, Pub. L. No. 100-690; 21 U.S.C. 1501; Subtitle A–Death Penalty, Sec. 7001, Amending the Controlled Substances Abuse Act, 21 U.S.C. 848.

132. Eric Jensen, Jurg Gerber, and Ginna Babcock, "The New War on Drugs: Grass Roots Movement or Political Construction?" *Journal of Drug Issues* 21 (1991): 651–667.

133. U.S. Department of State, *1998 International Narcotics Control Strategy Report,* February 1999.

134. David Hayeslip, "Local-Level Drug Enforcement: New Strategies," *NIJ Reports* (1989, March/April): 1.

135. Mark Moore, *Drug Trafficking* (Washington, D.C.: National Institute of Justice, 1988).

136. Peter Rossi, Richard Berk, and Alec Campbell, "Just Punishments: Guideline Sentences and Normative Consensus," *Journal of Quantitative Criminology* 13 (1997): 267–283.

137. Robert Davis, Arthur Lurigio, and Dennis Rosenbaum, eds., *Drugs and the Community* (Springfield, Ill.: Charles Thomas, 1993), pp. xii–xv.

138. Saul Weingart, "A Typology of Community Responses to Drugs," in *Drugs and the Community,* eds. Robert Davis, Arthur Lurigio, and Dennis Rosenbaum (Springfield, Ill.: Charles Thomas, 1993), pp. 85–105.

139. Earl Wyson, Richard Aniskiewicz, and David Wright, "Truth and DARE: Tracking Drug Education to Graduation as Symbolic Politics," *Social Problems* 41 (1994): 448–471.

140. Ibid.

141. Dennis Rosenbaum, Robert Flewelling, Susan Bailey, Chris Ringwalt, and Deanna Wilkinson, "Cops in the Classroom: A Longitudinal Evaluation of Drug Abuse Resistance Education (DARE)," *Journal of Research in Crime and Delinquency* 31 (1994): 3–31.

142. Mareanne Zawitz, *Drugs, Crime, and the Justice System* (Washington, D.C.: U.S. Government Printing Office, 1992), pp. 115–122.

143. John Goldkamp and Peter Jones, "Pretrial Drug-Testing Experiments in Milwaukee and Prince George's County: The Context of Implementation," *Journal of Research in Crime and Delinquency* 29 (1992): 430–465; Chester Britt, Michael Gottfredson, and John Goldkamp, "Drug Testing and Pretrial Misconduct: An Experiment on the Specific Deterrent Effects of Drug Monitoring Defendants on Pretrial Release," *Journal of Research in Crime and Delinquency* 29 (1992): 62–78. See, generally, Peter Greenwood and Franklin Zimring, *One More Chance*

(Santa Monica, Calif.: Rand Corporation, 1985).

144. See, generally, Greenwood and Zimring, *One More Chance.*

145. Tracy Beswick, David David, Jenny Bearn, Michael Gossop, Michael Sian Rees, and John Strang, "The Effectiveness of Combined Naloxone/Lofexidine in Opiate Detoxification: Results from a Double-Blind Randomized and Placebo-Controlled Trial," *American Journal on Addictions* 12 (2003): 295–306.

146. George De Leon, Stanley Sacks, Graham Staines, and Karen McKendrick, "Modified Therapeutic Community for Homeless Mentally Ill Chemical Abusers: Treatment Outcomes," *American Journal of Drug and Alcohol Abuse* 26 (2000): 461–480.

147. Michael French, H. J. Jeanne Salome, Jody Sindelar, and A. Thomas McLellan, "Benefit–Cost Analysis of Ancillary Social Services in Publicly Supported Addiction Treatment," February 1, 1999, data supplied by the Center for Substance Abuse Research (CESAR), College Park, Md. 20740.

148. The following section is based on material found in Jerome Platt, "Vocational Rehabilitation of Drug Abusers," *Psychological Bulletin* 117 (1995): 416–433.

149. The National Center on Addiction and Substance Abuse, *Shoveling Up: The Impact of Substance Abuse on State Budgets* (New York: Author, 2001).

150. Office of National Drug Control Policy, *National Drug Control Strategy: FY 2004 Budget Summary* (Washington, D.C.: Author, February 2003).

151. Charlie LeDuff, "Cocaine Quietly Reclaims Its Hold as Good Times Return," *New York Times,* August 21, 2000, p. A1.

152. Nadelmann, Ethan, "The U.S. Is Addicted to War on Drugs," *Globe and Mail,* May 20, 2003, p. 1; Ethan Nadelmann, "America's Drug Problem," *Bulletin of the American Academy of Arts and Sciences* 65 (1991): 24–40.

153. See, generally, Ralph Weisheit, *Drugs, Crime and the Criminal Justice System* (Cincinnati: Anderson, 1990).

154. David Courtwright, "Should We Legalize Drugs? History Answers No," *American Heritage* (1993, February/March): 43–56.

155. Kathryn Ann Farr, "Revitalizing the Drug Decriminalization Debate," *Crime and Delinquency* 36 (1990): 223–237.

Chapter 14

1. For a detailed analysis of this work, see Samuel Walker, "Origins of the Contemporary Criminal Justice Paradigm: The American Bar Foundation Survey, 1953–1969," *Justice Quarterly* 9 (1992): 47–76.

2. President's Commission on Law Enforcement and the Administration of Justice, *The Challenge of Crime in a Free Society* (Washington, D.C.: U.S. Government Printing Office, 1967).

3. See Public Law 90-351, Title I—Omnibus Crime Control Safe Streets Act of 1968, 90th Congress, June 19, 1968.

4. Federal Bureau of Investigation, *Crime in the United States, 2002* (Washington, D.C.: Government Printing Office, 2003), p. 208.

5. Brian Reaves, *Felony Sentences in Large Urban Counties, 1998* (Washington, D.C.: Bureau of Justice Statistics, 2001).

6. Bureau of Justice Statistics Web site [Online]. Available: http://www.ojp. usdoj.gov/bjs/sandlle.htm#personnel (accessed October 29, 2003).

7. See Albert Reiss, *Police and the Public* (New Haven, Conn.: Yale University Press, 1972).

8. Patrick A. Langan, Lawrence A. Greenfeld, Steven K. Smith, Matthew R. Durose, and David J. Levin, *Contacts between Police and the Public: Findings from the 1999 National Survey* (Washington, D.C.: Bureau of Justice Statistics, 2001).

9. Joel Garner, Christopher Maxwell, and Cederick Heraux, "Characteristics Associated with the Prevalence and Severity of Force Used by the Police," *Justice Quarterly* 19 (2002): 705–747; William Terrill and Stephen Mastrofski, "Situational and Officer-Based Determinants of Police Coercion," *Justice Quarterly* 19 (2002): 215–248.

10. Colin Loftin, David McDowall, Brian Wiersema, and Adam Dobrin, "Underreporting of Justifiable Homicides Committed by Police Officers in the United States, 1976–1998," *American Journal of Public Health* 93 (2003): 1117–1121.

11. James Hawdon and John Ryan, "Police-Resident Interactions and Satisfaction with Police: An Empirical Test of Community Policing Assertions," *Criminal Justice Policy Review* 14 (2003): 55–74.

12. Matthew Durose and Patrick A. Langan, *State Court Sentencing of Convicted Felons, 2000* (Washington, D.C.: Bureau of Justice Statistics, February 2003).

13. Cassia Spohn, Dawn Beichner, and Erika Davis-Frenzel, "Prosecutorial Justifications for Sexual Assault Case Rejection: Guarding the 'Gateway to Justice'," *Social Problems* 48 (2001): 206–235.

14. *Powell v. Alabama,* 287 U.S. 45, 53 S.Ct. 55, 77 L.Ed. 158 (1932); *Gideon v. Wainwright,* 372 U.S. 335, 83 S.Ct. 792, 9 L.Ed. 2d 799 (1963); *Argersinger v. Hamlin,* 407 U.S. 25, 92 S.Ct. 2006, 32 L.Ed. 2d 530 (1972).

15. *Wiggins v. Smith, Warden,* No. 02-311 [Decided June 26, 2003].

16. Herbert L. Packer, *The Limits of the Criminal Sanction* (Stanford, Calif.: Stanford University Press, 1968), p. 159.

17. Barbara Boland, Catherine Conly, Paul Mahanna, Lynn Warner, and Ronald Sones, *The Prosecution of Felony Arrests, 1987* (Washington, D.C.: Bureau of Justice Statistics, 1990), p. 3.

18. See Donald Newman, *Conviction: The Determination of Guilt or Innocence without Trial* (Boston: Little, Brown, 1966).

19. Paul Cassell, "How Many Criminals Has Miranda Set Free?" *Wall Street Journal,* March 1, 1995, p. A15.

20. David Garland, *Punishment and Modern Society* (Chicago: University of Chicago Press, 1990).

21. The most often cited of these is Douglas Lipton, Robert Martinson, and Judith Wilks, *The Effectiveness of Correctional Treatment: A Survey of Treatment Evaluation Studies* (New York: Praeger, 1975).

22. "Many State Legislatures Focused on Crime in 1995, Study Finds," *Criminal Justice Newsletter,* January 17, 1996, pp. 1–2.

23. Daniel Nagin, "Criminal Deterrence Research: A Review of the Evidence and a Research Agenda for the Outset of the 21st Century," in *Crime and Justice: An Annual Review,* ed. Michael Tonry (Chicago: University of Chicago Press, 1997), pp. 126–158.

24. "Crime and Punishment in America: 1997 Update," National Center for Policy Analysis, Dallas, 1997.

25. David Fogel, *We Are the Living Proof* (Cincinnati: Anderson, 1975). See also David Fogel, *Justice as Fairness* (Cincinnati: Anderson, 1980).

26. Travis Pratt, "Race and Sentencing: A Meta-Analysis of Conflicting Empirical Research Results," *Journal of Criminal Justice* 26 (1998): 513–525.

27. Packer, *The Limits of the Criminal Sanction.*

28. Eric Lotke, "Hobbling a Generation: Young African-American Men in Washington, D.C.'s Criminal Justice System—Five Years Later," *Crime and Delinquency* 44 (1998): 355–366.

29. Roy Austin and Mark Allen, "Racial Disparity in Arrest Rates as an Explanation of Racial Disparity in Commitment to Pennsylvania's Prisons," *Journal of Research in Crime and Delinquency* 37 (2000): 200–220.

30. Anthony Petrosino and Carolyn Petrosino, "The Public Safety Potential of Megan's Law in Massachusetts: An Assessment from a Sample of Criminal Sexual Psychopaths," *Crime and Delinquency* 43 (1999): 140–158; "New Laws Said to Raise Demands on Justice Information Systems," *Criminal Justice Newsletter,* September 17, 1996, pp. 3–4.

31. Jim Yardley, "Convicted in Murder Case, Man Cleared 7 Years Later," *New York Times,* October 29, 1998, p. 11.

32. "DNA Testing Has Exonerated 28 Prison Inmates, Study Finds," *Criminal Justice Newsletter,* June 17, 1996, p. 2.

33. Richard McCorkle, "Research Note: Punish and Rehabilitate? Public Attitudes Toward Six Common Crimes," *Crime and Delinquency* 39 (1993): 240–252.

34. For example, see D. A. Andrews, Ivan Zinger, R. D. Hoge, James Bonta, Paul Gendreau, and Francis Cullen, "Does Correctional Treatment Work? A Clinically-Relevant and Psychologically-Informed Meta-Analysis," *Criminology* 28 (1990): 369–404; Carol Garrett, "Effects of Residential Treatment on Adjudicated Delinquents: A Meta-Analysis," *Journal of Research in Crime and Delinquency* 22 (1985): 287–308.

35. Mark Lipsey and David Wilson, "Effective Intervention for Serious Juvenile Offenders: A Synthesis of Research," in *Serious and Violent Juvenile Offenders: Risk Factors and Successful Interventions,* eds. Rolf Loeber and David Farrington (Thousand Oaks, Calif.: Sage, 1998), pp. 39–53.

36. Francis Cullen, John Paul Wright, Shayna Brown, Melissa Moon, Michael Blankenship, and Brandon Applegate, "Public Support for Early Intervention Programs: Implications for a Progressive Policy Agenda," *Crime and Delinquency* 44 (1998): 187–204.

37. Shawn Bushway, "The Impact of an Arrest on the Job Stability of Young White American Men," *Journal of Research in Crime and Delinquency* 35 (1998): 454–479.

38. Edwin M. Lemert, "The Juvenile Court—Quest and Realities," in President's Commission on Law Enforcement and the Administration of Justice, *Task Force Report: Juvenile Delinquency and Youth Crime* (Washington, D.C.: U.S. Government Printing Office, 1967).

39. Craig Hemmens and Katherine Bennett, "Juvenile Curfews and the Courts: Judicial Response to a Not-So-New Crime Control Strategy," *Crime and Delinquency* 45 (1999): 99–121.

40. James Austin and Barry Krisberg, "The Unmet Promise of Alternatives to Incarceration," *Crime and Delinquency* 28 (1982): 3–19. For an alternative view, see Arnold Binder and Gilbert Geis, "Ad Populum Argumentation in Criminology: Juvenile Diversion as Rhetoric," *Criminology* 30 (1984): 309–333.

41. Herbert Bianchi, *Justice as Sanctuary* (Bloomington: Indiana University Press, 1994); Nils Christie, "Conflicts as Property," *British Journal of Criminology* 17 (1977) 1–15; L. Hulsman, "Critical Criminology and the Concept of Crime," *Contemporary Crises* 10 (1986): 63–80.

42. Larry Tifft, "Foreword," in Dennis Sullivan, *The Mask of Love* (Port Washington, N.Y.: Kennikat Press, 1980), p. 6.

43. Robert Davis, Barbara Smith, and Laura Nickles, "The Deterrent Effect of Prosecuting Domestic Violence Misdemeanors," *Crime and Delinquency* 44 (1998): 434–442.

44. John Braithwaite, "Setting Standards for Restorative Justice," *British Journal of Criminology* 42 (2002): 563–577.

45. Christopher Cooper, "Patrol Police Officer Conflict Resolution Processes," *Journal of Criminal Justice* 25 (1997): 87–101.

46. Lois Presser and Patricia Van Voorhis, "Values and Evaluation: Assessing Processes and Outcomes of Restorative Justice Programs," *Crime and Delinquency* 48 (2002): 162–189.

47. David Altschuler, "Community Justice Initiatives: Issues and Challenges in the U.S. Context," *Federal Probation* 65 (2001): 28–33.

48. Elliott Currie, *Crime and Punishment in America* (New York: Henry Holt, 1998). See also Elliott Currie, *Confronting Crime: An American Challenge* (New York: Pantheon, 1985); Elliott Currie, *Reckoning: Drugs, the Cities, and the American Future* (New York: Hill and Wang, 1993).

acquaintance robbery A robber whose victims are people he or she knows.

active precipitation Aggressive or provocative behavior of victims that results in their victimization.

actual authority When a corporation knowingly gives authority to an employee.

adolescent-limited Offender who follows the most common criminal trajectory, in which antisocial behavior peaks in adolescence and then diminishes.

adversary system U.S. method of criminal adjudication in which prosecution (the state) and defense (the accused) each try to bring forward evidence and arguments, with guilt or innocence ultimately decided by an impartial judge or jury.

aggravated rape Rape involving multiple offenders, weapons, and victim injuries.

aging out (desistance) The fact that people commit less crime as they mature.

alien conspiracy theory The belief, adhered to by the federal government and many respected criminologists, that organized crime is a direct offshoot of a criminal society.

American Dream The goal of accumulating material goods and wealth through individual competition; the process of being socialized to pursue material success and to believe it is achievable.

androgens Male sex hormones.

anomie A lack of norms or clear social standards. Because of rapidly shifting moral values, the individual has few guides to what is socially acceptable.

anomie theory View that anomie results when socially defined goals (such as wealth and power) are universally mandated but access to legitimate means (such as education and job opportunities) is stratified by class and status.

antisocial personality Combination of traits, such as hyperactivity, impulsivity, hedonism, and inability to empathize with others, that make a person prone to deviant behavior and violence; also referred to as sociopathic or psychopathic personality.

antisocial potential (AP) An individual's potential to commit antisocial acts.

apparent authority If a third party, such as a customer, reasonably believes the agent has the authority to perform the act in question.

appeal Taking a criminal case to a higher court on the grounds that the defendant was found guilty because of legal error or violation of constitutional rights; a successful appeal may result in a new trial.

appellate court Court that reviews trial court procedures to determine whether they have complied with accepted rules and constitutional doctrines.

arousal theory The view that people seek to maintain a preferred level of arousal but vary in how they process sensory input. A need for high levels of environmental stimulation may lead to aggressive, violent behavior patterns.

arraignment The step in the criminal justice process when the accused is brought before the trial judge, formal charges are read, defendants are informed of their rights, a plea is entered, bail is considered, and a trial date is set.

arrest The taking into police custody of an individual suspected of a crime.

arson The willful, malicious burning of a home, building, or vehicle.

assault Does not require actual touching but involves either attempted battery or intentionally frightening the victim by word or deed.

attention deficit hyperactivity disorder (ADHD) A developmentally inappropriate lack of attention, along with impulsivity and hyperactivity.

authority conflict pathway Pathway to criminal deviance that begins at an early age with stubborn behavior and leads to defiance and then to authority avoidance.

bail A money bond intended to ensure that the accused will return for trial.

battery Offensive touching, such as slapping, hitting, or punching a victim.

behavior modeling Process of learning behavior (notably aggression) by observing others. Aggressive models may be parents, criminals in the neighborhood, or characters on television or in movies.

behavior theory The view that all human behavior is learned through a process of social reinforcement (rewards and punishment).

Bill of Rights The first 10 amendments to the U.S. Constitution, including guarantees against unreasonable search and seizure, self-incrimination, and cruel punishment.

biosocial theory Approach to criminology that focuses on the interaction between biological and social factors as they relate to crime.

bipolar disorder An emotional disturbance in which moods alternate between periods of wild elation and deep depression.

booking Fingerprinting, photographing, and recording personal information of a suspect in police custody.

booster Professional shoplifter who steals with the intention of reselling stolen merchandise.

brutalization effect The belief that capital punishment creates an atmosphere of brutality that enhances rather than deters the level of violence in society.

bucketing Skimming customer trading profits by falsifying trade information.

burglary Entering a home by force, threat, or deception with intent to commit a crime.

capable guardians Effective deterrents to crime, such as police or watchful neighbors.

capital punishment The execution of criminal offenders; the death penalty.

cheater theory A theory suggesting that a subpopulation of men has evolved with genes that incline them toward extremely low parental involvement. Sexually aggressive, they use deceit for sexual conquest of as many females as possible.

Chicago School Group of urban sociologists who studied the relationship between environmental conditions and crime.

child abuse Any physical or emotional trauma to a child for which no reasonable explanation, such as an accident or ordinary disciplinary practices, can be found.

child sexual abuse The exploitation of children through rape, incest, and molestation by parents or other adults.

choice theory The school of thought holding that people choose to engage in delinquent and criminal behavior after weighing the consequences and benefits of their actions.

chronic offenders A small group of persistent offenders who account for a majority of all criminal offenses.

churning Repeated, excessive, and unnecessary buying and selling of a client's stock.

classical criminology The theoretical perspective suggesting that (1) people have free will to choose criminal or conventional behaviors; (2) people choose to commit crime for reasons of greed or personal need; and (3) crime can be controlled only by the fear of criminal sanctions.

Code of Hammurabi The first written criminal code, developed in Babylonia about 2000 B.C.

cognitive theory Psychological perspective that focuses on mental processes: how people perceive and mentally represent the world around them and solve problems.

cohort A group of subjects that is studied over time.

collective efficacy Social control exerted by cohesive communities, based on mutual trust, including intervention in the supervision of children and maintenance of public order.

commitment to conformity A strong personal investment in conventional institutions, individuals, and processes that prevents people from engaging in behavior that might jeopardize their reputation and achievements.

common law Early English law, developed by judges, which became the standardized law of the land in England and eventually formed the basis of the criminal law in the United States.

compensation Financial aid awarded to crime victims to repay them for their loss and injuries; may cover medical bills, loss of wages, loss of future earnings, and/or counseling.

concentration effect As working- and middle-class families flee inner-city poverty areas, the most disadvantaged population is consolidated in urban ghettos.

confidence game A swindle, usually involving a get-rich-quick scheme, often with illegal overtones, so that the victim will be afraid or embarrassed to call the police.

conflict theory The view that human behavior, and thus crime, is shaped by class conflict and power relations. Laws are created and enforced by those in power to protect their own interests.

conflict view The belief that criminal behavior is defined by those in a position of power to protect and advance their own self-interest.

consensus view The belief that the majority of citizens in a society share common values and agree on what behaviors should be defined as criminal.

consent The victim of rape must prove that she in no way encouraged, enticed, or misled the accused rapist.

constructive possession A legal fiction that applies to situations in which persons voluntarily give up physical custody of their property but still retain legal ownership.

convictability A case that has a good chance of a conviction.

corporate or organizational crime Powerful institutions or their representatives willfully violate the laws that restrain these institutions from doing social harm or require them to do social good.

courtroom work group Prosecution, defense, and judges working together to resolve criminal cases quickly and efficiently through plea bargaining.

covert pathway Pathway to a criminal career that begins with minor underhanded behavior, leads to property damage, and eventually escalates to more serious forms of theft and fraud.

crackdown The concentration of police resources on a particular problem area to eradicate or displace criminal activity.

crime control model View that the overriding purpose of the justice system is to protect the public, deter criminal behavior, and incapacitate known criminals; favors speedy, efficient justice and punishment.

crime An act, deemed socially harmful or dangerous, that is specifically defined, prohibited, and punished under the criminal law.

criminal justice system The agencies of government—police, courts, and corrections—responsible for apprehending, adjudicating, sanctioning, and treating criminal offenders.

criminal law The written code that defines crimes and their punishments.

criminology The scientific study of the nature, extent, cause, and control of criminal behavior.

crisis intervention Emergency counseling for crime victims.

critical criminology The view that crime is a product of the capitalist system.

critical feminism Approach that explains both victimization and criminality among women in terms of gender inequality, patriarchy, and the exploitation of women under capitalism.

cross-sectional research Interviewing or questioning a diverse sample of subjects, representing a cross-section of a community, at the same point in time.

cultural deviance theory Branch of social structure theory that sees strain and social disorganization together resulting in a unique lower-class culture that conflicts with conventional social norms.

cultural transmission Process whereby values, beliefs, and traditions are handed down from one generation to the next.

culture conflict Result of exposure to opposing norms, attitudes, and definitions of right and wrong, moral and immoral.

culture of poverty A separate lower-class culture, characterized by apathy, cynicism, helplessness, and mistrust of social institutions such as schools, government agencies, and the police that is passed from one generation to the next.

cyber crime People using the instruments of modern technology for criminal purposes.

cycle of violence Victims of crime, especially childhood abuse, are more likely to commit crimes themselves.

date rape A rape that involves people who are in some form of courting relationship.

death squads The use of government troops to destroy political opposition parties.

deconstructionist Approach that focuses on the use of language by those in power to define crime based on their own values and biases; also called postmodernist.

defendant In criminal proceedings, the person accused of violating the law.

defense attorney The person responsible for protecting the constitutional rights of the accused and presenting the best possible legal defense; represents a defendant from initial arrest through trial, sentencing, and any appeal.

defensible space The principle that crime can be prevented or displaced by modifying the physical environment to reduce the opportunity individuals have to commit crime.

deliberation Planning a criminal act after careful thought rather than carrying it out on impulse.

delinquent subculture A value system adopted by lower-class youths that is directly opposed to that of the larger society.

demystify To unmask the true purpose of law, justice, or other social institutions.

determinate sentencing Principle that all offenders who commit the same crime should receive the same sentence.

developmental theory The view that criminality is a dynamic process, influenced by social experiences as well as individual characteristics.

deviance amplification Process whereby secondary deviance pushes offenders out of mainstream of society and locks them into an escalating cycle of deviance, apprehension, labeling, and criminal self-identity.

deviance Behavior that departs from the social norm but is not necessarily criminal.

deviant place theory The view that victimization is primarily a function of where people live.

differential association theory The view that people commit crime when their social learning leads them to perceive more definitions favoring crime than favoring conventional behavior.

differential opportunity The view that lower-class youths, whose legitimate opportunities are limited, join gangs and pursue criminal careers as alternative means to achieve universal success goals.

diffusion of benefits An effect that occurs when efforts to prevent one crime unintentionally prevent another, or when crime control efforts in one locale reduce crime in other nontarget areas.

discouragement An effect that occurs when limiting access to one target reduces other types of crime as well.

discretion The use of personal decision making by those carrying out police, judicial, and sanctioning functions within the criminal justice system.

disorder Any type of psychological problem (formerly labeled neurotic or psychotic), such as anxiety disorders, mood disorders, and conduct disorders.

displacement An effect of crime prevention efforts in which efforts to control crime in one area shift illegal activities to another.

disposition Sentencing of a defendant who has been found guilty; usually involves a fine, probation, or incarceration.

diversion programs Programs of rehabilitation that remove offenders from the normal channels of the criminal justice process, thus avoiding the stigma of a criminal label.

division of markets Firms divide a region into territories, and each firm agrees not to compete in the others' territories.

dizygotic (DZ) twins Fraternal (nonidentical) twins.

drift Movement in and out of delinquency, shifting between conventional and deviant values.

due process model View that focuses on protecting the civil rights of those accused of crime.

economic compulsive behavior Drug users who resort to violence to support their habit.

edgework The excitement or exhilaration of successfully executing illegal activities in dangerous situations.

egalitarian families Husband and wife share similar positions of power at home and in the workplace. Sons and daughters have equal freedom.

ego The part of the personality developed in early childhood that helps control the id and keep people's actions within the boundaries of social convention.

eldercide A murder involving a senior citizen.

embezzlement Taking and keeping the property of others, such as clients or employers, with which one has been entrusted.

enterprise crimes Crimes of illicit entrepreneurship.

enterprise theory of investigation (ETI) Model that focuses on criminal enterprise and investigation attacks on the structure of the criminal enterprise rather than on criminal acts viewed as isolated incidents.

equipotentiality The view that all humans are born with equal potential to learn and achieve.

eros The life instinct, which drives people toward self-fulfillment and enjoyment.

ex post facto law A law applied retroactively to punish acts that were not crimes before its passage, or that raises the grade of an offense, or that renders an act punishable in a more severe manner than it was when committed.

exclusionary rule The rule that evidence against a defendant may not be presented in court if it was obtained in violation of the defendant's rights.

experimental research Manipulating or intervening in the lives of subjects to observe the outcome or effect of a specific intervention. True experiments usually include (1) random selection of subjects, (2) a control or comparison group, and (3) an experimental condition.

expressive crimes Offenses committed not for profit or gain but to vent rage, anger, or frustration.

expressive violence Acts that vent rage, anger, or frustration.

extinction The phenomenon in which a crime prevention effort has an immediate impact that then dissipates as criminals adjust to new conditions.

false pretenses or fraud Misrepresenting a fact in a way that causes a deceived victim to give money or property to the offender.

felony A serious offense that carries a penalty of imprisonment, usually for one year or more, and may entail loss of political rights.

felony murder A killing accompanying a felony, such as robbery or rape.

fence A receiver of stolen goods.

first-degree murder Killing a person after premeditation and deliberation.

focal concerns Values, such as toughness and street smarts, that have evolved specifically to fit conditions in lower-class environments.

front running Brokers place personal orders ahead of a large customer's order to profit from the market effects of the trade.

gay bashing Violent hate crimes directed toward people because of their sexual orientation.

general deterrence A crime control policy that depends on the fear of criminal penalties, convincing the potential law violator that the pains associated with crime outweigh its benefits.

general strain theory (GST) The view that multiple sources of strain interact with an individual's emotional traits and responses to produce criminality.

general theory of crime (GTC) A developmental theory that modifies social control theory by integrating concepts from biosocial, psychological, routine activities, and rational choice theories.

globalization The process of creating a global economy through transnational markets and political and legal systems.

grand jury A group of citizens chosen to hear testimony in secret and to issue formal criminal accusations (indictments).

grand larceny Theft of money or property of substantial value, punished as a felony.

group boycott An organization or company boycotts retail stores that do not comply with its rules or desires.

hate or bias crimes Violent acts directed toward a particular person or members of a group merely because the targets share a discernible racial, ethnic, religious, or gender characteristic.

homophobia Extremely negative overreaction to homosexuals.

homosexuality Erotic interest in members of one's own sex.

human capital What a person or organization actually possesses.

hung jury A jury that is unable to agree on a decision, thus leaving the case unresolved and open for a possible retrial.

hypoglycemia A condition that occurs when glucose (sugar) in the blood falls below levels necessary for normal and efficient brain functioning.

id The primitive part of people's mental makeup, present at birth, that represents unconscious biological drives for food, sex, and other life-sustaining necessities. The id seeks instant gratification without concern for the rights of others.

incapacitation effect The idea that keeping offenders in confinement will eliminate the risk of their committing further offenses.

incarceration Confinement in jail or prison.

index crimes The eight most serious offenses included in the UCR: murder, rape, assault, robbery, burglary, arson, larceny, and motor vehicle theft.

indictment A written accusation returned by a grand jury charging an individual with a specified crime, based on the prosecutor's presentation of probable cause.

infanticide A murder involving a very young child.

influence peddling Using one's institutional position to grant favors and sell information to which one's co-conspirators are not entitled.

information-processing theory Theory that focuses on how people process, store, encode, retrieve, and manipulate information to make decisions and solve problems.

insider trading Using one's position of trust to profit from inside business information.

institutional anomie theory The view that anomie pervades U.S. culture because the drive for material wealth dominates and undermines social and community values.

instrumental crimes Offenses designed to improve the financial or social position of the criminal.

instrumental Marxist One who sees criminal law and the criminal justice system as capitalist instruments for controlling the lower class.

instrumental violence Acts designed to improve the financial or social position of the criminal.

interactional theory A developmental theory that attributes criminal trajectories to mutual reinforcement between delinquents and significant others over the life course—family in early adolescence, school and friends in midadolescence, and social peers and one's own nuclear family in adulthood.

interactionist view The belief that those with social power are able to impose their values on society as a whole, and these values then define criminal behavior.

interdisciplinary Involving two or more academic fields.

international terrorism Terrorism involving citizens or the territory of more than one country.

interrogation The questioning of a suspect in police custody.

involuntary or negligent manslaughter A killing that occurs when a person's acts are negligent and without regard for the harm they may cause others.

jail Institution, usually run by the county, for short-term detention of those convicted of misdemeanors and those awaiting trial or other judicial proceedings.

just desert The principle that those who violate the rights of others deserve punishment commensurate with the seriousness of the crime, without regard to their personal characteristics or circumstances.

justice model View that emphasizes fairness and equal treatment in criminal procedures and sentencing.

La Cosa Nostra A national syndicate of 25 or so Italian-dominated crime families.

landmark decision A ruling by the U.S. Supreme Court that serves as a precedent for similar legal issues; it often influences the everyday operating procedures of police agencies, trial courts, and corrections institutions.

larceny Taking for one's own use the property of another, by means other than force or threats on the victim or forcibly breaking into a person's home or workplace; theft.

latent trait theory The view that criminal behavior is controlled by a "master trait," present at birth or soon after, that remains stable and unchanging throughout a person's lifetime.

latent trait A stable feature, characteristic, property, or condition, such as defective intelligence or impulsive personality, that makes some people crime prone over the life course.

law of criminal procedure Judicial precedents that define and guarantee the rights of criminal defendants and control the various components of the criminal justice system.

left realism Approach that sees crime as a function of relative deprivation under capitalism and favors pragmatic, community-based crime prevention and control.

life course persister One of the small group of offenders whose criminal career continues well into adulthood.

life course theory Theory that focuses on changes in criminality over the life course; developmental theory.

lifestyle theories The view that people become crime victims because of lifestyles that increase their exposure to criminal offenders.

longitudinal research Tracking the development of the same group of subjects over time.

Mafia A criminal society that first originated in Italy and Sicily and now controls racketeering in major U.S. cities.

mandatory sentences A statutory requirement that a certain penalty shall be carried out in all cases of conviction for a specified offense or series of offenses.

manslaughter Homicide without malice.

marginalization Displacement of workers, pushing them outside the economic and social mainstream.

marital exemption Traditionally, a legally married husband could not be charged with raping his wife.

masculinity hypothesis The view that women who commit crimes have biological and psychological traits similar to those of men.

mass murderer A person who kills many victims in a single, violent outburst.

merchant privilege laws Legislation that protects retailers and their employees from lawsuits if they arrest and detain a suspected shoplifter on reasonable grounds.

middle-class measuring rods The standards by which authority figures, such as teachers and employers, evaluate lower-class youngsters and often prejudge them negatively.

minimal brain dysfunction (MBD) An abruptly appearing, maladaptive behavior such as episodic periods of explosive rage.

Miranda rights Rights of criminal defendants, including the right against self-incrimination and right to counsel, spelled out in the case of *Miranda v. Arizona.*

misdemeanor A minor crime usually punished by a short jail term and/or a fine.

monozygotic (MZ) twins Identical twins.

moral entrepreneur A person who creates moral rules that reflect the values of those in power rather than any objective, universal standards of right and wrong.

moral entrepreneur A person who creates moral rules, which thus reflect the values of those in power rather than any objective, universal standards of right and wrong.

Mosaic Code The laws of the ancient Israelites, found in the Old Testament of the Judeo-Christian Bible.

motivated offenders People willing and able to commit crimes.

murder The unlawful killing of a human being with malice aforethought.

naive check forgers Amateurs who cash bad checks because of some financial crisis but have little identification with a criminal subculture.

narcissistic personality disorder A pattern of traits and behaviors that indicate infatuation and fixation with one's self to the exclusion of all others and the egotistic and ruthless pursuit of one's gratification, dominance, and ambition.

narcotic A drug that produces sleep and relieves pain, such as heroin, morphine, and opium; a habit-forming drug.

National Crime Victimization Survey (NCVS) The ongoing victimization study conducted jointly by the Justice Department and the U.S. Census Bureau that surveys victims about their experiences with law violation.

nature theory The view that intelligence is largely determined genetically and that low intelligence is linked to criminal behavior.

negative affective states Anger, frustration, and adverse emotions produced by a variety of sources of strain.

neglect Not providing a child with the care and shelter to which he or she is entitled.

neurophysiology The study of brain activity.

neurotic In Freudian psychology, a personality marked by mental anguish and feared loss of control.

neurotransmitters Chemical compounds that influence or activate brain functions.

neutralization techniques Methods of rationalizing deviant behavior, such as denying responsibility or blaming the victim.

neutralization theory The view that law violators learn to neutralize conventional values and attitudes, enabling them to drift back and forth between criminal and conventional behavior.

noninterventionist model The view that arresting and labeling offenders does more harm than good, that youthful offenders in particular should be diverted into informal treatment programs, and that minor offenses should be decriminalized.

nurture theory The view that intelligence is not inherited but is largely a product of environment. Low IQ scores do not cause crime but may result from the same environmental factors.

obscenity Material that violates community standards of morality or decency and has no redeeming social value.

occasional criminals Offenders who do not define themselves by a criminal role or view themselves as committed career criminals.

offender-specific The idea that offenders evaluate their skills, motives, needs, and fears before deciding to commit crime.

offense-specific The idea that offenders react selectively to the characteristics of particular crimes.

organized crime Illegal activities of people and organizations whose acknowledged purpose is profit through illegitimate business enterprise.

overt pathway Pathway to a criminal career that begins with minor aggression, leads to physical fighting, and eventually escalates to violent crime.

paraphilia Bizarre or abnormal sexual practices that may involve nonhuman objects, humiliation, or children.

parental efficacy Parents who are supportive and effectively control their children in a noncoercive fashion.

parole A conditional early release from prison, with the offender serving the remainder of the sentence in the community under the supervision of a parole officer.

passive precipitation Personal or social characteristics of victims that make them "attractive" targets for criminals; such victims may unknowingly either threaten or encourage their attackers.

paternalistic families Father is breadwinner and rule maker; mother has menial job or is homemaker only. Sons are granted greater freedom than daughters.

patriarchal Male-dominated.

peacemaking Approach that considers punitive crime control strategies to be counterproductive and favors the use of humanistic conflict resolution to prevent and control crime.

penology Subarea of criminology that focuses on the correction and control of criminal offenders.

personality The reasonably stable patterns of behavior, including thoughts and emotions, that distinguish one person from another.

petit (petty) larceny Theft of a small amount of money or property, punished as a misdemeanor.

pilferage Systematic theft of company property.

plea bargain An agreement between prosecution and defense in which the accused pleads guilty in return for a reduction of charges, a more lenient sentence, or some other consideration.

population All people who share a particular characteristic, such as all high school students or all police officers.

pornography Sexually explicit books, magazines, films, or tapes intended to provide sexual titillation and excitement for paying customers.

positivism The branch of social science that uses the scientific method of the natural sciences and suggests that human behavior is a product of social, biological, psychological, or economic forces.

postmodernist Approach that focuses on the use of language by those in power to define crime based on their own values and biases; also called deconstructionist.

posttraumatic stress disorder Psychological reaction to a highly stressful event; symptoms may include depression, anxiety, flashbacks, and recurring nightmares.

power The ability of persons and groups to control the behavior of others, to shape public opinion, and to define deviance.

power–control theory The view that gender differences in crime are a function of economic power (class position, one- versus two-earner families) and parental control (paternalistic versus egalitarian families).

precedent A rule derived from previous judicial decisions and applied to future cases; the basis of common law.

preemptive deterrence Efforts to prevent crime through community organization and youth involvement.

preliminary hearing Alternative to a grand jury, in which an impartial lower-court judge decides whether there is probable cause sufficient for a trial.

premeditation Considering the criminal act beforehand, which suggests that it was motivated by more than a simple desire to engage in an act of violence.

premenstrual syndrome (PMS) The idea that several days prior to and during menstruation, excessive amounts of female sex hormones stimulate antisocial, aggressive behavior.

price-fixing A conspiracy to set and control the price of a necessary commodity.

primary deviance A norm violation or crime with little or no long-term influence on the violator.

primary prevention programs Programs, such as substance abuse clinics and mental health associations, that seek to treat personal problems before they manifest themselves as crime.

prison or penitentiary State or federally operated facility for the incarceration of felony offenders sentenced by the criminal courts.

pro bono The provision of free legal counsel to indigent defendants by private attorneys as a service to the profession and the community.

probable cause Evidence of a crime, and of a suspect's involvement in it, sufficient to warrant an arrest.

probation The conditional release of a convicted offender into the community under the supervision of a probation officer and subject to certain conditions.

problem behavior syndrome (PBS) A cluster of antisocial behaviors that may include family dysfunction, substance abuse, smoking, precocious sexuality and early pregnancy, educational underachievement, suicide attempts, sensation seeking, and unemployment, as well as crime.

professional criminals Offenders who make a significant portion of their income from crime.

Prohibition The period from 1919 until 1933, when the Eighteenth Amendment to the U.S. Constitution outlawed the sale of alcohol; also known as the "noble experiment."

prosecutor Public official who represents the government in criminal proceedings, presenting the case against the accused.

prosocial bonds Socialized attachment to conventional institutions, activities, and beliefs.

prostitution The granting of nonmarital sexual access for remuneration.

pseudomaturity Characteristic of life course persisters, who tend to engage in early sexuality and drug use.

psychodynamic (psychoanalytic) Theory originated by Freud that the human personality is controlled by unconscious mental processes developed early in childhood, involving the interaction of id, ego, and superego.

psychopharmacological relationship The direct consequence of ingesting mood-altering substances.

psychotic In Freudian psychology, a personality marked by complete loss of control over the id, characterized by delusions, hallucinations, and sudden mood shifts.

public defender An attorney employed by the state whose job is to provide free legal counsel to indigent defendants.

public order crime Behavior that is outlawed because it threatens the general well-being of society and challenges its accepted moral principles.

racial threat view As the size of the black population increases, the perceived threat to the white population increases, resulting in a greater amount of social control imposed against blacks.

Racketeer Influenced and Corrupt Organization Act (RICO) An act that created new categories of offenses in racketeering activity, which it defined as involvement in two or more acts prohibited by 24 existing federal and 8 state statutes.

rape The carnal knowledge of a female forcibly and against her will.

rational choice theory The view that crime is a function of a decision-making process in which the potential offender weighs the potential costs and benefits of an illegal act.

reaction formation Irrational hostility evidenced by young delinquents, who adopt norms directly opposed to middle-class goals and standards that seem impossible to achieve.

recidivism Repetition of criminal behavior.

recognizance Pledge by the accused to return for trial, which may be accepted in lieu of bail.

reflected appraisal When parents are alienated from their children, their negative labeling reduces their children's self-image and increases delinquency.

rehabilitation model View that sees criminals as victims of social in-

justice, poverty, and racism and suggests that appropriate treatment can change them into productive, law-abiding citizens.

rehabilitation Treatment of criminal offenders aimed at preventing future criminal behavior.

relative deprivation Envy, mistrust, and aggression resulting from perceptions of economic and social inequality.

reliable Producing consistent results from one measurement to another.

restitution Permitting an offender to repay the victim or do useful work in the community rather than face the stigma of a formal trial and a court-ordered sentence.

restorative justice model View that emphasizes the promotion of a peaceful, just society through reconciliation and reintegration of the offender into society.

restorative justice Using humanistic, nonpunitive strategies to right wrongs and restore social harmony.

retrospective reading The reassessment of a person's past to fit a current generalized label.

right to counsel The right of a person accused of crime to have the assistance of a defense attorney in all criminal prosecutions.

road rage Violent assault by a motorist who loses control while driving.

robbery Taking or attempting to take anything of value from the care, custody, or control of a person or persons by force or threat of force or violence and/or by putting the victim in fear.

role exit behaviors Strategies such as running away or contemplating suicide used by young girls unhappy with their status in the family.

routine activities theory The view that victimization results from the interaction of three everyday factors: the availability of suitable targets, the absence of capable guardians, and the presence of motivated offenders.

sampling Selecting a limited number of people for study as representative of a larger group.

schizophrenia A severe disorder marked by hearing nonexistent voices, seeing hallucinations, and exhibiting inappropriate responses.

secondary deviance A norm violation or crime that comes to the attention of significant others or social control agents, who apply a negative label with long-term consequences for the violator's self-identity and social interactions.

secondary prevention programs Programs that provide treatment such as psychological counseling to youths and adults after they have violated the law.

second-degree murder A person's wanton disregard for the victim's life and his or her desire to inflict serious bodily harm on the victim, which results in the victim's death.

seductions of crime The situational inducements or immediate benefits that draw offenders into law violations.

self-control A strong moral sense that renders a person incapable of hurting others or violating social norms.

self-report surveys A research approach that requires subjects to reveal their own participation in delinquent or criminal acts.

semiotics The use of language elements as signs or symbols beyond their literal meaning.

sentencing circle A peacemaking technique in which offenders, victims, and other community members are brought together in an effort to formulate a sanction that addresses the needs of all.

serial killer A person who kills more than one victim over a period of time.

Sherman Antitrust Act Subjects to criminal or civil sanctions any person "who shall make any contract or engage in any combination or conspiracy" in restraint of interstate commerce.

shield laws Laws that protect women from being questioned about their sexual history unless it directly bears on the case.

shoplifting The taking of goods from retail stores.

situational crime prevention A method of crime prevention that seeks to eliminate or reduce particular crimes in narrow settings.

situational inducement Short-term influence on a person's behavior, such as financial problems or peer pressure, that increases risk-taking.

snitch Amateur shoplifter who does not self-identify as a thief but who systematically steals merchandise for personal use.

social altruism Voluntary mutual support systems, such as neighborhood associations and self-help groups, that reinforce moral and social obligations.

social bonds The ties that bind people to society, including relationships with friends, family, neighbors, teachers, and employers. Elements of the social bond include commitment, attachment, involvement, and belief.

social capital Positive relations with individuals and institutions, as in a successful marriage or a successful career, that support conventional behavior and inhibit deviant behavior.

social class Segment of the population whose members are at a relatively similar economic level and who share attitudes, values, norms, and an identifiable lifestyle.

social control theory The view that people commit crime when the forces binding them to society are weakened or broken.

social development model (SDM) A developmental theory that attributes criminal behavior patterns to childhood socialization and pro- or antisocial attachments over the life course.

social disorganization theory Branch of social structure theory that focuses on the breakdown of institutions such as the family, school, and employment in inner-city neighborhoods.

social learning theory The view that people learn to be aggressive by observing others acting aggressively to achieve some goal or being rewarded for violent acts.

social process theory The view that criminality is a function of people's interactions with various organizations, institutions, and processes in society.

social reaction (labeling) theory The view that people become criminals when labeled as such and when they accept the label as a personal identity.

social structure theory The view that disadvantaged economic class position is a primary cause of crime.

socialization Process of human development and enculturation. Socialization is influenced by key social processes and institutions.

sociobiology The view that human behavior is motivated by inborn biological urges to survive and preserve the species.

sociological criminology Approach to criminology, based on the work of Quetelet and Durkheim, that focuses on the relationship between social factors and crime.

sodomy Deviant forms of sexual intercourse.

specific deterrence The view that criminal sanctions should be so powerful that offenders will never repeat their criminal acts.

spree killer A killer of multiple victims whose murders occur over a relatively short span of time and follow no discernible pattern.

stalking A course of conduct directed at a specific person that involves repeated physical or visual proximity, nonconsensual communication, or verbal, written, or implied threats sufficient to cause fear in a reasonable person.

status frustration A form of culture conflict experienced by lower-class youths because social conditions prevent them from achieving success as defined by the larger society.

statutory crimes Crimes defined by legislative bodies in response to changing social conditions, public opinion, and custom.

statutory rape Sexual relations between an underage minor female and an adult male.

stigmatize To apply negative labeling with enduring effects on a person's self-image and social interactions.

sting or swindle A white-collar crime in which people use their institutional or business position to bilk others out of their money.

strain theory Branch of social structure theory that sees crime as a function of the conflict between people's goals and the means available to obtain them.

strain The anger, frustration, and resentment experienced by people who believe they cannot achieve their goals through legitimate means.

stratified society People grouped according to economic or social class; characterized by the unequal distribution of wealth, power, and prestige.

structural Marxism Based on the belief that criminal law and the criminal justice system are a means of defending and preserving the capitalist system.

subculture of violence Violence has become legitimized by the custom and norms of that group.

subculture A set of values, beliefs, and traditions unique to a particular social class or group within a larger society.

successful degradation ceremony A course of action or ritual in which someone's identity is publicly redefined and destroyed and they are thereafter viewed as socially unacceptable.

suitable targets Objects of crime (persons or property) that are attractive and readily available.

superego Incorporation within the personality of the moral standards and values of parents, community, and significant others.

surplus value The difference between what workers produce and what they are paid, which goes to business owners as profits.

systematic forgers Professionals who make a living by passing bad checks.

systemic link A link that occurs when drug dealers turn violent in their competition with rival gangs.

target hardening strategy Locking goods into place or using electronic tags and sensing devices as means of preventing shoplifting.

target removal strategy Displaying dummy or disabled goods as a means of preventing shoplifting.

temperance movement The drive to prohibit the sale of alcohol in the United States, culminating in ratification of the Eighteenth Amendment in 1919.

terrorism Premeditated, politically motivated violence perpetrated against noncombatant targets by subnational groups or clandestine agents, usually intended to influence an audience.

terrorist group Any group practicing, or that has significant subgroups that practice, international terrorism.

testosterone The principal male hormone.

thanatos The death instinct, which produces self-destruction.

three strikes and you're out Policy whereby people convicted of three felony offenses receive a mandatory life sentence.

trait theory The view that criminality is a product of abnormal biological or psychological traits.

transitional neighborhood An area undergoing a shift in population and structure, usually from middle-class residential to lower-class mixed use.

truly disadvantaged The lowest level of the underclass; urban, inner-city, socially isolated people who occupy the bottom rung of the social ladder and are the victims of discrimination.

turning points Critical life events, such as career and marriage, that may enable adult offenders to desist from crime.

tying arrangement A corporation requires customers of one of its services to use other services it offers.

underclass The lowest social stratum in any country, whose members lack the education and skills needed to function successfully in modern society.

Uniform Crime Report (UCR) Large database, compiled by the Federal Bureau of Investigation (FBI), of crimes reported and arrests made each year throughout the United States.

USA Patriot Act (USAPA) An act that gives sweeping new powers to domestic law enforcement and international intelligence agencies in an effort to fight terrorism, to expand the definition of terrorist activities, and to alter sanctions for violent terrorism.

utilitarianism The view that people's behavior is motivated by the pursuit of pleasure and the avoidance of pain.

valid Actually measuring what one intends to measure; relevant.

victim precipitation theory The view that victims may initiate, either actively or passively, the confrontation that leads to their victimization.

victimless crime Public order crime that violates the moral order but has no specific victim other than society as a whole.

victim–offender reconciliation programs Mediated face-to-face encounters between victims and their attackers, designed to produce restitution agreements and, if possible, reconciliation.

victimologists Criminologists who focus on the victims of crime.

victimology The study of the victim's role in criminal events.

victim–witness assistance programs Government programs that help crime victims and witnesses; may include compensation, court services, and/or crisis intervention.

virility mystique The belief that males must separate their sexual feelings from needs for love, respect, and affection.

voluntary or nonnegligent manslaughter A killing committed in the heat of passion or during a sudden quarrel that provoked violence.

white-collar crime Illegal acts of people and institutions, whose acknowledged purpose is profit through legitimate business transactions. White-collar crimes may include theft, embezzlement, fraud, market manipulation, restraint of trade, and false advertising.

workplace violence Violence such as assault, rape, or murder committed at the workplace.

SUBJECT INDEX

PHOTO CREDITS

This page constitutes an extension of the copyright page. We have made every effort to trace the ownership of all copyrighted material and to secure permission from copyright holders. In the event of any question arising as to the use of any material, we will be pleased to make the necessary corrections in future printings. Thanks are due to the following authors, publishers, and agents for permission to use the material indicated.

Chapter opening images

3, 27, 51, 73, 97, 125, 155, 181, 207, 235, 269, 289, 317, and 349 are all © 2004 Turner Broadcasting System, Inc. CNN is a trademark of Turner Broadcasting System, Inc. Licensed by Turner Learning, Inc. All Rights Reserved.

Chapter 1

5: The Image Works
8: AP/Wide World Photos
16: A. C. Cooper Ltd; by permission of The Inner Temple, London
21: © Joe Raedle/Getty Images

Chapter 2

36: © AP/Wide World Photos/courtesy of Court TV
40: © 2003 AP/Wide World Photos
41: © 2003 AP/Wide World Photos
45: © 2003 AP/Wide World Photos

Chapter 3

54: © Stefan Zaklin/Getty Images
60: © 2003 AP/Wide World Photos
64: © 2003 AP/Wide World Photos

Chapter 4

78: © 2003 AP/Wide World Photos
81: © 2003 AP/Wide World Photos
90: © AP/Wide World Photos
91: © 2002 AP/Wide World Photos

Chapter 5

104: Dr. Alan Zametkin/Clinical Brain Imaging, courtesy of Office of Scientific Information, NIMH
107: © 2003 AP/Wide World Photos
114: © 2003 AP/Wide World Photos
115: © 2001 AP/Wide World Photos

Chapter 6

127: © Kevin Fleming/Corbis
135: © Eric Fowke/PhotoEdit
142: © David H. Welles/Corbis
150: © 2003 AP/Wide World Photos

Chapter 7

157: © 2003 AP/Wide World Photos
160: © 2000 AP/Wide World Photos
173: © 2003 AP/Wide World Photos

Chapter 8

188: © 2003 AP/Wide World Photos
192: © 2000 AP/Wide World Photos
194: © A. Ramey/PhotoEdit
197: © 2000 AP/Wide World Photos

Chapter 9

210: © Chris Rank/Getty Images
216: © 2000 AP/Wide World Photos
219: © 2003 AP/Wide World Photos
227: © 2003 AP/Wide World Photos

Chapter 10

239: © A. Ramey/PhotoEdit
247: © 2003 AP/Wide World Photos
249: © 2003 AP/Wide World Photos
254: © 2003 AP/Wide World Photos
256: © 2003 AP/Wide World Photos

Chapter 11

270: Roy 20 CVii f. 41v British Library/Bridgeman Art Library
276: © 2000 AP/Wide World Photos
280: © 2000 AP/Wide World Photos
283: © 2003 AP/Wide World Photos

Chapter 12

292: © Frederick M. Brown/Getty Images
296: © 2003 AP/Wide World Photos
304: © 2003 AP/Wide World Photos
309: © 2003 AP/Wide World Photos

Chapter 13

323: © 2003 AP/Wide World Photos
328: © 2003 AP/Wide World Photos
330: © 2000 AP/Wide World Photos
343: © Ron Wurzer/Getty Images

Chapter 14

353: © 2003 AP/Wide World Photos
363: © 2003 AP/Wide World Photos
367: © Shannon Stapleton/Reuters Newmedia Inc./Corbis
371: © 2003 AP/Wide World Photos